EXPRESSIVE
SINGING

BROWN
MUSIC SERIES

Edited by FREDERICK W. WESTPHAL, *Ph. D.*
Sacramento State College, Sacramento, California

EXPRESSIVE SINGING

VOLUME II

Correlated Advanced Theory, Technic, Pedagogy, and Repertoire

**A Textbook
For School or Studio
Class or Private Teaching**

Complete In Three Parts

Part I — Technics in Singing and Vocal Teaching Applied to Specific Problems

Part II — Basic Principles and Methods in Singing and Vocal Teaching

Part III — Select Literature for Solo Voice and Duet

VAN A. CHRISTY, Ph.D.
Professor of Music
University of California
Santa Barbara, California

WM. C. BROWN COMPANY PUBLISHERS
135 SOUTH LOCUST STREET ● DUBUQUE, IOWA

Other books by the same author:

EXPRESSIVE SINGING, SONG ANTHOLOGY, VOLUME II

(Medium Voice Edition)

EXPRESSIVE SINGING, VOLUME I

(Basic Principles)

EXPRESSIVE SINGING, SONG ANTHOLOGY VOLUME I

(Medium Voice Edition)

Manufactured by WM. C. BROWN CO. INC., Dubuque, Iowa

Printed in U.S.A.

Foreword

COURSE ORGANIZATION AND CONTENT

This complete vocal course is arranged in four volumes: *Expressive Singing Volume I* for the student and teacher; *Song Anthologies Volumes I and II* for the student; and *Expressive Singing Volume II* for the intermediate and advanced student, the class and private teacher, and teacher training classes in vocal methods, vocal production theory, and vocal literature. The four volumes in this course are designed to meet completely the needs of both the student and teacher in either class or private voice study. It is the first course in the vocal field to provide complete song content, theory, exercise and methods for four or more years of normal study as well as a complete "professionalized" textbook for the teacher and student.

Authorities who have previewed *Expressive Singing Volume I* agree that it provides in 16 chapters all the vocal exercises and most of the vocal theory needed in developing technic in singing. Volume II supplies the remainder of needed theory for the intermediate and advanced student. Although Volume I can be used separately with any other song sources, it will be found that when accompanied by *Song Anthology Volume I* for the *beginning student and Song Anthology Vollume II* for the intermediate and advanced, it furnishes a carefully coordinated, graded, and complete vocal course for colleges, conservatories, and private study.

Expressive Singing Volume I concerns itself chiefly with the HOW of singing. The details of HOW, and the WHY, progressive teaching methods, listing, classification and grading of solo and duet vocal literature, and a large amount of other pertinent information are in this professionalized textbook, *Volume II*. *Volume II* goes into more detail on the HOW of singing with Part I correlated, chapter by chapter and lesson by lesson, with Volume I. Part II, chapter 23 also outlines a full four-year, eight semester vocal course, listing objectives, content covered each semester in *Expressive Singing*, and suggesting supplementary song volumes from other sources. A high school age level course, or a college or adult course with either more limited or more extensive objectives, can also follow this outline with slight revision.

This textbook, *Volume II*, is organized in three parts. Part I is correlated chapter by chapter with Expressive Singing Volume I, the basic student manual. Value of the content is independent of correlation, however, while educational methods recommended are fully applicable to integration with any other student manual or teacher outline that might be used. Part II deals with general methods and basic principles in singing and vocal teaching and also covers thoroughly the problems concerned in organization, administration, and teaching of class voice. Part III lists and classifies solo voice and duet song literature, both collections and sheet music; includes some graded material and various song lists from the National Interscholastic Music Activities Commission of the Music Educators National Conference, the American Academy of Teachers of Singing, and the National Association of Teachers of Singing; a list of songs used in the Rochester, New York, high schools, and many useful types of song classifications often needed.

EDUCATIONAL OBJECTIVES EMPLOYED IN DETERMINING CONTENT

Five over-all objectives were employed in organizing the content of this complete vocal course: comprehensiveness, authoritativeness, clarity, attractiveness, and usefulness.

We agree with Fields that "There is certainly no lack of printed material on the subjects of singing and voice culture. But it is inaccessible to teachers because it is extremely diversified and fragmentary and rather diffusely distributed throughout a variety of books, periodicals, scientific papers, reports of experiments and published interviews that have never been correlated from the standpoint of definite vocal pedagogy. Furthermore, what is written about the singing voice is so often overlaid and interwoven with conflicting theories and extravagant conjectures that misinterpretations are inevitable."[1] It is our purpose to collect available information on each phase of singing through careful research, resolve conflicting theories according to the preponderance of evidence, and organize into one available authoritative source all the most useful ideas bearing upon the problem.

Most texts in English and all articles on singing available in professional magazines and periodicals were read before writing on the course began. Ideas bearing on each phase of study were filed together, conflicting viewpoints were analyzed carefully for the true or most practical solution, and contents of readings were synthesized, summarized, and organized into the most useful form for presentation and study. It is the purpose of this course to present proven methods and theory endorsed by the preponderance of recognized vocal authorities. These methods and theory have proven successful in wide practice and are as standard as it is possible to determine. They present the fewest hazards to safe progress and the most direct way toward artistic singing.

Pronouncements of the American Academy of Teachers of Singing, of the National Association of Teachers of Singing, and recommendations of vocal committees from the Music Educators National Conference, are used as the basis for much of the theory and methods outlined. We are indebted particularly to these organizations, and to the many authors of texts, vocal teachers, and authorities on voice and music education for quotations used and the many ideas obtained. We are indebted also to the large number of publishers of vocal literature who submitted song collections and sheet music for consideration in the recommended materials section, Part III of this textbook.

We have endeavored to include all useful and needed theory and methods about the art and science of singing and the teaching of singing, concentrating the most valuable ideas into one source, plus a great deal of needed organization of information into a usable form heretofore unavailable in any publication. The task has been monumental. The time and effort expended will be well repaid, however, if this vocal course makes possible an adequate training of teachers of singing; develops more and better students of singing; and serves to standardize in considerable measure a profession that long has been seriously confused and handicapped by many conflicting theories of the so-called experts.

The experienced instructor may find some recommended methods or theory in this course contrary to his own opinion or experience. It has been demonstrated conclusively in the field of voice teaching that there is often more than one way of arriving at the same goal. There is certainly no necessity for slavishly following the course outline, theory, and methods recommended if a way is found that works better for the individual instructor. In case of a conflict in views, however, we do urge the teacher to give the method outlined a fair trial.

It is self-evident that comprehensiveness, clarity, and brevity are three worthwhile objectives in a vocal course. Brevity must not be achieved at the expense of clarity and comprehensiveness, however, or the student and inexperienced teacher will be confused and flounder. In a field as broad as the vocal, no single text of even large dimensions could possibly do more than scratch the surface, omitting much needed information and song content or reducing clarity in explanation in order to reduce size and cost. Our aim has been to avoid compromise and superficiality; to organize logically in the necessary number of volumes of reasonable size the content needed; and to avoid wordiness. We have tried to present each phase of singing with sufficient discussion to make ideas clear to both student and inexperienced teacher, using plain language supported by quotations representing authoritative opinion and modern educational philosophy, and reflecting, in general, the most successful current practices. Considerable care has entered into the selection of the most standard and meaningful terminology, and into sufficient explanation of meaning, so that theory involved can be transferred into intelligent action.

Much thought and a great deal of time over a number of years was devoted to the selection of song literature in the two song anthologies in this series. Four criteria were used for selection: (a) Attractiveness to the student and teacher, (b) musical worth, (c) practical suitability and usefulness, and (d) variety in type and mood. Most of the songs have been used successfully and recommended by various authorities and teachers as outstanding for the purpose and level of advancement needed.

A majority of the songs are also favorites of leading concert artists today. They not only fulfill the purpose of being practical and interesting study material but also provide excellent literature for building a permanent basic repertoire. Nearly all songs are appropriate for both sexes. *Song Anthology Volume I* includes simple art songs in English, folk songs, ballads, spirituals, and sacred songs. *Song Anthology Volume II* adds emphasis on the Old Italian, Old English, German Lieder, and French Impressionistic literature, with an introduction to oratorio and opera.

---

[1]Fields, Victor Alexander. "Training the Singing Voice." Kings Crown Press, 1947, p. 1.

NEED FOR A PROFESSIONAL TEXTBOOK

In the past, experienced teachers of class voice and private voice work have organized their own course from many scattered sources of information, supplementing and organizing what they learned from their own teachers and from reading. Inexperienced teachers, especially of class voice, were forced to follow as best they could published texts designed for the student, none complete in much of the information required for proper guidance and vocal progress, none supplemented by a professionalized textbook to further clarify student manual theory and suggest proper teaching methods, and none inclusive of songs needed over a four-year period of study.

It is commonly recognized that standards in the vocal teaching field have been needlessly low and that the crying need is for better-equipped teachers. This condition is often attributed to the fact that no professionalized basic text on organization, educational philosophy, methods, and materials for class or private voice teaching has ever been published which could be used as a complete guide by the individual teacher in the field, or employed as a fundamental text in methods courses on voice teaching in teacher training institutions. It is generally agreed that class voice teaching in the high schools and colleges and vocal methods courses in the colleges have demonstrated inferiority to similar instrumental offerings. It is agreed furthermore that many well equipped and successful teachers of private voice either have been ineffective in teaching class voice or have refused to attempt the undertaking because of lack of specific information on methods to guide them in group teaching technics.

For the first time, inexperienced teachers with adequate private voice study background will find in this complete course the needed detailed information on methods of teaching and vocal theory; as well as vocal exercises and song material required for immediately successful class voice teaching at any level.

There appears little doubt that high school and college class voice work would have been as well developed and generally practiced as instrumental class work if a comprehensive and effective professionalized textbook, correlated with a complete vocal course for the student, had been available for guidance as a basic text in teacher training courses.

As early as 1930 Callan[2] called attention to the lack of a professionalized text in vocal instruction as partially responsible for the fact that class voice instruction had not spread as rapidly as instrumental instruction in the schools. Haywood says, "There is great need for teachers who know the fundamentals of voice culture theories, as well as those who have had experience in singing."[3] In surveying the weakness of class voice teaching in high schools, Lee concludes that there is great need for class voice teachers to obtain methods courses on how to teach voice in the colleges and universities during the summer sessions, and that "Until many schools do offer such a course, there will be few voice teachers adequately equipped to give group instruction in voice."[4]

Since authorities who know the field are in agreement on the foregoing, it is amazing that a comprehensive text for vocal study of the type needed has never been published to meet the long recognized need. This professionalized textbook is intended primarily to achieve these five major objectives:

1. To furnish more detailed explanations and additional vital information on the technics and principles of singing, supplementing the material in *Expressive Singing Volume I* to further assist the ambitious vocal student and the prospective future teacher.

2. To provide a basic professionalized text on vocal production theory and methods of teaching voice for use in teacher education.

3. To provide an invaluable guide to effective teaching for the inexperienced teacher of either class or private voice.

4. To furnish suggestions and compile information that may prove helpful to even the experienced teacher of either class or private voice.

5. To list and classify for study and teaching what authorities consider to be choice solo and duet song literature, both collections and sheet music.

Van A. Christy, Ph.D.
Professor of Music
University of California
Santa Barbara, California

---

[2]Callan, E. J. "High School Voice Classes." School Music, Nov. 1930, p. 14.

[3]Haywood, Frederick. "The Value of Voice Culture classes for Senior High School Students." Etude, April 1929, p. 276.

[4]Lee, M. E. "Voice Classes in the Secondary Schools." Master's Thesis, University of Illinois, 1946, p. 77.

Table of Contents

PART I

TECHNICS IN SINGING AND VOCAL TEACHING APPLIED TO SPECIFIC PROBLEMS

(Correlated Chapter by Chapter with Expressive Singing, Volume I)

PART II
BASIC PRINCIPLES AND METHODS IN SINGING AND VOCAL TEACHING

PART III

SELECT LITERATURE FOR SOLO VOICE AND DUET CLASSIFIED AND GRADED

PART I

TECHNICS IN

SINGING AND VOCAL TEACHING

APPLIED TO SPECIFIC PROBLEMS

Orientation and Guidance

RECOMMENDED TEACHER USE OF THIS VOCAL COURSE

EXPRESSIVE SINGING is a complete vocal course for both students and teachers. To obtain the maximum help from this textbook, teachers are advised first to carefully read the student manual, Volume I, in order to obtain the complete educational philosophy and over-all picture of problems involved. Second, read carefully Lesson 1 of Chapter 1 in Expressive Singing Volume I and then the corresponding lesson and chapter in this volume before starting to teach. It is well for inexperienced teachers to review Part II of this textbook, "Basic Methods and Principles and Methods in Vocal Teaching," from time to time after teaching starts to check methods and refresh the mind concerning fundamental principles.

VALUE

A brief survey of the eight lessons in Expressive Singing, Volume 1, dealing with the various phases of pupil orientation and guidance, will present convincing evidence of the unusual practical value of this chapter to the student and the time and effort it will save the teacher in guiding practice and informing students concerning many important ideas pertinent to vocal study. In spite of the fact that all experienced vocal teachers recognize that attitude and practice guidance are two of the most important elements in teaching singing, previous vocal methods have done little but present a few cursory instructions to students on these vital factors.

*GENERAL ADVICE IN TEACHING CHAPTER 1

Students should realize the unique value of this chapter to their pleasure and success in singing. It is advisable to urge careful reading of each lesson as well as review of lessons involved that are needed most. Assigned readings and written examination over the most pertinent content is sufficient for most

lessons. For obvious reasons, however, two of the lessons of Chapter 1 need much greater initial and continued attention: Lesson 2, "Fear and Self-Consciousness," and Lesson 6, "Practice Guidance." It is advisable not to begin individual practice until after Lesson 6 has been read, discussed, and well understood. Individual topics in some of the lessons other than 2 and 6 may justify some class discussion as well. Subject matter considered most important will be indicated in the following discussion of each lesson in this chapter.

PSYCHOLOGICAL APPROACH TO VOCAL STUDY

Some colleges and most teacher training institutions have beginning voice classes composed almost entirely of those required to take the subject in order to satisfy a degree program. These students may be instrumental music majors, music minors, elementary or kindergarten-primary education majors, or public school music majors required to take a minimum amount of voice for certification in teaching. This program is usually administered in voice class work. For various reasons, many feel inferior vocally, lack confidence, are ill at ease and have an inferiority complex about singing to such an extent that singing efforts are fearful and inhibited. No pleasure and little progress is possible until such attitudes are corrected. From somewhere in an unfortunate early experience, many of these students have gained the impression that solo singing is a difficult, highly complex, theoretical act; that no one can be successful in vocal study unless already possessed of a good singing voice; and that worthwhile achievement and pleasure in singing are impossible without a long theoretical course in vocal training.

---

*It is recommended that the teacher read at this point the material in Part II, p. 140, "Twelve Basic Factors in Creating and Maintaining High Interest and Favorable Attitude."

Although they speak normally and can carry a tune, some have been told by a misguided teacher, or some other source, that they cannot sing or have no voice for singing.

This results in an attitude all too common — a psychological block to progress which must be recognized and corrected immediately in the approach, methods, and songs employed in teaching. An inferiority complex regarding singing, or any other subject, not only will cause a dislike for that subject but also is frequently accompanied by an associative dislike for the instructor. Confidence cannot be developed in such persons by plunging them immediately into technical phases of vocal study, solo singing, or by attempting vocal literature foreign to the student's interest or of considerable range and difficulty. If this is attempted, any interest in singing or chance for pleasure and success is destroyed.

It is most important that the instructor do everything possible to encourage, guide, and give confidence, pleasure and some degree of success in the singing of easy songs together in class as a preliminary step to the formal study of vocal theory, technic, or solo singing. Fearful students are first assured that everyone who can carry a tune and can speak resonantly on a few tones has the nucleus to start development of the singing voice. They are sold first on the proposition that *they can sing, that singing is natural, that singing is fun, and that satisfactory progress is possible.* Most successful teachers of singing agree that the study of singing must be fun or it will be futile.

The orientation information in the eight lessons of this chapter has been virtually neglected heretofore in vocal texts. It will assist the instructor immeasurably in this important task. Even vocal majors with an established interest, confidence, and a good background will gain greatly through an improved awareness of the over-all problems involved, the suggestions regarding practice habits, and the ideas concerning elimination or reduction of fear, selection of a vocal instructor, suggestions on self-guidance, etc. The highly proficient student interested in singing as a career will more than make up for the small amount of time necessary to study the eight lessons, time that could have been spent in intensive technical or song study, and will have the basic information necessary to guide safely all future practice and progress in his chosen career.

Technical study always gains in efficiency when students are made aware first of what they are about and the long range goals involved. Every educator agrees that favorable attitude is prerequisite to a satisfactory degree of success in any subject. It is certainly far more vital in the expressional arts than in ordinary academic subject matter, since the very life of artistic expression depends on free emotional projection and this can occur only through a favorable attitude of confidence and pleasure. *An act of art is an act of love.* The student is led first to like to sing before any significant progress can be expected.

It is highly vital, therefore, that the first lessons in either class or private voice teaching arouse an enthusiastic desire to sing. This can be accomplished best by choosing easy and attractive introductory songs; by *putting the emphasis on natural expression*; by having a brief overview experience with the various types of style and mood in interpretation; and by *building confidence and pleasure in the use of the singing voice,* preferably in a preliminary group experience. This is both psychologically and musically the best orientation into the art and science of singing. The vocal instructor cannot afford to forget that *ability to sing depends first of all upon self confidence and enjoyment.*

EMPHASIS ON EXPRESSION

(Note — See also Chapter 12, "Interpretation," p. 92)

It is necessary above all to emphasize pleasure in natural, free expression in the approach to vocal study, avoiding a technical emphasis or approach. "As a foundation for musical development, attitudes, interests, and directed awareness are worth more than all specifics conceivably obtainable."[1] There is no doubt that emphasis on expression and enjoyment is phychologically sound in the initial stages of vocal study. Neither can emphasis on joy in singing and expressive significance be discarded later for it stimulates and gives purpose to technical study. Without this stimulus drill itself is sterile of progress.

Detailed illustrations of the larynx, pharynx, lungs, etc., are informative and perhaps interesting to the teacher but may be confusing to the student, causing more, rather than less, self-consciousness in the singing act. Consequently, only illustrations of correct and incorrect posture and basic mouth position for vowels are included in Volume I of this course. We agree with Fields that "The study of the physical structures of the larynx and its functions belongs in physiology . . . singing as a form of self-expression demands psychological treatment."[2]

Confident interpretation is the outcome of healthy growth with emphasis on expression. Hesitant response is due usually to consciousness of mechanical technics or other externalistic factors. The influence of desire for expression or interpretation is incalculable in creating enthusiasm for technical study. Without doubt, emphasis on expression is both the psychological approach and the abiding stimulus for

---

[1]Mursell, James L. "Music in American Schools." Silver Burdett and Co., 1943, p. 58.

[2]Fields, Victor Alexander. "Training the Singing Voice." Kings Crown Pres, 1947, p. 123.

natural and correct technical controls. Beginning students therefore should be oriented into the primary importance and function of expression as the fundamental goal and guiding factor in all following theoretical and technical study. *The only vital way to do this is through the song approach.*

"The idea that one first builds a voice and then studies the singing of songs indicates a thorough lack of understanding the process of learning and art and, in the end, inhibits creative expression. With inexperienced singers a few vocalises are appropriate for various aspects of building a lovely voice but here, in turn, they should be applied immediately to the singing of songs."[3] Lawrence Tibbett recommends that interpretation and vocal techniques should be learned simultaneously: "It is inconceivable that one could first learn to sing the notes of a song and then graft a layer of 'interpretation' over them. . . I am inclined to approach the entire question of study from the interpretive rather than the purely vocal standpoint."[4]

Helpful interpretive suggestions on all songs concerning the basic factors of style, mood, and tonal color, and specific hints on expression are included to assist the student and teacher as a valuable part of the two Song Anthologies accompanying this course. It is hoped that these suggestions will be studied carefully before singing the song involved.

THE SONG APPROACH

Motivation factors are the most important in the initial stages of training the singer. Student interest and natural love of expression are impelling forces that can be utilized best through emphasis on the expressional qualities of well-chosen and presented songs. The best advice that can be given to those who wish to maintain a high level of interest, as well as maximum progress in singing, is to *use a song, or songs, from the first day on in each normal class period.* The "Song Approach" stimulates both the technical and creative abilities of students. Alfred Spouse states the philosophy of the "Song Approach" most strikingly: "Here the song is the thing from start to finish. Its proponents ask, why waste time on any drill whatever, until a problem is confronted in the actual song being studied. For instance, as interesting an artist as is before the American public today, Louis Graveure, says that if he had a coloratura soprano to whom he wished to assign agility study, he would take a cadenza containing the particular problem from some great aria, and use that as an exercise. When it is mastered, the student has learned something which she would have to study anyhow; whereas if she studied pages of vocalises, when she had mastered them, she would still have the cadenza in the aria to learn."[5]

Many successful teachers and singers agree with the foregoing viewpoint. "Avoid the traditional voice-lesson procedure for exercises, vocalises, and then songs. . . . When a song presents a difficulty, develop an exercise which will help to overcome the difficulty."[6] The beginning singer first should be allowed to sing "Before he is bewildered by counsels and methods."[7] "Singing should be taught by the whole rather than by part methods. This means a minimum of local action techniques and a maximum of singing songs involving the whole coordinations of the physical instrument."[8] "Experience . . . . in my own studies and in those of my students has convinced me of the value of presenting each new principal of singing by means of a portion of some standard song rather than through the comparative abstraction of a mere exercise."[9] "We should develop the voice in and through actual song material. The intense and careful study of worthy song material is the best and most central means of good voice building, which means making musical voices, and through them, musical students."[10] "There are no special practice rules. Use the material at hand. A musical phrase or extract from an aria or lyric will provide excellent practice material for exercising the voice."[11]

The often-quoted statement of great philosopher and educator, John Dewey, "We learn by doing," applies to study of singing. *The best way to learn to sing is to practice singing songs.* No separate exercises, no study or knowledge about physical function can do more than exercise the instrument, verify, and explain. They cannot substitute for basic psychological expressional controls. The right kind of fundamental exercises should be used by most students, but their use is supplementary rather than primary to actual song singing. Normally a well-balanced and coordinated use of songs and exercises is employed, with songs receiving by far the greater emphasis.

Music educators and leading voice class exponents, as well as most private voice teachers, no longer

---

[3]Wilson, Harry Robert. "Establishing the Resonance." Choral and Organ Guide, Feb. 1952, Vol. 5, p. 18.

[4]Tibbet, Lawrence. "There Is No Open-Sesame." (an interview) Etude, 1940, Vol. 58, p. 820.

[5]Spouse, Alfred. "Voice Classes in the Senior High School." Music Supervisors Journal, Feb. 1930, p. 57.

[6]Wilson, Harry Robert. "The Solo Singer." Carl Fisher, 1941, Vol. 1, p. 5.

[7]Castagna, Bruna. "Good Singing Must Be Natural." (an interview) Etude, 1939, Vol. 57, p. 159.

[8]Witherspoon, Herbert. "Thirty-Six Lessons in Singing for Teachers and Students." Meisner Institute of Music, 1930, p. 14.

[9]Waters, Crystal. "Song, the Substance of Vocal Study." G. Schirmer, Inc., 1930. p. 1.

[10]Murrsell, James and Glenn, Maybelle. "The Psychology of School Music Teaching." Silver Burdett & Co., 1931, p. 281.

[11]Anderson, Marion. "Some Reflections on Singing." (an interview) Etude, 1939, Vol. 57, p. 631.

subscribe to the Mechanistic Theory that a student must spend months or years in perfecting technical controls on vocal exercises before it is safe to allow singing of a song. There is still a remaining residue of this traditional concept, but it is pure educational nonsense and does not stand up under critical examination or in practice. Students will make many mistakes in the early singing of songs, but they are not fatal or necessarily injurious. If they were, all voices would be ruined in public school music singing long before formal vocal study began. Why should there suddenly be a different educational philosophy about the safe use of the voice when formal study does start? It is the same singer with the same throat and same interests and emotional reactions. Modern educational philosophy and experience in the past indicate that the student will advance most rapidly and normally if interest is first kept high through song singing with emphasis on expression, while mistakes and weaknesses are pointed out and technics developed gradually, as they need to be, for correcting and strengthening production.

It is expected that technics in each song and exercise bear some fruit in progress at once, but authorities agree that it requires further practice and study, perhaps years, to perfect them. Vocal training, like all other education, is a developmental process which progresses most rapidly through experience in doing to the best of the student's ability and understanding at the time. In this developmental process, *the wise teacher will use easy, interesting song material as the most important source for developing technic itself.* It would be possible to dispense with separate exercises entirely if exactly the right song material, or excerpts from songs, were readily available to increase technic progressively. However, this is difficult and not considered as practical for most teachers as the use of a limited number of carefully-chosen exercises to supplement song literature, such as the exercises in the last chapter of Volume I, Expressive Singing.

THE MECHANISTIC VIEWPOINT

A statement in a thesis on class voice training by a candidate for an advanced degree in one of our leading universities illustrates a viewpoint still prevalent, unfortunately, by a lingering minority regarding the best way to teach voice. "Just before the close of the first semester, the student is given a chance to sing the other vowels." (Note — The class had been confined previously for the whole semester to exclusive practice on the vowel *Ah.*) While this is, no doubt, an extreme example, it illustrates a fundamentally unsound educational policy which still lingers in voice teaching.

To take the viewpoint in voice training, or any other type of applied music study, that we must begin with the most fundamental step, perfect it before moving on to the next, etc., is known as the

Mechanistic System in education. It has long been discarded in favor of the Developmental Method by educators in other fields and, more recently, by modern music educators. "Mechanistic teaching deliberately stresses the routines, although it is as clear as day that any real efficiency depends on getting away from them . . . . it assumes that each lesson in a series is learned to the point of mastery. Obviously this does not happen in fact, and most teachers do not even seriously try to make it happen. But beyond this, it could not happen anyhow."[12]

In practice the Mechanistic Theory falls down immediately in the process of voice teaching because teachers do not, and probably never will agree, on what the most fundamental step is and what the progressive order of successive steps should be. It is a false philosophy in learning because there is no order of difficulty which is the same for all students, and the human mind responds best to the psychological rather than the logical approach. Those who wish further information on this basic problem are urged to read Chapter I of the Mursell text cited in the foregoing quotation.

The Mechanistic System is still followed, at least in part, by a considerable number of vocal teachers, however. Most of them, as a result, inevitably discourage a large number of students, with a resulting high mortality in dropping vocal study and a permanent destruction of joy and enthusiasm in singing. Unfortunately, the evil effects are not confined to the poor and average students, but affect the able and highly talented as well.

EMPHASIS ON AN OVERVIEW OF VARIOUS EXPRESSIONAL STYLES

Closely allied to emphasis on expression and for quite similar basic educational reasons, is an early overview experience with various typical styles, moods, and tonal colors employed in singing, using the easiest available song material for the purpose. This procedure not only emphasizes the vital importance of expression and makes the study of singing more enjoyable, but also gives the student a needed early orientation into fundamental styles and tonal colors involved in singing. It furnishes a few "Basic Type Songs" which may be employed in the future as models for style in interpretation on all song literature. Overview in style not only is desirable psychologically, to create a greater interest and awareness in the art of singing and a desire to master fundamental technics needed in expression, but also furnishes a basic and much needed musical and intellectual background for all future interpretation. After these "Basic Type Songs" are studied in the manner suggested, students certainly have had re-

---

[12]Mursell, James L. "Education for Musical Growth." Ginn and Co., 1948, pp. 14-17.

vealed to them the necessity for greater technic in inproving expression and the basic areas in which improvement is needed. They are then ready to work for it with more enthusiasm and purpose toward more definite and well-understood goals. In comparison with these values, the fact that students can be expected to sing the florid type song inadequately, and the dramatic song and those requiring extremely bright or dark tone quality with more tension than easier lyric material with normal tone color, is of minor importance.

The following six "Basic Model Songs," selected for overview purpose from EXPRESSIVE SINGING, Song Anthology Volume I, are all easy enough so that beginning classes, although technically inadequate on some, nevertheless, with the instructor's help and example, can be successful in achieving the overview and in obtaining "Song Models" for guidance in interpretation of most future vocal literature. It is suggested that the "Basic Songs" be studied and sung in the following order during the time that the first six lessons in Chapter I, Orientation and Guidance, are being studied and discussed:

1. Drink to Me Only with Thine Eyes (Old English), p. 42. (Legato lyric style with normal tone color)

2. All Through the Night (Welsh Air), p. 143. (Legato sostenuto style with dark tone color)

3. Passing By — Edward Purcell, p. 54. (Legato lyric style with bright tone color)

4. Mister Banjo (Creole Folk, p. 155. (Light accented lyric style with bright tone color)

5. The Miller of Dee (Seventeenth Century English Air), p. 134. (Accented robusto dramatic style with dark tone color)

6. The Old Woman and the Peddler (English Folk-Ballad), p. 116. (Narrative lyric legato style with normal tone color)

To complete the survey of song styles, it is suggested that classes having access to sufficient copies of EXPRESSIVE SINGING, Song Anthology Volume II, also sing a seventh type of "Basic Song," "Love Has Eyes" — Bishop, p. 5, featuring florid lyric staccato style with bright tone color.

After having been sung in order in a number of previous periods, it is suggested that these "Basic Model Songs" quickly be reviewed in one or two lessons following Lesson 6 so that the great variety in production style and tone color be thoroughly impressed before undertaking other songs of a similar style. It is recommended that most beginning students make no attempt to study more extensively and memorize the more difficult of these songs, numbers 5 and 7, until later, after technic is more secure. Since these songs are intended to be introductory, they can be taught quickly and effectively to achieve only their overview of style purpose. The remaining part of the first semester can be devoted chiefly to easy lyric legato songs requiring, on the whole, neither very bright nor very dark tone color and no great extremes of dynamics. *Vocal authorities concur that easy legato songs should form the backbone of vocal literature for beginning study.*

ORDER OF LESSONS

Actually, after the first two lessons in Chapter 1 on "Orientation and Guidance," and Chapter 2 on "Posture," it does not appear to be a serious consideration which of the next three chapters comes first in the order of study. In fact, instructors and texts on voice disagree considerably on the logic of order desired in the various topics to be studied. Truth of the matter is that posture, breath control, tone, and diction (the technical foundations for singing) are so inextricably allied and coordinated in the act of singing that full understanding and correct use in one involves understanding and skill in the others. Howerton states in this regard: "Each (factor) has its role to play and must have its proper development. Each, however, must be developed in relation to the others, and the various integrants must. be developed simultaneously."[13]

Frequent review by the student of past lesson content, and reference at times to ideas in more advanced chapters than those yet covered, is therefore a necessity for best understanding and growth. For example, students should refer to Chapter 16 in Expressive Singing Volume I as soon as the teacher is ready for them to start vocalises. It is important that much of the information in the three chapters on Interpretation, Stage Deportment, and Memorization in the latter part be read and used as soon as the pupil starts independent memorization and solo singing.

It is recommended that the study and practice of Chapter 2, Posture, be started almost immediately, and that the eight lessons in Chapter I accompany the study of Posture and Breath Control which follow. It is not necessary to follow the exact order of chapter or lesson as listed, if the teacher prefers another order. The various chapters are arranged by the author, after consultation with a number of experienced vocal teachers, in the sequence generally preferred. It was found impossible to maintain both the most preferred order in chapter headings and in the content of the various lessons which belong logically under the chapter headings, however. It is recommended therefore, in some instances, that certain lessons in some chapters be delayed until study of later chapters has been completed. For order of lessons preferred by the author, see "Outline of a Four Year Vocal Course," pp. 191-196.

---

[13]Howerton, George. "Technic and Style in Choral Singing." Carl Fischer, Inc., 1957, p. 3.

Students should read ahead of class discussion, covering all the vocal theory content in Expressive Singing, Volume I, on their own initiative as soon as possible, for the sake of a clear orientation into total problems involved and to locate information to which they may need to refer. It is also important for students who desire complete information and understanding of problems involved to supplement information in Volume I with that provided by the correlated materal in this professionalized textbook, Volume II. Obviously, the serious student of voice, even in the beginning stages of study, should either own, or have ready access to, Volume II through the school library or the vocal studio.

COMPARATIVE TIME TO SPEND ON LESSONS

Time devoted to any particular lesson before progressing to the next depends upon a number of factors. These include comparative importance; difficulty; comparative proficiency of the class, student, or teacher; amount of time devoted to supplementary exercises and song material; and size of the class. There are so many variable factors that no cut and dried rule can be given. Some lessons are so important that several periods are required before enough understanding and gain are achieved to warrant continuance. Other lessons can be covered quite adequately by assigned reading and short discussion in one period.

It is well to remember that *only a working grasp, and not perfection, should be expected before advancing to the next lesson.* Progressive teachers today agree that it is a mistaken idea that a song or exercise must be done perfectly, or nearly so, before progressing further. Lessons should be done as well as possible at the time, mistakes and weaknesses noted, and higher standards set for future achievement, as the principles that are involved are reviewed from time to time and technic strengthens from usage. The important objective is further refinement of ideas and technics in additional song material as they are supplemented and coordinated with new concepts.

It is generally agreed, however, that *basic understandings, a workable knowledge and some technical gain must be established before progressing to successive lessons;* otherwise time that has been spent is wasted and only superficial learning at best will result. Actually, various chapters that relate to tone production are so closely interrelated that it is impossible to understand thoroughly and master the technics involved in one until a number of other chapters also are covered. "A knowledge of the various processes involved in singing is like a disjointed skeleton until their interrelation is understood."[14] It is vital that functional ideas of each lesson be carried over into successive lessons until

technics involved are coordinated and mastered thoroughly. *Thus for such basic technics as breath control, legato, and beauty and freedom of tonal production, emphasis will continue in all future practice and singing toward ever-higher standards of perfection.*

SUGGESTED SONGS

(*Note — See also pp. 167 and 211-216*)

Selection of improper vocal material can do irreparable harm to immature voices. It is agreed that, in most cases, beginners are restricted in range and lack power and resonance, while breath control and physical endurance are weak. Gradual physical development is a corollary to vocal growth for the high school age student and is a vital factor at the college age level in many instances. It is therefore important to choose songs judicially for beginners in regard to range, length of phrase, and dramatic requirements. Choosing songs for the individual pupil's repertoire ought to be a cooperative matter between the student and the instructor. "Guided supervision in the choice of song repertoire is to be advised rather than slavish dependence upon the teacher's choice."[15]

Carefully-chosen folk songs or ballads are ideal beginning material for most students. No great power or beauty of voice is necessary but, through this medium, the singer most easily can develop desirable basic technics and qualities of naturalness and directness often lacking on the concert platform. Emphasis is on telling the story of the text with clear articulation, natural, unforced tone, and good intonation — all basic fundamentals for later singing of art song literature. Actually, choice folk songs with imaginatively arranged piano accompaniments are superior musically to many art songs. They well deserve their traditional place at the end of concert programs of outstanding artists.

After folk songs, "The old classic music with its great demands upon the musical knowledge of the singer, and its lesser physical demands, affords the best medium for study and development, with the least danger of forcing the voice."[16] The young singer is advised to study the Old Italian, Old English and classic literature before attempting the more dramatic works of the later composers, opera, or oratorio. "In fact, no works of intensity should be attempted until the voice is thoroughly trained and developed and inured to hard work by much practice."[17]

---

[14]Vennard, William. "Singing, the Mechanism and the Technic," Edwards Brothers, 1950.

[15]California-Western Music Educators Conference Curriculum Committee. "Voice Training in Classes." Music Educators Journal, May-June, 1945, p. 40.

[16]Witherspoon, Herbert, "Singing." G. Schirmer, Inc., 1925, p. 49.

[17]Ibid, p. 49.

A number of songs, which may be sung either as solos or in two parts, are included in each of the Song Anthologies of this vocal course. Duets are not only attractive program material and interesting to students, but also provide the basic training for skill in ensemble singing. They are an easy preliminary to solo singing which many students welcome. One or two duets may normally be allowed to substitute for solo song requirements during the semester. It is desirable for every soloist to become also a skilled ensemble singer. Excellent ensemble singing demands everything tonally and technically that solo singing does, furnishing, in addition, training in musicianship factors of blend and balance that soloists need sooner or later. Unison singing is the foundation of two-part singing, and skill in two-part singing is basic to singing in many parts.

In intermediate and advanced classes it is well, when time allows, to assign particular students to carefully-selected music in trios, quartets, quintets, etc., which they may prepare, receive help in class on interpretation, and do in recitals. This greatly enriches the interest and musical value of solo voice training. *In all duet and ensemble work particular attention is given to the factors of blend, balance, and intonation.* Since none of the duets in the first song volume of this course range beyond the average voice, it is suggested that voice classes divide equally on the parts, with only the very low or high voices definitely assigned each time to the part which best fits their range. Low and high parts can be alternated from song to song for the average student.

Certain specific songs are suggested at the end of each lesson in Expressive Singing, Volume I. Personal experience has indicated that these songs are particularly appropriate at the time to correlate with the lesson. It is not necessary however for the instructor to follow the order of songs suggested if other songs, which serve the purpose equally well or better at the time, are preferred. In any case, classes and individual pupils progress at different rates and vary in ability, making considerable variation from any printed lesson scheme sometimes desirable.

Song literature in the two anthologies has been tested thoroughly and proven highly interesting and beneficial to most students. That mistakes and weaknesses in technic and undesirable tonal tension will occur in class singing of even the easy song material provided is inevitable for beginning students. This is not of serious consequence in a long range view, however, since technic is developmental in any approach and many mistakes will be made. The highly important factors in studying singing are: first, that the student enjoy the process, and second, that mistakes are recognized, some progress achieved, and a way for further improvement be evidenced.

TIME TO START THE FOUR BASIC EXERCISES FOR VOCAL DEVELOPMENT

(Note — See p. 126)

The Four Basic Exercises for Vocal Development given in Chapter 16 of Volume I may be started in the warm-up procedure (after two or three lessons) if desired, although it is suggested that they be delayed until after several songs have been sung. Each exercise has been suggested for practice at the end of the particular lesson where we have usually found it appropriate to be introduced. They may be started sooner than suggested, however, providing the instructor is sufficiently experienced to explain briefly, and illustrate plainly, the correct production desired.

Lesson I.   You Can Sing

(See Volume I, p. 1)

In studying this lesson, it is suggested that brief class discussion be held about the topics, "The Truth About Who Can Sing," and "Directions for Using This Vocal Course."

AN OPTIMISTIC ATTITUDE IMPORTANT

The importance of establishing an optimistic attitude, confidence, and dispelling inferiority complexes, which many students have about singing, need not be "sold" to the music educator. This lesson in the Volume I provides the initial step in the right direction. It must be followed by teaching methods designed to provide the pupil with confidence and pleasure in individual singing. By using very easy, attractive songs in the beginning, building confidence through ensemble class singing, and employing short phrases or parts of songs before whole songs are attempted by the individual, fearful students are led by natural and easy stages to success.

Experienced vocal teachers are generally agreed that neither beautiful singing of songs nor free, correct, tonal production is likely until the student has the attitude that singing is fun. "Effective singing must be associated with pleasant emotion."[18] Scott declares that the best singing results "From the sheer joy of singing."[19] Fields also emphasizes that "Carefree attitudes are more conducive to natural, spontaneous vocal release than are meticulous techniques; or the conscious manipulation of breathing and vocal muscles; or the planned 'placing' of each tone . . . . optimal vocal conditions for singing can be induced by first promoting right thinking and feeling conditions in the student."[20]

---

[18]Mursell, James L. "The Psychology of Music." W. W. Norton, 1937, p. 229.

[19]Scott, Charles Kennedy. "Word and Tone." J. M. Dent & Sons, 1933, Vol. 1, p. 126.

[20]Op. cit. p. 64.

Many students, especially instrumentalists, believe that they have a poor vocal instrument and it is therefore a waste of time to study voice. It is vital that this defeatist attitude be corrected. Actually, quality of the vocal instrument is apparently not nearly as important in singing as knowledge of its proper use and musical imagination, according to most authorities. Negus states, "Of two human beings one will possess a far better voice than the other, although both are apparently equally well equipped anatomically."[21]

APPRAISING VOCAL POTENTIALITIES

It is unwise for a teacher to be dogmatic about a first impression of the limitations of beginning voices. Douglas Stanley says, "Every healthy vocal apparatus can, theoretically be trained to produce tones which have formerly been thought to be the special characteristic of only 'great natural voices.' "[22] Amazing development and change often occur with proper practice and mastery of technic, providing the student has persistence, intelligence, and satisfactory native music capacity. This is especially true of bigger, dramatic, or heroic voices that often at first exhibit short range, poor breath control, a rough, breathy quality and out-of-tune production. It may give the vocal instructor pause to realize that some of the greatest singers of all time, including Caruso, were told by teachers of the highest reputation that their instrument was too poor to contemplate a professional career. It is impossible to estimate the myriad others wtih potential greatness who have been discouraged mistakenly.

On the other hand, the voice teacher dare not lean too far in the other direction. He should be realistic and honest with all students or he is subject to the justifiable criticism of being a charlatan. He could be accused of being more interested in the money concerned, or in the size and popularity of his classes, than in guiding the hopelessly weak and natively lacking in talent into some more rewarding pursuit before valuable time, energy, and money have been wasted. In actual practice, only exceptionally talented pupils with attractive personality, persistence, vital health, and high ability for learning songs and the principles of singing reasonably can hope to reach highest professional standards. All normal students can benefit from the study of singing, however.

While amazing growth and improvement is possible in muscular strength and coordination, physiological studies reveal that, for an adult, the structural instrument does not change. One has a fine, average, or poor vocal instrument for singing and there is no structural growth or improvement through practice. "So far as voice training is concerned, providing the vocal mechanism is normal, the improvement in voice therefrom is almost wholly neuro-

muscular. No structural changes are wrought in the larynx as the result of training."[23]

After a few months of vocal training and contact with the pupil as a personality, the signs of hopeless weakness should be fairly conclusive. The conscientious and honest teacher will then have the integrity to notify the pupil of this fact.

Lesson 2. Fear or Self-Consciousness
(See Volume I, p. 5)

It is well to emphasize the importance of this entire lesson to the student's future success. It does very little good just to read and agree with the psychology outlined: *the principles recommended in Expressive Singing, Volume I are to be adopted by the student and followed persistently to guarantee reduction or elimination of fear.*

ELIMINATION OR REDUCTION OF FEAR VITAL TO SUCCESS

Shaw declares that "It is the general experience of teachers of singing that fear, in the mind of the student . . . . is the greatest and most persistent obstacle to overcome. . . . The first requirement of the teacher is to eliminate this apalling and almost universal sense of fear."[24] The first and often the greatest problem facing the voice teacher in beginning voice work is establishment of confidence and pleasure in singing. "Mentally, the singer must have an inner calmness, confidence and self-control."[25] *This means reduction of fear until it no longer exists in a degree sufficient to cause rigid tensions in the control muscles of singing.* Since fear is often the cause of tension, it is evident that elimination of rigidity or undue tension is frequently a basic psychological, and not a physiological, problem. We can be absolutely certain that few, if any students, will enjoy singing publicly until fear is reduced to the point of pleasant excitement, and as a result they can experience success, pleasure, and promise of satisfactory progress in singing.

CLASS PROCEDURE SUPERIOR FOR REDUCING FEAR

The class situation is the best possible laboratory in which the student can learn to reduce or eliminate fear. Frequent appearances as a regular

---

[21]Negus, V. E. "The Mechanism of the Larynx." C. V. Mosley Co., 1929, p. 437.

[22]Stanley, Douglas. "Your Voice." Pitman Publishing Corp., 1945, p. 52.

[23]Anderson, Virgil. "Training the Speaking Voice." Oxford U. Press, 1942, p. 10.

[24]Shaw, W. Warren. "Modern Trends in Voice Class Instruction." Music Educators National Conference Yearbook, 1936, Vol. 29, p. 217.

[25]Peterson, Paul W. "Natural Singing and Expressive Conducting." John F. Blair, 1955, p. 12.

part of class routine eventually give the student the necessary poise and ease for public performance. It is a common observance of music critics that products of voice class work usually demonstrate much greater ease and poise in recital than do comparable students from private studios. Many private teachers recognize this fact and arrange to have their students meet regularly in recitals for one another in order that they can gain the necessary experience in performance before others.

Lesson 3. Technic, Musicianship, and a Broad Education

(*See Volume I, p. 7*)

Content in the lesson title above is covered adequately in the Volume I. The development of technic is necessary. Its relation to emphasis on pleasure and confidence has been discussed previously. (Note — See also discussion on p. 17)

Although improving, the vocal teaching field is still shamefully infested with quacks. There are those who claim to have some magical or mystical secret, or system, and who neglect emphasis on sound training in expression, musicianship and technic for some cure-all system of vocal gymnastics or direct physical manipulation of the tongue, larynx, hyoglossus muscle, etc. There can be no quick or quack system of learning to sing, or developing musianship and a high degree of technical proficiency. The facts prove that it is a long and difficult road at best. The wise and conscientious teacher will tell pupils the truth and point out the safest and most direct road. Short-cuts are few and always the result of common sense method, not some magical or secret system, or technical formula for success. The conscientious teacher of either class or private voice cannot fail to strongly advise students of the value of a broad college education as the best basis for success in both life and the art of singing.

Lesson 4. Health and Physique

(*See Volume I, p. 11*)

Of paramount importance to the singer is vital health, a vigorous coordinated physique, and desirable hygienic habits. A physician's advice is needed in some instances, for significant vocal progress is impossible for pupils whose vitality and endurance are woefully weak. Primary responsibility for improving health and vitality weaknesses belongs to the student, who must practice proper health habits and corrective vocal and physical exercises. The New York Singing Teachers Association recommends that "Body building exercises should be practiced *apart* from singing."[26]

Careful reading of this lesson in the student manual by students, a brief class discussion, and

individual conference and advice with particular students needing help, are necessary for proper guidance.

Lesson 5. Self-Guidance

(*See Volume I, p. 16*)

This lesson is a great time saver on the road to mastery of singing if students will read carefully and follow the advice faithfully. Sound recommendations on many phases of singing and practice will enable pupils to promote their own progress effectively.

The teacher is obligated, first of all, to make clear the vital importance of self-discipline and to point out that, to a considerable extent, progress and success in singing depend upon personal responsibility by the student. An important factor is that students recognize the high value of recording to check on how the voice sounds, and the mirror to check on posture, facial expression, excessive visible tension, and appearance. When possible, students should purchase their own tape recording machines and use them often. It is strongly advised that they be taught in class how to use them effectively. Every effort should be made to have the vocal studio, or classroom, and pupil practice rooms equipped with full length mirrors, and to have a good tape recorder, not only in the classroom but also elsewhere in the school for student use. Some school libraries supply recorders for student use.

Lesson 6. Practice Guidance

(*See Volume I, p. 23*)

This lesson in Volume I is of paramount importance to all students and is also a valuable time saver for the teacher. Extra time during class periods given to discussion, clarification, and illustration of some of the topics will be well repaid in more efficient student practice. Students are urged not only to read this lesson carefully in the beginning but also to review some of the content from time to time.

PRACTICE HABITS

Proper practice habits are among the most vital objectives in vocal study for safe and rapid technical progress. The voice will "make or break" according to whether or not safe practice routine is established. Many promising voices are ruined, or fail even to approach their potentialities for progress, because of improper or ineffective practice habits. Many otherwise excellent vocal instructors achieve only mediocre results because they fail to guide and

---

[26]New York Singing Teachers Asociation. "Its Story." Theodore Presser, 1928, p. 29.

supervise student practice properly. *Proper practice guidance is one of the "musts" for success in vocal teaching.*

The teacher is obligated to ascertain that the student not only knows when and how to practice effectively but also to make sure that he is doing so by checking each student in class and studio. It is important that warm-up and practice routines employed in class be the model for student use when practicing alone. Establishment of safe and habitually correct routine in practice without doubt is one of the most important factors in success, and the one point most often neglected by instructors.

A large percentage of successful vocal teachers believe that *practice alone might impede growth or actually be injurious until after the student has acquired a correct tonal concept in the studio or class lesson.* "The beginning student cannot practice alone,"[27] declares Clippinger, since his concepts of free production and tone are as yet indefinite and unformed. . . . "Therefore, he will be strengthening his wrong habits."[27] Wilson qualifies this idea somewhat believing "It is the duty of the teacher to establish habits immediately that will enable the student to practice by himself."[28] It is agreed the student should be cautioned that *frequent short periods of practice are preferable to extended sessions for a number of reasons.*

It appears preferable not to allow a student to vocalize alone until it seems as if he can do so without undoing what has been done for him in supervised class or private instruction. With most beginning classes, individual practice could not start safely before four to six weeks have passed. Even then, there will probably be some pupils who should be requested to refrain until they can demonstrate to the instructor that it is safe to allow practice alone. *No individual practice at all is better than incorrect practice which can only further habitualize fault.*

Practical factors such as age, health, physical vitality and endurance of the vocal organ, home requirements, and amount of study on other subjects enter into consideration when recommending individual frequency and amount of practice. "Another contributing factor to the deterioration of voices is the desire nowadays to master difficult accomplishments with a minimum of time and effort."[29] Young singers frequently injure or ruin the youthful freshness and beauty of their instrument either by impatience in attempting to force progress beyond technical limitations at the time, or by persistent attempts to imitate the tonal volume and timbre of the instructor or an artist with mature voice, who may be their ideal.

FOUR FUNDAMENTAL WAYS FOR GUIDING PRACTICE

The vocal instructor is limited to four fundamental ways in which he can guide a student to free, beautiful, and emotionally expressive production in singing. He can only tell students:

1. How they should think.
2. How they should feel.
3. How they should sound.
4. How they should practice.

Wise guidance in how to practice is by no means the least of these. If this is not undertaken other values will be lessened in effect or destroyed.

THE WARM-UP

It is urged that teachers be careful to illustrate correct warm-up practices and principles during class warm-up vocalises, and *insist that students follow the same procedure when practicing alone.* Directions given in Volume I for this lesson, particularly under the topics, "Ten Commandments for Vocal Practice" and "Technical Control," together with instructions and specific suggestions in connection with Chapter 16, "Four Basic Exercises for Vocal Development," present most of the ideas the inexperienced teacher needs in order to have efficient warm-up procedures. They are the fundamental core for student guidance in practicing for technic.

After the principles of the two basic exercises in Chapter 16 on "The Long Tone" and "The Scale" have been studied and practiced successfully in class, many periods may well normally begin with a short 5 to 10 minutes of warm-up exercises previous to song singing. The arpeggio and combination exercises can soon be added. Students themselves usually will request a warm-up period previous to singing songs after they discover that it functions very much like oil on machinery; it makes the technic of singing following songs easier, expression improved, and, therefore, more pleasurable.

HEARING AND FEELING AS GUIDES

We must admit, for the practical purposes of singing, that we are completely dependent upon our sensations (hearing and feeling) to perfect our instrument."[30] Some teachers and singers claim that the initial training of the singer should be confined exclusively to sound sensations, while a smaller group maintains that feeling sensations are even more important. Most authorities hold the sensation of hearing is the primary guide; however, the role of feeling is secondary but, nevertheless, important in singing.

---

[27]Clippinger, David. "The Human Instrument." Etude, 1929, Vol. 47, p. 212.
   [28]Wilson, Harry R. "The Solo Singer." Carl Fischer, 1941, Vol. 1, p. 5.
   [29]Litante, Judith. "A Natural Approach to Singing." Wm. C. Brown Co., 1959, p. 6.
   [30]Roma, Lisa. "The Science and Art of Singing." G. Schirmer, Inc., 1956, p. 35.

A singer can progress technically and artistically only as discrimination is improved in the two senses that function in singing-hearing and feeling. Neither is a reliable guide for the beginning student, but since they are the only guides, the quicker discriminations can be developed, improved, and habituated, the quicker progress is made. *Progress is in direct proportion to development in these two senses.*

It is vital for satisfactory progress to impress on students that one of their major objectives is learning to hear themselves as others hear their production, and to refine continually their tonal concepts from within. In initial stages, pupils have to depend on the judgment of their teacher and recordings to determine when tone is best. *This superior tone should be analyzed in reference both to how it sounds and to what feeling sensations accompany it.* Only then can it be habituated in practice.

INVERTED HEARING

A beginning student is obliged to accept the fact that it is necessary to depend on the instructor for guidance. He cannot depend on his own ear in initial development since hearing of the singer is largely through the eustachian tube and inner ear and, because the instrument is a part of him, he may hear inverted, i.e., the tone which sounds best to him actually sounds worst to the listener and vice versa. *Acuteness and accuracy of hearing their own production varies greatly from student to student.* In any case, after the student has made tonal development under the guidance of the teacher, *he must analyze the sound and feeling sensations involved and make every effort to remember and duplicate the effect when practicing alone.* Rapidity of advancement depends absolutely upon aptness in this respect.

RATIONALIZATION AS A GUIDE

We cannot rationalize from the experience of any one great teacher or great singer and use their recommended vocal method as safe for the average student. For example, some artists recommend warm-up on soft dynamics and a certain vowel, while others, equally successful, recommend that the warm-up should always be a vigorous *forte* with an entirely different vowel. The only conclusion that can be drawn from such conflicting statements and practices regarding many technical matters is that some highly successful singers have succeeded in spite of their method, or that the method used was best adapted in each case to the particular individual and type of voice. The latter conclusion seems more reasonable in the majority of cases. Actually, it is desirable that both loud and soft singing be practiced but always within the limits of safe technic. Exclusive use of either loud or soft singing will lead to one-sided development. *The pupil is advised to find the dynamics and range at which he sings with the best quality and emphasize that at the beginning of each practice period.*

COMMONLY EXPERIENCED FEELING SENSATIONS

This vocal course is unique in that it emphasizes consistently the common associative feeling sensations which the student should experience as one of the two basic guides in judging production. Establishment of the "Tonal Sensations" and "Posture Sensations" described in the Expressive Singing, Volume I for this lesson is fundamental to future progress. Students are urged to read and review this section until it is understood thoroughly and the feeling sensations described are established. They are common, communicable feeling sensations which most students and skilled singers report experiencing when tone is best. They are not unique to individuals and, therefore, *should be standard objectives in practice.* Descriptions are couched carefully in simple, non-technical terms that will generally be within pupil experience and understanding.

Because of the great difference in sensivity and reaction between individuals, however, there is no guarantee that all students will experience some of the sensations described, or experience them as soon, or in such pronounced degree as others, especially in regard to balanced resonance. Nevertheless commonly-experienced sensations should be a basic objective of all students, unless the student concerned is already producing a free, resonant, balanced tone, and does not experience the common resonance sensation, as sometimes happens. In that case the student may be told to forget the whole matter and go ahead with whatever thought and feeling sensations he happens to have, since they are obviously effective.

Silva makes the following observations regarding feeling sensations. "While singing we can feel distinctly, and more strongly than the vibrations of the vocal cords, the phenomena of internal resonance, namely, the sonorous vibrations of the various parts of the resonant apparatus of the voice; and we can also distinctly feel certain muscular contractions of the vocal organ. All these sensations can serve as legitimate aids for the training of voice during the study of singing. By means of judicious control of these sensations the singer can verify the results of control which he exercises over his own voice chiefly through the sense of hearing."[31]

"Students learn best in the actual doing. More often than not they are hazy about even clear explanations until they have actually experienced the

---

[31]Silva, Giulo. "Advice to Beginners in Singing." G. Schirmer, Inc., 1917, pp. 11-12.

proper sensations personally."[32] Many students have more trustworthy feeling than hearing sensations, especially in the initial stages of study, and can develop more rapidly in the technic of free tonal production if attention is given to establishment of proper feeling associations. If both the student and teacher had the musical taste and ear of the artist, neither of which is common, the voice no doubt could be controlled successfully entirely by concepts of sound. Those possessed of only mediocre musical discrimination and sensitivity in hearing nevertheless may have high feeling sensitivity, and can develop more rapidly by giving early attention to a sense that is, to them, more likely to be a more reliable guide for the time being.

A mechanistic system is by no means implied in the foregoing emphasis on feeling as a guide. *Instruction in tonal sound can never be divorced from accompanying feeling associations, but hearing should always have the final ascendency.* At the same time that the student is attempting to control tonal emission by means of proper feeling sensations, he should be striving to develop aesthetic judgment regarding quality and beauty. What pleases his artistic sense today must not satisfy tomorrow; if it does, no gain has been made. A patient, understanding instructor is necessary to guide and aid the student in determining progress in both feeling and hearing associations.

DIFFERENCES IN INDIVIDUAL SENSITIVITY

An often-expressed saying is that no one ever masters a vocal principle on one hearing. It is agreed that fundamental concepts and principles must be repeated over and over in simple language pupils understand until content is absorbed. This is especially true of the slow pupil for, apparently, there are some so mentally unreceptive to essential vocal concepts that it is most difficult or impossible for ideas to penetrate and be transferred into action. No matter how good the basic quality of the vocal instrument, such a person is ill-advised to study voice seriously.

While all singers have feeling associations during the act of phonation, there is a tremendous difference among individuals in awareness of tension and degree of sensitivity. This is due in many instances to long established muscular rigidity that has become so habitual the student is unconscious of abnormality. It is much better, in such an instance, to have a pupil with no vocal training whatsoever than one who has had incorrect feeling and sound concepts so firmly established that they have become habitual. Correction is always difficult. Sometimes it is possible only by making the student first aware of the fault through recording. Attention must then be focused intensely on feeling and hearing associations that should accompany correct production,

gradually replacing former concepts with new and more reliable sensations.

In a few rare instances, correction can be made only by focusing attention on specific muscular rigidity like a set tongue or mouth position. Corrective exercises are given to obtain relaxation that, (in the initial stages,) are perhaps not even associated with singing until a proper feeling sensation first is established consciously and then repeated until it becomes more or less reflex or habitual. *This corrective procedure involving conscious specific muscular control is recommended only in rare instances of long established and stubborn abnormality that will not respond to the usual indirect methods of control.* It is never recommended as a normal class or individual procedure.

LIMITATIONS OF FEELING SENSATIONS

In spite of the undoubted value of feeling sensations as a guide, the fact that tone is easy is never a guarantee that the tone is right. For example, production can be easy in the throat and still have a horribly nasal hillbilly twang; however, the student can depend on the assumption that *no tone can ever be right unless it is easy in the throat. A free, open, relaxed feeling in the throat is an obsolute requirement for maximum beauty of tone.*

SAFE PRACTICES FOR THE AVERAGE STUDENT

"The easiest volume for singers in the upper half of the range is best vocalized *mezzo forte . . . .* successful *piano* and *pianissimo* singing are more difficult and require training and guidance."[33] While this statement does not say anything about easiest dynamics in the lower range, it does imply that intensity is different from *mezzo-forte.* It is the opinion of the great majority of successful vocal teachers that volume should be reduced gradually as the singer approaches the lower part of the range until, on the lowest tone, there is a feeling that breath energy is reduced to a minimum.

It would appear that the voice teacher must analyze the situation realistically for the sake of determining safest practices for the average student. He also must recognize that other procedures may result in more rapid progress for the unique individual or type of voice. It is generally agreed that all voices should warm-up at the dynamic level, with the type of vowel, and in the range most likely to produce free and efficient tonal resonance, for that particular voice. It is also believed by most that all voices will sing more easily if they increase breath energy and dynamics somewhat for high tones, reducing these factors in the low compass.

---

[32]Litante, Op. cit. p. 11.
[33]American Academy of Teachers of Singing — (A pronouncement)

Voices can be classified roughly into three types for the sake of practice procedures. Common sense reasoning, based on physiological factors and observation, would appear to indicate the soundness of the following recommendations for the warm-up:

1. *Average voice* — Emphasis on *mp* to *mf* dynamics with an *Oh* or *Ah* vowel.

2. *Voices with a tendency to be "white" or shrill* — Emphasis on *p* or *pp* warm-up with the *Oo* or *Aw* vowel.

3. *Voices with the tendency to be "spread," out of focus, breathy, or lugubrious* — Emphasis on *Mf* to *f* dynamics with *Ay* or *Ee* vowels.

The foregoing recommendations seem sound for the following reasons:

1. The average voice, because it is between the two extremes, had best use an average dynamics, *Mp* to *Mf*, and the *Oh* and *Ah* vowels more nearly in the center of the color range. *Ah* is preferred, as the exact center, *after* the student has solved the problem of attack with the larynx in a relaxed low position and enough forward resonance has been established. In the beginning stages, *Oh* will be produced more freely and properly by the average student. (Note — The color range of the pure vowels from bright to dark is *Ee-Ay-Ah-Oh-Oo*. The English vowel *Aw* is the broadest vowel of all, and excellent for obtaining more freedom and sonority in the tight, "white," shrill voices, especially when attempting to sing loudly.)

2. The tight, "white," shrill voice is most likely to achieve more spacious resonance and freedom on the darker, rounder, more spacious vowels without using too much breath pressure and force to balance resonance.

3. The spacious, breathy, out-of-focus and lugubrious voice is most likely to resonate efficiently in the reduced space of the brighter *Ay* and *Ee* vowels and at the louder dynamics.

One of the reasons why *Mf* is the easiest and most desirable warm-up dynamics for the average voice is found in scientific tests of breath expulsion rate for well-produced voices; the least amount is at *Mf*, more at *pp*, while the rate rises considerably for *ff*. This fact may be surprising to many who have assumed that the least amount of breath is used at *pianissimo,* and that the rate of expulsion would rise gradually and evenly as dynamics is increased.

It is well to warn the student continually that only harm, and never benefit, can accrue from persistent practice of tones known to be wrong; such practice can only habituate fault. Attainment of extensive range, wide dynamic extremes, and great tone color variety can be safely and rapidly accomplished only by songs and exercises for gaining control *in the limitation of a situation where the tone can be produced easily and properly.*

The easiest pitch that can be sung by the average student should be the note on which to start vocalization of sustained tone. This will lie between *E* flat and *G* above middle *C* for treble voices, and an octave lower for male. As a rule, a unison long tone or scale exercise can begin on *G* and work downward to *C* or *B* flat before working up to *C*, possibly *E* flat, somewhat later, in the octave above. Easiest range for most beginning voices is from *C* to *C* above. It is necessary that warm-up exercises be confined to this easy range for the first few weeks and until the group demonstrates that a more extensive range can be attempted safely. High voices can be segregated and carried higher, and low voices lower, by insisting that students drop out as soon as straining for pitch is evidenced. *Is is highly inadvisable for a vocal warm-up ever to begin in high range or on extreme fortissimo.* There is never any advantage but only harm in exercising either a class or an individual beyond easy production range. Authorities concur that *singing exercises must be free from inordinate tension or they should never be undertaken.*

GROWING TIRED

Beginning students often become alarmed after vigorous singing when they grow tired, or their throats grow tired, and fear that they are practicing incorrectly. They may be assured that growing tired after vigorous practice is a normal expectation for beginning students, whose laryngeal and breath support muscles are naturally weak and undeveloped. Their endurance is very limited, and exercises should be neither too taxing in range or difficulty nor should vocalization be extended over too long a period without rest and relaxation. Because of many variant factors, there can be no definite answer as to the number of consecutive minutes or total amount of time in one period or day that students can practice. Only intelligent experimentation on the part of the student under teacher guidance and checking can determine maximum limitations. As a rule, academic demands on the time of the student are so severe that the difficulty lies in finding appropriate time for regular daily practice, and the problem of time limitation is non-existant. Some beginning students actually need to stop and relax after every exercise before repetition; others can practice 15 minutes or more before resting the instrument.

GROWING STALE

Two factors cause students to lose interest and "grow stale" in vocal study: too much continuous concentration on one exercise or song, and wrong type of song to challenge continued interest. It is inefficient use of practice and lesson time, and much less interesting to the student, to learn one song completely, then another, etc. Such a procedure is extremely deadening to pupil interest, the frequent cause of "staleness," and is the slowest and least effective way to learn a number of songs. Repertoire to be memorized for the semester, or an entire concert program, should all, or nearly all, be selected by the instructor and student as soon as possible. These songs then can be alternated in the practice period, with those they wish to finish first receiving the most attention. This is the "whole method of learning" applied to the practice period.

It should be self-evident that a song must be adapted to student interest and background to capture initial enthusiasm. It is also important to have abiding musical value and sufficient challenge to keep the student from growing stale with continued practice. When a pupil chooses to practice habitually on saccharine, obvious, "ear-tickling," or entertainment songs that he has heard often, there is little real musical challenge to stimulate continued work. Growing stale on such literature is to be expected.

*Some Principles in the Care and Development of the Human Voice from Childhood through Adolescence to Maturity

"Among teachers in charge of the training of the child and adolescent voice there is at present serious disagreement concerning the nature of the physical structure of the voice mechanism, its use, and its treatment during these periods. The American Academy of Teachers of Singing presents the following beliefs regarding this important subject, which beliefs, in consultation with various authorities, have received definite substantiation.

1. WE BELIVE that the functioning of the voice of the child, of the adolescent, and the adult is governed by identical physical laws; that the principles governing the use of the voice are the same in all three stages. From childhood to maturity there is development of the body structure, but no change in position or muscular action.

2. WE BELIEVE that these principles demand balance in the posture of the body, in the position of the vocal organs, and in their muscular activity, and, a coordination of the whole. The ideal procedure is to teach the child correct habits in these matters during the early years. The habits of the early formative period then will carry through the various changes as the individual and the voice grow mature. In any physical activity, golf, swimming, etc., correct form in childhood is retained as the child matures.

3. WE BELIEVE that the principles of balance in the posture of the body, in the position of the vocal organs and in their muscular activity should be taken up in that order, as the first steps in formative training at any stage of the individual's development, whether child, adolescent or adult.

4. WE BELIEVE that, notwithstanding the significance and benefits of mass singing and the need for it, the primary stress in the early years in vocal

matters should be on the correct use of the voice. This will not necessarily be brought about by mass singing. In fact, all too often the contrary is true; the stress on effects from the group — with little regard to the use of the voice — generally proves antagonistic to the welfare of the singer. We submit that only through sufficient attention to the correct use of the voice may the joy of singing, the chief aim of mass singing, be fully realized. It is axiomatic to say that a certain degree of skill in any physical endeavor is necessary for any considerable degree of pleasure.

5. WE BELIEVE that the practice of inducing young people to sing in a way commonly and inaccurately described as *soft,* which should be termed *devitalized,* will result in the presence rather than in the absence of strain; and therefore, children and adolescents should be taught the vitalization and coordination of the body in singing.

6. WE BELIEVE that the director of a choral group should know the technic of voice. No dean of music or school principal would think of putting a choral director in charge of the training of an orchestra or band but it is a common practice to place the chorus under the direction of a band leader, orchestra conductor, organist or pianist who has no technical knowledge of voice."

VOCAL EXERCISES

Four categories of vocal exercises are found in Volume I: Fundamental or basic exercises (See Chapter 16); supplementary exercises dealing specifically with the problem of the particular lesson; select phrases from famous song literature illustrating the problem of the particular lesson; and select exercises from the standard Vaccaij to assist in sight reading, musicianship, and technic. The vocal instructor is advised to select judiciously from these the amount and types of exercises needed in each situation.

It is generally agreed that much emphasis should be placed on selecting and using appropriate vocal exercises chosen from phrases of songs being sung, that these exercises *follow* and not precede the original singing of the song, and that such exercises always be put back into context of the song in order that improvement can be noted. As a rule, an exercise derived from a phrase of a song being studied also can be transposed upward and downward to cover suitable ranges.

FOUR BASIC EXERCISES FOR VOCAL DEVELOPMENT

(*Note* — See also p. 126)

Many vocal authorities agree that a few highly select basic vocal exercises, chosen carefully and used intelligently for what they will do for the voice, are

---

*Quoted with permission of the American Academy of Teachers of Singing.

highly desirable and quicker and better in developing vocal technic than extensive use of numerous published vocalises, no matter how excellent. The author subscribes to this veiwpoint and has provided four simple basic types of exercises in Chapter 16 of Volume I, with careful directions for their use and variation.

These basic exercises cover the types of technical problems commonly encountered in all melodies for voice. Since the singer finds only single notes, scales, arpeggios, and combinations of these in songs, the four basic exercises are: (a) The Sustained Tone, (b) The Scale, (c) The Arpeggio, and (d) Combination of the Scale, Arpeggio, and Sustained Tone. No other exercises actually are needed in the process of voice building, except later work on the trill in connection with agility study. The Basic Exercises are highly desirable for the following reasons:

1. They furnish for ready practice the major types of technical problems encountered in song in simple, easy to understand, and most convenient form.

2. They furnish a safe and quick method for warming up the voice, vitalizing the body, and "toning" the muscles used in singing. In this way they are comparable with oil on machinery.

3. They furnish a simple, convenient tool, the use of which is understood, and are easily memorized for aid in development of specific skills necessary to expressive singing.

It is important that the instructor acquaint himself throughly with these exercises and the directions for their use. It is well that the more select of the exercises, marked with an asterisk, be memorized by the teacher so that they can be used more readily as the normal basis for the warm-up. The student, in turn, is urged to memorize these few select exercises and to understand thoroughly the various directions for most effective use at the time, as well as later, when technic improves. No exercise can be produced with concentrated attention on freedom and tonal beauty unless it is memorized; *sight reading of the finest exercises ever devised is alien to developing free technical control rapidly.*

The long-sustained tone is the most fundamental of these exercises, and is especially valuable when practiced *crescendo-decrescendo.* Dodds and Lickley[34] claim that this exercise, the *messa di voce,* is the best of all. They state that it should be practiced assiduously in the middle compass with as varied an extent of dynamics as can be sung freely, and that duration should increase gradually with growth in technic.

TECHNIC, EXPRESSION, AND EDUCATIONAL EMPHASIS

"Singing is taught as a soul-satisfying experience, rather than a laborious self-conscious performance of vocal gymnastics."[35] This does not by any means imply that technic can be disregarded for "An artist who labors under technical difficulties cannot express faithfully what is in his mind."[36] Although the approach to stimulating development of technic is through emphasis on interpretation, we must not forget that really fine interpretation is impossible without the presence of a fine technic also. McClosky states the case for technic well: "To my mind, good interpretation can begin only when voice mechanics have been so thoroughly mastered that they have become second nature and need not be thought of consciously."[37]

It is human nature to enjoy any artistic act more as technical control over expression increases. When technical power remains woefully weak, fear and dislike of the subject are almost inevitable. There comes a time when promotion of progress and pleasure on the part of the student demands attention to increasing technical mastery. Then appropriate drill procedures on vocal exercises require more emphasis in supplementing the singing of songs. Technic has its place, and a most important place, when properly understood — that of revealing and clarifying the musical form and desired expression without mechanical interference or distractions.

While adequate technic is absolutely necessary, it cannot be a fetish, exalted as an end-all of art or a substitute for the deeper verity of feeling. Music and the values of music reside first of all and fundamentally in *expression* — a cry in the night, a prayer at twilight, a shout of exultation, a lullaby to a sleeping child, a challenge to battle, or an avowel of love. *Music is primarily an expressional art.* This fact can never be even temporarily lost sight of in the confusing complex of emphasis on the technical and the intellectual.

A liberal college education of the right kind is a very valuable, indeed an almost prerequisite asset, for the fine concert singer today. Some colleges and universities have mistakenly gone too far toward exclusive emphasis on intellectual values, however. They approve as respectable material for college study those aspects of music that are historical or theoretical only and appear on the surface to offer most in improving the mind. Any attempt to spiritualize music or the arts, or to maintain that their greatest educational value and contribution is emotional and expressional, is frowned upon as sentimentalism. Many promising music students are being led astray down the paths of futility under this false philosophy. It fosters the belief that a great

[34]Dodds, George and Lickley, James Dunlop. "The Control of Breath." Oxford U. Press, 1935, 2nd ed., p. 48.

[35]Fields, Op. cit. p. 127.

[36]Litante, Op. cit. p. 85.

[37]McClosky, David Blair. "Your Voice at Its Best." Little, Brown and Co., 1959, p. 106.

musician is one who knows primarily all about theoretical and historical facts, or in some institutions, with emphasis on the other extreme, one who displays an amazing technical dexterity.

SUMMARY FOR GUIDING STUDENT PRACTICE

Authorities, in general agree that:

1. The teacher's own singing voice, when used in illustration and example, should be above reproach.
2. Objectivity, insight, freedom from self-consciousness and rigidity, and self-discipline cannot be over-emphasized.
3. The student must understand:

(a) That a definite time should be set aside for vocal practice and followed faithfully.

(b) That correct practice habits result, sooner or later, in worthwhile progress.

(c) That the causes of vocal difficulty must be understood and corrected before a cure is possible.

(d) That auditory and feeling concepts should be refined gradually and continually.

(e) That aesthetic tonal concepts and associative feeling relationships must be coordinated for maximum progress.

(f) That control of technic is based fundamentally on concept of *sound* and secondarily on *feeling* associations.

(g) That a desirable warm-up method, and an effective system for technical development through basic exercises such as recommended, are desirable for rapid technical progress.

(h) That songs themselves, or phrases from songs, are in themselves the richest and most satisfactory source for technical development.

(i) That technic itself, although valuable and necessary, is but a means to an end — *expression*.

(j) That the secret of effective practice is primarily intelligent method ánd not time spent.

(k) That concentrated effort in short periods, with rest or variation of activity in between, and not a long continuous practice, is most efficient.

Lesson 7. Ethical Conduct

(*See Volume I, p. 32*)

Reading of this lesson in Volume I by the students, supplemented by the statement by the instructor that ethics suggested be adopted as guides for all in the future, should be sufficient. This lesson is intended to aid the teacher considerably in obtaining better attitude and conduct, and in helping prevent future trouble on ethical matters with some thoughtless students.

RECOMMENDING ANOTHER TEACHER

The vocal instructor, especially of school voice class groups, is asked at times to recommend a certain teacher with whom the student is contemplating private study elsewhere. Professional ethics should be followed, of course; nevertheless, principle responsibility belongs to the student in this instance.

*It is unethical to exploit as one's own the results of another teacher's instructions, to proselytize the pupil of another teacher's instructions, or to criticize adversely the work of a fellow teacher, unless statements can be substantiated by proof.

What kind of a vocal teacher is safe to recommend? Litante puts it this way, "A teacher's skill is apparent if he is able to make good singers out of defective material."[38] In commenting on singers and teachers of singing, Bernard Shaw once said, "He who can, does; he who cannot, teaches." This pungent observation is too often true today regarding former professional singers whose age is such that they should still be singing well before the public, rather than teaching the gullible beginner. Ability of such a teacher should always be suspect. How can they transmit necessary vocal fundamentals which they obviously never learned?

Unfortunately, there are still many charlatans who attract, damage, or ruin promising voices. They usually advertise themselves highly as proponents of some unique, mysterious, secret, or magical system of voice training, and base their reputation in most instances on the professional success of one or two students. It may be necessary for the conscientious teacher to express doubt about the advisability of studying with a teacher of the aforementioned types.

Students often ask: Should I study with a man or a woman teacher? "Experience has shown that the teaching of vocal technic is largely theoretical, and so the teacher's sex and vocal range mean little."[39] Other things being equal, however, it is probably best for a tenor to study with a tenor, a soprano with a soprano, etc.

Above all, beginning students are advised not to study with noted vocal coaches for finished interpretation before the rudiments of free and even production over an adequate range have been mastered. To do so is futile and dangerous. Fortunately, famous vocal coaches are seldom interested in instructing any but the more advanced students.

SUCCESS IN SPITE OF METHOD

The pupil may well ask, "If reputed methods are so wrong, how does it happen that a certain success-

---

*Excerpted from "Code of Ethics for the Guidance of Its Members," National Association of Teachers of Singing.

[38]Op. cit. p. 145.

[39]Brown, Ralph Morse. "The Singing Voice." MacMillan Co., 1940, p. 161.

ful singer is the product of the teacher in question?" It should be pointed out that uniformly favorable results with many average students is a better criterion for judging a teacher; one or two successful pupils is never a sure indication of teaching competency. A few highly intelligent and highly gifted students with unusually sturdy voices survive almost any system of voice training, succeeding in spite of, and not because of, instructions received. In some instances, the naturally free qualities of such voices are recognized by the teacher, and they have enough intuition to leave production alone.

Quite often excellent fundamental technic has been established previously by the sterling work of a comparatively unknown teacher, and the charlatan reaps the reward because the student studied with him last. In this connection it is necessary to distinguish between the vocal coach and the voice instructor. There are numerous successful and competent vocal coaches who advertise misleadingly as vocal instructors. It is well that the student be alerted to this fact, and avoid such instructors until after his technic is secure.

Experienced teachers also recognize that some students with abnormal personalities and abnormal mental and physical characteristics may respond to abnormal teaching methods. In many instances, the gifted vocal student has an unusually sturdy vocal instrument that will withstand a number of years of destructive practices before breaking under the strain. No matter how renowned they may be for a time, however, they eventually pay the price for vocal abuse, ending careers at a time when the voice should be in its prime.

When the voice is used correctly, singing is "on the interest and not on the capital" of the voice. It grows more rich, powerful, and expressive until the setting in of physical deterioration in advanced years. Lilli Lehman, Heinrich Schlusnus, Oscar Siegel, George Henschel, Battistini, and Guiseppe De Luca are outstanding examples of artists who sang with undimmed opulance until around seventy years of age.

Lesson 8.   Singing as a Career

(See Volume I, p. 34)

Students in vocal classes often think that they would like to make singing a career. For them, and for the private lesson pupil, the information given in Volume I is a most valuable guide. Others also should read the lesson because of its educative value and relationship to high standards. The practical value of a college degree needs special emphasis for those impatient to short-cut the time necessary to enter professional singing. In this age of speed and hurry, students are inclined to think in months rather than years of study necessary to prepare for

a successful career. The concientious teacher advises students that there are no quick, "sugar-coated" paths or formulae that will lead to success in technic and repertoire, and that a fine cultured mind and a sensitive appreciation for beauty in the arts are prerequisites that they cannot afford to short-cut.

Experienced voice teachers realize that, while development of vocal ability is physical as well as mental, *voice teaching is almost 100 per cent psychological*. In guiding a pupil intent on a career, it is usually necessary to emphasize over and over that there is much more to singing than the voice. Owning a Stradivarias is an advantage, but a far cry from the various understandings and abilities required to play it well professionally. Before embarking on a singing career, students usually question themselves seriously regarding whether or not they have enough *voice*. Actually they should be more concerned with the more important elements of *native musical capacity, aesthetic sensitivity, musicianship, and personality qualities*. Personality is a most vital factor in success. Those with superior musical talents are not always the ones who survive. Most successful singers are extroverts, durable, hardy, determined individuals constitutionally fitted to the vicissitudes of a professional career.

MUSICIANSHIP

The vocalist can no longer expect to have a career in singing without adequate musicianship, no matter how beautiful his voice. "It is not enough to develop proficient technique and interpretative powers; the concert singer must also be enough of a musician to utilize vocal abilities."[40] There is no market today for mediocrity of this kind in a highly competetive profession where sight singing ability and knowledge of style are "musts." In fact, the singer of only fair attainments, but fine musicianship, will go infinitely farther than one who possesses a magnificent voice but lacks musicianship.

The voice teacher has a major responsibility in regard to musicianship. In most instances the fundamentals of theory, sight singing, piano playing, study of history and appreciation of music, and foreign language are taught in special classes in the schools devoted to these subjects. All needed musical background cannot be gained in the voice class or private lesson, but the foregoing subject matter areas should be supported and advanced there. When no other special classes in music training are available, it is desirable that more of the content of sight singing, theory, etc., be included in the vocal class.

EDUCATION

The singer needs not only adequate technic and musicianship but also usually finds it necessary to

---

[40]Wilcox, John C. "The Living Voice." Carl Fischer, Inc., 1935, p. 49.

be a sensitive, discriminating, and cultured person to excel in concert work. That type of education which contributes most to a balanced physical, mental, cultural, and spiritual environment is the best possible preparation. A broad, liberal college education, with an accompanying vocal major emphasis, would seem to offer most as the best type of fundamental preparation for the professional singer.

Professional Guidance

The National Association of Teachers of Singing list the following 12 prerequisites as desirable to justify study of singing as a career. It is well to point out, however, that it is possible to develop a number of these factors while studying singing.

1. *"Intelligence* — Mental alertness, the power to understand, and readiness of comprehension.

2. *Concentration* — Ability to give exclusive attention and to sustain the effort of close mental application to any activity.

3. *Healthy physique, vocal apparatus, and hearing equipment* — Freedom from physical malformations, organic lesions, or chronic illnesses that would interfere with artistic vocal development.

4. *Ambition* — Patience, the willingness to work hard, and the desire for advancement and self-improvement.

5. *Mental health* — Ability to relax mentally and physically, freedom from chronic inhibitions and neurotic tendencies.

6. *Emotional Stability* — Sense of joy and buoyancy of spirit; singing is impossible under conditions of pessimism, melancholia, or chronic depression of spirit.

7. *Good memory* — The faculty of absorbing, retaining, identifying, and reproducing what has been learned and experienced.

8. *Musicianship* — A good general knowledge of music fundamentals, including innate sense of rhythm, a fine sense of pitch, and a love of music.

9. *Personality* — Poise, self-confidence, stage presence, and a pleasing appearance.

10. *Capacity for languages* — The ability to acquire the vocabulary, pronunciation, phraesology, and manner of expression of foreign languages.

11. *Good diction* — A free and flexible tongue, with ability to produce clear-cut and intelligible vowels and consonants in any verbal combination.

12. *Interpretational sense* — The ability to absorb, understand, and express the meaning, intent, or mood of an idea."

After a year of vocal study, under personal supervision, the competent vocal teacher is in a position to have learned enough about a student's personality, intelligence, musical sensitivity, and vocal capacities to be able to give sound advice on his future — whether or not it is worthwhile to continue study with the idea of becoming a professional and, if so, in what professional field to specialize. These fields are discussed in Volume I (see p. 36). However, "even the greatest expert cannot prophecy with certainty how long it will take a singer to reach his vocal goal."[41] There are roughly three types of students who can be advised as follows:

1. Those with charming personality, good voice, and high exhuberance of spirit, but not inclined to study intensively over a long period of time. Such students have best chance for success in light opera, musical comedy, radio, and television productions.

2. Those with analytical minds who understand and like people, but do not have either a natively fine vocal instrument or the burning desire or aggressiveness necessary to push themselves in the professional field. These students should be advised to seek a teaching credential emphasizing vocal music. Even those in category 1, and in 3 following, well may be advised to consider obtaining the teaching credential also during their college career. It would be the best possible insurance in case a professional career does not turn out to be as successful or desirable as anticipated.

3. Those with the rare combination of high native talent, a fine natural voice, magnetic personality, physical vitality, perservering ambition, and artistic sensitivity. To such few belong the most difficult goal — a concert and possibly an operatic career. Those aspiring to opera must be willing to spend the time necessary not only to learn the traditional languages of Italian, German, French, and English, but also to master acting technics.

---

[41]Litante, Op. cit., p. 28.

2

Posture

BASIC PRINCIPLES

(See Volume I, p. 39)

There is little if any disagreement among vocal authorities regarding the fundamental value of proper posture as a prerequisite for singing. In discussing the problem of posture with students, however, it is highly important that the personality and health values of good posture be stressed also. Ferguson maintains that "The consideration of posture comes first among fundamentals of training the voice."[1] The author agrees that it is the first *technical* consideration but would place posture second following establishment of an attitude of confidence and pleasure in singing, a necessary psychological condition.

Continued insistance on good posture is one of the "musts" in vocal teaching. Vocal authorities agree that it is one of the first major responsibilities of the voice teacher to insist continually on proper postural conditions until they are habituated. Correct singing posture seldom happens by chance; it has to be practiced until habitual. "The singing teacher should apply the physical principles of correct posture to every voice lesson, requiring daily practice of postural controls as a means of enhancing breathing and breath controls."[2] Posture for the singer should be upright and expansively vital, in a state of readiness to function; it must not be tense or rigid, nor can it be completely relaxed. Litante explains this seeming paradox as follows, "Your body must be relaxed, but not flabby; erect but not stiff in posture."[3] Whether standing or sitting, the body should be held in an alert, erect position conducive to free and coordinated physical and mental activity.

It is basic that the singing instructor understand that the necessary physical development for singing begins with posture and proceeds through breath control and strengthening of the vocal organs through singing practice. This is a long and patient process in which the beginning student needs continual checking and guidance to make sure that proper habits are established early and that careless practices do not return.

The three most basic fundamentals to emphasize in obtaining good posture are:

1. *The upper chest must be lifted first BEFORE inhalation starts.* This is the first prerequisite of breath control and, if it is not followed, the chances are that the student will always be a "chest-breather." If the chest is mistakenly raised by inhalation, a pumping of the chest action is started which is followed inevitably by collapse of the chest on phonation. Breathing should be deep (diaphragmatic), and the only way to guarantee it is to *raise the chest before inhalation and keep it high and quiet thenceforward.*

2. *The chest must remain comfortably high and quiet during singing.* The words "comfortably high" should be stressed; rigidly high, such as the soldier assumes at attention, is too much. If the expansive muscles around the waistline (the costal muscles) do not hold outward, or resist and are allowed to relax, the diaphragm is blocked at the waistline and only inadequate chest (clavicular) breathing is possible. When they do resist to the end of the phrase, the diaphraghm can sweep up into the chest cavity from below, utilizing all the breath in the lungs for well-controlled tone.

3. *The spine, through the neck downward, should be kept flexibly stretched.* A straight spine supplies the supporting structural foundation upon which most coordinated body activity depends. In singing, a slight expansion around the lower rib line combines with the comfortably high and quiet chest and the stretched spine to serve as the basic structural

[1]Ferguson, George. "Singer's Basic Equipment." Musician, 1940, Vol. 45, p. 5.

[2]Stephens, Percy Rector. "Fundamentals That Govern Singing." Musician, Jan. 1934, Vol. 39, p. 5.

[3]Litante, Judith. "A Natural Approach to Singing." Wm. C. Brown Co., 1959, p. 29.

framework for diaphragmatic-costal breath control. Only a slight expansion around the rib-line — to the point of gently firming the stomach muscles — is needed: too much will cause rigidity. Straightening the neck in the spine-stretch process also automatically levels the head to its proper balanced position. (The stretched spine automatically induces correct breathing and establishes the most favorable condition for singing.)

There is a basic interaction between posture and breathing; correct posture is fundamental to easy, vigorous breath control, while correct, expansive breath control, without nervous rigidity, is necessary for maintaining proper posture. Upright posture is necessary not only because the lifted chest and erect spine enable the diaphragm and lower rib and back muscles to hold back the breath properly, but also because proper neck and head position help prevent harmful neck tension. *The over-all importance of the stretched spine and neck cannot be overemphasized* as a prerequisite and accompaniment for steady breath support and to bring the neck, head, and rest of the body into alignment.

A proper head position perpendicular to the shoulders and body is a basic postural condition. Head too high or a jutting chin causes whiteness and shrillness in tone; head too low tends to cause a dark and "thick" production. *Most beginners tend to carry the head tilted up too high* and perhaps sidewise. The chin tucked too low is seldom encountered.

PSYCHOLOGICAL VALUE

There is no doubt that tonal thought is the control stimulus for all technical skills which enter into the complex act of singing, and that balanced coordination depends on a mental attitude of confidence, pleasure, and buoyancy induced by a feeling of physical well-being. Proper posture not only makes it possible for muscles concerned in singing to coordinate and function correctly, but also stimulates a buoyant feeling and a more confident mental attitude. Physiologists maintain that a high chest and a straight spine, in particular, are also posture essentials for promoting a healthy nerve supply to muscles controlling singing.

STANDING POSTURE BEST

It is easier to maintain good posture while standing than when seated. The seated posture is "more or less unnatural."[4] There is too much of a tendency to slump immediately, lie down in the chair, or cross the legs when seated; therefore, *the warm-up and most vocal exercises and solo singing should be while standing.* A class may sit when discussing vocal theory and details of interpretation, or in the preliminary stages of learning a song and when tired after extended practice when standing. Soloists are

advised to stand in almost every instance; at their seats when singing a short passage and at the piano in traditional concert position when singing a solo. The sooner these directions are understood and routined the better.

From the first lesson in which correct posture is taught, the vocal instructor's eternal vigilance is required in watching and checking individual students and insisting on habituation. Habit of poor posture is established so firmly with most students that they have to be watched constantly and corrected with kindly but firm insistence. *Fundamentals to watch in particular are the slumped spine, deflated chest, raised chin, and crossed legs when seated.*

SINGING WITH POOR POSTURE

Is it possible to sing well with poor posture? That depends on several factors. For the beginner, the answer is usually *no!* If the singer has built up enough reserve technic in tonal production and breath energy, however, he can sing successfully and still not conform to all phases of good posture. For him, it is possible to sing well in spite of poor posture; however, it is more difficult. The operatic singer may be required to sing in a reclining position because of dramatic requirements — presumably dying, for example, according to the libretto. A reclining position is certainly not conducive to good singing, but many professionals appear to be able to sing lustily in spite of the imposed handicap. We may be sure, however, that they could sing easier and better if they were in a more favorable standing position.

Even the finest professional is obliged to maintain the two prime essentials of posture to sing his best under any and all circumstances — a high, quiet chest and a stretched spine. Some concert artists are not perfect examples of good posture on such details as evenly balanced head position and relaxed shoulders, but the high, quiet chest and erect posture are common to all fine technicians.

As far as the beginner is concerned, it is evident that vocal freedom with tonal vitality is unlikely to exist as long as poor posture prevails. Even the best possible posture is insufficient in providing all the assistance needed at times.

THE HANDS

What to do with the hands is often a difficult problem, especially for awkward and shy boys with large hands. Some feel more at ease if allowed to hold a small piece of paper. Girls sometimes hold a handkerchief.

All students need coaching in several acceptable hand positions; both hands down and relaxed at the

---

[4]Laine, Juliette. "A Cure for Hoarseness After Singing." *Etude,* 1934, Vol. 52, p. 374.

sides; both hands up in front of the waist with the back of one loosely placed in the other; one hand down at the side and the other up in front of the waist; or one hand resting easily on the piano. This latter position should never be leaning, lying, or "lolling" on the piano, as is often seen. It should be used mostly for more informal type of songs. interchanging position of the hands is perfectly acceptable during singing if it is done quietly and naturally.

This policy seems to help relieve tension with many students.

If the hands are clasped at all during singing, they should be relaxed and at ease. No nervous twitching or gripping is allowable. *It is much safer to place the back of one hand in the palm of the other than to interlace the fingers.* It is almost impossible to interlace the fingers without creating excess of tension there; and tension in the hands is almost invariably transmitted to the throat.

3

Breath Control

Lesson 1. Preliminary Considerations and Clarification

(See Volume I, p. 46)

STANDARDS FOR GUIDANCE

The fundamentals of breath control are agreed on by the American Academy of Teachers of Singing and are quoted by permission in full as follows.

"BREATHING —

    1. Believes in teaching the pupil how to breathe.

    2. Believes that the correct practice of singing in itself tends to develop and establish the mastery of the breath.

    3. Believes that the singer should stand comfortably erect, with the chest medium high, and with a feeling of flexibility and well being.

    4. Favors the method of breathing which is known scientifically as 'Diaphragmatic-Costal', colloquially as 'deep breathing.'

    5. Believes that in inhalation the upper abdomen expands, owing to the descent of the diaphragm, and the ribs expand; in exhalation the abdomen tenses and contracts, owing to the pressure of the abdominal muscles and to the gradual ascent of the diaphragm, and the ribs contract. Thus the greatest observable effect in both inhalation and exhalation is at the sides and in the region of the waist-line.

    6. Believes that either the mouth or the nose may be used in inhalation.

    7. Recommends the daily practice of calisthenics or setting-up exercises."

The foregoing pronouncements form the basic core for the theory content regarding breath control used in Expressive Singing, Volume I. There is no accepted standard method for teaching, however, and it appears that there are a number of successful methods. The basic theory and methods for developing breath control, advanced by the author in the four lessons following on this topic, are subscribed to and used by many successful teachers. They not only work effectively in practice, but also are supported soundly by the sciences of psychology and physiology.

IMPORTANCE OF CONTINUED PRACTICE

Actually, there is no such thing as perfect breath control; perfection can be only approached. Breath control is not something that, once understood and mastered, can be neglected. Never-ending, patient work to maintain and extend breath control is one of the main objectives of the skilled vocalist's practice. Muscles controlling phonation are not only complex in number and balanced coordination factors, but also are apparently extremely sensitive to physical or emotional state and to lack of sufficient regular practice.

FUNDAMENTALS IN TEACHING BREATH CONTROL

    1. *Proper erect posture,* as described in detail in Chapter 2 of *VOLUME I*, Expressive Singing, *is a prerequisite.*

    2. *Tonal efficiency is a basic requirement to emphasize.* "Economy of breath is much more important than volume of breath."[1] No matter how much breath can be inhaled, it will not avail if tone is breathy and wasteful. To be efficient, tone must have a ringing quality.

A prevalent misconception is that one must inhale a large quantity of breath to sing. It is the quality and efficiency of tone that are most important; a comfortable breath, properly resonated, will last through the longest phrase. In analyzing the reason for Caruso's incomparable singing, Marifioti concludes, "He always employed only the exact amount of breath required for producing each tone, and no more; and this was responsible for his precise into-

---

[1]Herbert-Caesari, Edgar F. "The Science and Sensations of Vocal Tone." J. M. Dent & Sons, 1936, p. 17.

nation, his remarkable legato, and his long sustained tones."[2]

3. *Breath control is actually expansive breath-holding* as far as the singer's feeling sensations are concerned. Abdominal muscles should be firm but not rigid. They should never collapse and the abdomen protrude; *neither should they be consciously drawn in or lifted as is sometimes taught.*

4. *Emphasis is placed continually on THOUGHT and FEELING* — how the correct tone should sound and how breath control action should *feel* in supporting it. "Never consciously control the breath, but rather control the tone."[3] *Proper diaphragm action is a result of proper tonal concept.* On inhalation there is a resultant slight expansion around the lower rib-line and the back muscles. *This postural feeling is a constant during phonation and is maintained from the tonal attack to the very end of the phrase.*

5. *The most effective stimulus to adequate breath control is concept, before inhalation, of how the whole phrase should sound.*

6. It is basic that the pupil understand that *breath control cannot be accomplished by body relaxation but rather through flexible, expansive, balanced tension.*

BASIC FALLACIES

There are two prevalent fallacies regarding breath control, indicating that many teachers are either poorly informed or careless in their thinking. These are first, that breath control in singing will be successful if students only will breathe as naturally and in the same way as in life; and second, that the pupil should be entirely relaxed in singing. Actually, anyone who counsels a student that he must breathe in the same manner for singing as for normal respiration, or that he must be entirely relaxed in singing, is indulging in a form of fakery. It is time that we stop kidding ourselves and students in these two respects and teach the truth, if most rapid advancement is desired.

DIFFERENCES IN BREATHING FOR SINGING AND NATURAL BREATHING

In singing the action of the muscles on inhalation should be relaxed, deep, and gentle (never tense) — quite similar, it is true, to natural, relaxed, deep breathing in reflex respiration. *Only the feeling of inhalation is the same,* however. Everything else must be different, for the muscular action demands of phonation in singing are actually contrary and in conflict with automatic reflex respiration. Since most inhalation in singing must be *quicker* than that in normal breathing, and exhalation *slower*, it is obvious that the singer cannot breathe as he does in life. For phrasing, "the singer will have to be able to breathe as slowly as four or five times per

minute if necessary. Therefore this (breath) control must be developed."[4] In life, exhalation follows inhalation immediately, rhythmically, and fortunately for our continued existence, automatically.

The fundamental difference in singing resides in the artistic necessity for sustaining tone in long phrases, with no opportunity for inhaling regularly and rhythmically as in normal respiration, or even in the act of speaking. This requires the setting up of breath *resistance* controls to *hold back* the breath and "meter" it to tone over the whole phrase. "Ordinary breathing is an automatic business. But singing requires extra breath and therefore extra breathing control."[5] Actually, the term "breath-holding" is more descriptive of muscular function in singing than either "breath control" or "breath support." The skilled singer, in fact, is a professional resister against the natural rhythmic tendency of the diaphragmatic muscles to contract immediately following inhalation. These resistant controls are never used in the life process of natural breathing, and to only a comparatively minor extent by any except the most skilled speaker.

Since the reflex contractive muscles used in breathing are used continuously in the life process, they are naturally strong through development. On the other hand, the holding back or resistant muscles are naturally weak since they are used only in crying, yelling, and speech, where no artistic demands compel long and sustained effort. The pupil therefore must build up these normally weak muscles by singing practice until they are strong enough to hold successfully against the normally much stronger contractive muscles. To develop the necessary amount of strength, endurance, and balanced control with *flexible tension*, but no rigidity, requires years of practice to perfect.

It is evident that correct breathing for singing cannot be the same as breathing for living, and that it is not automatic or "natural" but a developed process. On the other hand, if we interpret the term "natural breathing" as meaning "normal and unconscious activity without any attempt at voluntary control," breath control is "natural" in singing. Certainly, the singer learns to breathe naturally *as a singer* in the same fashion as the dancer or fencing master learns to function naturally in his field — by patient work under correct postural principles to

[2]Marifioti, P. Mario. "Caruso's Method of Voice Production." Cadica Enterprises, 1950 (original copy 1922), p. 5.

[3]Wharton, Florence C. "Rotary Voice Method." Augsburg Publishing House, 1937, p. 21.

[4]Combs, William Walker. "The Voice in Singing; Its Care and Development." The Author, 1938, p. 9.

[5]Storey, Barbara and Barnard, Elsie I. "A Key to Speech and Song." Blackie and Son, 1940, p. 17.

develop balanced and coordinated technics whereby control is accomplished.

The singer is advised never to try consciously to control breath while singing. *Breath control is accomplished "indirectly" through mental concentration on tone and phrasing desired, and through establishing habitually the postural expansive resistance feeling sensations which accompany proper breath control.* The singer should not think at all about his breath while singing; he should concentrate on expression. The American Academy of Teachers of Singing maintains that the correct practice of singing itself tends to develop and establish the mastery of breath. Jussi Bjorling,[6] Metropolitan opera tenor, believes that the singer becomes short winded the moment he begins to think about breath function while singing. This view is supported by practically all singers of repute. *The student needs to be reminded continually that the length of the phrase and its expressional demands should be clearly in mind BEFORE inhalation as the best known means for obtaining breath control.*

A normal and natural way to develop breath control is to assign songs gradually increasing phrase lengths. Abstract breath control exercises without tone, such as the few in the Expressive Singing, Volume I, for this chapter, are useful only in the very preliminary stages. After that, the student is advised to improve breath control principally through songs and through extending length of the basic vocal exercises in Chapter 16 of Volume I.

THE TRUTH ABOUT RELAXATION AND TENSION

Rigid muscular tension is the greatest physical enemy of most vocal students. If rigid tension is in the vocal bands, the pharynx, or the tongue, it must be eliminated or successful singing is impossible. If in the extrinsic muscles (those not involved in singing), it will transfer soon to the throat. The only antidote for rigid tension is relaxation. Relaxation, like all other impulses, has its origin in the mind. We *think* relaxation to the affected area to correct rigidity and keep on thinking it until the habit of relaxation is established.

Actually, the problem of many students is to *unlearn* rather than *learn,* since most have harmful habituated tensions of which they are unaware. These habituated tensions, with very little doubt, are the result of school, home, and church choir influences. If all students could have good teaching and examples of correct singing in their early environment, labors of vocal teachers later in obtaining free tonal production would be practically eliminated.

Voice teachers are usually aware that the basic cause of strain in singing is often psychological, not physiological, and that improvement in the physical manifestation is often impossible until the psycho-

logical cause is removed or alleviated. Emotional disturbances such as fear, worry, jealousy, grief, and hatred may cause physical strain so severe that normal free singing is impossible. Seasoned singers who have developed mental discipline and a reserve of secure technic are able to overcome even the most severe emotional handicaps, however.

Relaxation is much talked about and urged on the student, but it is frequently misunderstood by both teacher and student to the detriment of proper breath control and development of vital tone and endurance in singing. To urge a student to "entirely relax" may be beneficial at times for certain areas of the body where stubborn and extreme rigidity exists. For example, teachers of singing repeatedly tell their students to "completely relax the throat." When given such directions the student often relaxes the surface muscles of the neck which had been rigid and not the throat, resulting in a beneficial condition to phonation. It would be better for the sake of accuracy for the teacher to have used the terms "neck" and "pharynx" instead of throat, since obviously it would be impossible to produce tone if the larynx itself were completely relaxed.

A relaxed muscle is a dead muscle; it has no energy and, therefore, can do no control work. Like all other control muscles in the body, the throat muscles producing singing function best when under *balanced tension. Flexible, balanced tension in all breath and larynx muscles concerned in phonation furnishes abundant tonal power without rigidity.* From a scientific physiological standpoint, balanced tension must occur for properly-controlled action. As we have emphasized previously, however, control is accomplished *indirectly* through establishing correct posture, the mental stimulus of proper tonal concept, and the associative feeling conditions that accompany correct breath support.

To urge complete relaxation of the body as a general principle in singing is both physiologically and psychologically unsound. If the student actually could achieve complete relaxation of the throat and body, he would be not only impotent vocally but also would collapse to the floor. Relaxation in singing is a relative matter requiring the absence of abnormal tension, but not looseness of any of the organs involved. According to Witherspoon,[7] singing demands correct physical *action*, not relaxation, and instructions to relax completely are misleading. Wilson also comments that "When a fine singer delivers that thrilling climax, he is not relaxed; he just looks and acts relaxed."[8] *Muscles used in singing should*

[6]Bjorling, Jussi. "Good Singing Is Natural." (an interview) Etude, 1937, Vol. 55, p. 603.

[7]Witherspoon, Herbert. "Thirty-Six Lessons in Singing." Meissner Intitute of Music, 1930, p. 16.

[8]Wilson, Harry Robert. "Artistic Choral Singing." G. Schirmer, Inc., 1959, p. 168.

be under flexible balanced tension. This is *flexible,* never *rigid,* tension; there is always a sharp distinction between the two. Rigid tension destroys all possibility of artistic control.

The teacher is unwise to assume that every student of singing needs to be relaxed. Most do, it is true, but people vary greatly in this respect from the overly-tense, nervous, highly strung, perhaps neurotic type to the extremely placid person who is habitually over-relaxed and needs, therefore, stimulation to a more vigorous and flexibly tense physical vitality. Indeed, it is usually more difficult to obtain sufficient energy and body vitality, or "muscle tone," from the over-phlegmatic person than it is to secure sufficient relaxation from the over-tense. Difference between these two extreme types is both biological and psychological; there is a radical difference in temperament and personality as well as in physical response. The phlegmatic, lethargic pupil is often, but not always, overweight.

When anemic or lethargic vocal response is due entirely to etreme physical weakness, the right kind of body building exercises, hygenic health habits, and singing itself will improve and probably correct the condition. When the cause is psychological, however, i.e., emotional or temperamental and not physical, improvement involves a change in personality to greater alertness, intensity, and emotional sensivity. This is a slow and difficult procedure.

The temperamentally lethargic person can never become an inspiring interpreter; the best that can be hoped for is mechanical excellence in free tone production. On the other hand, the concert and operatic stage is filled with artists who have high emotional sensitivity, are intense and "high strung" in their reactions. Such a person is usually self-conscious, nervous and highly tense physically in the early stages of training — a time when the lethargic student often sings with greater relaxation and supperior tonal freedom.

CAUSES OF RIGIDITY

Constriction, rigidity, interference, and undue tension all mean the same thing in practice — blocking of freedom in muscular action. We cannot control the effect of extreme tension without reaching the cause. It is a mistake to blindly tell a pupil to relax his throat when the tone is tense. Such directions may, in fact, merely call attention to the throat and make it more rigid. It is necessary to reach the cause of tonal tension to effect a cure. Origin often can be found in fear, sometimes in direct conscious attempts to control specific muscular response, sometimes in improper imagery concept for freeing and balancing tonal resonation, and sometimes in a combination of causes. Fortunately, most causes of rigidity are corrected, or improved greatly, by normal class instruction procedures without re-

course to individual attention in the beginning stages of vocal study. Realization of this fact makes possible an enormous saving of time and acceleration in the training process. Some of the principal causes of rigidity that the teacher may bear in mind are:

1. Fear or self-consciousness.
2. Poor posture.
3. Nervous inhalation.
4. Poor aesthetic concept of tonal quality.
5. Either too little or too much breath for the demands of the phrase.
6. Sluggish articulation.
7. "Setting" the jaw, tongue, or lips rigidly.
8. Incorrect breath support — either nervous, inadequate inhalation or "chest" breathing are frequent causes.

PRINCIPLES REGARDING RELAXATION AND TENSION

Several basic principles and laws are evident regarding relaxation and tension in singing:

1. Free production demands that the arms, hands, shoulders, legs and other parts of the body not involved in singing *always be relaxed.*

2. The chest remains quietly and comfortably high at all times as a basic postural condition. It is necessary to maintain enough expansive, flexible, outward tension around the lower rib-line to secure this position.

3. No muscle can tense properly for controlled action unless it is relaxed the instant before action takes place. "The law is: Any tension in muscles prior to functioning makes freedom of function of these muscles impossible."[9] This law signifies that *the vocal cords, tongue, lips, jaw, diaphragm, and any other muscles involved in singing be relaxed before action in singing.* Tension occurs only at the moment we sing and this tension is flexible not rigid.

4. *Controlled* action demands flexible, never rigid or "set" tension, the kind of tension in a rubber band. A flexible feeling of firmness is necessary in all control muscles involved. It is relaxation in that there is absense of rigidity or tightness, but it is tension in that there must never be a condition of looseness or "let-go" during phonation.

5. Ideally controlled function for all muscular action in the body, whether it be walking, singing, or anything else, *occurs only when opposite sets of muscles are in balanced tension.* Physiologists have established the fact that no muscle works alone — it must always have another to work against. "No muscle acts by itself, it is always acting against an opponent."[10] This is known as the principle of mus-

---

[9]Bachner, Louis. "Dynamic Singing." L. B. Fischer, 1944, p. 45.
[10]Shakespeare, William. "Plain Words in Singing." Putnam, 1938, p. xiv.

cular antagonism. In view of this principle, "Relaxation means the freeing of (any) positive movement from the pull of antagonistic muscle groups."[11] Like a tug-of-war, tension of muscle resisting against muscle, or sets of muscles resisting against sets of muscles, creates the breath pressure necessary for tonal volume and balanced control in singing.

Concerning antagonism Stanley writes, "When the voice is produced properly, the breathing muscles are in equilibrium: Expiratory tension is balanced by inspiratory tension; also the 'forward and out' pull of the diaphragmatic muscle is balanced by the 'backward and out' pull of the lower ribs."[12] Perfection of control in singing depends upon the degree of balanced antagonistic equilibrium existing between and within these two groups of breathing muscles, as well as balanced resistance that the vocal bands must achieve against the controlled breath pressure from below.

Meyer states in relation to vocal cord resistance, "For it is the quantity of steam that cannot escape that makes the train go; it is the quantity of gas that cannot get out that makes the balloon ascend; it is the quantity of wind that cannot pass through a sail that propels the ship; and it is the quantity of breath that cannot escape that results in controlled tone."[13] *Feeling that the high, quiet, chest wall, rather than the vocal bands, is the focal point of resistance against breath pressure, helps free the tone, provides more vital dynamics and more secure breath control, however.*

Antagonistic function of muscles is easily verified in certain parts of the body. In other places, like the muscles involved in singing, the muscles are so complex and hidden from view that it is difficult or impossible to determine their exact function. This explains many of the contradictory theories advanced by physiologists and vocal specialists regarding exact physical function in singing; however, the principle of muscular antagonism remains sound and undeniable. This principle explains why the comparatively weak resistant muscles in the diaphragm and around the lower rib-line, and the comparatively unused falsetto register muscles in the larynx, have to be strengthened before satisfactory breath control is possible in the first case, and extensive range and tonal control in the second.

The teacher will find it necessary to remind students often that *after inhalation there can be no relaxation or "let-go" in breath resistance and that the feeling of flexible, yet firm and expansive outward lift of the chest and around the waist line, continues to the very end of every phrase.* The teacher should never be led astray by methods emphasizing direct or localized muscular development and action in singing. The indirect method of controlling breath support, and vocal action on emphasis on how the tone should *sound*, and how breath control should *feel*,

is the only successful method — the natural, musical method used by all artists.

TYPES OF BREATHING

The two types of breathing, clavicular (chest), and diaphragmatic-costal, are described sufficiently in Volume I. To prevent clavicular breathing, it is advisable to check beginners continuously in the initial stages of establishing diaphragmatic-costal breath control. Clavicular breathing is the breath of exhaustion and, as long as the chest is heaving on inhalation, proper breath control never can be established. Chest breathing is inefficient because only a small amount of breath in the upper part of the lungs can be phonated, and even that is under poor control. Diaphragmatic-costal breath control is a matter of expansion and contraction in the *bottom* of the lungs; control of expulsion is *below and around the lower sides of the lungs.* In this way pressure is where it belongs and all of the breath can be used if necessary. In practice, a small amount of breath is always held in reserve in the upper part of the lungs when singing is correct.

The principle of diaphragmatic-costal breath control can be graphically illustrated to students by comparing the lungs full of air to a rubber bottle full of water. The way to force all of the water out the neck of the bottle would be to exert pressure from *below* and at the *lower* sides. Squeezing from above and the upper sides, as in clavicular breathing, would generate pressure in the wrong place, the bottom of the rubber bottle.

The keys to correction of clavicular breathing are:

1. Raising the chest comfortably high *before* inhalation.

2. Habitually maintaining the feeling of outward lift of the chest and outward expansion around the waist line to the very end of the phrase. (Note — The stretched spine postural condition described previously is a prerequisite.)

If these two principles are observed, diaphragmatic-costal breath control is inevitable — no other type is possible. The breath has to be deep and the diaphragm has to function without the singer's needing to attempt conscious control in any manner.

The diaphragm is a large dome-shaped muscle stretching across the floor of the rib cavity and separating it from the abdominal area. Inhalation causes it to flatten out and move downward, pressing against the viscera which, in turn, cause the vis-

---

[11]Mursell, James and Glenn, Maybelle. "The Psychology of School Music Teaching." Silver Burdett, 1938, p. 244.

[12]Stanley, Douglas. "Your Voice." Pittman, 1945, p. 3.

[13]Meyer, Edmund J. "Vocal Reinforcement." Boston Music Co., 1913, p. 43.

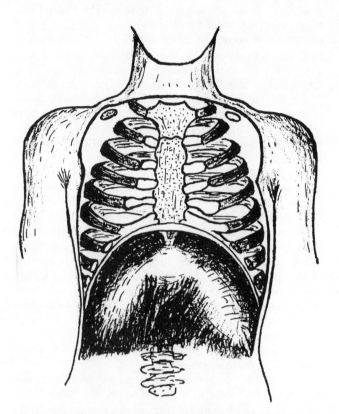

Cut-Away Illustration Showing Diaphragm as a Dome-Shaped Muscle Separating the Chest and Stomach Cavities

ible outward movement of the belly. When the stomach and intestines are full after eating, downward action of the diaphragm is limited and breath control, therefore, more limited. Visible evidence of diaphragm function is a tensing and outward "push" of the belly just below the "V" of the ribs. The bottom of the abdomen is not relaxed and protruded as some believe. *There should be no visible moving in of the lower wall of the stomach immediately after the attack.* If there is, resistance has not been established.

BREATHING AND SETTING-UP EXERCISES

Abstract deep breathing and setting-up exercises have little value in actual tonal production, but are often highly beneficial and necessary to general health and vitality. *They are urged as a daily ritual for all those with flat chests or general physical weakness.* Any exercise which improves health, vitality, and strengthens physique also promotes singing. The lack of vitality and presence of fatigue prevent many students from singing well even though they have fine structural instruments and are excellent musicians. The abdominal and inter-costal (waist-line)

muscles need strengthening in particular. Any calisthenic exercise for strengthening and flattening the abdomen, strengthening the expansive muscles around the waist-line and attaining a high chest posture, straight spine, neck and head position, is a valuable aid to the singer. Deep breathing can and should be practiced while walking with the chest up, inhaling and exhaling by counts for a number of steps, with a gradual increase of the number that can be covered without discomfort or rigidity.

The few selected breathing exercises recommended in *VOLUME I, Expressive Singing,* are not entirely abstract in function. They have a direct relation to establishing proper posture and the flexible feeling for slow emission of breath necessary in singing. They are introductory measures to establish proper postural conditions and feeling sensations, which are to be maintained in the simple singing exercises that follow.

One of the difficult problems for many beginning students is to get the muscular action and proper feeling for intercostal rib and back expansion. These are necessary to vital breath control, and to permit complete diaphragmatic action. Exercise I, if properly taught as outlined, will help accomplish this objective. Exercise II, the panting exercise, causes the pupil to become aware not only of the feeling for vigorous diaphragm action but also for staccato and accented attacks. During the panting exercise, vary the cadence, slow, medium and fast, but do not let speed become so excessive that control is lost. Be sure to check that students maintain proper posture — chest high and quiet, lower abdomen in, and the spine straight. Number of counts for the several steps in the exercises may be increased gradually *only* as students are able to sustain posture without collapse or rigidity at the end. *Insist on students first raising the chest and straightening the spine, and then starting to inhale slowly at the very beginning of the count.*

It is comparatively inefficient use of precious time to spend several minutes at the beginning of each period on breathing exercises. After careful introduction and class practice until the principles are understood and used with success, it is recommended that little or no further class time be devoted to them. *Continuation of breathing and calisthenic exercises should be the responsibility of the individual student,* and is recommended especially for those who obviously need it most. Unlike beginning tonal exercises, such exercises can be safely turned over to the conscientious student immediately after class introduction.

Exercises in breath control, except in the very initial stages, *normally are associated with tonal production.* "The capacity for breath will grow in the singer as it does in the athlete, by practicing the activity for which breath is required."[14] Continuously more exacting breath control exercises, involving both songs and vocalises, are basic to rapid development of technic and are an essential part of most lesson periods.

Lesson 2. Four Phases of Breath Control for the Singer

(See Volume I, p. 54)

It is quite evident that the four phases of breath control for the singer as listed in *VOLUME I*, "Inhalation, Suspension, Exhalation, and Recovery," are two more than are present in natural inspiration. Suspension and Recovery are not involved in normal breathing. The four phases are convenient and useful to the teacher in explaining necessary physical action and feeling associations, and for stimulating correct thought on the part of the student in habituating the necessary feeling associations. Rather than emphasis on memorizing the four steps involved, in the false hope that this will help in the breathing act, it is recommended that *emphasis be on establishing the accompanying postural and feeling associations as habitual for each of the phases concerned.* Attempts to directly and consciously control specific muscle action in any of the four phases will weaken or destroy necessary coordination for proper breath control. Control must be natural and *indirect*, based on the stimuli of how tone production should *sound* and how it should *feel*.

INHALATION

Proper inhalation is the basic key to success in the three phases of breath control which follow. Singers who inhale nervously or inadequately are always troubled with interference in the vocal act. The New York Singing Teachers Association[15] maintains that the chest always remain high and stationary in respiration for singing. A comfortably high, quiet chest is not only fundamental for proper inhalation, but its continuance is necessary for successfully controlled phonation. In regard to breathing it is the first technical aim of sound pedagogy, with relaxed inhalation second.

The high, still upper chest is a postural control, and not a direct attempt at physical manipulation. The chest is first raised by the stretched spine action *before* inhalation starts; *it should never be raised while breathing in.* It is well to quote the old saying to students, "We raise the chest to breathe, we do not breathe to raise the chest." When students learn that the act of raising the chest before singing is quite independent from breathing, and practice it first entirely separate from singing, they have taken the first step to successful breath control.

Normally, breath is taken simultaneously through the nose and the mouth. This gives the most breath in the quickest and quietest manner. If inhalation is unduly noisy or "wheezy," *it is nearly always due to opening the vocal bands insufficiently.* This action causes their edges to wheeze noisily. Experimentation by the student will usually prove this point. Too much inhalation through the nose, and too little through the mouth, also will cause noisy breathing.

A deviated septum or enlarged turbinate bone in the nose might need surgical operation for correction of blocked passage. This operation results not only in quieter, more effortless breathing, but also in increased resonance space. Students who have continued colds or severe blockage of the nasal passage are urged to consult a specialist and follow his advice regarding need for treatment or an operation.

When the singer has a head cold, he must learn to open the throat and mouth more to compensate. Unduly cold temperature, or air laden with tobacco smoke, may irritate the throat and cause coughing. If singing under these conditions, it is well to inhale mostly through the nose even at the cost of more noisy breathing. Breathing through the nose is generally considered more conducive to a relaxed throat preceding the attack, and is encouraged as the major means of breath supply, especially for those addicted to extreme tension.

A sigh-like beginning of a yawn feeling is the recommended sensation for inhalation. "The freedom of deep breathing for singing is exemplified by a contented sigh."[16] This type of gentle inhalation relaxes the throat and all phonation muscles; induces deep-breathing; and automatically brings the larynx into an ideal, moderately low position for the tonal attack. The deeper and lower one imagines the filling sensation, down into the pelvis or even into the very toes, the fuller inhalation will be and the more the throat will be opened.

Although often confused, deep-breathing and amount of breath inhaled are not the same thing. Deep-breathing (diaphragmatic-costal breathing) is the *manner* of breathing for breath control, not the *amount*. In fact, too much breath for the demands of the phrase overloads resistance muscles, perhaps causing their immediate collapse, a breathy tone, or, at best, eventuates in unnecessary exhaustion. Physiologists claim that excessive breath, left unused in the lungs, sets up a metabolism, forming carbon dioxide gas and weakening or poisoning the system. *Learning to take and control a deep, full breath is a developmental process, and should not be hurried unduly.* It is well to advise the student first to practice full deep-breathing in exercises without tone. He

---

[14]Jones, Archie N. "Techniques in Choral Conducting." Carl Fischer, 1948, p. 24.

[15]New York Singing Teachers Association. "Its Story." Theodore Presser, 1928, p. 31.

[16]Waters, Crystal. "Song, the Substance of Vocal Study." G. Schirmer, Inc., 1930, p.5.

should refrain from too much inhalation in singing until the resistant muscles are strong enough to endure the strain of holding back a large supply of breath. "That the quality of sound is better where superfluous air is not inhaled is unquestionable."[17]

Actually, the amount of breath one can inhale is relatively unimportant, especially in the beginning. *Deep breath action, the establishment of resistance or "hold," and efficiency of tone are absolutely vital to singing, however.* It is always a mistake, no matter how strong the resistant muscles, to inhale a much larger amount of breath than needed for the phrase — just enough and a little more for reserve is ideal for both tone and control. The eminent soprano, Lilli Lehman, discovered eventually that she had been laboring for years under the handicap of inhaling too generously for the demands of the phrase. When corrected, both tone and endurance improved.

Economy of breath is much more important than volume of breath, according to Herbert-Caesari.[18] The ability to sing long phrases is not a matter of lung capacity but "It is in knowing how to control the breath after it is taken."[19] Taking too much breath for a short phrase is as incorrect as taking too little for a long one, according to Jessica Dragonette.[20] "In singing never attempt to fill the lungs to their utmost capacity."[21] *The basis of fine breath control is pure resonant tone and not a great amount of inhalation.*

On the other hand, *timid, tentative, and scared beginners often have to be urged to breathe generously, to be positive and "physical" about inhalation, and to take time to breathe.* Short, inadequate, tense inhalation is the first by-product of fear. When music allows, students are strongly advised always to take plenty of time for a slow, deep, gentle inhalation, but never more than they feel comfortable in sustaining. Places to habituate this practice are before beginning, when there is no introduction, on introductions, and interludes. *The pupil is wise who establishes the habit of starting a slow inhalation a number of beats before the attack.* Instructors who are vigilant in checking students to make sure these principles are observed will be most successful in teaching breath control.

The physiological reason why breath must be deep and never shallow, or nervously "gulped," is simple. The lower part of the lungs not only is far larger than the upper part, but also is adjacent to comparatively strong diaphragmatic-costal control muscles. Since the upper part of the lungs employs clavicular (chest) action, it is never involved in proper singing, or a throaty and poorly-controlled tone results. It is far better to take a catch-breath if enough low breath has not been taken.

SUSPENSION

Suspension of the breath is merely the initial establishment of "hold" in the diaphragm muscles around the waist-line (a gentle outward lift), with a consequent "firming" of the belly wall. *After inhalation there is a sensation as if breath were continuing to be taken in when "suspension" starts.* This feeling holds the air column in balance, moving neither in nor out, until the attack. *The vocal bands remain open as established on inhalation.* The sensation for a free, open, throat is best described as that experienced when breathing deeply and easily, mouth closed, but with very relaxed jaw and lips, as if about to go to sleep. It is necessary for the student to learn that suspension of breath, and the following attack, are not accomplished by closing the vent in the larynx but by a gentle, holding-back and out action of the diaphragm and waist-line muscles, while the throat is kept open and lax.

EXHALATION (PHONATION)

The Old Italian Masters continually advised their students to "Hold back the breath." *The feeling of holding back the breath is essential to establish "Suspension," and continues through the attack and the entire phrase following.* It prevents collapse of the resistant breath muscles and establishes a steadiness of control, necessary for all good legato singing. When posture is correct, and all the muscles function properly in singing, there is a feeling of flexible, expansive openness in the body. Students are advised in phonation (singing):

1. *That the chest never collapses nor do the shoulders move up or down when singing even the longest phrase.* The feeling of continuous outward lift of the ribs around the lower waist-line and the high, quiet chest must persist to the very end of the phrase.

2. *That they not attempt to sing too long phrases on one breath,* but always maintain good quality of tone and sufficient breath reserve first, with the long ideal phrase second in importance. An experienced singer never uses all the breath in the body, no matter how long the phrase. There is always a small reserve in the upper lung area which is maintained by high chest position.

3. *That efficient tone is basic for efficient breath control.* A breathy, leaky tone makes futile all the good qualities of posture and diaphragm action.

4. *That under no circumstance should the singer try to "pull in" the diaphragm or control its action*

[17]Graves, Richard M. "Singing for Amateurs." Oxford U. Press, 1954, p. 45.

[18]Op. cit., p. 17.

[19]Christy, Van A. "Glee Club and Chorus." G. Schirmer, Inc., 1936, p. 17.

[20]Dragonette, Jessica. "The Mental Approach to Singing." (an interview) Etude, 1940, Vol. 58. p. 510.

[21]Henderson, W. J. "The Art of Singing." Dial Press, 1938, p. 44.

consciously. The function of the diaphragm in singing is resistance.

RECOVERY

Recovery is primarily physical — a moment, no matter how brief, of relaxation in the breath control muscles and larynx before the new phrase is attacked. It is also at times, however, a difficult mental problem. For example, a high register, dramatic *fortissimo* climax followed by a legato, low register *pianissimo* phrase is one of the most difficult tests of a singer's technic. Recovery is mental in order to meet the new style demands. It is also physical in order to recover from the intensity and "drive" of the previous loud, dramatic phrase sufficiently to sing with the soft, simple legato now demanded. Composers are aware of the extreme difficulty and sometimes follow such a climax with a rest, or *fermata* over a rest, in the score, indicating that a pause for recovery is in order.

Singers learn gradually to speed up recovery between phrases until it can be done with amazing rapidity. In beginning practice it is best to take it in "slow motion," rather than start the next phrase tense and exhausted. A series of long phrases without any rests in between is especially difficult for the beginner, straining endurance ability. Authorities advise that such songs never be assigned to beginning students. Phrasing requirements gradually can become more requiring as technic and endurance progress.

Lesson 3. The Attack

(See Volume I, p. 58)

It is of primary importance that *the attack should always be natural, coordinated, and as spontaneous as in speech.* The jaw is never opened first and the lips set in some fancied position for the vowel; opening the mouth and lip formation for the vowel are simultaneous with breath impulse for tone, just as in speech.

Most students have difficulty mastering a smooth attack right in the center of pitch with a free, ringing, sonorous quality. The explanations and exercises given in Expressive Singing, Volume I, clarify the matter and simplify the problem for the teacher. Vocal methods normally recognize that there are two improper attacks, the Glottal, and the Aspirate (breathy). They rarely deal also with the distinction among the three correct types of attack: Normal Legato, Staccato, and Accented. These all are explained clearly, and practical exercises provided to inaugurate mastery. In the beginning, it is recommended that these exercises be practiced only in the middle range, where tones are easiest.

The attack may be incorrectly adjusted in four respects: pitch, dynamics, vowel color, and resonance (tonal focus or balance). It is important that *clear concepts regarding these factors be in minds of students preceding the attack, or tone will be faulty.* There is a tendency to "slur" or move all these factors into adjustment *after* the attack. Proper attack demands that they be correctly adjusted in exact timing with breath impulse.

STROKE OF THE GLOTTIS

A great deal of confusion exists in vocal writings regarding the meaning of "stroke of the glottis" on the attack. Most authorities believe it should never be permitted under any circumstances. They apparently are interpreting the term as "shock of the glottis," to be avoided at all times, of course. A "shock of the glottis" is caused by closing the vocal bands after inhalation to stop the breath from rushing out again, then opening them on the attack with a harsh, explosive "shock" of an unpleasant throaty quality. It cannot occur if the vocal bands are not closed after inhalation and preceding the breath impulse. *It can always be prevented if the student learns habitually to "Suspend" the breath with the vocal cords left open,* regardless of vowel, style, or degree of force desired on the attack.

Students are prone to attack with a shock of the glottis, particularly when first attempting the *staccato* and the accented types of attack. They are less likely to employ this harsh and injurious effect when singing the rounder *Oo* and *Oh* vowels; the *Ah* and *Ay* are common offenders. Legato style requires a very neat and gentle attack, staccato a sharp, neat impulse, and accented style a heavy, weighty breath impulse. On the attack it is vital that movement of breath and glottal adjustment be synchronized exactly, and regardless of style or force of tone, *there never should be a throaty glottal sound.*

MEANING OF OPEN THROAT

Authorities agree that the throat should be open for tonal production. "The expression *open throat* is used to describe the sensation of freedom or passivity (or space) in the throat region that is said to accompany good singing."[22] Caruso, Chaliapin and the greatest artists of the past and present endorse the theory that "The more open the throat is, the more full-throated, vibrant and generally desirable the tone is likely to be."[23]

The completely open throat does not mean either forcible conscious distention, or relaxed, flabby vocal cords that do not resist sufficiently to resonate breath efficiently. In addition it does not mean dropping the jaw to the maximum, in the mistaken belief that

[22]Fields, Victor Alexander. "Training the Singing Voice." Kings Crown Press, 1947, p. 118.
[23]Austin-Ball, Thomas. "Answers to Some Vocal Questions." Eastman School of Music Publication No. 7, 1938, p. 14.

this will completely open the throat. Although an open throat is accompanied in proper singing with a feeling of loose and limber lower jaw and a receding rather than a jutting chin, *an open throat and an open mouth are not synonomous.* The throat can be either open or constricted, with the mouth either open to the maximum or closed to the minimum. "It must not be imagined that to open the mouth wide will do the same for the throat. If one is well versed in the art, one can open the throat perfectly without a perceptible opening of the mouth."[24]

There are those who mistakenly interpret the idea of the completely open throat as meaning a consciously controlled, distended, or spread condition. This theory of direct control is opposed by most teachers as extremely dangerous and is well summed up by Clippinger. "It is physically impossible to hold the throat open consciously without a considerable degree of tension."[25] To do so would be in direct contradiction to the principle of relaxation, the basic requirement for an open throat. It is certain that if a student is instructed to open his throat without knowing what it means, he almost invariably attempts to spread and distend the pharynx. This results in harsh, tense production.

Three important facts need to be stressed in learning the proper concept for the "open throat:"

1. *Open throat means,* first of all before the attack, *open vocal bands on Inhalation, and Suspension.*

2. *Open throat means a relaxed, long shape of the pharynx;* it never means a distended or "spread" pharynx. The throat is *relaxed* open but not consciously distended or held open. Sensation of an open throat is that of relaxed "drop" or depth in the lower throat and a gently arched upper throat.

3. *Opening the throat and opening the mouth are two quite different things.*

In correct singing the palate has a feeling of *gentle* lift upward when the pharynx is fully opened. The open vocal bands, low larynx, forward, relaxed tongue base position, and the feeling of gentle lift of the soft palate, are all attributes of the open throat. This is undoubtedly what Jan DeReszke, internationally famous tenor and one of the world's greatest teachers, meant when he admonished his students to "sing with a smile in the throat." This feeling causes not only easier production but also a lift of the soft palate and upper pharynx. Like most good things, however, it can be overdone if misinterpreted to mean conscious and extreme distention of the throat. *The lift feeling should always be gentle and relaxed and is highly necessary for the high compass and louder sonorities.* It causes a roundness and "blooming" quality to the tone as the upper pharynx and head spaces are opened up fully for resonation.

Again we wish to warn that this lift of the upper pharynx is achieved through a long, *relaxed,* arched feeling in the throat and not by conscious distention. Conscious distention or forcible "spread" of the throat causes the walls of the throat to become tense and hard, resulting in a tense, hard tone. The consciously raised soft palate and unnaturally distended throat are held responsible by authorities for ruining many voices and cutting promising singing careers short. "Perhaps the first rule on which the good teacher will insist is that the throat will be left so open and free from interference that the singer will not be conscious of its existence."[26]

FREE TONE

To obtain a free and efficient tone on attack, several fundamentals are to be observed:

1. Tone is thought free and ringing.
2. The throat is open as described previously.
3. Tone is attacked with assurance, positiveness and as naturally as if it were being spoken.
4. All attacks are tonal attacks first and vowel production second. (Note — See also p. 58, "Tonal *uh* Basis").

Proper posture and a complete mental concept of the tone are basic, of course. Kortkamp advises that during inhalation "Imagine you can hear your voice singing the first note . . . .*before* actually singing it."[27] Jeffries says, "The basic preparation is very simple. First there should be an upright position; second, an easy, relaxed intake of breath; and third, a normal opening of the mouth with a feeling of opening the whole channel down into the chest."[28] (the yawn feeling). Ferguson maintains that an assured and positive attack, "Permits the involuntary, natural, and consequently correct action of those muscles which are employed in the production of tone. The tone then 'places' itself without any artificial or localized aid; the tongue and jaw are free from constraint and the articulation of syllables and words is as easy and natural as in speech."[29] It is obvious that any studied attempt to control or place the tongue, lips, or jaw in any specific position first, and then attack the tone, is contrary to the above philosophy. Most vocal authorities agree that such attempts result inevitably in more rather than less tension.

---

[24]Marafioti, Op. cit., p. 157.
[25]Clippinger, D. A. "The Clippinger Class Method of Voice Culture." Ditson, 1932, p. 8.
[26]Graves, Op. cit., p. 50.
[27]Kortkamp, Ivan A. "Compensation for Flattening." Educational Music Magazine, Sept.-Oct. 1940, Vol. 20, p. 46.
[28]Jeffries, Arthur. "The Natural Voice." Etude, 1934, Vol. 52, p. 430.
[29]Ferguson, George. "Class Instruction in Singing." Music Supervisors Journal, Feb. 1932, p. 39.

A quick tonal attack should precede the vowel. The vowel "mold" (place and space for resonation) is then kept in the *same space* as the fundamental preceding tone *Uh.* This method for attack is explained thoroughly in the student manual, with explicit directions and exercises for achieving it. A rough "glottic shock" is impossible when all vowels have a common denominator of uniform tonal attack to promote both free production and uniform vowel color, so necessary in legato. The natural tone of the human voice, *Uh,* demands neither shaping of the lips nor forming of the pharynx, and is therefore ideal to induce the relaxed, open throat condition necessary for the following vowel.

All vowels are "man made" and demand forming of the pharynx for their production. *Uh* is the natural sound of the human voice when produced involuntarily in the groan, the last death gasp, or when we are punched in the "wind." The Normal Legato Attack exercise in Expressive Singing, Volume I starts with the *Uh* tonal attack in slow motion preceeding the vowel in order to enable the student to grasp the idea easily. This is speeded up gradually until the tonal inception cannot be heard by the listener and, after some practice, the method becomes an habitual reflex with the singer.

Leading authorities concur that there should be a feeling of "singing on the breath" *through* the vocal cords and not *with* them. Although flexibly tense on and after the attack, in order to function, all muscles concerned with tonal production in the throat in correct singing are relaxed *prior* to the attack. *Any previous tension is sure to be reflected in tense tone.* This concerns the larynx, pharynx, tongue, jaw, and lips. Preparation for the attack is therefore setting up relaxation in these areas previous to the attack.

In addition, other interference muscles which should *not* be used in phonation are relaxed prior to the attack, and continue that way throughout the phrase. Either we keep rigidity out of the neck, chest, shoulders, arms, and hands or tonal freedom suffers. If the chest muscles become rigidly tense by nervous inhalation before the attack, inevitably they cause the resistant muscles of the diaphragm and waist-line to become rigid, destroying all possibility of proper breath control and free production. Learning to take time to inhale deeply and easily and set-up "Suspension" before the attack is a fundamental for free tone production. To obtain unanimity of attack in class singing, a beginning group is taught to inhale together rhythmically by the use of a slow count such as, "One-two-ready-sing."

NORMAL LEGATO ATTACK

If the vocal bands are adjusted too loosely, the result is a wasteful, breathy tone lacking in vitality, and a "scooping" of pitch. If tone is thought exactly on the center of pitch and attacked mentally from above, the vocal bands will automatically adjust to the right tension at the outset, and prevent the unpleasant "scooping" slur so common with amateurs and the crooning profession. This scooping attack may be proper and legitimate at times in popular singing of blues songs, or when the effect of laziness or helplessness is desired. It should be a means of departure for an occasional special effect, however, and not a norm for singing.

If the glottis is closed preceding the attack or adjusted too violently at the moment of attack, tone will be tense. The ideal attack is neat and precise, never violent or explosive. It varies in crispness and strength according to whether the style is legato, staccato, or heavily accented.

Legato attack is best induced first by the hummy "N-uh"; the "N" is then omitted using only the tonal "Uh" sound before the vowel; and finally, by speeding up the preceeding tonal "Uh" so that it, like the aspirate "H" recommended for starting the staccato attack, is not heard by the listener.

It is normal to sustain, or even *crescendo-decrescendo* tones in legato passages after the attack. It is well for the singer to be prepared to do this by taking sufficient breath on inhalation, therefore, and not wasting it on the attack. "On starting a vocal tone, the attack should be made confidently and lightly, so that the voice shall sound full and sonorous, and shall be ready, instantly after the attack, to increase in strength according to the singer's will, and without effort."[30]

STACCATO ATTACKS

Staccato and accented attacks are a danger to beginners in that they are inclined to change the open throat and free resonation established in legato. In proper staccato attack, vowel production and resonance form remain the same as in legato, breath support is kept flexibly vital, and the same principles of free upward and downward scale adjustments are maintained.

Staccato attack should be sung *lightly.* No attempt to sing a series of staccato notes quite rapidly, or in an extended range, is made until it can be executed easily and freely at a slower pace in the middle voice range. Because the breath must move with a sharp, precise impulse, danger of "shock of the glottis" also is increased. Staccato practice is excellent for developing agility, quick responsiveness, free production, extensive range, efficient phonation without breath wastage, and perfect intonation in attacking tone squarely in the center of pitch. While staccato agility technic is used most often in concert

---

[30]Silva, Giulo. "Advice to beginners in Singing." G. Schirmer, Inc., 1917, p. 3.

by sopranos, it is equally necessary as a practice habit to make all types of voices more flexible.

ACCENTED ATTACK

Accented attack is not the same as staccato attack. In staccato, each tone is attacked lightly and sharply, and is stopped immediately so that a definite interval of silence is heard before the next tone starts. In an accented attack, the tone is started with a heavier breath impulse and is held for indicated rhythmic length.

It is well to delay any except introductory practice on the accented attack until the other two easier types are mastered and the vocal instrument stronger. Most early attempts to achieve a strong *sforzando* accent result in extreme constriction, poor tone and, if persisted in, injury to the voice. There also is greater danger of the student's attempting the harmful "shock of the glottis" attacks because of the weight and force of tone required.

Weight of accent must not come from the glottis but from breath impulse. There is no difference among the three types of accent in the basic method of attacking tone with a free, open throat. The pupil need be conscious only of the difference in sound desired and in the relative strength and weight of breath impulse. In practice the consonants "V" and "Y" before vowels will be found even better than an "H" for the approach before vowels to induce a strong accent. They are especially useful in bringing vowels out of a gutteral throat position and giving them maximum space and sonority.

TONGUE ACTION

The tongue is one of the most important muscles used in phonation and articulation. Its improper use can destroy any possibility for free and beautiful tone. The proper use of the tongue determines the opening and shaping of the throat that make possible the necessary pharyngeal adjustments in producing the various vowels, as well as affecting the proper low position of the larynx.

The objective is to get the tongue out of the way on the attack. In order to do this, it lies loosely well forward in the mouth with the tip close to, or barely touching, the base of the lower teeth. This recommended position conforms with the outline drawn by the great soprano and vocal teacher, Lilli Lehman, in her text, "How to Sing." It conforms also with the outline used by Caruso, according to Marafioti,[31] who was the great tenor's personal physician and an eminent authority on vocal production.

The tongue tip should never be curled up, or drawn down rigidly. The base may move forward and roll slightly upward with the attack, further lengthening the pharynx, but it can never be consciously forced high or tensed. "Grooving" the tongue is favored by some authorities, but the ma-

jority frown on consciously attempting this position if it does not appear with natural, free tonal production. *Base of the tongue is never tensed rigidly* in free production because it is connected directly through the front wall of the pharynx with the muscles that control vocal band action, and will cause a hard tense tone. The flexible tension, which occurs when the tongue base moves naturally forward out of the pharynx on the attack, is sufficient to set up any necessary resistance for controlled phonation.

Proper tongue position and action is a subject over which controversy continues to rage. On the one· hand, we have those who make one or all of the following claims:

1. That in the beginning proper action of the tongue should be consciously controlled and exercised by observation while looking in a mirror.
2. That the tongue base should be pulled forward, "grooved," and raised upward in a high arch at the back and held firmly in this position.
3. That the tip of the tongue should be curled downward and drawn solidly back against the pull of the larynx muscles.

The author and the majority of successful vocal teachers believe that the aforementioned methods are injurious and the reasoning behind them false. Tongue control is accomplished through the mind, "not through voluntary effort or physical force."[32] It is no wonder that the inexperienced vocal student is often hopelessly confused by the extensive reading written by so-called vocal authorities. Let us examine the evidence briefly and attempt to bring order out of confusion on this issue.

There are three major fallacies in the foregoing assumptions:

1. In spite of the fact that the tongue can be observed and controlled by conscious action, this procedure is unnatural, and unnecessary and most students will obtain results more quickly, easily, and safely by indirect tonal and feeling stimuli. There is no doubt that normal action of the tongue in artistic singing is involuntary and reflex, and that such action is best induced by thought of desired diction and tone. It is only the abnormal student who ever needs conscious control methods, and then only after the normal indirect approach has failed.
2. Excessive pull of the tongue base will upset the ideal flexible tension balance which normally is created involuntarily by thought stimuli regarding the nature of tone desired. It overpowers the counter pull of the larynx muscles, causing unstable con-

---

[31]Op. cit., p. 113.

[32]Skiles, Wilbur Alonza. "Learning to Rule the Unruly Tongue." Etude, 1934, Vol. 52, p. 675.

trol and a harsh, constricted tone. By adding more than normal pull to the tongue base, tension passes beyond the flexibility stage and goes over into the rigid. It is our belief that the student should not be even conscious of the *normal* flexible tongue base tension which occurs automatically on the attack, let alone attempt to create more tension by conscious control.

3. Curling the tip of the tongue back, and "folding" it solidly against the base, not only adds further to rigidity of tone, but also interferes with the free action of the tip of the tongue in its principal function while singing — articulation of consonants. Laws of physiology require that *a muscle must be relaxed previous to its use for controlled, flexible action.* Tip of the tongue could not be relaxed previous to articulating consonants if it were "folded back solidly." We have never heard an exponent of the tense, folded-back tongue tip position who articulated freely and clearly. This theory for singing has to be discarded therefore, even if we could accept it for vowel production. In singing the consonants also must be articulated.

What if an occasional student does not respond to normal indirect methods for inducing proper tongue action, and has an aggravated low tongue base position which prevents the throat from being properly opened? It must be admitted that this happens in rare instances. Then the direct method can be tried. The pupil is instructed to look in a mirror, place the tongue tip loosely forward, and move the base in an arching forward and upward position at the exact moment tone is attacked. It is suggested that this action be done without tone a number of times before tone is attempted. We can expect that tone will be more or less tense until the postural forward and high base position can be habituated through practice and forgotten. In habituating, students are instructed to analyze and aim to reproduce naturally the *associative feeling sensations* while concentrating on producing a free, spontaneous tone. This is a much longer and more tedious approach and is certainly not recommended for the average student or class procedure.

JAW ACTION AND MOUTH SPACE

Since shape and size of the various resonators vary radically among individuals, each singer is a law unto himself regarding mouth space needed for a given pitch and dynamics. Certainly no "rule of the thumb," like placing a number of fingers between the teeth, will work ideally for all as a principle in obtaining proper mouth space for maximum tonal freedom and beauty. Such procedures may be quite injurious in fact, causing rather than alleviating tension. After the student understands certain fundamental principles for free tonal production in obtain-

ing an even scale, particularly those outlined in Chapter 16 of the student manual, he can experiment under the teacher's guidance to discover just the right amount of "jaw drop" needed for best production on any given scale degree and volume.

It is definitely wrong to exaggerate opening of the mouth to the point of rigidity in the jaw muscles. The jaw should not be stretched, pulled, or forced down by conscious muscular effort while singing. After the pupil has *let* the jaw drop as far as it will go without forcing, and mouth opening is still not sufficient to emit sonorous tonal volume, stretching exercises without tone are recommended for awhile.

For all tones there is an ideal mouth opening which varies with compass, dynamics, and tone color desired. Exaggeration either horizontally or vertically is undesirable. Normal mouth shape lengthens vertically for high tones; there is very little "jaw drop" and mouth space for low. Beginning singers tend to keep mouth opening too restricted, especially for high tones. On the other hand, we agree with Haywood's contention that "Opening the mouth too wide is the most common error"[33] that afflicts the concert singer, and, in most instances, all other vocalists in the low compass. A forced or "locked" wide open jaw position is undesirable in any register and especially fatal in the low. *What is needed is more throat and less mouth opening for maximum beauty and freedom of tone.*

The head is not to be tilted up to drop the jaw as seen frequently; *the jaw should be allowed to drop loosely of its own weight.* Directing students to *relax the muscles over the cheek bones* is one of the most effective devices for correcting insufficient jaw drop, or a "jaw-lock" condition, which plagues many pupils. Because of the efficacy of this thought, it is evident that there is close coordination between the muscles over the cheek bones and those that lock the hinges of the jaw. When maximum opening is desired, the jaw should feel as if it drops easily *down* and *back*. This prevents a rigid and jutting-out chin position that always creates harsh tone. If students will concentrate on dropping the jaw loosely and easily of its own weight, and relaxing the muscles over the cheek bones, opening will usually be adequate and will develop gradually without strain.

LIP ACTION AND SHAPE

It is necessary that the lips be loosely and easily formed for all vowels and be flexibly mobile in action. It is a mistake to set them in a fancied position for the vowel first and then attack the tone. *A moderately long, somewhat rounded or "square" position of the lips is recommended with but slight*

---

[33]Haywood, Frederick H. "Universal Song." G. Schirmer, Inc., 1933-1942, Vol. II, p. 14.

variation for particular vowels. A "spread," "grinning" position of the lips usually causes a "white," strained tone. "Exaggerated mouth and lip action is totally unnecessary and spoils many a good singer."[34]. Volume I for this lesson has a clear explanation of lip shape and action and excellent illustrations of lip shape for the vowels.

LARYNX AND VOCAL CORD ACTION

The vocal cords are a pair of muscular bands or folds that project into the laryngeal cavity. Tone is produced by the upward pressure of breath against the bands, causing them to vibrate. The so-called "false cords" above the "true vocal cords" do not affect phonation directly but are for fixation and distention of the laryngeal ventricles.

In spite of invention of the laryngoscope by Garcia, the exact action and function of the complex muscles in the larynx for singing is still a subject about which anatomists disagree. Fortunately, "It is as unnecessary for the student to know the different muscles and cartilages of the larynx as it is for the dancer to have a detailed anatomical knowledge of the muscles of the legs."[35] In any event, attempts to manipulate or control the attack of tone through conscious attention to any action of the larynx are doomed to failure. "The healthy activity of the muscles of the voice box lies below the level of consciousness in a realm that still awaits new techniques of investigation. Only when something is painfully wrong do we become conscious of the function and never do we control it directly. . . . If you feel that you are manufacturing tone in it, you are feeling something that is wrong. It is only when you seem to let go in the larynx, and the tone begins to seem as if it were in the resonators, that production will be right."[36] When questioned about her singing, the great prima donna, Emmy Destinn, is quoted by Marafioti as having said, "When I sing I feel as if I had no throat."[37]

It is agreed generally that a normal low position of the larynx is desirable, and is induced by proper, relaxed inhalation and dropping the jaw loosely for the attack. A larynx that is too high tends to produce a shrill, "white," constricted tone; one that is too low, a muffled, "dark," gutteral tone that also is constricted. "Elevation of the larynx during singing is a faulty mechanism."[38] A long, open position of the pharynx induces a normally low larynx.

The two greatest faults of students in regard to proper position of the larynx are:

1. They do not relax the jaw, tongue base, and frontal neck muscles sufficiently on inhalation to allow the larynx to sink to its normal low position.

2. They immediately close the throat and tense rigidly on the attack, pulling the larynx upward in the process. (Signor Lamperti,[39] one of the leading exponents of Bel Canto singing, warns us to take care that the larynx does not rise while singing.)

It is incorrect ever to have a feeling that the voice-box is held, but rather that it is free and "floating." Any rigidity or "setting" of the jaw, lips, tongue base, or front neck muscles is usually reflected immediately by grip in the larynx, preventing free production. When the larynx persists in rising on the attack, constricting tone, students can be helped by placing a finger lightly on the Adams apple after relaxed inhalation; they should be instructed to keep the larynx in the same position as they sing "Uh — — Oo," while maintaining a feeling of gradual transition from neutral tone to vowel. The other vowels can be added in like manner. This procedure induces a freer tone on the attack, a low larynx, and corrects attempts to *pronounce* vowels locally in the glottis, a frequent cause of a raised larynx and throat constriction. This method again is for correction of the abnormal student, and is not recommended for normal class procedure.

BEST VOWEL FOR INITIAL STUDY

It is possible to begin the attack and study of vowel production with any of the particular vowels, as many successful teachers have demonstrated. Authorities do not agree, but the usual choice is either *Ah* or *Oh* for initial study and as a model for comparison. Many teachers prefer the *Ah*, arguing that it is naturally the most sonorous of the vowels and lies in the middle of the tonal color scale from bright to dark — *Ee, Ay, Ah, Oh, Oo*.

The author and many other vocal teachers find, however, that the *Ah* generally is produced very badly by beginning students. It "sticks" in the throat and often is accompanied by tongue base depression, "jaw-lock," and too excessive mouth width for balancing with the other vowels. It takes too long therefore, to cure all these evils before it can be used safely as a model for improving the other vowels. "The sound of *Ah* often gives trouble. Students can find more different ways to sing it incorrectly than any other sound that I am acquainted with. They sing it too far back and nearly always sing *Aw* rather than *Ah*"[40] "Many singers do not realize that

---

[34]Lloyd, Robert. "The Robert Lloyd Tone System." Herr Wagner Publishing Co., 1929, p. 9.

[35]Marifioti, Op. cit., p. 79.

[36]Vennard, William. "Singing, the Mechanism and the Technic." Edwards Bros., Inc., 1949, p. 44.

[37]Op. cit., p. 79.

[38]Negus, V. E., "The Mechanism of the Larynx." C. V. Mosby Co., 1929, p. 383.

[39]Lamperti, G. B. "The Technics of Bel Canto." G. Schirmer, Inc., 1905.

[40]Downing, William B. "Vocal Pedagogy." Carl Fischer, 1927, p. 27.

the vowel *Ah* is most difficult to master."[41] Philip agrees with this opinion, claiming that the *Ah* is the most difficult vowel for the beginning student to place in balanced resonation and therefore, "It is inadvisable to start with *Ah*."[42] Both the *Ah* and the *Ay* are particularly poor choices in beginning practice on the attack. Students are more inclined to try to pronounce them than other vowels deep in the glottis with a closed vocal cord "glottic attack."

Since the *Oo* is produced with a muffled, dull, devitalized resonance by most beginners, *Oh* is the safest vowel for initial class study. It is our experience that the average student produces it more nearly correct without study, and can be taught to produce it freely, sonorously, and in pure quality quicker than any of the other vowels, when instructed to sing it with a ringing, exclamation-like, upper inflection quality.

The teacher will find that the tonal *Uh* attack idea described previously will act as a "persuader" allowing open throat attack on any of the vowels, which ever is preferred first. When the *Ah* can be gotten out of the low glottal area and into a foreward speech area, it can be used more safely as a desirable norm for comparison when the objective is to develop sonority. Voices that have a tendency to be breathy and too "spread" or spacious with throaty qualities should usually avoid the *Ah* as a model to improve their singing, however.

Lesson 4. The Catch-Breath

(*See Volume I, p. 67*)

USEFULNESS

The catch-breath is really a partial or half-breath, in which only breath supply in the lower part of the lungs is replenished sufficiently to allow the phrase to be completed. It is a temporary device for allowing beginning students to sing long phrases, that for them would be either impossible or possible only at the cost of exhaustion and poor tone quality. It is also a necessary technic for even the skilled professional to master in rapid tempo songs that do not allow time or rests between phrases to take a normal full breath.

The student is advised always to take a catch-breath, rather than end up a phrase in an exhausted condition. Normally, the singer should be able to sense inadequacy of breath supply to complete demands of the phrase either before beginning or immediately after the attack. If singing publicly, he can handle the phrasing so that it is possible and sounds natural to take a catch-breath at an appropriate point.

The artist, as well as the pupil, is faced with the problem of where to breathe. The artist, with his reserve of technic, normally need be troubled only with aesthetic considerations. The student often has not only the aesthetic problem but also a practical physical problem of inadequacy. In general, it is well to avoid the catch-breath when it is possible to do so with poise and some breath reserve left. However, the singer is ill advised who attempts to "last out" a phrase because it is ideal to do so at the cost of wavering or collapsing breath support and exhaustion for the succeeding phrase. Ideal phrasing should be plainly marked in the score, preferably by a colored pencil that is easily seen. Optional places for a catch breath in long difficult phrases can be inserted with a different kind of mark.

In oratorio arias and long runs in florid music, sometimes it is necessary to take a catch-breath in the course of an agility passage, indicated to be sung on one word or syllable. In that case, avoid breathing on major accents or obvious points, choosing a place that will interfere as little as possible with flow of the vocal line. Near the end of such a phrase is usually the least desirable spot. *When a catch-breath has to be taken usually it is best somewhere near the beginning or in the middle of the phrase rather than near the end.*

Some singers become so clever at taking a catch-breath that only the most critical in an audience is aware of inhalation and the broken musical phrase.

RULES FOR TAKING A CATCH-BREATH

The four rules following are the keys to success in taking a catch-breath cleverly:

1. Take breath at an appropriate point; usually after punctuation marks, nouns, or verbs, but never between the syllables of a word or after an article, preposition, or conjunction.
2. Take a quick half-breath simultaneously through both the mouth and the nose.
3. Keep dynamics of the tone just before the catch-breath the same as the tone just after it.
4. Keep tone color of the tone just before the catch-breath the same as the tone just after it.

Taking a *quick* catch-breath is actually not as necessary in slow and moderate tempos as is observance of points No. 3 and 4, in creating the effect that the phrase line has not been disturbed artistically.

One last warning is desirable — *Do not allow students, who are capable but too lazy or careless to sing the ideal phrase, to take catch-breaths.* This is the one hazard of study and mastery of the catch-breath. As soon as the pupil is capable of singing the ideal phrase, it is advisable that songs be reviewed and phrasing adjusted accordingly.

---

[41]Tkach, Peter. "Vocal Technic." Neil J. Kjos, 1948, p. 8.
[42]Philip, Frank. "Philosophy of Vocal Culture." Schribners, 1930, p. 101.

4

Tone

FUNDAMENTAL TONE

Fundamental tone of the human voice, *Uh*, belongs logically under this heading. It was found desirable, however, to introduce it in the previous chapter on the "Attack." It also will be discussed later in the lesson on "Evening the Vowels" where application of the idea is needed most by students. (See p. 58)

OUTLINE OF TONAL THEORY

The following "Outline of Tonal Theory" has been adopted by the American Academy of Teachers of Singing and is used by permission:

"Good vocal tone depends upon concept of beautiful sound and upon a sensitive and educated ear. It results from consequent coordination of the following:

1. Controlled breath.
2. A larynx whose normal position, neither locally raised or lowered, is insured by correct inhalation, and allows freedom of action of the tongue to which it is attached;
3. Vocal cords in unhindered vibration.
These three produce a fundamental tone, proportionately reinforced by —
4. The resonance chambers of the chest and the head (mouth and nasal cavities), and issuing through
5. a free throat;
6. Tongue, palate, lips, and jaw, all freely active in pronouncing without rigidity, and with no locally specialized effort for supposed aid to the tone.

This tone, easy flowing, smooth, permits every variety of expression in singing. Its inception, following inhalation, is the Attack; that is, the immediate application of breath to the vocal cords, after pitch and vowel adjustment of the whole apparatus."

IMPORTANCE OF TONE AND TONAL CONCEPT

Attention to tonal quality is basic to freedom, beauty, and expressiveness in singing. Roma advises students that "Every word should be sung as though you were in love with it."[1] "It is useless to expect the student to produce a good singing tone unless it first exists in the mind."[2] "The beautiful and satisfying tone associated with artistic singing must first be heard as a vocal image. The vocal image, in turn induces automatic actions on the part of the vocal mechanism."[3] We never sing more beautifully, freely, and significantly than we think. Students therefore, are strongly urged to saturate their minds with the finest of both live and recorded singing as a basic prerequisite to production of good tone.

In an interview published Jan. 7, 1951, in the Santa Barbara News Press, the eminent baritone, John Charles Thomas said, "While my career has been diversified and full, I have concentrated on one thing all my life — beauty of tone and line. As John McCormack used to say, 'if it ain't a pretty noise, it ain't worth nothing.'" Kagen also emphasizes the importance of tonal concept, "The greater the singer's concentration on the complete sound image, the more relaxed his body seems to become. The more the singer tries to concentrate on the muscular activities involved in his singing, the more tense these very muscles he is trying to control may become."[4] In discussing tone Henderson says, "Melba had an ideal conception of tone. She is seeking all the time for pure, velvety, luscious quality — not for a huge volume. Secondly, she makes her exquisitely conceived tone carry by the rational process of focusing or forming it correctly and floating it out to her hearers on the surface of a thin, steady, solid column of breath. She sings always within her limits and

[1]Roma, Lisa. "The Science and Art of Singing." G. Schirmer, Inc., 1956, p. 45.

[2]Clippinger, David Alva. "School Music" (Vocal Department), Chicago, Jan. 1935, p. 9.

[3]Peterson, Paul W. "Natural Singing and Expressive Conducting." John F. Blair, 1955, p. 5.

[4]Kagen, Sergius. "On Studying Singing." Rinehart and Co., 1950, p. 59.

that is one reason why her tones are so rich, so smooth, so mellow."[5]

What then must the student do to obtain such a free and beautiful tone? Would that the answer could be as brief as the question. While this chapter deals specifically with the problem, practically every lesson, in both Expressive Singing, Volume I and in this Textbook, has some bearing.

Lesson 1. Freedom and Vitality

(*Note — See p. 33 where the topic, "Free Tone," has already been discussed in relation to the "Attack." See also Volume I, p. 70.*)

How can the instructor and the student intelligently go about the task of building freedom, beauty, and expressiveness in tonal production? *By continuously applying and refining analytical judgment in reference to how the tone sounds and how it feels: that is the only way.* The author has broken down this basic generality into a discussion and listing of "Fundamental Criteria for Students to Use in Judging Their Own Singing." (Note — See p. 71 in Volume I) These criteria are the fundamental judgments in reference to tonal production which both the instructor and the student must use. Importance to progress of continual emphasis on their refined application cannot be overemphasized. The beginning student cannot keep all of the criteria listed in mind while singing; therefore, each must be stressed from time to time in song and exercises until all are automatically and subconsciously applied. Since aesthetic taste and discrimination are a developmental matter, students are reminded to seek continually to raise their standards as the surest way to speed up musicianship and technic.

Within certain limitations of volume and range, the vocal instrument of most students is capable of surprising beauty at an early stage of vocal study if challenged sufficiently by proper concepts of tone. *Students do not sing beautifully within these limitations because they do not think beautifully.* The problem is thus largely a psychological-aesthetic problem.

Physical progress follows along rapidly after mental stimuli; it can never be expected to precede it. *The vocalist will sing no more freely and beautifully than he thinks;* therefore, the principal way to improve tone is to improve thought. Authorities are in general agreement on this principle. "In the case of most singers, beautiful tone is evoked not by conscious attempts at manipulating the vocal organs, but by mentally conceiving the type of tone desired and thus bringing about automatically the proper physical adjustments. Criticism of the tone thus produced as to its adequacy in terms of what the ears of the teacher and pupils hear serves as a check upon the singer's concept and hence of resulting tone."[6]

The two most essential qualities of the singing tone are that it be free and ringing or vital. Students are advised always to question their tones first while practicing in terms of: (a) *Does it feel easy in the throat?* (b) *Does it sound ringing?* Such a tone has vitality, beauty, and resonance to carry regardless of dynamics, and is the basic norm desired. If in addition it has even vibrato, appropriate tone color and force, it has everything desired. The singer dare not be dulled into complacency when he has only one or the other of the aforesaid necessary fundamentals of tone. Any one factor can be present without the others; all should be questioned. It is possible to obtain a free and ringing tone at an early age. A ringing tone has no reference to dynamics. If anything, the student is instructed to *think soft tones even more intense in ringing quality than loud tones*, in order to counteract the tendency to think all soft tones dark, breathy, and devitalized.

"Faulty tone production is due to one of two factors, either the concept of tone is not correct, or the conditions of the vocal instrument are not conducive to good tone. In the case of the beginning singer, both of these factors may be the cause of faulty tone production."[7] "Having the conditions right means freeing the vocal instrument from all restriction, interference, resistance, tension, intrinsic and extrinsic, and properly managing the breath."[8] (Note — We have discussed in the previous chapter the intrinsic muscles [those actually used in singing] and relaxation of the extrinsic [those not used in singing]).

EASE IN PRODUCTION

It is necessary that tonal concept include more than pitch and volume; quality, ease, and proper associative feeling sensations are an essential part of the imagery. Since the imagery concerned deals with both how the tone should *sound* and how it should *feel*, it is the soundest method for developing proper physical coordination and growth in the muscles involved for singing. Methods for developing isolated muscles, with exercises dissociated from the actual act of singing, are to be regarded with suspicion at best.

The right way to produce tone is always the easy way. Technic without ease is imperfect technic. It frequently requires months of patient study before the student becomes conscious of small degrees of

---

[5]Henderson, William J. "The Art of Singing." Dial Press, 1948, revised edition, pp. 245-246.

[6]Dykema, Peter and Gehrkens, Karl. "The Teaching and Administration of High School Music." C. C. Birchard & Co., 1941, p. 199.

[7]Lee, Marjorie E. "Voice Classes in Secondary Schools." Masters Thesis, University of Ill., 1946, pp. 61-62.

[8]Clippinger, D. A. "Collective Voice Training." Music Supervisors National Conference Yearbook, 1935, p. 58.

tension in the throat and habitualizes a free, relaxed, spontaneous tonal production in the easy middle register. Ideals for tone production in the more difficult extremes of the high and low compass must be based on previous concepts and perfection of control in the more easily-produced middle range. Since a small amount of tension is most difficult for students to detect in their own voices, they must depend for a long time on the ear and advice of their instructor.

Extreme tension should be evident tonally to all but the most insensitive ear. It can be detected also by feeling the muscle of the under jaw and tongue base (Hyoglossus), or by looking in the mirror to check rigid jaw, set lips, and strained neck muscles. Once detected, *the best cure is thought of a perfectly free and beautiful tone with habituation of proper posture and expansive, steady breath support.* Quite often tones are tense because they are not fed enough breath to resonate them properly. "When the tone is correctly produced through the use of a free automatic action of the vocal cords, you will hear good tones and you will also be conscious of a lack of feeling, or sensation, in the larynx."[9] The habituated or subconscious feeling of ease and openness in the throat is there, of course, as if singing *through* the vocal bands and not *with* them, but there should never be a direct awareness of tension or function of the larynx.

In spite of the fact that source of tone is the larynx, *sensation of resonance should not be there.* A characteristic of tense production is the specific sensation of "placement" in one area only. The free tone has a general, balanced feeling of resonation, primarily in the upper pharynx and head and, secondarily, in the mouth and nose. The perfectly balanced tone has a feeling of *depth* (fullness in the open relaxed throat), *height* (upper throat and head space), and *forwardness* (front of the mouth, and nose). If pitch is low, there also may be an associative feeling of vibration in the chest. Sensation of head and nose vibration is more pronounced in the upper compass and that of mouth resonance in the middle and low range. *The singer is advised never to try to direct the voice to any specific resonance area, but to let it go where it will naturally seek its proper balance and attain the greatest possible freedom, beauty, and opulence.*

MAJOR TYPES OF TENSION TO AVOID

There are four principal types of tension or rigidity to avoid:

1. *Phlegmatic thought tension.* A tone which is allowed to "stand still" in mental development always becomes less interesting to the listener and probably more tense. A sustained tone, unless a monotonous effect is desired, should be developed in thought concept to more and more beauty, freedom, and emotional significance until released. Continual mental development of the tone is the best guarantee of flexible and free vocalization. A changing tone is much easier to sing freely than one that is held to a monotonous level.

2. *Articulation tension.* The jaw, lips, and tongue are articulating organs that are never "set" or held in one position but should move flexibly, continuously, not only from consonant to consonant and syllable to syllable, but also to a slight degree in the singing of a sustained vowel.

3. *Throat tension.* It frequently takes months of patient study under the supervision of a competent teacher, first, for the pupil to become conscious of small degrees of tension in the larynx, pharynx, tongue base, and neck muscles and, second, to habitualize a free, relaxed, spontaneous tonal production.

4. *Body and Breath Tension.* This type of tension is caused by a rigid chest and diaphragm, and by clavicular (chest) breathing. It often is induced by nervous, inadequate inhalation, the fundamental cause of which is fear. It is basic that students learn to take time to inhale in a relaxed manner, and to maintain a flexible expansive posture to guarantee proper control of breath energy.

FIVE CHARACTERISTICS OF TONAL FREEDOM

Besides sounding free with an even vibrato, tonal production in properly developed voices can be tested by five other criteria:

1. There will be an even, smooth, and fully usable range of at least two octaves.

2. There will be ability to sing both loud and soft with good quality and distinct dynamic gradations from *ppp* to *fff*.

3. Production will be flexible — agile in fast passages and quickly responsive to changes of pitch, dynamics, and tone color.

4. The voice is durable, capable of singing for long periods of time without exhaustion, and of maintaining its freshness over the years.

5. There will be ability to sing extremes of both sombre and bright tone color freely and easily. No voice is truly flexible that cannot meet this test; it may be free and agile but is not truly flexible.

RESERVE TECHNIC

Reserve technic is a characteristic of all truly fine singing. It is a necessity for free production and one of the most fundamental factors in reducing fear. Although a great artist appears to be singing

---

[9]Bowen, George Oscar and Mook, Kenneth C. "Song and Speech." Ginn and Co., 1952, p. 7.

everything with consummate ease, he is still burning up a great deal of energy. The energy used, however, is most skillfully and flexibly controlled and directed in a manner in which it will be most effective; reserve always is available. Artistic singing requires endurance, vital physical energy, and intense mental concentration. It is truly no undertaking for a weakling or a lazy person. The ambitious student will become so strong in reserve technic that, like the artist, singing is no longer an exhausting effort nor does it seem difficult to an audience. *It is a mistake to assign a beginning student a song for public performance that demands all the technic the student has in practice.* A reserve in respect to range, long phrases, etc., is necessary.

HIGH TONES AS EASY AS LOW

It is ridiculous to assert that high tones can be produced as easily as low. They always require more breath energy for comparable volume; however, *the throat will feel just as easy and comfortable,* and the necessary increase in breath energy should not constitute a "struggle." A more vigorous feeling is to be expected and the additional breath energy will have an easy, flexible, expansive muscular sensation as well.

DYNAMICS AND A FREE TONE

Many teachers in the public schools apparently still mistake a full, powerful, ringing tone for a "forced" tone, and insist on soft singing as the only method for attaining tonal freedom and safe physical development of the instrument. Nothing can be farther removed from the truth. Actually, attempts by beginners to sing too softly produce either a flat, devitalized tone injurious to the voice, or even more constriction than a normal vigorous *mf*.

Conversely, attempts to sing too loudly also result in excessive rigidity. It is *how* we sing, not *how loud* or *soft*, that is important. A correctly-produced *fortissimo* is the foundation for a *pianissimo* and vice versa. There is no change in quality or ease of production in the throat; only a change in breath energy and, perhaps, but not necessarily, in mouth vibration space. *Both extremely soft and very loud singing are good for the growth and quality of the vocal instrument, providing the production is free.* Any correctly-produced voice can safely sing loudly or softly, high or low, regardless of age, without fear of injury. Vigorous use of any of the muscles of the body is necessary for a maximum healthy growth. Why should the muscles concerned in singing be any exception to this physiological law? Most vocal authorities, including the American Academy of Teachers of Singing, agree that continual soft singing over a period of years will gradually weaken and devitalize the voice for the demands of expressive singing. (Note — See p. 16)

Children, of course, are expected to use the so-called softer type of "head tone" for most of their singing, but why limit them to soft dynamics and, especially to the breathy, devitalized *pianissimo* heard so often? Many choirs and glee clubs, and especially madrigal singers, still use soft, devitalized tone almost exclusively. It is easy in this manner to get blend and balance, and it sounds good to most listeners. Such ensembles are greatly limited and sound anemic when dramatic quality and loud intensities are required for expression, however. *The real test of a choral group's technic and versatility is ability to sing both loud and soft, high and low, with maintenances of fine blend, balance, intonation, and freedom of production.*

It is unwise to urge great power of tone as an immediate objective for any student or group. A ringing, free, *fff* of great volume is the legitimate resultant of freedom of production for a considerable time on vigorous but lesser intensities. It requires little teaching skill to obtain a loud, blatant tone, in a short length of time, from any student with a strong physique and normal vocal instrument; who wants to hear such production? It certainly can do only injury to the voice. In addition, teachers must recognize that the light, lyric type of voice can never develop huge volume. Attempts to do so merely counteract the tonal sweetness and fine quality characteristic of the light, lyric voice.

When students first open up the mouth and throat and sing vigorously with proper utilization of nasopharyngeal resonance, they usually believe that the resultant tone is too loud, "brassy," and nasal. It is difficult for them to believe that this new tone can possibly be beautiful and right, while the old weak, thin, and immature tone, which habit had made sound beautiful to them, could be wrong. Persistent assurance by the instructor, classmates and others, and recording of the two types of production are methods to convince the student.

THE VIBRATO

"The vocal *vibrato* is defined as a periodic oscillation of vocal tone above and below its normal pitch level, occuring at a rate of about 6.5 variations per second and is always *within* a semitone interval. It is not to be confused with a *tremolo* effect which usually varies more than a semitone or with the vocal trill which is the rapid alteration of two distinct pitches in the interval of a semitone, whole tone or third."[10] According to Seashore, "A good vibrato is a pulsation of pitch, usually accompanied with synchronous pulsations of loudness and timbre, of such

---

[10]Fields, Victor Alexander. "Training the Singing Voice." Kings Crown Press, 1947, p. 109.

extent and rate as to give a pleasing flexibility, tenderness, and richness to the tone."[11]

The vibrato is caused by an intermittent supply of nerve energy, resulting in regular fluctuation of muscular energy in the vocal bands. No willed concept of pitch interval is involved. Nerve energy fluctuation is a normal phenomenon of free, controlled action of any muscle in the body. In the vibrato, this fluctuation affects pitch, quality, dynamics and beauty of tone. If the vibrato is free, even, and not too slow or wide, tone usually is beautiful. If vibrato is uneven and too slow or wide, tone is always off-pitch and displeasing to the listener.

Vibrato is an essential concomitant for beauty and freedom of vocal tone. *Every great voice of all time has had a vibrato.* Choral authorities contend that it is an impossibility to make a proper portamento without moving on the vibrato pulse, and that voices with no vibrato always slur, destroying true Bel-Canto legato. It also appears impossible to sing a very fast scale or arpeggio passage without first developing a vibrato. Thus agility and freedom of production both seem to be distinctly correlated with the freedom and controls induced by vibrato.

Choral directors who seek to eliminate vibrato for the sake of more steady and perfect ensemble pitch, merely succeed in making the voice mechanical. They destroy the vitality, vibrancy, freedom, and pleasantness of tonal production natural to the human voice. *A voice which is freely produced will always have a vibrato.* If muscles are not allowed to flex naturally from nerve energy fluctuation, but are held rigidly in order to produce a "straight tone," constriction is inevitable.

The ideal vibrato is regular — neither too slow nor too rapid — and does not swing above or below pitch center in excessive amplitude. A vibrato rate of near six per second, and a semitone deviation from center of pitch, usually are considered ideal for normal expression. An eight to ten rate is considered maximum for pleasing quality. Caruso's average rate was rather rapid and, according to studies by Metfessel,[12] was 7.25. Both Metfessel's and other studies reveal that opera singers, specializing in a style that demands more dramatic qualities than normal, have a somewhat faster vibrato rate and greater amplitude from pitch center than does the average concert singer. This makes production more exciting but not so smooth and legato.

Speed of vibrato, to a certain extent, is inherent in the particular voice. If too slow or too rapid to be pleasant, however, it is subject to limited control through corrective exercises. Speed of vibrato should be uniform in respect to compass, i.e., both low and high tones will have the same rate. Amplitude of vibrato varies unconsciously with change of mood and tonal volume, however, and is one of the most important factors in emotional expression. Very little amplitude is present in *pianissimo* and a great deal in *fortissimo*.

Students often think the vibrato is wrong when it first appears in their voice. They may try to consciously eliminate it unless the phenomena is explained to them, and they are urged to let the tone sound absolutely free. They may be assured that vibrato is natural and desirable, and urged to let it alone to find its own speed and absolute evenness through singing with the maximum of ease. Those who try to consciously control either the rate or amplitude of vibrato often make it worse, resulting in a pronounced tremolo. When the singer forces, or becomes too excited or tense, vibrato either disappears entirely or swings over into a tremolo.

THE TREMOLO

Tremolo has already been defined and discussed briefly in the previous topic of Vibrato. Wilcox[13] further defines the tremolo as an irregular unsteadiness or faulty trembling in pitch, resulting from interfering tensions, muscular weakness and the inability to maintain a stable adjustment of the laryngeal mechanism during phonation. Many beginners have some form or slight degree of tremolo until the voice is freed and the vibrato takes over. It is the teacher's responsibility to detect the difference between the two and not allow tremolo to continue. It will inevitably grow worse until there is a pronounced "billy-goat-like" quaver. This pronounced type of tremolo-wobble is quite unmistakable. The weak tremolo is similar to a weak vibrato and more difficult to differentiate, however, especially when it has the same rate. The tremolo-wobble, normally more violent and jerky, covers a greater pitch amplitude and its frequency is usually too slow or too fast for a true vibrato.

Young singers are seldom afflicted with the tremolo-wobble. It usually is the result of poor fundamental training and a number of years of incorrect singing habits. Efforts to mature a voice too quickly in wide range and loud dynamics are often the cause of tremolo. These efforts create habitual imbalance between breath pressure and vocal cord resistance, with the resultant tension and unsteadiness in resonation.

Tremolo usually is the result of forcing or constriction; vibrato is the natural result of freedom. An habitual tremolo may be due to many causes.

[11]Seashore, Carl E. "Psychology of Vibrato in Both Voice and Instrument." University of Iowa Studies in the Psychology of Music, Vol. III, 1936, p. 7.

[12]Metfessel, Milton. "The Vibrato in Artistic Voices." University of Iowa Studies in the Psychology of Music, 1932, Vol. I, p. 47.

[13]Wilcox, John C. "The Living Voice." Carl Fischer, 1935, p. 39.

These include muscular strain; unsteady or rigid breath support; nervous inhalation; fear; unbalanced laryngeal adjustment; or lack of awareness that it is a tremolo instead of a vibrato. Obviously, the first step in correction is to determine the cause and treat it. A return to the fundamentals of free tone production exercises with patient, *calm* practice will often correct the fault. In most cases, correction is a slow and difficult process for the mature singer who has sung for years with the tremolo. *Much emphasis on a calm and peaceful mental state and the singing of easy, quiet, legato songs is the correct procedure.*

Correction of tremolo and control of an even vibrato are based primarily upon inducing a calm emotional state. A student who is over phlegmatic is inclined to have no vibrato at all or too slow a vibrato rate. One who is overly intense tends to have a rapid vibrato or, perhaps, a tremolo. The overly-intense pupil must be calmed emotionally, the phlegmatic student stimulated. Speeding the tempo for the phlegmatic, and slowing it for the excitable, often has a beneficial effect.

The properly-produced vibrato tends to reduce in amplitude as tonal volume decreases, until it disappears entirely. On the other hand, either the rapid tremolo or a quavery, jerky vibrato, will persist at the softest *pianissimo*.

THE TRILL

The trill is a rapid willed alternation of two distinct pitches. Garcia defines it as "A rapid, equal and distinct alternation of two notes at the distance of a major or minor second, according to the position of the trill on the scales,"[14] and adds that it is induced "by a very loose and swift oscillation of the larynx."[15] It sounds like an exaggerated vibrato with an amplitude of a major or minor second and a fast frequency rate of around 20 per second. It is smooth, even, and not jerky, as is the tremolo.

Even vibrato and free tonal production are prerequisites for the trill. In practicing to acquire the trill, or the shake, the singer starts with a slow, consciously controlled pitch alteration of a major or minor second. He speeds up gradually to the point where rapidity is so great that indirect, or unconscious, oscillation control takes over through mental concept of the sound desired.

Because public taste has changed and no longer requires the trill in lower voices, very few singers, with the exception of sopranos, use it in performance. Sopranos must master it or be severely limited in appropriate repertoire; however, practicing the trill is excellent to develop flexibility in all types of voices. Students who learn to trill are advised to be careful that they do not use it in place of the vibrato, substituting a psuedo-trill on all sustained notes when only a vibrato is appropriate.

Lesson 2. Tone Color and Beauty
(See Volume I, p. 76)

The most vital element of expression in singing is tone color; if it is not appropriate, excellence of all the other factors in interpretation cannot avail in producing a thrilling performance. Unless singers master a satisfactory range of tone color from sombre to bright, and develop sensitivity for just the right shade to use, they are seriously limited in repertoire and expression.

"The human voice is an instrument capable of producing the most astonishing range of sounds, colors, emotions and musical tones."[16] "We must face the fact that tone is the dominating emotional and artistic requisite in artistic performance."[17] The singer who achieves a wide palette of tonal color, without disturbing freedom of resonation, has an established basis for artistic performance over a wide range of vocal literature. Those with a meagre palette are reduced accordingly.

In spite of the proven need for a wide range of tone color, many instrumentalists, and even some singers, appear to be unaware of the possibility and desirability for tone color variation. We have heard even the philosophy that the singer should master a clear, free type of pure tonal production and use it exclusively. This idea is ridiculous in face of the evidence from all great voices of the past and present. Stature of a concert artist has always been closely associated with the artistic use of a wide range of tone color variation.

The important point in vocal education is that even those with high potentialities may never use tone color variation intelligently and effectively to the maximum, *unless urged and taught to do so in study and practice.* This course emphasizes interpretation with stress on appropriate tone color from the very first song in the two manuals to the last. Exactly the right tone color shade to portray any desired mood is stimulated largely through penetrating understanding of the meaning and mood of the text. Intelligent analysis, practice and mastery of degrees of head, mouth, and chest type resonance qualities also are contributing factors.

Some believe that sensitivity to use of tone color is entirely an inborn trait. This is also a false concept, although potentiality for training is limited by native capacity and sensitivity. *We cannot produce suitable tone color unless it exists first as a mental ideal.* This ideal can be stimulated by the teacher

---

[14]Garcia, Manuel. "Hints on Singing." A. Ascherburg & Co., 1894, p. 42.

[15]Ibid.

[16]McClosky, David Blair. "Your Voice at tIs Best." Little, Brown and Co., 1959, p. xii.

[17]Wilson, Harry Robert. "Artistic Choral Singing." G. Schirmer, Inc., 1959, p. 138.

and, once it is clearly in the mind, achievement is possible by most students. "The more we have experimented, listened, imitated; the more mental concepts we have of good, bad, and indifferent tone qualities — that much more readily will our unconscious and conscious vocal adjustments take place in us. And we can paint multiple-tone-color pictures with our songs. We can be tone color artists. And that is the real fun in singing."[18]

Tone quality and color variety is a more important factor in evaluating a beginning student's potentialities than extensive range, great volume, or perfect pitch. Most teachers believe that if there is quality and ease of production first, sufficient quantity of tone and range will come. Fory states that he is in agreement with W. J. Henderson that there would be no further difficulties in voice production "If singers would devote all their attention to securing a round, mellow, beautiful tone."[19] We agree with the school of vocal teaching maintaining that tone should first be easy, ringing, and "balanced" between pharynx and mouth resonance. We agree also that mouth space backward and additional tonal volume be added as the student is able to support and maintain balanced production without throatiness. In this manner more opulence and "room" are added gradually, in which the tone can develop or "blossom" to maturity. In the beginning considerable range of tonal color is not expected; eventually, the pupil should be able to sing wide extremes with ease, according to just the shade required for expressing feeling most significantly.

IDEAL TONAL NORM

There always has been and, undoubtedly, will continue to be, disagreement as to what constitutes the best tonal color norm. Some maintain that it should be bright, some dark, and the majority of successful vocal teachers an average color between the two extremes. Some even argue that the voice should be produced instrumentally, with the most free production that can be established on one stable tonal color. This philosophy results, of course, in purely mechanical production, arid in all the thrilling varieties of tone color characteristic of really great singing. It robs the voice of its most outstanding characteristic and superiority over all other types of instruments — extremely flexible control of infinite shades of expressive tone color.

It is time that vocal teachers discard entirely the idea that there is only one ideal tone color and that all others are imperfect. "The very vowels themselves are only different tone qualities, each having its characteristic arrangement of high-lighted overtones just as do individual voices. . . . The coloring of tone is largely effected through modification of vowels. We do not hold with the 'pure vowel' idea as the ultimate virtue."[20] The "pure" Italian vowel,

leaning slightly toward bright tone color, is usually accepted as the best norm for practice. A darker modification is certainly required when a solemn, subdued, or grandiose effect is desired, and a brighter color when mood of an opposite character is indicated.

Aesthetically, there can be no argument; the best tone is the one that expresses emotional intent most perfectly. Since the ultimate aim of singing is generally agreed to be to make the hearer feel, and feel deeply, it is well to advise the student early to seek, with utmost diligence, the mastery of a wide range of tone color, *the most potent factor in expression.* Extensive listening and analysis of tone coloring employed by famous interpreters will help educate the student's ear and greatly stimulate sensitivity in this respect. A library of choice records for this purpose is invaluable.

Common sense reasoning and experience justify the use of an intermediate tone color, neither very bright nor very dark, as easier for the average vocal student to use freely in vocalization, and as a safe norm from which to depart for most singing. *The most beautiful and free sonority is to be sought first as a model, of course.* The idea often expressed, however, that a student should confine himself entirely to a normal in-between tone color for at least a year or more in all practice and singing, is as unsound educationally as not allowing any singing of songs until perfection of technic is achieved in vocal exercises. *It is highly desirable that students be oriented early into the paramount importance of tone color, guided in how to go about achieving it, and urged to produce as wide and suitable variety as they can achieve safely at the time.* When this type of approach is carried out, pupils soon develop sensitivity and discrimination in choosing appropriate tonal color, together with corresponding awareness of the deeper meanings of songs and heightened pleasure from the intriguing business of tone-painting in vocal expression.

It is well to advise students, however, that a variety of tone color should not be "forced" into the singing of a song just because a wide variety is necessary for greatest emotional effect on the listener. Tone color variety must not be an abortion, but the result of deep and sensitive feeling appropriate to the word and consistent with prevailing mood and style. Technical inadequacies at the time will also wisely limit extent of tone color variation attempted. Like other technics, tone color mastery is a developmental process that is undesirable to force or hurry unduly.

---

[18]Kortkamp, Ivan. "Tone Color Artistry." Choir Guide, May-June, 1949, p. 11.
[19]Fory, Gordan A. "The Need of Soft Practice." Etude, 1935, Vol. 53, p. 45.
[20]Kortkamp, Op. cit., p. 11.

METHOD FOR INDUCING PROPER TONE COLOR

After reading the text, *mood and appropriate style and tone color will be factors discussed habitually as a necessary part of the introduction of each song.* After the song has been sung through once with the text to obtain an over-all concept of the musical setting, it is recommended procedure to select the vowel that has the most appropriate tone color affinity for the mood of the song, and vocalize through the entire song with this. If a contrasting section demands a different mood, it is advisable that the vowel, or neutral syllable be changed accordingly. In rhythmic songs the vowel should be preceded by a consonant such as *l*, singing *lah, loh, loo, lay,* or *lee*, according to which vowel color is most appropriate to mood. *The Old Italian masters invariably recommend the vocalization of all songs on an appropriate vowel.* After singing through with the vowel or syllable, there is normally a return to the text, endeavoring to obtain a *similar* tone color and melodic flow with the words, regardless of changing vowels and articulating problems on the consonants.

The following vowels are suggested for song vocalization as most appropriate for the mood indicated:

1. Solemn, mysterious, sad — *Oo* and *Oh*.
2. Gay, happy, merry — *Ay* or a bright *Ah*.
3. Dramatic, tragic, theatrical — *Oh* and *Ah*.
4. Dignified, majestic, grand — *Ah*.
5. Complaining, crying, whining — *Ee* and *Ay*.

UNIFORM TIMBRE

Correctly-produced voices, whether high or low, should sing with the same timbre when expressing the same mood or idea. Tone quality norm will be the same; the only difference is the size and comparative range of the instrument. This principle does not mean that a tenor will have the identical quality of a baritone when producing the same tone any more than would a violin or viola. Instruments different in size naturally sound different to the ear. Basses and altos should · not consciously attempt to sing with an habitually darker tone because their voices are low, nor sopranos and tenors whiten tone because their voices are high. If this is done, inevitably it will reflect adversely on the ease, range, and control of the voice. It is not expected, of course, that a bass will have as much brilliance as a tenor, nor the tenor as much sombreness as the bass. The same principle applies similarly to contralto and soprano voices.

TONE AND ENVIRONMENT

The many harsh and unpleasant voices heard are not due, in most instances, to an inadequate physical instrument, but to a poor tonal ideal. Some ears are seemingly quite uncritical of poor tone because of unfortunate environmental association with others who produce poor tone. It is a well-known fact that habitual riders on noisy subways often develop unconsciously a high-pitched, harsh, penetrating nasal twang in order to penetrate the noise and make conversation easier. The quality becomes a habit affecting both the speaking and singing voice, and is sometimes most difficult to correct. On the other hand, children raised in homes where they always hear cultured, fine quality speech and beautiful, resonant singing, normally have excellent tonal qualities as a basis for further development.

Lesson 3.   Resonance and Sonority

(*See Volume I, p. 81*)

VOCAL RESONANCE DEFINED

Webster defines resonance as an increase, reinforcement, and enrichment of sound, due to the sympathetic vibration of some body capable of synchronous movement with the initial pulsations of the vibrator generating the sound. In other words, the vibrator (vocal cords) issue certain pitch frequencies which are in turn reinforced and increased by the vocal resonators (cavities of the mouth, throat, nose, sinus, and chest). The New York Singing Teachers Association[21] accepts this view. There is much controversy regarding the function, or alleged lack of function, of the head cavities and particularly of the chest, in reinforcing sound. There appears little disagreement or doubt that character and force of resonance are changed by shape and size of mouth and pharynx space and by relaxing or tensing the tongue and surfaces of the pharynx and the soft palate, however.

PHYSICAL NATURE OF THE VOCAL INSTRUMENT

It was commonly believed in the past that the human voice functioned like a string instrument; that the vocal cords were similar in action to stretched strings; breath energy to the bow; and resonance chambers of the head, pharynx, mouth, and chest to the shell or body. Research establishes the fact that vocal function is more analogous to an open type of wind instrument, such as the trumpet, however. Breath from the lungs generates sound in both, the vocal bands function as vibrators similar to the lips in a mouthpiece, and the resonance chambers of the human instrument serve the same purpose as the open tubing of a horn in amplifying and conditioning sound.

Although some research workers cast doubt on whether the chest cavities in particular actually

---

[21]New York Singing Teachers Association. "Its Story." Theodore Presser, 1928, p. 35.

function as selective resonators, there appears little doubt about the psychological value of conceiving not only of them, but also of the whole body, as a resonator of tone. Dr. Marafioti[22] subscribes to this theory, as have many of the most successful singers of the past and present. "I like to think of the singing body as a single large larynx. The throat gives out the sound, but the entire body sings."[23] Thus the muscular tone and vitality of the entire body, the balanced tension (tonus) of a healthy physique, is considered an important resonance factor. Authorities also generally agree that the singer normally should experience a sensation of head and nose vibration or resonance in order to achieve balanced tone, and that some feeling of sympathetic chest resonance is desirable for the low compass.

RESONATION

Whether or not the head and chest are actual resonators doesn't appear particularly important to the artistic act of singing. The value of *feeling* of head resonance and forward hum in the nasal area on the inception of attack, and to provide vital tone in balanced resonation, is questioned, however, by few singers and teachers of repute. In this respect it is well to point out to those who argue the matter that the actual scientific *presence* of resonation in an area, and the *feeling* for proper resonation to control tone, may not coincide, since *we do not always feel stimuli where they actually occur.*

The Old Italian masters insisted that the farther in and up in an arching curved line we imagine we can "drink in the tone" when singing, the more all the resonators of the pharynx and head are brought into full play. This induces the maximum of sympathetic vibration, richness of overtones and opulence in phonation. They urge that we always keep the head cavities "open" when singing any note so that the tone can swirl and vibrate freely through the head and nose. When matched by flexible, firm, and energetic breath support, this free, enlarged, and balanced resonation furnishes the amateur singer with a new and exhilarating experience rather than a confined and localized sensation to which he has been accustomed. The entire vocal instrument — motor, vibrator, and resonators — is now coordinated and functioning in one balanced unit, as is true of the best production of all instruments regardless of type.

There is no single area where resonance is directed in balanced singing, although the principal vibration sensation is above the roof of the mouth in the region behind the nose and the eyes. This sensation, however, is the result of correct resonation and not of an attempt to "place" or "focus" tone in the area. Feeling of proper singing is "in" and not "out," or as if inhaling the tone high up in the back of the throat. This sensation materially helps

obtain balanced resonation of the vowel in its proper form and place, high in the upper pharynx.

It is certain that if we block the nasal passages by pinching the nostrils and continue to direct resonance forward, the resulting tone has a terrible "nosey" twang through *lack* of head resonance. "Nasal twang, so-called, does not originate in the nose, but in the throat, and does not enter the nasal passages. It is *singing without any nose.*"[24]

There is confusion regarding meaning of the terms "head resonance," "nasal resonance," and "nasal tone." According to the dictionary, head resonance and nasal resonanec are synomous terms. A "nasal tone" and a "nosey tone" are often confused. A "nosey tone" is caused by *blocking* the head resonances entirely with the soft palate, an effect similar to that obtained when singing with the nostrils pinched together. The most horrible "hill-billy" types of voices are mistakenly called "nasal voices" when in fact they are "nosey-tone voices" without any nasal or head resonance.

Some head or nasal resonance is necessary for balanced resonation in any part of the voice; a maximum amount in the upper range normally is desirable. Some voices overnasalize, particularly in the middle register, causing too much rough, "buzzy" nose quality in the voice. An overly-nasal tone is caused by too much head resonance and not enough balance with pharynx and mouth resonance. Voices with the easiest and richest toned upper register sometimes make the mistake of carrying too much of the nasal quality necessary for their superior high range down into the middle compass, where more mouth and pharynx resonance is required for tonal beauty and balance.

How much nasal resonance (*m, n* or *ng* quality) should be used in tone is a matter of taste. We prefer just enough to obtain a balance with pharynx and mouth qualities to make a pianissimo safe without danger of the voice cracking, to induce the attack securely. Too much nasal (head) quality sounds unpleasantly "buzzy," especially close up, and will muffle bell-like clarity of the pharynx and mouth resonances in the middle register. The ideal tone is balanced — enough "head" mellowness to give freedom and suavity and enough "mouth" brightness and intensity to give "ring" and efficiency in phonation. *It is practically impossible, however, to obtain too much head or nasal quality in the extreme upper compass,* and this quality should be intensified when the singer has a cold or fears that the voice might

---

[22]Marafioti, Pasqual Mario. "Caruso's Method of Voice Production." D. Appleton, 1933, p. 102.

[23]Dragonette, Jessica. "The Mental Approach to Singing." (an interview) Etude, 1940, Vol. 58, p. 510.

[24]Weer, Robert Lawrence. "My Views on Voice Production." The Author, 1941, p. 41.

"crack." It is the principal secret of "singing through a cold."

EFFICIENCY

Ideal tone will maintain freedom and space but still be intense enough to be efficient. By "intense" we mean "concentrated" and not loud in this instance. We cannot have satisfactory tone, breath control, or sonority in the voice if the vocal bands are so leaky or loosely adjusted that only breath with very little tone emerges. It is a mistake to blame breathy tone and inability to sing long phrases exclusively on poor breath control; *more often than not it is due to breathy concept of tone or to leaky vocal bands.* Although a large chest and ample lung capacity are undeniable assets, the ability to sing long phrases does not depend primarily on the size of the person, his lung capacity, or the amount of air he is able to pack into the lungs; it depends on efficiency in resonation. Marafioti, and many eminent teachers of the past and present, believe that "Resonance is the most important factor in voice production."[25] It is necessary that vocal cords resist sufficiently against the breath to balance its pressure in order to achieve an efficient tone.

The properly balanced and resonant tone is also the most sonorous for the amount of breath used. *The greatest amount of volume for the least amount of effort is always the ideal tone containing the maximum of overtones.* In this regard Groves declares, "And here let me insist on the principle regarding which all authorities are agreed, that apart from maintaining a raised chest and flat abdomen, which becomes second nature in a short while, the singer should deploy the minimum of muscular effort required to make his effects. Just as the skilful golf player makes his longest and straightest shots without pressing, the accomplished singer will pour out a stream of song without any visible strain."[26] The objective for efficient resonance has been stated by the eminent English vocal authority, David Frangcon-Davies, as *learning to emit just enough breath to produce a whisper, and then converting it into tone.*

Ease, purity, and endurance of voice production depend on tonal efficiency in the economy of breath used for tone. Henderson[27] claims that effortless singing is based on the habit of quick but unforced inhalation and economical exhalation. Economy of breath is much more important than volume of breath, according to Herbert-Caesari.[28] Bruna Castagna declares, "The secret of the singer's breath lies in its conservation."[29] Lilli Lehmann[30] also believes that breath emission should be reduced to an absolute minimum, while Madame Schumann-Heink states, "I advise you to give supreme attention, not to the drawing in of breath, but to its budgeting."[31]

Habitual inability to sing long phrases is a sure sign of breathy and inefficient tonal emission for any normal student. On the other hand, ability to sing long phrases, while a favorable indication, is not a sure sign of free emission — the tone could still be tight and shrill. Unfortunately, ability to sing a long phrase does not necessarily imply freedom, but sometimes the exact opposite. In fact, when there is intense throat constriction, expulsion of breath is generally low. Most singers instinctively sense this fact, and tense up the throat when they feel that they have an inadequate breath supply to finish the phrase properly.

A voice cannot be tensely brilliant and also have freedom; nor can it be breathy, muffled, overly nasal, or "focused" to one area and still have desirable "ring" and sonority. The ideal balanced tone should contain the pharynx space, mellowness, and sonority of a properly sung *Ah*, plus an intensity and efficiency in phonation for which the closer *Ee* and *Ay* vowels are best adapted.

HUMMING

Huming is not valuable for developing loud sonority in the voice but is excellent for obtaining efficiency. In fact, unless freely and correctly produced in an open throat, humming will be detrimental. It is necessary that production of the hum be based on the vowel and not the vowel on the hum. Putting the cart before the horse may impede rather than develop freedom and resonance. While there is considerable controversy regarding the value of humming as an exercise, your author agrees with a great number of authorities that it is particularly beneficial for exercising the vocal cords in warming-up the voice quietly; in correcting breathy, "spread," and wasteful tonal production; and in establishing the feeling for correct vocal embouchure (adjustment of the vocal bands) for *pianissimo* and low pitch tones.

A light hum approach also is helpful to the male voice in making high pitch adjustment for the following vowel, particularly for soft attacks. It is quite difficult, however, for some trebles voices to hum above fifth line *f;* when required it may be necessary to open the lips slightly into the "open hum" in order to free production. *A quick way to learn to sing a pianissimo on pitch with efficient tone is first to hum*

[25]Op. Cit. p. 100.
[26]Graves, Richard M. "Singing for Amateurs." Oxford U. Press, 1954, p. 52.
[27]Henderson, Mrs. Archibald M. "Speech and Song." Macmillan, 1933, p. 54.
[28]Herbert-Caesari, Edgar F. "The Science and Sensation of Vocal Tone." J. M. Dent & Sons, 1936, p. 17.
[29]Castagni, Bruna. "Good Singing Must Be Natural." (an interview) Etude, 1939, Vol. 57, p. 159.
[30]Lehmann, Lilli. "How to Sing." Macmillan, 1929, 3rd revised edition.
[31]Schumann-Heink, Ernestine. "You Can Sing — If You Will." (an interview) Etude, 1934, Vol. 52, p. 11.

the passage lightly and then sing the text retaining the same close, intense vibration form.

The *m* and *n* are frequently-used "persuaders" in practice for inducing greater tonal intensity and efficiency on the following vowel. They are recommended in many vocal texts for this purpose. Singers use the hum as a favorite means for obtaining efficient phonation in exercising and warming-up the voice. Lily Pons, famous coloratura soprano, states, "This exercise is very helpful to me."[32] On the other hand, some teachers consider the hum an "instrument of the devil" — dangerous in its likelihood of excessive tension and reduction of spacious sonority.

What are the facts between these two apparently irreconcilable views and practices upon which the beginning teacher can safely base a method in vocal instruction? First, it can be stated unequivocally that humming, like a vowel sound, is injurious to the voice if produced, as it often is, with pinched rigidity in the throat. There can be no doubt that the hum, together with the "close" vowels *Ee* and *Ay*, has a tendency to be produced with too constricted a throat. Like the *Ee* and *Ay*, however, the student need merely learn to open up the throat on the hum to produce it freely. Then its values for improving resonance efficiency can be utilized safely. This can be done very simply by alternating the vowel *Ah* and the hum on a sustained tone thus, *Ah- m- Ah- m- Ah- m*, etc. The *n* type of hum can be treated likewise. To learn to produce the *ng* type freely, sing "Huh-ng" keeping the same open throat feeling on the "ng" as on the previous "Huh." *It is necessary to take care that the throat remain as open in feeling in producing any type of hum as it would be in singing a free and sonorous Ah.*

The hum undeniably does produce a maximum of frontal tonal "focus" and reduces spread, breathy tonal quality. If produced correctly, therefore, it is an excellent catharsis for breathy type voices lacking in forward balance and efficiency in phonation. This is true especially of the low compass, where closeness of resonation on the *m* or *n* is ideal for inducing the necessary compactness in throat space, and thickening of the vocal bands needed for efficient phonation. On the other hand, the *ng* type of hum on such words as "hung," "sing," "ming," freely produced in an open throat, is an excellent method for obtaining the sensation of sufficient nasal resonance in the etxereme upper register.

It would appear therefore that students having breathy or "spread" voices should use the hum habitually in the warm-up process and as a "persuader" consonant. It will induce sufficient resonance concentration on the dark, or broad vowels, *Aw, Ah, Oo,* and *Oh*, while all voices can extend the downward range of tone in the low compass through its usage. It is not recommended as a warm-up exercise for voices already tending to be overbrilliant or too tensely adjusted in the larynx.

BRIGHT VOWELS

Efficient resonance without wastage of breath is best obtained through the use of *Ee*, the closest and brightest of all vowels, while "ringing" tone is best induced by the bright vowel *Ay* as a model. Balanced tone will have space and sonority characteristic of the properly produced *Ah*, plus an intensity of resonation and efficiency in phonation found in the closer *Ee* and *Ay* vowels and the humming consonants *m, n,* and *ng*. The *Ah, Oh,* and *Oo* are most likely to be free but also spread and breathy, while the closer, brighter *Ee* and *Ay* are subject to overtension and rigidity in production. A balance between the two extremes produces the ideal tone. In most voices, however, freedom of production should be established first through preliminary practice on the rounder and more spacious vowels, *Oh, Oo,* and *Ah*.

SONOROUS PRODUCTION
(See also "Resonation," p. 47)

Students often appear afraid to open up the mouth, the pharynx and head, and to support tone vigorously in order to produce vital, ringing, and sonorous tone. They are apparently afraid to "let the lion roar" and think they are yelling when, after repeated urging, they produce a really free and robust tone for the first time. The student may be assured that *a really sonorous and resonant full-voiced tone can be expected to sound rough and, perhaps, even yell-like to him when it sounds the most free, resonant, and mellow to the listener.* Presence of a class helps to assure the pupil that the new tone is right and that the old inhibited, tense, thin type of production should be discarded. Recording both types of production is also highly valuable as the final proof for convincing the pupil.

It is unwise to urge pupils to sing loudly in order to sing sonorously, since this advice only produces more force in an already constricted tone. The result is achieved best by telling the student to *drop and relax the jaw* and to *ring* out the tone freely with a strong and vigorous feeling of *flexible expansion*, accompanied by high, quiet chest, spine-stretch, comparatively low head position on the axis of the spine (no lifting of the chin), and a loose, open position of the lips. A stronger, more sonorous tone is the result, but it is never a "yell-tone" if the chin is kept down and the resonance filtered properly through the head through the familiar "drinking in the tone" sensation. This "opened-up" tone becomes, from that time on, the model and ideal to establish

---

[32]Pons, Lily. "Fame Overnight." (an interview) Etude, 1931, Vol. 49, p. 394.

throughout the range. It is interesting to note that the small voice which is really opened-up produces more tone than the biggest voice that is inhibited and constricted.

Unless all voices are "opened" in this manner, the vocal instrument can never become really rich and sonorous, and the voice continues to sound immature. Tone will be inhibited in range and never resonant enough for anything except microphone singing and certain types of intimate recital work in a small room. Even then, if the voice is used much in the high compass, it will not last.

After the initial opening and freeing of the tone in the middle range, it is further refined in ease and mellowness, and the quality extended both upward and downward. The student also learns to produce all degrees of dynamics with the sonorous quality retained; however, the development process in this respect should not be rushed. Considerable practice on songs and exercises in the limited middle range and near a *mf* is the recommended procedure to first "set" and strengthen the new technic. If the voice is well produced in this fashion, it will continue to improve in ease, quality, and dynamic range. The teacher can be assured that *plenty of sonorous, vigorous singing is the best possible type of development for any adult*, providing the throat is opened and tone produced freely. If tone is only loud and constricted, the voice will soon be destroyed by persistent efforts to produce lusty tones.

The use of *Haw* and *Ha* in vigorous exercises throughout the easy compass is a favorite method of many teachers for increasing sonority. The exercise is accompanied by the fully-opened throat, a high arched sensation in the back of the throat, mouth opened generously with the lips extended slightly from the front teeth and a feeling as if the nostrils were somewhat flaring. Lips will not be protruded unnaturally, but the upper lip is raised sufficiently for the tip of the upper teeth to show in order to produce maximum resonance.

The opposite type of student to the tonally inhibited is encountered occasionally. They have no inhibitions about using the physique vigorously, but never have been taught to free the tone and filter it through the head in balanced resonation. Consequently, they shout and scream, especially in the upper register. It is necessary that these students be taught the principles of singing, urged to "take it easy," not to attempt to sing loudly, but always easily, and never to push dynamics beyond the limit set by freedom and beauty of tone. This advice will result temporarily in reduction of power, but the student will be on the safe road to opening up the voice legitimately. The ultimate result will be even more dynamic power accompanied by rich sonority and tonal beauty.

The principles of "Correct resonance should be established very quickly in the teaching of voice in order that the complete range of the voice can be developed in the early stages of training."[33] Tendency in the low register is to sing too dark, breathy and lugubriously and, in the high compass, too bright, shrill, and tense. Vocalization therefore should be designed to correct this by using the brighter, more intense vowels in the low register and the darker, rounder, and more sonorous vowels in the high as models for comparison.

-----

[33]Wilson, Harry Robert. "What! Another Voice Book?" *Choir Guide*, Vol. 4, No. 9, p. 23.

CHAPTER

5

Diction

Lesson 1. Preliminary Considerations
(See Volume I, p. 86)

The first part of this lesson in Volume I can be covered adequately by assigned reading with a brief discussion period following. However, adequate class time should be devoted to drill on speaking and singing together (chanting) the commonly mispronounced words, correction made, and individuals guided on future study and practice. We suggest that students be instructed to mark each section and word with which they have difficulty, in order that they can continue to practice them until corrected. The objective has been to list only types of problems and words that research has shown to be most faulty, and to avoid the interminable listing of all phonetic sounds and problems encountered in the English language.

As early as 1723 a celebrated maestro wrote, "Singers should not ignore the fact that it is the words which elevate them above instrumentalists."[1] "Much of the charm that lies in singing comes not alone from the beauty of tones, but equally from the proper and intelligent use of the elements of good speech."[2] Marafiote insists that "singers must sing words for their *meaning*, not for their tones."[3] They must place emphasis on word meaning first and not primarily on tone as had been the custom too often in the past.

Many eminent vocal authorities believe that emphasis on all the problems involved in correct and beautiful diction is the very basis of vocal production. They believe that vocal tensions disappear when diction problems are solved and that "Perfect diction means perfect singing."[4] If there is tension, it almost always finds its way into the area of diction. One can readily observe the tight jaw, protruding neck muscles, and strained facial expression of the student who forces the voice to sing. Vocally the tone can be recognized by its strident, unmusical qualities, confined resonance, and distorted diction."[5] Various types of faulty tone such as throaty, tight,

breathy and "nosey," are caused by faulty diction. When the student learns to enunciate clearly, easily, and beautifully, faulty tone is eliminated.

It is advisable to make clear to the pupil that precise, correct diction is an indispensable help and not a hindrance to beautiful, free tone. To purify the tone it is necessary to purify the vowel. Habitual speech habits inevitably condition and influence the singer's diction. Prevalence of poor diction in speech is surprising; its occurrence in singing is truly astounding. It is therefore necessary for the teacher to assist pupils to discover their diction faults and correct them before singing can progress far.

Students have inaccurate or confused concepts of the sound of many words, and of vowel and consonant sounds which need correction as a basis for freedom and beauty of tonal production. "The effectiveness of choral music is governed by the close relationship of diction and tone. . . . We must work in a manner so that diction will aid tone and tone will aid diction."[6] Slovenly articulation is common and mispronunciation of many words can be expected. *Correction cannot occur until the student first is made aware of his faults.* This corresponding lesson in Expressive Singing, Volume I is designed primarily to enable detection of major faults in pronunciation.

Individuals who study voice may be classified in the beginning as "poor," "average," and "good" in

---

[1]Henderson, William J. "The Art of Singing." Dial Press, 1938, revised edition, p. 104.

[2]Bowen, George O., and Mook, Kenneth C. "Song and Speech." Ginn & Co., 1952, p. vii.

[3]Marafiote, P. Mario. "Caruso's Method of Voice Production." Cadica Enterprises, 1950 (original copy 1922), p. 23.

[4]Oblensky, Alexis. "Passing from Conscious to Subconscious Control." Musician, April 1930, Vol. 35, p. 17.

[5]Peterson, Paul W. "Natural Singing and Expressive Conducting." John F. Blair, 1955, p. 22.

[6]Wilson, Harry Robert. "Artistic Choral Singing." G. Schirmer, Inc., 1959, p. 138.

their ability to speak English correctly. All need some correction of speech and aid in learning how to carry through the principles of good diction into singing, however. Even the best students are careless at times in precise articulation of consonants and in clear enunciation of pure vowel sounds, resulting not only in lack of word clarity but also in interference with free production.

Surprisingly beautiful singing for either solo or ensemble can be achieved by careful attention to eloquent diction alone. Many vocal teachers use the pure vowel and diction concepts as the core or basis for teaching all other technical factors relating to vocal production. Distinct and eloquent diction thrills an audience. It also gives the singer far more pleasure in expression, because it is the best guarantee that he understands and feels what is being sung about. *The importance of continued emphasis on perfection of diction for the singer or speaker cannot be stressed too greatly.*

Voice teachers who analyze carefully the text of songs, with a view to locating where indolent or incorrect diction is likely to occur, are forewarned in both detection and correction of mistakes. There should be neither under nor over-definition in singing, but naturalness and clarity. *The problem of the singer is to articulate consonants so precisely and rapidly that all words are clear without distorting rhythm or interrupting legato flow on the vowels.* Words in singing are to be pronounced exactly as in correct, cultured speech, but it is necessary to make sure that the speech model is correct, and not garbled or provincial.

CORRELATION OF SPEECH AND SONG

Speech and song are very closely related. Singing is merely elongated speech on carefully-chosen pitches to create a meaningful and artistically interesting melodic line. There is no difference between the speaking and the singing voice as physiological phenomena. Both are produced by the identical mechanism of the same vocal organs. It has been said that "well spoken is half sung." There can be no doubt that the student who starts to sing with the foundation of a rich, resonant, well-modulated and correctly-produced speaking voice has the most valuable asset possible. On the other hand, a poorly-produced speaking voice will continue to seriously handicap the singer, no matter how long the period of study. There are few who ever reach eminence in the art of singing who do not have a resonant and pleasing speaking voice.

There is no reason why a normal person who has a good speaking voice cannot also acquire a good singing voice. *If we desire to improve singing, we must study speech; if we wish to have a fine, resonant, and well-controlled speaking voice, we also should study singing.* Singers, therefore, will first

make sure that they are capable of reading great poetry and dramatic works with authority, depth of feeling, expressive rise and fall of inflection, proper word accent and clear, fluent diction.

Songs are approached through the text. The text first inspired the composer and, in turn, it must inspire the singer, furnishing an indispensible key to expressive interpretation. Absorption in projecting the story and mood of the text is also the most vital factor in eliminating self-consciousness. Without becoming sentimental, words in songs should always be significant in drama and emotion. *If it cannot be more beautiful and significant emotionally in song than in speech, however, it had best not be sung.*

To obtain best results in singing, approach "Should be made through the early cultivation of a beautiful speaking voice."[7] Lawrence Tibbett recommends that "It is helpful to think of singing as dramatic speech . . . . sustained on definite intervals of pitch."[8] The singer will endeavor to become an able speaker not only to promote good singing, but also for increasing chances of success in life. Nothing adds more to effectiveness of personality than a rich, resonant, well-modulated speaking voice.

All academic and music classes throughout the public schools, and even in college, should join in emphasizing the importance of clear, correct, and beautiful speech as a highly important supplementary objective to their own specialized subject matter. Certainly it is highly desirable and vital to do so in a voice class. Study of speech and study of voice go hand-in-hand. Each supplements the other and gains values obtainable in no other way.

Students of drama make a serious mistake if they do not also study voice as the quickest and best way to gain resonance, sonority, and tonal beauty on the vowel, adequate breath, endurance for long sentences, and a wider pitch inflection. Problems such as stuttering, that are more difficult and slow to correct by speech technics, are often relieved quickly in singing. Faults in speech diction also are magnified in singing to the extent that they become more audible and thus more readily detected. "When people begin to study singing they are astonished to find that they never learned to speak (correctly)."[9]

Ideal expression is achieved when we sing with the same spontaneity and naturalness and on the "same level" of resonation as the speech approach. Singing then becomes more natural; tone improves; the scale is more even; and previously difficult high

---

[7]Seashore, Carl E. "A Beautiful Voice." Music Educators Journal, Feb. 1938, Vol. 24, p. 18.

[8]Tibbett, Lawrence. "There Is No Open-Sesame." (an interview) Etude, Vol. 58, 1940, p. 820.

[9]Pease, E. R. "The Singing Voice." Pitman & Sons, Ltd., 1933, p. 64.

or low tones are more freely resonated. The advice, "sing like you speak," often is heard. Although it is obviously impossible to do this in fact, because of melody and rhythm dictated by the composer and the necessity for elongation of the vowel, nevertheless, it is a valuable approach for inducing a natural and spontaneous attack, and for calling attention to the paramount importance of projecting word meaning. The idea also has its dangers for the singer when the spoken word is not correct as a model. The approach has pedagogical merit, nevertheless, especially for its possible psychological effect upon freedom, spontaneity, and communicative expressiveness of the singing voice. Smallman insists that "We should sing with the same abandon that we use in speech."[10] There is no doubt that the idea is beneficial in preventing the student from trying to "make himself sing" by setting the lips and jaw in position, and then attacking the tone later in an unnatural manner. *The speech approach is also highly effective in obtaining sufficient brilliance and frontal resonance while singing in the low compass.*

It is desirable that students realize early that they have some, probably many, speech defects in pronunciation and articulation; that they possess some erroneous concepts of word and vowel sound no matter how fortunate their home and community environment. Because they grew up with these concepts, they naturally are accepted as correct and normal, even though incorrect or provincial in fact. The pupil needs also to realize that his voice, being a part of him, sounds differently to him than it does to others. Recording of either the speaking or singing voice usually reveals for the first time faults and qualities of which the student has been unaware.

DIFFERENCES IN SPEECH AND SONG

Some types of singing like chanting, the free recitative and the "patter song" are so closely related to speech that the differences are subtle. Hathaway says, "Speech at its best is spoken song."[11] We might well reverse the order and say, *singing at its best is more eloquent speech.* In speech, word emphasis, duration, inflection, and force are all determined at the will of the speaker. In singing these elements are intensified, augmented and artistically arranged by the composer to achieve greater beauty and emotional intensity. "In speaking, breath is taken without any thought just as often as is necessary to replenish the store in the lungs. In singing, it is necessary to look ahead and perceive where breath can be conveniently taken without disturbing the outline of the melody which is sung."[12] On the whole, however, the greatest difference between speech and song resides in the elongation of the vowel, necessary for greater beauty.

No reason exists why diction should be any different in singing than in speech except in *timing.* It is necessary that articulation of ending consonants be delayed, and the motion of the lips for vowel ennunciation be slowed, because of elongation of the vowel. *The singer has to maintain a sustained legato* in most songs — the speaker does not. No one is disturbed if the speaker drops his jaw to a maximum on the *Ah*, and on the following *Ee* sound closes the mouth to a very short space, producing a much thinner and more specific vowel sound. In fact, maximum differences in vowel characteristics are actually encouraged in some speech classes. To do this in singing is fatal to the basic requirement of legato, for radical change of either jaw or lip position alters vowel color and resonation characteristics so that sustained legato quality is weakened or destroyed.

VALUES OF WHISPERING, CHANTING AND RECITATIVE

Many teachers recommend practice of whispering through the words of songs as a means of improving clarity of diction and resting the vocal cords. Since the vocal bands do not vibrate in whispering, this technic is restful to the vocal organs at the same time that it vigorously exercises the articulators.

Practice in chanting or "intoning" is a natural transition to close the gap between speaking and singing, and to enlarge the area of speech resonance as an intermediary step to singing of songs. Greene[13] recommends selecting an easy pitch for vocalization and first intoning (chanting) an entire phrase, that presents diction difficulties, as a valuable means of overcoming singing faults. Wilson also emphasizes that "Chants are wonderful songs for singers to sing in order to gain a sensitivity to a flowing phrase line, to relate the verbal and musical accent and nuance, and to acquire a homogeneous, pure tone."[14] We commend his further recommendation that, in order to develop the dual ability to articulate easily and clearly and produce a free and natural tone, beginning singers should first chant through the words of a song on a single pitch in the rhythm of the music (scansion).

Easy, free recitative is quite similar to the chant in its technical values for the beginner, but changes pitch more frequently and is more dramatic.

Marafiote[15] contends that in the approach to singing we should first learn to talk on any pitch in order

---

[10]Smallman, John and Wilcox, E. H. "The Art of A Capella Singing." Ditson, 1933, p. 8.
[11]Hathaway, Helen. "What Your Voice Reveals." E. P. Dutton, p. 15.
[12]Henderson, Op. cit. p. 49.
[13]Greene, Harry Plunkett. "Interpretation in Song." Macmillan, 1940, p. 142.
[14]Op. cit., p. 103.
[15]Op. cit., pp. 134 2nd 270.

that the singing tones be mouthed naturally around the speaking pitch. Chanting is one of the oldest methods for obtaining free and natural production with emphasis on word clarity. Chanting or intoning combines "Speaking and singing in one unified . . . . phonation process."[16] Practice of chanting as a natural approach to singing is often overlooked by most vocal texts and many contemporary teachers. Grove[17] suggests practicing a chanting monotone treatment of all vowels. It will be noted that exercises in both chanting and recitative are included in Volume I, Expressive Singing.

NATURAL VERSUS CORRECT SINGING

"The two most important contributions to good singing are spontaneity and naturalness."[18] We agree with this statement providing the term "naturalness" is defined and qualified, for it is necessary that natural singing be *correct* singing also. Correct singing involves judicious and balanced use of both tonal and physical imagery. *A high level of excellence in these concepts has to be taught;* it is not the result of allowing the singer to sing naturally as he pleases. "A person doesn't sing naturally anymore than he walks naturally, or plays a violin naturally. With training, a person sings or walks correctly, or at least he should."[19]

It is time that voice teachers and choral conductors realize that natural singing, as often understood, and correct singing are not necessarily synonymous. The false concept of allowing pupils to "sing naturally" as the best way to develop technic is responsible for many of the liberties allowed in poor solo and ensemble singing heard today. In all the arts involving a high degree of technic, necessary skills first are taught and then routined by continued practice before they become "natural" on a high plane of expression. In order for faulty singers to sing naturally they "Must learn to perform *consciously* an act that in its ideal state is unconscious. Given enough time it will become automatic with them too."[20]

IMPORTANCE OF CORRECT THOUGHT

Since a sound exists first in the mind, pronunciation, enunciation, and articulation can never be right unless thought is right. It is evident that *establishing a vivid mental concept of proper sound is prerequisite to teaching proper diction.* The words listed in Volume I, p. 88, are those most often mispronounced in speech and need to be corrected before they will be sung correctly.* It is basic to beauty in singing that beginning students be given a correct concept of the *purity* and clarity of each vowel sound, and aided in achieving it as habitual. Unfortunately, beginners neither think the vowels *pure* nor produce what they think. For example, they nearly always sing *Aw* for *Ah,* shade the *Oh* with

some of the qualities of *Oo,* and anticipate the terminal sound of the dipthong vowels *Ay* (Eh-ee) and *I* (Ah-ee).

THE ENDING "R" PROBLEM

The hurdle of proper enunciation of the syllables, *ar, er, ir, or,* and *ur* in such words as "heart," "her," "bird," "word," and "fur" is the first major diction problem to correct. Most students attempt to use the *r* as a vowel for sustaining tone when it comes at the end of a word or syllable, rather than in its proper function as a consonant receiving only quick articulation at the end. The result is a sound similar to a dog's growl, certainly contributing nothing to beauty of tone. In speech the sound of *r* is so momentary that only the discriminating ear is disturbed when it is used like a vowel. In singing, however, elongation of the consonant *r* in substitution for a proper tonal sound becomes highly offensive to any discriminating listener.

Southerners, New Englanders, and some Englishmen often solve the problem of the ugly final *r* quite simply — they just leave it out. "Heart" becomes "haht," "her" is "huh," "bird" is "buhd," etc. Even some vocal teachers give up in despair and instruct their students to do the same; however, omission is a mere avoidance of the issue and is neither necessary nor desirable. *The only solution is to learn to sustain the preceding vowel or tonal sound to the very end of the indicated rhythm and then articulate the r with a quick flip of the tongue.* "Heart" then becomes "hah - - -rt," "her" is "huh - - - - r," etc., as described in the Volume I. If followed carefully, the instructions and exercises there should correct the student's concept of production and furnish the basic examples for proper production in all songs. However, it is necessary that the teacher be alert in all future singing to catch and correct this most insidious fault until pupils habituate correct practice.

The *r* problem furnishes an excellent example of how speech habit, being provincial and wrong with most Westerners and Middle-westerners, operates as a serious deterrent to beauty in song. Difficulty will often be encountered in getting some pupils to accept a concept so radically foreign to their speech practices. Proper sound appears affected and unnatural to many, especially in the speech drill appli-

---

*An excellent text to explore more fully than Volume I allows is "Notebook for Voice and Diction" by Lyle V. Mayer, published in 1953 by the Wm. C. Brown Co.
[16]De Bruyn, John. "The Oldest Authentic Voice Method." Etude, 1940, Vol. 59, p. 597.
[17]Grove, Grace J. "On the Development of the Vowel." Etude, 1937, Vol. 55, p. 534.
[18]Peterson, Op. Cit., p. 23.
[19]Wilson, Op. cit., p. 162.
[20]Litante, Judith. "A Natural Approach to Singing." Wm. C. Brown Co., 1959, p. 6.

cation listed. Most, however, will agree with the premise that *r* is a consonant, is ugly in sound and should not, therefore, be sustained in singing. If the instructor illustrates the wrong way and the right way in singing the exercises listed for practice in Volume I, then all will be convinced of the desirability of working for correction. The problem is largely psychological and is first a matter of convincing the student of the ugliness and absurdity of trying to sustain tone on the harsh consonant. When this is accomplished, the pupil is assisted thereafter in using the proper enunciation with careful checking for a long time before the fault is eliminated entirely.

Lesson 2. Vowels

(*See Volume I, p. 94*)

THE FIVE CARDINAL VOWELS

The principles of enunciation in English are based by most successful teachers on the traditional pure sound of the five "Cardinal Vowels" in Italian; *Ah, Ay, Ee, Oh,* and *Oo* (English equivalents). The proper English vowel sounds illustrated in words are: *Ah* as in "father," *Ay* as in "lady," *Ee* as in "see," *Oh* as in "no" and *Oo* as in "room" or in "tune." Considerable time and analytical practice are demanded before the student can establish habitually a *pure* and free Italian-like vowel production. Singers are advised *always to imagine vividly the sound of a free, pure, ringing vowel as the best method yet devised for improving tone.*

While tone is the basis for all singing, we produce tone only through the medium of the vowel. "The invariable medium for forming and sustaining the vocal tone is THE VOWEL. Therefore, the vowel should first be established in pure form and not changed until time for the next vowel or consonant."[21] The five pure Italian vowels are considered not only the most beautiful of the various English vowel sounds but also the most fundamental for beginning study. Other English vowel sounds are close variants and present no great problems after the five basic vowels are mastered. Simplicity of approach through the five basic Italian vowels is apparent when we consider that various authorities list an array of 18 or more English vowel sounds under such headings as "open vowel monothongs," "the short vowel monothongs," "the dipthongs," etc.

Vital keys to proper singing are the correct formation, resonation, and even connection of vowels. It is well to clarify a rather common misapprehension concerning the belief that a vowel is pure only when color is bright. *Tone color and purity of vowel have no connection; tone color can be either bright or sombre and the vowel still remain pure.*

Vowels are presented individually in Volume I in such a manner as to achieve not only pure quality and beauty, but also a type of production on each vowel that will blend or balance in the "Evening Principle" of resonation that is necessary for legato singing. In spite of the fact that each vowel has a characteristic all its own, *they must all sound evenly as if produced from the same resonating space.* Until this can be done the voice is uneven and a sustained legato, the basis of singing technic, is impossible.

Unless we purify and free the vowel the tone cannot be pure and free. Vowel sounds in English are produced as near to the pure Italian Cardinal Vowel sounds as possible, although they should never be distorted or fail to give the illusion of naturalness. For example, the harsh English short *a* as in "and" and "cat" will have a suggestion of the pure *Ah* quality to mellow the provincial harsh, blatant quality, but it should never be exaggerated to the extent of actually sounding like "ahnd" and "caht." The *o* sound as in the word "dog" is another example; it will be neither "dahg" or, even worse "dawg," but have only a slight shade of *Ah* for best production and correct sound. In like manner, "song" will be more "sahng," and "God" will be more "Gahd" than "Gawd," as often sung.

Research and analysis leave little doubt that the vowel *Ah*, when sung properly, approaches nearest to the tonal *Uh* and the open throat condition desired in singing. In this connection Fields states, "The *Ah* (sometimes called the Italian *a*) is the closest approximation to the matrix vowel (*Uh*) of the singing voice and therefore a favorite vehicle for practicing various vocalises and diction exercises."[22] We have discussed previously, in the lesson on the Attack, how the beginning student is more inclined to attack the *Ah* incorrectly with a throaty, "swallowed" production than is true of the rounder *Oh*. After the *Ah* has been mastered in a well balanced, "forward" resonation, however, it appears for the average student to be the most beneficial of all the vowels for practice in developing free and sonorous tone. An inducing vocal consonant, *m, n,* or *l*, preceding the *Ah*, will help greatly in bringing it out of the glottis and forward into balanced resonation. Shakespeare[23] recommends *l* while other authorities favor *m* or *n*. Actually, there appears to be little choice among the values of the three for this purpose.

Ah should be super-bright, hummy, and forward in feeling, but not to the extreme of sounding thin or "white." Its danger is that of nearly always being too dark (toward the Aw), throaty and guttural. *Ah* is most likely to have the greatest freedom, especially in the upper compass, once it is gotten out

---

[21]Pronouncement of the American Academy of Teachers of Singing.

[22]Fields, Victor Alexander. "Training the Singing Voice." Kings Crown Press, 1947, p. 202.

[23]Shakespeare, William. "Plain Words in Singing." Putnam, 1938, (new edition), p. 307.

of the glottis and properly balanced in a more forward resonation. The *Ah,* the *Ay* and the *Aw* are the vowels most likely to be produced too far down in the glottis. The good *Ah* has more forward mouth resonance than any other vowel except *Aw* in order to obtain balanced production.

Beginning students seldom have much trouble with a throaty attack and balanced resonation on the *Oh* once they have been given instructions that it is always thought free and ringing, like a rising inflection exclamation "Oh!" This thought of brighter color offsets its tendency to be somewhat dull and lifeless, and approach the quality of *Oo.*

Ay is inclined toward being too bright and shrill. If much of the tonal *Uh* foundation quality is retained, the *Ay* will be one of the most "ringing," as well as beautifully sonorous, of all the vowels. *It always can be sung properly if the student will first sing Uh and then merge it into Ay with no change of mouth space or shift of resonation into a shallow, forward mouth position.* The danger of both the *Ay* and *Ee* is the tendency toward a too shallow, forward mouth space resulting in a tense, overly-bright, or shrill tone. Singers are inclined to pinch or "choke" these vowels to death, with too high tongue base and too little mouth opening. When in addition, the lips are set in a grinning position, the crime is complete. More mellowness of either the *Uh* or *Ah* pharynx space resonation for the *Ay,* and the lip position of *Oo* for the *Ee,* will invariably improve or correct production.

The voice teacher also will need to urge students to give more breath support to the *Ee* and *Ay* than they think necessary when produced in the larger resonating space recommended. If dynamics, and legato effect are to be maintained evenly, the pupil will learn to feed these vowels more generous breath support than the *Ah* and *Oh.* The same principle holds for the dark *Oo.*

It is a surprise to students to find that the jaw can be dropped on *Ee* as far as a medium length *Ah* position, the lips slightly rounded toward the *Oo* position and the character of the *Ee* sound still maintained. It will be a freer, richer, and more sonorous *Ee* than that to which the student is accustomed and, consequently, difficult in the beginning to get them to accept as correct. Some cannot define the *Ee* well at first in the new and larger space, but definition will come later if pupils only will persist in applying the principle of *similar vibrating space for all vowels.*

The *Oo* is inclined to be dull, lifeless, and breathy. Just as the *Oo* is used to help the *Ee,* the intensity of the *Ee* resonation can be utilized to brilliantize the *Oo.* Achieving balanced resonation for each by comparison is to be expected, since both vowels are at opposite extremes of the tonal color range. The *Ee* pattern tends to give the *Oo* the necessary intensity and forward quality which it lacks. When

the student is instructed always to think the *Oo* super bright, to feed it somewhat more breath energy, and to open the lips more and move them far enough forward so that a feeling of added resonance is induced between the front teeth and the lips, the *Oo* takes on a surprising brilliance and volume. It is thus enabled to equalize with the other more brilliant and sonorous vowels. Another method favored by many for improving the *Oo* is first to sing an *Oh* and then gradually merge into *Oo* with as little change of jaw and lip position as possible.

OTHER ENGLISH VOWELS

Other English vowels than the five pure vowels are produced in the same position or form as the pure vowel to which they are most closely allied, as explained in Expressive Singing, Volume I.

LIP POSITION AND MOVEMENT

"So many teachers and singers consider the lips of prime importance in vocal emission, whereas actually they are secondary and subsidiary. In the last analysis, their shape reflects the adjustment of the pharyngeal parts for the particular vowel and pitch."[24] In fact, all the vowel sounds can be sung without moving the lips in the least. Moving the lips helps in defining the vowel more easily, however. Beginning students always have a tendency to change both lip position and mouth opening far too much between vowels. *Radical change is always wrong.* The basic law is: *lips are moved quickly and generously in articulating consonants, but only to a slight extent in forming the different vowels.*

It is necessary for correct singing that most of the change to establish sound of the different vowels be in the *pharynx,* and that it be reflex action induced entirely by proper thought of the sound of the various vowels. Even small variations in the shape and dimensions of the mouth strikingly alter the color and resonation of tone. Experimentation is necessary by the pupil to discover the way he can form each vowel with the greatest ease and beauty and *with the least disturbance of mouth opening and lip action. Lips should be relaxed in a semi-round position as a norm and adjusted from this shape to only the small degree necessary for obtaining definition of the various vowels.* (Note — see illustrations of mouth position for *Oh* and *Ah* in Expressive Singing, Volume I, p. 96)

Any movement of the lips in the initial shaping of the vowel should be simultaneous with the tonal attack. Lips will never be "set" previously in some fancied ideal position for the vowel and the tone attacked later. "Nothing should be held (rigidly)

---

[24]Herbert-Caesari, E. F. "Opening the Mouth in Singing." Etude, Jan. 1938, p. 46.

in singing! If singing means anything at all it means MOTION."[25] Witherspoon[26] also emphasized the importance of flexible movement of the lips and the fallacy of any stereotyped position of the mouth.

The method illustrated in some texts of "setting" the lips first, and then attacking the tone, is contrary to all laws of naturalness in speech and to principles of ease in tonal production. Muscles set in studied position previous to phonation are bound to be more or less rigid. Even if the authors of such texts do not subscribe to the belief that the lips and mouth be shaped previous to the tonal attack, they often fail to clarify the matter in illustrations presented. Consequently, the conscientious student is led astray in his zeal to follow directions explicitly by imitating exact positions shown and then attacking the tone.

Graves believes that the mouth is to be opened adequately but never forced or exaggerated. "A horizontal oval is the correct shape for the singer's mouth in action."[27] This position rules out the horizontal grinning position, as well as the exaggerated egg-shaped position, as norms in singing. "Santley was the first British singer to contest the efficacy of the wide open mouth, and now no good singers look as if they were going to swallow billiard balls."[28]

Most teachers and authorities condemn the exaggerated "grinning" or wide horizontal lip position. For example, Bachner says, "A very well known practice is to sing with the upper lip pulled up and back, the teeth showing in a sort of frozen smile. This causes abnormal tension in the soft palate, in the cheeks, and in the lips, which, in turn, results in throat clutch, giving a destructive rigid stability to the vocal box."[29]

In any case, illustrations of lip position for singing any vowel could express only one phase or stage, since after the initial slight adjustment of the lips which may follow the norm on attack, their position changes as tone is developed to the end of rhythm length. It is necessary that flexible feeling of motion in the proper direction for enunciation development be retained, even though motion be so slow as to be practically invisible.

The alert teacher will warn and check students continually to prevent the mouth from moving to its maximum position for the vowel long before the rhythm for the vowel is concluded. *For best production lips never assume their maximum ending position for any vowel until just the moment when it is released,* no matter how long the note. The reason is basic — NO MUSCLE INVOLVED IN CONTROL OF SINGING EVER CAN BE SET IN A FIXED POSITION. Muscles must be kept in motion or they will become rigid, and rigidity in the lips is reflected immediately in the throat. The wise teacher will watch the jaw and lip position of students and check any tendency to prematurely

close the vowel or syllable, or to "set" the lips or jaw, during the sustaining of any tone. Disappointing tone, bad diction, and poor legato are directly traceable to this fault and are improved immediately when it is corrected.

Danger of making lip and mouth action primary, and not secondary, in obtaining free and proper resonation will be recognized in teaching procedure and the tendency counteracted early. Lip position is never either set or changed so radically that the vowel is literally "pulled" out of the pharynx and transferred to the lips or mouth. *Pronunciation of vowels must be primarily in the pharynx and not in the lips.* Vowels are resonated primarily in the pharynx, while most consonants are articulated with the lips and the tip of the tongue. The sooner these functions are recognized and kept separated permanently, the more free and beautiful the voice will sound. In free and correct singing lips have no voluntary set position in formulating vowels; movement is an involuntary resultant phenomenan through association with proper vowel concept and pharyngeal action.

Lip shape, in general, starts from a loose, easy, neutral position, from which a small degree of flexible movement is made only in the degree necessary to define the vowel on attack. Lip motion is then continued either backward or forward, according to the particular vowel. Direction of motion is easy to remember, since only the "round" *Oh* and *Oo* move toward a farther forward position as tone is sustained and developed; all other vowels develop with a backward "swing" of the lips. This lip movement is exactly the same as for speech; *the only difference is that motion is slowed down in singing to meet the demands of an elongated vowel.*

Properly established pharynx enunciation of the vowels frees the lips and tongue for consonant articulation without interference with the vowel. That the pharynx, and not the lips or tongue, has primary action in producing vowels is proven conclusively. In fact, it has been discovered after operation on cancer patients that vowels can be produced with both the lips and tongue removed entirely. Clear definition of vowel color suffered, however.

The student is advised to develop the sensation that vowels are formed primarily in the pharynx, with only a secondary sensation in the mouth. "Each vowel must be carefully formed very close to the instrument (voice box), and the formation of the

---

[25]Weer, Robert Lawrence. "My Views on Voice Production." The Author, 1941, p. 72.

[26]Witherspoon, Herbert. "Thirty-Six Lessons in Singing." Meissner Institute of Music, 1930.

[27]Graves, Richard M. "Singing for Amateurs." Oxford U. Press, 1954, p. 50.

[28]Ibid, p. 50.

[29]Bachner, Louis. "Dynamic Singing." L. B. Fischer, 1944, p. 12.

vowel-sound should be felt in the rear mouth cavity, on a direct line between the vocal instrument and the cavities of the head."[30]   Stanley supports this viewpoint, "The pharyngeal, or back, cavities should be used as the resonators of tone.   The mouth cavity should be completely out of action (i.e., resonance adjustment).   In view of the fact that sound is communicated to the outer ear through the open mouth, this cavity must have some effect upon quality.   The vital point, however, is that, in good technic, the mouth is never used as a selective resonator — is never 'set'."[31]

Lesson 3.   Equalizing the Vowels

(*See Volume I, p. 100*)

Beginning students vary greatly in evenness of vowel production when singing a series of different vowels.   There is no such phenomena as a perfectly equalized and correct production of a series of all the pure vowels by the beginner; this is an end result after long practice.   Beginning voices are all more or less uneven; none are perfectly even.   In fact, some professionals never learn to sing certain vowels correctly, notably the extremes — the bright *Ee* and the dark *Oo*.   The only deduction that can be drawn from this is that a surprising number of vocal teachers and coaches do not understand the principles of vowel equalization.   Once these concepts are understood and given adequate practice, there is no good reason why one vowel cannot be about as freely and easily produced as another.

The previous lesson discusses the principles of production for the individual vowels that are basic to equalized tone for sustained legato singing.   Volume I for this lesson (See p. 100) states concepts clearly and provides the basic types of exercises for initial development, whose principles are to be furthered by observance in future songs.   Concepts involved in lesson 3 also help in further clarifying lesson 2 content in relation to individual vowel production.

TONAL "UH" BASIS

(*Note — See also pp. 33, 34, 39, 59, 129*)

In singing, tone functions, of course, through the vowel.   Tone is basic to the vowel and, when tone is poor, we look not only to the purity of the vowel but also to whether the vowel has retained its fundamental *Uh* tonal basis and free resonation space. Tone is a natural phenomenon; *vowel sounds are all man-made inventions*.   The natural tone of the human voice is *Uh*.   It is the sound produced by the vocal bands in the unformed, relaxed pharynx when we aren't thinking.   It is the sound heard in the last dying gasp, and when we are punched in the "wind."

Because it is natural, *Uh* is more relaxed as a tonal basis, or norm, for obtaining freedom and uni-

form production than any of the pure man-made vowel sounds possibly can be. *It should be the mold into which all the vowels fit in obtaining either a proper attack or a sustained legato.*   It is a valuable concept to help in achieving a number of objectives: free production; the maximum of relaxed pharynx space; a common method for attacking all vowels (the tonal *Uh* precedes the vowel); a smooth legato tonal transition between vowels; and a long relaxed pharynx space needed to achieve maximum "head" resonance for high tones.

Since the correct formation and "evening" of the vowels is the key to beauty in tonal production and a necessity for legato technic, it is necessary that the teacher devote a great deal of time in the beginning, and give continued attention, to this fundamental. The more nearly all vowels can be produced in the same "form," "mold," or resonation space, the more even, free, and simple phonation becomes and the finer the legato that can be produced.   One vowel will not be resonated spaciously in the throat and the next vowel of an opposite character thinly and far forward in the mouth.   *Legato demands that all vowels be sounded uniformly in resonation space and color from the same "mold."*   The "mold" or resonation space norm for all vowels is best found in *Uh*, the natural tone of the human voice; its primary resonance is in the pharynx where it belongs and is a safe basis for further development.   The concept of a common tonal denominator facilities uninterrupted flow of tone in spite of vowel change and prevents the voice from "breaking" or "cracking." When used in conjunction with the principle of sameness in mouth opening for all vowels produced on the same pitch and with the same force, the mastery of legato is tremendously accelerated. (Note — See next topic, "Jaw Position and Movement.")

Blending or evening the vowels implies the legato merging or "melting" of one vowel into another without break or wavering of tone between, and without sudden changes of dynamics or tone color.   In evening the vowels, "If *Ah* is taken for the normal vowel color, the *Ay* and *Ee* will almost invariably be brighter, thinner than the *Ah*, and *Oh* and *Oo* will be darker.   The singer must learn to produce these vowels as if they came from the same organpipe.   This means making the *Ay* and *Ee* a little darker and the *Oh* and *Oo* a little brighter."[32]   The common tonal denominator resonation space of *Uh* will accomplish this purpose better than *Ah* and any device we have yet discovered.

In general, the major ways to achieve the ideal of even vowel production are threefold:

---
[30]Taylor, Bernard U.   "Group Voice."   G. Schirmer, Inc., 1936, p. 14.
[31]Stanley, Douglas. ·"Your Voice."   Pittman Publ. Co., 1945, p. 72.
[32]Clippinger, D. A. " The Clippinger Class Method of Voice Culture."   Ditson, 1932, p. 12.

1. Learn, in the beginning, a concept and production space for each individual pure vowel which will match with the tonal color and resonation characteristics of the other vowels. (Note — Both Volume I and previous discussion of individual vowel production in this lesson cover this concept.)

2. Habituate the basic concept of tonal *Uh* as the method for attack inception, and as a continuing fundamental tonal "flow" underlying all vowels.

3. Habituate the principle of similar mouth opening for all vowels when sung on the same pitch and with the same dynamics. (Note — See next topic, "Jaw Position and Movement.")

In discussing the vowel *Ah*, Vennard says, "Authorities tell us that the glottal tone is probably more neutral than *Ah*, more like *Uh*."[33] *Ah* is the nearest of all pure vowel sounds in pharynx position to the neutral tone of the human voice, *Uh*, however. That is the underlying reason why it is generally preferred by many voice teachers as the best single vowel to use as comparison in correcting faulty production on other vowels. *Uh* itself is a better norm for comparison in the so-called process of "placing" (balancing) the voice, since it is more naturally and freely produced in an unformed, relaxed pharynx.

All vowels benefit by assuming the freedom and resonance space of the Uh and by a slight suggestion of its "general" or neutral sound in the upper register. The higher the pitch, the more benefit is derived from this principle. Henderson[34] indicates that Madame Lilli Lehmann had a similar idea in mind when she advised singers to keep the "u" sound always in mind, thus holding the vocal organs in position to give all the vowel sounds throughout the voice with equability. Weer states the concept quite plainly also: "Changes of molds (for the forming of various vowels) have nothing to do with the fundamental tone. . . . No matter what *shape* the vowel mold assumes, the substance of the vowel is always the same — the sound of the fundamental tone."[35]

Comparatively few texts emphasizes the basic importance of the natural tone *Uh*, and then chiefly or only in relation to the staccato attack in which "H" (sounding "huh") commonly is recommended to open the throat and induce proper freedom and precision. Some authorities mention that *Uh* is the sound which all vowels approach (or should approach) when singing in the extremes of the upper register. *This concept greatly simplifies vowel production on the attack and singing technic in legato, furnishing a common tonal denominator for the attack as well as providing an underlying basic factor for all phonation.*

JAW POSITION AND MOVEMENT

Mouth opening remains relatively the same for all vowels when sung on the same pitch with equal force. The jaw is a heavy, cumbersome bony structure, and should not be used for either enunciation of vowels or articulation of consonants when the work can be done by the far more flexible tongue and lip muscles. If the jaw is allowed to "flop" back and forth, changing mouth opening radically between vowels, an even series of vowels and a fine legato are impossible. Students have a tendency to sing the short and bright pure vowels *Ay* and *Ee* (and the short *e* as in "set," the short *i* as in "sit," and the short *a* as in "sat") with much too constricted mouth opening; and, conversely, the "broad" vowels *Ah* and *Aw* with too much space. The round *Oh* is usually produced about normal in jaw opening; the *Oo* is sung too confined and muffled.

Students can be taught to correct the common tendency to distort resonance space in a series of vowels by singing them on one pitch, preceding each with the neutral tonal *Uh*, e.g., Uh-Ah-Uh-Ay-Uh-Ee-Uh-Oh-Uh-Oo. (Note — See p. 102 of Volume I). Instruct the student to do this *while keeping the mouth opening the same* and with only *slight* modification of lip position for the different vowels. Somewhat more breath energy will be needed on the *Ay*, the *Oo*, and especially the *Ee*, in the fuller space now provided for these vowels.

Some will think that they cannot enunciate without changing jaw position and making a radical difference in lip shape. They will find eventually that they not only can, but that tone is now uniformly free and sonorous on all vowels. As a rule the short and bright vowels will need most attention because beginning students almost invariably sing them too bright, thin, and "mouthy." To insist on singing them in the *Uh* space, or with as much space as an *Ah*, will correct the difficulty.

It is important for the pupil to learn that *degree of mouth opening is controlled almost exclusively by range and dynamics* and not by the fact that different vowels are sung. The higher we sing the more mouth opening is used, the lower the less; the louder we sing the greater the opening, the softer the less. "There is and indeed can be, no hard and fast rule, and certainly no artifice, as regards the opening of the mouth in singing, for the simple and cogent reasons (a) that actual mouth opening (lip-to-lip aperture) is, or should be, determined solely by the height of the particular sound column, which height varies according to pitch; (b) that the degree of such mouth opening is essentially an individual one, as no two mouths are exactly alike in size and shape."[36]

[33]Vennard, William. "Singing, the Mechanism and Technic." Edwards Bros.. Inc., 1949 p. 76.

[34]Henderson, William J. "The Art of Singing." Dial Press, 1938, revised edition, p. 107.

[35]Op. cit., p. 70.

[36]Herbert-Caesari, Op. cit., p. 46.

The jaw is always relaxed in vowel production, i.e., never held or "set" in any fixed position. If the tongue base or jaw is set or tense, it will usually be apparent visually as well as tonally. Strained muscles and prominence of the cords in the neck are a sure indication of excess tension in production. Tension in the tongue base also can be checked and felt by placing the fingers on the hyoglossus muscle under the chin. Jan De Reszke, internationally famous tenor and vocal teacher, is reported to have advised his students repeatedly, "We should feel fat under the chin when singing" and also, "the singer should feel like he has a double chin."

Many teachers evidently have a fallacious belief that the mouth must be opened wide in order to open the throat, regardless of whether the tone be high or low, loud or soft. First, it has been pointed out previously that open throat means a relaxed open pharynx, and that the pharynx can be opened and relaxed with the mouth either opened fully or closed. Second, soft dynamics and low compass tones are sung much easier and in better balanced resonation with the mouth in a closer form than for normal *Mf* and middle compass tones. It is as much of a crime to easy production to open the mouth too much as too little. *Most students are inclined to open the mouth too little for high tones and fortissimo and too much for low tones and pianissimi.* To force the jaw open by conscious effort at any pitch or dynamics creates a degree of tension sure to be reflected in the tone.

Weer says, "It is definitely wrong to *pull* the mouth open by conscious muscular effort. One of the surest ways of removing all direct resonance from the head cavities is to forcibly open the mouth. When resonance is correct, the jaw will *drop* down loose and free and the jaw will open to any necessary extent without effort."[37] Herbert-Caesari concurs as follows, "Procedures such as employing wooden posts, showing six teeth, the lips smiling, a smiling form of mouth, mean absolutely nothing to the student seeking the truth; indeed they mislead because they teach nothing."[38]

To the foregoing objections the author places a device used by many teachers of two or three fingers between the front teeth to force the student to drop the jaw widely. This "rule of thumb" procedure may prove beneficial in the high register for those having a tight, thin tone, *providing they are able to drop the jaw to the opening demanded without excessive tension.* The practice is positively injurious as a generality, however, and especially so to students who already have breathy, "spread," and spacious types of voices. It cannot be emphasized too strongly that *correct amount of "jaw drop," or mouth opening, depends entirely upon the individual concerned, the range and dynamics involved.* As a rule, the student learns gradually to drop the

jaw more as ability to support a higher, or louder and more spacious tone is increased. This is a developmental process and, like other technics in singing, should not be forced.

CORRECTIVE QUALITIES OF THE VOWELS

Actually, there is no such thing as the best basic vowel to use in vocalization for all voices, and attempts to prove that there is are futile. *The best vowel depends on the individual type of voice and corrective needs at the time.* For example, a voice that is overly dark, breathy, and "spread" in quality should vocalize mostly on the brighter vowels *Ay* and *Ee;* one that is overly bright and tense should use the dark vowels *Oo* and *Oh* until a balanced resonation is established. The best vowel in each case is that on which the most desirable balance of tonal freedom, sonority, and efficient resonance are achieved.

In speaking about the beneficial values of various vowels, Vennard says, "In obtaining resonance and a balanced, even vowel production, the pointed vowels, *Ee* and *Ay,* are logical ones to use since this exercise is designed to give brilliance to the voice; but light voices also need 'focus,' and using the round vowels, *Oh* and *Oo,* helps to accomplish roundness and freedom at the same time."[39] It is apparent that the quality of a vowel should be balanced; that all vowels must have some of the fullness and sonority of the *Ah* and *Oh,* some of the suavity of the *Oo,* and some of the intensity, efficiency in resonation, and brilliance of *Ay* and *Ee.*

For the average voice, it is usually best to vocalize the upper compass with the broader and more spacious vowels, *Ah* and *Oh,* and the lower register with the more intense brighter vowels *Ay* and *Ee.* To achieve a suave *pianissimo* in the upper register, the *Oo* usually is preferred. *Oo* also generally is recommended for altos and contraltos as the vowel most likely to develop quickly the suave quality and rich, dark, tonal texture required for this type of voice. *Continued exclusive vocalization on any vowel is injurious to technic, however;* all need to be vocalized sufficiently to obtain balanced resonance and even production.

1. *Ah*

In class teaching, the problem is to choose the vowel that will be most beneficial for the majority of the class for initial emphasis in vocalization. In this case most teachers choose the *Ah,* with *Oh* running a close second. As has been stated previously, our preference is for the rounder *Oh* until the problem of glottal attack has been solved, and the pupil is able to produce the *Ah* in good balance forward

---

[37]Weer, Op. cit., p. 94.

[38]Herbert-Caesari, Op. cit., p. 46.

[39]Op. cit., p. 134.

with a brilliant, and not the swallowed *Awe* quality, usually heard. After that the *Ah* is preferred for a number of reasons. *Ah* has not only the greatest sonority of any of the pure vowels but also is closest of all the vowels to the unformed, relaxed pharynx position of the matrix tone of the human voice, *Uh*. When properly resonated, the *Ah* induces a desirable normally low pharynx position and the greatest sonority for amount of breath energy, providing a better pattern for imitation in developing the high compass.

2. *Oh*

"For many pupils this vowel readily becomes the first one placed properly."[40] Most beginning untrained voices will produce an *Oh* without the unpleasant "shock of the glottis" attack, and in better resonance balance than the *Ah* or any other vowel. *Oh is probably the best single vowel for most beginning students to use in vocalization that covers the entire compass.* After some study, *Ah* is likely to be best in the upper and perhaps the middle register but, because of its spacious quality, tends to be the worst in the low. *Ay* and *Ee* are too close and bright for easy upper voice production. The *Oo* is inclined to be too gloomy and muffled as a model for beginners.

3. *Ay*

The *Ay* is one of the most brilliant as well as sonorous of vowels when sung properly. It has a particularly pleasing quality when the "shrill edge" and mouthy quality often heard are eliminated by dropping the jaw and thinking a maximum of the tonal *Uh* quality in production. *Ay is an excellent vowel for vocalization to develop vitality and "ring" in the voice.*

4. *Ee*

Ee, being the brightest, closest, and thinnest of all vowels, will produce the most intensity or "focus" of tone forward with the least wastage of breath. *Ay* is next in this respect. *Ee* is simultaneously the most "pointed" and efficient of the vowels in resonating without wastage of breath, and the vowel most likely to be tight and constricted. When a throat specialist wants to obtain the *best* view of the action of the vocal bands, he requests the patient to produce *Ee*, the vowel with maximum glottic closure. *Ee, therefore, is the best of all vowels as a model in practicing to correct a breathy, "spread" tone quality and imparting intensity to the Oo through comparison. The singing of Ee - - Oo, Ee - - Ah,* etc., tends to improve the efficiency of resonation on all the broader and darker vowels when they are sung too spaciously.

5. *Oo*

The *Oo* has corrective qualities of a type which no other vowel possesses. Its use in rounding and freeing the *Ee* and in producing the high voice

pianissimo has already been mentioned. *It is highly beneficial in obtaining a suave, dark tonal quality and in resting and relaxing the voice.* A too habitual use of the *Oo*, to the exclusion of the more brilliant and sonorous vowels, will result in an anemic and artificially sombre quality, however. This fault has been particularly obvious in much public school singing of the past but, fortunately, has recently evidenced considerable improvement. It is desirable to produce the *Oo* so that it gains in brilliance and intensity as it descends into the lower compass, and to modify it toward a more open form as it is carried into the upper range. Like the *Ah*, it should be thought super-bright for best quality and blending with the other vowels.

Lesson 4.   Double Vowels and Dipthongs

(*See Volume I, p. 103*)

DOUBLE VOWELS

Beginning vocal students seldom are aware of the existence of compound vowel sounds until the matter is brought to their attention when they encounter difficulty with proper enunciation in vocal lessons. Maintenance of pure vowel quality and proper timing of double vowels and dipthongs is the objective.

In the compound vowels *Ay* (eh-ee), *I* (Ah-ee) and *Oh* (Oh - - oo), the initial sound is held in its *pure* form until the last possible moment before the "vanish" second part is sung. Most students either anticipate the vanishing part or sing an intermediary compromising tone with qualities of both the initial and vanishing parts. *Students must learn to sustain the pure vowel sound of the initial part.* In the compound vowel *Oo* (Ee - oo), the order is reversed with the initial sound being quickly enunciated and the final part receiving the length and emphasis. If there is lingering on the *Ee* part in such words as "few" or "new," the result is an unpleasant mewing sound, "fee - ee - oo," "nee - ee - oo."

The most troublesome of the double or dipthong vowels, and the ones most often produced incorrectly, are the *Ay* and the *I*. Beginners and many singers in the popular style enunciate as follows: "say - ee - ee" for "say," "dah - ee - ee" for "die," etc., with a premature closing and lingering on the vanishing part. Some even may argue that this is the proper and natural way to sing, since "we should sing like we speak." The point is that they are not singing like they speak, and the ridiculous nature of the argument is readily apparent with an illustration in speech of their manner of singing enunciation.

---

[40]Lamperti, Carlo. "Improving Your Voice." Vantage Press, 1954, p. 81.

DIPTHONGS

The most commonly encountered dipthong sounds, *oi, oy, ou* and *ow,* are illustrated and explained clearly in Expressive Singing, Volume I, with exercises given for correction. Dipthongs in effect are the same as compound vowels, e.g., "thou" (thah - oo), "low" (lo - oo), "boy" (baw - ee), "void" (vaw - eed). Both parts are always plainly sounded, but the shorter unstressed portion should be very short and not exaggerated in length as done by many untrained singers. The student needs to be checked and assited in timing dipthong production so that the major sound is sustained to the maximum and the unstressed part executed as quickly as if it were a consonant. With the exception of dipthongs involving the sound of *Oo,* in words such as "new," the unstressed part is always the second or "vanish" section.

When a dipthong, or double vowel, is written to be sung on two notes with a "slur" mark between, the second sound is never to be sung at the beginning of the second note in the interval concerned. The initial part is carried over to the second note of the interval before the vanishing part is sounded. (Note — See exercises 1 and 2, p. 105, in Volume I)

Lesson 5.   Consonants and Articulation

(See Volume I, p. 106)

The American Academy of Teachers of Singing consider the singing of clear and understandable English so important that they have issued a special pronouncement as follows:

"David Bispham, well-beloved American baritone, famous in opera and song-recital on both sides of the Atlantic, wrote these words: 'English is just as easy to sing as any other language — if we but know it, and know how to pronounce it. The only thing bad about English as a song-medium is bad English. To all American singers I say, sing your songs in well-chosen English if singing to an English-speaking audience, and sing them so that everyone understands your words; enunciate so clearly that the audience can tell even how every word is spelled. Get away from this foreign-language fad and you will find yourself nearer the heart of your public.'

W. J. Henderson, dean of American critics and an authority on the art of the singer, has this to say: 'Nine-tenths of the songs we hear are songs without words, they are either mangled in the formation or neglected in the matter of significance. We get tone, tone, and tone. To sing mere sounds is a senseless performance. Let it be understood that in song the music is not the end but the means. Singing is the interpretation of text by means of musical tones produced by human voice.'

After spending some ten years as teacher in New York city, the late Victor Maurel, international famous baritone, earnest advocate of opera in English, gave this in an interview: 'The most fundamental need of the American singer is to acquire the habit of more careful speech in his own home, at school, and in his private intercourse with men and women. With rare exceptions, singers know nothing about diction, enunciation, articulation. They are under the impression that the only essential of dramatic singing is tone. During my stay here I have had two thousand pupils. They treated consonants as though they were negligible both at the beginning and at the end of the words they sang.'

Feeling that there is much truth in these quotations, the Academy would ask its correspondents and co-workers to consider carefully if the prime cause of this lack of intelligibility is not too exclusive attention to vocalization, and a slighting of the consonant as being an interference or obstruction to be gotten over as lightly as possible. Vocalization deals only with vowels, is merely the making of sounds. Articulation involves words and demands clearly audible consonants. If we would retain in song that perfect balance between vowel and consonant which characterizes the diction of trained speakers, must we not give the consonant a strength proportionate to the strength demanded by the vowel?"

Both verbal significance and tonal freedom are essential for the singer. Tonal freedom is comparatively easy if the singer could vocalize only on vowels. Needless to say, it is necessary also to employ consonants in order to be understood. Consonants either partially or completely obstruct the vocal channel, causing more or less tension in production according to how rapidly and freely they are articulated. It is still the rare vocal teacher who realizes that the singer usually is required to practice as faithfully to perfect rapid, free, and precise articulation of consonants as he does to perfect purity, freedom, and uniformity of vowels. Clear articulation is a necessity if the art of singing is to be truly mastered.

With the advent of radio, motion pictures, and television, whose quality and appeal depend on words being understood, competition has caused a great renaissance in emphasis on the clarity and proper "timing" of consonants by some teachers in these fields. It is safe to say that the professional "microphone" singers of today are far superior in articulation of consonants to those singers of the so-called "Golden Age of Song" when vowel production received almost exclusive attention, according to most accounts.

ARTICULATION PROBLEMS IN SINGING

We often hear the idea expressed that consonants are the "bones" of speech and vowels the "flesh." Certainly consonants are the framework upon which the structure of intelligibility rests, for without consonants there is no meaning to words. Some singers merely vocalize on vowels — it would be better then if the song were played on a violin or some other instrument.

"Many singers vocalize freely on vowels but, when they attempt to combine vowels and consonants into words, tense production results. The vocalist must learn to articulate quickly and flexibly, for there appears little doubt that the conflict between vowel production and articulation of consonants demands refinement and skill in diction which explains, at least in part, the scarcity of fine singers in the world today."[41]

Understanding the many problems and difficulties of articulation is basic but it is only the first step; persistent practice is necessary for correction of faults and development of speed, precision, and clarity. "Just as a pianist shakes and loosens his wrists and fingers or plays exercises designed to relax the muscles for a more free and effective finger action, the singer likewise can sing vocal exercises that relax and activate the muscles of the jaw, tongue, lips and throat."[42] Quite often it is the slow and labored articulation of the initial consonant that causes the following vowel tone to be tense. Students need to practice to attain sufficient speed and flexibility on the consonant so that the following vowel is not distorted. A favorite and oft-recommended procedure is first to vocalize a troublesome passage only on a favorable vowel, or on the exact vowels involved, leaving out the consonants. Second, whisper through the text giving due attention to dramatic accent and clarity. Third, sing the song, attempting to retain the same resonation feeling for free tonal production as in step one and the consonant clarity of step two.

It must be admitted that it is much more difficult for the singer than the speaker to make himself understood. First there is the competition of an accompaniment that has to be "sung over." Primarily, however, the greater difficulty resides in the necessity for elongation of the vowel and greater mouth space which the singer uses for legato, greater sonority, and high compass tones. Singers are notorious for inaudible diction in the high register. Since lips are usually much farther apart in the greater mouth space required for singing, they have to move much farther and more quickly to achieve the same clarity as in speech. The same is true for both tip and base of the tongue action. The singer should, however, consider this added difficulty a challenge and not an insurmountable obstacle: *greater speed and flexibility in articulation can and must be developed through intelligent and faithful practice.*

Elongation of the vowel also inserts a psychological memory factor — the longer a vowel is sustained, the more likely the listener forgets the beginning consonant, thus failing to understand the word. *When long note rhythms are involved, more precision and force is required on initial consonants to impress them on the minds of the listener.*

The most common and pernicious diction fault of amateurs is an anticipation or running-together of the consonant and vowel. "The final consonant is anticipated and an effort is made to sound it long before it is rhythmically due. This results not only in distorting the vowel but also the consonant."[43] Anticipation of the consonant has a psychological basis also — the desire of the singer to time ending articulation in song with the same timing as in speech. Because of the frequent vowel elongation in singing this cannot be done and articulation must be delayed. To bring this about in legato singing *it is necessary to think of the consonant at the end of any sustained word or syllable as attached to the following word or syllable.* Actually this speeds up the total time involved in utterance of consonants, as well as making them more rather than less intelligible, as students are prone to think. When articulation does occur it will then be quick and precise.

"The consonant must be uttered with exactness but quickly, so that continuity and flowing tone suffer as little interruption as possible. Distinctness need never work injury to note sung. To preserve the legato and still make every word clean-cut is what staggers most singers. The secret of the whole thing lies first in perfect purity of vowel sounds and second in free and untrammeled articulation."[44] Free and untrammeled articulation is impossible if the singer attempts to use the jaw for action which can be more quickly and efficiently performed by lips and tongue. Those who struggle with articulation usually attempt to use too much jaw action. The lips and tongue can move rapidly and flexibly — the jaw is too ponderous. In addition, jaw action disturbs lower vowel form greatly, while lip and tongue action have comparatively minor effect.

When consonants demand jaw action, too much emphasis cannot be placed on the importance of quick, free, and flexible movement, since "Jaw tension brings tongue tension, and tongue tension brings throat tension, resulting in blocking the lower half of the resonator and destroying the true position of the vowels."[45] Exclusive jaw action is necessary on only two consonants, *y* and *h;* on a number of others it is supplementary and secondary to lip or tongue action — *it should never be primary when the lips* or tongue are involved. The singer practices to train lip and tongue action so that they are capable of quick and complete function over a much wider arc than in speech. *This is especially necessary in*

[41]Anonymous. "Academy Offers Sound Advice to Vocal Students." Musician, Feb. 1929, Vol. 34, p. 35.

[42]Peterson, Op. cit., p. 22.

[43]Dengler, Clyde. "Class Vocal Methods — High School Level." M.E.N.C. Yearbook, 1937, p. 214.

[44]Henderson, Op. cit., p. 117-118.

[45]Westerman, Kenneth U. "Modern Phonetization." Edwards Bros., 1945, p. 67.

the high compass where "jaw drop" needs to be more generous for free and sonorous tone.

Most singers use the jaw far too much, dropping it farther than normal in the articulation of certain tip-of-the-tongue consonants, *d*, *l*, *n*, and *t*, making easy and quick tongue action unnecessarily difficult. All consonants formed by tip of the tongue action or by the lips are easier to articulate quickly and precisely if the mouth is not opened unduly. *Extremely fast diction songs, therefore, are sung with less mouth opening than normal if words are to be intelligible.*

A factor which confuses the singer is reconciling the aesthetic requirements of a *pianissimo* vowel with what may need to be very forceful articulation of consonant at the same time in order to be understood. The natural tendency is to articulate consonants with very little force when singing vowels softly. *It is necessary to keep dynamics of the vowel and force of consonant separate in singing concept, however.* Vowels carry well and consonants do not. Even the softest tone will carry to the back of the largest auditorium if it is produced with vital resonance and there is no interfering noise, while only the most precise and forceful consonant will be heard.

The singer thus may be thinking *ppp* on the vowel and *fff* on the consonant in order to sing artistically and to be understood. Force on the vowel is determined very largely by aesthetic ideal; force on the consonant is dictated by the acoustic requirements for audibility in the back row. Tone of a small, clear voice is easily heard in a large hall, but the singer cannot be understood unless articulation is powerful. The same principle applies to speakers. Fortunately, force on articulation does not demand a powerful, resonant voice and *singers with "small" voices can make themselves understood if only they will learn to articulate, can keep the accompaniment subdued, and eliminate interfering noises.*

Initial and final consonants, especially the *b*, *g*, *d*, *p*, *t*, *h*, *k*, and *w* are often entirely omitted, or slighted to such an extent that audiences sometimes even wonder if the song is being sung in English. The vocal consonants *m*, *n*, *l*, and *ng* interrupt tonal legato less than other types. Although the general rule is to articulate all consonants rapidly, these may at times be "lingered on" at the beginning of words to give greater dramatic emphasis and, at the ending, to provide a grateful connecting link with the following word, or a continuous *diminuendo* following an extensive softening of the preceding vowel. These effects should always be completely appropriate to expression at the time, however, rather than being "dragged in by the heels" at the slightest excuse to display effect, as often heard.

After the gutteral *r*, the sibilants *s*, *z*, and cedilla *c* (sounding *s*) are the greatest offenders as noise makers, and always need to be articulated rapidly unless a harsh, ugly, and brutal effect is planned deliberately. The *h* is frequently weak or omitted in such words as "white," "when," and "whither." Both the *w* and a beginning aspirate *h* seldom have enough force for audibility. Substitution of one consonant for another is not uncommon, e.g., "bay" for "pay," "dake" for "take," "vine" for "fine," and "gall" for "call." Naturally such faults are a habit; students are unconscious of fault and need to be corrected and helped to overcome them.

Rolling or "trilling" the *r*, executed by fluttering the tip of the tongue, is often overdone unnecessarily by singers to the detriment of vocal beauty. There are so many exceptions to specific rules on rolling the *r* that it would seem best to give only brief generalizations and leave the matter to good taste. An excellent rule to follow is — *If you don't roll the r in speech, don't roll it in song!* In general, a strong rolled *r* adds dramatic effect when accent and roughness are desired, but should be avoided in soft, lyric style passages. A horrible example of the effect of rolling *every r* is found in the phrase, "Onward Christian Soldiers, riding as to war."

Articulatory tensions can be benefited, perhaps eliminated, through practice on rapid reading drills, chanting, recitative, intoning, whispering, counting rapidly, and rapid-word songs in an easy range. The "Patter-songs" in the Gilbert-Sullivan comic operas are unsurpassed for this purpose.

MEN SUPERIOR IN ARTICULATION

In spite of the fact that women are accused of being more loquacious than men, and thus have more practice in articulation, it is common knowledge that men seem to be more able and consistent than women in singing so that they are understood. This is undoubtedly one factor which explains why the average person prefers a male voice. A speech expert expressed the opinion to the author that perhaps the reason for masculine superiority in articulation is that the male voice is usually more powerful. Added power on the vowel would not affect understanding of words unless conflicting noises interfere, however. In fact, volume on tone which is carried by the vowel even may react unfavorably in an over-reverberant hall.

It is force and clarity in forming the consonant that is the principal determinant for intelligibility, and a powerful tone is unnecessary for that. Women with comparatively light voices, but with extremely precise and clean-cut articulation, have proven this point in the largest auditoriums. For further proof one need merely whisper — nearly all consonant and aspirate breath. A forceful "stage" whisper will carry for long distances, although tonal or vowel quality as we know it in singing is lacking. In any case, it appears that women do have to practice harder and give more attention to the force of articulation than men in order to achieve comparable results.

EXAGGERATION NECESSARY

Exaggeration in fancy and exaggeration in fact are two entirely different things. *Thought exaggeration is necessary in the developmental stages of articulation in order to obtain enough force on the consonant to be heard.* Actual exaggeration in fact is usually the result of poor timing in anticipating consonants, wrong word emphasis, and slow articulation or "struggle" with the production technic. Diction should never be labored or obtrusive. When the listener easily understands every word without giving it a thought — that is the ideal in articulation. Exaggerated articulation is seldom due to the fact that the word is too plain; but if articulation is too slow, labored, powerful in conjunction with being poorly timed, it will cause the effect of extra syllables, become unnecessarily noisy, and interrupt flow of tone to the extent that legato is impossible.

Cases of exaggeration in fact are usually just another form of poor articulation rather than excessive plainness of the word — labored action, anticipation of the consonant, lingering on vocal consonants, etc. Labored diction is often evidenced by struggling to move the jaw too much in functions which can and should be performed by the more flexible tongue and lips. Excessive rolling of *r's* and habitual lengthening of the vocal consonants *m, n, l,* and *ng* are heard more often than any other types of exaggeration. This is just "hamming," another form of bad diction that needs to be discouraged.

It usually amazes beginners to discover how much thought exaggeration on consonant force, speed, and precision is actually necessary to make words intelligible for some distance. They *think* they are articulating strongly enough to be understood when even the keenest ear is unable to detect what is being said or sung. *Nothing is so effective in the learning process as experimentation in a large auditorium* to reveal to the student the amount of force and precision actually required. It is well to scatter the class or listeners in various parts of the auditorium — a few in front and the remainder in the center and rear. Request listeners to raise their hands when they can't understand any word or syllable being sung on the stage. Pupils are invariably astounded at how precise and forceful articulation must be for clear audibility in the back rows. Patterns of diction weaknesses unique to each singer are thus revealed and the student then knows more exactly what requires improvement through practice.

VALUES TO PHONATION

All consonants are not enemies to vowel production, not always villains in interfering with vowel tone, nor are they always exclusively intellectual in function. In fact, some are often used for their "persuader" or "therapeutic" qualities in inducing more efficient and balanced resonation on the vowels. Some, when properly articulated, function quite often like "triggers" to provide more feeling, meaning, and beauty in the flow of vowel tone. For example, the "vocal consonants" *m, n* and *l* are particularly useful to employ previous to vowels in achieving more efficient forward resonance, natural attack, and precise rhythm. Dramatic accented passages are assisted by the accent and "bite" of such consonants as *b, d, p, t, k, w, y* and *ch* either on the attack or endings of significant words.

The strongly and rapidly articulated percussive consonant is like a hammer that strikes an anvil to "trigger" a ringing, dramatic tone on such words as "behold," "die," "take," etc. Conversely, consonants, when articulated with delicacy in such words as "softly," "pray," "splendor," etc., can color the following vowel with an emotional significance and beauty otherwise impossible. Many vocal teachers also maintain that the aspirate *h* is the best possible "persuader" to secure an open throat attack and rhythmic precision in staccato singing. It is thus quite clear that the consonant is not always a villianous impediment to beauty in singing.

FUNCTIONAL CLASSIFICATION

Numerous and confusing classifications of consonants such as pitch consonants, breath consonants, percussive consonants, sub-vocals, gutterals, labials, etc., etc., are found. Although informative and interesting theoretically, it is quite doubtful if these various types of classifications in themselves have any value to students in learning to sing. Volume I and discussion in this lesson, therefore, have been confined principally to the most troublesome problems and to specific suggestions for improving all articulation.

6

Legato and Sostenuto

IMPORTANCE

Legato style is both the basis of the singer's technic and the principal technical factor which causes the listener to have an impression of beauty in singing. The reader has no doubt had the experience of listening to voices whose peculiar quality he did not like for a time, but he enjoyed the singing later because of the skill with which the voice was used in significant interpretation. Since most songs are legato either in whole or in part, skillful use of the voice depends to a great extent upon fine technical control of legato style. A beautifully-toned vocal instrument is highly desirable, of course, but everyone cannot have lovely, rich quality of tone because of inherent structural limitations or peculiar overtone characteristics. Everyone who has normal musical capacities otherwise, and is intelligent and persistent, can learn to sing with a well-controlled legato and most people will then call the voice beautiful.

FINE LEGATO RARE

Extremely fine legato is rare and found to a high degree of perfection among only a few outstanding singers. This cannot be due to the fact that voices in our generation are not good enough, for there are many grand and beautiful voices. One is forced to the conclusion, after listening to these fine voices, that either sufficient emphasis on the basic fundamental of legato technic is being neglected by most teachers, or that they are not fully aware of all the factors involved in legato and how to teach and coordinate them. We strongly suspect the latter cause since apparently no vocal text up to the present has outlined all five factors in legato and made the teaching problems clear.

It is our belief that legato style is so fundamental to the art of singing that strong emphasis needs to be given to the problem by stating and explaining the five essential technics for mastery. These must be presented in sufficient detail to make the problems involved perfectly clear to both students and teachers. As outlined and discussed thoroughly in this chapter of Volume I, these five essential technics are: Portamento connection, sostenuto (obtained through steady breath support), homogeneity of vowel color, an even scale, and delayed articulation concept. Students first are led to understand the factors involved, helped to gain a working knowledge of each, and then checked continually for progressive refinement of each detail.

DEGREE OF LEGATO RELATIVE

It should be understood that the ideal degree of smoothness in connection between tones and level sostenuto effect varies with the expressional demands of each song or phrase. In other words, all legato songs do not require maximum legato-sostenuto effect — there are various degrees that need be used for most appropriate expression. Beginning students can be expected to have difficulty in achieving even a moderate degree of legato. *It is necessary that they be taught to appreciate and strive to attain the maximum degree as an aesthetic ideal for future attainment, and to judge the degree of legato most appropriate for each song and each phrase.* Most of the songs in Song Anthology Volume I, and many in Volume II of this course, require only moderate legato, as they should, for best vocal development. Some require supremely fine flowing legato involving the maximum of sostenuto for most effective expression, however, and will always constitute a challenge to improve legato skill.

Lesson 1. Portamento Connection

(See Volume I, p. 118)

PORTAMENTO AND THE SLUR

Confusion exists regarding interpretation of meaning of the terms *portamento, slur,* and *glissando* and their difference in execution in vocal music. Fields defines *portamento as,* "Singing from one note to another by means of a continuous gliding tone that passes through all intervening pitches. When the gliding connections between two tones is perceptible to the ear it is called a *portamento* connection. The *portamento* is usually indicated by a slur mark connecting two notes of different pitch."[1] It is evident from this definition that *portamento* effect in vocal music never means to slur or glissando.

What is the difference between a slur or *glissando* and *portamento?* Silva states, "Do not confound *portamento* (carrying over) with the *strisciamento* (slurring over) of the voice. The *portamento* is one of the finest attributes of the singer, and results from ease and lightness of emission; whereas the habit of slurring the voice from one note to another is one of the very worst defects."[2] *Portamento* technic produces definite, well-defined pitches on each note; the slur destroys any definiteness of pitch. Above all, *portamento* does not mean *glissando,* an abomination to legitimate singing, heard often in "crooning" or in "blues" songs. Confusion is due very largely to the fact that the "slur line" is used in vocal music printing to indicate when a portamento of moderate force is desired between two tones. If a true slur or *glissando* is actually desired, it will always be written in the score as *glissando* or as *gliss.*

When a curved line covers a whole phrase in vocal music it signifies not only the length of phrase desired but also that the phrase is to be sung legato style, i.e., with a light *portamento* glide between most tones. Composers and editors, however, often omit the use of the curved line over phrases in songs that are, nevertheless, of legato style and must be sung with a light, gliding connection.

Both the *glissando* (slur) and *portamento* are alike in that all possible pitches between the two intervals are sounded. The slur moves *slowly* and has a lazy, siren-like effect seldom appropriate, however, while the *portamento* moves rapidly and has an exciting emotional effect. *Portamento* is used often by the best artists; the glissando-slur is considered an abomination.

Principal differences between the slur and the *portamento* are:

1. *Rhythmic timing* — The slur robs the first note of time value, starting to move to the next note in the interval immediately or soon after the attack; the *portamento* robs the second tone of time value and does not start to move until the beat on which the second note occurs. (There is an exception occasionally when an anticipation of the second note is appropriate, in which case *portamento* is delayed until rhythm value of the first note is almost over before moving.)

2. *Speed* — The slur moves *slowly* with all intervening pitches clearly defined; the *portamento,* although varying in speed for expressive reasons, always moves more *rapidly* than the slur.

3. *Emotional* — The slur has a lazy, careless effect, or an impression of helplessness or exhaustion. *The slur is a legitimate device only when these emotional effects are appropriate.* The *portamento* has an emotionally intense, exciting effect, serves to emphasize important words, greatly augments the desired mood, and relieves a dry, plodding, and pedantic note-to-note delivery.

APPROPRIATE USE OF THE PORTAMENTO

In analysis of numerous examples of artistic singing, Seashore[3] reports that approximately 40 per cent of note-to-note pitch connections were accomplished by imperceptible (Light) *portamento* transitions. Edward Johnson,[4] former tenor and manager of the Metropolitan Opera Company, urges carrying the voice from vowel to vowel like a string of pearls with the consonants articulated quickly, firmly, and distinctly, but without interrupting the flow of sound.

Volume I is quite specific about the characteristics of the three classifications of *portamento* (Light, Medium, and Extreme) in explaining where each type is appropriate and in warning about taste in use of the effect. Nothing is more indicative of good taste in singing than the discrimination and skill with which the *portamento* is used. Overuse and inappropriate use easily can become an interpretive evil. It is a common fault of many singers exemplified in an habitual slipping, slurring, and "crooning" style. Correctly used in good taste, *the true portamento is the basis for fine legato in Bel Canto style.* If exaggerated it cheapens and oversentimentalizes expression. The vocal teacher needs to be alert first to whether or not the student is using true *portamento* or is slurring and, second, to whether the *portamento* is employed in good taste at the appropriate places with the right emphasis.

The three classifications or basic types of *portamento* are:

1. *Light* — Smooth, delicate, unemphasized glide used as the normal connection between tones in a legato phrase.

2. *Medium* — Moves with pronounced energy between two notes connected with a slur line, and at other significant intervals if desired by the singer.

3. *Extreme* — Strongly emphasized; moves with maximum energy and emotional effect. It is usually written in the score as *port.* to connect two climatic

[1]Fields, Victor Alexander. "The Singer's Glossary." Boston Music Co., 1952, p. 44.

[2]Silva, Giulo. "Advice to Beginners in Singing." G. Schirmer, Inc., 1917, p. 7.

[3]Seashore, Carl Emil. "New Approaches to the Science of Voice." Scientific Monthly, Vol. 49, p. 340.

[4]Johnson, Edward. "Styles in Singing." Doubleday Doran, 1941, p. 43.

notes, but also may be appropriate to express an emotional climax where only the slur line is used.

Vocal authorities declare that it is an impossibility to portamento properly without vibrato, and that voices without vibrato always give the effect of slurring between tones. (Note — see "The Vibrato," p. 42)

In learning the *portamento* the student or class should first sing a slur-glissando and then a true *portamento* in the three degrees of force described previously. Selection of good examples from song literature for the three types, and illustration by the instructor, are highly valuble as a preliminary to speed up understanding and mastery by the student. Careful listening and analysis of the device in select recordings by great artists is also a most valuable procedure.

Lesson 2. Steady Dynamics. Even Scale, and Uniform Tone Color

(See Volume I, p. 124)

In reference to legato, steady dynamics, even scale, and uniform tone color are explained clearly in this lesson in Volume I. They also are covered so thoroughly in other chapters and lessons of both Volume I and this text that only a brief supplementary discussion follows here.

HIGH-LOW PITCH FIXATION

The concept of learning to sing "on a level" is fundamental to success in producing an even scale without weak tones, sudden "breaks," or audible registers. One of the most insidious causes of tension and an uneven scale is the pupil's attitude toward pitch as a position — something to be reached or "squeezed" up to if it is a high tone, and "pressed" or "gargled" down to if it is low. The illusion of height and depth in tonal production to correspond to pitch change is a fallacy which should be corrected. Since high tones are produced in exactly the same place as the low (in the larynx), the concept of height is injurious to production.

"Students must lose their feeling of singing high and low and must learn to think of it (pitch) in terms of more or less energy."[5] *There should be a sensation rather that the voice is produced all the time on one level of tonal flow.* To recognize that singing is "Always produced on the same general level"[6] prevents trying to reach for tones of high pitch frequencies or "pressing down" for low tones. Waters recommends that in order to counteract high-low pitch fixation it is best to "Think ascent while singing down the scale and vice versa."[7] Shakespeare also quotes Lamperti as advising, "When rising to a note, think of the movement as being down and vice versa."[8] The higher the note the

more important it is to think low production; the lower the tone the more essential to think high.

Eye association up and down the staff undoubtedly causes this absurd mental and physical "reaching" for pitch. As far as tonal production is concerned, up and down the staff is no more significant than up and down the street to an automobile; smooth and flowing progress is necessary to both. *"Reaching" for the tone merely disconnects legato and changes quality and ease of production.*

It is normally easy to detect when a student is reaching up mentally and physically for a high tone by the presence of disconnected legato, shrill tone, and such signs as stretching the cords of the neck, tilting the head up, and arching the eyebrows. In reaching down the tone may be "gargled" or glottal, shallow and out of balance, while the chin is sometimes tucked too far down against the "Adams apple." Again there is the disconnected legato as a sure sign of radical change in production.

THE ONE-POINT SCALE

In the classic age of Haydn and Mozart, it is significant to note that professional singers all were purported to have three octaves or more usable range, and that separate registers such as chest, middle, and head were unknown in nomenclature. In the Bel Canto singing method used at the time, an idea called the "Voce di Mista," a term now obsolete, was employed in obtaining an even scale. Its theory was called the one-point scale: every tone from the lowest to highest originated from one undeviating point of vibration, using both chest and head resonance on every tone.

Modern teachers call this idea "singing on a level" with *balanced* and not locally shifting resonation as pitch changes. As the singer progresses from one pitch to another, he should produce tone on all pitches, high or low, *like a river ever flowing onward at one level.* Breath energy increases, and pitch rises and falls, of course, but *there is a feeling that tonal production is on a constant level.* In this respect Weer states, "If one sings on the speaking level in cooperation with proper chest and head resonance, correct breath control is achieved, a free open throat is assured and an even legato scale is not only a natural result but becomes entirely automatic."[9] Conklin also urges the singer not to think higher when singing octaves or upward interval leaps,

[5]Wilson, Harry Robert. "The Solo Singer." Carl Fischer, 1941, Vol. 1, p. 7.
[6]Austin-Ball, Thomas. "Answers to Some Vocal Questions." Eastman School of Music Publ. No. 7, 1938, p. 25.
[7]Waters, Crystal. "Song the Substance of Vocal Study." G. Schirmer, Inc., 1930, p. 26.
[8]Shakespeare, William. "Plain Words in Singing." Putnam, 1938, p. 31.
[9]Weer, Robert Lawrence. "My Views on Voice Production." The Author, Boston, 1941, p. 55.

but to imagine the tone on a level that is "straight ahead and on the same level with the mouth."[10]

Lesson 3. Delayed Articulation Concept

(See Volume I, p. 126)

DELAYED ARTICULATION

Many singers can demonstrate lovely legato if vocalizing on vowels but legato disappears when words involving articulation of consonants is attempted. This is because they have not learned the secret of timing articulation. Analysis reveals that the consonant is anticipated habitually: i.e., vowel sound is not sustained long enough, and the ending consonant of each sustained word and syllable is formed much too soon, breaking or punctuating melodic flow. *A prerequisite for legato is that the vowel must be sustained unchanged to the maximum length that rhythm allows.* This is accomplished only when the vowel of the first word or syllable is held to the maximum rhythmic length, then the consonant at the end of the first word or syllable is *quickly* articulated and *merged* with the beginning of the succeeding syllable or word. In this "merging" process, there is a neat and rapid combination of the two as if it were one articulation act. The singer actually must think the ending articulation of the first word or syllable *as on the beat of the succeeding word or syllable.*

Ending consonants and dipthongs are hitched onto the word or syllable which follows whether or not they belong there in normal speech syllabication. Thus "My country tis of thee" is sung as if written, "ma - - - - ee - kuh - - - - ntree - - - - ti - - - - zah - - - - vthee - - - -.

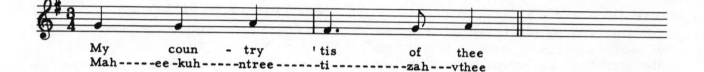

My coun - try 'tis of thee
Mah - - - - -ee -kuh - - - -ntree - - - - - -ti - - - - - - - - - -zah - - -vthee

Waring's Pennsylvanians owe much of their reputation to their remarkable diction, using this method of delayed articulation which they call the "Tone Syllable System." Waring did not discover the idea, as many seem to think, however, but merely has carried it farther in vocal ensemble in a highly successful business venture. Experienced and able vocal teachers and choral conductors have used the principle of delayed articulation for many years in order to obtain fine legato. This timing concept in diction not only allows the vowel to be sustained for maximum length and tonal beauty but also speeds up and, strange as it may seem at first thought, actually increases clarity of articulation on the consonant. The reason is clear: delayed articulation forces quick action when it does come, and quick articulation is one of the important rules for clarity. Explanations in Volume I and exercises given should make the idea of delayed articulation perfectly clear and the manner of practice for mastery well understood.

However, delaying or linking-over of the consonant has its dangers at times with certain words in that it may change word meaning or even produce a ridiculous idea. Thus "A soldier's tear" becomes "A soldier's steer," "The wondrous cross I'd bear" sounds "The wondrous cross eyed bear," and "Let us pray" is "Lettuce spray." Volume I lists 16 such classic examples (See p. 127). This dangerous effect on certain word combinations is easily prevented by not emphasizing the linking over consonant, but giving a slight accent to the beginning sound of the following word or syllable. For example, in "Let us pray," "s" in the word "us" should be sounded lightly and the "pr" beginning the word "pray" should be somewhat accented.

SUMMARY OF RULES FOR LEGATO SINGING

The "Summary of Rules for Legato Singing" at the end of this lesson in Volume I concentrates all of the necessary rules for singing legato presented in previous lessons of the chapter. It is important that this summary be learned thoroughly by all students. They should be checked subsequently both in examination over the content and in singing applications, to make sure that the rules outlined are understood and improved continuously. Nothing will prove of higher value in promoting smoothness, ease, and beauty in singing.

---

[10]Conklin, Maurice. "Fundamental Vocal Technic." Dorrance & Co., 1936, p. 103.

CHAPTER 7

Agility and Flexibility

Lesson 1. Agility and Velocity

(*See Volume I, p. 129*)

VALUE OF VELOCITY EXERCISES

All types of voices need to practice agility exercises, and the more rapidly moving florid type songs, if the complete range, freedom, and technical expressiveness of the voice are to be realized. Wilson states, "There is a high correlation between flexibility and quality because flexibility of the voice calls for free production. Free production means free resonance. Light flexible songs will tend to develop a more lyric quality of voice."[1] Proper execution of vocal embellishments such as the acciatura, appogiatura, mordent and turn or grupetto are necessary for all concert singers. Even the trill can be practiced to advantage in advanced study, although it may never be utilized in concert except by the more flexible treble voices.

Agility exercises improve the ease and quality of sostenuto but exclusive emphasis on slow legato will not improve agility — in fact, it will cause the voice to become progressively more ponderous in velocity ability. Singers who practice too long exclusively on sostenuto and the louder intensities always have inflexible voices, narrowed range, and considerable tonal constriction. Such voices always have difficulty in adjusting quickly and easily to demands of changing picth, tone color, and dynamics in either sustained legato or in dramatic, accented style songs. On the other hand, voices that are trained to move more lightly and rapidly are inevitably conditioned to move freely and flexibly, a necessary function for slow tempo singing as well.

Proper agility practice always improves freedom, control, range, efficiency, and lightness of tone for lyric singing. Any good thing can be overdone, however, and coloratura, lyric soprano, and some lyric tenors sometimes have needless lack of variety in tonal color and upper dynamic levels because of too exclusive concentration on light, velocity exercises, and light lyric song literature.

BASIC FACTORS TO STRESS

In developing an agile, flexible voice, the teacher should stress several factors:

1. An attitude of confidence, pleasure, and even gaiety.
2. Finesse and grace in style.
3. Precision in rhythm and pitch.
4. Observance of steady tempo, proper accent, and a light, free, clear tonal production.

It is well for the student to make sure that he has adequate experience in three styles of velocity exercises: *Legato*, *Semi-legato*, and *Staccato*. A mastery of each style is necessary to provide needed versatility for expression in songs. Staccato style should follow preliminary emphasis on legato and, although it is more difficult to master, it is definitely superior as a technic builder in development of quick, precise breath action and agile function of the vocal cords. *Staccato is also one of the very best exercises for eliminating breathy tonal quality and extending upward range.* In staccato song style, ending consonants should be articulated quickly and precisely, the ending consonant never delayed as in legato, but anticipated so that there is an effect of a rest between each note.

Velocity exercises are not to be attempted until after a reasonable degree of skill has been achieved at slower tempos. When taken at a fast tempo, basic exercises II, III, and IV in Volume I are ideal preparation for a more formal study of agility and embellishment.

[1]Wilson, Harry Robert. "Music in the High School." Silver Burdette Co., 1941, pp. 172-173.

70

Lesson 2. Ornamentation and Embellishment

(See Volume I, p. 135)

NEED FOR UNDERSTANDING TRADITIONAL EMBELLISHMENTS

Clear explanation and examples and sufficient exercises for the appogiatura, acciacatura, mordent, turn and trill are given in Volume I. Students need to become thoroughly familiar with the meaning and execution of all the various traditional signs listed if they ever expect to sing the music of the Baroque and Classic Schools from older manuscripts, and some European printing editions of today. Although they often write out the turn and seldom use the sign for the inverted turn, or the turn over one note, modern American and English printers also use the tradtional signs at times for all embellishments mentioned except the mordent.

VALUE OF THE TRILL FOR ALL VOICES

Some teachers assume erroneously that the trill or shake is a valuable technic and possible only for treble voices or those who are endowed naturally with unusual vocal agility. "The trill is an accomplishment possible for all singers,"[2] although not necessary as a concert technic for low, heavy, dramatic male voices. It is, nevertheless, a valuable exercise for these "loggy" voices, inducing more lightness, flexibility and an increased range — technical assets which such voices often need desperately. For example, a bass who aspires to sing oratorio arias should practice not only rapid agility scale and arpeggio exercises but also the trill, in order to develop necessary flexibility of the instrument.

SUGGESTIONS FOR DEVELOPING THE TRILL

Most voices have to develop the ability to trill through a slow and persevering approach, using such exercises as those suggested in Volume I, first in slow tempo, then in *moderato* and, finally, in *allegro*. It is easier to approach the trill at first through a wider pitch fluctuation than a major or minor second. Exercise No. 1 therefore suggests a third.

Lesson 3. Accent

(See Volume I, p. 156)

IMPORTANCE OF NORMAL ACCENT

The first section of this lesson in Volume I dealing with normal meter accent should be understood and employed by students as soon as song singing and vocal exercises are started, since *precision, cohesion, and vitality of all singing depend on proper observance of normal accent.* The latter section on "Types of Style Accents" may be delayed until such accents are actually encountered in songs, or until specific study on this lesson is undertaken, providing proper execution of accent marks is explained by the instructor at the time they are encountered in songs.

LACK OF STANDARDIZATION

There is an amazing lack of specific information in various music dictionaries and encyclopedias regarding the exact meaning and execution of the various accent marks. It is not surprising, therefore, that many musicians, instrumentalists as well as vocalists, often have an incorrect concept, or only a hazy idea at best, as to how to perform certain accent marks. Composers and arrangers also cannot be depended on to use the type of accent mark needed to achieve the result they obviously have in mind.

There is more general agreement regarding the meaning and execution of *staccato, pichettato, sostenuto, sforzando,* and *forte-piano* accents. No standardization of terminology, definition, and execution for the others listed in Volume I exists in practice, however. The generally accepted meaning, as understood by most vocal teachers and authorities, is the one given. It will be realized, therefore, that it is always well to question accent marks when found in print to determine just what style of accent appears to be most appropriate to the text and music. This is vital, for correct style in music is often dependent on proper execution of accent.

---

[2]Haywood, Frederick. "Universal Song." Haywood Institute of Universal Song, 1929, Vol. III, p. 12.

Extending Range

(See Volume I, p. 160)

VOCAL COMPASS REQUIREMENTS

Range of undeveloped voices varies considerably. As a rule, those with wide vocalization ranges of over two octaves also have distinct "breaks," or registration changes, that have to be corrected by training before parts of the compass are usable. Beginners who have over an octave and a fifth of fairly easy and usable range are fortunate indeed. An octave and a fifth of usable range, and a two-octave vocalization range, is a normal expectancy for the average student at the end of the first year of study, however, and will be found sufficient to cover compass requirement of the ordinary song.

Most beginning students 17 years of age or over should have a vocalization range of around two octaves after a year of proper study and vocalization. *Singing range of beginning songs sung by the class or by most individuals should seldom exceed an octave and a fourth in compass.* This limitation gives the student more confidence and pleasure in singing and is safer in establishing right habits that are the foundation for all future development. The great majority of professional singers and successful teachers subscribe to the belief that the basis for developing both the high and low range extremes is first to habituate a free production in the easy middle range. Extension of the middle voice downward is the next easiest and most logical step before developing the high compass.

Limits of range in vocalization and songs can be extended gradually as the voice develops in flexibility and strength. Development of agility, flexibility, and free production are an absolute necessity for achieving the full range of the singing voice. All students ambitious to develop range to the maximum therefore need to practice florid lyric agility and staccato exercises and lyric songs employing a light easy production. *Extensive sostenuto practice on loud dynamics tends to shorten range.*

"The vocal range of the singer should be built up carefully by degrees, exercising infinite attention to detail."[1] After the first year of proper vocal study, gaining additional range is usually a comparatively slow note-by-note process, resulting from gradually developing muscular flexibility and strength and from added finesse in coordinating and balancing resonation. Professional singers sometimes work for a year or more in daily practice in order to add one more note to their dependable range. A well-coordinated two octaves is sufficient to cover the compass of all but a very few of the songs and arias sung today, and normally is adequate for the amateur and even most professional needs. Unfortunately, the singer cannot always choose the proper key to fit his particular compass. Most leading professionals, therefore, learn to vocalize over a two-and-one-half to three-octave range in order to build an adequate technical reserve.

When both the extreme low compass, so called "chest voice," and the "head tone" production of the female voice are coordinated with the middle voice, a usable three-octave range can be expected in some voices. A usable range of over two octaves is more rare in male voices since falsetto adjustment, which extends the woman's voice one octave, is not considered a legitimate tone today for concert use by some teachers, even when produced with a maximum of "head" quality in what is generally termed "mixed-falsetto" or "mixed-voice" adjustment.

REGISTERS

Much controversy, misunderstanding, and antagonism continues regarding concepts of registers in the voice. Antagonism to concepts of more than one register come about largely through the unfortunate experience of many vocal instructors in the past, who followed the teachings of those maintaining that there were three or more registers in the

---

[1] Roma, Lisa. "The Science and Art of Singing." G. Schirmer, Inc., 1956, p. 37.

voice which should be strengthened and trained separately. Consequently, students sang with a different type of voice in each part of the range, had definite breaks between parts, and an uneven, uncoordinated production.

What are the facts? How many registers are there? How should we explain registers to students who obviously have them and know that they do? How can the registers be coordinated and balanced in training?

Much confusion exists because there are three concepts of register founded upon different premises. First, based upon audible differences in tone quality and sensations experienced in singing, there appear to be three registers — head, middle (or mouth), and chest. Voice teachers today generally agree that it is a dangerous procedure to develop each of these three registers separately and then attempt to smooth them together later, as some have done in the past. Such methods usually result in a disjointed scale and a permanently uneven voice. "Psychologically, it is wrong and often disastrous to think of three registers, and this may be the cause of 'breaks' in the voice."[2]

In spite of the fact that the voice has different *qualities* and resonation sensations in the low, middle, and high compass, these three qualities ought not to be confused with actual separate registers.

Second, based upon observable muscular action, scientific findings indicate that there are only two registers in the human voice, the lower and the upper (or falsettto). Briefly explained, the lower adjustment functions for low and loud tones; the high adjustment functions for high and soft tones. Lyric and coloratura sopranos normally use the upper adjustment, basses only the low. Tenors and altos use both, and must learn to smooth the register breaks in between. Tenors are obliged to learn to use the high adjustment in what is generally termed mixed-falsetto," or to develop the flexibility and strength of the low adjustment muscles to carry the voice higher. If soft singing is required in the high compass, it has to be done with falsetto upper adjustment. In general the lower register is associated with the "chest voice" and strong dynamic singing, the upper register with the "head voice" and light lyric production.

Third, based upon proper tonal production concepts, there are as many registers in the human voice

as there are notes, since each pitch ideally requires slight adjustments of breath energy, mouth space, and resonance "mold" from the note just above or below. Breaks or uneven qualities disappear when these adjustments are made properly and there are then no audible registers in the singing voice. This method of production retains some of the desirable qualities of both the lower and upper (falsetto) adjustments on all tones throughout the compass. Groves declares, "Nowadays it is generally agreed that the vocal line should be uninterrupted from the bottom to the top and that head resonance should be blended with chest resonance in the lower and middle ranges, while chest support should never be abandoned in the higher range."[3]

Bell Laboratories' pictures, and findings of a number of scientific investigators, have definitely established the fact that, from the standpoint of types of vocal cord adjustment, there only two registers for either the male or the female voice. One covers approximately the lower two-thirds of the compass and the other, the upper two-thirds, with about an octave of intermediate tones capable of being produced with either physical adjustment. In view of the great vocabulary confusion existing in regard to register terminology, Wilcox[4] suggests that it would be preferable to use the terms "Heavy mechanism" instead of chest or low register and "Light mechanism" instead of falsetto register.

How can we reconcile these scientific findings with the observation of many experienced teachers who know that crude, untutored voices and poorly-taught students often have two or even three breaks in their scale, and certainly sound as if they have three or four registers? It has been noted frequently in writings by authoritative vocal teachers in past generations that these "breaks" in average undeveloped voices usually occur from *e* to *f*, *b*, to *c*, and *f* to *g*, every tetrachord (fourth) upward from *b* below middle *c* as illustrated following. Low voices may have the breaks somewhat lower. Male voices have breaks, of course, an octave lower than written.

---

[2]Ibid, p. 36.

[3]Graves, Richard M. "Singing for Amateurs." Oxford U. Press, 1954, p. 54.

[4]Wilcox, John C. "The Living Voice." Carl Fischer, (revised and augmented edition) 1945, p. 9.

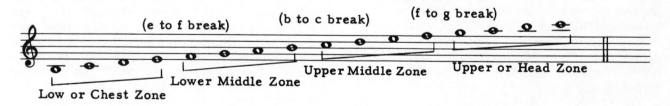

(e to f break) (b to c break) (f to g break)

Low or Chest Zone   Lower Middle Zone   Upper Middle Zone   Upper or Head Zone

For the average undeveloped voice, however, transition from the Upper Middle Zone to the Upper or "Head" Zone is reported by most authorities today as follows: Sopranos and tenors, *e* to *f♯*; altos and baritones, *d* to *e♭*; and bass, *c* to *d*. *The several lower notes just preceeding the transition need to be gradually modified to the unforced head quality, and no notes above the pitches indicated are sung with the heavy "chest" adjustment or forcing and shouting result.*

The break from *b* to *c* between the Lower Middle Zone and the Upper Middle Zone appears infrequently and, even then, seldom gives as much trouble in smoothing over as the other two breaks. Consequently, most teachers in the past have concluded that there were three registers in vocal production: The lower, or chest; the middle, or mouth; and the upper, or head. Actually, these are three zones with a characteristic quality of resonance, but from a physiological production standpoint cannot be considered three registers, since science has proven rather conclusively that there are only two.

There is considerable evidence to support the belief that breaks between *e* and *f* and *b* and *c* are caused entirely by accumulations of tension in the lower adjustment, by failure to progressively lighten the vocal mechanism in an ascending passage until forced to do so. There appears little doubt that *these breaks are caused by attempts to retain one adjustment of breath energy, mouth opening, and tonal form and character,* finally resulting in an accumulation of tension that makes an audible break imperative to further progress in range.

That this conclusion is valid is supported by the fact that so-called register breaks between *e* and *f* and *b* and *c* smooth out or disappear entirely when accumulations of tension are prevented by adjusting the three factors mentioned. The break from *f* to *g* (or *e* to *f♯*, according to most authorities today) appears, however, to be a true register break, especially in the male voice; it seldom yields quickly to proper singing concepts, but demands a considerable period of developing and strengthening the falsetto register before the break can be "bridged" over and the voice unified. Reasons for this are discussed later in this chapter under the heading of "The Falsetto Register."

Several factors add to the confusion in regard to registers. One in particular is that the male and female voices differ and even voices of the same sex and type often vary in characteristics regarding breaks and registers. The male voice seldom has difficulty with a break between the Lower Chest Zone and the Lower Middle Zone, but nearly always has trouble between the Upper Middle Zone and the Upper Head Zone.

On the other hand, the average female voice has compartively little difficulty with the upper break, but often has a distinct weakness or break between the Lower Chest Zone and the Lower Middle Zone from *e* to *f*. This is true particularly of the more powerful mezzo and contralto voices which appear at times to have as distinct and disconnected a lower "chest register" as the male voice has for the upper falsetto. *This low zone of the woman's voice must be smoothed and lightened,* the break eliminated, and production coordinated and balanced with the Lower Middle Zone before the lower compass is truly usable. Many light soprano voices apparently do not have this lower "Chest" zone, but carry the Lower Middle Zone down lightly around middle *c* and can go no farther. On the other hand, some male voices do not appear to have a falsetto register, or at least a usable falsetto. In this case nature usually compensates, enabling them to carry the Upper Middle Zone production somewhat higher than normal.

Proper practice in developing control of the so-called "unused" register (high zone for the male voice and low zone for the female voice) usually balances registers, improves quality of all zones, and eliminates breaks and uneven qualities in the scale. Thus when the man learns the falsetto tonal concept and sensation, other tones are brought forward out of the throat, lightened and resonated more freely. On the other hand, the immature female voice characterized by a child-like, thin, falsetto-like tone, can best add maturity, depth, and mellowness by strengthening the fundamental and lower partial overtones with the richer quality characteristic of the Lower Chest Zone. *This so-called "chest voice" never can be ground out with a throaty gutteral quality often heard, however.* Such forced production will never connect up and blend with the upper voice.

HOW TO TEACH BLENDING AND EVENING THE REGISTERS

Whether or not there are two or more registers in the voice is really immaterial to proper production and teaching method. "Nowadays nearly every teacher teaches the theory of one register developing a smaller number of breaks in both voices and singers."[5] As the quickest path to an even scale, the student is advised to think the entire compass of the voice as a consistent whole with no radical changes of production, freedom, and tone quality at any point. There is no advantage in discussing various theories and details of registers, "breaks" of the voice, or "placement" with beginning students. It is more likely to confuse and add to self-consciousness than to help. Actually, students interested only in learning to sing need never have any reading or discussion of either registers or placement. On the other

---

[5]Butler, Harold L. "Salient Changes in Voice Teaching in the Past 50 Years." Etude, 1928, Vol. 46, p. 220.

hand, those who may sometime be called upon to teach voice or direct choral groups should understand the factors involved.

For even production it is necessary that *the voice be one equalized register containing a balanced mixture of the various qualities and resonances.* It is only the tone produced for an unique interpretive effect that utilizes only one type of resonance chamber, or focuses toward a particular resonating area. Such a tone is sure to be harsh, muffled, shrill, or abnormal in some respect, because it is out of balance and will not "connect-up" in an even scale. When a voice sounds to the listener as if it had different registers, we can be sure it is the result of incorrect out-of-balance singing. "Registers are produced when a singer forces a series of tones, when ascending, upon one resonating point, holding the vocal mechanism in the same position instead of remembering that each tone requires a change of vocal organs."[6] *Breaks in voices are thus due to not making gradual adjustments of mouth space, breath energy, and resonation quality.*

On an ascending scale it is necessary to progressively lighten the pressure or "grip" feeling of the vocal cords, or when fourth space *e* or fifth line *f* are reached, the student will be screaming and unable to progress further without a "break" or sudden change of quality. The technic of gradually lightening is especially vital for the Upper Middle Zone pitches *c* to *f*. Lower voices may need to start the lightening process somewhat sooner. Since a lighter vocal band adjustment causes a decrease in tonal power, the singer is required to compensate by somewhat increased breath energy for each tone unless softer intensity is desired. At the place where the voice would normally "break" under a heavy type of adjustment, an even more generous "surge of breath" accompanies a lighter vocal cord approximation to achieve easy and smooth transition into the upper compass. Although the vowel then takes on some of the qualities of fullness, depth, and freedom of the neutral tone, *Uh,* it will never be made dull, muffled, breathy or "covered" in the process.

The principle of changing from *heavy* to *light* adjustment gradually as the scale is ascended, and vice versa when descending, as outlined in Chapter 16 under the heading, "Principles of Production in Tonal Progression" (See p. 127), will eliminate accumulations of tensions, breaks, and unevenness in the voice throughout the entire compass. The author never has had a student, among many hundreds taught privately and in voice classes over a period of over thirty years, whose technic did not respond favorably to these principles.

Thus in spite of the fact that we recognize, physiologically speaking, that there are two registers in the voice — the upper or *light,* and the lower or *heavy* — the problem of the voice teacher is to in-

struct in such a manner that these qualities will be blended and that the student will not be even conscious, in most instances, of the presence of different registers. Vennard suggests calling the two registers *light adjustment* and *heavy adjustment,* and gives the following valuable advise regarding registration. "Three generalizations may be offered, one as to pitch, one as to intensity, and a third as to quality. First, to develop the widest possible range without a break, the adjustment must be *heavy* in the lower part of the voice, and the balance should shift smoothly toward the *lighter* production as the scale is ascended. Second, on any given pitch, the softer it is, the *lighter* must be production without breathiness; and the louder, the *heavier.* Third, to produce rich timbre the adjustment should be *heavy;* to produce sweet timbre, it should be light."[7]

PLACEMENT AND FOCUS

Registers and placement concepts are combined inevitably in discussions of either topic. If anything, there is even more antagonism regarding the term "placement" than there is regarding registers. Much of the disagreement and confusion revolves around definition of what is meant by placement and what the pupil thinks it means. If we mean efficient and balanced resonation of the voice, most everyone will agree that placement is desirable and necessary. On the other hand, if we mean, or it is interpreted by the student as meaning, attempts to put, place, hurl, or direct the voice to a specific area such as the head, nose, mask, chest, etc., the principle of indirect muscular control is violated and self-consciousness, rigidity, and out-of-balance resonation are the result. The eminent English authority, David Frangcon-Davies, asserts, "The process of placing voices results too often in their being put on the shelf, where they are indeed useless."[8]

"The vocal tone has been directed to the nose, the sinus, the eyes, and practically every spot in the head. In each instance, any attempt to increase the resonance by direct control actually defeats its own purpose by producing tension in the throat, confining the tone, and disturbing the diction. True resonance can be attained only when the voice is allowed to sing."[9] "The singer must never direct the breath stream. Directing the breath stream into the mouth, the nose, or the masque simply causes tensions and a throaty quality of tone."[10]

[6]Tkach, Peter. "Vocal Technic." Neil A. Kjos, 1948, p. 62.

[7]Vennard, William. "Singing, the Mechanism and the Technic." Edwards Brothers, Inc., 1950, p. 38.

[8]Clippinger, D. A. "The Clippinger Class Method of Voice Culture." Ditson, 1933, p. 31.

[9]Peterson, Paul W. "Natural Singing and Expressive Conduction." John F. Blair, 1955, p. 42.

[10]Wilson, Harry Robert. "Artistic Choral Singing." G. Schirmer, Inc., 1959, p. 177.

It is thus apparent that the singer needs to be alert in order to avoid attempts to "place" the tone in the head, or any other area, or to "fix" or "set" the muscles involved in phonation and enunciation into any fancied position. Such conscious manipulation can result only in an unnatural or constricted tone lacking in individuality and balanced resonation. *In order to sound its best, resonance must be balanced and free, with a character unique to the particular voice.*

More chicanery, vocal vagaries, and magic formulas have been inflicted on hapless students by unscrupulous or ignorant vocal pedagogues, in the name of specialization on "voice placing," than in any other phase of vocal teaching. Many charlatans have victimized students purely on the basis of flamboyant advertising concerning their ability, often by a secret or little known method, to teach proper placement. Actually, *the voice places itself if resonation is free and balanced.* As a consequence, the term is in disrepute, and many honest and conscientious teachers are almost afraid to use publicly the word "placement" or the closely allied word "focus" in any sense, regardless of definition. Whether or not the terms are legitimate in voice teaching appears to hinge entirely upon meaning in practice. Certainly the voice teacher cannot avoid the issue of getting voices to resonate freely, sonorously, and evenly from top to bottom of the compass whether "placing," "focused," "balanced resonation," or some other term is used to describe the process.

If students are given the concept that "placing" the voice is an act of focusing or hurling the voice to one spot or area of resonance, then the connotation is highly injurious to production. On the other hand, if the student is carefully instructed as in Volume I, that "The only legitimate focused or placed tone is a *balanced* tone, a tone that has a *general balanced feeling* of free resonation in the upper pharynx with supplementary resonance sensations in the mouth, head and mask," the proper concept for free resonant production is implied and should benefit production. *Getting the voice to sound freely and beautifully balanced where it belongs may be called "placing" or "focusing" the voice, and is the only legitimate connotation.* It is a *balanced sensation of resonation,* not something that is done to the voice in efforts to "put" it anywhere. Defined thus as a sensation which the singer understands and experiences in the aforesaid manner, the term is acceptable in both theory and practice.

We control singing entirely by our hearing and feeling sensations. Since these sensations may not always conform to fact, it is sometimes difficult to choose descriptive terms for teaching that are both accurate in fact and practical in obtaining proper tonal result. For example, it is a fact that singing is produced by the vocal cords, yet every competent vocal teacher knows that the major sensation for vibration and resonation should not be there. Since action in the larynx is below the level of consciousness, the sensation of vibrating tone is experienced somewhere else, preferably anywhere else than in the larynx itself, unless we desire a glottic, "swallowed," constricted tone. This paradox between physical fact and sensation, experienced by the singer for proper control, is responsible for much of the disagreement between the scientific mechanists and the psychologic empiricists in voice teaching.

As the scale is ascended, properly we feel more of a sensation of resonance or vibration in the head and less in the mouth. To suggest that the student use more "head resonance" may be quite meaningful to him and result in more free and beautiful tone, *providing he has been taught the meaning, concept, and proper feeling and hearing sensations that accompany head resonance production.* To tell the student to "sing the tone in the head" or "place the tone in the head" would certainly be scientifically incorrect, and is not a terminology that is recommended. The author nevertheless has observed demonstrations of teaching voice in which such directions were given to students and excellent improvement resulted. The secret of that success was, of course, that the students' interpretation of terminology used was "correct head resonance sensation" and quite different from factual meaning.

Many vocal teachers are prone to instruct students to put or place the tone in the head, particularly for the high compass. These directions produce desired freedom and quality only if the pupil interprets such directions as really meaning that the upper head and pharynx spaces are to be opened up more generously; that the *major* sensation is upper pharynx and head vibration in a fuller space; that balanced resonation with some qualities of the lower production is still necessary; and that exclusive head resonance sensation produces only an unbalanced tone. *It is necessary for the teacher to emphasize over and over to students that they never feel that they have "hold of the tone" in the throat, or that they have an exclusive sensation of putting or placing tone in any definite place.*

There is common agreement that the pharynx and mouth not only are important resonators but also are capable of flexible adjustment through imagery of tone and vibration feeling sensations. Actually, any vibration felt in the chest appears to be the result of trachea vibration, since the chest has neither a resonating space nor a "sounding board" connection with the source of sound in the larynx. The presence and value of head resonance vibration also is denied by some scientific investigators. Nevertheless, those who emphasize "head" type of resonance sensation with their students actually obtain a better type of high pharyngeal resonance, as pointed out by Bartholomew.[11]

The fact that tone does pass through the spaces of the mouth and the head, and sets up certain sensations there, is incontestable. When tone is best, it has a characteristically balanced feeling. *It not only vibrates "round" and high in the pharynx and head, but also has a ringing sensation in the mouth and a "hummy" feeling in the mask and nose.* It is well to remember that the *pharynx sensation is primary* and the head, mouth, nose, and mask feelings *secondary* in the ideally-balanced tone. If too much emphasis is placed on forward mouth resonance through radical lip movements, the tone will be "pulled" out of the primary pharynx resonation and unbalanced. On the other hand, if thought is centered entirely on the pharynx sensation, the tone will most likely be throaty and "glottal," lacking the vitality of mouth "ring" and the forward "humming" intensity necessary for balanced resonation.

The voice will automatically "place" itself; that is it will phonate with balanced resonance when produced with maximum freedom in the open throat. The student will therefore make every effort to *let the voice place itself through obtaining as free a tone as possible.* When needed, however, character of tonal resonance can be consciously changed through varied adjustment of the tongue, the lips, and the jaw. These adjustments stimulate resonance feelings, as if the tone were forward in the mask, in the mouth or lips, or high back in the upper pharynx and head. If a student has too blatant and mouthy a tone without sufficient mellowness, he is advised to think more round space and resonation in the upper pharynx and head, drop the jaw more, and round the lips somewhat. If a student has a breathy, spacious or "whoopy" voice lacking in ringing quality and "hum" intensity, he is instructed to think the tone more ringing in the mouth with a humming "m" quality.

The foregoing are functional directions for obtaining a better balanced resonation, and much more desirable than instructions to "place" or "focus" tone in the head, mouth, or mask — dangerous ideas when used in this fasion. Functional directions also are meaningful to the student. The teacher is limited to terms and directions which create an imagery of sound and feeling in the understanding of the student. Anything else, no matter how accurate scientifically, is useless in practice.

THE FALSETTO REGISTER IN THE MALE VOICE

The falsetto register is generally understood to be the lightest and highest mechanism of the male voice. Because of its thinness, the pure-falsetto is not a pleasant tone to hear and is comparatively weak in dynamics, especially on the lowest notes

that can be sung in this adjustment. The falsetto break occurs between *d*, fourth line, and *g*, first space above in the treble clef. (Male voices sound, of course, an octave lower.) The break for average untrained voices can be expected from *e* to *f*. Falsetto range then extends approximately one octave above the break. There is an overlap of about a fifth, the Upper Middle Zone of the voice from *c* to *g*, in which the tones involved can be produced either with falsetto or lower "full-voice" adjustment.

Lack of standardization in vocal terminology, and many writings in the past based on conjecture, have resulted in a confused plethora of theories regarding the upper male voice and how it is produced. Understanding of the falsetto and development of the male voice upper register is especially baffling to the woman teacher, since she does not normally experience the same production difficulty in her own voice.

Actually, there are four types of tonal production in the upper part of the male voice that can be employed, and that the well-equipped vocal teacher must learn to differentiate among. They are as follows:

1. *The pure-falsetto.*

The pure-falsetto is produced with the lightest type of adjustment of the vocal bands. The tone is thin, "white," anemic sounding and not useful for legitimate solo singing. The pure-falsetto needs to be practiced as an *approach* to the proper use of the "head-voice" and as a means of strengthening and balancing muscular action in the larynx, however. The pure-falsetto also is used as an approach to the "mixed-falsetto" by those who believe in the latter type of production as legitimate solo tone. In any case, the falsetto adjustment appears harmless. It should be used by immature voices in high register chorus work to save the voices in practice until either the "mixed-falsetto," or the true light "head-voice," can be mastered with easy production.

2. *The mixed-falsetto.*
(*See also p. 80*)

The mixed-falsetto is used frequently in concert, radio, and microphone work by many tenors and some baritones, usually by the lyric rather than the dramatic or heoric type of voices. It is basically the same light type of vocal band adjustment as the pure-falsetto; however more depth and warmth of tonal color, maximum "head" space, and more breath energy are used so that the tone matches up with a light type of lower register adjustment. There is no doubt but that it is employed often by professionals — especially lyric tenors — with an effect

---

[11]Bartholomew, Wilmer T. "The Paradox of Voice Teaching." Journal of the Acoustical Society of America, Vol. II, 1940.

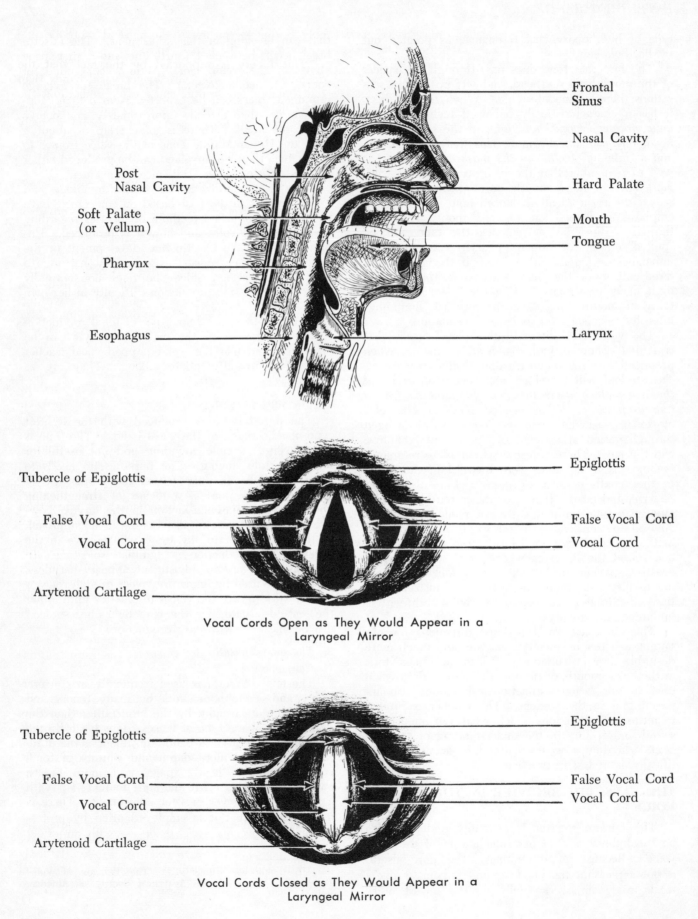

Frontal Sinus

Nasal Cavity

Post Nasal Cavity

Hard Palate

Soft Palate (or Vellum)

Mouth

Tongue

Pharynx

Esophagus

Larynx

Tubercle of Epiglottis

Epiglottis

False Vocal Cord

False Vocal Cord

Vocal Cord

Vocal Cord

Arytenoid Cartilage

Vocal Cords Open as They Would Appear in a
Laryngeal Mirror

Tubercle of Epiglottis

Epiglottis

False Vocal Cord

False Vocal Cord

Vocal Cord

Vocal Cord

Arytenoid Cartilage

Vocal Cords Closed as They Would Appear in a
Laryngeal Mirror

on *mezzo voce* especially pleasing to most members of an audience and many vocal authorities. On the other hand, its use is anathema, considered in poor taste at any time by some vocal teachers, who accept only the full-bodied head voice and a lustier tonal force as legitimate production for the male voice in public singing.

3. *The chest-voice.* (carried up)

Some men have unusually strong and enduring vocal bands and for a considerable time are able to carry the heavier, lower zone, "chest type" production much higher than normal before the voice breaks. Such production is always loud, "shouty," and strained in quality. A voice so abused cannot long endure. No vocal teacher of reputation recommends this type of production, but the unfortunate fact remains that many allow it in their students.

4. *The head-voice.*

The "true" head voice, which all agree is a legitimate and desirable production in the upper register of the male voice, especially for loud intensities, has the primary vocal adjustment of the lower register; but the singer has learned to lighten the vocal bands, singing more on the "edges" and compensating by using more generous breath energy. Head-voice production has a feeling sensation in the throat quite similar to the falsetto; but it is a more robust tone not capable of being sung with very soft dynamics on the higher tones, or of being carried as high as the falsetto or mixed-falsetto. For this reason, many vocal authorities contend that the mixed-falsetto must be mastered also if the singer is to complete the upper range of his instrument and be able to sing top tones with soft dynamics and maximum suavity.

Principles of voice production for male and female voices are the same, and types of song material and fundamental exercises needed in the early stages of training also are identical. The male voice, however, often has considerable difficulty getting into the head-voice without abrupt or audible change of quality. This involves a routine of practice and exercises for strengthening the falsetto register for many male voices.

Physiologists explain that there are only two sets of muscles in the larynx which control all singing and speaking, the Thyroid and the Arytenoid. There are, therefore, only two registers, the lower controlled by the Thyroid muscles and the upper (falsetto) controlled by the Arytenoid. These registers are present in all male and female voices; however, some male voices never experience or employ the falsetto adjustment, and in others it appears quite disconnected and useless. The high voice of all women singers is falsetto, but it is usually so easy to blend and coordinate with the lower production that neither the singer nor the listener is conscious of its use. The greater ease with which it is coordinated probably is due to the much shorter and more flexible vocal cords of the female voice.

This theory is supported by the fact that the deep-voiced contralto, with longer vocal bands than the soprano, has trouble more often smoothing the break into the upper register falsetto production. The light, flute-like, falsetto quality is traditionally accepted as normal concert production for treble voices in their upper register. In fact flute obligato is often employed with high sopranos because it blends so perfectly with upper register falsetto production.

The male voice is usually limited to a range of two octaves unless falsetto adjustment is employed to carry it up an additional octave. In the florid age of song there is no doubt that falsetto adjustment was accepted by audiences and all music critics as standard for the upper register. How else can we account for the frequent references in writings of the time to male singers with usable singing ranges of three or more octaves? Some of these male singers also are reported to have sung female arias and parts in operas with great skill. We may be confident, however, that the production that was accepted was not the pure-falsetto but rather what is generally known today as the mixed-falsetto, or mixed-voice.

According to physiologists, the falsetto register is the Arytenoid register, since the Crico-arytenoid muscles in the larynx, and not the Crico-thyroid which is used in the lower register, furnish the muscular resistance against breath pressure. There have been a number of theories in the past regarding the falsetto voice, frequently based more on fancy than on fact. Recently, scientific research in the Bell Telephone Laboratories, investigations by Douglas Stanley in New York University and Electric Research Products, Inc., and a number of other investigations, have revealed certain facts regarding vocal cord action previously unknown. Unfortunately, ill-considered interpretation and application of these scientific findings to methods in teaching, in many instances, have done so much injury to voices that many teachers have discarded all scientific findings as dangerous.

Facts in themselves are never dangerous; interpretation and application of fact often is. In this instance the mistake appears to be that teachers failed to understand that *vocal production inherently remains an indirect empirical or artistic process* controlled by psychology and not by physiology.

WHY DEVELOP OR PRACTICE FALSETTO IN THE MALE VOICE?

Many authorities today believe that, after the principles of production in the middle and lower range have been pretty well established, the only way to develop the full possibilities in range and control of the male voice upper compass is through practice and development of the falsetto register. This belief is held by not only those who accept the mixed-falsetto as legitimate, but also by many of those who will accept only the "head voice" production in concert. "As no constriction ever appears to accompany the singing of falsetto, it can be a help in demonstrating how to strive for an equal freedom in full, round tones that exploit all the overtones."[12]

The reason for falsetto practice and development appears simple, as explained by physiologists. The answer is found in the law or principle that all control muscles, including those of the vocal cords, must have resistant muscles that are strong enough to balance action to pull against. Since falsetto voice is used little, if at all, before vocal study, the Crico-Arytenoid muscles in the larynx that control falsetto and extreme pianissimo are unused, quite weak, and undeveloped. They must be developed in strength and flexibility not only to make possible a well-controlled mixed-falsetto, if this type of production is accepted, but also to balance the pull of the stronger Crico-Thyroid muscles, to make possible the emergence in the upper compass of the true "head voice" type of production.

In speaking of male students' using the falsetto, Clippinger writes, "The falsetto they can produce without effort, and there in lies its value. They become accustomed to hearing their high tones without association of effort, and after a time the real voice appears. The thing which prevented the head voice from appearing in the beginning was extreme resistance, and as soon as the resistance disappeared the head voice made its appearance. This was accomplished by practice of the very light register known as falsetto. When the head voice appears the use of the falsetto may be discontinued."[13] Weer states, "The so-called falsetto voice of the male must be developed and strengthened until it is no longer false, but strong and resonant and capable of cooperation with the lower process."[14] Stanley says, "All men who have no falsetto coordination force the upper tones."[15]

The chief value of the falsetto for many voices "Is in helping the student to find his 'head voice' when the chest type voice has been carried too high and the head voice has been almost destroyed. In such a case it is best to have the student sing in falsetto until he can gain some idea of the head tone, which is not unlike the falsetto in its lightness and effortlessness."[16] Practice of the falsetto to develop the voice is a traditional policy. A statement in this regard by the eminent authority, Dr. Leo Kofler, who lived in the nineteenth century, is recorded by Street, "From experience and from the testimony of the best singers of all time, I can state that falsetto practice is the fundamental work for developing the

high tones of all male voices and for equalizing them with the middle range."[17]

Standard type exercises for developing the falsetto are given in Volume I, p. 162. The objective should be to *learn to produce the falsetto as strong and resonant as possible, and strive to lighten the lower register production as it is carried upward farther and farther.* This type of practice develops the range and freedom of the true head voice production as rapidly as possible. The darker, rounder vowels and the *Ah* will be found easiest at first, but all vowels must be practiced eventually.

DEVELOPING THE MIXED-FALSETTO
(*See also p. 77*)

This topic can be disregarded in vocal training by those who believe only in the head-voice type of production as legitimate in the upper compass. Those who maintain this point of view will accept only the more powerful, resonant, "full-voice" type of tone; anything else is anathema. To them the mixed-falsetto is anemic and there is no effective answer, since taste is a personal matter.

The claim advanced by some, however, that use of the falsetto or mixed-falsetto is injurious and will eventually destroy the voice, or the vitality of the voice, is spurious. This is readily attested by the fact that all treble voices use this production in their upper compass, while many eminent male singers of the past have had long and successful careers, could sing in the high compass either very softly or very loudly, and used the mixed-falsetto habitually for suave, high, soft singing. Contemporary singers, especially lyric tenors, often use the mixed-falsetto or "mixed-voice" in concert, radio, and recording. It is an easy and effective way of performance in high compass for microphone technic. Its principal fault for concert singing, production of a real fortissimo, is overcome mechanically by the singer approaching nearer the microphone.

There can be no doubt that audiences are particularly fond of suave, well-controlled, mixed-falsetto tone. For example, in spite of insufficient power to sing operatic roles with great success, John McCormack was the most popular concert tenor of his generation. The one principle outstanding characteristic and technical superiority of his voice over

[12]Litante, Judith. "A Natural Approach to Singing." Wm. C. Brown Co., 1959, p. 42.

[13]Clippinger, D. A. "The Head Voice and Other Problems." Ditson, 1917, p. 26.

[14]Weer, Robert Lawrence. "My Views on Voice Production." The Author, 1941, p. 67.

[15]Stanley, Douglas. "Your Voice." Pitman, 1945, p. 9.

[16]Nicoll, Irene and Dennis, Charles M. "Simplified Vocal Training." Carl Fischer, 1940, p. 47.

[17]Street, George Hotchkiss. "Pure and Easy Tone Production." The Author, 1927, p. 84.

other lyric tenors at that time was the superlative evenness and tonal beauty of his high, mixed-falsetto; it was literally smooth as silk and cleverly integrated with lower production.

Without finesse in use of the mixed-falsetto, it is difficult to imagine any male singer interpreting with the utmost effectiveness some of the songs of Debussy, other French Impressionists, and some modern songs which require a delicate, suave, *pianissimo* tone on high notes. The singer, who has been trained exclusively on full-voiced dramatic operatic technic to habitually increase dynamics for each successive note in a rising scale, is as completely inept as an elephant dancing the minuet when confronted with the free, suave, high tones, the delicate *pianissimos,* and decreasing scale line intensity demanded at times in such song literature.

While there is no doubt that the mixed-falsetto is not practical or useful in some voices, especially basses and some dramatic or heroic baritones and tenors, many authorities believe that its proper development, blending with the lower register and proper use in extreme high *pianissimo* singing, *is the only way to complete the full vocal resources of the male voice.* In some male voices, blending with the lower adjustment is so perfect that it is difficult to detect whether many high tones are cleverly controlled head-voice or mixed-falsetto. Such singing is truly balanced and ideal production, according to most eminent authorities.

In any case, *the criteria for proper method in high singing is whether or not the tone is free and sounds well; whether it balances and blends with low register; and whether it is dynamic,* i.e., capable of smooth *crescendo-decrescendo.* The objective in teaching is to develop both a *light* and *heavy* production in one coordinated voice without involving consciousness of registers.

After all that is possible has been done to develop the head-voice, mixed-falsetto production will still carry into higher upper compass, make softer intensities easy on all high tones, and provide a degree of extreme *pianissimo not possible otherwise.* Many teachers feel that the mixed-falsetto is worth developing for these very reasons, even if the male singer is able to achieve an adequate range and control in head-voice type of production.

A number of principles are suggested in developing the mixed-falsetto and blending it with the lower register and with head-voice production:

1. *Seek similar quantity of tone for balancing the registers.* It is futile to try to produce mixed-falsetto as loudly as tone can be produced in lower adjustment, or the lower adjustment as softly in its overlapping range as mixed-falsetto. As a rule, mixed-falsetto can be sung in its high compass above f♯ with a spread of dynamics from *ppp* to *mf* when compared with the lower register force.

Even for an experienced singer, therefore, an approaching scale or arpeggio passage from below must be no louder than *mf,* or the two registers will not blend smoothly. If louder intensity than *mf* is desired, the singer must learn also to sing the upper tones in head-voice adjustment.

2. *The lower falsetto adjustment is carried, the less intensity is possible and the lighter the lower register adjustment must be to balance.* It is evident, therefore, that the singer is obliged eventually to learn, at the very least, to produce all tones in the Upper Middle Zone (*c* to *g* overlapping compass) in head-tone method; otherwise satisfactory dynamics and dramatic *forte* climaxes on these often-used notes would be impossible.

3. *Seek similar quality of tone for blending the registers.* The mixed-falsetto should be imbued with as much of the *weighty* qualities of the lower register, and the lower register with as much of the *light* qualities of the mixed-falsetto, as possible. Since the pure falsetto is throaty, thin, and "white" in tonal color, the mixed-falsetto is corrected by thinking the vowel rich, dark, and sonorous (toward the "*Uh*" in quality and full head space) with the jaw dropped loosely to generous opening and vigorous breath support applied. In spite of the necessity for maximum head space and quality, no effort should be made to focus or "place" tone in the head. A feeling as if drinking the tone deep into a spacious upper pharynx and head space assists in obtaining the type of tonal quality and full resonance necessary to balance and blend with lower production, however.

4. *Changes of register will be made by finesse and not by forcing.* Change is always abrupt or audible unless the principle of *lightening* the ascending scale just *before* transition is observed. The skilled male singer is able not only to manage the breath and adjustments so cleverly that scales and arpeggios involving both registers sound smooth, but also can start long high notes *ppp* in mixed-falsetto, crescendo, and when *mf* intensity is reached, transfer smoothly into head-voice for greater volume. He can then also reverse the process. This is one of the most difficult technics to master, requiring much practice and finesse for smooth execution. On the crescendo the tone appears to "bloom," or open up into head-voice, and is a most thrilling effect when done smoothly. The eminent operatic and concert recital tenor, Gili, was a past master in this regard. Preliminary training, to achieve a well-controlled crescendo-diminuendo effect in the high compass, should emphasize learning to produce the particular tone sung as *loudly* as possible in mixed-falsetto, and as *softly* as possible in head-voice.

5. *The greater the number of overlapping tones that can be sung in both mixed-falsetto and lower register adjustment, the easier transitions upward and downward can be made.* Practice, therefore, to

carry the mixed-falsetto as *low* and *resonant* as possible and the low adjustment as *high* and *light*.

6. *Manner of approach is most vital to conceal change of register and maintain balance.* It is especially necessary to observe the following:

(a) Sing tones in the Upper Middle Zone, *c* to *g*, with *light* lower register adjustment to smooth transition upward.

(b) Do not sing the last tone of lower register adjustment so forcefully that the first note of mixed-falsetto cannot be as loud or louder.

(c) Development and characteristics of the individual voice determine where transition should occur. In softer dynamics, however, the change should occur on lower pitches, and at louder intensities higher in the scale. This is due to the fact that mixed-falsetto adjustment can be produced only very lightly in the lower part of the overlapping range.

(d) Before singing a tone which is followed by a tone in the other register, *think the quality and dynamics of the second tone and match it as nearly as possible in the first.* Smoothest transition occurs when vowel character and tone color remain the same. *Transition is even smoother if it is possible to produce mixed-falsetto somewhat louder than lower register production.* To lean in this direction is wise; to err in the opposite is fatal.

DEVELOPING THE HEAD-VOICE

Success and reputation of a singer often depend upon whether or not he is able to develop sufficient range and control in the upper voice. Students and teachers recognize this fact, often with disastrous results to practice. They reason that, since it is a requirement, why not take a short-cut and start there. This reasoning is vocally as falacious as that of the carpenter, who decided to build the roof of the house first because it was most important in keeping out the rain.

Universally-accepted laws of learning specify that progress should be from the known to the unknown, and from that which is easiest and most correct to that which is next most easy and closely allied. Common sense suggests also that the logical place to begin developing the voice is the tone where the beginning student produces it most easily and naturally, as a basis for comparison and further progress. There is agreement by the majority of teachers that this tone normally will be found in the lower part of the middle range, around *e* flat to *g* above middle *c*, and that it is easier and more natural to carry the voice downward first. In other words, to practice establishing a good foundation before attempting to carry the voice into the more difficult high range should be the order followed.

Under this process *the head-voice is the culmination of a developmental process.* It cannot be had at once, but must be built patiently on a sure foundation through careful training. This approach is considered the safest and the most likely to retain the vitality, sonority, and strength of the fundamental tone without the upper partials in the overtone complex becoming overprominent.

Every singer, male or female, has an upper head-voice. By head-voice we do not mean falsetto adjustment for the male singer. To develop virile, high, dramatic tones the male must learn to sing high with the lower registration adjustment. The head-voice is not properly trained until upper limits of range and dynamic variety are adequate. Legato requires that the singer be able not only to progress smoothly into the head-voice from the lower range at different dynamics, but also to produce smooth *messa di voce* (crescendo-diminuendo) on any note in the upper compass. It is safe to say that the latter can never even be started with the forced, heavy, "chest-type" production as a base. *Rigidity and a weighty type of upper production must be eliminated;* the rigid "grip" or "clutch" of the vocal bands must be released, and the tone resonated on the thin edges of the vocal cords with generous breath support.

Vocal authorities agree that easy tonal production on the tone just preceding a high pitch is of vital importance, because it serves as a tonal base for high production. *Tensing-up on the low note in anticipation of difficulty on the high will always result in greater difficulty and tonal constriction, while emphasis on ease of production and maximum "head-like" quality on the low tone base inevitably makes the connection smoother and the upper tone more free and beautiful.* In this respect Caruso is reported as saying, "In the matter of taking high notes one should remember that their purity and ease of production depend very much on the way the preceding notes leading up to them are sung."[18] Many teachers also insist on the value of opening the mouth generously for high tones, e.g., Marchesi declares, "The higher the tone, the lower the jaw must drop."[19]

A voice that can sing only softly, or sing only loudly, is improperly produced. It must be so balanced that both dynamics are possible and smoothly coordinated. When the head-voice is properly resonated without rigidity it is dynamic, i.e., it can be developed in crescendo on long tones without break or change of quality into fortissimo production. This does not imply that it can be sung as softly as if the mixed-falsetto also were employed.

---

[18]Marafioti, P. Mario. "Caruso's Method of Voice Production." D. Appleton, 1933, p. 158.
[19]Marchesi, Blanche. "The Singer's Catechism and Creed." J. M. Dent and Sons, 1932, p. 34.

A criterion which the singer can always follow for safe development is, *never sacrifice ease and quality for power;* both the head-voice and the execution of an extensive *messa di voce* are based on the unforced light pianissimo. The singer needs to be able to sing both softly and loudly in head-voice and carry this production up to an adequate range. He can never sing as softly nor as high, however, as is possible through mastery also of the mixed-falsetto.

In male voices where falsetto production seems completely detached and unmanageable, nature usually compensates, giving the singer a naturally wider range in lower adjustment for carrying the voice upward. Those interested in developing the greater dynamics necessary for singing over an orchestra, or for dramatic operatic roles, are required to develop an adequate range and full power of the head-voice; mixed-falsetto is too light in dynamics to meet these demands in upper compass.

When falsetto practice is used purely as the basis for strengthening the Arytenoid muscles, in order that the head-voice can be carried higher and controlled more flexibly, most authorities agree that *it is not necessary to seek beauty of tone in the falsetto but rather to sing freely with vigorous dynamics.* It is particularly important, for developing coordination and ease in the head-voice, that overlapping notes capable of being produced with either low or high registration *be practiced easily and lightly in low registration, and as full bodied and resonant as possible in falsetto.* Such practice will strengthen and balance vocal cord action until eventually a well-controlled head-voice emerges, and can be carried up as far as needed for most voices.

In regard to coordination of the lower and upper voice, Vennard states, "There should never be a question as to which register to use. The answer is always: Both! The registration should be coordinated. It is not a matter of singing in one register up to a certain point and then shifting gears and continuing the scale in a different register. It is a matter of achieving a dynamic balance in which the best elements of both registers are functioning."[20]

The head-voice, sometimes called "mixed-voice," is therefore "mixed" with the light qualities of the falsetto and this blending process begins early in the Upper Middle Zone. Clippinger says in this regard, "In order to pass through the pitches C-F the pitches must be mixed-voice. If they are not mixed by the time the tenor or baritone reaches D or E♭ he will be shouting, and if he undertakes to go higher he must change suddenly to a dull, covered-tone and his scale will be destroyed."[21] Balanced coordination never can be achieved by forcing either the upper compass or the approach tones, but only through the finesse of free production, "floating tone on the breath." *The head-voice, when*

properly produced, must literally be blown open with fluid breath in a free throat operating through a long pharynx, an open head passage, and thin vocal cord approximation.

After strengthening the Arytenoid muscles in the larynx, through falsetto practice and through observance of the "Principles of Upward Tonal Progression," as outlined in Chapter 16 of Volume I, it will be found possible to carry the lower adjustment progressively higher, developing a light adjustment similar to falsetto in feeling sensation, but employing the lower register Thyroid muscles, rather than the Arytenoid, for control of resonation. Whether or not it can be carried high enough to meet completely the needs of the singer depends on development, the potentialities of the voice, and type or style of vocal literature to be sung.

FEELING SENSATIONS FOR THE HEAD-VOICE

While it is true that the major resonance sensation of a fine head-tone is spacious and high in the upper pharynx and head, the student must not try to force or place it there. Previous discussions have emphasized this point repeatedly.

When the upper octave compass is first experienced in free and energetic production, it often greatly stimulates nerve endings in the head cavities inducing a feeling of vibration, and perhaps even of "buzzing," sometimes accompanied by watering of the eyes and possible dizziness or a tendency to faint. In our experience these unpleasant symptoms are more likely to occur for treble than male voices. The student may be assured that watering of the eyes and dizziness are only temporary, and that these "head resonance" sensations for high tones are not abnormal; they are merely an indication of virile, resonant, and sonorous upper tone production.

Whether or not the sinus and head cavities actually function as resonators still is a moot question among vocal authorities. It is really not important to singing production, however, since the pronounced feeling of head space vibration and the open, free, spacious upper throat (pharynx) sensation associated with proper production in the high voice are scarcely debatable. In teaching, *it is the vital qualities of tone and associative feeling sensations that must be habituated to establish proper control.*

DEVELOPING THE LOW VOICE

Since most of the tones are already there, the problem of the student in building the low voice normally is confined to learning the principles of how to connect it smoothly with the Upper Middle Zone, and to give it the necessary "ring" and resonance

[20]Op. cit., p. 129.
[21]Op. Cit., p. 35.

without forcing. Low tones, especially, should have a ringing quality or "bite;" breathy, fuzzy, off-center production must be eliminated. This can never be developed by attempting to sing loudly, but is the result of ease and proper efficiency of resonation, first on the lower dynamic levels with a steady but "stingy" breath support. This basic ringing but soft low tone of good quality then can be slowly extended to louder dynamics, as the vocal bands are gradually strengthened to properly resist breath pressure in the low compass, without tone becoming breathy or spread. In comparison with upper tone dynamics, *the lowest tones in the compass never can be sung loudly.* Attempts to do so merely result in forcing, a lot of noisy breath, and even less tone than if unforced normal dynamics were attempted.

If head or nasal resonance is allowed to disappear entirely, low tones become thin and shallow. Although mouth space is reduced for easiest production, a feeling of forward "nasal" hum resonation is retained down to the lowest tone. Production is wrong if this sensation disappears at any point in the descending scale.

A break or weak part in the scale is seldom encountered for the male voice in progressing from the middle to the lower zone of the voice. Most sopranos do not have difficulty here either, although occasionally even a coloratura soprano will have a distinct break, usually from *e* to *f* above middle *c*, and a heavy "chest" quality which extends the voice to *g* below middle *c*. The heavier more robust-voiced contraltos and mezzo sopranos are more likely than high sopranos to have a distinct break, and a weakness between the Low Zone and the Lower Middle Voice Zone of the voice. The author has never had an instance, however, where the break would not respond favorably to persistent and proper practice.

Extension of range in the Lower Zone is an automatic by-product of establishing the fundamentals of singing first in the middle voice and the easier adjacent tones of the low compass. When the "Principles of Production in Tonal Progression," as outlined in Chapter 16, are mastered and gradually carried downward, proper resonation of most tones in the lowest compass develops with comparative rapidity — certainly much more quickly and easily than notes in the extreme high register. It can be expected that a few additional notes will be added gradually in the low range as the normal consequence of additional age, further technical maturity, and correct practice.

Volume I for this chapter lists eight rules for "How to Sing High Tones Easily" and seven for "How to Sing Low Tones Easily." (See p. 165) The vocal instructor, will make sure in the beginning that these rules are thoroughly understood, applied properly, and then check thereafter to see that they are being followed in vocal practice and the singing of songs.

CHAPTER 9

Extending Dynamics

(*See also "Climax and Dynamics," p. 105, and Volume I, p. 173*)

LEARNING DYNAMIC VARIATION

Few beginning students are conscious of the monotonous inadequacy of their tonal dynamic variation, either within the sweep of the phrase or between contrasting sections of a song. Awareness is the first step in correction, and this is the responsibility of the instructor. Many beginners, who are capable from the first of much greater dynamic variety within safe limits of free production at the time, sing monotonously on one power level.

GOOD TONE BASIC

"Good, strong, vigorous singing is not injurious to the voice; it is healthy. Much of the soft, anemic, mezza voce singing is undoubtedly more detrimental to correct production and the general welfare of vocal action."[1] Most authorities subscribe to the principle that the singer should endeavor to develop as wide a spread of dynamics as is consistent with good tone, and that enough reserve of breath energy and technic always should be present to maintain secure control, beauty, and freedom in production. Shakespeare quotes Hiller as saying, "Never force the voice so as to excite astonishment; never louder than lovely."[2]

Unfortunately, there are still those who insist on powerful intensity at any cost, in the misguided belief that tonal freedom will develop later. A few teachers, especially operatic coaches, will accept only *mf* to *fff* or louder as legitimate dynamic spread, rejecting the lower intensities as useless, anemic, and detrimental to the rapid development of utmost sonority. It must be acknowledged that the quickest way to learn to sing loudly is to concentrate on loud singing. However, to sing loudly without freedom, flexibility, and beauty of tone is both futile artistically and dangerous in the extreme to the vocal instrument.

The unfortunate fact that it is often possible to obtain quickly a big, loud, raucous tone in the high compass is probably responsible for more ruined voices, and voices with severely shortened range, than any other element in vocal training. The unwise teacher and the deluded student assume that they are getting somewhere quickly on the basis of rapid development of tonal force. It must be admitted that an occasional sturdy voice survives a training method based on *fortissimo* singing. The important fact is, however, that there are only a very few and, for even that few, maximum range, flexibility, beauty, and lasting quality of the voice are invariably affected adversely.

ACHIEVING POWERFUL TONE

The human voice is an instrument and follows the laws of other instruments regarding dynamics. Development of extensive *fortissimo* is, therefore, dependent on two factors: full utilization of resonance capabilities and increased motive force (breath pressure). For the best quality *fortissimo*, increased breath pressure cannot be carried to the extreme of forcing more energy against the vocal bands than they can balance and resist successfully, or quality of tone, as well as actual extent of dynamics, suffers. In fact, the best *forte* tones are produced with a comparative minimum of breath expenditure. It is always a mistake to increase breath pressure to achieve more tonal force unless we have first made sure that resonation factors are fully utilized. Throat and mouth must be opened generously, the head and nasal passages unobstructed, and concept of tone must be correct in freedom, ringing clarity, and sonority.

Jeffries states, "For loud singing a wide jaw opening is indispensable."[3] Scott agrees, "The oral cavity

---

[1] Wilson, Harry Robert. "Artistic Choral Singing." G. Schirmer, Inc., 1959, p. 219.

[2] Shakespeare, William. "Plain Words on Singing." Putnam, 1938, new edition, p. 81.

[3] Jeffries, Arthur. "For the Untrained Singer." Etude, 1933, Vol. 51, p. 44.

is an adjustable resonator. Hence, the larger the mouth, the more ample the sound will be."[4] Conversely, it must be noted that, to achieve soft singing, the smaller the mouth the softer the tone will be. We agree with Pease that "There is an ideal lip opening which produces the purest sound"[5] and the desired dynamics.

Controlled breath pressure necessary for the robust tone is generated by a vigorous feeling of "spinal-stretch," lifting chest and expansion around the waist-line. The concept of squeezing in the diaphragm, using it like a bellows, is a grave error. Instead of amplifying the tone, "Such forcing robs it of both color and volume."[6] Schumann-Heink[7] also believed that forcing the voice to attain volume or range is the surest way to ruin it. These testimonials and many others emphasize that "Power of the voice is secured as much, or more, through the use of resonance resources as through the increase of breath pressure."[8]

ACHIEVING SOFT TONE

Authorities generally agree that a fine *pianissimo* is more difficult to achieve than a *fortissimo*. Almost anyone with a vigorous constitution can gulp in a lungful of air, open the mouth wide, and blast out a loud tone; however, a beautiful, well-controlled *pianissimo* can be obtained only by the development of proper tonal concept and strong breath *resistant* muscles. Really vital tone in very soft singing requires the finesse of an extreme amount of steady but "stingy" breath, the very opposite of increased breath pressure required for loud singing.

It is fatal to good production for the student to associate *pianissimo* with a breathy, dark, dull, devitalized tone. Tone must be thought just as ringing, "hummy," and vital as a *fortissimo*. "The true *pianissimo* has the same qualities of resonance, vowel quality and throat adjustment as the more dramatic tones."[9] Only breath energy and mouth opening are reduced.

The freely-produced open-throat hum has the feeling of firm resistance and close approximation of the vocal cords needed as a model for students to learn to sing vowels softly. *Mee, May, Mah, Moh, Moo,* and particularly *Hm - - - ee, Hm - - - ay,* etc., on long sustained tones, are favorite types of exercises used by many teachers in developing the controlled, vital pianissimo. The student should be advised to retain the feeling of close, firm, "hummy" quality and small resonation space of the inducing *m* or *n* consonant throughout the following vowel, to open the mouth sparingly, and feed the vowel

with an extremely steady, but small amount, of breath. It is well always to bear in mind that *if the intense "ring" and hummy quality of the vowel is lost, vital, controlled pianissimo is lost also.*

BALANCED TRAINING

The human voice cannot be completely and adequately trained on an exclusive diet of either fortissimo or pianissimo. Too much concentration on fortissimo will produce a loud, strident voice that will not long endure; exclusive use of light intensity will result in free production over wide range accompanied, unfortunately, by an anemic, devitalized tonal instrument, incapable of suitable dynamic variety or dramatic expression. Mezzoforte should be the norm from which to depart in the singing of most songs and exercises, and for the introductory part of the warm-up period. Neither pianissimo or fortissimo can be neglected without unfortunate consequences, however. Development of vital pianissimo should come fairly early in vocal training, but *a powerful fortissimo normally should be developed slowly and carefully, always on the basis of freedom and beauty of tone.*

Extent of tonal power and volume on any pitch is definitely fixed during any particular stage of technical development. The teacher and student must determine limitations beyond which it is unsafe to go without resulting in loss of control and harsh tone. Breath energy, vocal cord resistance, and resonation factors must be kept in balance; one cannot overweigh the others.

Since Volume I is explicit in directions and exercises for developing safely both pianissimo and fortissimo (See pp. 173-179), fhrther detail is unnecessary here. It is one of the teacher's major responsibilities to guide the pupil in principles stated, however, and not permit forcing the voice at any time beyond the student's capacity for safe and easy tonal control.

---

[4]Scott, Charles Kennedy. "Word and Tone." J. M. Dent & Sons, 1933, Vol. II, p. 26.

[5]Pease, E. R. Garnett. "The Singing Voice." Pitman & Sons, Ltd. 1933, p. 69.

[6]Pons, Lily. "Fame Overnight." (an interview) Etude, 1931, Vol. 49, p. 394.

[7]Schumann-Heink, Ernestine. "You Can Sing — If You Will!" (an interview) Etude, 1934, Vol. 52, p. 11.

[8]Wodell, Frederick W. "The Proper Training and Use of the Voice of Persons of School Age." Etude, 1929, Vol. 47, p. 678.

[9]Peterson, Paul W. "Natural Singing and Expressive Conducting." John F. Blair, 1955, p. 76.

10

Intonation

(*See Volume I, p. 180*)

IMPORTANCE

There can be little doubt for those with an acute sense of pitch, that pleasure in listening to singing is destroyed unless the singer achieves accurate intonation. For many instrumentalists, especially, pitch is a religion, and the measure of a singer's artistry is often based almost exclusively on perfection in intonation. It is an unfortunate fact that most singers, even with the assistance of an accompaniment, sing slightly under pitch — some so obviously that it is readily apparent to even the untrained ear. Actually, no vocalist sings in perfect intonation all the time; perfection never is achieved entirely — it is a matter of relativity. No professional artist can ever gain or hold high reputation, however, unless degree of singing off pitch is held to a minimum.

VIBRATO AND PITCH

A tone cannot sound pleasant to the discriminating ear unless it is on pitch, which means centering the middle pitch point of the vibrato. Because of vibrato there is no such thing as perfect pitch in the freely-produced human voice. As explained previously, vibrato carries the voice periodically both above and below the true pitch; when the middle pitch point of the vibrato is centered, we call the pitch perfect. When a tone is off this center, although it be freely produced, the sensitive listener's concept of tonal beauty is destroyed. Either excessive vibrato or tremolo, although centered on the pitch, also always gives the impression of off-pitch singing. In choral ensemble, singers must produce a uniform type of vowel color as well in order to give an impression of good intonation.

CAUSES AND CORRECTION OF POOR INTONATION

What are the causes of off-pitch singing? Wilson says, "Off-pitch singing is sometimes the result of carelessness and habit, sometimes a matter of faulty ear, but most often it results from incorrect voice production and a lack of sensitive listening."[1] Wilcox agrees, "It is true of course, that many singers have failed to sensitize their pitch thinking through intelligent disciplinary practice and that their intonation suffers because of this failure; but the fundamental cause of such widespread deviation from pitch among singers is, nevertheless, an incorrect habit of voice production."[2] According to Seashore[3], a poor ear can be insensitive to pitch differences as large or larger than a semitone. On the other hand, the average person can hear pitch deviations as small as one-seventeenth of a tone, and those of superior acuteness may be able to detect one-onehundredth of a tone or less. With the exception of very few persons, everyone has the native capacity to sing fairly well on pitch.

When poor intonation is due to extremely low native capacity in hearing pitch change, there is nothing that a voice teacher can do to train the student to sing on pitch, regardless of how fine an instrument the student possesses or how enthusiastic and persistent he may be regarding the study of singing. The "Pitch" section of a standard native capacity music test such as Seashore's, plus a practical "tune-test," should give a significant basis for student guidance regarding whether or not further study of singing would be justified. Experience has demonstrated that if a student ranks in the lower ten percentile in a standard pitch test, and has great difficulty in matching pitch and "carrying" a familiar tune, he should be guided into some other undertaking, in which an insurmountable handicap is not

[1]Wilson, Harry Robert. "What — Another Voice Book?" Choir Guide, Dec. 1951, Vol. 4, No. 9, p. 23.

[2]Wilcox, John C. "Why Do They Sing Off Pitch?" Etude, Jan. 1937, p. 49.

[3]Seashore, Carl Emil. "New Approaches to the Science of Voice." Scientific Monthly, 1939, Vol. 49, p. 340.

present. Those with weak hearing capacity, but above the lower ten percentile bracket, usually can be helped to hear and produce pitch more accurately, if there is enough time available. One good device in voice class is to place them in front of, or beside, one or more superior students in intonation.

The fact that a student does not sing on pitch in class or on a "tune-test" is not, however, a reliable guide in itself regarding native hearing capacity. Outward and inward hearing are two quite different things, and acuteness of hearing pitch is greatly reduced when judging our own singing. Wilcox states, "Nor does the fact that the singer himself fails to sense that he is singing off pitch prove that his ear is at fault. The vibratory sensation conveyed to the inner ear of the singer by his own tone does not register the same accurate pitch impression that the auditor receives."[4]

The foregoing is attested to by the fact that some who rate high on native capacity in pitch tests, and are highly sensitive to off-pitch singing when listening to others, nevertheless sing out of tune atrociously and are apparently unaware of this error. As a rule in such cases, when production difficulty is corrected, intonation is greatly improved. Nevertheless, ability to hear their own voices varies greatly from student to student, and most pupils need assistance in learning how to think and hear the more difficult intervals accurately. Singers sometimes have only one area or "island" of two or three tones that are sung off-pitch habitually. This occurrence is most frequent on the several notes just below where "head registration" begins. It normally is corrected by more generous breath support and proper concepts of free and balanced resonation.

When pupils have at least an average ear according to native capacity tests, and are physically normal, singing off-pitch always can be improved significantly by learning correct production and habituating the accompanying associative feeling and hearing associations. *Tones will sound accurately on pitch when the singer thinks pitch correctly, supports the tone with sufficient breath, and eliminates muscular interference.* Mastery of the "Principles of Production in Tonal Progression." (see p. 127) will correct or at least greatly improve intonation, since establishment of these principles eliminates accumulation of tension, the major production cause of poor intonation.

In addition, many students need to be taught to hear the various intervals and types of melodic progressions accurately. They must be trained to associate both correct hearing and feeling associations, and make them habitual, before intonation in singing is reliable. After the student learns to sing throughout his range with comparative freedom and adequate breath support, he establishes a definite feeling association for each pitch. This feeling sensa-

tion often becomes fairly reliable unless the singer has a cold, is exhausted, or vitality is low for some reason. For the vocalist the feeling association is valuable in establishing what is known as a "relative sense of pitch." This usually happens eventually without the singer's being conscious of the process.

Relative sense of pitch can be greatly accelerated if the pupil will mentally tabulate each tone in the scale, checking pitch if necessary at the piano while singing, and making needed adjustments until sound and feeling imagery is accurate. This process of establishing relative sense of pitch may sound laborious, but actually can be established rather rapidly for many students. Even students with considerably below average hearing acuteness often can learn to sing in pitch by establishing correct feeling sensations as a guide for each pitch. Reliability of feeling sensation flutcuates noticeably with the physical vitality and emotional state of the student, however. In order to be safe for all pitch contingencies, we must develop accurate hearing of our own vocal production, also.

Minor mode is often neglected in the public schools and in training repertoire for beginning singers, with the result that some who sing well in pitch in major mode may flat atrociously when they attempt a song in minor. We cannot sing intervals accurately unless we hear them accurately. Some intervals and types of progressions are more difficult than others. Major troublemakers are listed in Volume I, and helpful exercises are included at the end of Lesson 10 as well as in Lesson 16.

Causes of off-pitch singing are both mental and physical. *Establishment of accurate, dependable pitch is contingent on first establishing endurance in a free production.* From the standpoint of physical production, singing flat usually can be traced to either insufficient breath support, or to too large a resonation space for available breath energy to fill. Correction is obvious — increase breath energy in the first instance and decrease mouth space in the latter. Production reason for singing sharp also is due to lack of balance — too much resistance or "rigidity" in the larynx, forcing the tone. It is nearly always evidenced by a tense or "locked" jaw or by insufficient mouth space. Again the cure is obvious — establishment of more relaxed vocal cord resistance and use of a larger resonating space.

MAJOR CAUSES FOR SINGING OFF-PITCH

1. *Faulty tone production.* This is admittedly the greatest single villain in causing poor intonation. If production is off-center, breathy and spread, pitch will be flat; if tone is too open, shrill, and tense, pitch is likely to be sharp. Flatting occurs in the lower compass when too much breath is driven

---

[4]Op. cit., p. 49.

against lengthened vocal bands vibrating in too generous a space; sharping occurs in the upper compass when the vocal bands grip excessively and when too much breath energy is forced through too small a vowel form. Such tones tend to be "white," shrill, and piercing in quality, and often occur when the pupil is trying to sing too loudly or to crescendo by mistakenly adding more throat constriction. Flatting occurs when too little breath energy is supplied to balance a large vowel form. Habitually too spacious a resonation form results in flatting. Tenors who imitate baritones, and sopranos who imitate contraltos, can expect this difficulty.

2. *Fatigue.* Flat singing is sometimes psychological fatigue because of becoming "stale" on a particular composition or exercise. If changing the key doesn't help, the song or exercise should be given a rest. If physical fatigue is to the point of exhaustion, singing should not be attempted. Principal causes for physical fatigue are:

(a) Lack of physical vitality or sufficient endurance.

(b) Phrases too long or demanding for technic at the time. (Taking a breath in the middle of some phrases may be possible and is always preferable to exhaustion.)

(c) Key of the song too high or low, or tessitura unfavorable. (When tessitura or a number of repeated notes lies around a weak part or "break" area of a voice, a key either lower or higher can be expected to improve pitch. Tessitura that is consistently too high causes exhaustion, while lack of tonal vitality and flatting result from tessitura that is consistently to low. Light, "fluty" type voices are more inclined to flat if the key or tessitura is too low. The heavier, "reedy" type voices are more subject to sharping when the key or tessitura is too high.)

(d) Poor ventilation or excessive heat.

(e) Singing too long or too loudly.

3. *Careless articulation.* Always vitalize diction when pitch is waning. Insist on consonants being quick, precise, and clean-clipped. *Initial consonants are always thought on the same pitch as the vowel that follows, or pitch starts flat.* A pitch that starts flat is difficult to lift into balanced resonation without undue tension.

4. *Weak musicianship.* Failure to imagine intervals and the demands of the whole phrase accurately before inhalation is a common cause of poor intonation. If the correct sound and interpretation requirements of a whole phrase are not in mind *before* breath is taken, breath support demands are not in mind. Consequently, either too little or too much breath is inhaled. Either fault causes pitch difficulty. *Time to concentrate on pitch and demands of the phrase is before inhalation.* In addition, there are some intervals that are more difficult for many singers to hear. They need first to be made aware of fault and then to have persistent help by the instructor until correct thought is established. Recording and playback is often beneficial. In extreme cases, use of the Conn Stroboscope, when available, is recommended. Drill in singing the various scale forms and the major, minor, diminished, augmented, and dominant seventh chords in arpeggio is basic to correction of pitch-hearing difficulty.

5. *Rigidity.* Rigid tension and "forcing" cause sharping. It may be due to fear, overexcitement; nervous or spasmodic inhalation; lack of flexible, expansive breath support; or failure to think the tone free. Rigidity manifests itself in throat "clutch," in set or "locked" positions of the jaw, lips, tongue, chest, in visible tension of the hands, hunched shoulders, and protuberant chords in the neck. Persistent rigidity eventually causes excessive fatigue, and a song which started with sharping may end up with the worst type of flatting.

6. *Inertia.* Flatting may express itself either through lack of mental concentration on pitch and the expressive and technical elements of the song itself, or it may be physical, i.e., slumped posture and weak breath support. As a general rule, when posture is slumped so is the mind. The cure is to obtain correct posture and breath support and stimulate attention to expression and technical demands.

7. *Reiterated tones.* Often-repeated tones on one pitch are a severe intonation hazard. Tendency is to grow careless in pitch concept, relax breath support, and sing each successive tone a little flatter. Correction is achieved by keeping breath support firm, initial consonants on pitch and, when necesary in stubborn cases, thinking a slightly rising level of pitch on successive tones.

8. *Tempo too slow.* Most students have a fatal tendency to take tempos slower and slower when they commence to get into trouble with adequate breath support, increasing difficulty in phrasing and the tendency to flat. A tempo that is too slow also has a depressing psychological effect on the singer, and might cause flatting even when breath support is more than adequate. Speeding up the tempo with attention to crisp articulation will cure most flatting.

9. *Lack of familiarity with the music.* Sight singing and inadequate memorization create insecurity, tentative singing, and flatting.

10. *Inadequate concept of tonal production.* Dull, breathy concept of tone is a frequent cause of flatting, especially in the low compass and for *pianissimo.* Tone should be thought vital, ringing, and resonant in all registers and for all dynamics.

11. *Acoustic difficulty.* Many rooms and auditoriums are over-reverberant; a few are comparatively "dead" in resonance. The singer must practice and

gain experience under varying acoustic conditions. These conditions vary so much that the voice not only sounds quite different to the singer, but also difficulty is encountered at times in hearing the piano accompaniment. Acuteness in hearing piano pitch needs to be trained. Tonal force may need to be reduced in over-resonant halls before the piano pitch can be heard adequately. It may also be necessary to request the accompanist to use the sustaining pedal sparingly and to play with a lighter, more legato singing tone, rather than the percussive pounding sometimes heard. A piano badly out of tune, or a very poor upright piano in the pit with the sounding board toward the singer, are crosses that most singers have to bear from time to time. They are handicaps that require excellent pitch acuteness to overcome.

DEVELOPING SENSE OF PITCH

While everyone cannot develop a perfect sense of pitch, the attainment of a satisfactory "relative" sense of pitch is well within the possibilities of achievement for most. Since correct intonation is closely wedded to proper tonal production, the teacher should not fret or fume and severely criticize beginning students because of slight deviations from pitch. Destructive criticism and focus of attention on bad pitch itself, rather than on its causes, frequently does far more harm than good.

Poor intonation is deplorable at any time — painful to the aesthetic sensibility of the musician, and needs to be eliminated as soon as practicable. It is nevertheless a cross that must be borne temporarily at times as the lesser of two evils — singing off-pitch or singing with excessive tension. The student first is urged to learn to produce a free tone properly supported by breath, and to discard old habits of throat "clutch," often used to "squeeze" the tone into pitch. In this preliminary process of transition, students often sing badly under pitch for a time. It is always a mistake to go back to the old method of "squeezing" the throat merely for the sake of correcting pitch.

Able teachers sometimes are severely criticized during this transition period because the student sounds worse to the uninitiated, since pitch is temporarily flat. The pupil should be informed, if not already aware of it, that he is singing flat, but that the only way to correct it, and also sing properly, is to learn as speedily as possible to support a more spacious free tone with an adequate amount of breath. Some, especially those with keener hearing acuteness for their own production, will respond rapidly, correcting major pitch errors in short order. Others, because of poor hearing capacity or inordinately weak breath control, never will sing consistently on pitch. Means of improving tonal production are well covered in this course. Correcting natively weak hearing capacity is another matter; when limitations are too great all efforts are wasted. Such students can and should be discovered early and their interests transferred to something more rewarding.

Concientious teachers will never be satisfied until their pupils sing on pitch. Students are taught proper hearing habits and production methods in their lesson periods, and urged in their individual practice to *learn to sing through the melodies of songs unaccompanied and end exactly on key*. It is stressed that *the only way to attain good intonation and pitch independence is to sing unaccompanied*. For this reason, as well as for quicker development of proper tonal concepts in free production, considerable class and individual singing will be *a cappella*.

Use of the piano or any other accompanying instrument should be dispensed with much of the time. The piano may well be used in the initial stages of introducing a song; for accompanying the song after it is well learned; and for the student to check pitch, if in doubt, when practicing alone. It is vital that teachers and students divorce themselves from the pernicious habit of depending or "leaning" on the piano for pitch concept, however. Pianists studying voice are especially prone to this fault. In severe cases it may be necessary to forbid use of piano for awhile, assigning the student to a studio with no piano and only a pitch pipe to check intonation.

11

Recitative

(See also pp. 53, 98, and Volume I, p. 186)

Recitative is a type of singing in which words are delivered in a manner resembling declamation. Good recitative, whether *strict* or *free*, "Gives with extraordinary fidelity the accentual value of the words which belongs to good speaking and emphasizes the broad sense of the text."[1]

Recitative style in singing, especially in the United States, is the most neglected facet of the singer's art today. It is so commonly misunderstood and neglected by teachers, conductors, and singers alike that one of the most stirring means of vocal expression is in danger of disappearing from the singer's technic. As usually heard, it amounts to little more than a meaningless matter-of-fact chant, a painful interlude which must be borne and hurried through until the aria begins. "Most singers and directors think that recitative is a nuisance, that it is too bad that it appears in the Oratorio, Opera, or Lieder at all, and they treat it, especially the singers, as a necessary evil, and what an evil it can be is very well demonstrated in actual performances which we hear today."[2]

It is not at all uncommon to hear conductors declare that all recitative should be sung pretty much *a tempo*. Certainly this attitude is contrary to intent of composers writing in this style, and is indefensible on artistic grounds as well. *Free* recitative must be sung *free* to sound well; *a tempo* production cannot fail to sound anything other than matter-of-fact. If conductors in the future only will make an earnest effort to understand recitative style, and the technics of how to conduct it, while the singers master the principles of declamation, which it demands, and when and how to change from *strict* to *free* recitative style, then what threatens to become a lost art will once again assume its rightful importance and significance in vocal expression.

Recitative style and the difference between *free* and *strict* recitative are described clearly in the student manual, and representative examples of recitative are included for practice. After study and discussion of the lesson content, it is well to listen to select phonograph records from oratorio and opera illustrating the style, while observing a copy of the score. This is recommended as the quickest method for approaching and teaching recitative style effectively.

Two recommended sources on recitative style and recitative singing are:

1. Corder, F. "Vocal Recitative." Associated Board of Royal Schools of Music, London. (Note — 54 examples of recitative from important works are given.)

2. Mabon, Charles B. "The Art of Recitative." G. Schirmer, Inc. (Note — Contains technic, history, usages, characterization, and interpretation discussions.)

---

[1]Grove's Dictionary of Music and Musicians. (Third Edition) Macmillan, 1941, Vol. IV. pp. 294 and 337.

[2]Hoffman, Franz. "Recitative." The Journal of the Choral Conductors Guild of California, Feb. 1953, p. 3.

12

Interpretation

(*See Volume I, p. 190*)

Part I — Learning Interpretation*

STRESS EXPRESSION FIRST AND TECHNIC SECOND

(*Note — See also p. 4, "Emphasis on Expression"*)

Modern technics and methods of teaching voice have demonstrated conclusively that the old idea of practicing vocalises and basic technics for years before the student is allowed to sing songs is an unnecessary, wasteful, and discouraging procedure. It is important to stress the vital importance of emphasizing expression continually from the first lesson to the last. "We should always teach songs on the broad basis of suggestion and imagination, and emphasize and work for interpretation and beauty."[1] In this manner the student always has the fundamental goal in mind; he is better able to see the woods of interpretation and not be lost in the trees of technic. He is stimulated to greater effort to improve technic through being made aware of inadequacies in expression, working thereafter with heightened enthusiasm and efficiency in corrective exercises and required technics, once need is revealed in song.

Both practical and psychological reasons appear conclusive as to why a class or private teacher should stress interpretation from the very beginning. Of course the student will be inadequate at first even on the easiest songs, but he will have enough success to have an enjoyable experience, and to furnish the most powerful stimulus to effort toward future improvement.

In emphasis on expression and stimulation of the imagination, *most singers do not place enough time and stress on word study* — dramatic meaning as well as precise diction with proper accent for maximum significance. This requires careful analysis, as well as a great deal of repetition and the looking up of

words in foreign language, so that the exact meaning of each is clear. Brines declares that, since interpretation is a form of "Story telling, the singer must forget himself in expression of the song."[2] Another common weakness is failure to work out and routine an artistic phrasing scheme. This fault is due no doubt, at least in part, to lack of insufficient musical background. Primarily it is due to little or no effort to applying intelligence and imagination to the problem of each song in the initial stages of study.

STRESS LISTENING EXPERIENCE

Interpretation primarily is *caught,* not *taught.* While it is necessary and useful to give students many suggestions, to point out principles in style and interpretation, and urge them to read the best sources available in regard to the matter, the fact remains that the most functional help is obtained through listening and analysis of fine interpretations. *The student must have a rich listening experience* in order to stimulate the imagination, to gain refined concepts of style, and the necessary understandings to project mood powerfully.

DEVELOP IMAGINATION AND SENSITIVITY TO MOOD

Singers must face the fact that success can be only strictly limited, no matter how beautiful the voice and erudite the musical knowledge, unless an active and refined imagination furnishes the neces-

---

*A storehouse of sensitive and penetrating suggestions on interpretation as applied specifically to a number of the greatest German, French, and Old Italian Songs will be found in Mme. Lotte Lehmann's text, "More Than Singing," published by Boosey & Hawkes, Inc. Judith Litante's recent text, "A Natural Approach to Singing," published by the Wm. C. Brown Co., also has many valuable ideas on interpretation and song literature.

[1]Mursell, James L. "The Psychology of School Music Teaching." Silver Burdett & Co., 1931, p. 281.

[2]Brines, Mrs. John Francis. "Supreme Test of Singing." Etude, 1930, Vol. 48, p. 816.

sary stimuli. Superb singing by great artists is always characterized by naturalness, artistic sensitivity, and a highly versatile and creative imagination. "It is usually said that one must have lived to be a good interpreter. Experience no doubt seasons the powers of the interpreter, but a vivid imagination, one of the attributes of dramatic talent, can make up in part for lack of experience."[3] Litante declares that the fundamental instinct for interpretation cannot be taught. "You are either born with it — or not. Nevertheless, it lies dormant or inhibited in many singers and often needs only the right kind of stimulus to bring it to life."[4]

There appears little doubt that a tendency toward artistic sensitivity and a creative imagination are inborn to a certain extent. The modern educator is well aware, however, that proper environment and training condition these factors to a great degree. Imagination is a faculty of the mind, and like all other faculties, is capable of growth through favorable environment and proper exercise. We cannot emphasize too much the *vital importance of developing power of the imagination in relation to visualization of mood and characterization in songs.*

It is basic that students be led to recognize that artistic singing is a product of the mind and the emotions, while technic is merely their obedient servant. Many youth are not artistically sensitive and imaginative because they have not experienced enough in life and art to make them so. The wise teacher realizes this fact and does his best to guide and direct the student in the paths that will supply desirable experiences. All types of experiences which stimulate imagery and dramatic response to mood are valuable; contacts with various styles and schools of music, vocal and instrumental, and poetry, drama, literature, art, and the dance are all beneficial. Outside of extensive music listening, study and practice, *the student, above all, will concentrate early on developing the ability to read prose and poetry eloquently and to effectively read various characterizations in plays.* This is the most functional and rapid means available for stimulating imagination, dramatic sensitivity, and ability to project mood. Rapid progress is often noted in expressiveness in singing after students study and read plays, or actually participate in dramatic productions.

DEVELOP STYLE DISCRIMINATION AND MUSICIANSHIP

What is the difference between interpretation and musicianship? Chambers expresses it well as follows, "Interpretation is the emotional and artistic portrayal; the summation of all music. . . . Musicianship is the science of music, interpretation is the emotional content. Interpretation demands musicianship, while musicianship implies interpretation."[5]

Style is is an important phase of musicianship. It is important that the student be educated as to appropriate style, and then assisted in the details of interpretation on specific songs within the limitations of good taste, which the particular style imposes. A well-educated and equipped singer needs to know all styles and be familiar with choice examples of music from all the schools of song literature, even though he may never use some in his public repertoire. Too often, if left entirely to their own preference, students, will choose to study and sing in a very narrow field of song literature limited to a style which they understand, or in which they naturally excel. Quite often that which they avoid is most valuable for their musical and technical development at the time. In such instances, a great deal of tact and persuasion on the part of the teacher, and a careful choice of songs in the particular area being neglected, are necessary.

The fundamental aesthetic factors in interpretation discussed in Volume I for this chapter (Unity, Variety, Proportion, and Dominance) also require considerable analysis, guidance of students, and discussion toegther on each particular song as a necessary musical and intellectual approach that is fundamental in determining other subsidiary details of expression.

DEVELOP INDIVIDUALITY IN INTERPRETATION

Interpretation is not a single item or skill but a complex sum total of many elements: experience, imagination, intelligence, emotional sensitivity, musicianship, technic, personality, and stage deportment. Each is subject to study and improvement. "Also of prime importance in the interpretational phase of vocal training is the emergence of the individuality of the singer in which he demonstrates his capacity for original and creative expression."[6] Even though a number of singers be coached on the same song by the same teacher, expression still will differ in detail, since personalities and emotional sensitivity differ. Artistic singing is the creative utterance of the whole personality; it is not the voice that sings, it is the singer functioning through his voice.

Finest details of expression are beyond the capacity of the composer to notate in the score; they are the result of the singer's projecting his own personality, his own individual thoughts, emotions, and understandings of the song. A young singer

---

[3]Ross, William Ernest. "Sing High, Sing Low." Brown & Ross, 1948, p. 58.

[4]Litante, Judith. "A Natural Approach to Singing." Wm. C. Brown Co., 1959, p. 89.

[5]Chambers, Lawrence B. "A Critical Survey of Unison Octavo Music for Voice Students." M. A. Thesis, Ohio State University, p. 18.

[6]Fields, Victor Alexander. "Training the Singing Voice." Kings Crown Press, 1947, p. 238.

cannot expect to be a mature interpreter since musicianship, knowledge, imagination, and poise in expression are the result of a maturation process. "Experience is the soil out of which interpretation grows and young people are deficient in that."[7]

OBSERVE THE BOUNDARIES OF GOOD TASTE

"Composers do not leave works of art to posterity as do painters."[8] The composer creates the idea of the song, the singer recreates it. A song is really not a song, but the blueprint of a song, until the singer recreates it. Thus the composer is the architect and the singer the builder. It would be most unusual for a reputable builder to change radically the carefully-drawn-up plans and instructions of a master architect. The singer should not change radically the plans and instructions of a master composer either.

It is, of course, both impossible and undesirable to attempt to standardize the interpretation of a song in details of expression. The style, melody, rhythm, harmony, text and general intent of a song by a master composer will never be wilfully distorted or garbled, however. Under no circumstances should a fine art song be individualized: i.e., made to fit the particular style or idiosyncracies of the singer. *The singer fits the style of the song, not the song the style of the singer.* There are limits of good taste in changing the traditional interpretation of a song. It is the responsibility of the performer to know and stay within these limits. If technic is inadequate to do so, the composition should never be programmed.

Our finest interpreters not only study and absorb every feature of the printed score, but also seem to possess an instinct for deep penetration of the score by "reading between the lines." This deeper insight will cause them to question, and at times disregard, certain dynamic and tempo markings often inserted by music editors who are better printers than authorities on interpretation.

A teacher is ill-advised who insists that there is only one way to interpret a song — his way, or some traditional way. A sincere and searching reproduction of the composer's intent by those of different temperaments should vary, and is the only worthwhile tradition. When the same song is sung by two sensitive artists, it is highly unlikely that the general style, tone color, and mood will be markedly different; however, dynamics, tempo, word accentuation, and innumerable details often are.

A conscientious interpreter seeks, of course, to recreate a score with maximum fidelity to the intent of the composer. This does not imply slavish compliance to the exact tempos, exact note values, and other factors indicated in the score, nor does it imply that nothing should be added not implicitly written in the score. If this were so, music interpretations would be stereotyped and deadeningly pedantic expressions indeed. "As a matter fact, no score, however accurate in notation and no matter how specific in the employment of directional terms, can indicate the exact performance intentions of the composer."[9] Even scores by modern composers, filled with a plethora of directions, still require that the imagination and musicianship of the performer fill in countless details before truly eloquent expression is possible. Some of these details are supplied intellectually through the background and training of the performer. Others come from an active imagination and a sensitive instinct for suitable expression.

A few geniuses possess musical insight in amazing degree. They make the outstanding artists of each generation. For instance, Mozart's teacher is reputed to have declared that it was difficult to teach him anything, since he already seemed to know the answers. More than anything else this intuition for eloquent and fitting expression in various styles is what is meant when we say that a person is highly musical. Such a pupil is a joy to teach, for he absorbs correct interpretive suggestions instantly and seldom needs a second reminder. The task, in this instance, is usually to promote technical facility so that it does not lag discouragingly far behind musical insight.

SET HIGH STANDARDS

The possession of a fine voice and high technical facility do not guarantee artistry. One must have something to give spiritually and musically. It is apparent that study of the art of singing should therefore devote itself not only to musical and technical study, but also to developing in the singer highest artistic ideals and the best elements of his nature.

"Perfection is a goal that has always been highly regarded — an unattainable ideal toward which you should strive. . . . And what is the ultimate goal? That is the large question — but one answer might be — the communication of some bit of beauty, of wisdom, of truth, some flash of inspiration, some richness of understanding from the perceptive artist to the receptive watcher and listener. It is the intensity and burning compulsion of the artist to convey his meaning that is important; not the suave mastery of all the technicians of the world. The creative artist is always inadequate to express, to communicate all that he envisions or discovers. But

    [7]Glenn, Maybelle and Spouse, Alfred. "Art Songs for School and Studio." Ditson, 1934, (quoted from "Introductory Teaching Procedure").

    [8]Wilson, Harry Robert. "Artistic Choral Singing." G. Schirmer, Inc., 1959, p. 38.

    [9]Howerton, George. "Technique and Style in Choral Singing." Carl Fischer, Inc., 1957, p. 112.

his struggle to convey some part of it is what makes, after all, master works of art."[10]

Part II — Elements of Interpretation

The various aesthetic, psychological, sociological, technical, musical, and practical elements entering into interpretation are so complex and far-reaching that many texts, essays, and articles have dealt with the subject without exhausting the content. It is the purpose of this course to cover briefly but clearly, in the combined Volume I and this volume, the principal factors involved. Content should prove a most helpful guide to effective interpretation and an excellent orientation for further study. Volume I deals primarily with the basic over-all aesthetic principles; discussion in this text covers chiefly the individual factors involved.

MOOD AND EMOTION

The underlying objective of music is the transfer of mood and emotion, the "feeling" of the song, in a manner as closely approximating the intent of the composer as can be determined. "Ultimately the significance of all music resides in its emotional content and meaning."[11] All textual and musical devices, all knowledge of style, theory, vocal and dramatic technics, principles of interpretation and stage presence, must be brought to bear in order to achieve this all-important goal. Song has the advantage over all other musical media in projecting mood since it not only works through the most flexibly responsive of all instruments, the human voice, but also has the further advantage of poetry and exact word meaning to amplify mood and emotional impact.

While striving to project emotion with maximum significance and beauty is the paramount objective, the young singer must beware of the pitfall of uncontrollable emotion and obvious exaggeration. Fine interpretation requires that *a song never be obviously interpreted or used as a means for technical display,* but that it appear a natural, spontaneous, and sincere projection of ideas and feelings concerned. *Sincerity is a necessary prerequisite for greatness in interpretation.*

While, on the whole, singing should be beautiful, the mission of the art song is not the making of pretty tones; rather it is the dramatic delivery of your emotional-intellectual-musical message as close to the composer's intent as can be determined. The great artist does not makes us conscious of his brush strokes; the master chef does not make us taste the ingredients. The singer should not make us aware of pretty tones or of any other display or technical factor to the detriment of over-all expression.

Controlled emotionalism is a great asset; undiscipline emotion can be carried to the extreme that it becomes overly sentimental, undignified, or even ridiculous. Uncontrolled emotions also frequently set up strong muscular interference, which result in unsteady tone of poor quality and increase the danger of lapse of memory. *Disciplined emotion is a powerful stimulant to highest artistic expression, but undisciplined emotion is at best dangerous and at worst disasterous.*

It is not enough for the singer to *feel* emotion; it must be *transmitted* to the listener as well. Principal factors involved in the transfer of emotion in song are: Sincerity; tonal shadings; clear diction and proper word accent; suitable dynamics, tempo, climax, and phrasing; facial expression, posture, gesture, and stage presence.

When singing a group of songs that are greatly varied in mood, a severe strain is placed upon the power of imagination to make the quick mood transitions required. In the short interval between songs, the interpreter has to make such abrupt changes as from passion to meditation, storm to calm, love to hate, joy to sadness, etc. Such transitions demand extreme mental concentration and flexibility that can be brought to the peak of perfection only through training and experience. No matter how beautiful the voice as an instrument, it will leave the hearer cold unless this challenge is met adequately. There can be no doubt that imaginative temperamental qualities are both inherited and developmental — singers can do nothing about the former but they can make the most of the latter.

Singing is a complete art, capable of expressing the full gamut of emotions common to the human race: Happiness, joy, exaltation, sorrow, despair, anger, hope, excitement, repose, peace, love, hate, fear, confidence, timidity, boldness, mystery, supplication, humor, tragedy, etc. *The wise teacher will classify songs also according to mood, assigning students songs in the process of study that will guarantee a variety of mood experience.* Four specific procedures for developing mood sensitivity in a particular song are:

1. Read the poem out loud dramatically. In situations where this might be embarrassing or interfere with the study of others, a substitute is to whisper the text as meaningfully as possible.

2. Carefully analyze the musical setting of the text — style, form, major and minor climaxes, appropriate tone color, interpretive markings, unique qualities and how best to obtain the basic aesthetic factors of interpretation — Unity, Variety, Proportion, and Dominance.

3. Vocalize through on the most appropriate vowel or neutral syllable to express the emotional

---

[10]Scofield, Ronald D. "Intermission." Music Editorial, Santa Barbara News Press, April 20, 1952.
[11]Mursell, James L. "Education for Musical Growth." Ginn & Co., 1948, p. 176.

content of the text; then sing the text with the same uniformity of tone color.

4. Encourage students to react freely through facial expression, posture, and gesture to the meaning and emotional quality of text and music. In this connection Greene emphasizes that "Mood and physical response are so interdependent that paradoxical as it may sound — the response can sometimes actually appear to initiate the mood."[12]

The able interpreter can relive in the imagination, and project vividly to an audience, any characterization encountered in the text in such a realistic manner that the listener, in turn, is induced to feel and think as do the characters projected. This is accomplished within the boundaries of good taste, musical integrity, and style of the period.

Several analytic approaches help in visualizing the qualities of a song as a prerequisite to expressive projection of mood and characterization. The singer first uses all available factual information as the basis for imaginative concept. The text and notation give a fundamental suggestive blueprint, but a great deal of detail will still come from the whole cloth of the singer's imagination. A useful device for pointing or directing the imagination into right channels is provided by answering questions concerning three factors: *environment, characterization* and *action.* Clarification of each idea follows.

1. *Environment — What are the setting, the situation, the surroundings and conditions in which we find the action and characters portrayed?* For example, in Schubert's "Die Erlkonig," (The Erlking), we are told that it is late on a stormy, windy night — a key to the dramatic mood and a fit setting for the feverish ride and the tragedy to follow.

2. *Characterization — Who are the actual, implied, or imaginary characters in the song, and what is their nature and feeling?* If no characterization is outlined by the text or it is only dimly implied, the singer imagines an appropriate type to accompany the ideas and feelings suggested in the text and music. For example, the characters indicated in "The Erlking" are the Father, whom we may picture as a large man with a deep soothing voice; the Child, small, frail, and feverishly ill; the Erlking, a sly, ugly and misshapen demon; and the Narrator, a sympathetic and deeply-moved person who tells the story. The singer identifies himself intimately with the feelings, actions, and manner of expression of each; he relives the song in the emotions of each character involved.

3. *Action — What are the activities of the characters, what do they think, what are their emotions and what do they do?* Again using the "Erlking" as an example, the Father is galloping furiously through the dark, stormy night with his son cradled gently but firmly in his arms. He rides in fear and

dread that home will not be reached in time to save his seriously ill child. He tries from time to time to calm the child's cries of fear which grow continuously more desperate, stating that the Erlking is trying to get him and carry him away. Deep underneath, the Father is not sure himself that the traditional demon is purely a figment of the sick boy's imagination. After the Child shrieks that the Erlking has him in his grasp, the Father clasps his son more tightly in his arms and rides even more desperately through the night to reach his destination. But when he reaches there, all is in vain, for the Child lies dead in his arms.

The Child is feverish, ill, and terrified by the ugly and sinister Erlking. He can see the demon at first lurking in the shadow and then plainly, although his father cannot; cries out with mounting fear and desperation for his father to protect him from the clutches of the demon; avoids at first the sly blandishments and promises of the Erlking but is finally seized brutally, overpowered and, in spite of his final despairing shriek of terror, carried away. (Carried away in the spirit, not the flesh.)

The Erlking slyly, silently, swiftly, and relentlessly follows the boy and the father, first approaching on one side and then on another, but revealing himself only to the child. He first tries to trick the boy into going with him by sly promises, but finally, when the boy is not fooled by his blandishments, reveals his true nature and seizes the child brutally in his grasp.

The Narrator lives and feels with all the characters, the Father, the Child and the Erlking, as each appears in the text. At the end the Narrator hastens the story with dread to the emotional climax, the final denouement, and grieves with the father over the tragic end.

The Father's voice is at first calm and reassuring, then it begins to show some alarm and, finally, dread and panic. Voice of the demon Erlking is at first slyly seductive, and finally cruelly harsh, as he snarls to the boy, "And willing or not, I'll take you by force." Voice of the Boy starts with tremulous fear and ends with a frantic cry of terror, "Erlking has me in his grasp." The Narrator starts in normal dramatic narrative tone but, on the last passage, his voice hastens and crescendos to the ending denouement with tragic portent. The slow ending phrase, "In his arms the child was dead," is breathed out in overwhelming grief.

Value to interpretive insight, mood, and characterization in the foregoing approach should be readily apparent. Schubert's "Erlkonig" was chosen because it furnishes an ideal vehicle for illustration of difficult characterizations and mood delineation. The

---

[12]Greene, Harry Plunkett. "Interpretation in Song." Macmillan Co., 1940, p. 16.

ordinary song is simple in comparison and would need only a small part of the imaginative treatment necessary in the complex "Erlkonig." The principles and implications are nevertheless the same; the song is created by the poet and composer, recreated by the singer, whose imagination supplies all appropriate details of characterization, feeling, environment, and action implied by the text and music, some of which may be pure phantasy, an idealized version on the part of the singer. In spite of the fact that the source of poetic and musical inspiration is the same for all singers, it is readily apparent that differences in interpretation are bound to arise in the details of an idealized version, that area where phantasy rather than fact predominates.

STYLE

"Interpretation involves two things, having something to say and knowing how to say it."[13] It is apparent that anyone with imagination and aggressiveness can and will have something to say in singing. The question is *how* and *what* he will say — and will it be worth hearing. To the discriminating listener, it will not be worth hearing unless it is an artistically refined and authentic expression of the song concerned.

The singer who can draw upon a rich cultural background imparts an intellectual understanding, an authenticity of style, and an emotional sympathy in his interpretations, which could never exist if study and background were restricted solely to the limitations of text and musical score. One needs to know about the life of the composer, the motives behind his composition, and particularly, the aesthetic style characteristics and influence of the age or period. It is the business of the well-rounded singer to understand the style characteristics of the Renaissance, Classic, Baroque, Romantic, Impressionistic, and Modern periods; to recognize in which period and style the particular song is written, and to interpret accordingly. The versatile singer masters all styles. If he is wise, however, he will avoid singing publicly any song that is too far removed stylistically from his understanding, or unsuited to his technic.

Originality or uniqueness of individual style is desirable only so long as it remains within the boundaries of good taste and traditional style. A Classic or Baroque song will not be sung with the same style and type of tone as the Romantic period German Lieder. An oratorio aria is not sung with the emotional abandon and dramatic excesses suitable to the operatic aria. In truth, secure knowledge of appropriate style clears away the clouds in order that the sun of interpretation can shine through.

The serious vocal student cannot afford to be narrow in his interest, neglecting familiarity with orchestral music, poetry, drama, art, and the dance. The more sensitive and understanding he is to other forms of art, the more sensitive and understanding his taste as a singer. Attendance at concerts, vocal or instrumental, should be considered not only a pleasure but also a necessity for maximum musical growth. *The best approach to understanding style is through extensive listening to great artists in concert and on records.*

Each period and school of composition has an unique style of singing best suited for its artistic interpretation. Knowledge is gained primarily by studying a number of songs of each period or school, and by hearing them sung by those who understand the style. Not only does each school of song have its individual style, but the three major types of songs (Lyric, Dramatic, and Florid) also demand a specific style of singing. Other minor song styles are Recitative, and Diction or "Patter." In addition, the period to which the song belongs induces its own unique modification.

Knowledge of appropriate style is a prerequisite for each song before determining additional details of expression. It is always a prime consideration in preliminary analysis. The first observation in taking up a new song or aria is to note the composer, the school of composition, and the style period. Then from previous study, or study at the time, listening, and knowledge of the style characteristics involved, the student is prepared to work out the remainder of the interpretation intelligently.

Some songs, especially shorter compositions, and many songs of the Classic Period, retain one prevailing style — lyric, dramatic, or florid — from beginning to end. Others, usually the songs of the Romantic and Modern periods, change these styles for different sections or even for contrasting short parts. A key to when change is appropriate normally will be found in either or both the text and notations in the score.

Although a composer's work is usually a product of his historical style period, it also may have stylistic features in details unique to the particular composer. The singer needs to know the featuers of this uniqueness and emphasize them in interpretation in order that the full flavor of the composition be revealed.

From one standpoint of production, there are only two general styles, *Legato* (or smooth) and *Accented* (staccato or marcato). Staccato means "detached lightly" and marcato, "strongly accented" or "punched-out" music. Legato singing requires that stress be on natural inflection and accent of the text with smooth connection between all intervals. It demands minimizing the feeling of pulse, flexibility of tempo, and reduction of strength in normal metric accent. Marcato involves a pronounced increase of pulse; staccato requires short and sharp accent with the effect of a rest after each note.

---

[13]Clippinger, D. A. "The Clippinger Class Method of Voice Culture." Ditson, 1933, p. 48.

Timing of ending consonants is a vital factor in style. In legato, maixmum length is given to the vowel, with ending consonants of words or syllables delayed until the beginning beat of the next word or syllable (delayed articulation). In staccato on the other hand, dipthongs and ending consonants are deliberately anticipated to give time for the rest effect which is required after each note. Legato also often is accompanied by rubato tempo.

With a thorough knowledge of the various factors which determine style, together with a deep insight into the meaning of the text, the singer is equipped to gaze into the Infinite, to commune with the master composer, and recreate the song in an authentic, emotionally-moving fashion. Great interpretation always conforms to this mold. The following discussion will suffice to describe briefly, and suggest expressive demands of, the principal styles in singing.

1. *Song Styles*:

(a) *Lyric Bel Canto* — This style is basic to the singer's technic since it is employed in the interpretation of all or parts of most songs. It emphasizes smooth legato connection between intervals; sustained and easy flow of tone; employs only the soft and moderate dynamic levels; leans somewhat toward the "bright" side of tone color; emphasizes vowel clarity and finesse in phrasing and diction. According to Grove's dictionary, a lyric legato style always is presumed in singing unless the text and notation in the music score indicate the contrary. In order to sing lyric-legato style, the vocal line will be "fine spun" and light in texture, e.g., baritone and basses imagine the free, light quality of a lyric tenor, altos and mezzos the texture of a lyric soprano. Almost all of the Old Italian, Old English, and Classic Period songs are of this type.

(b) *Dramatic and Declamatory* — This style requires wide variation of tonal color, dynamics, and tempo for descriptive reality, employs in general the medium and upper range of dynamics, strong word emphasis, and a darker and more sonorous tone. Much of operatic singing and a great number of German Lieder demand dramatic style.

(c) *Florid and Coloratura* — This style requires an agile voice capable of rapid scale or arpeggio movement in either legato or staccato passages. Dynamics and sonority are never great, tonal color is usually the same as for Lyric Bel Canto, and the voice is treated instrumentally, words being sparse and used as the vehicle for tone. Some of the songs of the Baroque Period and parts of most oratorio arias are of Florid style. Soprano arias in the Italian and French operas also are frequently in this style.

(d) *Recitative* — This style gives emphasis to the qualities of declamatory speech rather than the legato singing approach. It is characterized by great freedom on the part of the singer in choice of rhythm and accent to emphasize word meaning. In "Free Recitative," singing is either *a cappella* or the accompaniment is so simple and rhythmically static that the singer can give any rhythm value desired to any particular word or syllable. In "Strict Recitative" the declamatory word emphasis is retained, and a limited amount of rhythmic flexibility is expected *so long as it conforms to the rhythmic and harmonic changes in the accompaniment.* Recitative Style is found most often in oratorio and opera singing. Most arias open with a recitative passage and some even close with one. (Note — See also Chapter 11, "Recitative," p. 91)

(e) *Diction or "Patter"* — The Germans have a word, "Sprechstimme" (half speech and half song), for this style for which there is no English equivalent. It is usually taken in very quick tempo in a kind of "patter-talking" manner. A number of encore songs that feature a loquacious, conversational word content should be sung in this style. No more perfect examples of the style can be found than in the numerous Gilbert and Sullivan comic opera "Patter Songs." The comic operas of Mozart and others also have excellent examples. No better means for learning rapid and precise articulation can be found than through the study and mastery of such songs.

*2. *Historical Period Styles*:

"To understand music as we have it today, it is necessary to know something of the forces which have shaped and conditioned the various epochs of its growth. Music reflects the temper of the time that gives it birth and has a definite relationship to the political, economic and cultural conditions that surround its composers and practitioners."[14]

(a) *Renaissance*, 1425-1600 (Morley, Byrd, Lassus).

As will be noted, there are so few composers of this time whose songs are sung by solo voice in concert that we can practically ignore the period as a necessary background. In general, any songs found are sung in Lyric Legato style.

(b) *Baroque*, 1600-1750 (Monteverde, A. Scarlatti, Carissimi, Caccini, Legrenzi, Cavalli, Lotti, Caldara, Stradella, Durante, Giordani, Pergolesi, Dowland, Campion, Purcell, J. S. Bach, Handel, Rameau and many others).

---

*Dates of the following periods are approximate, corresponding in general to those listed in most music history texts. There is, of course, considerable overlapping of styles between periods.

[14]McKinny, Howard D. and Anderson, W. R., "Music in History." American Book Co., 1940, p. vi.

The Baroque Period style is characterized by widespread use of embellishment and ornamentation; steady and decisive rhythmic movement with only slight changes of tempo from the first note to the ending cadence of each part; impressive dignity; only moderate metric accent and quite limited use of crescendo and diminuendo in the phrase. Contrasts are between rather than within, sections. Ritardandos are normally appropriate only at the ends of sections and at the end, should not be too emphasized, but rather have the effect of a slight broadening to underline the cadential effect of the harmony. Dynamics are in the intermediate range from *p* to *f* with a real *pp* or *ff* seldom appropriate.

There is usually only a simple text with only one idea repeated often in a section. Change of mood is therefore infrequent and uncomplicated. Emphasis is on clarity of vowel and word projection in the Bel Canto singing style, with an instrumental-like impersonal, rather than an individual, emotional expression characteristic of later Romanticism.

Actually, two abilities are required in order to sing all the literature of the period: a severe, plain, legato style for slower moving music and a light, florid style for the faster and more complex music, which is usually high in range and rich in embellishment. The latter music is confined today largely to the repertoire of sopranos.

(c) *Classic,* 1750-1825 (Haydn, Mozart, Gluck, C. P. E. Bach, J. C. Bach, Beethoven).

Classic style is usually covered by what is known as the traditional lyric "Bel-Canto" technic. In order to interpret Classic music in good taste, it is necessary to understand the aesthetic objectives which were considered most important in this period, not only in music but also in all other arts and the ballroom dance. In the time of Haydn and Mozart, artistic emphasis was on form, perfection in design, grace, simplicity, and emotional restraint. The flamboyant, overly ornate, exaggerated, highly emotional and unconventional were considered in poor taste and vulgar.

Classic music and art were governed to a great extent by rules, formulae, conventional design and expression. Proper musical interpretation demands intimacy, elegance, the light, delicate "touch" with avoidance of emotionalism, the highly dramatic, strong dynamics, rich sonorities, and extreme or sudden changes in tempo or tone color.

Sentiment is *personal,* rather than impersonal as in the Baroque Period. Pompous formality, impressive dignity, and showy emotionalism are entirely out of place. While it is necessary that meter and tempo be precise and crisp, they should have less weight on normal accent than in Baroque music. Somewhat more tempo and dynamic elasticity within the phrase and section is appropriate, however, but never carries to the extreme of the Romantic style. Much emphasis is on prominence of the melodic line in the harmonic scheme, with Bel Canto technic employed almost exclusively. While long crescendos and diminuendos are employed, they are only moderate in degree of variation.

The main characteristics peculiar to the few composers of the Classic period are simplicity and clarity of form, depth of restrained feeling, suave serenity, and graceful flowing melodies. Actually, *all dynamics in printed scores of both the Classic and Baroque periods may well be graded downward, a forte meaning no more than a mf in later periods.* Unfortunately, very little dependence can be placed on today's editions of music composed previous to the nineteenth century, since many expression marks have been added by editors who vary greatly in their taste and musical judgment.

It is well also to keep in mind that Baroque and Classic music were conceived more instrumentally than songs of later periods, and must therefore emphasize the instrumental qualities of clear tone, careful phrasing and exactness in intonation, rhythm, and technical control. The voice is often treated as a flexible instrument, with the text furnishing a suitable vehicle to develop musical objectives. *Tone color and mood are comparatively static, being suitably varied to a limited degree only, while tempos are kept steady except for a broadening at the final cadence of a section.* Tempo changes, like in the Baroque period, are mostly between, and not within, sections. Singing is free, unaffected, tranquil (never theatrical), graceful and reflects the finesse in phrasing so characteristic of the Italian Bel Canto style. "It should be at once calm, elegant, correct, and expressive, yet without coldness and heaviness."[15]

(d) *Romantic,* 1800-1875 (Schubert, Schumann, Mendelssohn, Lowe, Brahms, Rossini, Donizetti, Bellini, Verdi, Grieg, Moussorgsky, Tschaikovsky, Sibelius, Wolf, Mahler, Berlioz, Faure, Debussy, Ravel, Puccini, Strauss and others).

The flowering of poetry and emphasis on romance quite naturally made the nineteenth century the "Century of Song." With the songs of Schubert, stimulated by the romantic poetry of the age, came a new aesthetic philosophy and style in song writing. The composer follows the thought of the poet line by line, adapting the music to changing mood and meaning. Music now be-

---

[15]Parisotti, Allessandro. "Anthology of Italian Song." G. Schirmer, Inc., 1894, Introduction.

comes primarily a vehicle for making the words significant, rather than the opposite philosophy which normally characterized the Classic period. Not only was the new "Thorough Composed" philosophy of song writing the first important innovation of the nineteenth century, but it also has wielded predominant influence in song composition down to the present day.

Objective of Romantic vocal music is to depict mood suggested by the text faithfully and intensely through all available technical, emotional, and musical means. This demands particularly intelligent analysis of the lyrics and their musical setting, with maximum use of the imagination and all vocal and stage resources to project mood with emotional fervor. There are, of course, still limits of good taste in emotionalism beyond which interpretation becomes cheaply theatrical, but these limits have become greatly extended over boundaries permitted in Classical style.

Songs of Romantic character demand not only active imagination and sensitive feeling but also sufficient technic to color tone expressively in a wide variety of moods, and to make extensive tempo and dynamic changes rapidly and smoothly. In the main, songs of this period do not place as great a demand upon agility and delicate finesse in phrasing and other instrumental-like qualities as do songs of the Classic era. Fortunately, nearly all the great composers in the Romantic Period have given us highly suitable songs easy enough for young voices.

There are many Romantic songs which demand both dramatic and lyric style for effective rendition. There is a wealth of literature also in which only lyric or only dramatic style is featured. *As a rule the period demands a warmer, darker and more sonorous tone quality; more varied dynamics and tempo; stronger climaxes; greater force on accents and portamentos* and involves wider melodic interval leaps, chromanticism, stressed consonants and more frequent harmonic modulation than do songs of the past. Some require an extensive range, very wide command of tonal color, strength and endurance of tone, and an actor's technic in dramatic utterance.

Emotionalism is king in the Romantic Period and all interpretative devices are utilized to achieve it. Syncopation, rubato tempo, ritardandos, accelerandos, extreme tempo changes and fermati are common, although the vitality of the onward flow of the beat pulsation should be maintained. Tremendous climaxes with a number of minor climaxes, and great range of dynamics from *pppp-ffff* both between and within sections, are characteristic. Extreme and subjective personal expression, strong accent emphasis, and great changes of tonal color are often

required to delineate word meaning and the intense mood demanded. Basic stylistic changes from legato to accented or marcato may be frequent and closely allied with the numerous ideas and emotions expresed in the text. The German Lieder and the French Impressionistic schools of song make this period the richest of all history in fine song literature.

There is a tremendous difference between Baroque style of the Bach and Handel period, and later Romantic composers, in philosophy of emotional expression. The former is impersonally objective, the latter personally subjective. "Tragedy is expressed by Bach with quiet resignation, in uncomplaining acceptance and patient submission. With the Romanticist, tragedy often calls forth the expression of violent emotional upheaval, the experience of an intensely personal and bitter grief."[16]

(e) *Modern and Contemporary*, 1875-to the present (Bacon, Barber, Bartók, Bax, Berger, Britten, Campbell-Tipton, Carpenter, Charles, Creston, Diamond, Dougherty, Finzi, Gibbs, Griffes, Hageman, R. Harris, Hindemith, Huhn, La Forge, Loefler, Menotti, Milhaud, Schonberg, Scott, Shaw, Speaks, Stickles, Stravinsky, V. Thompson, Treharne, W. Schumann, Walton, Warlock, J. Wolfe, Vaughan Williams and many others).

There is no agreement about what is meant by the term "Modern Music." Some accept all contemporary music as modern when, in fact, most of it is Romantic in style. Others insist that modern music and modern style only signifies music that is distinctly different from either the Classic or Romantic idioms. It is, they say, music that goes farther in exploring dissonant harmonies, new scale forms, unique texts and melodic progressions, irregular and shifting meters and new tonal combinations. We shall accept this latter definition for the term and "Contemporary Music" as all the remaining literature written during the period. Although contemporary song writers have produced examples of all types of style, most songs written and sung, especially those suitable to the immature student, still follow the Romantic idiom. The ultra-modern dissonant song is too difficult melodically, and from the standpoint of intonation, for any except the rare student and the more mature musician.

The "Modern Song" is characterized by much experimentation and a number of cults of expression such as "Impressionism," "Nationalism," "Neo-Classicism," "Realism," "Futurism," and "Mechanism." No one summary therefore can

---

[16]Howerton, George. "Technic and Style in Choral Singing." Carl Fischer, Inc., 1957, p. 161.

describe accurately all shifting styles of the period. In general, the following trends are characteristic:

(1). *Meter and Tempo — Strongly reitterant* and insistent rhythms and emphasis on vigorous motion for the love of motion.

(2). *Dynamic Scheme —* Emphasis on the upper dynamic levels intensified by reiterated percussive and dissonant accentuation; multitudinous devices employed to obtain variety.

(3). *Emotional Expressiveness and Structure —* Intense personal emotionalism of the Romantic Period is often replaced by intellectual objectivism. A tremendous experimental variety is evident; melodies are generally more angular and less obvious than previous periods. Accompanying harmonies and counterpoint explore all possible dissonances in a contrasting rhythm to the vocal line. These characteristics require a better ear and musicianship on the part of the singer in order to maintain accurate intonation and convincing phrasing.

3. *Schools of Song Style:*

(a) *Old Italian —* Almost exclusively lyric "Bel Canto" style with very few exceptions in Florid Style especially suitable to sopranos.

(b) *Old English —* Generally very similar to Old Italian in Lyric Legato style. Requires much emphasis on finesse in phrasing, clarity on the vowel, and precision in articulating consonants. The unique flavor of the Old English song is difficult to describe and had best be absorbed through listening to outstanding interpreters.

(c) *German Lieder —* Usually considered the most musically rewarding and most extensive source of really fine song literature. Songs are in the Romantic idiom, often dramatic in style and exacting in their demand for rich, sonorous tone and ability to sing long phrases. However, much of the literature is within the capability of the average student after some background study.

(d) *French Impressionistic —* Usually descriptive and Quasi-Romantic in Style. The French Impressionistic song is usually not so dramatic, however, requires more delicate finesse and pianissimo, uses Bel Canto lyric legato technic, and emphasizes a more suave nasal tonal quality than does German Lieder. It needs great delicacy and finesse in phrasing.

Meter and tempo are often characterized by a flexible, "floating," ephemeral indefiniteness in motion. Accentuation is delicate and sometimes even omitted on normally-accented pulses. Lower dynamic range is featured with a force louder than *f* very rare. Gradual, rather than sudden changes are more common, while ascending melodic lines sometimes require diminuendo rather than the normal crescendo.

Emotional expressiveness is characterized by reserve, restraint, and delicacy of statement. Like the Classic song, no sudden contrasts of dynamics, tempo, tone color, style, or mood normally are appropriate. Accompanying harmony consistently and delicately supports the mood which is often ephemeral, mystic, mildly descriptive, rich in subdued color effects and at times dissonant, but not consistently. Melodic line usually is lovely but not obvious or hackneyed. Tone color avoids the extreme darkness and dramatic warmth often required in the German Lieder and other Romantic songs, featuring rather the lighter translucent, cooler pastel shades, with characteristic nasality of the French language on certain vowels and syllables.

(e) *Russian —* Romantic in character. Very similar to German Lieder in dramatic vocal requirement and emphasis on strength of the consonant in articulation.

(f) *Scandanavian —* Romantic in character. Does not usually require as dark a tone or as extensive volume as the German Lieder.

(g) *Spanish and Latin American —* Romantic in character. Usually requires considerable emphasis on the insistent rhythmic qualities of the score but melodies are usually lyric in style.

(h) *Opera —* Usually dramatic in style but employs as well all other styles at times for maximum variety and effect. Heroic dramatics are painted with a bold brush, while little or no emotional reserve is characteristic. Principal operatic roles require a voice of etxensive range, power, and expressive tonal control as well as the possession of dramatic acting ability. The German Wagnerian operas require an unusually robust, heroic, and sturdy vocal instrument to withstand the heavy orchestration and long periods of dramatic singing wtihout rest.

(i) *Oratorio and Sacred Cantatas —* Quite antithetical to opera style, exercising considerable dramatic restraint and featuring lyric legato style more. Many of the more florid arias demand vocal agility of a high order as well as the ability to sing unusually long phrases on one breath. Tone quality needs to be somewhat richer, warmer, and more robust than the lyric or florid style songs of the Baroque or Classic periods. Profound sacred texts require beautiful, pure, noble tone with lofty interpretive concepts and perfection of finesse in the singer's art-unsurpassed, if indeed equaled, in any type or school of singing.

Although dramtic in the highest sense, the religious oratorio must be sung by chorus and soloist with reverent nobility of sentiment, reserved dignity, repose, and intense spiritual devotion. *The audience should be stimulated to pray rather than to applaud.* Because of its religious character, the oratorio, more than any other type of music, has certain traditional tempos and interpretation for each particular aria. The well-equipped singer must be acquainted with and guided by these traditions, but certainly should not feel bound to them in all details. Tradition is a valuable guide but must not be allowed to be a slave driver, stifling appropriate individualistic expression of truth and beauty.

(j) *Folk Songs* — Normally employ simple legato or narrative style.

(k) *Ballads* — Narrative in character and are usually more dramatic than the simple folk song.

(l) *Sacred Songs* — Employ lyric legato style in the main with a warm, rich tone similar to the quieter German Lieder. Recitative and declamatory dramatic passages are not uncommon, however.

(m) *Humorous Encores* — Normally employ the Narrative style but some feature the fast tempo "Patter" song idiom.

PHRASING

1. *Over-all Considerations.*

A well-considered interpretation is often an involved process, requiring preliminary consideration of style and careful study of text and music, followed by part-by-part attention to each phrase as it fits into the over-all complex. The over-all aesthetic fatcors involved in interpretation — Unity, Variety, Proportion, and Dominance — depend upon what is done in phrasing.

Unity demands that each phrase fit into a balanced structure in relation to the whole structure, the principal climax, and the minor climaxes. "Lack of awareness of the form and design of a composition will give a vague and often distorted interpretation. It will lack unity of expression."[17] Dominance requires that we never emphasize detail at the expense of the main idea and the principal climax. In order to obtain Unity and Dominance, the performer must recall at the very beginning the position and force of the climatic phrase and the relation of all subsidiary parts and phrases that lead up to it. When this type of artistic phrasing is accomplished, music has Unity, Variety, Proportion, and Dominance, a cohesive logic as if the interpretation were an inevitable unfoldment.

The musical phrase is somewhat like the surge and recession of an ocean wave on a smooth, sandy beach. It has *shape* and *life;* it must go somewhere and say something. Unless otherwise directed, *an ascending melodic phrase line normally is accompanied by crescendo and a falling line by a decre-*

scendo, the degree being relative to climactic position in the composition. Monotony results if this law is followed too slavishly, however. In rare instances there are exceptional phrases, especially in French Impressionistic songs, where the ascending phrase should be progressively softened. Fortunately, the score almost inevitably indicates any deviation from normalcy desired by the composer.

Most phrases ascend and then descend with a smooth, surging flow and ebb of tonal dynamics, often accompanied by a slight accelerando and ritardando as well, when suitable to the period style. This smooth sweep or "shape" of the phrase is a paramount consideration in expression; fragmentary, halting, note-by-note progression is a sign of the amateur and the unsure performer.

Audience comprehension of meaning and mood is of prime importance. Musically, in fine phrasing, there needs to be proper tonal color, style, dynamics and tempo; textually, it is necessary that articulation be clear, vowels pure, and the proper words given the right amount of accent. "Group the words together to give them a sense of meaning. Not all words or all syllables are equally important, so distribute the weight and create dynamics which give meaning to what you sing. A phrase not only moves up to important syllables and words but to important places in the music. Usually a phrase is shaped like an arch, but the exact shape depends upon meaning."[18]

2. *Textual or Musical Dominance?*

In case of conflict, which should prevail, natural phrasing of the text as in speech, or the musical phrase? Fortunately, this problem rarely, if ever, occurs in well-integrated compositions of most great song writers. It does occur, however, more frequently in translations. While a musical phrase is analogous to the sentence in literature and usually conforms, there are exceptions at times when musical structure obviously and appropriately demands different treatment from the standpoint of taking breath. *When the sentence and musical phrase do not coincide, the intent of the composer,* if it can be determined, *normally should be followed.* Intent is usually indicated by a slur line over the vocal or piano score or by the harmonic cadence. When no clear indication is present, as is the case at times, it is up to the judgment of the singer to determine whether text or music supersedes. In general, if legato style is highly important, the musical phrase should predominate; if the song is dramatic in style and the words highly significant at the time, they ought to be given preference in the phrasing.

---

[17]Wodell, F. W. "Choir and Chorus Conducting." Theo. Presser, 1919, p. 72.
[18]German, Francis. "What a Judge Has Learned at Contests." Music Educators Journal, Sept.-Oct., 1952, p. 34.

3. *Phrasing and Breath Control.*

Many successful vocal teachers subscribe to the belief that the best way to develop breath control is through assigning songs which demand progressively greater and greater length of phrase. For example, Coleman maintains that the amount of breath "Must be prompted emotionally by the phrase which is to be sung with that breath" . . . . and that the phrase really begins "Not with the first note but with the intake of breath before the note."[19] Clark supports this view, "Know what you are going to say and the breath will not fail."[20] "Therefore, if the singer is preoccupied with the thought of his song he will breathe in a manner that is appropriate to its expression."[21]

4. *Length of Phrase.* (See also p. 38, "The Catch Breath")

There is a tendency to chop up long phrases in legato songs into small fragments because of weak or lazy breath support. On the other hand, some singers appear to think that all phrases should be as long as possible when, actually, *it is no more desirable to sing all long phrases than it is to use all long sentences in writing.* There is monotony in either; artistic contrast is desirable. In general, it is desirable that *long phrases predominate in lyric legato style songs, while short phrases are more the rule in a dramatic agitated mood.*

Beauty and charm of legato music in particular depends on length and finesse in phrasing. The Old Italian and the Old English songs are especially fine literature for initial training in artistic phrasing.

Many vocal authorities emphasize that the key to phrasing choral music is found in the normal nuance and accentuation of the text as it would be discovered through expressive dramatic reading. The artistic scheme which fits the student's breath control at the time needs to be determined at the very beginning of song study and, together with the ideal phrasing for future reference, marked in the score and routined by practice. When this is done the singer is always aware of breath demands *before* inhalation. Unless phrases are marked in the beginning, phrasing will be haphazard and incorrect habits will be formed that are difficult to break later on. It is suggested that the ideal phrase be marked with an apostrophe, **,** , at the end, and in especially long phrases where a catch-breath might be needed, that an apostrophe with a circle be used, ⊙ .

Breaking the ideal phrase by use of the catch-breath never is to be encouraged; it is advised only for those having inadequate technic at the time. It is preferable to avoid such songs until **breath support** develops. Correction in any case should come as soon as possible. In this connection it is well to emphasize that a comma in the text doesn't neces-

sarily mean that breath should be taken there as we have heard some students declare; it is only a punctuation, a place where breath is taken only when aesthetically desirable, or where it *may* be taken if short on breath supply. If the student cannot take breath in performance as rapidly as some of the phrases may demand, he is advised never to sacrifice the onward flow of tempo for the sake of taking time to breathe, if some of the rhythmic length of the last note of a phrase can be forfeited to supply more time to inhale adequately for the succeeding phrase. This is the better choice of two evils.

A combination of two phrases on one breath will never be attempted merely for the sake of displaying technic. Carry-over or joining of two phrases is a matter deserving study and discreet use by the singer. *Once in a song is enough.* A suitable opportunity for carry-over sometimes occurs in the linking of the last verse with the beginning phrase of the chorus in A B Song Form, and the last phrase of the B section with the first phrase of the return of the A section in A B A Song Form. When the two phrases concerned in the aforementioned instances are too taxing on breath control, it may be desirable to take a catch-breath in the course of the first phrase if it results in a better artistic effect. Carry-over generally is more effective when it follows ritardando at the end of a phrase, to be carried over with an immediate return to indicated tempo on the following phrase. *Its most common use and most appropriate effect seem to be when associated with the last return of the first section or theme.*

TONE COLOR

(Note — See also Chapter 5, Lesson 2, of both this text and Expressive Singing, Volume I for further discussion.)

Emotion in singing is expressed chiefly through tone color variation, i.e., modification of the vowel color or quality. Kirkland states, "Change in the nature of emotion makes itself evident not through *crescendo* and *diminuendo*, *forte* and *piano*, as some, judging from their singing, would have us believe, but through various combinations of Quality and Color of voice."[22] Change in tempo, extent of dynamics, pitch, rate of vibrato, etc., have, it is true, secondary effect. A singer who has one standard tonal color that is used for all songs — whether it be a joyful expression of ecstatic love or a funeral dirge — can give only a mechanical, instrumental-like interpretation, unlikely to thrill an audience, no mat-

[19]Coleman, Henry. "The Amateur Choir Trainer." Oxford U. Press, 1932, p. 34.
[20]Clark, Wallace R. "Breathing." Etude, 1930, Vol. 48, p. 506.
[21]Fields, Op. cit., p. 79.
[22]Kirkland, H. S. "Expression in Singing." Richard G. Badger, 1916, p. 82.

ter how excellent all other technical and interpretive factors.

It is basic to good expression that color in tone be suited primarily to over-all mood and style and secondarily, to the word, phrase, and section of the song. The expressive voice is capable of freely producing a wide range of tonal color from bright to dark. It is as important a resource for a singer to use various shades of tone in interpreting songs as it is for the painter to have at his command the full range of the color chart. It is not enough for the singer or painter to have all shades of color available, however; *they must have the even more important artistic sensitivity to select just the right shade at the right place.* When the singer is able on a phrase, even on a single note, to express any divergent sentiment such as joy-sorrow, passion-apathy, love-hatred, dignity-frivolity, longing-indifference, tragedy-humor, he truly can move the listener to the core of his being. Then and only then is the singer a real artist.

All songs require an appropriate tone color to best express their general mood. They require also contrasting shades of color in places to add needed variety and to express the text most significantly. The greatest voices of all time have two outstanding characteristics which set them apart — ability to sing with utmost perfection in legato and with infinite variety and intuitive taste in tonal color. Degree of excellence in these two factors is undoubtedly the major determinant between the great and the near great.

DYNAMICS

In general, soft dynamics give an emotional effect of peace and calm; loud intensities produce excitement and turbulence in the emotions. Dynamics is one of the four factors, Tempo, Tone Color, Style, and Dynamics, which may be changed to achieve Variety in interpretation. *When a text consists of more than one printed stanza, a different dynamics is needed for successive stanzas unless monotony is desired.* In order to save space, a number of different verses often are printed on one page with only one dynamic scheme indicated. Obviously, such an indication can be only a generality, possibly suited to one verse only — usually the first verse. It is the responsibility of the interpreter in this case to analyze the text and decide a suitably artistic and varied scheme for each verse.

General degree of force calculated to give the most satisfactory interpretation is usually indicated in the score by the composer, arranger, or editor. Dynamics chosen by the latter two may or may not exhibit excellent musical judgment in every instance. It is also a well-known fact that many composers, including the most careful and meticulous Brahms, often changed their minds about both dynamic and

tempo markings after the music was printed and they heard it performed. It is safe to assume, however, that great composers would not wish later on to change radically — a *p* might better become a *mp* or a *pp* but seldom, if ever, a *mf* or a *ppp*.

In most instances, listed *dynamic marks are useful guides and should not be changed unless a sound aesthetic or practical reason can be given for doing so.* In addition to the printed dynamic marks there are many small variations of force not marked, the observance or neglect of which means the difference between good and mediocre performance.

Some of the most common and distressing faults of singers in handling dynamics are:

1. The habit of singing pianissimo phrases at a slower tempo than preceding phrases, a tendency which usually has a devitalizing effect upon interpretation.
2. Very little expressive variation of dynamics within a song or between songs.
3. Violent or sudden changes of dynamics with little *mf* as a norm and no smooth crescendo-descrescendo effects.
4. Inappropriate decrescendo of long phrases and breath exhaustion near the end.
5. Monotonous "punching-out" of accent without reference to style or word significance.
6. Habitually loud singing on high notes and devitalized, breathy tone on low.
7. The habit of singing loud or a little louder, with consequent loss of the value of soft singing for contrast and in the building up of effective climaxes. (On the whole, most concert singers fail to anywhere nearly approach realization of the degree of vital pianissimo of which they are capable.)
8. Habitual crescendo-decrescendo on all long notes and phrases without regard to a more suitable dynamic treatment for some.

A sustained tone needs development or it becomes monotonous. Even a short note should have adequate breath support and some tonal development. A *gradual* change of both dynamics and of tonal color often is needed for best effect. There is an old adage in music, "Do something with a long tone." The Old Italians believed this so thoroughly that Henderson reports their philosophy to be that "A true artist avails himself of the *messa di voce* (crescendo-diminuendo) on every tone."[23] This dynamic treatment would give "life" to each tone but it is patently incorrect when applied to all tones for all desired emotional effects. The following dynamic treatment of sustained tones produces the emotional effect described:

---

[23]Henderson, W. J. "The Art of Singing." Dial Press, 1938, Revised Edition, p. 104.

1. ———————— (*cresc.*)= Excitement and climax, emotional tension.

2. ———————— (*dim.*) = Rest, peace, emotional release.

3. ———————— (*messa di voce*) = Alternate effect of emotional tension and release. Two or three of such waves of dynamics are often appropriate and thrilling on *fermata* or long, sustained final tones.

In addition the *sfz*, the *fp* and other types of accents vary the emotional effect on the tone.

CLIMAX AND DYNAMICS

(*See also Chapter 9. "Extending Dynamics," p. 85*)

The two types of climax, dynamic and emotional, are achieved at the same time in most songs. Exceptions occur occasionally, however, and must be recognized if the highest artistry in expression is to be achieved. For example, the dynamic climax in Schubert's "Erlking" comes near the end when the boy shrieks, "Erlkonig hat mir in seinem Hand" (Erlking has me in his grasp), while the emotional climax comes on the very last phrase *pianissimo*, "In seinem armen das Kind war tot" (In his arms the child was dead). It is evident in this, as in some other instances, that *pianissimo* can achieve as effective an emotional climax at times as can a *fortissimo*.

A *fortissimo* climax is frequently the danger point, straining technic of the singer and spoiling the finish of an otherwise fine interpretation. It is vital to good interpretation that *fortissimo never be louder than can be sustained with good vocal quality and sure intonation.* "The secret in obtaining a good *fortissimo* climax lies not in striving to obtain a louder tone, but rather in obtaining a softer tone *before* the climax."[24] "A tone attacked *fortissimo* should always be the loudest, if it cannot be maintained, at the release. In this connection, it might be well to emphasize that a *crescendo* cannot be obtained from a fortissimo."[25] This is a truism which many singers fail to understand. It is well also to remember the often-quoted comment of the famous conductor, Hans Von Bulow, "*Crescendo* means piano; *diminuendo* means *forte*." By this he meant that *normally we begin crescendos softly and diminuendos with sturdy tone.*

In order to organize the comparative dynamic levels of sub-climaxes, and the total dynamic relationship of the various parts of a composition, so that singers realize fully the dramatic and musical effect toward which they are progressing, *it is strongly recommended that the major climax first be determined and then work backwards to relate all parts accordingly.* Dynamic climaxes are obtained very largely by a skillful development of tonal intensity, although height of pitch, climax of meaning in the text, and force of articulation on key words are important contributing factors. Regardless of dynamics written, *it is always wise to set the major dynamic climax as no louder than can be produced safely.* Other minor climaxes must be adjusted downward accordingly, remembering that "Mountains only appear high in comparison with the lower ground around them."[26] The singer always should work for ease of production, meaningful text, and expressive tone color, keeping in mind that great loudness is seldom necessary and may even be inappropriate to artistic expression.

While it is often appropriate to both crescendo and accelerando toward a climax, it is not necessarily so. All depends on the emotional effect desired. A well-graduated crescendo held at a steady pace, or perhaps even broadened, has a noble and grand effect. On the other hand, when accelerando accompanies crescendo, the effect is exciting and exhilarating. *Broad ritardandos normally are reserved for closing cadences where the effect of finality is most suitable.*

Even if aesthetically undesirable, it may be necessary for the singer with inadequate dynamic control to disregard some dynamic markings in favor of technical limitations. This action is unfortunate but preferable to tense "shrieky" tone, breathy devitalization, or poor intonation, which result when vocalists press dynamics beyond their ability to control. Even the great Caruso was forced to compromise in the high register and is famous, or infamous, whichever way we look at it, for reversing intensity, ringing out high tones with a tremendously beautiful *fortissimo* even when marked *piano*.

In any case *dynamics in music, insofar as they relate to effective expression and climax, are a matter of contrast*, varying with the intensity range limitations of each singer. Krone says, "A given degree of loudness will sound *forte* if it follows a *pp* but only *mf* if it follows *fff*."[27]

The objective is always to obtain appropriate and significant contrasts and to avoid the weakening effect of anticipating the major climax, or of having too many dynamic climaxes. *One major climax is enough in all short songs.* Even in long arias, one dynamic climax should be selected as the major climax and no other should be allowed to quite equal it in force. It sometimes helps the singer to mark successive sub-climatic waves of tonal force working up to a major climax with numbers, 1, 2, 3, etc., expressing relative degrees of desired intensity and

[24]Christy, Van. A. "Glee Club and Chorus." G. Schirmer, Inc., 1940, p. 56.

[25]Jones, Archie N. "The Basis of Choral Interpretation." The Supervisors Service Bulletin, Jan. 1932.

[26]Krone, Max T. "The Chorus and Its Conductor." Neil J. Kjos, 1945, p. 88.

[27]Ibid. p. 147.

reserving the largest number for the principal climax.

Location of the major climax is usually obvious because of the dynamics indicated by the composer and textual significance. The major climax is always found at or near the end of a composition. *Even if the same degree of force is noted in the score on previous dynamic peaks, it ought seldom, if ever, equal the final climax.* This aesthetic law takes precedence over indicated dynamics, no matter who wrote them. Failure to observe it throws the song out of proportion, weakening the climatic emotional impact.

Although eight dynamic levels from *ppp* to *fff* commonly are used, six levels that are distinctly different and well controlled are sufficient for most amateur soloists and vocal ensembles. Unfortunately, a *mp* to *mf* range is all that many students produce, resulting in monotonous and unimpressive performance, needless to say. Listeners lose interest when their ears are dulled by monotonous lack of dynamic conrtast. In some instances the fault is due entirely to lazy or careless musicianship; much more variety is possible with technic already developed. Even for the mature concert singer, possession of an adequate number of well-controlled dynamic levels is of far more importance than ability to sing with great force. There is a practical limit to the extent of pianissimo allowable, however; tone should always be vital, audible, and stronger than noise interferences, or the competition of a loud, heavy action piano, when played as softly as the accompanist is able.

TEMPO

Tempo and rhythmic factors are extremely important in artistic phrasing. In order to point out the importance of tempo, Wagner somewhat overemphasized the case: "The whole duty of the conductor is comprised in his ability always to indicate the right tempo."[28] One of the most common faults is making changes of both tempo and dynamics *suddenly* when such marks as accelerando, stringendo, poco a poco animato, rallentando, ritardando, slentendo, crescendo, diminuendo, morendo, and allargando are encountered. *All of these terms mean gradual and not sudden changes, with most of the change coming at the end of the phrase in which the term is found and no audible change at the start.*

1. *The Ideal Tempo.*

Music requires life in an ever-onward, pulsing movement. This results from proper handling of tempo, rhythm, and accent. Should an exact metronomic speed indicated by the composer or arranger invariably be considered the proper or ideal tempo? Usually, it is somewhere near the ideal tempo. Considerations of acoustics and technic of the particular vocalist are practical factors which must be given priority, if the music is to sound at its best to the listener. *An ideal tempo, generally speaking, allows the music to move fast enough so that vitality and energy are maintained, yet is slow enough to permit conveyance of each significant detail in the musical complex.* It is never so fast that words are unintelligible or so slow that diction is lifeless.

As a matter of fact tempo, as well as other interpretive factors, is relative. It is merely a means to the end of clarifying the musical content and form in such a manner that its expressive purpose will be most significant. It is often desirable to experiment with the tempo in new songs in order to find the most effective rate. *The rate of speed which gives the utmost in expression for the particular voice is the best metronome.*

Ideal tempo is determined by a combination of such factors as sentiment of the text and rhythmic, melodic, and harmonic character of the music. A happy text will have a sprightly tempo; a sad or serious text demands a slow. Tempo should not be so rapid as to prevent clear diction on every word or the sounding of every rhythm. In general, *the more complicated harmonic change and rhythmic detail, the slower the tempo needed.* Music with intricate rhythmic patterns or rapid diction passages requires slower tempo than ideal in over-resonant auditoriums. Powerful voices may find also that singing more softly benefits clarity in such a situation. Having emphasized the limitations on fast tempos, it is well to warn that most singers have a tendency to take tempos deadeningly slow. We agree with Thaddeus Gidding's often-repeated admonition, "If a tempo has to be incorrect it had better be too fast than too slow." At least the music will then retain some semblance of vitality.

It is a well-known fact that many singers and some choral conductors have a tendency to play fast and loose with the tempo and rhythm, while instrumentalists incline toward being monotonously pedantic, metronomic, and inflexible. If choralists only would distort less, and instrumentalists be more flexible and less mechanical, the art of musical expression would gain ineffably. In spite of the fact that ideal tempo is relative, there are latitudes of variations beyond which clarity, style, and mood are impaired seriously. The sensitive musician will not go beyond these boundaries of good taste.

2. *Practical Determinants.*

There is some dispute as to whether there is such a thing as an ideal tempo which can be inserted as a metronome marking at the beginning of music scores. There is always a most practical tempo, however, a speed that will achieve the most favorable effect upon the listener under existing concert con-

[28]Wagner, Richard. "On Conducting." Wm. Reeves, 1897, p. 20.

ditions. This is the tempo the realistic singer tries to discover, of course.

Tempo should be flexible but not erratic. Historical style and type of music have much to do with the amount of tempo variation which is in good taste. On the whole, Renaissance, Baroque, Classic, and contrapuntal music demand uniformly steady tempo *within* sections, although wide contrast *between* sections is in order. Music of the Romantic and Modern periods, dramatic and operatic music, waltzes, and some folk songs and ballads are usually more effective when characterized by broad tempo changes and flexibility in rhythmic note length. Determination of the amount and character of suitable tempo and rhythmic variation is undoubtedly one of the most important factors in phrasing.

Although concept of tempo and rhythmic flexibility can be obtained best through listening to outstanding professionals, even this cannot be adopted always as an infallible guide, since artists sometimes differ considerably in their preferences for tempo. In addition, the student may not have the technic at the time to take the tempo as slow or as fast as the mature artist.

Tempo at which a song should be taken varies according to the power and richness of the individual voice, breath energy to support long phrases, ability to articulate rapidly, and acoustic conditions. As a rule, *the lighter and more amateurish the voice the faster tempo will be* in order to maintain vitality, interest the listener, and to conceal inadequacies of breath control on long phrases. On the other hand, *an extremely rich, resonant, and well-controlled voice may well take tempos slower than normal to advantage.*

Very fast tempo songs or songs with many words per measure, may have to be slowed down below ideal speed because of inadequate facility in articulation. Acoustics are always practical determinants in relation to tempo. Comparatively dead acoustic conditions allow faster movement, while over-reverberant rooms and large, cathedral-like structures with considerable echo demand slowing down of rapid tempos, and perhaps less tonal volume or diction and musical details will be confused or lost.

Other keys for adjusting tempo can be found within the structure and character of the text, melody, and harmony as follows. Tempo quite often should be:

(a) Faster when the text is less interesting dramatically, slower and more emphasis is on key words when highly significant.

(b) Faster when the melody is comparatively inactive and uninteresting. (A highly interesting piano score may counteract this.)

(c) Faster when the piano accompaniment is sparse, uninteresting, and perhaps ill-adapted to the poor sustaining qualities of the instrument. (This is counteracted, however, if the melody is quite active and interesting at the time.)

(d) Slower when the accompaniment is quite complex, colorful, and interesting in harmonic change.

(e) Slower, with perhaps a broad ritardando on the measure just preceding a new section. (This helps reveal the form of the composition more clearly.)

(f) Somewhat slower on especially significant harmony progressions involving modulation to a new key.

3. *Common Faults in Handling Tempo and Rhythm.*

(a) A metronomic or rigidly inflexible tempo.

(b) Purposeless variation or unsteadiness of tempo.

(c) Exaggerated ritardando followed by failure to return to the original tempo.

(d) Breaking of tempo between phrases by slow or labored breathing.

(e) Habitually slow tempo and devitalized rhythm.

(f) Undue holding of high notes for display of technic, with little or no regard for appropriateness.

It is desirable to be particularly careful that tempo of sentimental music does not drag. Wedding songs, saccharine melodies, and over-sentimental sacred songs often used in church services must be sung at times by the vocalist, whether or not he cares for such requested numbers. In order to compensate for the obvious nature and musical weaknesses, it is well to remember to keep the tempo moving always. A slow tempo and too much emphasis on ritardando and fermatas can make songs of this type a sickeningly cloying experience, especially to any musician present.

Beginning singers often have a tendency to take a tempo that had been properly set by the piano introduction, slower and slower, until they "bog down," completely out of breath and exhausted by unnecessary physical demands in breath support for the phrase. Altos and basses are usually the worst offenders in wanting to drag tempos unnecessarily, since their voices are less agile. The wise teacher will correct these tendencies as soon as possible, insisting on a faster, rather than a slower, tempo than ideal for the time being.

The beginner also is likely to be ineffective in interpreting songs at either extreme of very fast or very slow tempo. If the indicated tempo is quite slow, he either has to speed it up, break long phrases intended to be sung in one unit, or "squeak" through to the end of the phrase in an exhausted condition, with resultant poor pitch and tonal quality. If the tempo is very fast or diction requirements quite rapid, he is unable to articulate all words clearly or to take sufficient breath rapidly enough between phrases, production suffering likewise from exhaustion, poor tone, and pitch. The amateur is advised in public performance to avoid songs in extreme tempos until adequate technic is developed. Such songs are more interesting than exercises, however, may be excellent pablum for making desired technical growth in studio practice and, once mastered, form a valuable addition to varied repertoire.

4. *Significance of Tempo Markings in the Score.*

This topic has had considerable coverage in previous discussions and only a few supplementary ideas are needed.

The singer who is a sensitive interpreter, and is well grounded in the principles of artistic expression, will never be a slave to tempo indications. Composers themselves change their minds later, so why should the interpreter feel absolutely bound. For example, Brahms is reported to have said, "I am of the opinion that metronome marks go for nothing. As far as I know, all composers have, as I retracted their metronome marks in later years."[29] Tempo terms such as *lento, moderato, andante,* etc., are merely relative, never absolute in meaning. In fact, music dictionaries and encyclopedias differ somewhat on the meanings of such terms as *andante*, while composers obviously differ even more in their concept of meaning. Metronome indications and terms used to designate tempo are significant and useful in indicating *relative* tempo, however, even if they cannot be relied upon to provide an ideal speed. They are, therefore, to be regarded as significant suggestions or approximations in determining proper tempo, and *should be observed unless there is sound reason for change.* Change for the sake of change is never justified unless expression is heightened. "Nothing can be more detrimental to a piece of music than arbitrary nuances of tempo."[30]

5. *Steadiness and Flexibility.*

Two of the characteristics observed through analysis of great interpretation are *steadiness* and *flexibility* of tempo. At first thought the two terms would appear to be antagonistic. Flexibility is obtained *within* steadiness of tempo, and *steadiness does not mean uniformly maintained metronomic tempo*, however. A steady tempo may involve great variety, providing changes are smooth, gradual, and the result of feeling for the natural ebb and flow of the phrase. *Thus tempo may be flexibly bent but never broken.* If this is done musically, the listener scarcely is aware of tempo changes within the structural sections of a composition when, in fact, they may be quite extensive. Tempo changes will not be obtrusive when

they are accomplished so naturally and smoothly that they seem always the result of an inevitable expressive urge for significant phrasing.

Above all, *tempo, style, and dynamics of succeeding sections will never be anticipated at the end of a previous section* or the whole value of contrast in interpretation is destroyed. For the same reason, these factors in the new section should be established immediately and not "eased into" gradually, as often heard.

Rubato tempo flexibly slows speed of some notes within the measure and compensates by increasing tempo on others. It should be used rarely, and then only to a slight degree in Classic music and music previous to that time, but is highly necessary for interpreting properly much of the Romantic and Modern music. The concert waltz and the waltz song probably have more *rubato* treatment than any other type of literautre. Composers often indicate that they desire a very flexible treatment of tempo not only by the term *tempo rubato* but also by other markings such as *ad libitum, espressivo, agitato, sentimento,* and *abandono.*

RHYTHM

Since rhythm is the backbone of all music and, to a considerable extent the backbone of the poetry which inspired the musical setting, it is as important to sing with rhythmic accuracy and vitality as to sing in tune. Most people are born with an instinctive sense of rhythm and learning to sing the more simple rhythms correctly is comparatively easy. The ability to accurately and expressively sing complicated rhythms needs considerable study and development, however. Carelessness and bad habits are easily acquired. It is highly desirable that the all too prevailing habit to "play fast and loose" with the rhythm be corrected in the very beginning and continually checked in many students.

No doubt the generally careless practices of singers in interpreting popular songs are responsible for a great deal of rhythmic difficulties. In most instances even the popular song would be more effective if sung either as written or close to it. If not, the composer did not know his business. Mistakes are particularly noticeable in singing syncopation, triplets, and dotted note rhythms and in carelessly dropping the last note of the phrase at will, regardless of the number of beats indicated.

If a singer can only "hear" the phrase and "feel" the tempo and rhythm, many of his technical difficulties disappear. Without a clear sense of rhythm, nothing but fumbling indecision can be expected. When a composition has rhythmic life and vitality, it can have many other faults and still maintain

---

[29]Wodell, Op. cit., p. 163.
[30]Wodell, Op. cit., p. 148.

some interest for the listener. If it lacks rhythmic vitality, nothing else can compensate for the loss. Rhythm gives systematic order to music and propels it persistently forward to the end in a pulsating flow of sound. This feeling of continuing pulsation is not broken but even continues right through rests and *fermatas*. Our aesthetic sensibilities are disturbed unless all attacks and releases occur in rhythmic unanimity with this onward moving pulse. A feeling of off-pulse attack following a *fermata* is as distracting as failure to maintain the right number of beats in the measure. In singing, words are the rhythm makers and consonants bear the chief burden; therefore, it is highly important that they be distinct and precisely on time with the pulse, or rhythm lacks vitality.

Three factors are involved in rhythmic concept: tempo, note value, and meter.

1. *Tempo* — Rate of speed, or pace of the fundamental rhythm. (Discussed previously)

2. *Note Value* — the relative duration or "time values" and characteristic rhythmic pattern of the notes themselves. The different notes and rhythmic patterns fall within the normal accent pattern of the basic measure or meter. Duration of indicated rests is of equal importance to note values. Dotted notes, triplets, and syncopations are most difficult for students.

Exact note values, like all other notational considerations, are a relative matter depending on appropriate style and expressive values. It has been established experimentally without doubt that the most careful, sensitive, and best-trained musicians vary continually from the exact indicated time values of notes. These are always *slight* variations for the sake of better expression and never distortions, however — merely a *bending* of the total length and not *breaking*. A quarter note never becomes an eighth or vice versa, and a beat is never subtracted from a measure or added unless a *fermata* is indicated.

It is a well-known fact that style of certain music results in traditional rhythmic change, e.g., bands usually play the military march rhythm ♩. ♪ more like ♩. ♪ In solo singing or playing of florid Baroque music, turns, quavers, appogiaturas, acciacaturas, etc., considerable freedom is left to the preference and taste of the performer in regard to exact note length, as long as the tempo and basic meter are not disturbed.

The student is urged to attain careful accuracy of rhythm first; appropriate variance, usually unconscious, will result inevitably when the demands of style and expression are allowed to dominate. If these slight rhythmic variations are in good taste, only the most ill-informed and didactic pedantic

might then object. It is not the arithmetical preciseness of the score that is important but rather its significance, naturalness, life, variety, and taste in interpretation. A music score indicates desirable central tendencies or averages, but not slavish exactitude.

3. *Measure or Meter* — Characteristic pulse and recurring accent pattern within the measure, indicated by the "time" signature, 2/4, 3/4, 4/4, etc.

The pulse or beat with its characteristic normal accent pattern for the particular "time" signature is the basic organizing influence in musical rhythm. The types of meter with their characteristic normal accent pattern follow. An accented beat is indicated with the accent, $>$, and unaccented beats with, $-$. Relative weight of the normal accent is indicated by the relative size of the accent illustrated.

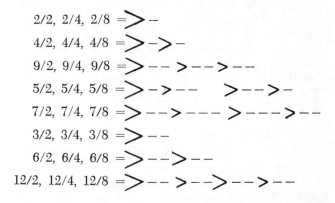

It is well to emphasize that *the lower figure of a "time" signature,* the beat note, *has absolutely nothing to do with speed of tempo.* For example, a 4/2 meter marked *moderato* should be performed at exactly the same speed as a 4/8 meter marked *moderato.* This fact is misunderstood more often than not by beginning students. The half note was used traditionally as the beat note until the eighteenth century. The quarter note is used today by most modern printers in the two, three and four beat measures, while the eighth is preferred in the six, nine and twelve beat measures. Superior visibility is undoubtedly the main reason for change.

Many singers, instrumentalists, and even conductors demonstrate in their performances that they do not realize the sovereign artistic importance of basic rhythm. Not only do they greatly distort rhythm values, but also appear to be lacking in a clear sense of the organizing beat, seeming not to understand that *all meters have a fundamental accent pattern normally expected in each measure.* Failure to observe this normal accent pattern, together with too slow tempo, will give any song anemia and, when accompanied by indefinite diction, the song expires.

The recurring normal accent pattern cannot be "punched-out" mechanically measure after measure in the same fashion, however, or monotony and unmusical expression result. "If the alternation of stress and slacks is followed too regularly and too rigidly then a dull, stilted, even awkward performance results. It is similar to reading poetry in a monotonous fashion."[31] *Either ignoring normal accent or slavish observance are fatal to fine interpretation.* Textual significance, style, tempo, and appropriate syncopation are factors operating continually in the complex to condition relative strength, or even the absence of normal accent. *Lyric-legato sustained singing demands less weight on the normal accent, dramatic accented style more; slow tempos usually require more force and regularity, while very fast tempos may omit normal accent except once or twice within the phrase on key words.*

Mechanical observance of normal accent, particularly in fast tempos, produces a monotonous effect and destroys flow of the phrase. In vocal music, the text provides the key to where normal metrical accent needs to be altered to conform to a stronger rhythmic urge intrinsic in the text and melodic line, and will even suggest where syncopation is appropriate. The anacrusis or pick-up note or notes before the bar line at the beginning of some phrases, are never to be accented in solo singing.

4. The Eloquent Rest

Too many singers not only blithely sing right through rests, but also inset them wherever they wish. We may be fairly sure that rests were inserted by the composer and were put there for as definite a purpose as the notes. It is often stated that "rests are eloquent silences." They function to provide desirable punctuation of the melody, to indicate phrasing, and are far more significant emotionally at times than any note that could be sung. For example, the emotional significance of a rest is well illustrated in Tschaikovsky's well-known song, "None but the Lonely Heart," (See p. 73, Song Anthology, Volume I, of this vocal course). A tremendous emotional and dynamic climax is built up near the end with a *crescendo* and *stringendo* marked in the score ending with the words, "Alone, and parted far from joy and gladness," and a crashing *ff* measure by the piano. This is followed by a quarter rest and the words, marked *pp* in the vocal score, "My senses fail, A burning fire devours me."

This quarter rest is one of the most eloquent parts of the song. It sets the stage for what is to follow and creates an almost breathless suspense. The rest ought never to be omitted or shortened but may well be lengthened to advantage, adding further intensity to the suspense. This climax and rest, with the following *pianissimo phrase*, is comparable in emotional impact and intensity of suspense to the effect of a gunshot in the forest, the sudden stark silence which follows and, finally, after suspense becomes almost unbearable, the quavering voice of a single bird. Fail to give the rest plenty of length and the illusion is lost.

How long is a rest? Certainly it should never serve as a loafing place where the singer can rest physically as well as emotionally. Normally, *we sing mentally right through the rests, continuing onward on the beat or pulse and never somewhere in between.* This rule applies as well to introductions, interludes, and postludes, which are merely longer forms of rests or punctuations for the melody. *Rests should usually be the exact,* or very near the exact, *duration indicated.* Certainly, in normal instances where rests are used to end phrases, there will be no feeling that a beat or a part of a beat has been either added or subtracted. Only when rests are used to create suspense following a climax, as in the Tschaikovsky song cited, can the length of a rest be extended as if there were a *fermata* over it. In such a passage, the singer judges the proper length to create the desired intensity of suspense without distortion or an awkward wait.

5. Holds (fermati)

Many soloists and choral groups have a tendency to sing straight through a *fermata* as if it did not exist, or merely treat it as a *tenuto. A fermata ought at least to add an additional beat to the indicated meter or it isn't a fermata.* Most *fermata*, or "holds," that are appropriate are indicated by the composer or arranger in the score, although this is not always the case. The *hold differs from the tenuto* (ten.) in that more beats are added according to taste when the *hold* is encountered. *Tenuto* merely gives the effect of a broad *ritardando* or lingering on the note so affected, without beats being added.

A *fermata* is used to accentuate highly important words, to achieve climaxes, to create suspense regarding what is to follow, and to break the monotony of rhythmic regularity. Overuse or abuse in number and length of *holds* is a pitfall to be avoided. *High notes should not be held or extended except when the effect is appropriate to over-all interpretation and not merely for exhibitionism.* The sustained *fermata* offers ample time for vocal coloring, dynamic variation, beauty, and significance in expression that reaches the ear and consciousness of the listener effectively. When employed with good judgment and restraint, the *hold* becomes a valuable means for heightened expression.

The Terminal "Grunt"

One of the outstanding characteristics of Caruso's powerfully-expressive dramatic singing is found in what has since been termed the "Caruso Grunt." It may be contended justifiably that Caruso employed the Terminal Grunt or gasp in some songs and arias more often than good taste would warrant. Caruso

---

[31] Wilson, Op. cit., p. 59.

was intensely emotional, however, and the frequent use seems more justified in one of his temperament than when "forced," as it often has been, by his imitators.

The terminal grunt-gasp is caused by a sudden and explosive ending of tone — the tone and breath support cease suddenly, and simultaneously a convulsive, sob-like intake of breath, which may be used for the next phrase, is taken. Like a sob, the effect has a powerful emotional impact on the listener.

The "Caruso Grunt" was, and continues to be, copied with more or less success. The effect has been so overused and abused that many vocal teachers have had a strong revulsion to the whole idea, condemning the practice at any time. Homer Henley, in an Etude article, "The Terminal Grunt," asserts, "The incomparable Caruso, with perhaps the most movingly beautiful tenor voice the world has ever heard, was the most capricious offender in the terminal shout-grunt; and it is notable that, with the rise of his fame, this, perhaps dramatically effective but wretchedly unmusical device, began to appear in the singing of nearly all of the vocal 'artists' of the last generation — tenors and baritones, sopranos and altos alike."

Nevertheless, the major purpose of singing is expression and not necessarily the production of beautiful sounds. Good taste demands that ugly tone or abnormal effect be justified dramatically and used with utmost caution. Our conclusion is that the Terminal Grunt-gasp may be used most sparingly at the right place to produce a powerful emotional climax, but then only by those who can produce it naturally without affectation. It should never be produced habitually in a "hammy" manner at the slightest excuse, and seldom to cover the fact that a breath had to be taken at the time.

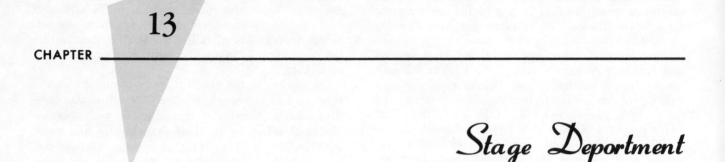

13

Stage Deportment

(*See Volume I, p. 198*)

LEARNING STAGE DEPORTMENT

The vocal instructor has a responsibility to check and guide the pupil in every phase of stage deportment as described in this chapter and outlined in detail for the pupil in Expressive Singing, Volume I. Items to watch especially are upright posture; a graceful walk; a modest, dignified manner; a resonant, unhurried speaking voice; and traditional manner in recognizing applause graciously. Members of a voice class normally should make suggestions each time one of their members sings. It is necessary to watch for and correct distractions in rehearsals which call attention to the singer or accompanist, and prevent audience concentration on the mood and messages of the song itself. Some of the most common distractions are:

1. *Awkward posture* — Standing with weight mostly on one foot, shoulders hunched up or quite uneven, rising on tiptoe, standing with weight too far back on the heels, teetering or unsteady stance, awkward hand position, lolling on the piano, hands in pockets or behind the back, etc.

2. *Extraneous movement or unusual mannerisms* — Swaying, beating time with the hands or arms, pumping arms upward for high notes, etc.

3. *Nervous manifestations and accentricities* — Gripping fingers or hands tensely, eyes shifting suddenly, quick erratic movement, clearing the throat nervously, strained or peculiar expression, lifted high-arched eyebrows, hesitant walk, indecisive gesture, wringing or twisting handkerchief or program held in hands.

4. *Inappropriate dress* — Extremely low-cut dress, very tight sweater, radical or extreme dress of any kind.

5. *Accompanist mannerisms* — Some accompanists are overly-theatrical or have distracting mannerisms, of which they are unconscious. Occasion-

ally, one may attempt to steal the spotlight by deliberately theatricalizing his playing and actions. Attention to posture is often needed. The vocal instructor often can help the accompanist in more than musical suggestions and should not hesitate to protect the singer from certain accompanists who overplay or "theatricalize."

It is well for the instructor first to demonstrate all factors and phases of stage deportment. Sometimes a demonstration of the wrong technic as a horrible example is not only amusing but also an excellent method for teaching. When students sing solos in class, the class members normally should furnish applause and react in the manner of an audience at a formal concert.

APPEARANCE

The poised singer will always give the appearance of confidence, naturalness, ease, and authority. According to Greene,[1] it is not enough to have a fine technic and interpretive ability; a pleasing stage manner and personal magnetism are also indispensable assets for the concert singer. *Good stage appearance must be practiced and routined until pleasing naturalness and traditional action are habituated.* The student, therefore, will frequently practice all the formal routine of concert singing in class with entrances, announcing songs, bowing in recognition of applause, exits, etc. Ease, relaxation, and naturalness can be established only by routine practice. If not established on entrance to the stage, the audience immediately has a prejudiced opinion regarding singing ability. On the other hand, if the singer looks natural, at ease and confident, an audience not only anticipates with pleasure a successful concert but also feels friendship and admiration for the singer as a person.

---

[1]Greene, Harry Plunkett. "Interpretation in Song." Macmillan, 1940, p. 4.

"Pupils should be taught to walk to a station in the front of the room without self-consciousness or bashfulness, assume the position of a singer, convey to the accompanist his or her readiness to begin, and in a perfectly natural manner perform the song as it has been learned. Every pupil in the class should be given this opportunity in regular order, the rest of the class observing, listening, and afterwards offering constructive criticism on the performance of the 'artist'.

It is strongly recommended that each soloist in turn be taught to bow when applauded, and to that end, the class should unfailingly applaud by hand-clapping when the soloist has completed the song. This should be a DAILY PROGRAM WITHOUT FAIL: applaud and bow each time. This cannot but provide the soloist with unassailable poise, which will not desert him when appearing in public.

The class should be aware that applause means 'we liked your singing'; the bow means 'thank you'. It is the wordless custom of the stage and should remain wordless. . . . Learn to bow easily and pleasantly more than once if the applause justifies. There should be no jocularity between 'audience' and 'artist'. The class as an audience should offer perfect attention to and encouragement of the 'artist'."[2]

While singing badly before an audience can never be condoned, the clever singer with an engaging stage personality can usually gain an encore, even following a poor performance. Unfortunately, stage appearance is more convincing than the sound of fine singing to many: i.e., more people still depend on sight rather than the evidence of their ears for musical judgment. The student can at least learn to *act* like an experienced artist, even if he does not yet *sound* like one to the discriminating ear.

There is much more to "selling" a song than students and many teachers realize. The singer needs to have not only an engaging personality but also to "look" the sentiment involved; facial expression, carriage, slight movements and gestures — all contribute toward making a fine performance. Without these and an attractive stage manner, efforts of the singer are mostly wasted on the average listener, even though the voice itself be most beautiful. Henderson and Palmer[3] list six rules for artistic singing performance; *naturalness, sincerity, convincing personality, clear diction, sustaining one mood throughout, and showmanship.*

Many a concert singer could learn much about stage appearance from the despised "crooner." The crooner usually sings with naturalness and simplicity, and his words are understood; he has no artificialities or stage mannerisms, and his appeal is direct. The greatest concert artists in public acclaim such as Fritz Kreisler, Roland Hayes, and Marion Anderson, are distinguished by a friendly earnestness, modesty, and absorption in their art as well as the naturalness, simplicity, and directness characteristic of the crooner.

SINGER-AUDIENCE RELATIONSHIP

There are two general types of singer-audience relationship to be mastered, the subjective and the objective.

1. *Subjective* — Most art songs, lullabies, and sacred songs are of the subjective type in which the audience is seen and sung to as a *mass* or unit only, and not as so many different individuals. In the serious art song, the singer lifts his eyes just over the heads of the members of the audience and avoids meeting anyone's eyes or noticing anybody. If not carried to the extreme, even closing the eyes is permissible at times, to shut out the distraction of individuals and allow greater concentration on interpretation. The singer should be conscious of the audience as a friendly and appreciative unit, to whom the spirit and message of the song are to be revealed with utmost significance and beauty. The impression given is that the artistic experience is shared with the audience and that entire concentration is on revealing the mood, meaning, and beauty of the song. This, in fact, is the case with all great artists.

Purpose is always to *reveal* rather than to *display*; to call attention to the meaning and beauty of the music rather than to the artist. It is important that the singer's expression and posture indicate the mood significantly, but emoting, posturing, theatricalism, and distractions are out of place on the concert platform. Gestures are more appropriate and will receive greater attention in dramatic operatic arias, humorous ballads, and popular entertainment type of songs.

In subjective relationship the audience stimulates highest interpretive efforts, but individuals in the audience should never intrude on the singer's consciousness or they become a distraction, preventing concentration on fundamental function in this type of serious music — projection of mood and meaning. Mood ought to be established when the accompanist plays the introduction and should be maintained throughout, without let-down of concentration during interludes or postludes by the piano. This power of concentration and self-effacement is often the deciding factor between great success and mediocrity.

In the serious art song no single individual ever is singled out or sung to at any time. Eyes remain steadily over the head of the audience, and care is taken that the chin is not lifted for this purpose. It is

[2]From the "1953 Outline of Voice Training in Senior High Schools" of Rochester, New York. Used by permission of Alfred Spouse, Director of Music.

[3]Henderson, Charles and Palmer, Charles. "How to Sing for Money." George Putnam, Inc., 1939, p. 30.

considered questionable stage deportment by most authorities — since it is obviously conscious studied action and interferes with concentration on interpretation of serious music — for the singer habitually to turn or swing head or body first toward one section of an audience and then another. *Direction of singing is normally straight forward.* Shift of direction is occasionally permissible between songs, or verses of a song, when the auditorium is quite large and difficulty in hearing is experienced by those seated on the sides.

2. *Objective* — Singer-audience relationship is quite different in the humorous encore, and in the ballad or narrative song, where music is essentially a vehicle for the words. "Getting over" the story is all-important, and the singer looks directly at individual members of the audience. *It is important that everyone feels that the story of the song is being told to him personally.* In this type of song, friendly relationship between the singer and each individual in the audience is most vital. The singer attempts to contact each member of the audience with a brief glance from time to time and *each person feels that he has been noticed, that the story of the song is being told to him, and that he is a part of the presentation.*

Failure of some concert singers to "put over" humorous encores and ballads often is due to incorrect singer-audience technic; it is as ridiculous to sing songs of this type as it would be to tell a humorous story with the eyes fixed over the heads of the listeners. Eyes and facial expression ought to be most suggestive in reflecting the humor or idea of the story, while somewhat more gesture and movement on the stage is appropriate for dramatization.

READING A TEXT OR MUSIC SCORE

Singing always appears more natural and is more expressive when the text is memorized. An experienced artist may be able to rise above the handicap of reading a text, but the begining student almost never can. In any case, no song should ever be sung in concert unless the text is well enough known so that only a brief glance at any phrase is all that is needed to recall the whole. No song can be interpreted expressively to an audience if the eyes have to be glued to the words or the score. After beginning students have gained some experience in singing memorized music publicly, then, and only then, can they be allowed to attempt singing solos with the words or score in hand.

Although memorization is always recommended when practical, we recognize that there are times when memorizing the text or music is of insufficient importance to justify the time and effort required. For example, solos in anthems for church services may not be of sufficient worth as a standard part of the repertoire or time is insufficient to allow memorization. It is also more traditional than otherwise for oratorio or cantata soloists to sing with a score, to which they refer briefly at times.

Considerable practice is needed to master the technic of singing with a text or score in hand so that interpretation appears natural. The singer who can make an audience forget that a text is even being held in hand has thoroughly mastered the art. *Unobtrusive reading of a text or music score depends principally on timing.* Observance of the two basic rules following will guarantee the least interference with an effect of naturalness and spontaneity:

1. *Never have the eyes on the text at the moment of attack.* Always read the succeeding phrase while finishing the one preceding.

2. *Under no circumstances should the head move up and down while reading.* Only the eyes glance down *slowly* and *naturally.* Any sudden or jerky eye movement is noticeable to the audience.

LEANING ON THE PIANO

Students will first habituate an upright, flexibly expansive, vital posture. After independent stance has been established they may at times for the sake of variety in less formal music, rest the hand and arm lightly on the piano. *Under no circumstances should they ever be allowed to loll or practically lie on the piano,* using it as a prop or place to drape the body, as sometimes observed. Some singers feel more at ease if allowed to hold a handkerchief or a small piece of paper rolled in the hand. This may well be the program for the concert. All objects have to be removed from students unable to refrain from twisting, tearing, or rattling them as a nervous manifestation, however.

PROJECTING THE VOICE

Stage presence, as well as technic in tonal production, are weakened by attempts to project or "hurl" the voice in order to get it to carry. The singer ought never to feel that he is squirting tone out the mouth in an attempt to project it somewhere far back in the auditorium. Such attempts merely result in a labored struggle and yelling. Singing is *inside* and not *outside;* efforts to project the voice inevitably create poor tone and tension. *The voice carries best when tone is resonated freely and clearly, and articulation is most crisp and forceful.* Wronski declares, "If the mouth is properly sonorized, the hall will also be fully sonorized."[4]

Singers often make the mistake of thinking that a big hall requires a big voice and that the voice must be projected or "hurled" forward in order to carry. From a diction standpoint, the singers needs

---

[4]Wronski, Thaddeus. "The Singer and His Art." D. Appleton & Co., 1921, p. 27.

only concentrate on telling the story of the text with precise, clean-cut articulation *to those in the back row*. From a tonal standpoint concentration is on a free, ringing, and sonorous production from *within* and not on projection of tone from *without*. If these directions are followed, singers with light voices need not worry or "struggle" to get the voice to carry. They have done everything necessary to make it possible within the boundaries of artistic singing.

THE BOW AND CURTSEY

The graceful bow and curtsey may seem simple technics to the observer but are actually difficult for many students to master. After the song has concluded, the singer should make no move of any kind to destroy the mood established until the last sound of the accompaniment has vanished. *After applause starts it is bad manners not to recognize it graciously by bowing or courtseying.* The male singer will always bow. Bowing should be from the *hips* while a *straight spine* and neck are maintained — *the neck and back are never curved.* A straight spine and neck seem stiff and unnatural to the student at first; however, he need merely observe how badly bending them looks in others to be convinced.

In bowing the singer needs to habituate several principles:

1. Bow slowly.
2. Bow from the hips.
3. Keep the eyes down.
4. Keep the neck and back straight.
5. Keep the hands relaxed and at the sides of the hips.

A pleasant nod and smile may be used in recognizing applause for humorous songs and for informal occasions. A curtsey is also proper for a small or a tall and graceful woman. A large and heavy woman often appears ridiculous when attempting a curtsey, however; instead of being graceful or "cute" it appears awkward and comical. A smile in recognition of applause isn't always necessary or desirable and should never be forced. The singer, however, will always look pleasant and never severe, distressed, or hostile in relationship with the audience.

An unforgivable *faux pas* in stage deportment is to bow toward only the center of a large hall or auditorium. A bow or curtsey to the center, to the left, and to the right is the minimum. If part of the audience is seated on the stage, they should be recognized also. Recognition of the accompanist is traditional at the end of a group of songs or after a particularly difficult accompaniment has been played especially well. The accompanist may be recognized by a nod, a handshake or by a gesture, indicating that he is to rise and bow also in recognition of applause.

WAIT FOR QUIET

Do not begin singing until the audience has been seated and a moment of quiet established. *If music is worth having it is worth hearing.* No singer deserves respect who does not first respect his art sufficiently to demand absolute quiet before beginning and reasonable quiet while performing. Banquets and school auditorium audiences often present difficult situations for obtaining quiet and attention. No agreement should be made to sing at banquets unless those in charge promise to arrange quiet from the waitresses and kitchen help during the performance. An appearance should not be planned by an amateur student at a school assembly where the students have a reputation for being noisy or "getting out of hand" unless authorities there promise to take care of discipline. An experienced concert artist usually has the reputation and poise to take care of adolescent rough-neck elements without assistance.

ENTERING AND LEAVING THE STAGE

The singer enters the stage from the wings briskly and quietly, going to a position about three feet in front of the piano before looking at the audience or recognizing applause on entrance. After bowing informally or nodding in recognition of applause, looking the audience over, and allowing them a brief time to satisfy normal curiosity regarding the singer as a personality, the vocalist steps back into singing position in the crook of the piano, nods or signals unobtrusively with some prearranged signal to the accompanist, and the song begins.

After finishing the song or group of songs, the singer recognizes applause first and then leaves the stage in the same manner as he came on, again without looking at the audience. Should applause continue, the singer comes back on stage, bows or curtseys, leaves again or presents an encore if he desires. When applause continues after leaving the stage a second time, it is good stage manners to bring the accompanist back to share in the applause. The accompanist will bow in the same manner as the soloist. If an encore is planned the singer ought not to wait too long, but present it on either the first or second entrance after leaving the stage. It is not good etiquette, however, to rush back immediately and give an encore before polite but unenthusiastic applause has had a chance to cease. *The signal for an encore is audience enthusiasm.*

Details of stage deportment and precedence on entrance and leaving the stage in relation to the accompanist will be found in Volume I for this chapter.

ANNOUNCING SONGS

All students need careful coaching on announcing songs. *Announcements are made slowly, clearly, with distinct articulation and sufficient force to be easily understood at the farthest distance by members of the audience.* It is a good policy to have students announce all solos with exaggerated force in class and to practice announcing and singing at times in any large auditorium or hall available. *A minimum of words to express the idea is considered best form in announcing a song.* For example, "Dedication by Franz," is all that is necessary. The words, "I shall sing," or any others are superfluous since everyone knows that is what the soloist is going to do, or he soon will. There always should be a slight pause between the name of the song and the composer for the sake of clarity. The author of the text is traditionally not given unless the poet is especially renowned. In such a case the technic is as follows, "Who Is Sylvia, the text by Shakespeare, the music by Schubert."

When songs are sung in a foreign language before English-speaking audiences, it is usually best to give a very brief and well-prepared resumé in English of the ideas involved. If it is an operatic aria, brief explanation of the dramatic situation is also desirable in order to orient the listener for fullest understanding and enjoyment.

14

Program Building

(*See Volume I, p. 207*)

Fine program building is an art and a science based on experience and musicianship. "A program should not only be composed of works of art but it should be a work of art itself. Throwing together a few numbers without rhyme or reason does not constitute a program."[1] It is necessary that programs have unity, variety, and balanced structure upon a definite plan which builds to a climax. The inexperienced student can learn the art only through study, observance, and guidance on the part of the instructor. Suggestions in Expressive Singing, Volume I, are quite explicit and detailed and should be most helpful. For an excellent discussion of repertoire and program making, as well as a generous listing of various types of concert programs, we recommend Chapter 5 of Judith Litante's text, "A Natural Approach to Singing," published also by the Wm. C. Brown Co.

It is suggested that advanced students be given an assignment outlining several concert programs according to suggestions in Volume I and that each program be discussed with the instructor, and in class, regarding the excellences and weaknesses. Guidance of the instructor will always be sought on program selection and arrangement when the student appears publicly.

There is never any necessity for programming poor music. If the best of music is performed beautifully, we need not fear an unfavorable response from audiences. If it is performed poorly or in an indifferent manner, however, we can expect listeners to perfer music of a more entertaining and transient character. It is desirable to have a judicious mixture of familiar favorites with less known or new music to please most members of concert audiences. A warning is in order, however — familiar favorites are always a hazard and should be done well if programmed. In these songs everyone becomes a critical judge; inadequacies will be more glaring than in less familiar music.

REPRESENTATIVE CONCERT PROGRAMS

Note — For the sake of discussion and example, some programs are purposely listed to illustrate departure from the ideal or traditional in the respect indicated.

Roland Hayes
Tenor

I

Ingrata Quanto Sei (from Cruda Irene)	Scarlatti
Pan Is Master (from Phoebus and Pan)	Bach
Wonne der Wehmuth	Beethoven
Warnung	Mozart

II

Fischerweise	Schubert
Erster Verlust	Schubert
Die Taubenpost	Schubert
Der Jüngling an der Quelle	Schubert

III

Danse Macabre	Saint-Saens
The Red Cockatoo	Fairchild
Scandalize My Name (Afro-American Folksong)	Arr. Burleigh
Mother to Son	Parham

IV

Afro-American Religious Folksongs:

Give-a-way Jordan	Arr. Hayes
By and By	Arr. Hayes
I Want Two Wings	Arr. Hayes
Ezekiel Saw De Wheel	Arr. Hayes

Note — The above program may be questioned in group III. In particular, it would be more traditional and logical to have included the Afro-American Folksong, "Scandalize My Name," as part of group IV.

---

[1]Wilson, Harry Robert. "Artistic Choral Singing." G. Schirmer, Inc., 1959, p. 305.

William Eddy
Baritone

I

Hera Me! Ye Winds and Waves
  (from Scipio) ....Handel
She Never Told Her Love ....Haydn
Breathe Soft Ye Winds ....Handel
I'll Sail Upon the Dog Star ....Purcell

II

Credo (from Otello) ....Verdi

III

Der Wanderer ....Schubert
Heidenroslein ....Schubert
Wanderers Nachtlied ....Schubert
Est Hing der Reif ....Brahms
Verrath ....Brahms

IV

Blow, Blow, Thou Winter Wind ....Quilter
O Mistress Mine ....Quilter
O Men from the Fields ....Hughes
Miranda ....Hageman

Elizabeth Ann Bollinger
Lyric Soprano

I

Depuis le Jour (from Louise) ....Charpentier
Air de Lia (from L'enfant
  Prodigue) ....Debussy

II

Le Temp des Lilas ....Chausson
Ils Etaient Trois Petits-Chats
  Blancs ....Pierne
Allerseelen ....Strauss
Cacilie ....Strauss

III

Micaela's Aria (from Carmen)· ....Bizet
Un Bel Di (from Madame
  Butterfly) ....Puccini

IV

In the Silence of Night ....Rachmaninoff
A Piper ....Head
Heather ....Warren
Miranda ....Hageman

Note — The above excellent program would have
been more traditional and have offered the singer an
opportunity to warm-up the voice on easier material if
there had been an introductory short group of Old Italian,
Old English, Handel, Bach, or Mozart songs.

Eula Beal
Contralto

I

Ah rendimi (from Mitrane) ....Rossi
Zwei Zigeunerlieder (Two Gypsy
  Songs) from opus 103 ....Brahms
  He, Zigenner, greife in die
  Saiten ein!
  Hochgethürmte Rimafluth, wie
  bist di so trüb
Der Tod, das ist die kühle Nacht ....Brahms
Ablösung im Sommer ....Mahler
Scheiden und Meiden ....Mahler

II

Infidelite ....Hahn
Fetes galantes ....Hahn
Soir ....Fauré
Fleur Jetée ....Fauré

III

Flidkan kom ifran sin alsklings ....Sibelius
Saf, Saf, susa ....Sibelius
Svarta rosor ....Sibelius

IV

The Ash Grove (Welsh Tune) ....Arr. Britten
Oliver Cromwell (Nursery Rhyme
  from Suffolk) ....Arr. Britten
Think on Me ....Scott-Perrenot
Holiday Song ....Schuman
The Bird of the Wilderness ....Creston

Note — It would have been more traditional and
ideal to present the first Rossi aria as a separate group I
and the Brahms and Mahler as group II.

Desire Ligeti
Bass-Baritone

I

Che fiero costume ....Legrenzi
Tu lo Sai ....Torelli
Pieta, Signore ....Stradella
Vittoria, mio core ....Carissimi

II

Die Himmel Ruemen ....Beethoven
In questa tomba ....Beethoven
Adelaide ....Beethoven

III

Der Wanderer ....Schubert
Der Jüngling an der Quelle ....Schubert
Die Post ....Schubert
Aufenthalt ....Schubert
Der Musensohn ....Schubert

IV

Catalogue Aria (from Don
  Giovanni) ....Mozart

V

Song to the Evening Star
  (from Tannhauser) ....Wagner

VI

Widmung ....Schumann
Talismane ....Schumann
Two Grenadiers ....Schumann
Die Mainacht ....Brahms
Standchen ....Brahms
None But the Lonely Heart ....Tschaikowski
Song of the Flea ....Moussorgsky

VII

Nobody Knows the Trouble
  I've Seen ....Negro Spiritual
Deep River ....Negro Spiritual
Hungarian Songs:
  I Rove ....Kodaly
  Which One Shall I Marry? ....Kodaly

Note — This was the impressive program listed. It had obviously proven entirely too long, however, and a number of the songs were omitted in concert. If only four or five songs from groups III and VI had been put in one group, and groups IV and V combined, the result would have been a more practical and simplified programming.

15

Memorization

(See Volume I, p. 211)

There is considerable evidence to support the conclusion that ability to memorize is not necessarily a corrollary to high intelligence nor a special gift possessed only by the highly gifted and talented, but rather a skill which can be acquired by any normal person.

Many intelligent students and some experienced musicians have difficulty with memorizing. This is due, usually, to the fact that they never learned how, although it must be admitted that the power of memory is a mental trait which psychologists believe varies about as much from person to person as any other trait. Nevertheless, the ability to memorize is distinctively subject to extensive improvement for almost everyone if only they will learn to apply the laws of psychology and common sense. There is no secret, no easy path, no royal road to memorization — only a number of methods or avenues which, if followed, can be expected to improve results. No matter what avenue or method functions best for the particular individual, there are fundamental laws for memorization from which all can benefit.

WHY MEMORIZE

"A performer who is constantly dependent upon the musical score is seriously handicapped in spontaneity of expression, creative interpretation and personal contact with his audience."[1] "There is no question that they (singers) will perform the music better if memorized thoroughly."[2] Litante declares that memorization is "An invaluable aid to vocal freedom."[3] Lamperti emphasizes that "Even an experienced singer will use more breath in learning (reading) a new song than in singing one already known."[4] Memorization develops both self-assurance and accuracy in singing, frees the individual to concentrate on expression, and eliminates mental concern with note and word reading. To pharaphrase Hans Von Buelow's often-quoted statement regarding the importance of the conductor's memorizing the score, *"The score should be in the singer's head and not the singer's head in the score"* if the song is to be interpreted most significantly and with maximum freedom in production.

"A song does not really belong to the singer until he or she has memorized it."[5] In this connection we warn that a singer does not really know a song until he is also aware of all the sound and characteristics of the accompaniment. Each note, including especially the introduction, interludes, postludes, and all the contrapuntal and harmonic devices used, should be a significant part of the singer's awareness in thorough preparation of a song. The pleasure of performing from memory anywhere and anytime is well worth acquiring. It is a habit easiest to acquire if practiced from the first in the process of learning to sing songs.

Most vocalists agree that, normally, a song that is to be sung publicly should be memorized. Nevertheless, there are teachers, especially among instrumentalists and those who have inordinate personal difficulty in memorizing, who are opposed to the beginning student's attempting to perform from memory. The two reasons most often advanced are:

1. The process is too time consuming and prevents acquaintance with a larger and richer variety of music literature.

2. There is too great danger of the beginning student's being embarrassed by forgetting and being discouraged from further study.

---

[1]Winslow, Robert W. "The Psychology of Musical Memory." Music Educators Journal, Jan. 1949, p. 15.

[2]Wilson, Harry Robert. "Artistic Choral Singing." G. Schirmer, Inc., 1959, p. 327.

[3]Litante, Judith. "A Natural Approach to Singing." Wm. C. Brown Co., 1959, p. 9.

[4]Lamperti, Carlo. "Improving Your Voice." Vantage Press, 1954, p. 23.

[5]Peterson, Paul W. "Natural Singing and Expressive Conducting." John F. Blair, 1955, p. 51.

Let us examine briefly some of the facts. First, it must be admitted that serious instrumental music of high quality is usually much longer than vocal compositions and places a greater burden on the memory. Even one movement from a sonata or concerto normally is equal in length to several songs. A disproportionate time, therefore, is required for the instrumentalist to memorize a selection for their repertoire. It would appear that memorization of everything studied would not be a wise educational policy for either the instrumentalist or the vocalist when a larger repertoire, and acquaintance with more extensive music literature, is an important goal.

Some class voice authorities insist that every song that is sung should be memorized by all. The author has found greater student interest and more over-all educational value by following a dual course, however — a few highly-select songs of common suitability and interest being memorized by all in beginning class procedure, with a larger repertoire being introduced and studied sufficiently for capable interpretation with score in hand. This procedure not only allows acquaintance with a larger repertoire, but also introduces choice songs from which the individual student chooses that which he wishes to memorize later for concert or class purposes.

Because of the nature of learning music it is self-evident that no composition can be learned with utmost thoroughness unless it is memorized. Thus the learning of music in thorough detail, which memory work imposes, is an important reason for memoriaztion. *Memorization can never be omitted when thoroughness of learning, highest standards in interpretation, and convincing public performance are major objectives.* There can be no doubt that use of the score is always a barrier between audience and performer, influencing the effect of spontaneity, and that greatest concentration on expression is possible only when the mind is not involved in reading notes and words. "Reading the music is like reading the lines in a dramatic performance. It may be adequate under intimate circumstances, but the presence of the printed page injects a barrier between the artist and his seemingly spontaneous creation."[6]

Objection to memorizing music number 2, that "There is too great danger of the beginning student's being embarrassed by forgetting and being discouraged from further study" is patently a weak argument. It is analogous to avoiding trying to learn to swim because of the danger of getting drowned. Obviously, the thing to do in the beginning would be to urge the swimmer to cover only a short distance in more shallow water. Likewise, the beginning singer or instrumentalist will not start public appearance "over his head," with music that is either too long or too complex for easy memorization. Students should not be assigned to perform at important public events where nervous pressure is likely to be great until after gaining confidence in calmer waters.

AN INTELLECTUAL AND EMOTIONAL PROCESS

Memory work is both an intellectual and emotional process. It is not a function of the brain alone, but of the total emotional personality. Defeatist attitudes and inferiority complexes are often the chief blocks to memorization and not low I.Q., as many believe. Bad memory often serves a neurotic purpose, a means of escape, helping the individual retreat from life experiences at which he is convinced he will fail. Some even use bad memory as an advance excuse to explain away their fear of inadequacy. *Confidence is best built up through class technic in learning songs thoroughly as a group, and through careful guidance in the lesson period in the fundamental steps and methods for using all the senses involved in the memorizing process efficiently.*

The emotions can be either a friend or an enemy to memorization. They are a friend when high interest and confidence are involved. They are an enemy when the student has an inferiority complex mind-set that he can't memorize, or if the distraction of fear is present. Pleasure and confidence are to be established and fear reduced before memorization can be trustworthy in the recall process. *Fear is the principal single cause of forgetting.* No memorization process, regardless of thoroughness, can be expected to function safely in public performance against the distraction of extreme fear.

The first way in which the instructor can help such students, therefore, is to establish pleasure and confidence in the singing act to guide and help in reduction of fear. (This topic has been discussed thoroughly in Chapter 1, Lesson 2, of both this Textbook and Volume I.) The second way in which the instructor can help memorization is to acquaint himself thoroughly with the process involved and the procedures for learning as discussed in this chapter and outlined in Volume I, and *specifically guide the student in the beginning until the process is well understood and the pupil can work efficiently "on his own."*

Confidence that one can memorize is the first prerequisite. Class memorization together of an easy song is often effective in breaking down lack of confidence in ability to memorize. In fact, some of the most effective class voice teachers have all songs studied sung from memory. They take the time in class to teach each song so thoroughly that by the time it is learned it is also memorized. Certainly, there is more educative and interpretive value to learning a few songs thoroughly than a large

---

[6]Rubin-Rabson, Grace, "The Psychology of Memorizing." Music Educators Journal, Jan. 1950, p. 22.

number superficially. After a few songs have been memorized in class under guidance of the instructor, memory work speeds up and the student then can be assigned to independent memorization.

FUNDAMENTALS OF MEMORIZATION

Highest efficiency in memory work first demands:
1. High interest and "noticing."
2. Intense and persistent attention.
3. Ceaseless enthusiasm.

The musical approach is always the best method for memorizing a song, i.e., first find the meaning of the composer through analysis of the words and the music as a whole, *noticing* particularly unique and salient features. Ability to memorize is increased in direct proportion to musical grasp and understanding of the composition.

Habit is a powerful force for either good or evil. Since habits are much easier to form than to reform, practicing incorrectly in the learning process is worse than no practice at all. On the other hand, it is just as easy to fix correct mental impressions as incorrect ones. *It is most vital that an accurate impression of the composition be obtained in the initial stages of learning.* We not only make sure that the first impressions of a song are correct but also that successive repetitions are done as nearly in the same manner as possible. After recall is secure, and only then, is it safe and desirable to vary interpretation somewhat at times. Unless the student is sure of his own ability to determine correct melody, rhythm, phrasing, accompaniment, and style, he is advised to secure competent help in the factors needed. *The services of an accompanist, a more experienced student, the instructor, or a recording will be of more value in the beginning formulation of correct impressions than at any other time.*

Complicated parts of the music or text require more careful analysis, frequent repetition, and use of more visual memorization than easier sections. In the process of "visual recording" of the score, a technic often recommended is first to closely and attentively scrutinize a short section, then close the eyes and attempt to see the score in the "mind's eye" as its sound is imagined in the "inner ear." If the impression is not clear, the passage should be scrutinized again until it is vivid. Another device, which some find effective to further "set" an impression on a particularly difficult passage, is then to write the score from memory.

The most facile memorizers are *sound* or *hearing* memorizers: those in whose inner ear the music and text unroll before the music is performed. It is the most musical, expressive, and natural approach, a method which cannot be by-passed by any singer, and the main avenue of the three available (*hearing, seeing,* and *feeling*) to be emphasized and developed thoroughly by all. *Seeing* in the "mind's eye" is valuable, however, especially for tricky or difficult parts. There is little doubt that *feeling* (kinesthetic process), involving habitual repetition in the same order of sensations and pattern responses, also will have some bearing on recall, although it does not appear as important a factor for vocal as for instrumental music.

Repetition should never be mere aimless going over and over the score, but rather purposeful concentration each time on specific objectives and improved expression. After the preliminary separate study and analysis of the text and music, it is well to combine them in the memorization process, since each serves to help recall the other because of their inherent association. This does not imply that the song is sung audibly all the time in either the "mental recording" process or on repetitions to routine the interpretation. In fact, *memorization is more rapid when the melody is "sung in the mind."* Higher efficiency results when the song — words and music — is repeated over and over in the imagination until routined memorization is established. Then, and only then, are the mental faculties concentrated entirely on the act of memorization. When a song is being sung audibly in the repetition process, attention is divided inevitably between the technical problems of production and the mental act of memorization. It is advisable, therefore, to *dispense with audible singing much of the time in the "recording" phase of memorization.*

FORGETTING

(*Note* — See also "Recall," p. 124)

Thoroughness of memorization and forgetting are closely allied and a consideration of what causes the one phenomena inevitably deals with the other. Forgetting, or failure of recall, has a number of causes. The three most important are: *distraction of fear, insufficient thoroughness in memorization and practice routine, and lack of continued concentrated interest.*

Forgetting is no sin and happens occasionally to the best of artists. With the experienced artist, however, it happens *only occasionally,* and then is usually of a nature that the disciplined musician is able to "cover-up" successfully from all except those acquainted intimately with the composition. When word substitutions, musical extemporization, and omissions occur through faulty memory, they are made so boldly and positively and in such good taste that the unitiated believe that all is well.

Why does the singer forget? Experienced artists will usually admit to one or more of the three basic causes:

(a) Lack of thorough memorization and sufficient routine in practice;

(b) The mind was allowed to wander from concentrating on the job of interpretation (lack of continued concentrated interest); or

(c) They were distracted momentarily by fear for some reason. Yes, even some experienced artists never completely overcome fear, and must guard against its dangers.

HELPING THE STUDENT LEARN TO MEMORIZE

(*See also p. 157, Part II, "Teaching a Song," for detailed instructions*)

In the initial stages, memory work requires careful and patient guidance from an instructor who understands and applies sound psychology to learning music. Many beginning students have a sense of futility and are utterly discouraged with the study of singing if assigned to memorize a song, without being guided and assisted in the complex problem. The voice teacher can encourage and assist in a number of ways. Nine of the more important follow:

(a) Establishing pleasure and confidence in the singing act.

(b) Selecting high quality songs that are interesting and not too difficult for the student.

(c) Getting the student to recognize the values of memorization in providing additional pleasure, freeing technic, and increasing spontaneity in expression.

(d) Assisting students in careful pre-analysis of the score.

(e) Making sure that the learner has a clear and correct aural-mental picture of how the music sounds by singing it for him, playing a recording, or assisting the class in an accurate sight reading of the score.

(f) Pointing out "tricky" or difficult places where the score should also be visualized and helping in guiding the process of "mental recording" by definite suggestions concerning "noticing."

(g) Pointing out "characterizations" and other pertinent word and music associations.

(h) Taking the class or student through each step of the "Whole Method" of learning a song until the principles and procedures are understood by all.

(i) Illustrating methods of practicing "Recall" in relation to memorizing the text, the melody, the accompaniment, and the total musical complex.

In order to assist the student efficiently as suggested in the foregoing, it is obvious that the instructor needs to be thoroughly acquainted not only with ideas in this chapter but also with the correlating content of Expressive Singing, Volume I, particularly material under the headings of "Underlying Principles and Suggestions," and "Learning a Song."

Involvement of all the senses concerned with memorization — *hearing, seeing,* and *feeling* — is a fundamental for efficiency. A strong motive desire to memorize is also basic. "The more definite, vivid, or interesting the goal towards which an activity is directed, the more quickly will it be reached. There must be more than just a desire to learn — there must be a desire to learn by a definite time and for a specific purpose."[7]

1. *Mental Recording*

In the process of mental "Recording," we first *notice* and *become aware* of the nature and characteristic features of anything we wish to memorize. The least trustworthy way to memorize is by mere parrot-like repetition without the assistance of various meaningful associations. A song so memorized is not really "learned" or understood, will sound mechanical, and be dangerously subject to memory lapses. The more vital and thorough knowledge about the song the student can have, or be given, the better; thorough understanding establishes vital relationships which make memorization not only easier but also more secure. Of what use is memorization if it results in mere "parroting" of the words and notes?

Understanding is based on careful analysis and noticing. All our intelligence, imagination, and background should be involved to the maximum for utmost efficiency. Intent of the composer, insofar as it can be determined, will be of paramount consideration. Understanding a song demands concentrated attention on characteristics of *text, melody,* and *accompaniment.* The instructor guides students regarding *how* and *what* characteristics to notice until they have developed sufficient musical insight and experience to be independent. First impressions are most important; they should be both *correct* and *vital.* Overall salient features such as outstanding characteristics of the text, melody, accompaniment, style, mood, form, and major climax are emphasized first. After over-all impressions are established, details of structure, unity, variety, proportion, minor climaxes, and phrasing may be undertaken.

Association and mental visualization are two faithful servants to memorization. "Recording" is effective and recall easier when we can hook-up what we wish to memorize with something already known or familiar. Strangely enough, the more ludicrous or far-fetched the association, the more likely recall becomes when needed. Vocal music has, however, a number of inherent associations which can be used to aid memorization and recall: form or structure,

[7]Drake, Raleigh M. "How to Memorize Music Economically." Music Educators Journal, May 1939, pp. 38-39.

rhyming scheme and definite ideas expressed in the text; text and mood, text and musical setting, and affinity of melody, rhythm, and harmony. *The greater the number and the more vital and interesting such associations can be made in the "Recording" process, the easier memorization occurs and the safer "Recall" becomes.*

Use of the imagination to create "visualization" is a shortcut in the process of memorization. Visualization may involve either concepts of "characterization" or an actual mental picture of the score. For example, in the previously cited Schubert's Erlking, to be able to visualize the appearance, actions, and innermost thoughts of the various characters involved — the worried father, the feverish and terrified child, the demon Erlking, and the deeply sympathetic narrator — is a most vital factor to both expression and memorization.

Ability to visualize the score, to mentally "draw a picture" not only facilitates Recording but also is a valuable safety factor in Recall. *It is especially important that students notice and visualize introductions, interludes, and unusually difficult or complex parts of the score.* The score should be imprinted on the "blackboard of the mind" together with the even more basic sound association — how it *looks* and how it *sounds.* At the important places mentioned, students will not only *see* the score in the "mind's eye" but also *hear* it in the "inner ear" at the same time. *Analytic noticing and visualization are worth innumerable repetitions in the memory process.*

Adequate repetition in practice is necessary, but *it needs to be meaningful repetition with a definite goal or goals,* not mere automatic going through the motions. Learning does not depend upon repetition alone, as some seem to think; thought must be active and directed toward definite interpretive or technical objectives. Attention of the learner is directed at challenges intrinsic to the material being used. This policy is educationally more effective when, after judicious questioning or stimulation on the part of the instructor, the group itself, or the individual concerned, sets their own objectives for improvement. Such a method develops initiative, musical self-sufficiency, and discrimination most rapidly. Number of suggestions for improvement to be borne in mind during repetition should be limited in number. Too many items generally confuse the student and more rather than less is accomplished. A good rules to follow is, the less advanced the class or student the fewer objectives before repetition.

Improved mental concentration toward more meaningful goals and taking full advantage of the three sensory avenues of hearing, seeing, and feeling are the keynote to efficient memorization. The sensory avenues are listed in their order of importance in memory work for most singers. We must recognize, however, that people differ in mental reaction characteristics and some, e.g., those who are "visually" minded, may prefer to place "seeing" first. In any event, *it is most important to memorize as naturally and easily as possible without hurrying the initial steps or unduly skimping in factors of interest and understanding.*

The best advice is for each student to experiment and find out which emphasis works best for him and use that method. While there is no doubt that "how it sounds" is musically the most important sensory guide, the singer who memorizes completely does not depend entirely on his "inner-ear" but takes no chances. He visualizes especially difficult or tricky spots and routines feeling associations through repetition. By using the three avenues for musical memory, the student will be well prepared for public appearance in case one or the other of them fails.

2. *Retention*

"Retention" is largely dependent on continued interest and practice from time to time. Unless there is an attitude of continued interest, caring about the particular composition, retention weakens rapidly. Once memorized, a song can best be kept in the active repertoire by a program of occasional rehearsing with an accompanist.

3. *Recall* (Note — See also "Forgetting," p. 122)

Effective "Recall" depends on a number of factors such as thorough learning and understanding, continued interest, number and vividness of associations, continued practice routine, and recency of practice. For safe recall, *routine practice extends beyond the point where music is first performed successfully.* The more all three senses — hearing, sight, and feeling — are involved in the process of mental "Recording," the more vidid associations are formed and the less chance there is for memory failure. Sufficient practice routine establishes also a kinesthetic association, a certain "feel" in production to the order of text delivery and to the succession of pitches and rhythms in any phrase. Words and music in a song are an unique, integrated complex, and there is no doubt that each stimulates recall of the other. For this reason, it would appear that separate and complete memorization of the text first and the music later, as separate entities, is not as efficient a method as combining the two in the "Recall" process after some preliminary analysis and study of each is made.

The vocal teacher will be alert to prevent a pupil from brooding over an embarrassing failure of memory in public performance. Brooding can only destroy confidence and reduce chances for success in the future. The student can be told that forgetting is no sin, that it happens at times to all performers, and that after analyzing why memory failed and learning a lesson from the experience, the incident should be "wiped" from the mind. The instructor, in turn, will question his own judgment to see if it was remiss in advising the student and learn also from the experience how better to guide others in the future. Was the song too difficult or complex for the particular student to attempt in public performance at that stage of development? Was it assigned in plenty of time for adequate learning and plenty of routine in practice? Was there plenty of checking in lessons to make sure that the student understood the song thoroughly and had it well memorized?

The "Whole Method," involving study of the whole song first, then the parts, and back to the whole, is generally agreed to be the most interesting, rapid, and thorough method of learning. In teaching songs to beginning classes or individual students, the details of the "Whole Method" as outlined in eight steps (see p. 158) normally will be found highly efficient. It is hoped, however, that neither the student nor teacher will follow slavishly this or any other plan. The individual song, musical ability, and advancement, and other practical and aesthetic considerations, rightfully demand variations in drill technic for the purpose of learning and memorization. For example, a short and easy song may well omit isolation of problems as in step No. 6 and deal only with the song as a whole. Use of recording to teach a song also places much more emphasis on an overall procedure for most rapid learning.

A long and difficult song will usually be started by pupils singing and memorizing the easiest section first; quicker success is achieved, and thereby greater interest and confidence generated to learn the more difficult parts. Emphasis on developing sight singing is also of necessity an important objective in some classes and conditions the approach and methods of memorization. In such classes, after a preliminary reading and analysis of the text and "noticing" of the key and salient features of the score, the next step for the easier types is normally an attempt to sight read the score. Only certain guiding principles are constant. When finest interpretation and speediest memorization are the paramount objectives, the most important of these principles is that students first be made aware of the character and sound of the song as a whole before it is taken up part-by-part.

16

Basic Exercises for Vocal Development

(See Volume I, p. 217)

MINIMUM EXERCISES NEEDED

Most class voice texts and modern teachers of both class and private voice agree that only a few carefully-chosen vocal exercises are really necessary to develop technic. Alfred Spouse states that in the highly successful Rochester, New York, classes, "Comparatively few exercises are used but these few are in definite order, systematically routined day after day."[1] "For though exercises have been written by the thousand, it is only the simple few with definite purpose and procedure that produce results. They must be fundamental and adaptable to every phase of voice-development."[2]

According to Frances Alda,[3] the simplest kinds of exercises, consisting of sustained single tones, slow scales, arpeggios, and other simple devices, were the basic elements of the renowned Marchesi's teaching to develop technic. Litante agrees with this principle, stating that "Ordinary graded books of exercises are utterly useless for the average student."[4] Wilson says also, "In the teaching of singing there is a place for exercises, but they should be functional to the student and not abstract drill, the meaning of which he fails to see."[5]

It is said that Porpora taught his famous pupil, Cafarelli, with a single sheet of exercises, sending him out finally as the greatest tenor of his generation. Whether or not this often-told anecdote is a myth or not is immaterial; the important fact is that for rapid vocal growth the principle of a few well-chosen basic exercises still applies as preferable to any or all of the vocalize methods ever published.

Some maintain that voices can be warmed-up through singing easy songs and that all exercises needed can be obtained from excerpts in songs being sung. There is much to be said for selecting exercises from song material to supplement standard basic vocal exercises used in the warm-up. Exclusive use of such exercises is, however, a successful pro-

cedure only when the teacher is experienced and thoroughly acquainted with just the right source of available material to meet the needs of the particular student at the time. These conditions are met so rarely that it is the normal procedure to employ also carefully-chosen fundamental vocal exercises, for both the warm-up period and to supplement songs and exercises from songs as the basis for developing technic.

Those who prefer to select all exercises from song material nevertheless will find this chapter and the comparable chapter in Volume I unique and valuable in the following respects:

1. To point out and illustrate the several fundamental types of exercises.

2. To explain how to use the basic types of exercises.

3. To outline clearly the underlying principles for vocal adjustment on upward and downward tonal progressions.

MEANINGFUL EXERCISES

To avoid meaningless practice, it is important that every vocal exercise have an express purpose or purposes which the student understands. "A vocalize should not be just a number of notes, but should be treated as a beautiful phrase in its own right."[6] "The intrinsic value of any exercise lies only in the manner

---

[1]Dykema, Peter and Gehrkens, Karl. "The Teaching and Administration of High School Music." C. C. Birchard, 1941, p. 510.

[2]Miller, Frank E. "Vocal Art-Science." G. Schirmer, Inc., 1917, p. 202.

[3]Alda, Frances. "Men, Women and Tenors." Houghton Mifflin, 1937, p. 299.

[4]Litante, Judith. "A Natural Approach to Singing." Wm. C. Brown Co., 1959, p. 30.

[5]Wilson, Harry R. "The Solo Singer." Carl Fischer, Inc., 1941, p. 5.

[6]Mursell, James L. and Glenn, Maybelle. "The Psychology of School Music Teaching." Silver Burdett, 1938, p. 294.

of performing it."[7] The singer needs to have a definite mood, style and tone color in mind, for "It is perfectly useless to practice technique in a mechanical fashion without any expression."[8] Students require guidance in class, and continual admonishment regarding their individual practice, to *always strive for variety of expression in exercises.* To mechanically plod through an exercise as a mere routine can achieve no advancement and do very little good except in the mechanics of warming up the voice. Even the warm-up is facilitated if imagination is used regarding variety of tempo, dynamics, style, mood, tone color, and length of exercise on one breath. "With vocalizes, scales, phrases, or longer passages from songs, the instructor, working with an individual or group, should frequently, if not constantly, vary the tempo, the type of tone, dynamics, and other factors of interpretation."[9]

PRINCIPLES OF PRODUCTION IN TONAL PROGRESSION

No claim is made regarding the originality of any of the guiding principles outlined under this heading, for they have been stated or implied in widely scattered sources by many vocal authorities of both the past and present. However, their compilation and presentation in easily understood form are invaluable to both students and teachers, whether in the singing of songs or of exercises.

A free technic in singing and an even scale require certain flexible adjustments of the vocal organs on *each* tone of the scale as pitch changes either upward or downward, in order to prevent accumulation of tension, unevenness, breaks, and shortened range. The adjustments concern amount of breath energy, mouth opening, pharynx space, vocal band approximation, and quality of resonance on the vowel. When coordinated in proper balance the goal of all legitimate voice training is achieved — *to sing the lowest tone in the compass to the highest evenly, freely, and with no sudden change of quality.* In this respect Wronski quotes Dr. Bonnier, "The human voice has as many registers as there are notes."[10] Marifioti also states, "Slight changes must take place in the vocal organs during the progressive adjustments for the ascending tones of the scale."[11] In other words, an adjustment is necessary on each tone for proper resonation.

When the following principles are habituated and coordinated in proper balance, low tones are seldom flat and never "spread" or breathy, while the high voice is free, sonorous, and smoothly connected with the low. *We cannot overemphasize the basic importance of mastery of these principles.* Both the student and teacher should understand them thoroughly and make every effort to continually refine their application. However, *study of these principles in exercises may have only slight benefit unless they*

also are applied immediately to song literature. Supervising immediate application to songs, and continual checking in the future to improve and perfect technics involved, is the responsibility of the teacher. This procedure will provide a short cut, if there is such a thing, to beauty and skill in tonal production and assuredly will pay rich dividends in time spent.

The five basic principles are:

1. *Use more breath energy for each degree of upward progression and less for each degree of downward.*

Every experienced singer knows that it is easier to sing an ascending passage with added tonal intensity and sonority. The greatest composers for voice recognize this fact in arranging their climaxes and writing their melodies in such a fashion that, in the main, this fundamental of easy production can be maintained. Beginners ought to follow the rule in practice until they have established tonal freedom, control, and coordination of the registers. Afterwards the much more difficult task of reversing the procedure can be attempted in order to sing the exceptional phrase in which it is sometimes required. This happens most frequently in some of the French Impressionistic song literature.

Henderson comments on the tendency of singers to overweight low tones with too much breath as follows; "The singer is always afraid that the tones of his low register will not carry. That is why he so often resorts to pushing."[12] If the tones are correctly formed while restraining breath pressure, they will carry. "The lowest register below the clef is that in which the vocal cords are least tense, and therefore the tones can never be given great sonority in that region."[13]

2. *Gradually release vocal band tension ("glottis-grip" feeling) for each degree of upward progression and progressively employ a more compact, smaller throat vibration feeling on the downward scale.*

It is necessary that the vocal cords in any register tense sufficiently to balance breath pressure or inefficient, breathy tone, without vital sonority, is bound to result. It is established scientifically that the vocal bands are more relaxed and thicker in vibration for low tones and more tense and thinner, vibrating on the edges, for the high. Superficial interpretation

[7]Judd, Percy. "Singing Technique." Oxford U. Press, 1931, p. 10.
[8]Bushell, Sidney. "Fifteen Minutes of Stimulating Vocal Practice." Etude, 1940, Vol. 58. p. 811.
[9]Dykema and Gehrkens, Op. cit., p. 102.
[10]Wronski, Thaddeus. "The Singer and His Art." D. Appleton & Co., 1921, p. 32.
[11]Marafioti, P. Mario. "Caruso's Method of Voice Production." Cadica Enterprises, p. 140.
[12]Henderson, Wm. J. "The Art of Singing." Dial Press, 1938, revised ed., p. 74.
[13]Ibid, p. 77.

of this fact is responsible for some very bad teaching. Some have assumed that the singer should assist this known vocal cord action by tensing the throat more for high tones and relaxing it for the low. *Exactly the opposite is needed* for the reason that the uniform tendency in the low register is to drive the breath too vigorously against an overrelaxed adjustment of the vocal bands in a spread pharynx. Conversely, tendency in the upper register is to use insufficient breath energy, to tense the vocal cords too rigidly, and to constrict the pharynx. Thus low tones are usually spread, flat, and overweighted with breath; high tones are shrill, constricted, and lacking in sufficient breath energy for balanced production. Scientific reason for rule number 2 is readily apparent.

3. *Gradually use more mouth opening for each degree of upward progression and less for downward.*

Previous discussions have emphasized that it is easier to produce high tones with the mouth opened generously; *the higher and louder the tone, the larger the mouth form needed.* Conversely, *the lower and softer the tone, the smaller the mouth form required.*

There is much confusion and more disagreement on the extent of mouth opening than on any other of the five principles listed here. Actually, there can be no set rules or "three-finger-formulas" appropriate to all ranges, all students, all types of music, all dynamics, or all tonal colors. *Correct amount of mouth opening is entirely a relative matter varying with all the factors mentioned.* Only general principles can be stated. The problem would be simplified if all vocal instruments were physically alike and all vocal music could be sung at one volume, tonal color, and tempo. Students are not alike, however, in physical structure of their resonators, expressional demands vary, while rapid or difficult articulation of consonants demands shorter lip aperature than normal for some songs.

Madame Marchesi[14] believed that the higher the tone the lower the jaw must drop for maximum ease of production. Most vocal teachers are in thorough agreement that the singer should use a more spacious resonance form, more ample breath support, and a more loose, "thinner-string" vocal cord sensation as the voice mounts into the upper compass. Strangely enough, however, many of these same teachers do not agree with the opposite adjustments for the descending scale and have obviously never thought the matter through to the only possible logical conclusion — *if certain adjustments are desirable and necessary as the voice progresses upward, these adjustments must inevitably be reversed when the voice progresses downward.* There is, without doubt, an ideal size of mouth opening for any specific pitch and dynamics, which produces best tonal balance,

and this adjustment will vary as pitch ascends or descends and tonal force is varied.

Some teachers mistakenly insist on all students' dropping their jaws widely in the low register as well as the high. It is admitted that eventually some students can learn to sing with good tone in a moderately low compass while employing a large mouth space. They learn in spite of and not because of too low jaw position, however, for this position always makes it more difficult to obtain an efficient low tone with clarity and intensity; the tone tends to be gloomy, breathy, and "spread;" an even scale as the voice progresses upward is made more difficult unnecessarily; and extreme lower range is shortened considerably. *The prevailing tendency is to overdo mouth space in the lower compass,* upsetting ideal resonation balance.

Why not teach the student first to habituate everything possible in technic to make production more natural, free, and easy? Later on when more volume and sonority are desired in the low register, the jaw can be lowered somewhat and more breath energy applied. *This adjustment had best be gradual and follow establishment of easy and correct production with shorter mouth space and softer dynamics when singing in the low range,* however.

Reasons for principle number 3 are clearly evident through brief analysis. Wide mouth opening makes balanced tone and sonorous head resonance easier in the upper register; reduced mouth space makes mouth and chest resonance qualities easier in the low compass. Thus for extreme high tones the jaw is lowered to its maximum position, since maximum head resonance quality is needed. Conversely, for extreme low tones in the compass, the jaw is almost entirely closed to a position closely approaching a hum. This close resonation form encourages needed compactness of the vocal bands for low tones.

A number of generalities may serve as valuable guides regarding proper mouth opening or "jaw-drop:"

(a) Small opening tends to produce a brighter, more concentrated, forward in the mouth tone; average space, a tone with normal tone color and balanced mouth and head resonances; wide space, a darker, more dramatic tone color with more pharynx and head resonance qualities.

(b) Jaw-drop remains the same for any series of vowels or syllables sung on the same pitch when sustained legato style is desired.

(c) Mouth opening normally should increase with *crescendo* and decrease with *diminuendo.*

---

[14]Marchesi, Blanche. "The Singers Catechism and Creed." J. M. Dent & Sons, 1932.

(d) Jaw-drop normally should increase on the ascending scale and decrease on the descending.

(e) Gay, rapid tempo songs, and all songs demanding rapid articulation, demand less jaw-drop in order that the tongue and lips are not forced to move over too wide a space for ease and clarity of articulation.

(f) The average song in medium range is best sung with average mouth space.

(g) The plaintive lyric song and bright tone color in any style require less than normal mouth opening.

(h) The dramatic song and dark tone color in any style demand more than normal mouth space for necessary tonal sonority and louder dynamics.

4. *Progressively think each higher note as having a more "general" and spacious tonal quality and each lower note a more defined and brilliant speech-like quality.*

Acoustically, when properly sung, all vowels gravitate toward the *Uh* form and resonation as the pitch ascends. While assuming warmer and fuller color, *vowels nevertheless retain their own sound identity characteristics.* Conditions of resonation and tonal freedom demand a gradual modification as the higher register is approached, e.g., if a soprano attemps to sing the vowel *Ee,* as in "see," on a high *c,* only an unpleasant scream will result unless the vowel is modified. It will still have an *Ee* sound to the listener but be rounder and mixed with more *Uh,* or an *Oo* quality, than is necessary in the middle voice range. In fact, all vowels in the upper compass are benefitted more or less by the resonance position of *Uh* and a suggestion of its sound; the higher the tone, the more vital for freedom and beauty that the principle be applied. *Ah* is the nearest of all vowels to the matrix *Uh,* which explains why it is preferred by most authorities for vocalization in the high register.

The principle of modifying the vowel toward greater post-nasal resonance as the scale is ascended was inherited from the masters of the Bel Canto singing according to Henley,[15] and appears to be accepted by most modern-day authorities according to Fields.[16] There is ample support for the principle from many sources. "It will be seen that all vowels tend to become more and more alike as the pitch ascends, but they never lose their own character. An *Ah* must always be an *Ah,* E must always be E, etc., but their formation is slightly modified."[17] Philip recommends modifying the vowels in the upper register in order "To reduce the physical strain of their production to a minimum."[18] Austin-Ball declares, "Some degree of vowel modification always takes place in the extreme pitches of the (high) register."[19] Wilson says, "In extreme high notes all

male voices gravitate toward this neutral color."[20] Armstrong also recommends that it is best to modify the vowel "At the point where discomfort sets in"[21] to avoid screaming or shouting the tone.

Many authorities particularly recommend modifying the bright *Ee,* the short *i,* and short *e* vowels in the high register toward the color of the dark *Oo,* a similar principle as modification toward *Uh.* For example, Lilli Lehman[22] urges that the quality of *Oo* always be blended with the ascending tone, while Bushell states, "Always think *Oo* in the upper tones, whatever the vowel."[23] Actually, the natural tone of the human voice, *Uh,* should be better adapted than *Oo* or any other vowel for modifying most vowels, since it achieves the maximum of relaxation and pharyngeal space desired for easiest resonation in the high compass. The *Oo* vowel is, however, in our experience, preferable for modification of the pure *Ee* and the short *i* and *e* vowels. This probably is due to the fact that it is normally desirable for the lips to assume that position anyway in enunciating these vowel sounds in any register in order to prevent them from being too shrill and "edgy."

The concept of modification does not signify that upper tones are then "covered," dull, or gloomy, or that the sound of the vowel becomes unintelligible. It implies rather that warmth, space and head resonance quality are added gradually to prevent upper tones from sounding "blatty" or "yelled." Most tenors and sopranos should start to modify the vowel around third space *c,* baritones and altos around third line *b flat.*

Conversely, vowels need to be thought consecutively more specific, pure, clear, and speech-like in quality as the pitch descends. Students should be advised always to use the speech-like approach on tones in the low compass, enunciating all vowels well forward in the mouth and lips with specific, pure, ringing vowel sound.

5. *Accelerate tempo on upward progressions and ritard it on downward in beginning vocal exercises.*

---

[15]Henley, Homer. "Training the Male Voice." Etude, 1936, Vol. 54, p. 46.

[16]Fields, Victor A. "Training the Singing Voice." Kings Crown Press, 1947, p. 79.

[17]Witherspoon, Herbert. "Thirty-Six Lessons in Singing." Meissner Institute of Chicago, 1930, p. 20.

[18]Philip, Frank. "Philosophy of Voice Culture." Scribners, 1930, p. 130.

[19]Austin-Ball, Thomas. "Answers to Some Vocal Questions." Eastman School of Music Publication No. 7, 1938, p. 52.

[20]Wilson, Op. cit., p. 208.

[21]Armstrong, William G. "On the Treatment of Vocal Registers." Etude, 1939, Vol. 57, pp. 532 and 598.

[22]Lehman, Lilli. "How to Sing." Macmillan, 1939, 3rd. revised ed., p. 81.

[23]Bushell, Sidney. "Covered Tone." Etude, 1939, Vol. 57, p. 739.

(Note — This technic cannot be used in some song literature that demands a metronomic steadiness of tempo.)

It is a well-known fact that it is easier to approach the high voice rapidly, to let the tone "ride" on a surge of breath accompanied by *accelerando*. On the other hand, it usually assists easy production in resonating low tones if we approach slowly with a *ritardando*, e.g., a bass soloist nearly always approaches his lowest tones deliberately, concentrating tone carefully to prevent "spread" or break of the voice.

FOUR BASIC EXERCISES

The four basic types of exercises given in Volume I, Expressive Singing, correlating with this chapter are: The Sustained Tone; The Scale; The Arpeggio; and combination of Arpeggio, Sustained Tone and Scale. It is quite easy to conceive how Porpora may well have selected exercises, identical or basically similar to some of these in each type, and have been able to place them on one sheet of manuscript as reported, to provide Cafarelli all the exercises he ever used. Actually, they are all that any singer will ever need to develop necessary flexibility and strength of the vocal instrument over a wide range. An asterisk in Volume I, Expressive Singing, is used to designate the most basic of the exercises listed for the purpose of memorization and continued use. The student needs other exercises for sight reading and musicianship, of course, but that is another matter and should be emphasized in classwork devoted to this objective.

In warming up the voice, exercises normally will be sung in the order of the basic exercises listed, i.e., sustained and reiterated tones on one pitch first, the descending scale second, etc. *The quickest and most efficient method of warming up the voice is to start exercises on the best vowel and the most freely-produced middle voice tone, then work downward first before extending practice into the upper compass.* In discussing the opinion of vocal authorities concerning the preferred direction of vocal movement in practice, Fields states that "13 agree that downward practice is preferable to upward practice,"[24] and, surprisingly enough, lists no dissenting opinion. *Length and difficulty of each exercise should be extended gradually as technic and endurance develop. Mf is the best choice for dynamics in the beginning.* When *staccato* and fast tempo scales or arpeggio are practiced, however, *p* or *mp* dynamics is preferable.

Exercises need never be mechanical. Students require continuous urging to sing exercises with as much beauty and freedom of tone and accuracy of rhythm, accent, and pitch as one would expect in the most beautiful song. *Variety of tempo, dynamics, tone color, and style are a continual objective* in order to make exercises more interesting and to gain the greatest technical benefit from their use. All exercises will be kept within the student's reasonably easy and correct production at the time. Only delayed progress and possible vocal injury can result if this rule is not observed.

The more difficult scale and arpeggio exercises listed at the end of each type of exercise normally should be delayed for most students and classes until technic develops. In class singing, students are instructed to drop out when exercises extend into a difficult range and tone becomes strained. At the end of the first semester with unselected college-age students, the majority can be expected to sing from *b flat* below middle *c* to *e flat* an octave and a fourth above with fairly good tone and ease.

1. *The Sustained Tone Exercise.*

In the warm-up period after the tone has become reasonably efficient, the inducing consonant *N* or *M* that is listed may be omitted and the various dynamic controls on sustained vowels practiced as in No. 4, (a), (b), (c), (d), (e), and (f) of *VOLUME I*, Expressive Singing. *Normal practice periods need some time devoted to gaining of free production and beauty of tone on long sustained notes* using all vowels, all comfortable pitches, and varying tonal color and dynamics from the softest *pianissimo* to the limit of a pleasantly-sounding and well-controlled *fortissimo*. The beginner will be watched carefully to prevent overdoing the *fortissimo* to the extent that it comes strained, raucous, blatant, or wobbly. *Safe limits in tonal duration, dynamic spread, tone color variation and range are to be determined by the technic of the pupil or class at the time.*

The aesthetic value of tonal beauty and dynamic control on long tones cannot be questioned. The listener is certainly more conscious of the singer's control and expressiveness on sustained tones than on the more fleeting scale or arpeggio passages. Both virtues and mistakes in production are more easily detected on long tones. It is the basis of the singer's technic in which he has the best opportunity to establish breath support and concepts of tone, pure vowel, and ease of production.

The most important of the long tone exercises and the one which demands the most time, patience, and skill to accomplish is the "swell" or *crescendo-diminuendo*, called *messa di voce* by the Old Italian masters. It is one of the fundamental training devices employed in the "Golden Age of Song." According to Henderson,[25] the *messa di voce* was a basic exercise practiced by singers as far back as the year 1638. It was believed that the singer could best attain mastery of breath in sostenuto and for all

---

[24]Op. cit., p. 157.
[25]Op. cit., p. 81.

degrees of dynamics through this practice. Many contemporary singers and teachers support the foregoing viewpoint. Dodds and Lickley[26] contend that the *messa di voce* is the best general vocal exercise, and that it should be practiced on all notes in a comfortable dynamic range. Lloyd declares that "You do not own any note in your voice"[27] until the *messa di voce* control on it is mastered. Lawrence Tibbett describes it as an "Acid test for the voice . . . . a singer who cannot do this cannot be said to have control of his voice."[28]

Henderson recommends that "In singing *messa di voce* the mouth naturally needs to be opened a little more fully at the *forte*. Otherwise the tones will sound compressed. On the contrary, as the tone is gradually diminished the mouth should be gradually permitted to diminish its opening."[29] In reference to mouth opening, the great teacher Mancini, according to Klingstead, declared, "The mouth was naturally opened more fully at the *forte*. . . . However, as the tone was gradually diminished the mouth opening became smaller so the tone would not scatter and lose its carrying power."[30]

When taken on a very long tone from the softest *ppp* freely and smoothly through all degrees of force to *fff* and back again, the *messa di voce* is unquestionably the most beautiful and thrilling effect in singing, and demands the utmost of control. Teachers must exercise a great deal of care in insisting that the student does not anticipate either the *crescendo* or the *dimenuendo*, but learns to execute the "swell" steadily and gradually. Most singers negotiate the *crescendo* with fair skill in a short length of time, but a great deal of practice is necessary to perfect a smooth *diminuendo*.

It is self-evident that the *messa di voce* should not be attempted until the student is able to start the tone freely, softly, and clearly. Neither can the *crescendo* carry to the point where it is forced or exhausts energy so that the much more difficult *diminuendo* is impossible of smooth and gradual execution. *The "swell" is accomplished by a feeling of gradually growing taller and expanding around the waist-line as the mouth opens more fully for the louder dynamics.* This feeling of lift and expansion cannot be discarded on the *diminuendo* as the mouth gradually closes or steadiness of breath is lost when most needed. *Purity of vowel, steady breath support, even vibrato, correct intonation, and free tone will be maintained at all times.*

Attack on *messa di voce* ought to be gentle but positive without any audible glottal stroke. It ought to employ a concept of tone similar to falsetto, but with enough "chest" quality so that it can be developed gradually without any audible shift into full-voiced lower registration on the *fortissimo*. The voice may break on the *diminuendo* until after considerable practice and mastery of the technic. Three

basic ideas can be employed in order to prevent the tone from breaking:

(a) *Let the jaw gradually reduce mouth space.* (This reduces vibration space and makes *ppp* easier.)

(b) *Gradually increase the sensation of intense, forward, nasal hum.* (This helps keep the resonance in the upper pharynx and mouth and prevents it from dropping down in the glottis, causing the break.)

(c) *Maintain a stretched spine and a high, quiet chest with gradually diminishing but steady breath energy.* (A *ppp* must be sung with very delicate but steady and firm breath support, requiring much more finesse than the loud intensities.)

Sustained tone exercises in Volume I are frequently given in thirds in order to accommodate both high and low voices in classes and provide opportunity for fundamental training in blend, balance, and intonation — objectives considered highly desirable in many voice classes. It is well to make it clear to the individual student that solo voices use the same exercises for warm-up and technical development when practicing alone but choose, of course, only one of the pitches given.

Three parts and the full four-part chord may be added for mixed voice classes if desired. Training in sustaining long tones and legato style in part singing on simple cadences also is recommended, using such chord progressions as I-V[7]-I, I-IV-I, I-IV-V[7]-I with various vowels and dynamics, always striving for perfection in legato, tone, blend, balance, and intonation. Such cadences had best be placed on the blackboard for all to observe. (Note — The author's text, "Glee Club and Chorus," published by G. Schirmer, Inc., lists such exercises with full directions for use on pp. 49-53.)

2. *The Scale Exercise.*

The rules for downward and upward tonal progression are listed in Volume I under the heading of "Basic Exercise II, The Scale." These rules are the same as "Principles of Production in Tonal Progression" on p. 127 of this text. They apply equally, of course, to the following basic exercises number 3 and 4, as well as in the singing of all song literature.

It is suggested that each of the five principles

---

[26]Dodds, George and Lickley, James D. "The Control of Breath." Oxford U. Press, 1935, 2nd. ed., p. 48.

[27]Lloyd, Robert. "The Robert Lloyd Tone System." Herr Wagner Publishing Co., 1929, p. 28.

[28]Tibbett, Lawrence. "Should I Change Teachers." (an interview) Etude, 1935, Vol. 35, p. 458.

[29]Op. cit., p. 83.

[30]Klingstead, Paul T., "Common Sense in Vocal Pedagogy as Prescribed by the Early Italian Masters." Edwards Bros., 1941, p. 28.

first be discussed, illustrated, and then applied separately on the scale and the arpeggio exercises following until the principles are understood and functional, before going on to other principles listed. To study all of them in one session, attempting to apply and coordinate all technics involved at once, involves too many new concepts and adjustments, and may result in confusion. After each new rule has been studied and practiced separately, another is added and the two principles coordinated, etc. To sing scales, arpeggios, and songs with the maximum technic, the student will learn eventually to coordinate and balance properly each of the principles involved. The singer continues to practice for more and more refinement in these as long as he sings.

It should be borne in mind that practice of any kind in developing new skill technics is always more or less conscious and labored in its early stages. Every effort is desirable, nevertheless, to make the approach and practice as natural, spontaneous, and musically expressive as possible and to transfer what may at first be labored, conscious effort to automatic habituation (free reflex action) as soon as possible. It is well to remember also that *the best possible assistant in establishing any correct physical adjustment for tonal progression in singing is expression — how it should sound.*

Scales for beginners normally should be sung at a moderately slow tempo, *mf* dynamics, and legato style first before either very slow or very fast tempos, dynamic variation, staccato, and semi-staccato style are attempted. In ascending or descending passages, either scalewise or by leaps, the student ought not to be conscious of any change in larynx position, but will feel rather that resonation for singing is "on one physical level" as discussed previously. In the beginning, however, there is consciousness of a feeling of greater surge of breath energy in a larger vibrating space on ascending passages and of restraining or holding back breath pressure, and resonation in a smaller vibrating space on descending.

3. *The Arpeggio Exercise.*

Arpeggio exercises are listed in Volume I with staccato dots, since their greatest contribution to technical development is probably in staccato style. The beginning student is advised to delay staccato, however, using the legato lyric style until free technic is first established. When staccato practice does begin it should be with a light tone on *p* or *mp* dynamics. Heavily accented style in practice will be delayed until a reasonably free production in both legato and light staccato styles is established.

4. *Combination of the Arpeggio, Sustained Tone, and Scale Exercise.*

These exercises ought not be undertaken until some skill is achieved in the three basic types separately. *If only one basic exercise for vocal development in future use had to be chosen and all others discarded, however, it would be this combination type.* The reason is obvious: it contains all the others done up in one package. Therefore, most of the technics which a student needs in singing songs can be developed through this exercise alone if it is varied as suggested in Volume I. While all basic exercises listed in this chapter are valuable for evening the voice and extending its range, the combination exercises under IV are particularly superior for extending compass.

PART II

BASIC PRINCIPLES AND METHODS IN SINGING AND VOCAL TEACHING

17

Resolving the Controversy on Vocal Methods and Teaching

WIDESPREAD DISAGREEMENT

There is general agreement that "Vocal teaching is less exact than any other branch of musical education,"[1] and that there is less understanding and more misunderstanding of the art and science of singing than any other area of music. Anyone who has read vocal literature extensively is acutely aware of the fact that widespread disagreement exists among singers and teachers of reputation regarding the nature and control of vocal action and how best to teach voice. The extent of disagreement is strikingly illustrated by a scolarly investigation by Victor A. Fields, "Training the Singing Voice,"* covering 702 sources and most of the literature of vocal pedagogy published over a period of many years. This study indicates that there are few points indeed upon which there was uanimous agreement by supposed authorities. For sake of illustration, a half-dozen of the major points of controversy follow:

1. Number of registers in the human voice — Opinions varied from one to three or more.
2. Breathing — Some maintain that the singer should learn to control tone through direct consciousness of diaphramatic action, others that only indirect control of tone through concept of sound is effective.
3. Position of the tongue — Forget it, keep it free, hold it low, hold it high, and groove it are various opinions expressed.
4. Larynx action — It is not agreed whether or not the vocal cords can or should be controlled consciously.
5. Resonation — The importance of head resonance is stressed by some while its value and actual existence are questioned by others.
6. Falsetto production — Whether or not to use or discard falsetto as a legitimate method of vocal production is debated.

SCHOOLS OF THOUGHT

Voice teachers can be divided roughly into two classes: those who believe that vocal control should be conscious, direct, and based upon the detailed scientific findings of physiologists, and those who believe that vocal control should be indirect, largely unconscious, automatic, or reflex and based on tonal imagery. One is physiological, the other a psychological-aesthetic approach. The first group are generally known as the "Mechanists" and the second group as the "Empiricists." Differences between the two are deep and basic. There is, of course, a large middle-of-the-road group composed of most successful vocal teachers who accept some of the findings of science as being quite practical, relevant to understanding of the vocal process, and useful to the teacher in some phases of instruction if properly interpreted. Together with the "Empiricists," however, they insist that the physical instrument used in singing, and the art of controlling it, are two different things and should never be confused; and that the only successful way to achieve control of artistic singing is indirectly through tonal imagery.

"Much as scientific data has contributed to the teaching of voice, there are still many controversial facts."[2] The fact that the physiologists or "Mechanists" disagree so much among themselves on interpretation of their findings is undoubtedly the reason that many teachers discard all knowledge of physical facts pertaining to muscular action in singing as dangerous and unreliable. In addition, the fact that some who appear to know the most about details of physical function, and stress it in their teaching with obviously poor artistic results, has further shaken

---

*First issued as a Ph.D. thesis, Columbia University. Published in 1947 by Kings Crown Press, New York City.

[1]Dassert, Dean (Mme.) "Sound Sense for Singers." J. Fischer and Brothers, p. 11.

[2]Wilson, Harry Robert. "Artistic Choral Singing." G. Schirmer, Inc., 1959, p. 167.

faith in the use of scientific findings in the art of singing.

There is disagreement also among vocal teachers in general as to what constitutes good tone, the detailed methods for achieving it, and in the meanings of many terms used in singing. Differences due to personal taste regarding tone quality will never be resolved, but much progress can be expected in the future regarding standardization of meaning in vocal terminology.* For example, such terms as "placement," "focus," "covered-tone," and "head-voice" have one meaning in some texts and quite a different implication in others.

Conflict regarding theory and methods for proper vocal development and control are so prevalent that it would be highly unwise to advise an ambitious student to read vocal texts extensively and indiscriminately as a basis for greater understanding and guidance in developing technic. The student most likely would become hopelessly confused, or adopt one or another of the extreme viewpoints expressed, with possible irreparable harm to technic or delay in normal progress. *Students can read indiscriminately with safety only after a secure singing technic is evolved as the basis for sane evaluation.*

Singing appears to be the field of music study wherein it has been said that the more you read, the less you are likely to know. Nevertheless, somewhere in the incredible welter of confusion and conflicting statements there are kernels of wisdom, rays of light, and trends of opinion toward the truth if careful analysis, common sense, and psychology of musical learning are applied to the problem. In many cases there is a middle ground between two extreme viewpoints wherein the right course of action can be found. In others, where compromise is impossible, prevailing evidence indicates that one or the other of diametrically opposed ideas is right and the other wrong, for the average student. No vocal text should avoid the responsibility for considering and resolving fundamental issues as the basis for theory and methods recommended to the student.

AGREEMENT ON BASIC PRINCIPLES

Agreement by important professional groups on certain basic principles needs greater emphasis than is given to the matter at present. For example, the pronouncements of the American Academy of Teachers of Singing on such subjects as posture, breath support, etc., are doing much in working toward standardization of a number of fundamentals. The degree of general agreement on teaching methods, appropriate vocal literature for beginners, and amount and type of supplementary vocal exercises also is surprisingly uniform in the various class voice texts now published. It is so uniform, in fact, that it appears on the basis of published ideas on the subject, and clinical demonstrations by recognized

authorities, that most of the fundamental features of class voice teaching are pretty generally standardized. Unfortunately, the same cannot be said for the private teaching field.

Fields comes to the conclusion that while "Unanimity of opinion rarely prevails among teachers of singing regarding any of the pedagogical questions raised, there is often sufficient agreement among authors on a given issue to indicate the basic argument underlying their contentions,"[3] and that "ultimately methods of experimental research and scientific testing can lead to standardization of most pedagogical procedures for training the singing voice."[4] He also concludes that "differences in opinion are usually differences in terminology."[5] Shaw agrees with this latter statement saying that, "More than anything else misleading terminology has served to confuse the vocal teaching profession."[6]

INDIRECT CONTROL FAVORED

It appears that the evidence is overwhelming in favor of the view that coordination of all the muscles concerned in singing is the very essence of free and successful tone production, and that attempts to directly control the action of any particular muscle can only interfere with coordination. Weer, in speaking about Manuel Garcia, the inventor of the laryngoscope and eminent vocal teacher, states, "In all the conversations I had with him, I never heard him say a word about larynx, pharynx, glottis or any other organ used in the production and emission of voice. . . . He was perfectly acquainted with their functions, but used his knowledge for his own direction and not to parade it before his pupils."[7] Garnetti-Forbes[8] believes that it is obvious from neurological evidence alone that the entire vocal masculature functions as one united system, governed only by thought controls, and that the training of the voice involves deep-seated coordinations that can be affected successfully only by a psychological teaching approach.

Many authorities, including Stanley,[9] concur in the belief that voluntary physical controls will obstruct the spontaneous mental processes which must

---

*In an effort to standardize vocal terminology, the "Singers Glossary" by Victor Alexander Fields, published in 1952 by the Boston Music Company contains 450 vocal terms defined as to the most commonly accepted meaning.

[3]Fields, Victor Alexander. "Training the Singing Voice." Kings Crown Press, 1947, pp. 242, 245 and 5.

[4]Ibid.

[5]Ibid.

[6]Shaw, W. Warren. "Authentic Voice Production." Lippincot, 1930, p. 518.

[7]Weer, Robert Lawrence. "My Views on Voice Production." The Author, 1941, p. 11.

[8]Garnetti-Forbes, Elena. "The Amazing Phenomenon of Voice." Rider and Co., 1936, p. 79.

[9]Stanley, Douglas. "The Science of Voice." Carl Fischer, 1939, 3rd edition.

invariably govern good tonal production, and that the vocal organs can respond freely only if let alone to seek their own natural coordination. Emphasis on any conscious direct control of any muscle or set of muscles used in the act of phonation is wrong. "Such training tends to impair a student's natural coordination, destroys whatever musicality he may possess, tends to promote the most sterile kind of self-analysis, and usually results in abnormal self-consciousness and, because of this, inefficient manner of singing."[10] Herbert Witherspoon concurs, "The most difficult thing to do is to leave the voice alone. Voices cannot be pulled, placed or squirted. They perform most effectively when free from conscious effort, mental or physical."[11] Mursell strongly supports this viewpoint, "Always remember, however, that any direct analysis, any direct attempt to control the action . . . . is sure to be extremely superficial, extremely empirical, and that it is certainly not based on any established doctrine of certain knowledge."[12] Klingstead concludes that "mechanical regulation of the vocal organs is impossible. Regardless of statements to the contrary, vocal problems cannot be solved along scientific lines."[13] Litante maintains that "singing is, ideally, a direct simple, spontaneous act"[14] and that "when the mind has been properly trained, it has a way of propelling the instrument."[15]

If we accept this philosophy as a basis for action in methods of teaching, as most teachers do, we employ only the indirect, aesthetic methods, which the Old Italian masters used so successfully, for muscular control. *The method is based on the art of expression, on how the student thinks and feels when producing the best technical results as judged by the ear, and on establishing as habitual the thought and feeling sensations associated with the best musical results.* The key to success in this method appears simple; continuous emphasis on expression — that is on concepts of beauty, significant phrasing, and naturalness of delivery — as controlling stimuli for proper technical response. The secret of rapid technical progress for the student lies very largely then in improvement of discrimination between the good and the bad, recognition of small degrees of advancement, and habituation of the best response.

Emphasis on the part of the student in applying critical judgment is always based on the question — HOW DOES IT SOUND AND HOW DOES IT FEEL? These two senses — sound and feeling — are by no means reliable for the beginning student but they must suffice and be gradually improved, for there are no other functional approaches. The student must recognize this fundamental fact. He must realize that technical progress is in direct proportion to growth in building reliable hearing and feeling discriminations. In turn, the teacher must realize that his pupils will progress most rapidly when continuous examples, explanations, and corrections are given with emphasis on how tone should sound and feel when most correctly produced. It is a distinct handicap for the teacher to be unable to illustrate vocally the proper sound; it is an absolute necessity to have the correct knowledge and vocabulary to describe and make meaningful to the student the proper aural and feeling sensations associated with superior results, or progress will be slow, halting, and insecure.

SCIENTIFIC KNOWLEDGE DANGEROUS

Famous old Italian master teachers believed that stimulus for the desired tone came from the mind and that muscular response followed automatically, without conscious effort, to produce the imagined sound. It appears that everything was known about singing in the year 1700 that is known today, except the physiological factors. It is contended by many authorities that we have inferior and not better singers than in the past. Can it be that the revelation of scientific knowledge of physical action in tonal production has worked injury to the vocal art? Or is the fault in unscientific aesthetic and psychological interpretation of the findings of physiology? We are inclined to the latter viewpoint, for it is common sense to assume that we cannot know too much about facts in any field. While the sensitive ear is the only true test or criterion for proper tone, every useful scientific fact, every pertinent physiological finding should be used — not to substitute for artistic control but to help explain it. Correct scientific findings, properly interpreted, can only complete and perfect knowledge about principles of vocal training arrived at through successful experience down through the ages. The soundest voice teaching, therefore, is psychological in nature but based on scientific physiological laws.

Those who interpret physiological findings incorrectly as a rule have started with a fundamentally false assumption: belief that analysis of the action of a particular muscle involved in phonation suggests that this muscle can then be consciously controlled and trained to function in the desired fashion

---

[10]Kagen, Sergius. "On Studying Singing." Rinehart and Co., 1950. p. 76.

[11]Witherspoon, Herbert. "Thirty-Six Lessons in Singing for Teachers and Students." Meissner Institute of Music, 1930, p. 15.

[12]Mursell, James L. "Education for Musical Growth." Ginn & Co., 1948, p. 229.

[13]Klingstead, Paul T., "Common Sense in Vocal Pedagogy as Prescribed by the Early Italian Masters." Edwards Bros., 1941, p. 43.

[14]Litante, Judith. "A Natural Approach to Singing." Wm. C. Brown Co., 1959, p. 145.

[15]Ibid., p. 98.

when singing. This assumption is physiologically unsound for two reasons. First, because all muscles involved in singing are part of an involved complex, one cannot be controlled consciously by concentrated thought without neglect of the others, with resultant blocking of necessary coordinate function. Second, the assumption does not take into account the fact that two principle areas of muscles concerned in singing, the throat and the diaphragm, involve muscles which are basically involuntary rather than voluntary in action. "There is the underlying difficulty of the fact that the vibrator, doubtless the most important (physical) element of the voice, functions below the level of consciousness and must be controlled indirectly through the resonators and by means of resonance imagery. This subjectively differentiates the voice from the instruments and makes vocal pedagogy highly personal."[16]

Finally the assumption is unsound psychologically and aesthetically in that it does not recognize that singing is first of all an art and, second, a science. As an art, expressive singing demands concentration of thought on sound desired rather than conscious control of muscles. Experience down through the ages indicates that the less the teacher says to a pupil about the details of vocal mechanics the better progress is likely to be. Students who desire to know certain facts about the physiology and mechanics of tonal production should be acquainted with them but, at the same time, earnestly admonished concerning the dangers of attempting *direct* control of muscles involved.

SUCCESSFUL TYPES OF DIRECT CONTROL

Does it follow, therefore, that all types of direct physical control should be discarded as injurious in the vocal training process? Not at all! Only attempts to consciously or directly control the *involuntary* muscles, particularly the vocal cords and the diaphragm, concerned with the act of phonation, should be discarded. We agree with Wilson that "Overemphasis on separate physical factors will only destroy the coordinated control absolutely necessary for good voice production."[17] Acceptance of the foregoing philosophy of indirect control in relation to the art of singing does not rule out the practicability of direct physical control both in relation to correction of persistent tension of *voluntary* muscles or parts of the body which should be habitually relaxed, and at times, the use of specific exercises for strengthening unusually weak or inefficient muscles. *Correct postural conditions, and jaw and lip opening for various dynamics, vowels, and tone colors are factors that will respond most rapidly at times to direct attention and control by the beginning student.* For example, students can be told safely to round the lips for a more free and less shrill pro-

duction of the *Ee* vowel. Such controls are primarily of a *postural* nature and, like the proper way to grip a golf club for best control, need to be habituated as rapidly as possible in order that they can be forgotten. They are actually the setting up of most favorable basic physical conditions as habitual in order that better coordination of all phonation muscles is possible and that expression can be realized more fully without muscular interference. *Such direct controls concern muscular adjustment or movement which can be observed, and are not exclusively involuntary muscles in normal life action.*

USE OF PHYSIOLOGICAL FINDINGS

Exact knowledge of what happens physically during proper singing undoubtedly gives the teacher a cue, based on scientific fact, for better analysis and formulation of safe empirical or indirect methods to guide the student in relation to habituation of desired sound and associative feeling sensations. Established scientific fact is fact incontrovertible. We cannot ignore it without closing our minds to the possibilities for improving and speeding up vocal training and being satisfied with the *status-quo* of present knowledge. There are a number of technical questions regarding vocal action which are still debated by the anatomists, however. It therefore would appear unwise to accept any statement on these controversial issues as fact until the mechanists can agree on what actually happens. Even then, no fact is to be trusted in singing when it is based entirely upon scientific physiological findings; reliance is justified on only the realities of experience in vocal training and production. *Scientific facts are valuable to the teaching of singing only when they help to explain, simplify, or verify experience in artistic expression.*

It would appear that a study of physical muscular action or condition in singing is valuable chiefly when it relates to desirable posture, relaxation of muscles which should not be involved in the act of singing, and, particularly, to the establishment of feeling sensations associated with the act of proper singing-sensations which can be described, felt, analyzed, and habituated as the basis for a more reliable technic. Drawings and illustrations of the anatomy of particular muscles and attempts to describe their exact function in singing, while interesting intellectually and perhaps valuable at times to the teacher, are often confusing to the students, a waste of valuable time, and sometimes a dangerous impediment to free and natural production.

Knowledge of the details of functioning of the individual muscles concerned in the singing act has

---

[16]Vennard, William. "Singing, the Mechanism and Technic." Edwards Bros., Inc., 1949, p. 94.

[17]Wilson, Harry Robert. "Music in High School." Silver Burdett, 1941, p. 167.

no more value to the singer in obtaining free tonal production than an awareness of the various muscles of the leg has to a runner in achieving free style in running. (Neither the singer nor the runner will perform one whit better for the knowledge). Both learn best by doing, by observing correct example, and by habituating proper feeling associations when results are best. Even the teacher of singing does not require a thorough knowledge of the anatomical details regarding the structure and placement of the various muscles used in singing. However, well-equipped teachers should thoroughly understand the function of the vocal organs, and all major muscles involved in the process of singing, in order to know whether or not the pupils work is normal or incorrect because of faulty mechanism.

Certainly the finest effects in singing, the most subtle nuances, are obtained empirically by *indirect* suggestion, by an appeal to the emotions and imagination with consequent automatic muscular adjustment. Free and beautiful expression cannot be dictated by attention at the time to direct controls, but is the result of unconscious reflex muscle work. We agree with those who maintain that science rather than tradition should determine vocal pedagogy; but *it should be the science of aesthetics and psychology* used to interpret the science of physiology, since singing is primarily a psychological expressive act, an art first and a science second. The teacher must never make the mistake of reversing the order.

CHAPTER 18

Basic Educational Principles for Teaching

TWELVE BASIC FACTORS IN CREATING AND MAINTAINING HIGH INTEREST AND FAVORABLE ATTITUDE

It may be well to summarize first the basic factors that are most important in creating and maintaining high interest and favorable attitude toward singing, without which maxium progress is impossible:

1. Breaking down or lessening the fear complex or inferiority complex of many students.

2. Emphasis primarily on expression and secondarily on technic.

3. Enthusiastic attitude by the teacher for songs used.

4. Understanding and sympathy of the teacher for the problems, desires, and preferences of the pupil.

5. Use of good song literature of a type to appeal to the interests of students and develop technic without creating discouragement.

6. Calling favorable attention to progress and to increasing technical and interpretive mastery which students might not notice. (Note — Recording helps greatly in this.)

7. Use of group motivation to promote the natural desire to obtain group approval, to cooperate, and excel.

8. Careful psychological approach to vocal study with selection of beginning songs that are sure to be interesting to the student and easy enough to build confidence and enthusiasm for singing.

9. Obtaining a competent, inspiring accompanist for the lesson period.

10. Making arrangements for an adequate accompanist to practice at times with the student.

11. Adequate opportunity for solo appearances before classmates and the public.

12. Wise use of praise and careful application of positive and constructive criticism.

Many of the above basic factors have been discussed in detail under various hearings in Part I of this manual.

TEACHING PEOPLE FIRST

The voice teacher has a greater responsibility than teaching voice: *he is teaching people!* "For effective instruction, the teacher should be conscious of vocal, physical and psychological problems of young students."[1] The finest type of teaching always is based on knowledge of background, interest, and needs of the student; method should be adapted to the student and not the student to stereotyped and inflexible method. Each pupil should be challenged according to his own ability and limitations. We should neither expect nor demand the same progress and goals from the less talented than from the more gifted.

Because the vocal instructor is working unavoidably with the emotions in artistic expression, he gets to know the pupil more intimately than a teacher in almost any other subject. Opportunity for good in influencing the philosophy, personality, and future welfare of the students is immense. The voice teacher must accept this responsibility conscientiously. Even in the private studios, most of the pupils will never become professionals. This is doubly true of high school and college vocal classes. "The singing lesson is a small part of what the student carries with him. The atmosphere of the studio which is the real personality of the teacher, his ideals, aims, the depths of his sincerity, in short, his concept and meaning of life, goes with the student and will be remembered when the lesson is forgotten."[2]

Each pupil, even the most inept and least talented, should be made to feel that his ideas and

---

[1]Turner, Louise. "A Study of Song Literature for Solo Voices in Secondary Schools." M. A. Thesis, University of Ia., 1939, p. 8.

[2]Clippinger, D. A. "The Head Voice and Other Problems." Ditson, 1917, p. 63.

opinions are important. The teacher should never be a dictator; he should encourage initiative and enthusiastic participation on the part of the student. Pupils must be given the self confidence to try, with the assurance that it is never a sin to make a mistake. The aim is to try to avoid making the same mistake twice or repeating mistakes until they become habitual. Discouragement, like the common cold, is contagious, and may spread in a class unless it is detected early in the individual, the cause determined, and positive help given in recommendations for correction.

Never assume that a pupil is totally unmusical because he cannot sing on tune at the beginning of vocal study, or even after a period of careful instruction. If unable to "carry a tune," the pupil is probably weak in other phases of musical ability as well. Musical ability has a number of facets, and a careful check sometimes is justified before the individual is advised to give up the study of music entirely for more fruitful pursuits. Even if they cannot sing, some pupils nevertheless will prove quite sensitive rhythmically — well coordinated for study of a keyboard instrument, and capable of discriminating judgment regarding music and its performance.

It is important at all times that music methods be so designed that students have a reassuring and stimulating experience and awareness of significant success, or the possibilities for success. It is doubly important that this be achieved at the very beginning of voice work. The teacher should avoid negative criticism, sarcasm, heckling, or impatience with a student who is really trying. We can be absolutely sure that a quick and never-failing way to reduce numbers of vocal students, and make the course disliked thoroughly, is to apply clever sarcasm and biting criticism in generous doses. *The best kind of teaching method is positive rather than negative.* The student is first told how to think and what to do rather than how not to think or what not to do.

Teachers who never allow students a thought or preference of their own in regard to interpretation are making a sorry mistake. It is well to avoid the pitfall of teaching every song and every phrase to the pupil by a dictatorial process. The student must be "put on his own" as quickly as possible if he is ever to develop initiative and independence in working out interpretations. Plenty of guidance and plenty of listening are necessary in the early stages of course but, even then, the student should be encouraged to study the problems, suggest interpretation, and be allowed some freedom of choice. Amount of freedom of choice should increase gradually or the singer can never become a real musician with necessary independence of judgment.

It is not enough to guide the pupil only while he is taking his lesson; *it is far more important that he*

be taught how to use his own intelligence and limited experience to best advantage while practicing by himself. Voice teaching needs the same thing that is now applied in more generous measure in some other subjects — careful attention to the psychology and technics necessary in teaching the student *how* to practice and study. For the first time in a published course, Expressive Sinigng, Volume I of this course goes a long way toward guiding the student, but the instructor must do his share also. It makes no difference whether voice teaching is private or in classes—*the biggest job of the teacher is to guide properly the practice of the pupil.* Careful attention to this principle will speed up vocal progress without fail.

When students are singing individually or with a group, they should be urged to sing with spontaneity and assurance. At the same time they should be urged to learn to *listen* and *feel* — listen to such factors as intonation, blend, and tonal freedom, quality and expressiveness, and attempt to habituate as rapidly as possible the associative feeling sensations that accompany the most beautiful and expressive results. Only in this way is it possible to speed up discriminations necessary for advancement of singing technic. *The student must learn that he is his own most effective critic;* i.e., only he *can* put criticism or ideas for improvement into effect.

At times it may be necessary to experiment somewhat in class with different songs, vowels, and exercises in order to discover a particular student's interests and needs for development. *No song or vocal exercise ever should be assigned for practice and memorization to an individual unless its influence for good is unquestionable.* Reason for an exercise should always be imparted and well understood. Trial and error in these respects is both unnecessary and unforgivable.

We can "catch more flies" educationally with honey than with vinegar. Nearly all pupils are stimulated and given more confidence to do their best work through well-chosen praise rather than criticism. This philosophy is particularly true of vocal study. Praise always should be honest and based on fact not fiction, however. It is well to remember that we can praise *effort* honestly even if we can't praise *product.* If the student is really trying, perhaps over-trying, and still botches production, we can praise his "good try" honestly as a preliminary to positive, constructive criticism regarding why product was poor. Few pupils resent criticism when given in this manner. They are not so likely to tense-up as they do when criticism is direct, severe, and not following praise of effort or some good point about their production. Censure is justified, of course, when the student fails to make a good try or is lazy. Nevertheless, the pupil should not be subjected to severe criticism publicly for lack of effort or trying until the instructor, perhaps after private conference, has ascertained the reasons.

KNOW YOUR STUDENTS

One of the outstanding characteristics of modern educational methods is emphasis on knowing the individual student. *We must not only know what to teach, but also those we are going to teach* if maximum interest and growth are to be achieved. The voice instructor should endeavor therefore to get to know each student as a person as soon as possible: likes and dislikes, progress in other subjects, demands upon time and energy, health, vitality, home and social background, study conditions, etc. All play an important part in the success of the pupil and in the choice of song material and assignments to promote proper growth. Attitude, general health, and freedom from colds and laryngitis are of vital importance. They often need the advice and wise counsel of the vocal instructor before satisfactory progress is possible.

VOICE RECORD FILING SYSTEM

It is well for the voice teacher to have a voice file index record for each student. Such a record might well have a place for listing personal factors such as those mentioned in the foregoing paragraph. Most colleges have an I.Q. and entrance examination ratings, as well as past academic record, that are available to college instructors. College music departments often have these records on file for each music major as well as each student's rating on a standard native talent music test such as the Seashore test. It is usually a simple matter for the vocal instructor to obtain the phonograph records and test forms for a native capacity music test and administer it himself when desirable. As a rule, only the sections on discrimination in pitch and in rhythm need

be given, since they are the most vital and significant factors in determining vocal limitations.

An index filing system for each pupil can be printed on standard letterhead, or better yet, on index cards. The first card, can contain general information, the second card voice classification and characteristics, and successive cards the pupil's repertoire and grade average for each semester of study. This system is concise, logical, inclusive of needed information, and handy for reference. Such a voice record file for college level students might well contain all or most of the following information. (High school age level would be similar, but usually needs somewhat less information).

INTENSIVE VERSUS EXTENSIVE STUDY

Educational psychologists agree in general on the desirability of a good balance between intensive and extensive study in voice classes. A too narrow concentration on memorizing and perfecting only a few compositions seriously limits variety of musical experience, gives only a meager acquaintance with song literature, and may result in discouragement on the part of the student. On the other hand, coverage of too large a number of songs in one semester causes superficiality of understanding, limits both expressional and technical progress; and also may result in loss of interest by the student. Both high standards and high interest therefore are served best by a balanced program; some songs should be selected early for memorization and continued attention while others may be studied and sung only once or twice.

No cut and dried answer is possible to the question of how many songs should be covered each semester because of many variable factors. These include academic credit allowed; number and length of lessons per week; difficulty of songs; general competence of the class or student; skill of the ac-

---

General Information (First Card)

Name _____ Age _____ Telephone No. _____

Address _____ Semester in School _____

I. Q. _____ Entrance Grade Average _____ Entrance Exam Rating _____

Former Average Grade in Music Subjects _____

Native Talent Music (a) Pitch _____ (b) Rhythm _____

Health _____ Vitality _____ Freedom from Colds and Laryngitis _____

Home and Social Background _____

_____

Speaking Voice _____ Personality _____

Comments _____

_____

Voice Classification and Characteristics (Second Card)

Name_____ Age_____ Semester in School_____

Type of Voice _____ Maximum Range_____ Usable Range_____

Production (Free or Tense) _____ Evenness _____ Flexibility _____

Quality_____ Power _____ Ability to Sing on Pitch_____

Control   (a) Breath in Phrasing _____ (b) Dynamic Range_____

Previous Background or Experience in Singing _____

_____

Solo Ability_____

Previous Background or Experience in Playing Instruments_____

_____

Comments _____

_____

*To be filled out after the voice has had some chance to develop and assume its true characteristics.

Repertoire, Grade and Recital Record
(Third Card and Successive Cards)

Name_____ Semester in School _____

Song Title	Composer	*School	Grade

Average Singing Grade

Effort Grade_____ Progress Grade _____ Final Semester Grade_____

Solo Appearances and Recitals (Place and Date) _____

_____

Comments _____

_____

*Classic, Romantic, Old Italian, German Lieder, etc.

companist; experience and ability of the instructor to teach rapidly and thoroughly, etc. Each voice teacher must survey his own situation and "cut the shoe to fit the last," always remembering to retain a reasonable balance between the factors of thoroughness and variety. Intensive study songs are memorized; extensive songs usually are sight read with accompaniment. Our experience in college classes has been that a beginning class can study 4 to 6 songs intensively, and 8 to 12 extensively, during a 16-week semester in which they meet two times weekly.

Effectiveness of teaching cannot be measured by the number of songs or exercises sung, or by the amount of vocal theory covered during a period or in a semester's work. *Thorough understanding of fundamentals is basic* and superficial work is a waste of time. Too many songs, too many ideas, and too many exercises during a period are confusing to the student and worse than too few. *Effective vocal teaching is reflected by understanding, grasp of the principles involved, and added enthusiasm and skill in expression.* Only as many workable concepts as the pupil can absorb should be presented in one period.

FUNDAMENTAL PRINCIPLES OR OBJECTIVES IN LEARNING TO SING

Ten great fundamental principles or objectives that are basic requirements for maximum progress and success in singing should receive major attention in the process of teaching voice. Neither teacher nor student can be unaware of or neglect them without injury to vocal progress. The key to success is continuous emphasis and improvement of these factors. Content of Expressive Singing, Volume I accompanying this course is based on these ten objetcives:

1. An attitude of enthusiastic interest, pleasure, and confidence.
2. Intelligent, regular practice habits.
3. Vital, upright, expansive posture.
4. Efficient diaphragmatic-costal breath control.
5. Freedom, vitality, expressive color, efficiency, sonority, and evenness in tonal production.
6. Mastery of correct, clear, and beautiful diction.
7. Mastery of legato technic.
8. Mastery of agility and flexibility technic.
9. Sensitive, intelligent, and movingly-expressive interpretation.
10. Natural, gracious, poised, and attractive stage presence.

BASIC PHILOSOPHY FOR DEVELOPING TECHNIC

1. *Mental Development*

Technic in vocal production is controlled indirectly by two senses — *hearing* and *feeling*. The student can judge his own production only in reference to the question, *"How does it sound and how does it feel?"* Both concepts are developmental requiring intelligent guidance on the part of the teacher for rapid growth. The major points which both the pupil and teacher should question are listed in Expressive Singing, Volume I (See p. 71, "Fundamental Criteria for Students to Use in Judging Their Own Singing.") Vocal instructors must keep the idea paramount that it is not enough to develop vocal technic; sound musicianship and discriminating taste are even more important and must be developed also. The voice is controlled psychologically through stimuli in which the factors of mental ease, motivation, and tonal and feeling imagery are stressed.

(a) *Mental ease* — Mental ease is established by convincing the pupil that singing is a natural and enjoyable expression, that he can sing, that fear and inhibitions can be reduced or eliminated, and that satisfactory progress is possible. Feelings of frustration, failure, and extreme shyness are lessened by first building confidence through starting with easy and attractive songs (the Song-Approach) and through group singing; stressing encouragement and positive natural expression; reducing criticism to a minimum; and gradually introducing and increasing amount of solo participation. (See also pp. 3-5)

(b) *Motivation* — No great amount of effective learning can be expected in any subject unless motivation is high. "Motivation controls phonation because it stimulates the proper desire to express, accompanied by the incentive of fruitful purpose. Those who favor indirect teaching methods believe that strong purpose, aesthetic feeling, interest, and joyous enthusiasm spell freedom of vocal action in singing."[3] The common sense approach to any problem appears to be one that enables us to reach our ultimate goal the quickest and easiest way with the least chance for accidents or casualties on the way. In the art of singing there is little doubt that beginning and continued emphasis on expression is the one sure road to interest and progress that all can follow safely. Technic is valuable and highly necessary, of course, but it should always be a by-product of expression and subservient to it.

High interest and motivation are achieved best in two major ways: placing strong emphasis in teaching methods on expression, on mood, on style, on spontaneity and naturalness, and building in the pupil as rapidly as possible some degree of success and pleasure in singing. When this is done, enthusiasm for further study and

[3]Fields, Victor Alexander. "Training the Singing Voice." Kings Crown Press, 1947, p. 128.

work to develop more proficient technic is not difficult to obtain. The pupil first must experience satisfaction in artistic vocal expression on a comparatively low technical difficulty level, and have or develop a minimum vocal skill before he can be expected to have pleasure and enthusiasm for vocal study. This is easiest to achieve for most students through introductory group singing.

It is obvious that vocal muscles can be strengthened and developed by either song singing or vocal exercises. Interest and motivation is usually higher when this can be done, at least in part, through song literature. When separate vocalises are used they should be short, easily memorized, and specifically designed for an explicit purpose of which the pupil is aware. When exercises are used, beauty and freedom of tone, as well as a variety of tone color, dynamics, and style should be emphasized as the surest way not only of retaining interest but also of advancing technic.

The most interesting and musical exercises are derived from phrases in song literature being studied. It is normal procedure also to vocalize the whole song on a vowel or neutral syllable as part of the learning process. Wilson recommends that the student practice songs by "singing them on a sustained vowel; especially *Ah, Oh,* and *Oo.*"[4] If a song is quite rhythmic or accented in character, it is best to vocalize it on a neutral syllable such as *lah, loh, loo,* or *lay.* Vocal authorities in general concur that this practice makes it easier to concentrate on the musical aspects of learning a new song without the hurdle of diction interference. This practice promotes beauty and freedom of tonal production, and establishes a concept of legato-sostenuto beneficial as a pattern when the text is sung. When a vowel in which natural tonal color fits the mood of the song is selected, an appropriate tonal color ideal, which has significant transfer to the singing of the text, also is formed.

(c) *Tonal imagery* — Discriminating tonal concepts are developed and musical taste is improved through listening and imitation of select singers of artistic merit in sensitive interpretations. This can be either in concert recitals or in the use of recordings. There is no substitute to listening to fine singing as a means of building high standards in technic and interpretation. *The student must be impressed with the fact that he can sing no more freely, beautifully, and significantly than he thinks and that vocal progress is in direct proportion to growth in aesthetic discrimination.* The student should be advised to imagine clearly the ideal sound of each tone and the complete expressional demands of each phrase *before the attack.* This results in better coordinated vocal reflexes, prepares the proper amount of breath, and puts the emphasis where it belongs — on expression.

2. *Physical Development*

It is self-evident that advance in vocal skill is dependent primarily on mental growth in aesthetic discrimination and, secondarily, on development of physical coordination, strength and endurance — neither can be neglected. Expressional concept furnishes the strongest possible stimulus for coordinated physical response. Nevertheless, there are other aspects of physical growth which need attention in teaching. Among them are developing vital health and strong physique, habituating correct posture, and establishing habitually reliable feeling sensations which accompany proper breath control and phonation.

The teacher of singing must realize that many students have to be built up physically before vital tone, adequate breath support, and endurance are possible. Feeling sensations which accompany erect, expansive posture, breath support, and phonation should be habituated as rapidly as possible as the basis for technical development. *No attempt ever should be made to directly control action of the diaphragm or vocal cords.* Their coordinated function is controlled successfully only through mental stimulation of tone desired and through establishing proper feeling sensations such as occur for the relaxed, open throat, the high, quiet chest, spinal stretch, and flexible expansive resistance around the waist-line.

3. *Coordination of Mental and Physical Controls*

It scarcely can be denied that singing is both a mental and physical act and that while the ear must be the most important and final arbiter, feeling sensations may be an even more reliable guide in the initial stages of developing free production and breath support. This is true especially for those whose aesthetic taste and pitch sensitivity are quite undeveloped. Contention of a few extremists, who maintain that a student should depend exclusively on either the sense of feeling or of hearing, denies the use of one of these important senses for assistance. It is also contrary to the testimony of most successful singers.

For examples of extreme viewpoints, Lilli Lehmann[5] is of the opinion that singing can be controlled indirectly only by listening and is devoid of physical sensation. On other hand, Louis Graveure

---

[4]Wilson, Harry Robert. "The Solo Singer." Carl Fischer, 1941, Vol. II, p. 20.

[5]Lehman, Lilli. "How to Sing." Macmillan, 1939, 3rd. revised ed., pp. 34 & 99.

insists that the correct way to learn to sing is "by the muscular feel of the thing,"[6] and that training should be "entirely through the channel of muscular sensation, and not by the ear."[7]

There is adequate support for the view that both mental concept and feeling sensation should be used in singing. "Sensation and hearing always go hand in hand with mental conception in producing a singing tone."[8] The formative years of vocal study should be devoted to persistent "listening for tones and feeling their sensations"[9] for the only way the singer can judge production is "by the way tones sound and feel."[10] Hall and Brown[11] declare that the student learns gradually to discriminate concerning the quality of his voice through both hearing and feeling sensations. Vivian della Chiesa believes that we should always make a concentrated effort to obtain the sensation of good tone so that they can be summoned at will "until they become second nature."[12] to assist in the reproduction of good tone again. Clippinger maintains that while the ear is the "final court of appeal."[13] nevertheless, it must frequently "be supplemented by the sensations"[14] which accompany voice production. Fields summarizes the opinion of most successful voice teachers as follows: "The view that both sound and sensation are effective guides to vocal action would seem to be a tenable compromise in the absence of objective evaluations of either factor."[15]

We agree with Mursell[16] that kinesthetic sensations should rarely be brought into conscious attention, especially during the act of artistic interpretation. It is quite another matter in the initial training process, however. Many feeling sensations in regard to posture, breath support, relaxation, dynamics, tone color, and resonation are desirable supplements to mental concepts for technical control. They are, however, of a type that are not associated with direct attempts to control specific muscular action of the vocal cords or diaphragm. They can be habituated comparatively early in the training process and become more a part of subconscious habitual reflex than of direct conscious control. Expressive Singing, Volume I, is quite specific in describing feeling sensations when tone is best.

THEORY OF MUSCULAR DEVELOPMENT

There are two opposed theories of muscular development in relation to vocal training. In practice there are teachers who adopt some of the training ideas of both systems in order to achieve a certain purpose or control in a specific register. Other teachers, in despair after reading a number of books or treatises on the subject by so-called authorities who disagree, adopt "lock-stock-and-barrell" whichever theory seems more reasonable to them. They then join the phalanx of those who claim this plan

as the *only* way and that any other is sure to injure or destroy the voice.

Unbiased observation of results obtained in various voices trained under the two diametrically-opposed systems, and application of common sense in relation to well-known physiological laws understood by any well-trained athletic coach, prove the fallacy of claims that there is only one way to develop the voice muscularly. Let us examine these physiological facts first as a basis for understanding what happens:

1. After a person becomes an adult no muscle can grow and develop muscular strength unless it is used.

2. Use of a muscle burns-up (oxidizes) old tissue and replaces it with new.

3. The new tissue is stronger than the old, providing practice was not so long or severe that more tissue was burned-up or severely exhausted than could be replaced before the next practice. (Notice the word *stronger* is used and not *stronger and more flexible*. Greater flexibility depends also on *how* the muscle was trained.)

4. Vigorous daily practice develops muscular strength most rapidly, providing again that practice is not too exhausting to allow recovery. (These facts support the claim of those who maintain that a student should practice voice vigorously, *mf*, and long enough to grow tired in order to obtain the maximum muscular growth from vocal practice. Louder than *mf* may be dangerous, however, since it is more likely to cause excessive tension and over-exhaustion, while too long periods of vigorous practice will certainly do so.)

5. There are three basic ways that muscles are trained according to the end result desired:

(a) *Powerful Rigid Tension* — This method results in slow, loggy response but will quickly develop enormously strong, bulging muscles for such acts as weight lifting. Much of a wrestler's muscular development is under powerful strain but

[6]Graveure, Louis. "New Theories of Vocalism." (an interview) Etude, 1931, Vol. 49, p. 128.
[7]Ibid.
[8]Key, Pierre Van Rensselaer. "Teach Yourself to Sing." Reader Mail, Inc., 1941, p. 65.
[9]Stueckgold, Grete. "If You Were My Pupil." (An interview) Etude, 1935, Vol. 53, p. 9.
[10]Ibid.
[11]Hall, John Waller and Brown, Ralph M. "What Every Singer Should Know." Vocal Science Publ. Co., 1928, p. 18.
[12]Della Chiesa, Vivian. "Successful Singing." (an interview), Etude, 1942, Vol. 60, p. 583.
[13]Clippinger, David Alva and others. "Vocal Forum." Music Teachers Natl. Asso. Proceedings for 1936, Vol. 31, p. 168.
[14]Ibid.
[15]Op. cit. p. 188.
[16]Mursell, James L. "The Psychology of Music." W.W. Norton, 1937, p. 227.

he must also develop adequate speed for the purpose. Powerful rigid tension results in huge, "knotty," locally-developed muscles *capable only of slow, powerful action.* If other sets of muscles are isolated and developed separately in like fashion, these also become powerful for slow action only; coordination remains poor between two sets of muscles *unless they are used together in the training process in some act which involves both.* It is therefore obvious that powerful rigid exercise, if used exclusively in vocal training, could never result in speedy, flexible action. It must be watched very carefully regarding amount of daily practice allowed to prevent excessive exhaustion and a tearing-down, rather than building-up, of muscular strength.

Few vocal teachers would admit that this is the type of muscular training which produces the end result they desire in singing. Nevertheless, many are doing just that in practice when they insist on starting vocal training on loud, long-sustained intensities above *mf* as a norm. Some also recommend isolating the upper register or the lower register and training students first on *fortissimo* dynamics. If the voice survives this dangerous tension system — and some do if the student has exceptional recuperative powers — and extent of practice daily is strictly limited, the vocal muscles become exceedingly powerful and capable of great tonal volume. If great power is the objective, it can be accomplished quickly by this system — but at what a cost in quality, flexibility, freedom of production, range, and probable lasting quality of the voice. Fortunately, the number of teachers advocating this system is less and less.

(b) *Light Flexible Tension* — This method of muscular training provides speed, coordination, and extensive range. It can be used exclusively for all sports in which a high degree of speed and coordination, but not power, is necessary. Fencing is an excellent example. Visible muscular development is smooth, never great, but uniform and coordinated. A boxer interested merely in sparring and piling up points could use this system exclusively. If he wishes to develop the power to knock out his opponent, however, he must amplify the light flexible training system by training also under powerful flexible tension described next.

It is evident that the light coloratura voice should emphasize light flexible tension training and that *all voices should be trained under this system when development of agility and more extended range is the objective.* This method allows easier coordination of the registers and longer periods of practice without exhaustion.

Like the boxer who also needs a knockout punch, however, singers desiring more power and a richer, dramatic quality in the voice also must practice under the powerful flexible system following.

(c) *Powerful Flexible Tension* — This system is closely allied to light flexible tension and is used where power as well as speed is desired. It develops large, smooth, coordinated muscles but not enormous, "knotty" growth. It is obvious that most voices need this type of vigorous training for a considerable amount of their practice in order to develop sufficient power and endurance to sing dramatic music effectively and to "carry over" an orchestral accompaniment. Powerful flexible tension results in slower action than light flexible tension methods and needs to be supervised more carefully in regard to safe limits of practice, however. If the two systems are judiciously combined in practice periods, the voice should be sufficiently agile, free and beautiful in tone. It should be well coordinated, have endurance, sufficient range, and become increasingly powerful and resonant with conitnued use.

In summary, it is obvious that the type of muscular training chosen should depend on the tonal ideal and objectives of the particular instructor. It is difficult to alter personal taste in this regard. The teacher of voice should understand, however, the type or types of training he is using, what their characteristics and limitations are, and what end result can be expected. The physiological laws for muscular development are unalterable. There is absolutely no reason to believe that the muscles used in singing will respond any differently to type of training than any other muscles in the body.

In organizing a standardized vocal course such as this, it is necessary to choose the type of vocal training and exercises needed by the average and not the exceptional singer. Methods recommended must be such that they can be applied by both the average teacher and the average student. Great power of voice is not an objective; freedom and expressive beauty of tonal production with adequate power, compass, and agility are. Those who wish to develop tremendous power in the voice quickly had therefore best seek some other vocal course.

DRILL

The gaining of adequate technical skill is extremely important in any expressive art. Drill cannot be avoided if high standards are to be achieved. However, an erroneous principle is involved in attempts to separate the study of technic from expression. When this is done, only mechanistic self-conscious production with limited meaning, beauty, and freedom can be expected. It is a fundamental misconception of many teachers that expressive singing is possible only after the details of technic have been perfected in vocal drills. This is placing the "cart before the horse;" *gaining of technic in singing is not achieved by blind, mechanistic drill but principally through stimulating intelligent, expressive intention.*

At just what point should systematic and formal drill begin in singing? There comes a time after the pupil has freed himself of major inhibitions, established a confident and enthusiastic attitude, and has a desire for more perfect and significant expression, when the systematic and formal study of technic is appropriate and most beneficial. *Emphasis on perfection of technic should not come suddenly but should be increased gradually, becoming stringent only toward the end of vocal study.*

Students always should be made aware of the purpose of a particular drill or exercise (what it will do for the voice) and have an immediate application of the principles involved in attempts to improve song interpretation. Direct benefit in some vocal drills, such as agility exercises, is not always strikingly or immediately evident, however. Like a tonic, they must be taken daily for some time before benefits are clearly apparent. Awareness of purpose of drill and recognition of progress always will serve to make exercises interesting and functional rather than pointless.

In initial lessons for beginning classes, it is best to start with an easy song. Follow that with a functional drill taken from context of the song, from the specific exercises at the end of each lesson, or from one of the appropriate exercises in Chapter 16 of Expressive Singing, Volume I. A good exercise is to select a phrase which is in particular need of improvement from the song being studied at the time. If necessary, transpose it first to an easier register and vocalize it on a vowel or neutral syllable. Then carry it back into the key and context of the song before continuing with other work. After a number of typical basic problems involving the sustained tone, the scale, and the arpeggio have been approached in this fashion through song singing, the student will recognize the value of such exercises and be ready to welcome the warm-up drill at the beginning of the class period.

EMPHASIS

It is best to spend most of the time in a class or lesson learning to sing by *singing*, rather than in long detailed theory discussions, most of which can be obviated by having students read Expressive Singing, Volume I, carefully. Some class discussion and illustration of major points plus mid-semester and final examinations, followed by a review and discussion of questions missed, should suffice in the ordinary class for covering theory of vocal production. Teacher training classes and classes composed largely of potential future voice teachers naturally should spend considerably more time in discussion of details.

REPETITION

Songs not only need to be repeated and gradually perfected but also it is axiomatic that *students never master a vocal principle on one hearing.* They may understand intellectually, but mastery does not come until the action implied by the principle can be correctly and habitually performed. Experienced teachers are well aware that they must explain and reiterate constantly, sometimes using a different approach or vocabulary to impress ideas on the minds of students. An effective teaching approach in empasizing important rules of vocal production is first to state the rule or principle positively (what to do) and then negatively (what not to do).

TERMINOLOGY

The instructor always should be on the alert for improving his vocabulary in explaining ideas so clearly that students can understand quickly and easily. Simple, clear-cut, non-technical language, followed by demonstration of the right and the wrong way, are best for helping the beginning student. Technically or scientifically correct language that has no meaning association is not only futile and a waste of time but also may be injurious.

The teacher should be absolutely clear in his own mind about meanings and never use terms glibly or loosely. There is seldom, if ever, an excuse for using terminology incorrectly or for endeavoring to impress pupils with erudite discussion in technical language that is meaningless and confusing. When there is any doubt about students' understanding terms used, they should be clearly defined at the time. "The Singer's Glossary," by Victor Alexander Fields, lists the standard definition of terms used in singing as understood by most vocal authorities today. The teacher should own this reference and be thoroughly familiar with its contents. An adequate number of copies should be available for use by students also.

Pupils should be urged always to disclose any confusion or uncertainty they may have regarding terminology, vocal theory, and methods in application until understanding is thorough. The teacher must realize that some are shy, proud, or do not wish to be considered "dumb-bells." It therefore is necessary to check to make sure that principles are understood, not only those presented in Expressive Singing, Volume I but also those given in lecture and demonstration.

FOREIGN LANGUAGE
(See also p. 213)

Common sense would suggest that the English-speaking students should first learn to sing English with good diction and control before attempting songs with the complication of a foreign language. It never is advisable to have pupils sing songs in a foreign tongue unless the teacher knows enough about that language to correct mistakes in pronunciation, or is confident that the pupil has an excellent background and can be trusted in this respect. If the translation is at all acceptable, *most songs should be sung in English before the average American audience.* If it isn't acceptable it usually is best to program another song. As a rule, when songs are sung in a foreign language, text meaning should be furnished either in program notes or verbally by the singer. *Such verbal explanations should never be left to chance but should be checked and coached carefully by the instructor.*

CLASSIFYING VOICES

Most informed authorities on class voice teaching, and many in private teaching, recommend that voices not be classified in the beginning. They contend that it is both possible and desirable, through first establishing proper basic principles and free production, to "eventually grow into healthy maturity and acquire normal characteristics of quality, range, etc., without any preliminary classification at all."[17] "In the voice class or private studio a common fault is the tendency to classify voices too soon. Young voice students, especially, should not be classified until the correct vocal habits have been established."[18] "Vocal teachers and choral directors should avoid cataloguing voices, particularly male voices, with any degree of finality, if the student is less than twenty-two years old. The young voice, and especially the untrained one, may not reveal its adult caliber in the early years."[19]

Vocal teachers frequently are puzzled over whether a youthful voice is a high baritone or a tenor in the making. There should be no worry over the matter for if the voice is allowed to settle into its own level, as it will if practice is in a moderate range, the voice will classify itself. *Only proper training and time reveal the true voice.* Actually, in close borderline cases — e.g., between a dramatic tenor and a heroic tenor, or between a coloratura and a light lyric soprano — the difference is frequently not clear, or if it ever is apparent, does not become so until after a high stage of technical proficiency has been established.

Voices should be classified primarily by natural timbre or quality and not by extent of range. *Vocal quality within the easiest produced middle octave of the particular voice is the safest determinant; range alone is deceptive and never should be used as the basis for classification.* "In classifying the untrained voice the existing range should be of the least concern. (Voices spoiled by wrong training have fre-

quently a false range.) The quality and color of the voice, and the ease with which certain passages are sustained, must first be considered."[20] The tessitura in which a singer can vocalize most easily and resonantly is a secondary factor in supplementing timbre judgment. Madame Marchesi states, "When in doubt, let quality be the deciding factor."[21] Gunderman and Schumacher agree, "Quality is the chief factor. Range is secondary."[22] Grace says, "Compass is variable whereas color is a more or less stable characteristic."[23]

Timbre, or characteristic quality of the voice, is determined by the size and construction of the physical organs of phonation and resonation. Thus soprano quality is soprano rather than alto because the instrument is smaller and produces, therefore, a tone characteristic of the soprano. This is so regardless of the fact that some soprano's voices may possess a "chest register," enabling them to sing lower pitches than many altos.

Mature voices are classified into four basic types according to quality of the voice and the characteristic tessitura and range in which they operate: soprano, alto, tenor, and bass. A number of sub-types are found within these four basic types. It must be understood that there is not just one distinct soprano timbre, alto timbre, tenor timbre, and bass timbre, but several. For example, within the basic soprano classification there are coloratura, light lyric, lyric, spinto, dramatic, and mezzo types, as well as perhaps others coined by some teachers. Differences between some of these closely-allied types are sometimes more imagined than real. Certainly, nature also makes voices so close to the line, or in between as it were, that even the highest authorities disagree in a fruitless attempt to classify them in an exact category.

In any case, the teacher's problem for several years with youthful voices is to select a varied repertoire for each individual voice which is *suitable at the time* in range and difficulty, rather than to worry over fine distinctions in classification. Even for mature singers authorities often disagree over this matter, especially in regard to voices of extensive range and versatile technic.

[17]Fields, Victor Alexander. "Training the Singing Voice." Kings Crown Press, 1947, p. 65.

[18]Peterson, Paul W. "Natural Singing and Expressive Conducting." John F. Blair, 1955, p. 7.

[19]American Academy of Teachers of Singing. "Problems of Tessitura in Relation to Choral Music." (A brochure)

[20]Wronski, Thaddeus. "The Singer and His Art." D. Appleton & Co., 1921, p. 16.

[21]Marchesi, Blanche. "The Singer's Catechism and Creed." J. M. Dent & Sons, 1932, p. 45.

[22]Gunderman, John and Schumacher, Bernhard. "Manual for the Music Reader for Lutheran Schools." Concordia, 1933.

[23]Grace, Harvey. "The Training and Conducting of Choral Societies." Novello & Co., 1938, p. 3.

The octave or two-octave major scale usually is employed in various keys as an exercise for classifying voices. It is well to check with songs also, however, for students often will sing more freely on a song than on an exercise, realizing more of the true quality of voice. A phrase of a song also may be transposed upward or downward until the compass limits of the voice are revealed without recourse to formal scale exercises.

In assigning individual songs and exercises to pupils, the teacher should be careful, of course, to select the most suitable keys in which range and tessitura will lie, so that the easiest and best quality of the voice will be emphasized. The wise teacher almost has an instinct for choosing just the right song material to interest and challenge the student without discouraging him with obstinate difficulties or a style completely alien to his understanding and taste at the time.

VOCAL RANGE AND TESSITURA

The best average singing range or tessitura of the individual voice at the time should determine the most suitable key in which a song is best sung. As voices develop toward technical maturity, tessitura may change; key then should be adjusted accordingly. In determining the safest range and tessitura for either solo or ensemble singing when dealing with undeveloped amateur voices, one of the most authoritative sources is the pronouncement of the American Academy of Teachers of Singing which follows.*

PROBLEMS OF TESSITURA IN RELATION TO CHORAL MUSIC

"It is common knowledge that a great many teachers of singing hesitate to permit their pupils to participate in choral singing because experience has proven that due to the usually high *tessitura* dominating the arrangements of many choral works, harm is done to the voice.

The subject of *tessitura* involves certain basic facts pertaining to the safe use of the singing voice. These, in the opinion of many teachers, have been and continue to be widely misunderstood and frequently disregarded by composers, arrangers and publishers. In order to clarify the basic principles involved, and their practical application, the American Academy of Teachers of Singing presents the following beliefs which have been reached through prolonged investigation and study, and confirmed by experience.

In this connection the designation *tessitura*, or 'heart of the range', is used in accordance with the definition of Grove's Dictionary as 'the prevailing or *average* position of the notes in relation to the compass of the voice, whether high, low, or medium', and is not to be confused with the word *range*. In the following tabulations the vocal limits allocated to the various voices are those of the *average amateur*

singer and not the professional artist, and refer *only* to *choral music*.

WE BELIEVE

1. That a general tendency exists among composers and arrangers to write voice parts in a dangerously high *tessitura,* and that continued singing in this high *tessitura* is apt to strain and permanently injure young and adolescent voices and prevent normal development of the vocal apparatus.

2. The safest and best *range* and the safest and best *tessitura* for the various vocies are as follows: (The *tessitura* limitations do not prohibit the composer and arranger from writing for the full *range* of the voice.)

Note — If composers and arrangers would keep within the designated range and favor the recommended *tessitura*, voices will be protected and choral music will be more effective when performed.

3. That although group singing tends to reduce the mental hazard, no singer can be expected to sing in ensemble a high tone he cannot sing reasonably well in solo. For example, the tenor section as a unit cannot be expected to negotiate high B flat if members of the group cannot sing it individually.

4. The easiest *volume* for singers in the upper half of the range is best vocalized *mezzo-forte*, and that successful *piano* and *pianissimo* singing are more difficult and require training and guidance.

It must be repeated — and emphasized — that the above beliefs refer to *choral singing* by *amateurs*. Directors will find in their groups individual voices of greater range than the ones cited above, but such individual cases cannot be considered as the standard in estimating the safe range and tessitura for the average voice.

GENERAL OBSERVATIONS AND SUGGESTIONS

Published music should provide some indication of *tessitura* as well as *range*. The range of a song may be conservative and yet the *tessitura* so high as to constitute a strain on amateur voices.

Voice teachers and choral directors should avoid cataloguing voices, particularly male voices, with any degree of finality if the student is less than twenty-two years old. The young voice, and especially the untrained one, may not reveal its adult caliber in the earlier years.

Chorus directors should assume the task of keeping in touch with the progress of individual voices, and because this involves frequent voice trials and the willingness to shift a singer from one part to another, it is frequently neglected. There is the endless temptation to encourage young people to sing certain parts, not because their voices are ready for this particular tessitura, but because the chorus needs more voices on the part. The choral director should restrain his ambition to produce a perfectly balanced ensemble and to perform over-ambitious

---

*Used by permission.

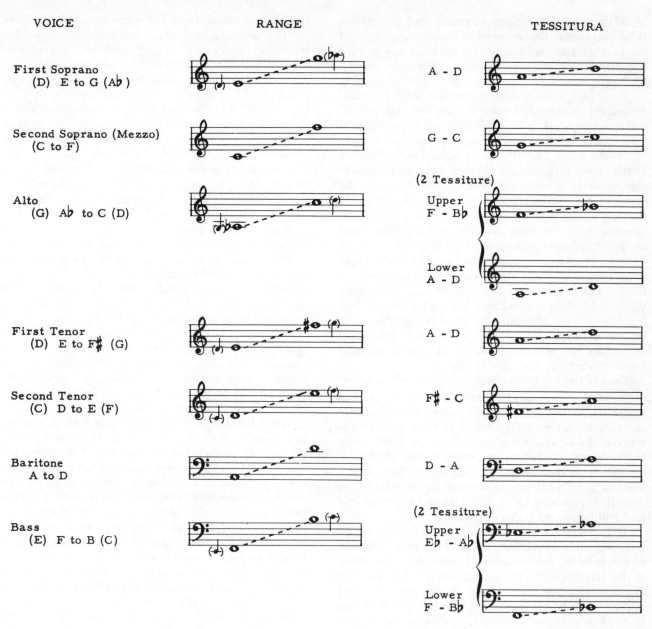

VOICE	RANGE	TESSITURA

First Soprano (D) E to G (A♭) — A - D

Second Soprano (Mezzo) (C to F) — G - C

Alto (G) A♭ to C (D) — (2 Tessiture) Upper F - B♭ / Lower A - D

First Tenor (D) E to F# (G) — A - D

Second Tenor (C) D to E (F) — F# - C

Baritone A to D — D - A

Bass (E) F to B (C) — (2 Tessiture) Upper E♭ - A♭ / Lower F - B♭

musical programs at the expense of the vocal welfare of his individual singers. This effort on his part would be minimized if composers and arrangers will consider carefully this important matter of *tessitura*, and confine their writings within the same compass of the average young voice."

THE CHANGING VOICE FROM CHILDHOOD THROUGH MATURITY

The voice changes physiologically during the normal span of life. First, from infancy to childhood; second, from childhood to adolescence; from adolescence to adult life; and, finally, from adult life into the muscular disintegration of old age. Before adolescence the range of boys' and girls' voices is the same, but the boy's voice is often warmer in color. After adolescence, the tenor voice is approximately one octave lower than the soprano and the bass voice one octave lower than the alto.

Be not deceived when male voices are said to be singing a melody in unison with treble voices; *the male voices actually are sounding an octave lower even if reading from the same score written in the treble clef.* On the other hand, when treble voices sing with male voices from a score written in the bass clef, the treble voices are sounding an octave higher than the actual pitch sung by the male voices. Adult mixed voices singing a melody together actually never really are singing in unison but in octaves. It is surprising the number of students, and even teachers in the public schools, who do not realize this basic fact and are amazed when it is proven to them.

The voice teacher deals principally with the post-adolescent or the adult voice but, in the high school, will have to work with some adolescent voices, perhaps many in the latter stages of the adolescent voice. In some cases the boy's voice has not settled to the extent of losing the characteristic reedy adolescent quality; it must be treated carefully from the standpoint of attempts to sustain loud dynamics or develop the high compass rapidly. Even at the college-age level the voice has not fully matured, and normally does not mature until the thirties.

After a voice has been trained to sing freely, there is no reason why the singer should not continue his singing career to age of sixty-five or more, providing the voice is not abused and the individual retains his health and physical vitality. When the body begins to grow old or lose its vitality, the vocal instrument, as a part of the body, grows old and loses its strength and vitality also.

One of the most distressing problems which sometimes faces the vocal teacher is rehabilitation of a singer whose voice finally has broken down because of years of misuse. Regardless of their past public success, those who have sung for years with faulty production must return to patient work on fundamentals for a considerable period before there is any hope of significant progress. Bad habits established over the years can be expected to yield only slowly and stubbornly to correct principles.

It is necessary to understand the changes which take place during adolescence, and the characteristics of the voice at that time and immediately following, if the student is to be guided safely and properly. Physical changes are usually more extensive and rapid for the boy than the girl, but this is not always true. For example sometimes, but very rarely, the voice of the girl who matures very rapidly drops an octave to a true contralto range during the high school age, making as extensive a change as that of the boy whose drop is down only to that of a high lyric tenor. When this occurs, the vocal cords greatly extend in length; the girl with such a radical drop in range never can be safely urged to sing with extensive volume in this new, lower "chest" range until the instrument is more physically matured and "set" with age and proper use.

Although there is some structural growth, the girl who remains a soprano continues to have vocal cords of approximately the same length and a voice of the same general range. The principal change that occurs is a physical strengthening of the muscles controlling the instrument, with consequent increase in power, warmth of tone, and some extension of range.

The public school music teacher's major problem in regard to choral singing often is knowledge of how to handle the adolescent boy's changing voice. Knowledge of what actually happens is a prerequisite. Physically the changes are as follows: First, the larynx enlarges and the vocal cords extend in length. There is considerable growth for a tenor and much greater development for the voice that eventually becomes a bass or counter-bass. Second, the extent of larynx and vocal cord growth occurs in proportion to extent of other physical growth. If physical growth is distributed over five or six years, as it usually is during adolescence, the voice lowers gradually and without marked loss of control. If physical growth is quite rapid, most of it during one or two years, as is infrequently the case, the voice lowers very rapidly and is sometimes quite unmanageable; so much so in fact that the speaking voice may sound like a child's on a few words and then drop suddenly an octave and rumble like a man's. Cartilage and bone structure outstrip muscular development and the boy is always awkward, gangling, and uncoordinated physically in other respects than vocal. In most cases of extreme vocal change the voice should be used, but only carefully in a limited range where tonal control is more secure.

Very few vocal authorities today believe that the boy should stop singing during the voice change period; rather they believe that it is both physiologically and psychologically beneficial to use the voice easily and naturally *within the limits of a changing range and dynamic variation.* In a very few rare instances when the boy seems to grow up almost overnight, and both the speaking and singing voice are extremely unmanageable and embarrassing to him, it may be advisable to discontinue singing temporarily. The adolescent age is the time when the proper kind of part music, arranged to fit the problems of the lowering voice, is especially needed. Some of the girls' voices that have a lower range and a richer quality often are assigned to sing the alto-tenor part with the boys. Even in adult mixed choruses, low altos frequently are used to supplement tenors on their part when it is weak or goes too high for their technic.

THE BOY VOICE

The boy soprano should be trained to sing in the same manner as any other soprano. Original emphasis on soft *Oo* vocalization to open the throat and prevent shrillness is justified. Exclusive and continued emphasis on a dark, hooty *Oo* vowel form, as exemplified in many church choirs, deteriorates vitality of tone and range in the middle and low compass, however. This practice, plus continued loud singing in the upper register, no doubt is the basic reason why so tragically few of the many potentially fine boys' voices trained in this manner are ever heard from later as outstanding adult singers. Exclusive use of any vowel form and color throughout the compass will deteriorate any voice, and boys' voices are no exception.

All the fundamental rules and principles regarding vocal production and training apply equally to the boy whether in the pre-adolescent or adolescent alto-tenor(Cambiata) changing stage. Curious common misconceptions still persist regarding the boy's changing voice. One is that it is injurious for the boy to sing during this period; another is that if he sings at all during the time, it should be in a very limited compass and always quite softly. Still another misconception is that boys' voices should be either hurried or delayed in the process of change. Actually, correct use of the voice is beneficial to the vocal instrument at any age level. Covering of as generous a range and dynamic spread as can be accomplished within the boundaries of free, unforced tone is equally desirable for complete and balanced development of the vocal instrument. Why either hurry or delay the physical change to a man's voice? It is more natural and safer to lower range of vocalization as nature dictates.

Most boys' voices, when correctly used and when physical growth is normal, actually lower and change slowly from around the age of ten up to twenty or more. Most of the change occurs between the ages of twelve and sixteen. It is beneficial for them to continue to use a normal wide range, employing the two basic registers of the voice, just as it is desirable for training any other voice. Most boys in the Cambiata period who have to be limited to the usual five-to seven-note range are thus limited because of improper use either previously or at the time. *Incorrect practice before and during the period of change is usually the direct cause of separation of high and low registers* rather than a condition to be expected because of physical change. *Physical change normally is gradual, and use of the voice in a wider range is possible and desirable in most instances.*

If the vocal instructor does not understand how to obtain free, well-connected tone over a wide compass, however, less injury will result to the alto-tenor voice by limiting ensemble singing to the five to seven tones traditionally employed in the junior high school song books. In addition, it must be recognized that when physical growth occurs very rapidly over a short period of a year or two, as it does occasionally, the boy is very awkward and un-coordinated in vocal as well as in all other physical responses. The voice of such a boy should be handled with special care to avoid forcing and strain, and may well be limited to a more restricted range.

EFFECT OF ENSEMBLE SINGING ON THE SOLO VOICE

Will choral ensemble singing harm the solo voice? A yes or no answer is impossible because so many factors are involved. In the first place, it should be remembered that it is not how high or low, loud or soft but *how* we sing that is important in improving and preserving the voice. An intelligently-used and freely-resonated voice never will be harmed but should be strengthened and benefited by the practice of normal ensemble singing. On the other hand, the immature singer with poor production, whose voice is in a critical formative period in vocal study, usually would be better off to avoid group singing for a time. This is true particularly of the individual who is tempted to strain and shout in order to hear his or her voice clearly above the body of ensemble sound, rather than to be content to allow the voice to merge into the mass effect. Choral directors who demand that immature voice groups sing any music chosen, regardless of difficulty, cannot fail to realize their ambition to program impressive literature for public performance at the cost of severe injury to voices. Students interested in preserving their voices should avoid such directors as they would smallpox.

The final answer depends on the individual conductor and his philosophy and practices in rehearsal, as well as choice of music with reasonable range and tessitura of parts. Those who understand the formative immature voice, and are more concerned with preserving it for the future with free tone properly resonated as the basis for all ensemble singing, and who choose music wisely from the standpoint of difficulty, seldom, if ever, will injure voices under their direction. In fact, the solo voice often shows marked improvement because of a high type of ensemble experience under the right kind of conductor.

Forcing in any part of the voice is bad but it is most likely to be injurious in music that demands *fortissimo* in continuously high tessitura. If the singer's throat aches habitually at the end of rehearsals and the voice fails to regain its freshness on the following day, it is time to call a halt, find out why, and correct the cause before irreparable damage results. Normal fatigue of the vocal instrument at the end of long strenuous rehearsals is to be expected and is beneficial to muscular growth, rather than injurious. However, extreme weakness, exhaustion, and pain in the throat are sure signs of dangerous strain that cannot be ignored safely.

Exclusive singing of a specialized type of ensemble literature featuring one type of production almost entirely is also a hazard for solo voice development. For example, one may say that, on the whole, madrigal singing is a noble form of small vocal ensemble specialization; it has high values in developing better musicians and singers able to handle light dynamics more skillfully. However, those devotees who persist for an extended time in singing the light, devitalized, rather dry tone mistakenly demanded by some directors, to the exclusion of balanced experience with other music requiring a warmer, more resonant, and sonorous tone, often find their solo technic deteriorating for recital singing, and especially so in dramatic works.

UNIQUE PROBLEMS OF EACH VOICE TYPE

Because of the characteristic tessitura in which they normally are required to sing in ensemble and other natural factors, different types of voices have their own unique problems as follows:

1. *Lyric and Coloratura Soprano.*

The lyric and coloratura soprano seldom has need to use her lower register in ensemble singing and it is normally best to carry the light "head voice" type of production down as low as required, around middle *c*. If matured too rapidly in persistent attempts to sing too loudly and dramatically with use of the low "chest" quality, tremolos and wobbles are likely to result and the voice may suffer irreparable damage. Sopranos, in particular, must open the mouth and throat generously on high tones, or the voice will be shrill and strident, blending badly in the choral ensemble. The neutral *Uh* or the vowel *Oo* is best in introductory soft singing to obtain a concept of free, open throat and a "head" tone without shrillness. Vocalization then should emphasize the *Ah* in the upper register as the best practice vowel for most voices.

When singing in the high range it is well to urge sopranos to "chew" each word and syllable with a quick and generous drop of the jaw; they must develop a sensation of spacious, relaxed, high-arched pharynx with pronounced resonation feeling behind the nose and eyes. Such production will result in free, mellow, and beautiful high register, a tone that is best not only for solo but also will blend best in choral ensemble.

2. *Altos, Mezzo-sopranos, and Contraltos.*

These voices find the center of much of their singing in ensemble lying just between the middle voice and the low register. Since they often have a break or weak area around *e* to *f* above middle *c*, they must learn to smooth the registers for both ensemble and solo singing. This is accomplished best by carrying the lighter quality of the high voice lower before the low "chest voice" takes over, and by not trying to carry the low register too high on the ascending scale. When the "chest voice" is in operation, power never should be the objective but rather ease and suave quality, otherwise the voice will become rough

and raucous. The *Oo* vowel generally is considered the best vowel for emphasis in practice in developing the rich, suave alto quality. Real contraltos, and altos in the making, are most likely to have trouble in the beginning stages with a distinct register shift in tone quality. They normally need much more work than sopranos to obtain a smooth transition into the lower compass. The deep, strong contralto voice rarely develops until after 25 years of age.

Singers in the alto section of choruses and glee clubs in the high schools and undergraduate colleges consist mostly of a very small number of future altos and contraltos. The majority are mezzo-sopranos and undeveloped dramatic, or even lyric, sopranos assigned to the alto part because they have never learned to use the upper compass. This preponderance of undeveloped sopranos in the alto section poses a number of problems. Voices must be protected by not requiring too much dynamic power in the low compass; by vocalizing in the warm-up period as high, or nearly as high, as sopranos; and by insistence that tone production in the low voice be correct and easy. The mannish, heavy, raucous "chest" quality characteristic of the popular "blues" singer, and at times of mature contraltos, should not be permitted. The light "head" quality of production, as described previously, should be carried down, permitting the low adjustment to function when it seems natural (around middle *c*) without a sudden transition or shift into a heavy, forced tone.

3. *Tenors.*

Tenors in ensemble singing find that most of their work lies in the upper part of the low adjustment, with only occasionally a high note which can be sung either comparatively softly in the falsetto register or loudly in the low registration. Because the general tessitura lies fairly high in the upper part of the low adjustment, there is a greater tendency in tenor than in other voices to tire, and the tone become tense and strident. Flatting occurs with continued forcing and its resultant exhaustion. Immature tenors therefore, should be encouraged to use the lighter falsetto adjustment and carry it lower to eliminate forcing and smooth the registers. Young tenors especially should be urged to sing lightly, lyrically, and to "take it easy" in practice and rehearsals. As the voice develops, more virile tone and dramatic power can be added gradually without injury. Development of the mixed-falsetto and the true "head voice" is covered thoroughly in Part I, Chapter 8, "Extending Range;" (see pp. 80 and 82.)

Even more tenors than sopranos will be found singing in lower voice parts in our high school and college choirs and glee clubs. Failure to find enough tenors to balance the other sections is common, and due to the fact that tenors are not discovered and developed early enough. It is rare when amateur tenors sing naturally and easily in the tessitura required; they must be trained to do so. Class voice instruction at the high school level appears the most practical solution for discovering and developing enough tenors to meet our choral needs.

Embyro tenors normally are convinced that they must be baritones or bases because they cannot sing high tones as easily as low. It is best to discover tenors as soon as possible and transfer them to the tenor section. It will not injure their voices to use falsetto in ensemble for the time being, and they will be making the necessary start in developing technic for the high compass.

It is not difficult to detect tenors in the baritone or bass sections. First, their speaking voice is not bass in quality but light and higher. Second, they have little power and sonority below second line *B flat* in the bass clef. Third, and most important, their singing voice has the typical lightness and character of tenor and not bass. Listen for this quality in undeveloped male voices in the octave *d* to *d*. If it is there, assign them to the tenor section and do not worry if they cannot sing higher or have considerable difficulty in singing higher at the time. When this is done there usually will be sufficient tenors, since their tone quality is such that not very many are needed to balance other sections once they are taught to sing easily and properly.

One of the chief reasons for recommending soft singing most of the time in learning new music is to protect immature tenor voices. Soft singing enables them to sing their relatively high tessitura parts in falsetto adjustment without strain or injury to the instrument. Full voice singing, as demanded at times in concert, should be alternated judiciously with soft singing in rehearsals after a composition has been learned; but it should be introduced carefully and not allowed to extend over long periods with immature voices. In any case, *good tenor quality and ease of production, and not quantity of tone, always should be the objective.*

Since top tenor voices are hard to find and take time to develop, junior high school and many high school choruses will do well to select a few low altos to assist the tenors in loud and high tessitura passages. However, to assign altos to sing all the time with tenors is a questionable procedure; it might result in injury to the alto instrument if required to sing low tenor passages also. A high tenor part well sung by altos, or assisted by altos, is much better for all concerned than loss of necessary part balance or, even worse, having the part screamed by inadequate tenors. We believe that the use of a few altos on the high tenor part is justifiable for awhile. This device is a vocal crutch and should be discontinued as soon as the tenor section can be developed adequately, however. Junior high school and some

weak high school groups also are advised to use some of the most select and musically satisfying S A B and S S A B arrangements that are now becoming more available, rather than demanding too much too quickly from adolescent tenors.

4. *Bass and Baritone.*

The bass, and to some extent, the baritone parts in choral singing lie in the middle lower part of the low register. Because of this tessitura, basses especially are inclined to sing with a ponderous, heavy, forced quality, tending to eliminate the top resonance values in their production, and to flat. This is particularly fatal to unaccompanied singing, since the fundamental pitch of the chord found most often in the bass section is the foundation of the choir intonation. Keep the basses firmly on pitch and the other sections are not likely to wander far or for long.

The secret of easy production and good intonation for the bass voice is development of a lighter, more flexible top voice production that can be carried down without forcing into the low compass. Basses and baritones, therefore, should emphasize light flexibility exercises, opening up the top voice through the use of falsetto to develop a free, light conception of high tones in the same manner as tenors. When this conception of lighter production is carried downward, better pitch, more flexibility, and improved tone result. Wilson declares, "Upper tones are developed just as with tenors. . . . The vowel formation must not drop (into the lower throat) with the pitch in singing low tones. The vowel should actually seem to come forward and become brighter. The mouth is relatively closed and the lips rounded. Without this resonance and mouth position the low tones will be breathy and 'fuzzy'."[24]

It has been said that one who throws a stone into a male gathering is almost sure to hit a baritone. Real second basses are tragically rare in the public schools, however; they develop later with time and proper training. Since most voices singing in the bass sections of high school, and to a considerable extent in college vocal groups, are really baritone, more numbers are needed in the bass section to obtain that wonderful organ-like quality and pitch security without forcing than would be the case if real second basses were available. Music that does not require forceful singing below first line *G* in the bass clef has to be chosen carefully. Some of the best school choirs, in order to achieve ideal balance, have more voices assigned to the bass section than any other. One legitimate, mature-voiced second bass can easily balance four average sopranos, however.

---

[24]Wilson, Harry Robert. "Artistic Choral Singing." G. Schirmer, Inc., 1959, p. 215.

*RECORDING, LISTENING, AND IMITATION AS TEACHING AIDS

There appears to be uniform agreement on the value of imitation and the aural approach as one of the best means for building high ideals concerning expression and vocal production. Pupils should do much listening to fine singing, whether it be "live" singers in class or concert, or choice recordings. Lyric style and lyric voices as a rule can be imitated safely within reasonable limits of range and dynamics. There is grave danger of injury to the young vocalist who persists in imitating powerful, mature, dramatic voices, however, especially when the youthful voice is of a light lyric type. For example, the budding young lyric tenor who idealizes a dramatic baritone or a mature bass voice, and persists in imitating this type of production, will force and strain the voice seriously with likelihood of permanent injury.

Until voices have progressed beyond the formative stage and are classified as to type with a reasonable degree of assurance, they should imitate only lyric models. After this they should be urged to purchase and listen to many fine records of their own particular voice type. No more effective self-help is available than through listening to select records by fine artists and through recording and listening to their own production. Records are well suited to the whole-method "Song wise" approach favored by many vocal instructors. The pupil or the class should first listen while observing the score, then join in with the record and, finally, sing the song independently with their own accompanist. The amateur will often find it necessary, however, to adjust phrasing in order to accommodate weaker technic.

The vocal instructor must do more than set up a model to be imitated; an inspiring ideal must be created also. Imitating the vocal instructor's voice has similar values as well as dangers present in imitating recorded music. *Students should be taught to imitate the style, phrasing, diction, and freedom of the teacher's voice rather than its mature sonority of exact quality.* In spite of the undoubted value of the imitative process in the formative stages of learning to sing, this method of teaching must not be the exclusive approach or students will not develop personal initiative. They will tend to give parrot-like interpretations and not develop the unique characteristics and complete freedom of production and expression inherent in their own voices. *The best type of teaching encourages initiative in expression from the very beginning.*

A teacher with a very good voice should use it frequently for quick example in teaching and in introducing some songs. It should never become the exclusive or habitual method used in teaching a new song, however. It is well to remember that students grow tired eventually of hearing the same voice over and over, regardless of how good it is, or the teacher thinks it is, and that a "new broom" in method of teaching often sweeps cleaner. Much added interest and educational value accrue from use of select recordings; it is seldom that the vocal instructor can match the over-all interpretation and technical skill in recordings of a fine professional singer.

APPROACH TO A SONG

Considerable controversy exists concerning whether songs should be taught by rote (listening) or by sight reading. Actually, both methods should be used in judicious balance for maximum interest and musical growth. Some extremists claim that all songs should be taught by the sight reading method in order to promote reading. On the other hand, some claim that sight reading has little or no place in the voice class if highest interest, maximum technic, and interpretive skill are to be achieved. A compromise is usually in order, since educational methods and procedures should be determined by circumstances and needs. It would appear that neither the ear nor the eye approach should be neglected entirely under normal circumstances.

There is no doubt that a few of the most outstanding interpreters with the most thrilling voices of the past either could not read music at all or could sight read only very slowly and inaccurately. Such singers depended on hearing someone else sing or play the music first, or on phonograph recordings, in order to learn the music. This is the aural or "rote" approach and undoubtedly has educational superiority in some respects in promoting uninhibited, natural, and free expression. It is probably preferable as the normal approach under the following conditions:

1. For beginning students until sufficient interest, confidence, and spontaneity are established.
2. For very difficult music.
3. For basic "model songs" to be memorized in which the very highest interpretive skill is an important objective.
4. For introduction of songs in a new style, idiom, or foreign language.
5. For the most rapid, thorough, and lasting memorization.

With the urgent demands of radio, television, motion pictures, etc., today, however, a professional singer is under almost insurmountable handicaps unless he or she can read and sing at least an easy

---

*Vocal Students Practice Aid Records, Box 209, Madison Square Station, New York 10, New York, have a continuously expanding list of select recordings of standard song literature to aid the vocal student and teacher. List of songs and prices of recordings will be sent on request.

score by sight. The vocalist must be a musician as well as a singer, and musicianship properly includes ability to read music. Even the amateur, who limits his singing to that for his own and his friends' pleasure and to singing in a church choir or community chorus, will find that sight singing is well worth the time and effort spent in its mastery. In most colleges and some secondary schools, special classes in solfege or musicianship are set up for this purpose and it is here, rather than in voice classes, that the main emphasis should rest. Voice classes should continue the work in approach to much of the easy song literature covered, however.

Major emphasis in the voice class on sight singing music of more challenging difficulty counteracts inevitably two of the major aims of vocal study — to obtain free tonal production and spontaneous, confident, expression. Neither of these objectives is normally possible to attain in sight reading music of considerable difficulty. Attainment is impossible because of the necessary mental concentration on the technical act of reading and the insurmountable difficulty in getting a complete concept and proper physical preparation for the demands of the phrase *before* inhalation. Either too little or too much breath is taken, and indecision of rhythm and interval also reflect inevitably on the quality and freedom of tonal production. Of course, the better the sight reader, the less difficulty is experienced in tonal production and appropriate expression. It is also obvious that a voice instructor should be assigned to teach solfege classes in order to protect the voices of future soloists as much as possible.

In some high schools where voice training classes are rapidly becoming more popular, students often have no opportunity in vocal music, except in the voice class itself, to gain sight reading ability. It appears in cases of this sort that part of the class periods normally should be devoted to this objective, using not only the easy songs in the vocal text but also one of the special sight reading and fundamentals of music texts designed especially for the purpose. Value must be weighed against value and, in spite of sight reading's being alien to best vocal production, over-all good and musical education of the students should be the determinant of method.

It must not be inferred that sight reading excludes all expression or emphasis on interpretation; it merely limits attention to these factors. Reading through a new song does not infer concentration on interval and rhythm values to the exclusion of expression. On the contrary, *emphasis on observance of at least the indicated dynamics, overall phrase lengths, word meanings and mood should have at least equal emphasis with the traditional factors of pitch and rhythm.* Unfortunately, theory teachers who often are assigned to teach all solfege classes are usually negligent in this respect.

In sight reading it should be normal procedure to note and discuss briefly interpretive factors of most importance in each song just before reading it through for the first time. Students always should be urged to sing confidently, freely, and expressively first, then, secondly, to read the notes as accurately as they can. The actual reading of note values and intervals not only will gain by this emphasis but also interest in reading will be fostered and better freedom in technic maintained. Students should be urged to try to imagine the sound of the complete phrase as they glance at it rather than undertaking the laborious process of reading from interval to interval.

Sight reading will be more free if new songs are vocalized first on a vowel or neutral syllable. The *sol fa* system also may be employed if students have had an adequate background in its use. Method of sight singing is not so important as long as it can be used effectively and musically with good tone, and there is transferrence back in the end to singing through with the words. Eventually, sight reading with the text becomes the principal method used.

*TEACHING A SONG

It is best to let the song itself do as much teaching as possible. Under no circumstances is it wise first to "pick the song to pieces" analytically and then sing it. Preliminary exercises on tonal patterns found in the song should not precede the singing of the song as a whole. Time for analysis, for detailed attention to any particular section or part, and for technical exercises involving problems in the song, comes after pupils are able to sing through the song as a whole with some degree of satisfaction.

While a common, over-all, reasoned interpretation for each song should be worked out and routined carefully, *it should be emphasized that there is nearly always more than one way to interpret a song beautifully.* Variations in details, therefore, should be encouraged in the interpretations of students after they learn the song in order to avoid monotonous sameness, increase interest, and develop individual initiative. The singing of a composition rarely should become so stereotyped that some new turn or detailed effect is impossible even after several performances.

Care in word meaning analysis, clear articulation, proper tempo, and accent are most vital for obtaining the proper concept of a song's meaning and style. Students should obtain a secure feeling for tempo, pulse, and the *exact* rhythm in the beginning phases of study. Failure to sight read intervals correctly when learning new music in many instances is due

---

*See also Chapter 15, "Memorization," in Part I, pp. 120-125.

to a fundamental difficulty with the rhythm. Regardless of the method used in learning a song, rote or note, *inaccurate rhythmic response should be one of the first objectives for immediate correction.* In order to get a strong feeling for pulse, meter, and tempo, it is often a good device to have singers beat time as they listen to a song and follow a score. This procedure is excellent also as an introduction to attempts at sight reading. Particularly difficult rhythms can be mastered by isolation — writing the rhythm on the board and singing it on a neutral syllable while clapping or tapping the exact note lengths. Rhythm cannot be accurate in songs unless attacks on releases of words and syllables are timed correctly. *Words are rhythm makers;* articulation of consonants in particular must be watched to guarantee unanimity and accuracy of rhythm.

Procedure in teaching a song should differ from time to time in order to avoid monotony, and from song to song because of varying difficulty and character. On the whole, the easier, more obvious songs can be sight read; more difficult songs require more careful analysis of the text and score and an aural introduction for best results. The following eight steps are suggested as a normal procedure in teaching a song:

1. Notice the composer's name and identify the school of composition and historical period in which he lives. (For some songs students should be assigned readings and a summary report to the class regarding the composer, period, and the song's style in order to achieve a better understanding of the song's background. This report normally would follow in a later class period after the song had been introduced.)

2. Read, or have the song read aloud, with dramatic quality to establish meaning, mood, and to provide a key as to the probable tempo and climax in the musical setting.

3. Sing through the song as a whole, or listen to it first while following the score carefully. (If the instructor sings the song through for the class, it is highly vital that the model be a good one, that intervals and rhythms are accurate, and tempo, style, tone color, and mood are suitable.) Learn the song in the "rough." Do not stop for minor mistakes and only if the student or class gets hopelessly lost rhythmically or tonally. Repeat the song as a whole several times, aiming to make at least two or three improvements on each repetition.

4. Analyze the song in detail. Discuss style and interpretation; mark in phrasing, dynamics, and tempo changes; plan the climaxes and sub-climaxes; determine tone color and style of each part; analyze the piano accompaniment and how it fits the text.

5. Vocalize the song through on the most suitable vowel or neutral syllable to express the mood of each part. (Suggested vowels — *Ah, Oh, Oo,* and *Ay;* suggested syllables — *Lah, Loh, Loo,* and *Lay*). Dispense with the piano except when necessary to give pitch.

6. Return to practice with the text singing unaccompanied. Make every effort to maintain a similar tonal color and freedom of production as when vocalizing through on the vowel or neutral syllable. Emphasize clear, precise, and forceful articulation and meaningful word accentuation. *Isolate and solve difficult rhythmic, tonal, phrasing, and diction problems that remain,* but do not break the song down for drill into smaller segments than necessary.

7. Return to singing through the song as a whole with the piano accompaniment added, first with the whole class and then individually, further refining interpretation with each repetition. Check for perfect balance and integration of piano and voice.

8. Memorize and repeat from time to time; continue to polish the song musically and keep it in the repertoire by sufficient practice routine with the accompanist.

19

History and Success of Class Voice

HISTORICAL PROGRESS

Although one of the newest music subjects to find favor in the curriculum, class voice is no longer in the pioneer stage in the United States. It is no longer a questionable experiment but a proven success, especially in the fundamentals or beginning stages of vocal study. That class voice study is here to stay and is expanding is attested by the fact that approximately twenty elementary type textbooks or methods, some of them in wide usage, have been published for this purpose.

Voice study in class groups had already been accepted in the high school for 25 years according to a statement by Alfred Spouse[1] in 1944. There is evidence, however, that experiments were being made even before 1919. The Music Supervisors National Conference Yearbook for 1927 records a statement by George Oscar Bowen as follows, "It has been my privilege to conduct voice classes in the Northampton, Massachusetts, High School some twenty years ago and again for four years in the Ann Arbor, Michigan, High School over a period of four years just preceding my coming to Tulsa."[2]
As early as 1935 an investigation by A. Deamer, "A Study of Public School Music Practices," Music Educators Journal, Oct. 1935, p. 13, disclosed that 28 of 62 cities reporting in a limited area of high schools in the North Central Association of Secondary Schools and Colleges, already had regular classwork scheduled.

Even as early as 1930, "High school voice classes were offered in the high schools of the following cities: Rochester, N. Y.; Philadelphia, Pa.; Pittsburgh, Pa.; San Francisco, Calif.; Oakland, Calif.; Providence, R. I.; Cedar Rapids, Ia.; Cleveland, Ohio; Kansas City, Mo.; Lancaster, Pa.; Detroit, Mich.; Montclair, N. J.; East Orange, N. J.; and New York, N.Y."[3] Since that time group solo voice teaching has spread to most large city systems and to thousands of progressive small town and rural high schools throughout the United States and Canada. Study of college catalogues reveals that it is offered in a great number of colleges and universities and in most teacher training institutions.

Choral singing made rapid progress in schools throughout the United States shortly after World War I. In order to have chorus and glee club work of better quality, it was necessary to develop good singers. It was found impractical if not impossible to accomplish this through private teaching alone. The class movement was the answer and spread rapidly into thousands of schools. Inaugurated in the high schools principally for the purpose of raising the standard of singing in select choral groups, it was soon found that class voice work had high educative values as well as surprising effectiveness in training pupils to sing solos.

College and private voice instructors at first looked upon the class voice movement with skepticism and critical disapproval. The proven excellent results achieved in some high schools, however, plus the impossibility of obtaining enough budget and facilities to accommodate students who wished to study voice, forced some teacher training institutions to try the system as a substitute for private vocal study. This movement in the colleges was most pronounced in the depression years following World War I. In spite of many classes taught by private voice teachers untrained in the specialized technics of class voice teaching, it soon became evident that class voice training not only was practical for the beginning phases of college vocal training, but also actually superior to private teaching in a number of respects.

---

[1]Spouse, Alfred. "Voice Classes in the High School." Music Publishers Journal, March-April, 1944, p. 19.

[2]Bowen, George Oscar. "Voice Training in the High School." M S N C Yearbook, 1947, p. 399.

[3]Callan, Emily Jean. "High School Voice Classes." School Music, Nov. 1930, p. 14.

Since that time group training in fundamentals of voice more often than not has become the standard practice in teacher training institutions; it is firmly established in many colleges and universities and, when combined with individual lessons, in some conservatories. More and more music conservatories are beginning to recognize its superiorities in some phases of work over exclusively private voice training, and the trend is to offer a combination of private and class voice training as the most effective method.

STATUS IN THE SCHOOLS

"No vocal program can be considered complete without voice classes. . . . It is entirely proper to offer such service in connection with the music program of a public school system."[4] Thousands of progressive high schools now offer class voice for one year, a considerable number for two, and some have even a three or four year course. Most colleges and universities with a music major curriculum offer either private or class voice training, or a combination of the two, for two to four years. Almost all teacher training institutions offer class voice for kindergarten, primary, elementary, and secondary teachers required to have voice credit in their teaching credential. More often than not, it is the standard practice and accepted norm for first and second year vocal study, especially where large groups have to be handled at comparatively low cost. The tendency is to emphasize class study in the fundamental stages while private lessons, or a combination of private and class lessons, are favored in the third and fourth year of study.

"Vocal training will be offered in every high school in America in the near future is prophesied by many."[5] That this prediction made in 1928 has not come to pass is due chiefly to five factors: school budget limitations; inadequate music staff; practical limitation on teacher time and energy; curriculum scheduling difficulties; and an insufficient number of qualified vocal teachers who understand the methods and procedures of class voice training. This latter factor is due very largely to the lack, until the present publication, of a "professionalized" text about class voice teaching methods and procedures to guide vocal teachers, and to serve as a text book in college classes in methods of class voice teaching.

Lack of opportunity for vocal training during the impressionable late adolescent years of high school no doubt is responsible for lifetime loss of development in singing for many thousands in the past. Need is imperative for more well-equipped class voice specialists in the high schools and colleges. There is no doubt that many more general students on both levels would elect voice, and be greatly benefitted by its musical and general educative value, if more and better-trained teachers were available.

Vocalists who have received their training, or part of their training, in class voice work usually have some knowledge of teaching procedures if they, in turn, become teachers. It is too often sketchy and inadequate, however. In addition, a well-organized special course in methods of class voice teaching is needed for the well-equipped teacher. Such a course should be required of vocal and secondary school music majors as an essential for the teaching credential and be open to private voice teachers as well. Both high schools and colleges should have sufficient facilities and a well-trained vocal staff in order to open up the educational advantages of class voice work as an elective to the entire student body. It is evident, in spite of the many thousands now studying voice, that the surface has barely been scratched as far as expansion into the future is concerned.

Many attest to the fact that class voice, when properly taught and scheduled in the schools, has been more successful than even the most optimistic of its supporters originally believed possible. The statement made in 1930 by Alfred Spouse, director of class voice instruction in the Rochester, New York, schools, is typical of reports from schools where the subject has been well taught and administered. "Our five high schools are carrying on this type of training, and it is one of the most popular courses in the entire curriculum. Our vocal classes have been in operation for nearly twelve years, and have clearly justified themselves by the results obtained. The singers who graduated from our first classes, nine years ago, are singing well today, many of them professionally, and it appears certain that many of them would never have done anything with their voices — indeed would not have suspected their own ability — had it not been for classes offered in their high school days."[6]

In high schools and colleges where class voice has long been an established subject, public support and interest of the student body and community are often as high for vocal solo recitals as for the *a cappella choir or glee club concerts*. Most high school principals approve of the idea and the educational advantages of the work. Nevertheless, it is not offered in many schools for practical reasons already mentioned. As these difficulties are being overcome gradually, class voice instruction is expanding. Some schools with limited funds and facilities still maintain a minimum educational program involving only courses designed for the traditional subject matter

---

[4]Mursell, James L. "Music in American Schools." Silver Burdett Co., 1943, p. 269.

[5]Hesser, Ernest G. "Historical Data-High School Voice Classes." Music Supervisors Journal, Dec. 1928, p. 65.

[6]Spouse, Alfred. "High School Voice Class Demonstration." Music Supervisors Natl. Conference Yearbook, 1930, pp. 138-139.

needs of the general student body. This condition, until corrected, naturally rules out class voice work together with other subjects of a more specialized nature.

There has been a recognized need and an ever-growing demand in the high schools and colleges for the development of a choral training program on a par with that in the instrumental field. It is a well-known fact that pupils in the past three decades have benefited greatly from a tremendously expanded program of class work in the instrumental field. In fact, the practical limit of instrumental technical development has been pretty well achieved in some of the most progressive schools, but this is not so for the vocal program. The instrumental group training program has advanced more rapidly principally because of the number of excellent published methods, including adequate needed information for the teacher to guide instruction. Until the issuance of the present volume, no "professionalized" teacher's manual worthy of the name has been available in class voice work. There are sound reasons why even more students elect to study voice than instrumental work when efficient and interesting class voice work is available.

Under prevailing conditions, the quality of work done in the vocal ensembles in many schools has reached a practical limit that can be extended only by developing better individual singing ability, better technic, and more tonal maturity than exists in untrained voices. Teachers in the public schools cannot possibly find either the time or the energy to do this in private teaching. The taxpayer is not willing to provide funds for the expensive procedure of furnishing enough additional teachers for private music lessons in the public schools; most of the students cannot afford private lessons even if they could be persuaded to take them from local teachers. On the other hand, boys and girls interested in chorus or glee club work, or in learning to sing, usually can be easily persuaded to take class voice, since in the group technic they learn to sing without their shortcomings being singled out immediately for public attention. Class voice seems to be the only practical answer to both raising choral standards and developing solo ability.

High school conductors, in particular, complain continually that there are too few tenors for their choral groups. Actually, there are plenty if they are discovered and developed through class voice work. This seems to be the only permanent and practical solution to the ever-present tenor problem. Most boys, after their voices change, think they are baritones or basses and, since they sound so strained and weak tonally in the upper compass, the instructor may erroneously agree with them. In any case, they often are allowed to continue injurious "gur-gling" with the basses when there is insufficient time and opportunity for training in the tenor range.

VALUES OF CLASS VOICE FOR CHORAL ENSEMBLE

"The requirement of a year in voice class before the pupil may become a member of other vocal organizations would have an immensely beneficial effect upon the singing of glee clubs, choirs, and small vocal ensembles, and such a requirement — which already exists in some schools — is strongly advocated by the authors for most schools."[7] Proper class voice work does more than develop range essential for singing choral parts. It promotes every type of technic needed for effective production — blend, balance, intonation, dynamic and tone color variety, clarity of diction, and agility. All of these technics are improved chiefly because of two basic developments common to class vocal work: growth of tonal freedom and promotion of homogeneous tonal production.

Presence of a number of voices with a vastly different type of tonal production — some dark, breathy and spread, and some bright, shrill, and tense — together with many different versions of pure vowel quality, makes it difficult or impossible to obtain excellence in the four major technical factors determining high standard ensemble singing: blend, balance, intonation, and diction. There is insufficient time to accomplish the necessary vocal corrections and establish proper concepts of vowel purity and tonal production in the number of rehearsals ordinarily assigned to choruses and glee clubs; time available must be used in "roughing over" and learning the music to be sung. Class work in voice is the most practical solution to the problem yet discovered.

CRITICISM AND DEFENSE OF CLASS VOICE TRAINING

Some private teachers of voice are still antagonistic; they resent and criticize the teaching of voice in classes in the schools. They mistakenly assume that most of what has been taught with this method will have to be relearned, and that the livelihood of the private teacher is endangered through students' obtaining free voice instruction at the taxpayers' expense. Neither assumption is correct in most instances. Where instituted properly into the curriculum at a high level of efficient instruction, fundamentals are taught properly and do not have to be relearned, while class voice has been proven to be the best possible source for stimulating greater interest and a larger clientele interested in continued or supplementary private study.

---

[7]Dykema, Peter W. and Gehrkens, Karl W. "The Teaching and Administration of High School Music." C. C. Birchard, 1940, p. 97.

"It has been proved that *Group Voice* is a stimulus to the private teacher. When the interest of the student has been aroused, he usually desires to know more about the voice; consequently he soon seeks to continue his study with a private teacher. Group vocal instruction feeds pupils to the private teacher. Teachers who have taught voice privately are realizing the advantage of teaching at least one lesson a week in groups. As a result they have not only added to their field of activity and usefulness but increased the number of their pupils as well."[8]

Critics of voice class work, and skeptics regarding its efficiency, base their stand principally on the contention that voices are extremely individualistic and therefore need individual attention. We agree that voices are individualistic and do need more individual attention than can be given if attempts are made to teach advanced voice in large classes. However, even the most individual vocal student needs to understand and master the fundamentals of vocal training as well as any ordinary pupil, and it has been demonstrated conclusively that this can be done efficiently through concerted class technics with a minimum of attention to individual idiosyncracies.

Haywood answers critics of the voice class method as follows: "How much can the individual achieve in actual vocal results as a member of a group, studying a subject that is conceded to be so strongly individualistic? Unqualifiedly I say, much more than the most enthusiastic supporter of the plan ever expected could be realized. For the reason that the fundamental laws of vocal technic are common to the human race at large."[9] Clippinger supports this view. "The perfecting of an artist is an individual matter, and can be done only by means of individual study; but the principles of voice production, the elements of the pure singing tone, the perfecting of vowel formation, the principles of breath control, gaining of freedom, the correct delivery of words, the principles of interpretation, can be taught successfully in groups."[10]

Bowen emphasizes the psychological influence of the class situation as a definite advantage. "The value of the class lesson, and the rapid progress made by the students, may be attributed, at least in some measure, to the element of competition and comparison, which always helps to motivate a subject; but more especially is class work valuable and successful because each student has an opportunity to learn to differentiate between what is good and that which is bad. Most people can tell the difference between good and bad tones, but to say why the tone is poor, and provide a remedy for its correction is another matter. That is what members of a voice class may learn to do, to a considerable extent, and its help to each member is of inestimable value in mastering his own difficulties."[11]

Ward favors class voice for developing poise and concert deportment. "Timidity in solo singing soon disappears in the voice culture class. The students are also perfectly at home before public audiences, since their singing experience has always taken place before an audience composed of the class. Critics generally agree that students whose voices have been cultivated through the school vocal classes manage their recital singing with much greater poise and dignity than many privately instructed students. In fact, the poised control shown at the school recital is often the envy of adult vocalists."[12]

The American Academy of Teachers of Singing is convinced of the values and success of voice class work and says, "The feasibility of group voice training for high school students has been demonstrated to the complete satisfaction of many educators in the school music field as well as to many private teachers of voice. It is logical to put voice training in the foreground of all solo and choral development. The voice achievement of the individual in the correct use of the voice will guarantee the best of choral as well as solo singing. The first requirement of the instrumentalist is that he know the instrument which he is to play."[13]

Mursell represents the viewpoint of music psychologists on class voice instruction, "That singing can be successfully taught, even to a high level of proficiency, in group situations has been amply demonstrated."[14] Private teachers who believe otherwise are now much fewer in number. They consist mostly of those who never have observed properly-handled class work, but may have reaped the result of poor; of those who base their opinion on others' prejudices or hearsay; and of those who have had an unfortunate experience in attempting to teach group voice without understanding its special method and technic. Experienced and able instructors who teach both class and private lessons generally recommend a combination of both for maximum progress. If the average beginning pupil has to drop one or the other, however, most of these teachers say it had better be the private lessons. On the other hand, the opposite is recommended for the more advanced pupil.

---

[8]Taylor Bernard U. "Group Voice Instruction." Music Teachers National Asso. Proceedings for 1937, pp. 107-109.

[9]Haywood, Frederick. "Voice Culture Classes." Music Supervisors Journal, Feb. 1929, p. 73.

[10]Clippinger, D. A. "On Becoming Musical." Music Supervisors Natl. Conference Yearbook, 1933, p. 96.

[11]Op. cit., pp. 399-400.

[12]Ward, Arthur E. "Music Education for High Schools." American Book Co., 1941, pp. 112-113.

[13]American Academy of Teachers of Singing. "The Reason Why the American Academy of Teachers of Singing is Interested in Group Voice Training for High School Students." (pronouncement on the fly-leaf of a contest brochure).

[14]Op. cit., p. 269.

Competent private teachers of voice who achieve poor results when they attempt to teach in groups do so because they neglect the advantages of using group technics for speedy and effective teaching of many common problems. They do not organize the advantages of social learning so that the group itself is used as a powerful agency for obtaining the desired objectives through mutual example, imitation, friendly rivalry, constructive criticism, and sympathetic interest. In most instances they make the fundamental mistake of regarding the voice class as a group of separate voice students, each of whom is to be separately apportioned as often as possible a short share of time in the assigned vocal periods for an individual lesson in a semipublic environment. While this technic and philosophy can be used to some extent with advanced pupils in very small classes, it is fatal to pupil interest and adequate progress in large or average size classes.

20

Class Voice - Its Character, Method, Values, Advantages, Weaknesses, Activities, and Objectives

CHARACTERISTICS AND BASIC PRINCIPLES IN TEACHING

1. *Use Group Educational Technics*

In voice classes the recommended procedure is basically different from private teaching in that, for the large part, *songs and vocalises are learned and sung together.* Voice class should not be taught in the traditional technics suitable to the private studio as a series of private lessons, with so much time allotted to each student in turn. "The relation of teacher to his class is quite different from the relation of the teacher toward the private student. To be successful he must organize the lessons and proceed along pedagogical lines. Digression from this plan means destruction."[1] *Most of the time in early stages of instruction should be spent with the entire group.* This does not signify that the beginning student never will be taught individually but that when he is, the whole class is always "in on the teaching," observing and ready to comment or demonstrate that they have gained in the instruction also.

The voice culture class is never to be treated as a typical chorus, since *the major objective should be to develop the solo voice.* Although little if any effort is made to classify voices during the first year of study, proper class voice method, especially after students have gained some confidence and a more relaxed and resonant production through singing together, incorporates the giving of considerable attention to the individual voice.

Certain basic songs and vocalises should be practiced together, memorized and learned thoroughly by the entire group, singing in a medium or medium-low key. This is followed by individual participation, by phrases, by verses or sections, or with the whole song. If there are any extremely high or low voices in the group and the class key lies in an uncomfortable range for them, a more favorable key should be used for these students, or they should be excused from singing the parts where range is difficult. An accompanist able to transpose is a most valuable asset when a suitable published key is not available. In some circumstances especially-assigned songs suitable in range to the particular pupil can be substituted for the common repertoire songs. In addition, if the common repertoire songs are insufficient in number or difficulty to challange more ambitious and advanced students, they should be assigned supplementary song literature according to their needs.

It is an easier introduction to solo singing, and more individuals can be heard and helped in a given period, by assignment first to singing short parts or sections of a song. Duet, trio, and quartet work also help to instill confidence in initiating the student gradually into solo singing, as well as adding interest and variety in recitals and teaching valuable concepts of blend, balance, and intonation.

Individual problems by no means are ignored. The instructor must be alert — listening and watching as the group sings — for evidence of individuals with abnormal physical difficulties in production or unique personality or musical problems that require brief suggestions, or perhaps personal conferences. Emphasis in the beginning should not be upon studying intensively a few solos for the sake of public performance as some assume. *Rather it is upon development and welfare of the individual student* with specific attention to health, vitality, care and development of the immature voice, general musicianship, principles of interpretation and style, and fundamental concepts and skills for improvement of both solo and ensemble singing.

A curiously mistaken concept of many voice teachers accustomed to individual voice lessons only is that the vocal lesson must always include individual coaching if it is to have value. Actually, in the early

---

[1]Haywood, Frederick H. "The Values of Voice Culture Classes for Senior High School Students." Etude, April 1929, p. 276

stages of group voice training — a semester or even a year — many of the leading authorities in this field maintain that it is a waste of time to classify voices and even unnecessary to give any time to the individual's *technical* difficulties. This opinion is based soundly on the observation that major technical, and often psychological, problems disappear from the normal pupil through typical class procedure and advancement. Thus much larger groups can be handled effectively in beginning classes than later when more time and attention needs to be given to individual performance and the correction of remaining minor vocal difficulties.

Few reputable teachers maintain that the entire time and attention always can be given to class procedure only; even in the early stages there are usually a few students in a class with abnormal psychological and physical problems that need individual attention. These problems are usually of a nature that can be handled briefly by occasional classroom help, but some may demand outside conference.

"The striking of a suitable balance between teaching the class and teaching the individual in the class is the very touchstone of successful group instruction — both vocal and instrumental."[2] It is easy to go from one extreme to the other. For example, some become so concerned with teaching the class as a whole that they never become aware of individual problems and difficulties that brief attention could correct or improve. On the other hand, others habitually spend the entire period in short lesson sessions for individual pupils, causing the remainder of the class to become restless, bored, and lose interest in the work.

After a song has been learned fairly well by the group, the skillful teacher will find ways for frequently helping the individual and holding the interest of the class as well. For example, the individual can be helped on a particular phrase or passage which the teacher notes is giving trouble in group singing, or can be assigned to sing parts of the song before attempting the whole. In the meantime, members of the class are urged to listen attentively to one another's singing, and be ready at any time to offer constructive suggestions and criticisms for improvement. Interest is maintained, critical judgment about singing and teaching of singing developed, and the social values of group instruction utilized.

Emphasis shifts from a purely group approach to more and more individual attention as confidence and technic improve. In advanced classes, numbers are kept small so that much more time comparatively can be given to individual singing and instruction. Even in advanced classes of the fourth year, however, the advantages of group technic should be maintained in familiarizing students with new vocal literature, style and interpretation; in teaching foreign language pronunciation; in vocalise activities for the warm-up at the beginning of the period; and in discussion of the individual's stage deportment, singing technic, and interpretation. *A basic aim is the development of intelligent, discriminating, and capable musicians.* Emphasis, therefore, should not be placed on technic or sheer skill as an end in itself but rather as a necessity for eloquent and correct musical expression. *Asking opinions and inviting discussion about singing performance and principles of interpretation and style are standard procedures.*

2. *Take Advantage of Group Suggestion and Criticism*

After solo work starts and the student has gained some confidence and ability to take criticism more easily, written comments may well be required from time to time. It is best to duplicate or mimeograph a form for this in order that the student's thought will be directed toward the most significant items for judgment, and more constructive criticism for improvement of individual singing will be received. This procedure — amplifying suggestions and criticisms from the instructor — keeps students alert about vocal problems, builds discrimination rapidly, and informs the pupils' pretty conclusively about the qualities of their production, stage appearance, and progress being made.

Students gain secure poise through subjection to analytical, friendly criticism and, when listening, develop eventually through rating and discussing others' singing, a keener sense for diagnosis of vocal problems and workable methods for improvement. Classes so conducted become the best type of clinical laboratory for developing more able future vocal teachers. Written criticism followed by discussion should be employed more frequently in classes where all or many contemplate future teaching of voice or choral groups.

3. *Vary the Approach and Order of Classroom Activities*

A routine practice of assigning so many minutes to warm-up exercises, to class singing of new and familiar songs, to individual singing, and to vocal theory discussion from assigned lessons in Expressive Singing, Volume I is desirable as a norm in most periods, but is deadly to interest if followed slavishly in every period. *Most periods should have several varied activities;* but some may be devoted entirely at times to one activity such as recital singing by individuals, recording, play-back and discussion of singing by class members, and listening to select records of vocal artists.

---

[2]Dykema, Peter W. and Gehrkens, Karl. "The Teaching and Administration of High School Music." C. C. Birchard, 1941, p. 98.

A form for suggestions and criticism that has proven very practical follows.

VOCAL PERFORMANCE CRITIQUE

(Note — Please mention first the good points and improvements noted and then criticize faults)

Student's Name _____ Song Sung _____

Posture and Breath Support _____

Stage Deportment and Appearance _____

Interpretation (Note — Comment on such items as mood establishment, intensity and projection; maintaining proper style; tempo; skillful phrasing; preparation and achievement of climax; expressive tonal color; dynamic variety; word emphasis; and balance and integration of accompaniment.) _____

Technic (Note — Comment on such items as free, even, and resonant production; tone quality; clarity and correctness of diction; accuracy of pitch and rhythm; skill in legato, flexibility, and agility.)

Comments and Suggestions on Points to Empasize Most for Future Improvement _____

4. *Avoid Formal Conducting*

Formal conducting is neither necessary nor desirable in the voice class. A baton or any formal type of conducting is entirely out of place. When sight reading new songs no conducting, except initial setting of the tempo, starting the group, and indicating changes of tempo, holds, and releases, is needed. In repeating familiar songs, informal conducting of the same type is recommended; time beating as such is unnecessary. An individual student's singing should seldom if ever be conducted. Students should be taught independence as soon as possible in such elementary matters as maintaining a steady tempo, rhythmic accuracy, and observing expression marks in the score. This cannot be done if the instructor indicates continually the tempo by conducting and all musical effects such as dynamics, rhythm, and phrasing. Singing loudly to lead the group is even worse for the same reason. It is a quick way to teach songs accurately and develop a group of followers, but *it is not a quick and efficient way to develop musicians.*

5. *Utilize Your Own Singing Voice Wisely*

Singing *for* but not *with* a voice class in the teaching of some difficult songs, and to give examples, is the accepted procedure for instructors with good solo voices. This is not an inflexible rule but a generality. For example, in going through a song for the first time in a sight singing approach, it is better to help a group over a particularly difficult spot than to let them flounder helplessly. It is also better in the very beginning to help a group considerably until they have established some degree of confidence and pleasure in singing. However, continuous singing with a group, and dominance of class resonance with a powerful mature tone, not only destroys the group and the individual's chance for developing musical initiative, but also makes it impossible for the instructor to listen analytically for places that need correction or improvement. *It is a major responsibility of the voice teacher to listen and watch carefully and make suggestions for improvement on the basis of what he hears and sees.* This cannot be done effectively if the instructor is involved in singing also.

Singing by the instructor, by advanced students, and playing of select recordings are valuable supplementary teaching devices when used judiciously to create interest; illustrate style and interpretation; reveal certain technics; speed memorization; and develop discrimination about good singing. The wise teacher never will neglect carrying of *example* or the *rote* process to the higher levels of learning as one of the valuable technics in teaching. Even if a class is fairly expert in sight singing, the aural approach by hearing the song well sung has certain natural and artistic advantages that are lacking in the reading approach. It should be used from time to time on songs where the highest degree of excellence is especially desired. "You need never feel any doubts about the value of 'rote' singing or 'rote' playing, because control both of singing and playing by ear is fundamentally right."[3]

Like all good things, example and the rote process can be overdone, however. It is well to remember that *most of the time in the normal period should be devoted to singing by the class or members of the class* if maximum progress is to be made. Many teachers who love to sing make the mistake of using consistently too much of the class time in singing songs, or even song recitals, for their students. This practice of singing recitals for students may be commendable at the proper time and place but not as a habit during scheduled class periods.

It is regrettable if the instructor has to serve also as the accompanist, since attention is unavoidably divided, making it more difficult to hear analytically and practically impossible to see what is going on. Every effort should be made, therefore, to secure or develop competent accompanists in order that the instructor can be free for concentration on his main task.

6. *Choose the Right Type of Song Literature for the Voice Class*
(*See also p. 8 and pp. 211-216*)

Group voice class work in beginning classes should center around folk and art songs in English. Most specialists in the field recommend considerable emphasis on the Old Italian song during the second year. The lyric Bel-Canto style — its pure vowels and wealth of interesting music of limited difficulty — makes the Old Italian song literature superior to all other types as a basis for tonal development and concept of lyric legato style. Far more interesting to students than vocalises, they also become an excellent addition to song repertoire when well learned. When a number of years of study are planned, specialization in each of the later semesters on one or two specific schools or types of song literature such as German Lieder, French Impressionistic, Classic, Old English, Modern and Contemporary, Operatic, and Oratorio is desirable. Specialization will guarantee a well-rounded repertoire and a broad, high quality vocal education. Such a plan will be found outlined in Chapter 7 following — see p. 192.

7. *Prepare Lessons Carefully*

Voice culture, like any other academic subject in the schools, requires careful planning and organization for outstanding results. "Specific aims and objectives must be set forth before undertaking to teach a voice class, and all work presented should be a step toward achievement of some goal."[4] Not only should over-all objectives for each semester be well worked out but also each lesson should be planned carefully, with the various types of activities that are suitable in mind. Careful daily lesson planning for the inexperienced teacher is a necessity for satisfactory progress. Even those who have learned their methods well through extensive experience in class teaching will find at least a minimum amount of lesson planning in three categories essential for most efficient work:

(a) Notes listing each song covered and the date sung last.
(b) Technics and interpretive phases completed or fairly well completed in previous lessons, and phases that are still weak or need further work to polish results.
(c) Types of activities planned for a specific lesson, songs and exercises to be covered, and specific objectives for accomplishment or im-improvement.

Brief lesson plans of the foregoing nature are valuable guides but *they never should be taken as inflexible procedures when worthy class interest leads in another direction.* On the other hand, voice teachers should not allow themselves to be led into "will o' the wisp" directions, that waste time and promise very little educational value at the whim of some student. The skillful teacher is not dogmatic but, through clever suggestion, leads a class to want to go in the direction planned.

8. *Promote Musicianship*

While sight singing and fundamentals of music study should not be the major function or aim of typical group voice work, the voice class cannot avoid its responsibility for further developing the general musicianship of all its members. The exclusion of this type of study as a major objective cannot be justified if the voice class furnishes the only curricular opportunity for students to obtain this basic asset. In such an unfortunate eventuality, musicianship, including a strong emphasis on sight singing, becomes an objective secondary only to the safe development of the voice and maintenance of enthusiasm and interest in singing. Musicianship study should cover principally note and rest values, sight singing, ear training, keys and key signatures, and most commonly-used music terms. While much of this can be taught incidentally together with songs

---

[3]Mursell, James L. "Music and the Classroom Teacher." Silver Burdett Co., 1951, p. 168.
[4]Lee, Marjorie Evelyn. "Voice Classes in Secondary Schools." M. A. Thesis, University of Illinois, 1946, p. 15.

and exercises, a supplementary text designed for the purpose, and extra rehearsal time for the specific content, are highly desirable.

FUNCTIONAL CARRY-OVER

Content and effect of class voice work should not be limited to class activities and an occasional recital in connection with them. The alert teacher will take advantage of the school assembly and other activities in the school, home, church, and community to expand the work and integrate it effectively into the lives of the students and the society of which they are a part. Nature of many of the songs assigned for individual study should be such that there is promise of a very high functional carry-over.

In this respect there is far too great neglect of sacred song literature in most class voice methods and collections for the purpose. This is no doubt due in part to the inferior musical quality of most sacred songs; exceptions are the oratorio and cantata arias that are usually too difficult for any but the more advanced pupils. It also is caused by the lack of printed sources listing the best available sacred song literature and the apparent general unawareness of many vocal teachers that the sacred song probably has the greatest carry-over value of all. Most students belong, or will soon belong, to some church choir where solo repertoire is in great demand as a regular feature of church services. Time spent in beginning classes to include some emphasis on sacred songs is therefore justifiable educationally, even at the expense of learning more established classics of higher musical value.

Students should be encouraged, assisted, and supervised, insofar as practical and possible, in extending their solo and ensemble vocal activities into school assemblies and functions of the home, church, and community. If high school students in the future obtain the right kind of training and guidance in class voice work, we can be confident that they will constitute a powerful influence, not only in raising the standards of singing in the public schools and colleges but also in promoting the quality of music and music performance in general.

SPECIFIC ADVICE ON METHODS

The following are specific educational methods which experienced class voice teachers recommend for maximum efficiency:

1. Keep major emphasis on expression and not on theory or vocalises.

2. Do not spend too much time on vocalises or preliminary warm-up. Five to seven minutes at the beginning of a period is usually sufficient for warm-up. Students normally should *stand* during this time, since it is easier to initiate vital posture, proper breath support, and a free, ringing tone when stand-

ing. Tendency is to slump both psysically and mentally when seated. Students are usually seated in the process of learning a new song or during discussions, but should stand for singing after songs are learned.

3. Enthusiasm is catching. If you are enthusiastic about the music sung and progress made, it is likely that students will be also.

4. Endeavor to become acquainted with each student as soon as possible; treat them as *persons* and not as faulty impersonal instruments that need repair. Listen and watch for abnormal individual difficulty and give such pupils early advice for correction.

5. Beginning students need encouragement more than anything else; therefore, do not fail to praise them for progress noted. Even if no progress is evident, sincere effort is deserving of praise, which encourages the pupil.

6. Students should be kept busy; if not in class or individual singing, then in listening analytically, in writing critiques on performance of others, and in oral suggestions and discussions. It should be emphasized in the first class period, and not lost sight of, that *group vocal study is a cooperative enterprise in which all contribute to mutual benefit.*

7. If possible, obtain one or more competent accompanists as assistants, in order to free the teacher's attention for listening, watching, and teaching. Members of the class often can do this work with proper coaching. In this case it is best to have more than one in order that the accompanist is not robbed of adequate singing experience with the class. An experienced paid accompanist is the best solution for classroom work, while student accompanists occasionally fill in and help other members of the class in routining songs in outside practice.

8. Spend more time in the singing of songs than on all other activities combined. The great majority of time in the class period should be devoted to singing with just enough review and discussion of theory in Expressive Singing, Volume I, to make sure that the principles are understood and being employed properly.

9. Do not spend too long a period in beginning voice classes on continuous singing without resting voices. Rest voices by changing to another of the various classroom activities suggested which do not involve singing. (Note — See next topic) Beginning voices seldom, if ever, should sing continuously for more than 10 or 15 minutes without some kind of break.

10. At least one-half of the period normally should be devoted to group singing in beginning classes. The ratio of time given to individual singing increases gradually as confidence and technic develop.

11. More advanced and confident students should be encouraged to start individual singing as soon as they are ready. They should not be permitted to monopolize the class time unduly, however.

12. Avoid monotony in class procedure. "Warm up at times with a song. Change the order of routine. Intermingle the various phases of study. A lesson may be devoted (at times) entirely to individual work. A period given over entirely to drill is a doubtful procedure. Students should have at least one genuine musical experience in every lesson."[5]

13. While procedure chosen to introduce most new song literature should be conditioned by the students' background and abilities and by educational objectives for the course, some variation to avoid monotony should be practiced. Various means are: The reading approach, performance by the teacher or an advanced student, listening to a phonograph record or tape recording by a soloist or by a previous class.

14. The lesson should be well prepared, varied in activities, and interesting. Although normally it is best to start a period with some type of singing, the value of surprise should not be overlooked at times.

15. Songs used in class should be introduced and taught in such a way as to benefit everyone. Most songs should be in a medium-low range and taught in unison. It is neither necessary nor desirable for those with extremely limited ranges — very high or very low voices — always to sing all pitches. *Students should be cautioned to stop singing either on vocalises or songs when they begin to strain or force on extended ranges.*

16. Normally, after songs have been learned in the rough with piano accompaniment, they should be vocalized through on a suitable vowel or neutral syllable, first accompanied and then *a cappella*, until phrasing and technical problems are solved.

17. The most interesting and vital vocal exercises often can be found by selecting particular phrases from songs during the latter procedure mentioned in No. 16.

18. Solo singing should be designated at random, rather than alphabetically or by adjacent seats, in order to keep all alert and to reduce fear build-up, which occurs more when pupils are able to figure out the exact order or day they can expect to sing. For timid students, anticipation is often worse than the actuality.

19. All fundamental or basic exercises used in the warm-up should be memorized, as should a reasonable number of the best songs studied each semester. Except for sight singing and ear training, a vocalise can be of very little value in promoting technic unless it is memorized. No song can be learned thoroughly or interpreted most freely and expressively until it is memorized. In this regard Mursell states, "If we want to derive spiritual and aesthetic nourishment from any piece of music, if we want music study to be a satisfaction of deep natural hunger, if we want to build our work on an assured psychological foundation, then we should remember that one can derive infinitely more insight and delight from one piece beautifully learned than from ten pieces miserably learned."[6] Superficial running through a song several times cannot be expected to result in more than superficial learning.

20. Except in the very beginning stages, students normally should be required to practice the routine of stage deportment when singing solos before the class. This should involve entrance, bowing, announcing songs, recognition of the accompanist, etc., just as in an actual formal concert situation. The class should be instructed to react with applause as would a recital audience. Routine in stage deportment is one of the distinct advantages of class study on which the teacher should capitalize fully.

21. Songs normally should be repeated through as a whole the first few times, without stopping for minor errors. The objective in repeating is to increase awareness of the significance of the whole; to improve in several designated respects; and to challenge students to correct as many errors as they can on their own initiative before breaking the song down into smaller segments for drill on the more difficult parts. It is seldom that a class can be given more than three or four objectives for improvement in this process without confusion in keeping them all in mind.

22. Do not be "wordy," give long-winded dissertations on theory of vocal production, or monopolize too much class time by example or solo singing for the class.

23. Use concise language and terms that students can understand when giving explanations or directions. Employ a few well-chosen words for directions; there is virtue in brevity and nothing so tiresome to students as a pedantic, long-winded instructor who uses much of the class time for lecturing or reminiscing. *Be careful to articulate plainly and speak slowly and resonantly enough to be understood easily.* When very important points are covered in lecture, outline major ideas on the blackboard, and insist that students keep a well-organized notebook for review.

24. Students can and should be studying, memorizing, and perfecting several songs at the same time without fear of confusion. Class work is more interesting; more vocal literature can be learned in

---

[5]Wilson, Harry R. "The Solo Singer." Carl Fischer, 1941. Vol. I, p. 5.
[6]Mursell, James L. "We Need Music." Music Supervisors National Conference Yearbook, 1932, p. 17.

a given period by this method. It is neither necessary nor desirable to delay class discussion of successive lessons and the introduction of new songs and vocalises, until songs, vocalises, or ideas introduced previously are mastered entirely.

25. Do not attempt to complete interpretation and technical finish of a new song in one period; make some progress, go to another song or activity, and return to the song in subsequent periods as technic and interpretative concepts grow.

CLASSROOM ACTIVITIES

Variety and nature of activities and comparative emphasis depend of course upon objectives selected for the class. (See p. 172) The following are commonly-encountered activities in well-organized classes:

1. Class study and discussion of problems in vocal production and theory, interpretation, style, and stage deportment. This activity is usually based on specific assignment in Expressive Singing, Volume I.

2. Class practice of vocal exercises for "warming-up" the voice and developing technic in the fundamentals of production.

3. Study and singing of solo or duet songs as a group.

4. Solo singing of an entire song or parts of a song. (Note — When possible, classes should be held at times in a large hall or auditorium, observing all problems of stage deportment and acoustics — "getting the words across" effectively.)

5. Occasional singing of part songs as a group.

6. Specific solo voices singing duets, trios, quartets, etc., and parts from operettas, opera, oratorio, etc.

7. Recording, listening playback, and study of effective microphone technic for broadcasting, recording, etc.

8. Writing critiques and discussing strong and weak points of solo singing. (Note — See "Vocal Performance Critique" form p. 166) In an alert class, students learn much from the mistakes and virtues of one another's performance and from the suggestions and criticisms of classmates. Written comments given to the performing student often are more effective than verbal.

9. Study of methods of class voice teaching. This can be omitted in some classes and emphasized strongly in others, where many or all of the students expect to become vocal teachers. In the latter, case methods presentation, theory, and song interpretation should be "professionalized:" i.e., explain the *why* for procedures used at the time.

10. Study of sight singing and musicianship. This may be purely incidental to other activities or a major emphasis, taking considerable class time for

groups having no other opportunity to obtain the information and skills involved.

11. Presentation of recitals from time to time. These may be informal concerts in the voice classroom itself or formal appearances in the auditorium or elsewhere.

12. Listening to the instructor or to select recordings for style, interpretation, technic, memorization, and acquaintance with vocal literature.

VALUES OF STUDYING SINGING*

1. Promotes deep breathing, better general health, and physical development of the lungs.

2. Develops a richer, more resonant and correct speaking voice, expressiveness to the countenance, and animation to the mind.

3. Furnishes a worth-while emotional outlet and activity.

4. Provides opportunity for worth-while self-expression.

5. Promotes good bodily posture and graceful carriage.

6. Increases self-confidence and poise, reduces self-consciousness, breaks down fear inhibitions, develops character, and strengthens personality.

7. Strengthens power of concentration, imagination, and ability to memorize.

8. Acquaints with a rich cultural heritage.

9. Provides a worth-while leisure time activity for all, and a vocation or supplementary income for many.

10. Awakens and stimulates appreciation of fine singing, of better song literature, and of music in general.

11. Develops musicianship.

12. Stimulates a deeper insight into poetry and prose and a better understanding of the fundamentals underlying all types of art.

13. Makes life more worth living, giving pleasure to one's self and, in many instances, to others.

14. Provides opportunity to contribute a needed service in the school, home, church, and community.

15. Has exceptionally high "carry-over" educative value into adult life.

16. Provides a valuable social asset for those who attain skillful solo or ensemble ability.

GENERAL EDUCATIVE VALUES OF CLASS VOICE

The high value of group voice training for promoting higher standards of ensemble singing and providing economical training for solo singing is generally recognized. However, the excellence of either private or class voice study as a subject with

---

*See also "Reasons for Studying Singing" as outlined by the American Academy of Teachers of Singing, p. 3 of Volume I.

exceptionally high general educative value is not generally known; it is not emphasized sufficiently by music educators. With the possible exception of speech and drama study, it has no equal in such matters as developing self-assurance, poise, leadership, quality of the speaking voice, and desirable personality characteristics. Effective contribution to our cultural heritage is also unquestionable.

Class voice enthusiasts, therefore, have very sound reasons for recommending the study on a "solid" basis as a subject available to all on an elective basis in the general education scheme in the high schools, state colleges, and universities. Cost is amply justified on a comparative basis of value to the individual and society. Widespread recognition of this fact by school administrators should provide a tremendous impetus to study of the subject on both the secondary and college levels in the future.

ADVANTAGES CLAIMED FOR CLASS VOICE INSTRUCTION OVER PRIVATE LESSONS

1. It is more economical and efficient in reaching large numbers of students who could not afford private instruction. While it is true that no two persons can sing in exactly the same way, they nevertheless may sing profitably by the same method or fundamental laws of vocal production which apply equally to all voices. Basic technical needs of all beginners in voice training are universal: it has been demonstrated conclusively that fundamental technics can be taught more economically, and in most instances more efficiently by the class method.

2. It provides a constant audience situation, a laboratory for study and experiment in expression, resulting not only in greater incentive and progress in the early stages of training but also in making singing before people a natural thing to do.

3. It lends itself very well to a broad and not a narrow musical approach, setting up more favorable conditions for control of standards and presentation of a rounded and uniform program in vocal study.

4. The instructor is inclined to organize and prepare lessons more carefully, and is not so likely to omit subject matter or repeat needlessly.

5. It develops confidence and ability to sing with poise in public more rapidly than private study.

6. It provides a more effective and economical method for initial presentation and practice of fundamentals such as posture, breath support, legato, diction, stage deportment, style, interpretation, etc.

7. It provides the elements of friendly competition and social pressure to stimulate progress and raise standards.

8. It is a laboratory in which future voice teachers learn to teach by observing the mistakes and virtues of the singing of the others by participation in, and discussion of, vocal problems and faults, and by noting the effective methods of correction used by the instructor. It develops power of diagnosis and analysis of vocal difficulties, making students better critics and better teachers.

9. It allows for academic credit toward graduation often denied to private study, since class study involves text material, examination, and pedagogical class procedures convincing to school administrators.

10. It tends to raise personal standards of many students through hearing and observing superior work by others.

11. It acquaints the pupil with a wider range of vocal literature, and knowledge about its style and interpretation, than private study normally provides.

12. It facilitates development of more discriminating and appreciative listeners to vocal music and performance.

13. It provides a text and organized pedagogical procedure for studying voice that is more likely to provide an adequate mastery of the fundamentals.

14. It gives a better chance to evaluate one's vocal assets and vocal difficulties by comparison with other voices in class.

15. It is preferred over private study by the great majority of students.

16. It allows for shared teaching values in which the students themselves, especially in the more advanced classes, assist valuably with constructive ideas and suggestions.

17. It creates a valuable social situation in which musical viewpoints, common knowledge, and problems are shared, technical problems are illustrated and analyzed, and the best condition for the development of appreciation and discrimination in expressional values is present. The music lesson is socialized by encouraging cooperation, self-reliance, and good sportsmanship. A student learns to stand on his own two feet, to contribute to group development, and assume his share for class progress. Music is essentially a social art, an experience to be shared. Though the student may be nervous or frightened when called upon to perform before the class, this usually reduces soon to the point where the experience really is enjoyed, although many students are reluctant to admit it.

MAJOR WEAKNESSES OF CLASS VOICE STUDY

1. The problem of discipline arises because of the class situation.

2. Difficulty is encountered by the instructor in finding time and opportunity to become acquainted with so many individual students and in discovering their needs — personal, educational, and vocal.

3. Exact and immediate application of vocal literature, exercises, and proper keys used in songs to specific needs and interests is difficult or impos-

sible for some pupils with abnormal problems, such as extremely low or high voices.

4. Vocal literature used in group study together must be limited, in the main, to a general nature, and is not specifically adapted to a certain type of voice such as coloratura soprano, low bass, contralto, etc.

5. Many fine songs are appropriate only to one sex or the other. In mixed classes, therefore, they must be omitted, learned by only one sex, or if learned by both, omitted from the repertoire of one with consequent waste of time. (Note — This objection is eliminated when classes are segregated according to sex.)

6. It is impossible to give the amount of personal attention and guidance to the individual student that private lessons allow. A large amount of personal attention is needed by some beginning students with abnormal difficulties or problems. In addition all advanced students require considerable individual attention for perfection of details in their singing technic, to polish interpretation, and to give adequate consideration to the most suitable and varied concert repertoire.

7. A purely group study method does not permit advancement or retardation in technical study at a pace exactly suited to the needs of the individual student.

SPECIFIC OBJECTIVES*

The following are specific objectives, aims, or goals mentioned by various authorities on class voice teaching:

1. To develop solo singers with excellent stage deportment.

2. To provide basic fundamentals for improving ensemble singing.

3. To preserve and develop the adolescent or post-adolescent voice.

4. To develop and provide soloists to serve the school and community.

5. To develop musical leaders and vocal teachers for the future.

6. To combat the evils of vocal neglect or misuse that often prevail during childhood.

7. To free pupils from the shackles of ignorance concerning the care and development of the voice.

8. To promote health, strength, and endurance through singing.

9. To develop independence in judgment between harmful and helpful technics and practice routines.

10. To provide a basic foundation for future private study.

11. To increase the number who will wish to pursue private study.

12. To develop greater aesthetic sensitivity and a basic introduction for greater understanding and higher appreciation of all the arts.

13. To encourage singing in the home, church, and community, particularly of the better music.

14. To encourage the joining of school vocal organizations, church choirs, and civic choruses.

15. To raise the general standard of solo and ensemble singing.

16. To establish poise, reduce fear, correct inferiority complexes, develop leadership ability, and a more attractive and forceful personality.

17. To establish pleasure in singing as a natural expressive medium.

18. To habituate good singing posture and breath support.

19. To develop a free, resonant, even, and expressive tone over an adequate range.

20. To emphasize correct and eloquent diction in both speech and song.

21. To reveal and encourage vocal talent otherwise hidden.

22. To provide opportunity for vocal study for many who could not afford private study.

23. To develop sight singing, an accurate and sensitive ear, and general musicianship.

24. To increase the number who will wish to study singing for its cultural and educative value.

25. To provide opportunity for students to evaluate ther own vocal gifts by comparison with others.

26. To provide adequate opportunity for use of the voice in solo singing before the class and in recitals.

27. To furnish a needed laboratory for a performer-audience situation and for discussion of common problems, both technical and expressional.

28. To develop a cooperative social attitude and a sense of responsibility.

29. To develop ability to sing as a worthy channel for emotional outlet.

30. To stimulate a desire to use the voice correctly in both singing and speaking.

31. To study and memorize a repertoire of desirable songs.

32. To become acquainted with a wide range of vocal literature.

33. To develop enthusiasm for both solo and group singing.

34. To promote fine taste in song literature and discrimination in judgment of singing.

35. To habituate proper physical and mental conditions for beautiful singing.

36. To reduce or eliminate fear and develop poise in solo singing.

---

*See also "General Objectives," p. 192, and "Specific Obectives" for the various semesters as outlined in Chapter 7.

37. To produce clear, resonant, pleasing tones of expressive quality.

38. To guide and establish habits of proper practice.

39. To promote knowledge about style and principles of interpretation.

40. To guide pupils in how to study and memorize songs.

41. To provide knowledge about class voice teaching methods and how to classify voices through practice and discussion. (To be emphasized in teacher training classes)

The Vocal Committee of the Music Educators National Conference state that the most fundamental purposes of voice training are:

1. "To present correct use of the singing and speaking voice, with a progressive study of good song literature and its intelligent interpretation.

2. To lay the groundwork for an appreciative concept of the art of singing and of fine repertoire, from the standpoint of the listener as well as the performer.

3. To provide further training and individual help for the more talented student who may become a professional singer and teacher."[7]

The National Association of Teachers of Singing state that "The four primary purposes or objectives of any basic system of training the singing voice are:

1. *To liberate the voice* — To build flexibility, range, resonance, fluency, and freedom from tension or restraint throughout the entire vocal compass; and to acquire spontaneity, buoyancy, and joyous release of the innate moods and impulses that seek self-expression through song.

2. *To strengthen the voice* — To amplify and improve the vigor, volume, and the intensity of vocal expression without strain or fatigue; and to develop consummate health, physique, and endurance in the entire body, the breathing apparatus, and the vocal organs, and the ability to sustain without strain or fatigue, the most challenging types of vocal expression.

3. *To beautify the voice* — To acquire aesthetic awareness and keen sensitivity toward the musical and dramatic expressive qualities of the singing voice; also to increase the capacity to understand and interpret beautiful music vocally and to widen the range of expressiveness and control of the vocal organs as a medium of artistic self-expression.

4. *To develop a singing repertoire* — To acquire experience and skill in the rendition and interpretation of vocal masterpieces, as a preparation for public performance."[8]

---

[7]Music Educators National Conference. "Music Educators Source Book." 1947, p. 109.

[8]National Association of Teachers of Singing. "Methods of Teaching Singing." (a pronouncement)

21

Organization and Administration of Class Voice

The teacher of a voice culture class in college or high school has problems to consider other than musical and vocal development. He must consider organization, administration, scheduling, physical facilities, and educational objectives. Practical conditions and outside pressures, like the desire to use class voice also as a basic class in musicianship, or as a required training medium for membership in advanced choral organizations, enter into the complex in determining the exact nature of group vocal training in any particular institution. In fact, an ideal situation for the most efficient work is seldom encountered; teachers must do the best job they can under certain limitations or handicaps which they often cannot alter.

As a rule, voice class work should be taught by a regular member of the school faculty who has both an educational and a vocal background. Such an instructor is more likely to understand the educational objectives, psychology of teaching, and care and development of the youthful voice than are private teachers without an educational and academic background. The average private voice teacher also is more accustomed to dealing with the somewhat more mature voice; he is inclined to demand more forceful resonance and extensive range than are safe for the adolescent or post-adolescent voice still in the formative period.

No fee normally should be charged for group voice culture in the schools other than regular tuition rates similar to all other academic classwork. Unless the school supplies all textbooks, students should be expected to purchase their own student manual or textbook and any needed song anthologies or separate songs in sheet music. The school music department library should supply enough copies of supplementary anthologies and vocal textbooks, and suitable phonograph records, storing them in an accessible locked cupboard in the vocal classroom for convenient usage.

AGE FOR INAUGURATING FORMAL VOCAL STUDY

It was believed in the past that formal study should not begin until the voice was more matured than the high school age. It has been discovered, however, that the voice of the high school boy or girl can be developed safely under the right instruction. Some effective work of a less formal nature is being done even in the junior high and upper grades, but the desirability of emphasis on maturing the voice before or during early adolescence is highly questionable. It is well to remember that habitually fully resonant production over a wide range — perhaps beneficial to a mature throat — usually is disastrous to the immature. We cannot recall any case on record of a so-called "wonder child" who sang extensively with mature quality and power and became a truly great singer after adolescence.

However, certain fundamentals like posture, breath control, free tonal production, diction, legato, and interpretative principles can and should be taught at an early age, in either normal choral work or a special voice class. Such basic training would greatly speed formal vocal study when it does start and is perfectly safe *if emphasis on loud singing, too extensive range, wide tone color, and maturity of production is deleted.*

"At present the majority of well informed music educators take the attitude that there is much about singing that a boy or girl of 16 or 17 ought to be learning if they are to be a singer later on, and that if they are put in charge of a wise and well prepared teacher, there is little danger of harming the voice."[1] Haywood concurs, "It is commonly agreed that boys and girls in secondary schools are sufficiently developed mentally, physically, and musically

---

[1]Dykema, Peter W. and Gehrkens, Karl W. "The Teaching and Administration of High School Music." C. C. Birchard, 1940, p. 96.

to understand and profit from intensive vocal training."[2] (Note — It is evident that Haywood meant the high school, and not the junior high, in the term "secondary schools.") Fields concludes, "Singing as a form of self expression should begin at an early age, but artistic voice culture commences in earnest during the early post-adolescent period (i.e., from 16 to 19). The younger, formative years of the pupil's life may be used advantageously for general education, physical culture and general musical development as a background for later voice work."[3] Since the girl normally matures physically a year or two earlier than the boy, she also can start formal singing lessons earlier to advantage — at the age of 14 or 15 in most instances — providing the right kind of teacher is available.

ORGANIZING GROUP VOICE CLASSES

The musical and general education values and advantages of voice class work often need to be "sold" to the administration, funds and facilities made available, and a scheduling and membership plan adopted before presenting the offering to students. It may take considerable time, patience, persistence, and a convincing presentation to school officials before necessary finance and physical facilities are made available, and schedules adjusted to make room for a new subject in what is usually an already overcrowded curriculum. The "Values of Studying Singing," as outlined on p. 170 of this text, with the following topic on "General Educative Values of Class Voice," and "Reasons for Studying Singing" on p. 3 of Expressive Singing, Volume I, should provide plenty of sound reasons to help convince the administration of the unique musical and the general education values of class voice training for the student, school, and community.

Limitations on budget and insufficient instructional staff in vocal music usually impose membership restriction in high schools to those who are especially interested and talented. This is unfortunate, because high general educational values justify the availability of class voice to any student who can "carry a tune" and has enough intelligence to profit by the instruction. Membership on an elective basis more often is available to the general college student. Even in college, however, exigencies of the situation usually limit enrollment to music majors, minors and those working for teaching certification in the elementary and kindergarten-primary field where some voice often is required.

"In a high school where voice culture is to be offered for the first time, the course should be thoroughly explained to the students during the spring of the year previous to the introduction of the course. An announcement that a voice class is to be offered can be made during assembly and home room periods. The explanation of the course may appear in the school paper, or a printed slip of paper which bears a description of the proposed voice class may be handed to each student in school."[4] Bulletin boards also are mediums for getting information regarding the new course before the student body. When class number has to be limited, announcements should state clearly that the course is for only those with good or fairly good voices who want to learn to sing better.

If the vocal instructor has a good solo singing voice, he or she can add to enthusiasm for the course by singing two or three carefully chosen songs in assembly. Once started on an effective basis, enthusiasm for group voice training is often one of the joys of the teacher. It also becomes a severe problem at times to limit membership to those who can be handled with the time, facilities, and staff available. Haywood says, "After beginning the first year work with a small group of ten or twelve skeptical youngsters, it is a rule to have four times the number enroll for the second year class, thereafter it is not uncommon to have a waiting list."[5] Girls are expected to have a high interest in cultural subjects, but one of the surprising things is the fact that boys often have even greater enthusiasm once they discover that it is possible to become solo singers through group voice training.

It is highly vital to success of voice class work to get it started on a high plane of inspiration and efficiency in the very first week of school. This includes having a competent accompanist who either is a good sight reader or is familiar with the accompaniments to the songs being used; well-planned and interesting variety of activities during the class period; and the necessary song litertaure available. *The most critical period for developing interest and preventing the subject from being dropped is the very first week it is taught.*

SELECTING MEMBERSHIP

It would be desirable educationally to allow not only the gifted few but also those of ordinary ability to participate in class voice work. Educational values, personal satisfaction, development and advancement in singing skill are not limited to the fortunate few, although the highest reaches of the art are. Because of the undoubtedly very high health, general educational, and personality development values in the study of singing, it would be desirable to accept to membership all who are not

---

[2]Haywood, Frederick. "Voice Culture Classes for Senior High School Students." Etude, April 1929, p. 276.
[3]Fields, Victor Alexander. "Training the Singing Voice." Kings Crown Press, 1947, p. 61.
[4]Lee, Marjorie Evelyn. "Voice Classes in Secondary Schools." M. A. Thesis, University of Illinois, 1946, p. 39.
[5]Op. cit., p. 276.

tone deaf. Unfortunately, the practical situation is such that this seldom is possible. Try-outs are then necessary to limit membership to those with superior vocal, musical, and intellectual equipment. In colleges priority often is given to music majors, minors, and credential requirement students; after them the various class sections may then be opened to other students on the basis of "first come first served."

In try-outs to select membership, procedure should be as informal as possible with every attempt to put the student at ease. The greater the competition for membership, the more thorough try-outs need to be in details and records for making comparison. The voice record index filing card No. 2 (See p. 143) is excellent for use in try-outs. No attempt should be made at this time to ascertain any except the most pertinent information in comparing vocal ability, however. Students may be given the card and asked to fill in the upper part in order to save time. The testing of each student in solo ability, using a very easy familiar song or a song of the pupil's choice, plus evaluation of the voice on some or all of the items listed on the voice record card, will furnish sufficient basis in most instances for prelminary selecton of the most promising students. If additional reduction in numbers is necessary, a native talent music test on the pitch and rhythm sections and information regardng the pupil's I.Q., past academic, and social cooperation record can be used as final determinants for membership.

Students should be requested in announcements of the tryouts to bring some song they like to sing. In addition to a "Tune Test" on a familiar song, voices should be tested for quality, flexibility, power, evenness, and range of voice on scales and arpeggios and on ability to sustain and control long notes with *crescendo-diminuendo effect.* A tonal memory test can be given by playing short musical figures or phrases of gradually increasing melodic difficulty and asking the student to repeat immediately after hearing. Ths is a practical test for native capacity in tonal memory and pitch which, when well administered, may be superior to the results of a standard native capacity music test using phonograph records for selecting potential singers. A sight reading test can be given also, or omitted if the pupil admits no experience or ability in reading.

It should be recognized that a number of motives may cause students to take class voice other than an earnest desire to sing well. These may include ambition for distinction through self-display, social fellowship with a particular gang, or amorous interest in some member of the opposite sex. These motives can be kept in mind for checking when attempting to weed out membership. It should be borne in mind, however, that initial ulterior motives on the part of the student often can be transferred, through

stimulating vocal class work, to sincere interest in singing.

Other things being equal, the older students with more mature voices should be given preference. As a rule a boy whose voice is still very markedly in the adolescent stage should be denied membership until later, when study will be of greater benefit. Girls usually mature early enough so that formal study in any year of high school is safe and practical. It is desirable to wait until voices have changed or "settled," but not at all necessary or desirable to wait until they have reached final maturity. This does not occur for many until after the twenties. If it is demonstrated conclusively that a student cannot "carry a tune in a basket," do not encourage him to study voice. Inability to carry a tune and singing off-pitch are two entirely different matters, however. Some of the finest, most robust voices sing atrociously flat at the beginning because of production problems which proper vocal training corrects.

SEGREGATION

There is some disagreement regarding the desirability of segregation of voices but not a great deal of difference in actual practice. Because of difficulties in administration of scheduling, mixed voices and those of various degrees of musical and vocal background and ability are usually placed together in beginning classes. Voices are segregated in some schools by sex, by ability, by class (Freshman, Sophomore, etc.), by major chosen, and classification as low or high in range.

Each type of division has some arguments in its favor and some against. There is little doubt that superior students in a class by themselves will make faster progress. On the other hand, as potential teachers, they do not become acquainted with the problems of the average student. The inferior student, if segregated with others of the same type, lacks the stimulation to higher standards that association with those of superior ability would provide. Boys and girls like to sing a somewhat different type of material in some cases but careful choice of songs that are appealing to both sexes obviates this problem. Students in mixed classes hear and learn to judge all types of voices, become acquainted with a greater variety of song literature, and at times have opportunity to sing in mixed voice duet, in trios, quartets, etc.

Segregation by range allows opportunity for group singing in more suitable key for all. In addition it eliminates much need for the accompanist to transpose songs to accommodate individuals when they sing. Since accompanists are usually ill-equipped for the job of transposition, it is a real advantage to have range segregation, especially in more advanced classes where song anthologies are published in both high and low key editions. However, only a very few extremely low voices have trouble singing select songs in a medium key, the range favored in songs found in most class voice texts.

Medium key group practice and song singing in a medium range from *B* flat below middle *C* to *E* flat, fourth space treble clef, is seldom a handicap to many students, but pupils should always sing their solos, if possible, in the key best suited to their particular voices. After the fundamentals have been covered and voices roughly classified (usually the second year), work progresses faster in some respects if membership in voice class sections can be determined on the basis of range — high, medium, and low. Altos and basses can be scheduled together as can sopranos and tenors, and baritones and mezzo sopranos.

In colleges often it has been found desirable to segregate beginning music majors from minors and elementary and kindergarten-primary students, who are best served by a consistently different emphasis in training. Standards in terms of achieving educational aims suffer for both groups unless they can be segregated, while the instructor labors under a very trying situation musically as well as in assigning grades. The elementary and kindergarten-primary group should be given a different type of course adapted specifically to their needs, with emphasis on the light type of tone best adapted for children to imitate in the rote process.

The majority of high schools and many colleges prefer to have no sex or range segregation in beginning classes for several reasons:

1. All beginning students need the same basic type of fundamentals, whether they be soprano, alto, tenor, or bass, and these can be taught equally well in mixed classes with all types of voices represented.

2. Most high schools offer only one year of fundamental vocal training and since classification of the voice is not considered of major importance the first year, all voices use a medium key with limited range for group singing.

3. As a rule, vocal methods courses designed especially for beginners in class voice are available with songs in one key only — medium key. These songs are usually appropriate to both sexes.

SCHEDULING

Scheduling problems in a "tight" school program is often the most difficult hurdle, especially in consolidated high schools with fewer than normal periods in the day to accommodate transportation to and from school. Students coming from a distance on busses rarely can participate in an extra period before 9 a.m. or after 3 p.m., leaving only the middle of the day periods available, and these are consigned traditionally to required academic subjects. Every school must work out the scheduling problem in reference to its own program and needs. Adjustments can be made and a more or less suitable time for class voice work can be found in most instances, once the administration is convinced thoroughly of its value. The tendency today is to enrich the program in high schools by increasing the number of periods in the school day.

1. *Time* — If possible, it is best to schedule class voice during regular school hours. It may be necessary, however, to start the project before or after school hours, during activity periods, or some other undesirable time until its value in the curriculum is apparent to the administration. For obvious reasons, when there is a choice in the matter, group voice work should be scheduled in the two periods before lunch or at 2 or 3 p.m.

2. *Number of Meetings* — The most successful arrangement in large schools where there is an established demand for the subject is scheduling of several sections for five days per week each in the choice periods mentioned. This ideal setup often is impossible or impractical. Group voice study has proven popular and successful even when limited to two or three periods per week and scheduled at the most undesirable hours. "The class should be scheduled for at least two periods each week and outside practice should be expected."[6] It usually is offered as a "solid" subject when sufficient outside study is required. It is feasible, however to offer it also in the beginning courses as a "lab subject" (no outside preparation required) if four or five class meetings per week are allowed. "The average number of meetings each week in schools offering voice classes is probably two or three."[7] In such cases, it usually fits in with, or between, other part-time subjects such as chorus or glee club.

3. *Length* — Length of class period is determined by scheduled practices of the individual school. A fifty-minute or hour period is not too long for class voice if singing is varied with other activities as suggested.

SIZE OF CLASS

Various schools report from 10 to 35 in beginning classes with an average of 15 to 20. Dykema reported in 1931, "Class voice lessons are successfully carried out in a number of schools with from sixteen to thirty students."[8] Most authorities favor 15 to 25 students the first year, 10 to 15 in the second,

[6]Wilson, Harry Robert. "Music in the High School." Silver Burdett Co., 1941, p. 159.

[7]Lee, Op. cit., p. 31.

[8]Dykema, Peter W. "Music for Public School Music Administrators." Bureau of Publications, T. C., Columbia U., 1931, p. 88.

and 5 to 10 in the third and fourth years of study. Numbers in classes often will be governed by policy of the school authorities and pressure for the course. We have observed efficient work in beginning classes of 30 to 35 students, but it could have been better if numbers had been reduced somewhat to allow more attention to the individual.

Practical limits for enrollments in each class should be conditioned also by such factors as number of meetings weekly, skill and experience of the instructor and the accompanist, and background and ability of the class. A fine accompanist is an invaluable assistant, allowing the handling of much larger classes than would be possible with an inexperienced and fumbling beginner in the work.

An effective scheduling plan sometimes is worked out whereby large groups, up to even 60 or more, meet together once or twice weekly and then separately in smaller sections two or more times. Efficiency in teaching is possible for very large groups in such phases of the work as learning common song literature and vocalises, presentation and discussion of vocal theory and methods of production, listening to phonograph records of artists, and listening and discussion of recital programs by students in the class. In fact, all phases of class work except solo singing and coaching of the individual can be presented as effectively to very large groups as to small.

When a two- to four-year sequence of vocal study is planned, many teachers prefer maximum size beginning classes in order that normal dropping from the course will not leave too few to justify advanced class offerings. School authorities often allow small advanced classes on the basis of averaging a teacher's pupil load with large choral groups which the choral teacher also conducts, however.

PACE

No set rule can be made as to how many chapters of theory in the vocal text should be covered, how many songs memorized, and how many sung individually during a semester. There are too many variable factors involved such as number and length of class periods, general ability of the class, number in the class, length and difficulty of the songs chosen, experience and ability of the instructor and the accompanist, etc. Practice ranges all the way from four to a dozen or fifteen songs memorized during the semester of 16 weeks. Somewhere in between would seem the wisest minimum requirement for most classes. Usually five to eight songs are chosen to be memorized as a basic common repertoire to guarantee thoroughness. As many others as possible are studied briefly for broader acquaintance with vocal literature and as exercise material to illustrate particular technics discussed in the various lessons. This plan appears best in order to have the advantages of thoroughness and diversity in learning.

It is obvious that only meagre experience with a variety of song literature is possible when all songs studied must be memorized. On the other hand, the building of high standards in interpretation is impossible and adequate technic is difficult or impossible unless throughness is carried to the point of memorization of a reasonable number of fine songs.

As a rule students choose the optional individual songs they wish to sing from the song literature that is studied briefly by the class. They even may be allowed to substitute some of these songs for memorization in place of songs in the common repertoire list. Other songs, even popular songs which the student expresses a desire to sing, should be allowed as optional for individual solo singing if range and technical problems are not too difficult for the pupil at the time. Students are going to sing popular music anyway and *it is far better that they be helped to choose it wisely and sing it well rather than to ignore or forbid it.* We have had a number of good singers who could be interested only in this manner, and who later preferred the classics and sang them well. After all, far more singers earn a living in the popular song field than in any other.

In any case it is much better to know and learn to sing a few songs well than a large number superficially. Four to six common repertoire songs well learned are plenty for most large and medium sized classes meeting two or three times weekly; six to eight are about right for the second semester. As students grow in experience and ability, more songs are memorized and reviewed each successive semester. When songs are taken up in a foreign language new to the student, however, memorization requirements obviously should be less than for songs of compraable length and difficulty in English.

A general principle to follow in regard to how fast to progress on theory lessons is — do not go from one lesson to the next until students understand the content and have developed sufficient mastery to guarantee a practical working knowledge for future application and improvement. We can be sure that, in the long run, it is thoroughness and not speed that counts and that if any of the basic fundamentals of production are slighted and not understood, the student is sure to pay the price sooner or later. On the other hand, it is unnecessary technically and undesirable educationally to demand perfection of each technic and lesson before advancing to the next. Such a philosophy is no longer considered sound educationally. It results in a training program that is interminable in length, deadly in interest, and fatal to rapid progress, whether it be group culture or private lessons.

ACTIVITIES AND TIME APPORTIONMENT

Twelve activities are listed on p. 170 as being appropriate to class voice instruction. An average class period, however, would have three well-distributed activities:

1. Presentation and study of the lesson topic with illustration and practice of the principles involved.
2. Warm-up and developmental vocalises.
3. Group and individual singing of songs.

Most authorities agree that the latter activity should be allotted at least one-half of the class time for beginning groups and two-thirds for more advanced. The warm-up vocalises may well be limited to 5 and not more than 10 minutes, with the lesson topic averaging 20 to 25 minutes. Some periods at times may be devoted, of course, entirely to singing and listening to singing, while entire periods spent in recording and play-back may be well spent, especially in intermediate and advanced classes. In solo singing of average length art songs, from 4 to 6 students are the maximum number that can be heard and given much practical individual help during a 50-minute period.

For this reason, in large beginning classes individual singing should emphasize drill on parts of songs, so that time essential to training the group as a whole on fundamentals is not disrupted for long periods. Class singing as a whole continues even in advanced classes in the process of introducing new vocal literature, studying principles of style and interpretation, and in developing technical and expressional finesse in any common repertoire selected. Common repertoire is gradually reduced as classes grow more advanced.

Songs chosen for solo singing by the pupil normally are selected from the new literature introduced previously and sung by the class as a whole. Study of vocal theory in the lesson topics of Volume I usually is more concentrated during the first and second semesters. There is more emphasis in successive semesters on style, interpretation finesse, stage deportment and on checking and applying basic principles toward the development of continuously improving technic and interpretation.

ACADEMIC CREDIT

(*Note — See also "Number of Meetings," p. 177*)

Group voice classes should be subject to standard educational practices for other subjects in regard to such matters as academic credit allowed and grading. There is no sound reason why class voice should not be scheduled like any other academic class and receive comparable credit for comparable work. Some high schools and most colleges schedule group voice training as a "solid" when sufficient outside preparation is required. When little or no outside preparation is required, credit usually is assigned on a "lab" basis. Crowded schedules and other practical factors usually limit high school of-

ferings to a two or three times weekly schedule, and a half rather than a full credit per semester. Colleges, as a rule, offer the course two or three times weekly and allow either one or two units of academic credit, according to the amount of required outside preparation and songs memorized.

When full "solid" credit is granted in high school and regular practice and homework are required, it is necessary in some schools to check carefully in order to determine if sufficient time and home preparation are being given by the pupil to justify the credit. Progress and number and difficulty of songs memorized for class presentation are the best indications of adequate time spent. As an additional check, however, some instructors use cards signed and turned in each week by the parents, indicating time spent in daily practice.

DISCIPLINE

Classroom order, a severe problem in many music classes in the public schools, is seldom difficult in the voice class. It need never be if the class is challenged with interesting work, kept busy, and a psychology of mutual help and respect is followed. One argument against large classes in high school is the added difficulty they impose in maintaining good discipline.

It is highly important to have the liking, respect and attention of every student and to know him as a person. (Note — See discussion relative to this topic on pp. 142 and 197.) It should be made clear to students in the beginning that they are expected not only to give their full attention to the instructor when he or she is talking or singing, but also to listen with attention to fellow classmates, showing courtesy and good sportsmanship no matter how poor the singing. In this respect it is well to point out that students can at times benefit as much, or more, from hearing poor singing corrected as from listening to a near-perfect production, and that we learn to sing from observing "what not to do" also.

If difficulty in discipline occurs, the teacher should first check his own methods by a review of certain fundamental principles. Such questions as the following may well be asked: Is there sufficient variety of activities during the period? Does the lesson "move" or does it "bog down" in details? Is emphasis primarily on expression? Is there highly enjoyable artistic experience in group song singing and not too much time and emphasis given to theory, vocal exercises, and individual singing? Are methods employed democratic or are they dogmatic? Does each period have at least one thrilling artistic experience for the students? Are songs used suitable to the ability and present taste of the students? Quite often indifference of a group and discipline problems arise from poor choice of music from the standpoint of student appreciation and technical development at the time. Musical taste of a group should be challenged to develop quickly, but never should be pushed so rapidly that students are discouraged, resentful, or lose interest in the process.

If a soul-searching review of methods and efficiency in teaching reveal no significant weaknesses, then the fault usually will be found in particular students who are trouble makers. A private interview with the students concerned, a frank discussion regarding the cause for their actions, and securing a promise for future cooperation is then the recommended procedure. Incorrigible individuals, who do not conform and interfere continually with class progress, should be dropped from the course.

CORRELATION

Group voice at times can be integrated with many subjects and activities with mutual benefit. Such subjects as solfeggio, dramatics, speech, English, foreign language, history, and social science offer worth-while correlation. In addition activities such as chorus, glee club, and assembly programs offer excellent public outlet for talent in the voice class.

While the vocal class period in general should retain its own identity, its own concept of unison and solo work in a class activity, it can to advantage, be flexible enough to introduce integrated work as related or incidental to the main objective. The wise vocal teacher should be eternally alert to organize singing opportunities outside the classroom, where students who are ready can gain the necessary poise, routine, and stimulation essential for greatest progress. To share the joy of singing with others and reveal one's achievement are natural desires and powerful incentives for greater effort.

In a way, the voice teacher often becomes a miniature concert bureau which the school, church, and community organizations are quick to recognize and use. The vocal instructor needs to exercise care and judgment in selecting the better students for appearances before larger and more important groups. He must limit demands upon time and energy of more popular singers to prevent them from being exploited unreasonably to the extent that other important work or health suffers.

Within reason, vocal students should be encouraged and helped to appear as soloists in church choirs, school organizations, assembly, etc., and to organize small ensembles in school or home in order to obtain a varied and rich type of musical experience. Solos required in such appearances should be sung in voice class first, receive the suggestions and criticisms of the instructor and the class, and be credited as part of the work of the particular student in earning an "effort" grade in class. Such integration into school and community life will do

more than anything else to make the work vital, promote the value of the class to the public and the school administration, and guarantee popularity with the student body.

RECITALS

Not only informal recitals within the classroom itself but also occasional formal recitals before the public are desirable for the more advanced pupils. In colleges and conservatories where there are several vocal teachers and many intermediate and advanced students there should be many informal recitals and a number of carefully organized and presented formal recitals each semester. Devices that are not used often enough to stimulate interest are for a whole class (usually beginning) to appear in a recital demonstration of group unison singing, and for classes on the same campus to sing for one another at times. Well-taught unison singing can be surprisingly beautiful and musically satisfying. These class recital demonstrations also may involve the preliminary warm-up exercises as well as some solos by pupils who may be advanced enough. In many schools these demonstration recitals are of high interest to school patrons.

To emphasize their importance, and for the sake of the most desirable type of experience for the students participating, formal recitals should be dressed for properly, have ushers, be supplied with attractive printed programs, and duplicate professional concert conditions as closely as possible. Special invitation cards can be sent (before the concerts) to parents and relatives of the performers and school patrons. Both the printed programs and the special invitation cards often can be printed at little or no cost to the students in the school print shop as a special project of the class in printing.

STANDARDS AND GRADING

Both interest and progress will be facilitated by avoiding emphasis on the "pressure" system to frighten students into working hard in order to obtain high grades. The student should earn his grade because he loves to sing and gives as much time and attention to the matter as the pressure of study and other outside commitments will allow. *Study of singing should be a happy undertaking if it is to have lasting value.* High grades should be a by-product and not a primary aim or threat dangled continually before the student, as practiced by some teachers.

Although students should be made aware either of satisfactory progress or the lack of it from time to time, they never should be threatened or "pressured" by harping on the fact that they are making a low grade or failing in the course. The pressure system still is mistakenly used by many teachers in all subjects that they teach as a means for attaining what they deem to be high standards. We can be confident that it is the surest way to discourage love of singing and continued interest in its study, however.

Students should be notified at the beginning of the semester as to the minimum requirements for achieving an average grade in the course. Then they should be told how they can *earn* a higher grade through additional effort, advancement of technic, and memorization and singing of more songs than the minimum required. In intermediate and advanced classes, pupils should be urged and aided to select the repertoire of songs they propose to prepare and to sing as early as possible in the semester, in order that they can get busy on the repertoire. Study on only one song at a time is not only comparatively uninteresting but also highly inefficient when a number have to be learned in a given time. If possible all songs sung by the individual during the semester should be studied and practiced from the beginning, or near the beginning, with more concentration on the particular song selected to be memorized and sung first for a grade.

To the common repertoire that all students normally are required to learn must be added the choice songs of the individual. The instructor should notify students early concerning the names of common repetoire songs in order that they can start working on them independently if they choose and are able. *Songs usually are sung by students at least once for help and criticism before being sung for a grade.* Beginning students in large classes may have only a common repertoire to be memorized; intermediate classes about an even balance between common repertoire and songs to be chosen by the student; while most songs in advanced classes may be chosen by the student. The instructor, of course, advises the student on each individual song to make sure that it is worthy of the time and effort spent and that it is suitable at the time for the pupil's development.

Since the intermediate and advanced students in classes normally select the majority of their choice songs from the particular school or type of song literature reviewed in class, most of this review work should be concentrated in the first part of the semester. This will aid students in selection of their song repertoire as early as possible. *Students should be admonished at the outset not only to select and memorize their songs early, but also to distribute their solo singing so that the minimum number of songs required are completed considerably before the end of the semester.* This plan counteracts procrastination, common with most students. It allows completion of at least minimum solo singing requirements in time to pass the course in case of laryngitis or illness at the end of the term. It also allows for better distribution of suggestions and criticisms in class solo appearances, increasing technical advancement. In addition, it provides opportunity for those who wish to do more than the minimum requirements to memorize and sing more songs, thereby improving their grade on effort.

Inevitable differences in ability are present in any voice class even when students are segregated carefully at the beginning. Under normal circumstances, differences can be expected to continue. *The important educational objective is not to attempt to make everyone achieve the same advancement or standard but rather to challenge each pupil to maximum growth according to his own limitations.* Methods in class teaching and grading practices should reflect this philosophy.

In order to prevent aimless study, to reveal progress and understanding of the subject, and to furnish a reasonable means for assigning grades, the vocal instructor must plan a logical and constructive grading system. *Students should be graded on their comparative vocal skill and progress, their knowledge of vocal theory read and presented, and on the number and difficulty of songs memorized and sung.* Pupils generally agree that comparative singing skill should be given the most weight in a final grade; 50 per cent on singing, 25 per cent on effort or application, and 25 per cent on advancement or progress is the method we have used to determine the *applied* grade in the singing phase of class work. In determining the final grade in the course, this singing grade is given a weight of two and grades in the knowledge of theory of vocal production a weight of one. In general, students are satisfied as to the fairness of this system for determining final grade.

Theory and methods of vocal production in Expressive Singing, Volume I, should be read carefully by the student, presented and illustrated clearly by the instructor in class, and the information from the various lessons covered, organized into an objective type of true-false, multiple choice, and completion examination similar to those used in other traditional academic subjects Expressive Singing, Volume I, for this course is replete with ideas from which objective examinations of this type can be fashioned on a par with any academic subject. This should prove useful in helping to "sell" class voice offerings to an administrator who is impressed chiefly with the intellectual and academic qualities of curricula. (Note — Teachers adopting this course in classes can obtain free from the publisher objective examination questions completely covering the entire content of Expressive Singing, Volume I, with reference to the exact page where each question is discussed. These questions have been prepared carefully by the author. The same free service also is available for classes using this textbook.)

It is suggested that at least two vocal theory tests be given in a 16-week semester, one in mid-semester and a final covering the entire term. The final may well count twice as heavily in weighting as the mid-semester exam in determining vocal theory grade for the semester, and the final theory grade, in turn, only one-third as much as the singing effort and progress grade.

Students in beginning classes should not be graded formally on singing ability for at least half a semester. They must be given time to gain pleasure and confidence in singing before facing the hard fact that, after all, a semester grade must be given and that in an applied subject like singing, it must be based partially on comparative skill in performance in order to be significant. Even in the performance factor, however, the grade should be *earned* and not the mere resultant of a natively superior voice or a better musical background.

The three criteria following present a grading method that helps assure that a high grade in singing must be earned. They have been accepted by nearly all students as eminently fair. It will be evident from examination of each of the criteria listed that if singing grade is determined on the basis of 25 per cent effort, 25 per cent progress, and 50 per cent comparative singing skill (Note — See following), even the most talented student with the best background must still work to earn 50 per cent of his singing grade based on effort and progress. In addition, the case of the vocally deficient student isn't entirely hopeless, since 50 per cent of his singing grade can be an "A" grade if suffcent effort and progress are evident. He is also under no handicap in the vocal theory grade, which has a weight of one-third in the final average.

Comparative singing skill grades are recorded each time the student sings a solo for credit. These are averaged at the end of the semester and combined with the instructor's estimation of effort and progress in singing for the final singing grade. In order better to determine advancement, it is suggested in smaller more advanced classes that a final singing examination be given at the end of the semester. It should consist of at least two or three songs which the student has prepared most carefully. This examination may also be set up as an informal recital if desired, or appearance in recital may be accepted in lieu of a song examination.

THREE CRITERIA FOR DETERMINING SINGING GRADES IN CLASS OR INDIVIDUAL STUDY

1. *Effort and application* 25 per cent, as evidenced by:

   (a) Work on assignments.
   (b) Number and difficulty of songs memorized.

   (c) Thoroughness of memorization and preparation of songs sung.
   (d) Understanding of vocal theory and methods studied as shown in singing, vocal theory examinations, and readiness in discussion.

2. *Advancement* 25 per cent, as evidenced by growth in:

   (a) Technical progress — Posture, breath control, tone, diction, legato, flexibility, range, dynamics, etc.
   (b) Confidence, poise, and assurance.
   (c) Skill and understanding in interpretation.

3. *Singing ability* 50 per cent, as determined by comparison with those in the same class or semester of training in:

   (a) Quality and freedom of production and interpretive ability.
   (b) Stage presence and poise.
   (c) Versatility in style and repertoire.

In determining the final semester grade in singing, it is suggested that:

1. Students must rank *A* in comparative singing ability and in at least one of the other two criteria in order to receive an *A* in singing for the semester; the remaining criterion should be at least a *C* to earn the *A* grade.

2. It is possible for a student to receive a *B* grade with only average singing ability if advancement and effort are *A*.

3. A failure grade will not be given if criteria 1 and 2 (effort and advancement) are *C* plus or better.

4. A grade of *C* is the average grade for beginning classes if students are unselected, but the average should be higher when only superior students are allowed to enroll, and in intermediate and advanced class in which only the better pupils remain.

In addition to teacher judgment, two methods can be employed if desired in determining final semester grade:

1. Ask each student to rate himself with others in the class in reference to the three criteria listed. (Some teachers record the two or three examination songs sung by each student on a tape recorder. They then play them back to the class in order that each student can obtain a more objective judgment regarding how he really does sound in comparison with others.)

2. Ask all students to rate one another in terms of the three criteria. (This can be done only after students have been in class together long enough to form opinions based on evidence. Students are often more severe than the instructor in judging one another and in assigning grades.)

22

Classroom Facilities, Equipment, and their Use

While knowledge and teaching skill of the instructor, competence of the accompanist, and the intelligence, persistence, and vocal potentiality of the pupil are undoubtedly the major factors in success of class voice, progress can be greatly retarded unless needed physical facilities and equipment are available. Many teachers could be much more successful if only they were alert to opportunities or persistent in insisting on improvements in equipment and facilities. "There are some necessary props in any vocal classroom. If possible, each teacher should have, or have access to: A good victrola or radio-victrola, plenty of fine records including foreign diction records, a recording machine to show the student his progress or glaring faults, bulletin board for musical events, mirror, metronome for marking tempo, pictorial material or replicas of chest and larynx, dictionaries and reference material, song library, a good piano which is tuned regularly."[1]

CHECK LIST OF FACILITIES

A check list of physical facilities, some essential and some that can be gotten along without, follows:

1. Suitable Student Manual and Songs for study.
2. Suitable vocal classroom.
3. Piano (preferably a good grand).
4. Organ.
5. Phonograph-radio-recorder.
6. Tape recorder.
7. Student practice rooms.
8. Full length mirror.
9. Metronome.
10. Blackboard for writing exercises, illustrations, and examinations.
11. Bulletin board.
12. Phonograph records.
13. Tape recordings.
14. Straight back chairs.
15. StroboConn (Stroboscope).
16. Vocal library consisting of —

(a) Vocal collections sufficient to study any period, style, or type of song desired.

(b) Classified and graded vocal solo, duet, and ensemble material.

(c) Scores of standard oratorios, operas, and operettas.

(d) Librettos of operas.

(e) Vocal music magazines.

(f) Pictorial material concerning vocal composers, great singers of the past and present, and illustrations of the larynx, diaphragm, mouth, and chest.

(g) Musical dictionaries, encyclopedias, and histories, and foreign language dictionaries.

(h) Mimeograph material such as bibliographies of vocal books with reference to specific topics; pronunciation hints for foreign language; classified bibliographies of vocal collections for each type of voice; phonetic sound of foreign language texts for songs sung in class; and vocal exercise sheets.

THE VOCAL STUDIO AND SEATING ARRANGEMENT

The vocal studio should be located in a quiet place and have good light, heat, ventilation, and proper acoustical treatment. It should not be barren or severe in appearance, but attractive in color and design with pictures on the wall and an atmosphere of relaxation. Ceiling should be higher and the room larger than that needed for the same number of students in academic work. For voice classes of 20 to 30, the room should ideally have an academic seating capacity of at least 60 in order to allow proper semicircular seating, wider spacing be-

---

[1]California-Western Conference Curriculum Committee. "Voice Training in Classes." Music Educators Journal, May-June, 1945, p. 40.

tween pupils, and favorable acoustics for group singing. A foot or more spacing between chairs is desirable since the instructor then can distinguish each voice better and can walk around between chairs, helping individual pupils when they are singing songs together. It must be remembered that seating arrangement for a voice class is quite different from the concentrated arrangement preferred for chorus or glee club. When using the choral room, in which the seats are permanently arranged, for class voice also, it is desirable to use alternate seats.

An exception to wide spacing may be made in the first few weeks and for pupils with pitch difficulty or excessive timidity. They may be seated either close to one side or directly in front of a singer with good intonation and a sonorous voice. After voices are classified, or perhaps merely segregated as *high* and *low*, high voices should be placed on one side and low on the other, in more or less permanent seating assignments. This plan improves duet singing in ensemble, facilitates use of supplementary song collections available in high and low key editions, and seats together the group that can carry vocal exercises either higher or lower than for average voices. The low group may well listen to the high group at times and vice versa.

An ideal arrangement is to have seating in a one to three row semicircle or horseshoe arrangement, with the teacher and piano well forward in the center of the opening. (See following illustration) Pupils should be close enough to the instructor so that each voice can be heard when singing together. In classes larger than 20 with more than two rows involved, this is more difficult. Window light preferably should come from back of the students, while electric illumination should be adequate but not glaring — indirect lighting is best.

Walls and ceiling of the voice classroom should be acoustically treated to prevent reverberation, and the room soundproofed with double doors and windows if near other classes or activities. An over-reverberant room is especially bad for recording and the ensemble singing in *forte* passages of a large class. In a comparatively "dead" room, each voice is heard more easily by the teacher and is not distorted, jumbled, or magnified by reverberation. The slightly under-reverberant room is excellent for clarity in recording, allows students to hear and judge their own voices more realistically, and gives better preparation for concert, radio, and television work.

In some schools where expenses in building must be kept to a minimum or a separate voice classroom is not available, an all-purpose vocal organization rehearsal, voice class, and a small, intimate recital room is the best answer. Such a room is illustrated on the next page. This specially-constructed room should have permanent semicircular seating on different levels or tiers. A voice class would occupy not more than two or three of the front tiers and its members normally would be seated in alternate chairs. Seating capacity of the room never should be less than the maximum number of students expected in the largest vocal organization in the school. The piano is moved forward for recitals and, in order that it can be rolled back and forth easily, it should have large casters. The stage area should be either on a floor level or only slightly higher, with a gentle ramp incline leading up. This room, properly designed and acoustically treated, is also an excellent small, intimate recital hall for solo vocal and instrumental concerts, contains one or two offices for vocal instructors, and adequate storage space for the vocal library, choir robes, etc. The curtain to the stage normally should be kept closed for voice class work and choral rehearsals. For those interested in modern music building plans, an excellent 96-page, 113-illustration publication, "Music Rooms and Equipment," list price $4.50, is available from the Music Educators National Conference, 1201 Sixteenth Street, N.W., Washington 6, D.C.

THE AUDITORIUM

Members of the voice class should practice singing solos at times in the school auditorium in order to become accustomed to its acoustics, to learn to articulate with sufficient strength in a large hall, and to discover the best stage position for singer and piano. Some consideration has been given to good acoustics in most auditoriums built in recent years. Few are ideal or have uniformly good acoustics throughout, however. The voice teacher and class first should find out by experimentation the position on the stage where sound carries most clearly and uniformly, and if there is a distinct deadline back of the proscenium arch from which the voice will not carry well.

In nearly all auditoriums, the best position for solo singing will be found in stage center and well forward on the apron. Side positions usually tend to devitalize the tone to the listener or create "dead" spots or uneven acoustics conditions at some locations in the auditorium. A position back of the proscenium arch is likely to deaden or muffle the voice unless the arch is generous in height and a hard reflecting surface is directly behind the singer.

ACOUSTIC CONSIDERATIONS

Auditoriums and concert halls that are satisfactory acoustically give the singer little trouble. It is the extremely over-reverberant and the over-dead halls that cause the singer to have difficulty in intonation, diction clarity, balance with the piano, and tonal quality. The experienced concert artist and

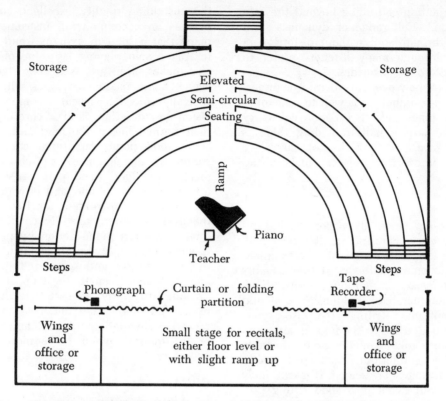

Illustration of Combination Choral Rehearsal, Class Voice, and
Small Recital Hall with Piano in Position for Class Voice

accompanist usually can judge the acoustic qualities of an auditorium or room pretty accurately after trying a few phrases in it, and know approximately what to do in order to make the best of the situation. The amateur singer and accompanist need help, guidance, and considerable rehearsing there before attempting to appear in recital. A few hints may help.

Over-reverberant halls need extreme care, precision, and force of diction, since echo tends to muffle the words. Tone may carry well but it is often distorted, especially in *fortissimo*. The voice and the piano will sound louder to the singer and accompanist than they do in a normal or a "dead" hall. Very loud singing or playing increase reverberation and muffle clarity to the extent that the singer may not be able to hear the piano pitch clearly, resulting in off-pitch singing. The singer needs to be close in the crook of the piano — it must not be underneath in the stage pit — or he is inviting trouble with intonation. Fast tempo or fast word songs should be taken at a somewhat slower tempo than normal in order to increase listening clarity. The most effective songs under such handicaps are the slower legato types that do not demand great tonal force from either the singer or accompanist. An accompanist easily can overpower a singer in

such a hall. He must be especially careful to "keep under" the voice in volume and never to pound. A *pianissimo* will carry providing tone is pure, articulation crisp, the piano subdued, and there are no interfering noises. Safest and best sounding dynamics are *p* to *mf*.

"Dead" halls, especially some of the older broadcasting studios, sometimes give the singer a sensation similar to that of singing into a wet sack, producing what appears to be disappointingly little resonance. This often results in the amateur singer's starting to force the voice in order to hear more tone, resulting in both poor tonal quality and pitch. Do not be deceived about sound carrying in the under-reverberant hall, however. It usually carries to the listener so well that the slightest error in articulation, unevenness in breath control or vibrato, or roughness in tone quality is audible immediately to the listener. Diction need not be exaggerated in force, as in the hall with echo, and it is always a fatal mistake for either the singer or accompanist to force tone until it sounds loud to him. Ease and finesse pay dividends, while tempos can be taken faster than normal to advantage. Fast word or fast tempo songs and those requiring a quiet intimacy of style are particularly effective. The slow, sustained dramatic song also sounds well providing the singer can avoid the temptation of forcing beyond the safe point in production. Full range of dynamics from *ppp* to *fff* comes through well without distortion in the "dead" hall, although many listeners prefer to hear more "liveness" to the acoustics.

In either the extremely over-reverberant or under-reverberant acoustic condition, it is well to remember that well-produced tones and crisp diction will carry to the back of the largest hall, providing there is no noise intereference. If they do not carry, we can be sure that a forced tone only can make a bad situation worse.

CHAIRS

If the recital room is an all-purpose choral rehearsal hall, voice classroom, and small recital hall, as it often is, or if the voice class will take examinations or make notes on vocal theory at times, *chairs should be straight backed with folding arms*. Such chairs are now manufactured. Folding arms should be kept down except when writing. It is also preferable if chairs can be attached to the floor in a permanent position. Loose folding chairs or comfortably padded, slant-backed auditorium chairs are a handicap to singing when singers are seated. It is extremely difficult to obtain and maintain a good sitting posture from a voice class rehearsing in folding chairs or any type of tipped-back chair.

STUDENT PRACTICE ROOMS

Schools should provide an adequate number of vocal music practice rooms for students. Some students do not have the time, opportunity, or facilities to practice at home. Practice rooms should be soundproofed, acoustically treated, adequately lighted, heated, and ventilated, and not too small for best results. They should contain a good piano kept well in tune. A full-length mirror should be provided also. While a piano is desirable for checking pitch and learning songs, the student should be continually cautioned to use it as little as possible in practicing vocalises and in singing through songs once they are learned. There is no other way to develop independent musicianship and good intonation.

PIANO

A fine-toned grand piano in the voice classroom is a distinct advantage. The grand piano is more convenient if the teacher also must function as the accompanist, as they often must, since it allows facing and observing the class over the piano. Some of the recent better tonal quality spinets are next in desirability for the same reason. The most important features of the piano are its tone and sustaining quality, however — better a fine quality upright than a poor quality concert grand. Tone should be deep and mellow rather than shallow and brilliant, and the sustaining quality excellent, in order to blend best as an accompanying instrument for voice. A piano that is loud in dynamics and voiced brilliantly for piano solo playing, as some of the most expensive makes often are, is a poor choice for the voice class. Some piano companies will provide a piano specially voiced for vocal accompanying, radio, television broadcasting, and recording if the tone of their normal line is too loud and brilliant.

A good piano repairman can move the whole action of the hammers up closer to the strings, making the loud-toned piano easier to play softly, toning down its volume, and providing a much better accompanying instrument for the amateur singer in the average classroom. He can improve the harsh tone of a worn piano action by picking the felt, or if worn too badly, by replacing the hammers with those of thicker and softer felt, producing a more mellow tone. Even the best makes of pianos should be tuned regularly, at least twice a year under light usage and more often under heavy. Excessive use, excessive fluctuations of heat and cold or humidity, or an inferior piano make more frequent tuning necessary.

ORGAN

While an organ is not an essential in the vocal room, it is undoubtedly an asset. The well-equipped vocal room will have both an organ and a piano. Electric organs are now more reasonable in price than concert grand pianos and have been perfected to the extent that they are satisfactory musical instruments. Some vocal studios have the traditional pipe organ, but a good one with many stops is too expensive and impractical for the comparatively small vocal studio. Organ accompaniment is preferable to the piano for most sacred solos, and because of its sustaining qualities, for songs in which the accompaniment is sparse in rhythmic movement, containing mostly long, sustained tones. Sometimes piano and organ can be combined or used alternately at different parts on the same song to artistic advantage.

RECORDER AND RECORDING TECHNICS

The use of recording and play-back of the student's solo singing offers the best means available for the student really to hear and objectively study his own singing. Recording tends to make what is heard so impersonal that the soloist himself is usually the first to criticize imperfections freely. Private teachers should own a good recorder and use it frequently in their teaching. Schools should supply an excellent tape recorder and keep it in good repair for their vocal classes. If they do not, the individual teacher, who is ambitious to attain maximum pupil interest and progress, can scarcely afford not to purchase one to use out of his own funds. In choosing a recorder, it is wisest to purchase a well-known make that is sturdy and reliable, easily and quickly operated and adjusted, and has good acoustic reproduction and ready local repair service.

Three principal types of recorders are available: the wax or plastic disc, the wire, and the tape. The tape recorder has a number of features which make it the favorite of most vocal teachers for instructional purposes, and has become justly popular as a highly valuable asset. High fidelity acoustic quality, mechanical reliability, and ease in operation are now satisfactory, and are being improved from time to time. The bulky, high-priced professional model tape recorder is not recommended for the ordinary classroom situation. Under ideal conditions, where the instrument can be left set up ready to record and with an expert technician at the more complex controls, it will give the best reproduction obtainable. Controls are not simplified as in the portable commercial models, however; the machine is bulky, heavy, and requires a considerable amount of time and labor to move and set up for use.

The comparatively low-priced portable tape recorder usually can be improved considerably in acoustic quality, if desired, by purchase of a more expensive microphone with a long, standing base, and also by installing a large separate speaker in the vocal room. A competent recording engineer should be consulted before purchase of either the microphone or speaker, however, since they must be of a type capable of being balanced with the recorder. In any case, purchase or construction of a standing base upon which the microphone usually furnished can be mounted is a convenience and is comparatively inexpensive.

Intelligent use of a recorder under teacher guidance can be of inestimable value as a teaching aid. Enthusiastic classes and students who are confident of their progress is the rule. After students have gained confidence and pleasure in the use of their voices through singing with the class, they should be urged to record and play back frequently as the quickest way in which to learn how their voices really sound.

The teacher should be careful not to use solo recording too early or in such a manner as to add unnecessarily to an already severe inferiority complex about singing. Some modest pupils may be pleasantly surprised at how well they sound but, on the whole, students are disappointed at the sound of their voices and the many technical faults revealed. Some will have their worst fears confirmed; others will be pleasantly surprised; some will be awakened to faults they never perceived; but none are likely to recognize their voices as they thought they sounded. A common reaction is the amazed, "Is that the way I really sound?" In any case, after the introductory phases of voice study, it is well for the pupil to know the truth, even if it hurts, since *correction and progress depend first upon awareness of fault.*

When a tape recorder is available in the classroom, each student should purchase as his own at least one spool of tape, upon which he can record and play-back frequently. Extra spools are desirable for permanent recordings of outstanding excellence and for keeping a record of progress. Many teachers keep their own carefully-filed library of such recordings.

Tape recordings can be transferred to phonograph discs if desired. While tape recorders are still scarce in homes, phonographs are plentiful and playbacks of the discs can be repeated at home as often as desired. One or more tape recorders are usually available in most modern school systems. These recorders, and that in the vocal studio, should be made available under careful regulations to vocal students whose competence in using the machine has been certified by the vocal instructor. It is a comparatively easy matter to teach all students the mechanics of playback on any type of recording machine. However, competence in recording to the very best advantage takes considerable study even with the comparatively simple and less "touchy" tape recorders. The following suggestions may prove useful:

1. As a condition for purchase, insist on an adequate demonstration of vocal recording by a salesman or representative of the machine being considered. The teacher and members of the class should make certain that they understand the controls and mechanics of the particular machine before the demonstration is finished. Anyone using the machine also should read carefully the directions and illustrations for operation issued by the company.

2. Make sure that a competent repairman and replacement parts for the machine you purchase will be readily available. All such electrical equipment, even the best, needs service and parts at times.

3. Do not allow students who have not been trained in its use to operate the machine, or damage may result. The best solution for the classroom machine appears to be to teach all the comparatively simple operation of the playback but allow only those to run the machine in recording who are especially interested, have been more carefully trained, and are competent for the work. Most classes normally will have several students who are especially apt and interested.

Two problems in recording should be given the most attention from an acoustic standpoint: achieving the best and most realistic tone quality for the particular voice, and balancing the voice with the accompaniment. It is usually necessary to experiment to some extent in determining the best distance of the singer and the piano from the microphone, and to determine the maximum volume setting that is safe on peak dynamics. The following steps are suggested in order to obtain best results in tape recording:

1. First test the voice alone at the *maximum* tonal volume expected on the dynamic climax of the song to be sung. Adjust distance from the mike until the best tonal quality is achieved at normal volume adjustment of the machine. Average voices should be tried first at the distance recommended in instructions, weaker voices closer to the microphone, and powerful, resonant voices farther away. Set the volume control so that the electric eye barely closes on peak dynamics, or if the machine has a light that flashes to indicate peak, so that the light barely flashes. Best recordings are usually at the maximum volume the machine will handle without ever going over the danger line indicated by the electric eye's closing or the light's flashing.

2. Do the same with the piano alone, playing the loudest dynamics encountered in the accompaniment. Leave the volume setting at its best point for the voice and move the microphone farther away from, or closer to, the piano until volume is stimulated somewhat less by the piano than it was for the voice. This microphone position should guarantee proper balance between the voice and piano when the two record together. As a rule the piano accompaniment is too weak with the singer in normal position in front of the curve of the piano, with the microphone placed directly in front of him. In this case, first try lifting the lid of the piano; and second, move the microphone closer to the piano by having the singer stand sidewise to the piano.

3. Finally, check dynamic peak again with both the voice and piano recording together at the dynamic climax. The volume indicator usually will have to be moved back slightly from the setting for voice alone and should be ideal or close to ideal for a stable setting for the particular voice and accompanist, if the recording machine is properly adjusted internally at the factory.

The preceding method of adjustment normally should result in good tone, satisfactory balance, and maximum safe volume adjustment on recording. To make sure of best results before permanent recording is attempted, however, it is best to record first a short part of the softest portion of the song and follow that with the loudest. If the softest portion is inaudible, or nearly so, the volume indicator will have to be adjusted upward somewhat in the *pianissimo* passages by someone at the controls while the song is being sung. This adjustment is not necessary for the best portable recorders if they are in proper working order. Another solution to "fadeaway" on *pianissimo* is to instruct the singer and

pianist not to reduce dynamics to such a great extent. *Most cheap recorders work best when either extreme ppp or fff dynamics are avoided.* A good technician, who understands the safe limitations of the particular machine and knows the music and how the performers will interpret it in dynamics, can manipulate volume controls during performance to offset the inadequacies of some machines and obtain more satisfactory recordings acoustically.

Teachers should keep a recording log for each student, indicating the conditions of microphone placement under which his voice recorded best, in order that they can be duplicated without loss of time in experiment in future recordings. Students also should be instructed to remember as nearly as possible their distance from the mike and the mike's position in relation to the piano. This plan usually works well as long as the same recording machine, microphone, piano, and piano accompanist are used; if any of these factors are changed, some additional experimentation may be necessary again to obtain best results. After some experience with recording, the alert and analytical instructor usually can guess pretty closely what the best microphone position and control settings will be for each student.

In judging excellence of recording from playback, if quality is good at normal or medium playback volume, there is no problem. If play-back volume is too weak, recording was at too low a volume or the microphone was too far away. If recording is harsh or raucous in quality and the machine is a good one, it is probably due to too high a volume setting or the microphone was too close. If adjustments in these respects are tried in re-recording and the tone is still harsh, the probability is that the recording equipment is out of adjustment and needs repair. If diction is not clear, it is usually the fault of poor articulation by the singer, he was too far from the microphone, or the microphone was too close.

Students in voice class should understand both the advantages and limitations of recording as a true means of estimating vocal production. They should know how to experiment in order to obtain best conditions for recording and how to perfect microphone technic. Recording has many values for assisting the singer in hearing his own faults, particularly in regard to diction, intonation, breath control, vibrato, and phrasing. It must be recognized, however, that any system of microphone amplification, whether it be recording, radio, television, or loud speaker, has its limitations and dangers as well.

Weak, somewhat throaty and perhaps breathy production is minimized, while volume output is dependent on engineering and not on actual fact in production. Students thus can be grossly deceived into believing that they have satisfactory technic in these respects when actually the opposite is true. It is a well-known fact that some microphone performers are immensely popular radio, recording, or dance band stars, but have such tiny and poorly-produced voices in the foregoing respects that they are entire "flops" if they attempt public performance without microphone amplification. Before the appearance of the microphone and the amplifier, such voices could not have "gotten to first base" in a public career.

The student, therefore, should not be deceived when listening to his own voice. He can place credence on only those factors in which recording can give a reliable picture; other factors mentioned must be ignored or questioned. They can be judged only by a competent teacher or critic in a "live" performance. There is no doubt, however, that recording helps to reveal and correct errors in intonation, diction, vibrato, steadiness in breath support, and phrasing. In fact, these errors appear to be magnified on play-back. It is obvious that recording has its weakness in preparing for "live" public performance since the weaker voices often sound much better than they actually are, while the stronger, more vibrant, and sonorous dramatic voices sound worse.

The following principles apply regarding the general rules for effective microphone technic:

1. The microphone is quite sensitive regarding clarity of articulation in relation to distance of the singer from the mike. Diction is plainest when the singer stands close and sings with comparatively little volume; as distance is increased, the more crisp and forceful articulation must be in order to be understood. Singing softly and close to the mike also gives the effect of intimacy.

2. A powerful, dramatic voice overstimulates the microphone and makes the sound over nasal or raucous to the listener if position is too close. Such voices must either reduce dynamics or stand farther away from the mike with resultant loss in clarity of articulation. The former, or a combination of the two solutions, is usually preferable for best results in recording.

3. Light lyric voices can be built up mechanically either by turning up the volume in recording or in the process of playback or broadcasting. On the best machines, thin and overbright voices can be benefited in both recording and playback or broadcasting by adjusting the fundamental and bass controls to the maximum, thus reducing the shrillness of upper overtone partials. Such voices then may sound much better than they actually are. Unfortunately, a powerful, rich, dramatic voice cannot be helped by the technician; this type of voice only can suffer through microphone transference. Thus recording and radio may be kind and flattering to the weak-toned, lyric voice and cruel and unfair to the powerful, rich, dramatic voice.

4. It is well to remember that no microphone or recording adjustment can conceal or correct poor diction, wavering or off-pitch singing, excessive vibrato, tremolo, unsteady or inadequate breath control, poor phrasing, or rough, glottic attacks. Regardless of the singer, the microphone is cruelly consistent in revealing, or even augmenting, such faults. All singers, therefore, can learn much from listening to recordings for weaknesses in these factors.

PHONOGRAPH AND SUITABLE RECORDS

The vocal studio should have a fine, modern, high fidelity phonograph and an excellent library of select records. Regardless of the claims that might be advanced by an enthusiastic salesman, it is impossible to get top quality from a small portable or any phonograph with a small loud speaker. It also is convenient if the machine is equipped with a recording device for students who wish disc recordings made in order to play them at their homes. However, much better results usually are obtained by first recording on tape and then having a commercial recorder make the transcription to disc.

There are an immense number of solo voice recordings available. The judicious use of some of these records is highly valuable at times to teach a composition, foreign language pronunciation, diction, and to illustrate certain vocal technics, style, tone color, and general interpretation factors. When the score is available, students usually should follow it carefully as they listen to the record.

The most important type of records to be purchased first should be those that directly illustrate song literature being studied at the time and those that exemplify technical problems being stressed. Fame of the artist is comparatively unimportant for teaching purposes, but an equally good recording by a well-known singer is to be preferred, of course, if it illustrates what is desired as well as other recordings do. Sometimes records illustrating what not to do are equally valuable in proving a point.

The instructor should be alert to building up and filing an excellent practical library of both tape and wax recordings of the songs that classes and individual pupils are most likely to sing. Interpretations should be like those desired by the instructor, with the exception of an occasional "horrible example" thrown in to illustrate what not to do. In addition to available commercial records, needed recordings can be supplied by several methods:

1. Recordings of excellent solo singing by advanced pupils.

2. Recordings by a whole class, or select members of a class, singing in unison.

3. Recordings by visitors or outside artists who consent to help in the project.

4. Recordings of the voice of the teacher.

Vocal teachers and advanced students interested in studying interpretation and the technic of teaching interpretation should investigate "The Art of Song Interpretation," 24 records including 66 separate songs recorded by John Scott Campbell, 540 South Hill Avenue, Pasadena, California. These are recordings sung by students of Madame Lotte Lehmann, a master interpreter and teacher of interpretation, and include her comments to each student as she works to improve expression on each composition. While it is sometimes difficult to understand the spoken instructions, there is a great deal of value to be obtained from the illustrations, from the outstanding song literature itself, and from the concepts of style, tempo, phrasing, tone color, and mood portrayed. The repertoire is particularly rich in German Lieder in which Madame Lehmann is recognized as a superlative interpreter.

"Vocal Students Practice Aid Records," Box 209, Madison Square Station, New York 10, N. Y., have a continually expanding list of select recordings of standard song literature to aid the vocal student and teacher. Brochures containing a list of recordings, prices and information regarding the nature of the recordings will be sent on request.

VOCAL LIBRARY

First of all a sufficient number of student manuals and song anthologies covering needed vocal theory, exercises, and songs either should be purchased individually by the student or should be available through the vocal library for the student to check out for the entire semester in which the material is used. It is much better for the students to own this material in order that they can underline statements as they choose and retain the volumes for future study and practice of exercises and songs. As explained previously, classes using this vocal course also should have available a sufficient number of copies of this textbook for more detailed reference on many topics.

Suitable supplementary song volumes or anthologies also may be desirable for advanced classes. Either the vocal library of the instructor or the school library should contain one copy each in the available key additions of the more choice song volumes and anthologies of the various types of song literature for ready reference. This is in order that the student, with the advice of the teacher, can examine and select most readily and wisely any song

volumes that are needed. While separate sheet music is sometimes of more interest to the student, and should not be neglected by those who can afford the cost, most of the great solo voice literature is available in collections at a minor fraction of the expense per song. There is little doubt that it is far more practical to organize class work in voice around available song volumes or anthologies.

Extent of supplementary vocal library is dependent on the needs of classes in reference to how advanced they are, the variety of interests, and what funds are available. An adequate vocal library should be either in a filing cabinet or cupboard in the voice room under lock and key or in a library close by, where it is readily obtainable for reference. Where voice work covers a number of years, the reference library should be more extensive. The instructor should own his own constantly-growing sheet music and song volume library, so classified, graded, and catalogued with card index by title, composer, and voice suitability that it is most useful for quick and efficient reference.

MIRROR

A full-length mirror should be installed permanently on the wall or on a movable standard near the piano in the vocal studio and vocal practice rooms. Students having difficulty with bowing, posture, improper mouth, jaw, or lip action, wrinkling the forehead, arching the eyebrows, or any other visible abnormality should be urged to use the mirror persistently until correction is made. To see one's self in such errors is better than many words of criticism by the instructor and class members.

VISUAL PITCH INDICATORS

The StroboConn, or Stroboscope, and other recent rather expensive and clever electrical instruments, indicate exactly and visually the slightest deviation from pitch in such a manner that the student can tell at a glance whether he is flat or sharp, and adjust upward or downward until perfect pitch is attained. It is our opinion that these instruments are most valuable for pupils having great difficulty with hearing their own offpitch singing, but are of questionable value for students having an average or good ear until after other normal means for improving pitch have been tried and failed. When used judiciously, they may prove useful in making the pupil more conscious of exact pitch and of the mental and physical adjustments necessary to attain it.

23

Outline of a Four-Year Vocal Course

THE IDEAL PLAN

In colleges where both private vocal lessons and group class work are offered by the same vocal staff, educators usually reach the conclusion that a combination of class and private lesson instruction is the ideal plan for maximum progress by most students. Private vocal teachers and some music conservatories report that even advanced students progress best if it is possible to organize at least one group meeting a week.

High school vocal culture is organized almost exclusively under the class plan, but seldom covers more than one or two years. There is today little remaining doubt about the effectiveness — many maintain the superiority — of class voice teaching in the lower levels of instruction for one and possibly two years. Experienced teachers in college usually prefer to start some private instruction at least during the second year, however, and increase the ratio of private to class lessons in the third and fourth years. An ideal scheduling plan, in which either private or class lessons five times per week are possible, follows:

1. First year — 4 class lessons and 1 private lesson weekly.
2. Second year — 3 class lessons and 2 private lessons weekly.
3. Third year — 2 class lessons and 3 private lessons weekly.
4. Fourth year — 1 class lesson and 4 private lessons weekly.

THE PRACTICAL PLAN

For economic and scheduling reasons the foregoing ideal plan is seldom feasible. We usually have found the following organizational set-up in college more practical and still productive of excellent results when voice is taught by a competent staff:

1. First year — 3 class lessons weekly.

2. Second year — 2 class lessons and 1 private lesson weekly.
3. Third and fourth years — 2 private lessons and 1 class lesson weekly.

It is our considered opinion that colleges and conservatories of music that schedule either private or class lessons exclusively normally cannot expect as high standards in vocal performance, and as well-educated a student for the same time involved, as the foregoing type of mixing the two plans will produce.

RECOMMENDED FOUR-YEAR VOCAL COURSE

In the following outline, Prerequisites, General Objectives, Specific Objectives, Text, Song Collections or Anthologies, Vocal Literature Emphasis, and Minimum Individual Memorization and Solo Singing Requirements, are suggested for an eight-semester four-year vocal course. It is designed primarily for college or conservatory classes meeting at least two or three times weekly and requiring some outside study and preparation. High school classes will find, however, that they can use exactly the same outline for their beginning courses providing they meet at least three or more times weekly, or that the personnel is fairly select. In any case, the outline is still suggestive and valuable to those organizing vocal work in either more fortunate situations, where it is possible to do more, or in more restricted situations, where it is impractical to do as much as outlined for each semester.

The course as outlined can be administered successfully either as:

1. A combination of class and private lessons.
2. Class lessons exclusively.
3. Private lessons exclusively.

When administered as a class voice procedure, it is assumed that beginning classes normally will not exceed 20-25 students, and that enrollment will be limited to a maximum of 15-20 in the second semester, 10-15 in the third and fourth, 8-10 in the fifth and sixth, and 6-8 in the seventh and eighth, in order that increasing attention can be given to the individual. The first number listed is preferred enrollment in each semester.

"Minimum Individual Memorization and Solo Requirement" listed for each semester is to be interpreted as the requirement of songs of average length and difficulty of the type suggested for an average grade of C in effort. Students who wish to earn a higher grade on effort should understand that they can do so by memorizing and singing more songs, or longer and more difficult songs or arias. More songs should be expected from superior students or from college-age level classes meeting more than three times weekly. Relative length and difficulty of songs must be a consideration in number required: e.g., a student might select three or four very long songs or arias that would distinctly require more time and effort to memorize and sing well than eight songs of average length and difficulty. Outside study requirements and number of meetings and credit allowed per semester necessarily are determining factors in selecting the minimum number of solo songs to be memorized and sung each semester.

GENERAL OBJECTIVES

The following general objectives apply to *all* semesters of vocal study:

1. To promote greater enthusiasm, pleasure, and spontaneity in singing and a desire for progress in singing skill.

2. To establish poise, correct inferiority complexes, and reduce or eliminate fear of solo vocal expression.

3. To provide adequate opportunity for use of the voice in solo singing in class, recitals, etc.

4. To develop a cooperative social attitude and sense of responsibility.

5. To study and memorize a desirable repertoire of songs.

6. To guide and establish habits of proper practice and music memorization.

7. To develop refined taste and discriminating knowledge and understanding of song literature and the art of singing in the various styles and schools of literature.

8. To supplement the work of other music classes in improving sight singing, musicianship, and discrimination in musical taste.

9. To provide the necessary foundation, guidance, and individual help for the more talented and advanced student who wishes to continue study privately and achieve professional standards.

10. To understand the function of vocal accompaniment and the cooperation of singer and accompanist necessary to achieve highest standards.

11. To present the necessary basic vocal fundamentals of theory and practice to enable the student to:

(a) Obtain habitually correct and pleasing use of the singing and speaking voice by establishing correct posture, breath support, diction, and vocal habits.

(b) Sing solos and vocalises with good intonation, quality, and expression.

(c) Become an efficient and intelligent member of a choral group.

(d) Establish a natural, poised, and gracious stage presence.

(e) Understand how to classify voices, diagnose vocal difficulties, and teach voice, either in classes or privately. (Note — This objective applies only to classes involving prospective teachers of voice.)

VOICE I

Prerequisite — Solfeggio I or equivalent.
Texts:

(a) For theory and technic content — *Expressive Singing* Volume I by Christy. Chapters I, "Orientation and Guidance;" 2, "Posture;" 3, "Breath Control;" 4, "Tone" (except Lesson 3); 5, "Diction" (except Lesson 5).*

(b) For song content — *Expressive Singing Song Anthology* Volume I by Christy.

Minimum Memorization and Solo Singing Requirement — five songs.

Vocal Literature Emphasis — Folk Songs, ballads, spirituals, sacred songs, and easy art songs in English. (Note — the art song may be sung in the original foreign language, providing the student is thoroughly familiar with the language involved.)

Practice Emphasis — Practice guidance, proper posture, breath support, ease, naturalness, free tone, tonal color variation, mood and style orientation through listening to and singing the six suggested "Basic Model Songs." (Note — See p. 7)

Specific Objectives:

1. To properly orient the student into the study of voice.

2. To promote poise, pleasure, and spontaneity in singing.

3. To reduce or eliminate fear of individual performance.

---

*The correlated lesson-by-lesson content in Part I of this Textbook also is recomended for suplementary reading.

4. To obtain correct and pleasing use of the singing and speaking voice.

5. To establish correct habits of practice, posture, breath control, diction, principles of relaxation, and easy tonal production.

6. To introduce and preview the major principles of style and interpretation in simple, easily-mastered vocal literature.

7. To understand folk song, spiritual, ballad, sacred song, and art song characteristics and start a basic repertoire of songs of this type sung with good tone, satisfactory technic, and style.

VOICE II

Prerequisite — Voice I.

Texts:

(a) For theory and technic content — *Expressive Singing* Volume I by Christy. Chapters 4, "Tone" (Lesson 3, "Resonance and Sonority," only); 5, "Diction" (Lesson 5, "Consonants," only); 6, "Legato and Sostenuto;" 16, "Basic Exercises for Vocal Development."*

(b) For song content — *Expressive Singing* Song Anthology Volume I by Christy.

Minimum Memorization and Solo Singing Requirement — five songs.

Vocal Literature Emphasis — Folk songs, ballads, spirituals, sacred songs, and simple songs in English. (Note — the art song may be sung in the original foreign language providing the student is thoroughly familiar with the language involved.)

Practice Emphasis — Legato and sostenuto, efficiency in tonal production, clarity of articulation, and application of the "Principles of Production in Tonal Progression" in Lesson 16.

Specific Objectives:

1. To improve the basic technics studied in Voice I.

2. To understand and apply the principles of efficient resonance in tonal production.

3. To understand the problems in articulation and make satisfactory progress in solving them.

4. To introduce and obtain a workable grasp, as a sound basis for future progress, of the principles and practices pertaining to legato and sostenuto singing.

5. To understand the "Principles of Production in Tonal Progression" and apply them efficiently in both exercises and songs.

6. To understand folk song, ballad, spiritual, sacred song, and art song characteristics and extend a basic repertoire of songs of this type sung with good tone, satisfactory technic, and style.

7. To be able to classify voices as to type. (Note — This objective applies only to classes involving prospective teachers of voice.)

VOICE III

Prerequisite — Voice II.

Texts:

(a) For theory and technic content — *Expressive Singing* Volume I by Christy. Chapters 7, "Agility and Flexibility;" 8, "Extending Range;" 9, Extending Dynamics;" 10, "Intonation;" 11, "Recitative."*

(b) For song content — *Expressive Singing* Song Anthology Volume II by Christy.

*Suggested Supplementary Song Collections:***

1. Old Italian:

(a) *Classic Italian Songs for School and Studio* by Glenn and Spouse. (Ditson edition)

(b) *Twenty Four Italian Songs of the 17th and 18th Centuries* (Schirmer edition).

2. Old English:

(a) *Reliquary of Old English Song* — Ed. Potter, Vol. II, G. Schirmer.

(b) 55 Art Songs — Ed. Spaeth, Summy-Bichard. (Note — Contains a number of old English songs at the beginning).

Minimum Memorization and Solo Singing Requirement — Six songs.

Vocal Literature Emphasis — Old Italian and Old English songs, art songs in English, or foreign language if the individual student is conversant with the language.

Practice Emphasis — Agility and flexibility, Lyric Bel-Canto style, extending compass and dynamic range, perfecting intonation, recitative style, and delivery.

Specific Objectives:

1. To improve the basic technics studied in Voice I and II.

2. To develop agility and flexibility of the voice and a knowledge of florid style and embellishment.

3. To develop an adequate vocal instrument in range and dynamics, smoothly connected, freely and correctly produced with the lyric Bel-Canto characteristics of the Old Italian and Old English songs.

---

*The correlated lesson by lesson content in Part I of this Textbook also is recommended for supplementary reading.

**Suggested for some classes and pupils wishing to become familiar with a more extensive repertoire or to select solos from a larger amount of song material of this type than found in Song Anthology Volume II.

4. To develop staccato technic.

5. To introduce and teach the principles of free and strict recitative in singing.

6. To understand the special problems unique to the male voice.

7. To gain a good workable concept of pronunciation in the Italian language.

8. To understand the Old Italian and Old English song style and obtain a basic repertoire of songs of this type sung with appropriate tone, satisfactory technic, and style.

VOICE IV

Prerequisite — Voice III.

Texts:

(a) For theory and technic content — *Expressive Singing* Volume I by Christy. Chapters 12, "Interpretation;" 3, "Stage Deportment;" 14, "Program Building;" 15, "Memorization."*

(b) For song content — *Expressive Singing* Song Anthology Volume II by Christy.

Suggested Supplementary Song Collections and Sources:**

(a) Salabert Collection of Beethoven Songs, or Augener Complete Edition of Beethoven Songs.

(b) Peters, or Kalmus Editions of Handel, Bach, Mozart, Haydn, and Lully Collections.

(c) Gems of Antiquity — Edited Nietzel, John Church Co.

(d) Individually-assigned sheet music songs by the Baroque and Classic Composers listed in (a) and (b) above.

Minimum Memorization and Solo Singing Requirement — Six songs.

Vocal Literature Emphasis — Songs of the Baroque, and Classic Periods, principally by Haydn, Mozart, Handel, Bach, Beethoven, and Lully. Songs to be sung in English unless the student is conversant with the original language. Extension of the Old Italian and Old English Song repertoire.

Practice Emphasis — Principles of song analysis and working out artistic interpretations, stage deportment, program building, and memorization.

Specific Objectives:

1. Progressive mastery of basic technics listed in previous semesters.

2. To understand the principles of interpretation and how to employ them in analysis and singing of songs.

3. To understand the factors involved in stage deportment and how to employ them skillfully in recital.

4. To understand the principles involved in program building.

5. To understand and employ efficiently the principles of memorization.

6. To understand and sing the Baroque and Classic Period songs and obtain a basic repertoire of songs of these types sung with good tone, satisfactory technic, and style.

VOICE V

Prerequisite — Voice IV.

Texts:

(a) For theory and technic content — *Expressive Singing* by Christy; both Volume I and this Textbook emphasizing more advanced vocal exercises and lessons covering interpretation, style, mood, tone color, sonority, etc., particularly in relation to German Lieder and the Romantic Song Style.

(b) For song content — *Expressive Singing* Song Anthology Volume II by Christy.

Suggested Supplementary Song Collections:*

(a) *German Art Songs* — Edited Taylor, Ditson.

(b) *100 Songs by Ten Masters*, Volume II, Ditson.

(c) Standard Schubert editions published by G. Schirmer, Oliver Ditson and others.

Minimum Memorization and Solo Singing Requirement— Eight songs.

(Note — Suggest that six of the eight required songs be from the German Lieder School and two elective songs be chosen by the student and instructor from any type or period of song literature preferred. They may be modern songs or ensemble numbers for solo voices; duet, trio, quartet, etc. Russian, Scandanavian, and Spanish songs may be explored. Number of songs sung in German will vary from eight for those conversant with the language to two to four for those with either no background or a weak one.)

Vocal Literature Emphasis — The German Lieder Art Song.

Practice Emphasis — Resonance, sonority, dramatic quality, warmth and variety of tonal color, phrasing and style characteristics of the German Lieder.

Specific Objectives:

1. Progressive mastery of basic technics studied in previous semesters.

2. To understand the Romantic German Lieder style and obtain a repertoire of songs of this type

---

*The correlated lesson by content in Part I of this Textbook also is recommended for supplementary reading.

**See previous footnote for Voice III.

sung with appropriate tone, satisfactory technic, phrasing, and style.

3. To obtain a good workable concept of pronunciation in the German language.*

4. To obtain the broadened dynamic range, warmth of tonal color, sonority, long phrasing technic, and dramatic quality of the German Lieder Art Song.

VOICE VI

Prerequisite — Voice IV.

Texts:

(a) For theory and technic content — *Expressive Singing* by Christy; both Volume I and this Textbook emphasizing more advanced vocal exercises and lessons covering interpretation, style, mood, tone color, etc., particularly in relation to the French Impressionistic Art Song.

(b) For song content — *Expressive Singing* Song Anthology Volume II by Christy.

*Suggested supplementary Song Collections:***

(a) *French Art Songs* — Edited Glenn and Taylor, Ditson.

(b) *Anthology of Modern French Songs* — Edited Spicker, G. Schirmer.

Minimum Memorization and Solo Singing Requirement — Eight songs.

(Note — Suggest that six of the eight required songs be from the French Impressionistic School and two elective songs be chosen by the student and instructor from any type or period of song literature preferred. They may be modern songs in English, Russian, Scandanavian, or Spanish song literature, or ensemble numbers for solo voices; duet, trio, quartet, etc. Number of songs sung in French will vary from eight for those conversant with the language to two or four for those with either no background or a weak one.)

Vocal Literature Emphasis — The French Impressionistic Art Song.

Practice Emphasis — Flexibility, mood projection, nasal resonance, and delicacy in phrasing characteristic of the French Impressionistic song literature.

Specific Objectives:

1. Progressive mastery of the technics listed in previous semesters.

2. To understand the Impressionistic French Song style and obtain a basic repertoire of songs of this type sung with appropriate tone, satisfactory technic, and style.

3. To obtain a good workable concept of pronunciation in the French language.***

4. To obtain the finesse in phrasing, nasal resonance, light dynamics, and flexible delicacy of tonal color characteristic of the French Impressionistic song style.

VOICE VII

Prerequisite — Voice IV.

Texts:

(a) For theory and technic — *Expressive Singing* by Christy; both Volume I and this Textbook emphasizing more advanced vocal exercises and lessons covering interpretation, stage deportment, style, recitative, mood, tone color, etc., particularly in relation to oratorio.

(b) For song content — *Expressive Singing* Song Anthology Volume II by Christy plus one or more of the following:

1'. *Oratorio Songs,* John Church publication.

2'. *Oratorio Repertoire* — Edited Douty, Theodore Presser.

3'. *Anthology of Sacred Songs* — Edited Spicker, G. Schirmer. (Note — Contents are all oratorio.)

Minimum Memorization and Solo Singing Requirement — Eight arias and songs. (Note — Requirements may include two ensemble numbers for solo voices from oratorio, duet, trio, quartet, etc.)

Vocal Literature Emphasis — The oratorio aria and recitative.

Practice Emphasis — The restrained, deeply emotional religious quality of oratorio style and the long, florid style phrase characteristic of many oratorio arias.

Specific Ojectives:

1. Progressive mastery of basic technics studied in previous semesters.

2. To gain an insight and practical experience in the restrained but deeply emotional religious quality of the oratorio.

3. To obtain a repertoire of arias, songs, and ensemble numbers from oratorio and the best sacred song literature, and experience in singing recitative.

VOICE VIII

Prerequisite — Voice V and VI, or Voice IV and adequate pronunciation knowledge of German, French and Italian.

---

*Students either should have studied German previously or be studying it in a German class at the time in order to facilitate vocal study during this semester.

**See previous footnote for Voice III.

***Students either should have studied French previously or be studying it in a French class at the time in order to facilitate vocal study during this semester.

Texts:

(a) For theory and technic — *Expressive Singing* by Christy; both Volume I and this Textbook emphasizing more advanced vocal exercises and lessons covering interpretation, stage deportment, recitative, style, mood, tone color, etc., particularly in relation to opera.

(b) For song content — *Expressive Singing* Song Anthology Volume II by Christy plus one or more of the following opera anthologies for individual voice, Soprano, Alto, Tenor, or Bass:

1'. *Songs from the Operas* (Musicians Library), Ditson.

2'. *Operatic Anthology* — Edited Spicker, G. Schirmer.

3'. *Opera Songs*, John Church publication.

4'. *The Modern Operatic Album*, G. Ricordi publication.

Minimum Memorization and Solo Singing Requirement — Eight arias in the original language, or four in the original language and six in English for those with language difficulties. (Note — Requirements may include two ensemble numbers for solo voices from opera, duet, trio, quartet, etc.)

Vocal Literature Emphasis — The opera aria and recitative.

Practice Emphasis — The dramatic theatrical quality, variety of mood, and intensity of emotional projection characteristic of operatic style.

Specific Objectives:

1. Progressive mastery of basic technics studied in previous semesters.

2. To gain an insight and practical experience in the dramatic and theatrical quality of operatic style.

3. To obtain a repertoire of arias, experience in recitative and ensemble numbers from opera sung with appropriate style, tone, and satisfactory technic.

24

The Voice Teacher

DUTIES

Major duties of the voice teacher are: to stimulate interest and pleasure in singing; to explain and illustrate information given in the text; guide discussion; present suitable illustrations or examples when needed; informally direct group singing; praise, criticize, and help the student in individual singing; guide mental, physical, musical, and career development of the students; and assign songs and exercises.

Songs are more interesting than exercises and, if well chosen to meet the individual needs of students at the time, can either partially or wholly take the place of formal exercises. "Songs for Specific Teaching Purposes" (See p. 217) are listed to assist the teacher in this respect. Every teacher is advised to also develop his own list, however, cataloguing and classifying songs as to difficulty and under specific use headings such as those on pp. 217-223. A growing list of songs with which the voice teacher is well acquainted is the most useful type.

Students are sometimes overly ambitious. They insist, and the teacher mistakenly complies with their desire, on appearing prematurely in recital or on singing a song too difficult, or beyond their understanding at the time. Results are usually unfortunate for both the students' progress and the teacher's reputation. Early public singing, before a reasonably free and easy production and an adequate range are acquired, had best be in the confines of a class situation or informal singing before a few understanding friends.

EDUCATIONAL PHILOSOPHY

"The teaching of singing is a very individual business. The teacher who treats all his pupils alike may have some successes but he will have many failures."[1] The well-equipped teacher is thoroughly acquainted with basic fundamentals and approaches in teaching which experience has demonstrated function well with nearly all students. He must not be an extremist, concentrating on only one idea or method of approach. Vocal development has too many coordinative facets to allow concentration on one factor or approach with the assumption that it is so basic that, sooner or later, all other factors will fall in line. We must recognize also that there is occasionally the exceptional pupil who, for psychological or physiological reasons, needs an approach different from the average or normal.

Certain basic principles of vocal training remain constant but methods must vary to meet varying needs and conditions. Approaches may be empirical through emphasis on emotional stimulation, imitative through emphasis on example and tonal imitation, or intellectual through analysis of various factors involved. As a rule, the expert teacher mixes and uses all the approaches judiciously when dealing with either the individual or the class.

TEACHER-PUPIL RELATIONSHIP

"The ideal teaching contact requires mutuality of participation between teacher and pupil."[2] The teacher should not consider the lesson merely as a setting for something to be learned by the pupil, but rather as *the creation of a situation in which both pupil and teacher can share in a worthwhile, significant enterprise.* The vocal teacher should be first a sympathetic, understanding person genuinely interested in the pupil's welfare, and second a sound, imaginative choral musician. One of our most respected early music educators in the United States, Thomas Tapper, stated in one of his addresses, "Teaching of any kind is an art, a science and a sacred trust. Keep it ever in mind that you are honor bound to be, above all else, a friend to your pupils. Sympathize; never be arrogant; never ridicule. Be worthy and trustworthy."

[1]Graves, Richard M. "Singing for Amateurs," Oxford U. Press, 1954, p. 34.
[2]Mursell, James L. "Human Values in Music Education." Silber Burdett & Co., 1934, p. 278.

It is most important for the teacher of voice to be honest and fair with students, not only regarding their possibilities and limitations but also in regard to the teacher's own limitations. For example, do not pose as an authority in pronouncing a foreign language you do not know well, or as an expert in the interpretation of certain styles or schools of vocal composition in which you have had very little or no training and background. *Students will have far more respect for their teacher in the end if he has been honest with them in the beginning.* If the teacher doesn't know the answer to a question, he should admit it, or say that he will look up the answer. It is even better to refer the pupil to a source or sources where he can find the answer readily and report back to the class or teacher. Questions irrelevant at the time may well be postponed, with the promise that they will be taken up in the particular lesson covering that point at a forthcoming period.

A friendly, natural relationship should exist between the teacher and members of the class. The better the instructor can get to know each pupil as a person, the more effectively each can be taught. A student never should be considered as an inanimate vocal instrument in the class mass, but rather as an individual with viewpoints, musical preferences, and the ability to suggest ideas worthy of careful consideration by the instructor. "The forcing of interpretive formulae upon a student may distort his natural inclinations and make it unlikely he will ever think for himself."[3] Once beginning students have been taught the principles of how to make intelligent decisions about expression, they should make them for themselves. The student also should assume a growing responsibility for class conduct and always be ready to help the instructor and fellow classmates. This friendly, cooperative, understanding relationship in the class is one of the most valuable educative factors. *It can be fostered only if the instructor first sets the pattern, however.*

Vocal teachers must be particularly careful of their speech, their posture, their manners and their dress if they expect their students to be careful. If the teacher slumps the pupils can be expected to do likewise, etc. In fact, the vocal instructor usually has more influence on pupils under his care than any other classroom teacher. This is to be expected in view of the intimate nature of the subject.

"The teacher who scolds and nags constantly, going only so far as to announce mistakes without suggesting a helpful corrective, probably does not know what he is talking about. . . . A teacher who flatters constantly may or may not know what he is doing, but such a one is dishonest."[4] The good psychologist praises first, when praise is due, and criticises second. However, criticism is always positive and helpful, never destructive and discouraging.

Teaching methods should accent the positive. We should never imply to a student that an assigned song or problems encountered are extremely difficult and perhaps cannot be mastered. Once the student senses this negative attitude, confidence is lost and enthusiasm wanes, while mental hazards and physical tensions make progress a practical impossibility.

Robert Shaw frequently emphasizes an important truth in his rehearsals with amateur choral groups, "You don't need to be a great singer to do great singing." This basic truth is apparently either disbelieved or misunderstood by many vocal teachers who cater only to pupils possessing "God-given" voices, neglecting the great number of less gifted. They are interested only in the highly talented, and have neither patience nor success with others. They apparently believe that only highly-talented pupils can comprehend musical content and perform with intelligent expressiveness. In many instances this attitude is merely a confession of ineptitude in teaching. Even a poor teacher sometimes can succeed with highly talented pupils; but it takes vastly more understanding and skill to instruct the inept, and even the average student, to sing well. This is the acid test and the sure sign of the competent teacher.

QUALIFICATIONS

"It is the quality of the teacher that counts far more than everything else put together. There may be a large and perfectly equipped music room; . . . a cooperating high school principal; full credit for the work, and a large class of pupils; but if there is not a thoroughly trained — and highly inspired — teacher these things will avail nothing."[5] It is generally agreed that the reason class voice training has not become a common offering in every high school where the physical facilities and budget could be arranged is that there are not enough well-qualified teachers available.

The American Academy of Teachers of Singing listed the broad general qualifications for vocal teachers in a pronouncement issued in 1924 as follows:

1. "A good general education, including a thorough knowledge of the correct pronunciation and use of the English language.
2. An ear, accurate in judging pitch and quality of tone.
3. At least five years of study with competent teachers.

---

[3]Litante, Judith. "A Natural Approach to Singing." Wm. C. Brown Co., 1959, p. 90.

[4]Brown, Ralph Morse. "The Singing Voice." Macmillan Co., 1940, p. 160.

[5]Dykema, Peter W. and Gehrkens Karl W. "The Teaching and Administration of High School Music." C. C. Birchard, 1941, p. 97.

4. Musicianship, including knowledge of the history of music, elementary harmony, form, analysis, style, and the ability to play the piano.

5. Ability to demonstrate vocally the principles of singing.

6. Ability to impart knowledge."

In commenting on the qualifications, Alfred Spouse states, "Finally, supplementing the above requirements, *teachers expecting to teach classes in this subject should have special training in class presentation.* It is different in many ways from the private lesson. Its technic is different. There is a difference between watching one pupil at a time, and watching twenty. There is a difference between listening to twenty voices at a time and detecting faults everywhere in the room, and detecting faults in one voice. For the entire class must sing their exercises at the same time. It would be denying the practibility of the class idea to listen to the voices one at a time, so this must be done very sparingly. Often the ensemble tone is so good to hear that the teacher may not be aware that the individual contribution to this tone may be wrongly produced here and there in the room. The ear of the teacher must be quick to detect these wrong tones."[6]

How can the prospective vocal teacher know what is involved in some of the six broad generalizations listed? "Ability to impart knowledge" requires a number of factors, most of which are common to all teaching success:

1. Pleasing speaking voice, personality, and leadership ability.

2. Health and vitality.

3. Enthusiasm, naturalness, and kindly understanding.

4. Patience, persistence, and high standards.

5. Intelligence, imagination, and versatility.

6. Liking for people and desire to understand and help them.

7. Ability as a sensitive and intelligent diagnostician regarding both visible and audible faults in singing.

8. Knowledge of the psychology and methods for class voice teaching.

The voice teacher should be a person of culture, sensitive to the values of the other arts, have a good speaking and singing voice, and be an able reader of poetry. A good vocal model is one of the best teaching devices, since students must have the proper tonal imagery to guide their efforts. It should be supplementary, however, and never the exclusive method, as many misguided vocal instructors seem to believe. Teachers who are also skilled singers have an immense advantage over those who are not. In the latter case, it is especially vital for pupils to have ready access to suitable recordings and the opportunity to hear much fine singing in concert. Even this is unlikely to compensate fully for the advantage of a skilled teacher's voice in illustration of specific examples and problems.

It is apparent that the voice teacher should be a singer well trained in the art and various styles of singing, and a musician capable of commanding respect in the community and among other musicians. He should be able to demonstrate any phase of technic and give examples of the principles of interpretation in all styles and for the various schools of vocal literature. He should have acute sensitivity for pitch deviation, for rhythmic accuracy, for presence of even small degrees of tension in production, and have a refined taste and imagination in interpretation. Although it is a valuable asset, the vocal teacher does not have to be a pianist if a capable accompanist is available. He should know enough about piano to play accompaniments adequately if necessary, and to coach student accompanists in style, finesse, and balance necessary for effective accompaniments.

Vocal instructors must know not only the *how* of singing but the *why* as well, in order to answer the many questions that students ask and to give intelligent reasons for methods and procedures followed. It also should be self evident that the teacher should read most carefully and be thoroughly conversant with the theory, exercises, and song content of the vocal method chosen for the class, and be ready to explain or illustrate whenever necessary or desirable.

Success in class voice teaching depends not only on clear ideas about basic principles of singing but also on a practical educational philosophy and a well-defined plan appropriate to class and not private voice technic. Conductors of choral groups who obtain good but not really fine tone in mass ensemble are, in the main, seldom equipped adequately in the production and teaching of solo singing. They lack enough study of solo singing and, until this is corrected, cannot be expected to make first class teachers in a voice culture class where skilled solo singing is a vital objective.

On the other hand, skilled private voice teachers are usually unsuited to voice class work because they lack the necessary general educational background, and the proper knowledge of group methods, to apply their vocal knowledge effectively in a group situation. Their class periods too often degenerate into a series of short private lessons, while the remainder of the class "twiddle their thumbs."

The vocal teacher also should have an adequate knowledge of anatomy and physiology of vocal function in order to explain why a certain posture or type

---

[6]Spouse, Alfred. "Voice Classes in Senior High Schools." Music Supervisors Journal, Feb. 1930, p. 69.

of physical response is best, why certain feeling sensations should be experienced, and why certain physical responses, with their associative feeling sensations, should be habituated.

Careful planning of class lessons is necessary. Only the most experienced and inspirational teachers can expect to obtain satisfactory results in a class period without preliminary planning; even their work is benefited in proportion to the care given its organization, planning, and preparation.

With a combination of the foregoing traits, or a goodly modicum of them, success in group voice culture teaching is assured. The teacher will not only arouse enthusiasm in his or her pupils but will also be able to work amicably with other instructors, with the school administration, and with other musicians in the community.

FAULTS OBSERVED IN CLASS VOICE TEACHING

The 12 most common faults observed in teaching methods are:

1. Consistent application of individual lesson studio technic.

2. Consistent application of chorus technic with too much class singing as a group and neglect of urgent individual problems.

3. Too much pedantic lecturing about theory or reminiscing, and not enough singing by the class and by individuals.

4. Too much singing by the instructor for or with the class.

5. Too much formal time beating and conducting, as if the voice class were a chorus.

6. Too much use of the piano and not enough unaccompanied singing.

7. Piano accompaniment consistently too loud.

8. Sarcastic, critical manner, and lack of sufficient praise and encouragement.

9. Lack of enthusiasm, honesty, naturalness, and friendliness in teaching technics.

10. Superficial coverage of lesson content with little or no class understanding, practical application, and gain.

11. Interminable concentration on one exercise, one lesson, one song, attempting to attain perfection before going on to another activity or song.

12. Failure to develop initiative, courage, and responsibility on the part of students by insistence on own ideas in every detail. This dogmatic attitude and the "pressure" method of teaching too often result in the student's passing the test and flunking the future as an imaginative, intelligent singer.

DIAGNOSING VOCAL FAULTS

The competent vocal teacher must become an alert and accurate diagnostician of vocal faults.

Without proper diagnosis, he can no more expect to cure vocal ills than a physician can expect to cure physical ills. Like the physician, the vocal teacher needs a clinic in order to learn the technic by observing its application by an experienced practitioner. The voice class experience, when taught properly by an competent teacher, plus a methods course in class voice teaching and vocal problems, give the prospective teacher an ideal clinical background for diagnosis and cure of vocal ills. Two general types of vocal faults must be diagnosed — the visual and the audible. Unfortunately, many vocal teachers neither see many visible faults nor recognize strained production when they hear it. This is true particularly of teachers who cannot sing freely themselves and of instrumentalists in small high schools, who are frequently assigned to conduct choral groups or even teach a class in beginning voice culture.

The Music Educators National Conference Vocal Committee Report for 1945 lists all physiological faults as related to one or more of the three major physical phases of singing:

1. "Management of breathing.
2. Management of the resonating system.
3. Management of the articulating system."[7]

Vocal instructors should understand the detailed factors involved in these three physical phases of singing. *If they know what to look and listen for they have made the first step toward diagnosis of fault and its correction.* The following lists of "Visible Faults" and "Audible Faults," with brief suggestions as to major causes in the latter, cover the principal factors concerned but are by no means inclusive of all problems.

VISIBLE FAULTS OF STUDENTS

1. Mouth open too much horizontally — "grinning smile" position.

2. Small trumpet lip opening; insufficient opening longitudinally.

3. Cords standing out on the neck.

4. Throat enlarging, veins swelling, and face reddening.

5. Trembling throat or chin.

6. Wrinkled forehead and strained expression.

7. Excessively arched eyebrows and staring eyes.

8. Flared or wrinkled nose.

9. Tongue curled up at tip.

10. Tongue tip pulled back and bunched tensely.

11. Tongue tip curled down under base of lower teeth.

12. Rigidly high larynx.

[7]Novahec, Hazel B. (editor) "Music Education Source Book." Music Educators Natl. Conference, 1945, p. 110.

13. Protruding jaw, locked rigidly forward.

14. Needless disturbance of jaw opening in forming a series of vowels and in articulating consonants.

15. Non-active lips and tongue in articulation.

16. "Setting" the lips in a fancied position and then attacking tone.

17. Head thrust forward.

18. Head held too high habitually.

19. Raising head for high tones.

20. Spinal slump; spine relaxed and not flexibly stretched.

21. Chest not raised before the attack.

22. Chest habitually too low before the attack.

23. Chest too rigidly high before the attack.

24. Chest pumping on inhalation and collapsing on phonation; clavicular breathing.

25. Pushed down and protruding abdomen.

26. Weight not balanced forward.

27. Standing with weight mostly on one foot.

28. Sitting with legs crossed.

29. Sitting with back against chair.

30. Hands gripped tensely or held awkwardly.

31. Hands held behind back or in pockets.

32. Shouders hunched up or uneven.

33. Eyes shifting nervously.

34. Eyes not over the heads of the audience for a serious art song.

35. Eyes over the heads of the audience for a humorous encore.

AUDIBLE FAULTS OF STUDENTS

Note — Any of the following faults might be due to improper thought concept.

1. *Tonal Quality Faults*:

(a) Throaty and gutteral — resonance too deep in throat.

(b) Mouthy, pinched, thin, metallic, shrill, or "yelly" — To much constriction and mouth resonance.

(c) Hollow or "hooty" — Forcibly spread pharynx.

(d) Breathy, spread, and out of "focus" — Resonance form too spacious, leaky vocal cords, too much breath pressure.

(e) "Nosey" (Often incorrectly called over-nasal) — Blocking head and nasal opening with the soft palate and directing resonance forward.

(f) Over-nasal — Too much nose and mask resonance for balanced tone.

(g) Tremolo, shake, or excessive vibrato — Forcing, constriction of throat muscles, too much breath pressure, excitement.

(h) Straight-line tone with no vibrato — Lack of complete tonal freedom in the throat.

(i) Overly sombre or muffled — To large a resonance form, upper lip down too far, not enough mouth resonance for balanced tone.

(j) Improper intonation — Incorrect concept of of interval, lack of free production technic and adequate breath support.

2. *Breath Support Faults*:

(a) Inadequate breath to finish phrase properly — Inefficient, breathy, tonal production; failure to inhale enough breath; endurance.

(b) Nervous, wavering, or jerky breath control, perhaps causing the tone to "break" — Fear, nervousness, constriction, clavicular breathing.

(c) Lack of sostenuto on long tones — Concept of legato-sostenuto style, reduction of breath energy after tone is attacked.

(d) Lack of precision on staccato or accented tones — Logy muscular response, failure to think the effect clearly.

(e) Grunt or gasp on release of tone — Habit, over-emotionalism.

3. *Diction Faults*:

(a) Impure vowel color — Pure concept not established.

(b) Lingering on the vanishing part of compound vowels and dipthongs — Failure to habituate proper timing in enunciation.

(c) Bright vowels too thin and shrill and dark vowels too spacious and breathy — Common resonation space not habituated.

(d) Radical change in resonating space and vowel color in a series of vowels destroying legato — Common resonation space not habituated.

(e) Tonal color on vowels habitually too white or too dark — Concept of normal tonal color in error, habitually too little or too much tonal resonation space.

(f) Radical change of vowel quality at certain parts of the scale — Accumulations of tension, failure to apply the principles of gradual adjustment.

(g) Improper pronunciation — Provincialism, habit.

(h) Slovenly or inaudible articulation — Habit, carelessness, failure to recognize need for crisp articulation.

(i) Omission of some consonants — Habit, carelessness.

(j) Substitution of one vowel or consonant sound for another — Habit, carelessness.

(k) Prolonged or exaggerated consonants — Habit, carelessness.

(1) Anticipation of consonants destroying legato — Improper concept of delayed articulation for legato.

(m) Insertion of extraneous sounds such as aspirate "H" before attacks and "Ah" after and between words — Habit, carelessness.

PROFESSIONAL ETHICS IN TEACHING SINGING

In an early pronouncement of the American Academy of Teachers of Singing, "Code of Ethics and Practice," the following points regarding teacher-pupil relationship are particularly applicable:

1. "Any specific promise by the teacher that leads the student to false hopes of a career is a breach of ethics and integrity.

2. In publicity of any kind a minimum of one year of continuous instruction shall warrant the teacher claiming the student as a pupil. But fairness must be practiced in the proper recognition of helpful services rendered by former teachers, and derogatory statements avoided. Furthermore, dignity and a scrupulous adherence to facts in advertising shall always be observed.

3. Teachers should treat their pupils with consideration and patience, inculating in them respect for their art.

4. In voice trials the duty of the teacher is to diagnose the case impartially. Therefore, it is suggested at the outset the student be requested not to disclose the name of any former teacher. In all instances an honest opinion should be given the student.

5. Punctuality is incumbent upon teacher and pupil. Pupils should be held responsible for the time originally reserved, except in rare emergency."

The remaining part of this chapter is quoted directly from a pronouncement, "Ethics in the Field of the Teaching of Singing," adopted by the American Academy of Teachers of Singing, and is used by permission.

A. *"Professional Relations Between Vocal Teacher and Student.*

1. A teacher should not only be an instructor but, as far as possible should also act as a mentor, advisor and friend of the student. It is important to both teacher and student in order to obtain the most satisfying results, that throughout their relationship there should prevail a spirit of mutual respect and confidence.

2. It is unfair, and therefore unethical for a teacher to assume a domineering and possessive attitude toward a student.

3. It is unethical for a student to study with two vocal teachers at the same time. It is obvious that with a two-way approach, confusion and uncertainty in the mind and work of the student must result, and that no properly integrated objective can possibly be achieved. The pupil should not allow himself to commit so grave an error, and no self-respecting teacher should become involved in such an unethical procedure.

4. A student should at all times feel free to bring to the teacher all problems, either professional or personal, pertaining to the former's studies and career. In turn the teacher should give to the student the benefit of his best judgment, advice and experience. It is unethical for a teacher to advise a student on professional matters in a manner detrimental to the best interests of the latter.

5. It is unethical for the teacher to deduct any portion of the regular lesson fee of a student who may be responsible for the introduction of new pupils to the studio, since such a reduction would constitute the equivalent of a commission paid for services rendered. Further, it is unethical for the teacher to extend financial credit to the student who may bring new students to the former.

6. It is unethical for the vocal teacher to engage in any form of proselyting, or to make an attempt of any nature to attract to himself in any way, the students of a colleague. Unfortunately, proselyting can be, and is employed in numerous, varied and subtle forms. In all social and professional contacts the teacher should be constantly on the alert, in order to avoid any gesture or action that approaches a breach of professional ethics.

7. In the event of a student's decision to change from one teacher to another, accepted ethical procedure should be strictly observed by all parties concerned, especially those relating to personal and professional courtesy and financial obligations on the part of the student towards the former teacher.

B. *Professional Relations Between the Teacher of Singing and Collaborating Associates.*

1. It is unethical for vocal coaches, accompanists, language and diction teachers and other assisting associates to offer advice or attempt to instruct the student in matters pertaining to voice problems. All such matters should be referred directly and specifically to the vocal teacher for proper and final solution.

2. It is unethical for language and diction teachers to advise the student on matters of style and interpretation. These phases of training should be directed by either the vocal teacher or the designated coach.

3. All financial arrangements between the student and assisting teachers should be understood thoroughly and arranged for prior to the first lesson, thus fixing the responsibility for payment, and avoiding the possibility of future misunderstanding and complications.

4. Mutual respect for work being performed by an associated colleague is incumbent on the part of all teachers concerned.

5. It is unethical on the part of one teacher to criticize either by suggestion, innuendo, or in any

other fashion, the work of any other associated teacher.

C. *Professional Relations Between Teacher, Student, and Manager and/or Agent.*

1. Where teachers have singers under contract with managers and/or agents, all should work together in close cooperation in solving the varied and complex problems involved in the promotion of a professional singing career.

2. Managers and/or agents, who represent the direct contact between artist and public, if and when they have criticism to offer regarding the singer's work, should discuss such criticism directly with the vocal teacher. This courtesy and consideration on the part of the manager and/or agent is due the teacher at all times. As a result of this joint cooperative effort, the vocal teacher should then be allowed a reasonable time in which to overcome the causes of the manager's criticism. If at the end of a given period the vocal or artistic problem remains unsolved, then, and only then shall the manager assume the initiative of recommending a change of teacher.

3. It is unethical for vocal teachers to advise their students in matters relative to their managers, to accept any fee or commission for engagements obtained by the singer. Any contract or agreement of a financial nature, written or otherwise, made between vocal teacher and student shall be based upon remuneration for lessons given, and shall in no way involve any form of reimbursement to the teacher out of the professional singing engagement contracts.

D. *Professional Relations Between the Vocal Teacher and the Public.*

1. There is a definite obligation on the part of the vocal teacher to instruct and guide the student in the latter's professional, personal and business relationship with the public.

2. The vocal teacher should be honest and frank in all contacts with those connected with the careers of his students, such as sponsors and prospective employers. These include, among others, an honest opinion of the student's ability and his fitness for a particular engagement, and a careful estimate of the scope of and expenditure for publicity and other details of public performance.

3. Although a vocal teacher does not function in the capacity of manager for his students, the obligation rests with him to do everything in his power to bring in legitimate fashion to the attention of managers, agents and the general public, the potentialities and artistic assets of any student recommended by the teacher as being ready for public appearance. At the same time it is detrimental to both singer and teacher for the latter to promote or exploit any student obviously not yet ready and equipped for public appearance.

4. Should a vocal teacher desire to advertise himself as a teacher of a singer who in turn may have, from time to time, studied in various studios, he should make a specific statement covering the exact period during which the singer in question received from the teacher his or her vocal training. For example — "John Doe studied with Richard Doe from March 1940 to May 1943 inclusive."

25

The Accompanist

IMPORTANCE

Among the most vital factors in the success of the voice class or of the individual pupil are the skill, musicianship and dependability of the accompanist. A fine, sensitive accompanist is indeed a jewel without price. A poor accompanist can torpedo the technic of even the experienced singer. Unfortunately, skilled piano soloists do not always qualify as acceptable accompanists. They are often inadequate as sight readers or prima-donnas who cannot bear to have the piano part subservient to the vocal line. "It is imperative that both accompanist and singer practice together to acquire a 'oneness' of phrasing and breathing. . . . The accompanist must learn how to phrase and breathe with the singer. Both must feel the rhythmical surge of musical phrasing known as melodic line. Both must be sensitive to the 'give and take' of rhythm, ritards and other changes of tempo that affect breathing."[1]

PROVIDING A SUITABLE ACCOMPANIST

The problems of a suitable accompanist often affects both the private voice and the class voice teacher. There is no doubt that an experienced and dependable professional accompanist, able to sight read well and transpose readily, will greatly speed up vocal progress. Unfortunately, in voice class work in schools, sufficient funds are seldom available to hire a professional accompanist and the work has to be done by either the vocal instructor or by students. Student accompanists as a rule are quite fumbling and insecure until they have been coached and trained at the expense of class time and interest. If the teacher is to be relieved of this responsibility as he should be, however, the best accompanists available will be trained and used.

Unfortunately, students rarely receive the type of instruction they need from piano instructors who are more interested in making concert soloists than skilled accompanists out of their pupils. The vocal

teacher in schools often has to assume this responsibility. The vocal teacher is obliged to realize also that it is important for music education to train accompanists as well as singers through the only way that they can be trained — experience in doing under expert guidance.

Cooperation between the voice teacher and piano teachers in both the school and community will work to mutual advantage when organized properly. The voice class, and accompanying individuals in the voice class in their practice and recital work, offers the most practical type of outlet for pupils of piano instructors if only they can be "sold" on the idea that it is more important and practical for piano students to become skilled sight readers and accompanists first, and piano soloists second. The facts are that piano soloists are a "dime a dozen" in many communities, while a good accompanist is always in demand.

The ideal set-up is an arrangement whereby the most advanced piano students available are assigned regularly to accompany voice class and individual students in the voice class. The most skilled accompanist available is assigned to assist in class voice periods, while a number of the other less-advanced pianists play for vocal students in their individual practice periods.

An adequate accompanist will be able to play fairly easy song accompaniments in a musical manner by sight, with correct tempo, rhythm, dynamics, and phrasing. This is seldom possible with the average student who needs adequate practice and help before attempting accompaniments in class, however. The usual practice, therefore is to select the songs before hand and give the scores to the student accompanist in order that he can be coached on the material during his regular piano lessons.

---

[1]Peterson, Paul W. "Natural Singing and Expressive Conducting." John F. Blair, 1955, p. 19.

Hints on tempo, phrasing, and dynamics desired should be marked in the score in order that the piano instructor can teach more efficiently. Some students will need assistance only on the more difficult accompaniments. Before a student accompanist appears on a recital, the vocal instructor and the piano teacher should be satisfied that accompaniments are being played acceptably.

When the piano instructor is thoroughly convinced of the importance of sight reading skill and the competent playing of accompanists as a required fundamental for his pupils, practice of the accompaniments used in the voice class is required as basic training for all pupils. Suggestions and illustrations are made by the piano teacher on how to play accompaniments accurately and artistically. Some piano instructors in the colleges and conservatories set up a special course in piano accompaniment playing: it is required of all their pupils at a specified time. Both the vocal and the instrumental instructors collaborate with the piano teacher in suggesting repertoire and content of this course in order that it be most practical. Competent students who have completed the course then are assigned to assist in the vocal and instrumental classwork and individual student practice, receiving credit and a grade for their work as part of the piano requirement. This cooperative plan works most admirably to the benefit of all concerned when well administered and taught.

In college or conservatory vocal classes for music majors, a sufficient number of accompanists normally are available from among the personnel of the vocal class. However, it is regrettable and unfair to the student enrolling for a vocal course to be occupied nearly all the time in playing accompaniments. Two or more students can alternate the work to advantage, the most skilled accompanist doing only the most difficult numbers while others are assigned to the easier grade.

Some schools find the best solution to providing suitable accompanists for both their vocal and instrumental classes in a student assistant financing program. The most capable accompanists are paid a fee of so much per hour for services rendered. This fee is often a godsend to deserving students who otherwise could not finance their way through school.

THE TEACHER AS ACCOMPANIST

There are some school situations and times in others when the available accompanists are so poor and inexperienced that the vocal teacher either must hire an accompanist or assume part or all of the responsibility himself. In any case, many teachers prefer, especially during the warm-up period, to sit at the piano in order to speed up the work. The vocal instructor also will play for students in recitals if the student accompanists are too poor or unreliable.

Use of student accompanists is desirable for educational reasons, however. They should be used in the school systems if they can meet reasonably high standards with help from their piano instructor and the voice teacher.

A few vocal teachers, who are also skilled pianists, learn the accompaniments of songs used in class so well that they are almost automatic and can be played by ear in several different keys. If accompaniments are played lightly and are well learned in such a fashion, hearing of vocal tone is not destroyed or impeded too seriously, and the teacher is able to rise above the handicap of divided attention. Nevertheless, to do a fine job of both accompanying and teaching voice is most difficult; it is not to be recommended when an adequate accompanist is available or can be developed in a reasonable time. In any case, an assistant accompanist or accompanists are especially desirable for a large class or for the several classes that the voice teacher often instructs.

USE OF ACCOMPANIMENT IN VOICE CLASS

The piano, or an organ when available, is placed close to the class in such a position that the accompanist can see both the teacher and the class easily. The piano never will be stuck in some out-of-the-way corner as often seen. It ought to be an important and integral part of the tonal ensemble — balanced, blended, and phrased in such a manner that it is a highly valuable supporting expressional factor. *It cannot have the necessary unity with either the class or individual students when wide distances separate the musical forces.*

The piano is a highly valuable adjunct to vocal study but it also can be a danger and discouragement when accompaniments are badly bungled or pounded-out. It had best be dispensed with, and all singing done entirely unaccompanied, if the piano part is "butchered" in rhythm and accuracy or banged-out so loud that it kills all pleasure in singing or covers the vocal line entirely. The best advice is to *do without the accompaniment unless it stimulates the class or the soloist to sing more easily, expressively, and correctly.*

Efficient accompaniment for singing is natural, unaffected, and never theatrical, showy, "poundy," or so loud that the singer's voice is drowned out in a flood of crashing piano chords. If balance between singer and the accompanist has to be less than ideal, *it is better to underplay than overplay.* The spirit of accompaniment playing, and accepted standards in practice, is opposed to "showing off" or indulging in certain acceptable concert artist solo mannerisms, even when playing introductions, interludes, and postludes. It is true that these furnish opportunity for solo pianistic expression, but good taste and relative balance must take precedence. On the whole, accompaniment is to be considered as background and support for the solo voice, and should not be played with the pianistic abandon and concert mannerisms of a solo performance.

The relation of piano accompaniment to compositional structure needs to be considered also in determining proper dynamics to balance the voice. Since piano is a poor instrument in sustaining tone, a sparse harmonic-style accompaniment with long sustained notes over a number of beats usually requires both louder dynamics from the piano and a faster tempo in interpretation than indicated. Reduced orchestral scores, or organ-like parts with long notes tied over for a number of measures, may even sound best if the chord is struck again on an accented beat in order to maintain some audible tonal support for the voice.

Accompaniment can easily overweigh the voice if it is harmonically "thick" and changing on each beat. If the accompaniment is polyphonic, the separate tonal lines should be clearly delineated so that they "sing" distinct melodies with the voice. A counter melody in the accompaniment should at times balance the voice as a duet and, when the voice is sustaining a long note or has very little melodic movement and interest, may even predominate to artistic advantage. In general, the piano may be played firmly and sonorously but not pounded when the singer is on high notes with *mf* or louder intensity, but should be played much more lightly for most singers in the low compass, regardless of dynamic markings. Range of pianistic dynamics used depends, of course, on the relative power and penetrating quality of the voice being accompanied.

The accompanist will be especially alert to reducing dynamics when the singer is in the low register. It is easy to overplay most singers here or cause them to force tone. In fact, forcing the voice in any register is often caused by overplaying, or percussive playing by the accompanist. *Introductions, interludes, and postludes are never played so powerfully and dramatically that the climatic effect of the voice is destroyed.* Unless they are scaled down for a light, lyric voice, the expressional effect is grotesquely out of balance.

In any case, a great deal of class and individual singing on exercises and the details of practice in vocal phrasing should be worked out *a capella*. Only then can the teacher and pupils hear what they are doing most analytically. Continual "leaning" on the piano for concepts of pitch, rhythm, and expression will never develop the independence and musicianship necessary for artistic singing. Although it may lightly furnish the chordal background at times, *piano should be used very little if at all in playing melodic line in vocal exercises.* Insult is added to

injury if the melodic part is banged-out loudly, or the sustaining pedal flirted with through a scale passage. Style and dynamics of an accompaniment should be not only suitable to the style and dynamics of the exercise (when it is used at all) but also always subdued under the voice. Accompanists who cannot easily fill in a simple and straightforward harmonization of a vocal exercise by sight either should allow it to be done unaccompanied or jot down a suitable chord progression and practice it beforehand until proficient in playing.

Other instruments than the piano are often suitable or even preferable for accompaniment. The organ and its advantages has already been discussed. (See p. 186) Other instruments such as guitar, accordian, and solo banjo are superior to piano in certain types of informal folk songs and ballads when played well. A string quartet, string ensemble, or woodwind ensemble provides a beautiful accompaniment for either solo or ensemble singing on many compositions. A considerable number of songs with special instrumental obbligato are published and add color and variety of interest to recital programs. We have provided a generous listing of these in Part III of this text.

Special obbligatos and instrumental arrangements often can be made by students studying composition, arrangement, or orchestration, and the vocal and instrumental forces can be combined for school recitals. When such obbligatos or accompaniments are well arranged and played, they should be featured in publicity and the printed programs for recitals. The foregoing policy provides coordination and correlation among the vocal, instrumental, and theory departments in a school system, with consequent gain to all.

BALANCE BETWEEN VOICE AND PIANO

This topic has had considerable incidental discussion previously. The piano is a percussive instrument which does not blend and balance well with voice, as do most sustained tone instruments. This is true especially if the piano is played percussively and not lyrically, or if it is a poor instrument with a bright, metallic tone or poor sustaining quality. Touch in accompaniment playing normally should be light, legato, sustained, and as lyric as possible in order to blend best with the voice. There are exceptions to this rule, of course, in accompaniments marked staccato or accented. Accent should seldom, if ever, be an excuse for pounding, however. Staccato and accent marks should be done, as a rule, with a lighter touch than employed in piano solo work. Fingers may be kept near the keys to prevent playing too loud. If there is still too much piano tone, the soft pedal will be used also.

Extemporization in poor taste is another mistake made by many accompanists who play readily by ear. Extemporization, when well done, might be superior at times to many of the hackneyed four-part harmonizations or "stock" accompaniments printed for folk songs, ballads, and popular songs. *It is never in good taste to extemporize the accompaniment of an art song by a recognized master composer, however.* These ought to be played as nearly as possible as they are written.

ACCOMPANIST-SINGER RELATIONSHIP

A song normally does not consist of a melody for voice alone; rather it is an ensemble, a duet involving both vocal and instrumental tone. Each needs to be learned and given carefully balanced consideration in artistic interpretations. Perfect or near-perfect ensemble will be maintained between singer and accompaniment. This does not imply that the balance of tone should be even or equal between the two forces for perfection. (The voice is normally louder and the accompaniment subservient, although in some few instances the opposite may be true.) It does mean that the accompanist should be neither ahead or behind the singer, that each will complement the other, and be thoroughly aware of the character and demands of each other's parts.

The skilled accompanist figuratively, if not actually, breathes with the singer, hears every part of the singer's melody before it is sung, and is highly sensitive and responsive to making adjustments of tempo, dynamics, and phrasing to assist the singer when slight indications of approaching difficulty occur. The experienced and sensitive accompanist actually is a better coach on interpretation than many voice teachers. He or she needs to be more than a pianist with adequate technic; in addition, it is necessary to be a musician and have also a highly attuned sensitivity to the mood and characteristic technical weaknesses and strengths of the particular singer. *A fine accompanist often has made a surprisingly successful singer out of a voice that was no better than ordinary.*

The artist accompanist knows where, when, and how to subdue the piano or make it prominent in order to achieve the maximum interpretive effect. He knows how to adjust the accompaniment to help the insecure singer to hold or restore pitch when intonation is "shaky." He establishes the correct mood, sets the proper tempo and dynamics on the introduction, and inspires the singer to do his best before a note is sung. He continues to inspire the singer, give him confidence, and stimulate him to achieve his best interpretation throughout the song.

On the other hand, the singer's obligation is to understand that it is not artistically wise always to "take" and not "give" in relationship with the accompanist. It is not a one-way street. Each learns to take his cue from the other; neither can be dogmatic or have to drag the other along. The singer needs to be thoroughly aware of the melodic, harmonic, and rhythmic character and qualities of the piano part, the technical limitations of the particular accompanist and of the piano being used. He will "cut the shoe to fit the last" in designing interpretation. The vocal soloist should:

1. Come in at exactly the right time after introductions or interludes.

2. In public performance, accept the tempo and dynamics suggested by the introduction if artistically feasible. (If it is not right the matter should have been settled in previous rehearsals.)

3. Allow the piano part to be predominant when the vocal line is static and comparatively unimportant and the accompaniment is active.

4. Consider carefully suggestions on tempo, phrasing, dynamics, and interpretation in general made by an experienced accompanist. (The accompanist should be famSvith the desires of the vocal instructor and not make suggestions contrary to his wishes, however.)

5. Work as one with the accompanist for the finest possible ensemble effect.

In the give-and-take between an accompanist and the singer, a motive or theme may start with one and be continued by the other. In this case, dynamics, tempo, and continuity in style will be consistent and the part entering last ought to be temporarily predominant. However, a phrase may be stated by one, repeated in exactly the same way by the other, or it may be repeated louder, or echoed softly according to the artistic effect desired. When there is a principal melody in either voice or piano and there is another counter melody, *the principal melody should be predominant.*

The wise teacher will capitalize on the help an experienced and capable accompanist is able to give by requesting suggestions and criticisms. In addition to the ways in which accompanists can be of assistance mentioned previously, they can be of great benefit and a source of assurance to the singer in rehearsals and concert as follows:

1. *In Rehearsal.*

   (a) Call attention to mistakes in rhythm, omission of rests, wrong words, wrong notes, off-pitch singing, and failure to observe phrasing, tempo, and dynamics as written in the score. (Accompanists for ethical reasons should never question before the student a direction for interpretation given by the vocal instructor, however.)

   (b) Make suggestions regarding clarity of diction, tempos, dynamics, and interpretation when not contrary to instructions of the voice teacher.

2. *In Concert.*

(a) Speed tempo when sensing that the singer is running out of breath on a long phrase.

(b) Double the bass fundamental in octaves, play the right hand an octave higher, and roll chords if the singer starts to go off pitch badly and has trouble hearing the piano.

(c) Be alert to assist the singer by "mouthing" or whispering words if the singer starts forgetting and signals for help.

(d) Whisper the name of the next song to the singer when there are no printed programs, the singer is announcing the songs, and forgets the order or name. It is much better for the singer and accompanist to whisper together about such matters when in doubt than to risk an unfortunate error regarding the next song to be sung.

Some singers and their accompanists have an artistic affinity for one another, each appearing to sense the other's expressional intent to the smallest detail. The singer should make every effort to find such an accompanist. On the other hand, personalities of singers and accompanists sometimes clash, and it is difficult or impossible to get along together. The reason can be found in most instances in the assumption by one or both of a dogmatic or domineering attitude instead of humbly approaching the matter of song interpretation together with an open mind and willingness to listen to suggestion.

RECOMMENDED READINGS

The accompanist will find a number of helpful suggestions in the following texts on the subject:

Bos and Pettis. "The Well-Tempered Accompanist." Presser, 1949.

Evans, Edwin. "How to Accompany." Reeves, (No date given).

Lindo, Algernon H. "Art of Accompanying." G. Schirmer, Inc., 1916.

Moore, Gerald. "The Unashamed Accompanist." Macmillan, 1946.

Winn, Cyril. "Do You Accompany." Curwen, 1929.

PART III

SELECT LITERATURE

FOR SOLO VOICE AND DUET

CLASSIFIED AND GRADED

Select Literature for Solo Voice and Duet Classified and Graded

RECOMMENDED VOCAL MATERIAL
(*See also p. 8 and p. 167*)

It is estimated that there are more than 100,000 separate published songs. Obviously, it would require a large text to list all worthy published songs by reputable composers. A scholarly text of a historical and comprehensive type of listing is Sergius Kagen's, "Music for Voice," published by Rinehart and Co., 1949. The majority of teachers, and those interested in purchasing songs for their own use, are desirous of obtaining a more highly selective graded and classified listing, however — songs which have proven most successful in voice teaching, concert, recital, contests, and church work. They desire information regarding the most select song collections and anthologies of the various types to meet the needs of the several kinds of voices in the various fields of song literature. Teachers and students also wish to know select songs appropriate for particular types of voices; graded songs for first year, second year, etc.; songs especially suitable for contest or festival purposes by immature voices; songs for special occasions; songs with accompaniments by one or more select instruments other than piano, duets, etc. Such information has long been needed in one published source, and it is hoped that the following listings in great measure will meet that need.

We wish to make it clear that the sacred song collections recommended, although the best available, and separate songs recommended by various authoritative sources, contain not only much of the best sacred song literature for solo voice, but also a large number of songs that are practical and popular in church services, without comparing in musical worth with the generally higher level of the secular art song listings. Anthologies and song collections recommended are those chosen by the author from a very large number of publications as the best available of that type; quality varies considerably. It should be understood that separate songs listed under the various categories are a compilation from those suggested by many experienced teachers and more than a half-dozen authoritative sources, and that standards of musical worth fluctuates considerably. The fact that any song, sacred or secular, is listed in the pages following does not signify necessarily that it bears the personal endorsement of the author regarding musical worth. Title, composer, keys, voices, and publishers for vocal material in Part III in general are as given by the various sources. While we have corrected a number of obvious errors, no responsibility is assumed for any remaining errors.

Only collections or anthologies containing songs by a number of composers are listed in the materials section following. Those desiring anthologies by individual composers such as Schubert, Brahms, Schumann, Faure, etc., can locate them easily by consulting the catalogues of leading American firms such as Theodore Presser, G. Schirmer, Carl Fischer, M. Witmark, and Arthur P. Schmidt, and foreign companies such as Boosey Hawkes, Boosey, Oxford, Novello, Ricordi, and Peters. Collections for the bass voice, such as they are, are listed separately because of the exceptional difficulty reported by many teachers in locating materials for this particular voice.

CRITERIA FOR SELECTING SONGS

What constitutes "good" music for the vocal student? Obviously more enters into its consideration than the aesthetic quality of the music itself. The problem of finding just the right song material to meet the interests and technical needs of students at the time is a highly important one. "Selecting teaching material is a serious business and should be given a great deal of thought and consideration by vocal teachers."[1] Many enthusiastic young sing-

---

[1]Klingstedt, Paul T. "Common Sense in Vocal Pedagogy as Prescribed by the Early Italian Masters." Edwards Brothers, Inc., 1941, p. 49.

ers are discouraged early by being required to sing vocal literature ill adapted to their interests, taste, and understanding at the time. Countless other aspiring and promising students injure their voices permanently by attempting difficult dramatic songs and operatic arias, assigned or permitted by their instructor before the voice has been developed and a safe technic established on less taxing music.

The following criteria are suggested in choosing songs for developing young voices:

1. Is it music which the pupil will sincerely and enthusiastically enjoy and understand at the time? (Music should not be entirely foreign to the taste, understanding, and experience of the student.)

2. Is it music which, although challenging to further progress, is still well adapted to initial success in performance, to instill confidence, and to build fundamental concepts and skills for more difficult music to follow?

3. Is it music which, in spite of being of a comparatively easy grade and presenting little complexity, nevertheless is considered good music of its type? (Sound advice to the beginning singer is tastefully to choose the more simple songs for public singing, rather than those that are, as yet, both vocally and musically "over their heads.")

4. Is it music with a strong aesthetic appeal and character of originality? (Songs should be chosen first with regard to their textual and aesthetic appeal and, second, to their expressive uniqueness.)

5. Is the text attractive and of a type that emphasizes a mood or moods that is normal and desirable for young people such as joy, grief, hope, love, ectasy, courage, humor, devotion, contemplation, and exaltation? (A text should be of high interest in itself as a poem when read aloud, and so "wedded" to the music that the proper tempo and mood for singing are suggested.)

6. Is there an attractive and singable melodic line in a comfortable vocal range? (This range for the average beginning student or first-year class should be not wider than *b* flat below middle *c* to *e* flat an octave and a fourth above.)

7. Is the accompaniment of a type to add rhythmic, contrapuntal, and harmonic interest as a background to the vocal line, but still is not too difficult for the average accompanist to do effectively with some practice? (Accompaniments of the best type do not plod along in a pedestrian fashion, duplicating continuously the melodic line and rhythm of the voice part, as is the case with most popular song accompaniments. The accompaniment should be independently interesting and beautiful.)

CHOOSING THE BEST MUSIC

Immature students with beautiful natural voices often are assigned taxing songs and opera arias by ambitious or unthinking teachers with results that are sometimes tragic. The teacher of voice cannot afford to be dogmatic in respect to using music which he himself prefers most, but can learn a great deal from the reactions of his students if only their opinion is sought in the matter. After a few years, he may no longer be surprised to find that most beginning students dislike, or are not enthusiastic about, some of the more profound or stylistic songs dearest to his own fancy. It is the rare teacher who has sufficient inspirational force to persuade most beginning students to start working with enthusiasm on such music as the arias of Bach or much of the Old English song literature, the texts of which are now foreign to our way of expression. Liking for these normally is the result of development and maturity. Music must be close to the experience of the student if his interest is to be captured so that eventually he can be led to prefer the less obvious, more profound, and stylistic songs. The teacher must be realistic in this regard and understand that it is often necessary for "Mohamet to go to the mountain."

It is evident, therefore, that the "best" music for a particular student to study at the time may not conform to the highest aesthetic standards. It is far more important educationally that music conform to criteria 1 and 2 listed previously, than that the song receive the highest rating by musicologists. In addition, if a student expresses a strong desire to sing popular music, he should be allowed not only to do so but also should be assisted in selecting some of the best music of this type and in giving it an effective interpretation.

It should be self-evident that ability to sing and progress in singing are based on interest, enjoyment, and understanding of what is sung, that musical taste is a developmental process, and that students can be led but seldom driven toward higher standards. In the beginning the factor of *what* the pupil sings is not nearly as important as *how* he sings and the confidence, enjoyment, and freedom of production established. We can be sure that maximum progress will result from using music within the student's capacity for enjoyment and understanding and technical limitations at the time. If necessary, taste for better literature can wait until more important objectives are satisfied.

As a rule, women ought not to sing songs in recital obviously intended for male voices, or vice-versa. Such factors as physical appearance, age, flexibility of the voice, command of foreign language and dialect, and understanding of style involved are determinants or limiting factors in choosing songs for recital, or even those to be sung informally for one's friends. It should be obvious, for the beginner, that it is highly important for the song to fit the singer and not the other way around. "A light voice should never sing a heavy song. A heavy voice can sometimes manage a light song, but not often."[2]

The foregoing does not imply in any sense that the use of inferior song material is recommended at the start or as a norm. On the contrary, cheap songs are a waste of time and energy. It is well to remember, however, that good music is not always difficult music and that complexity is not the same thing as excellence. There is an all-too-prevailing attitude that easy songs are necessarily weak in musical value. This concept is entirely erroneous. Worth of a song is determined by the quality of text and artistic sensitivity of its musical setting. Many fine texts of simplicity or nobility would be utterly ruined by either an involved, difficult vocal setting or a complex accompaniment.

Quality of songs is a vital factor in enjoyment; the selection of vocal material demands diligent search for the best available music of the right type to fit the student's needs and interests. In one real sense, good appealing music tends to be easier than poor, since it carries within itself the incentive to achieve. There is little or no excuse for not following this policy with the wealth of good song literature available today in any grade of difficulty. Mursell states the philosophy regarding ideal type of vocal material well. "We must have a wealth of songs of high emotional and aesthetic value. It is better to have the song somewhat ahead of the child (or adult) aesthetically than to have one that is devoid of musical meaning and interest. The introduction of musically worthless songs to teach reading or drill of voice control is definitely antagonistic to our leading principle."[3]

Songs in extensive ranges, or with long phrases which cannot be broken conveniently with a catch-breath, will be avoided for the beginning pupil. On the whole, songs for classes involving mixed sexes should be interesting to both boys and girls and worthy of inclusion in their permanent concert repertoire. Some excellent songs are easy in both range and length of phrase but are, nevertheless, difficult to interpret well, involving high finesse in sostenuto, or perhaps demanding extensive dynamic and tonal color variation and dramatic technic. Only a few such songs can be justified in early study and they should be introduced only then, with the intent of return later from time to time as technic develops.

For the most part, lyric-legato style art and folk songs in English, requiring moderate to light dynamics with an occasional *forte,* are the proper pablum for beginning singers. A few of the easier-accented style dramatic songs demanding a somewhat louder intensity level should follow in the second year. They are necessary for balanced vocal development to prevent the student from having only a "pretty" voice, with little or no dramatic capabilities. However, songs assigned to the individual pupil for solo singing in public ought never require the maximum dynamics, range, phrase, length, etc., that the pupil is barely able to negotiate successfully in the studio or class; *recital songs always will be limited enough in technical requirements to leave a reserve upon which to draw when fear or self-consciousness reduces ability.*

We agree with many authorities that good folk songs are an ideal type of vocal literature for introductory phases of vocal study. While no folk song is considered a great song by some critics, others disagree. Certainly, the best examples with sensitively arranged accompaniments, nevertheless, can qualify as good music. It is apparent that the American Academy of Teachers of Singing consider folk songs an important literature area for both vocal training and repertoire, since they spent so much time and research on the matter. They issued an extended list, "Arrangements of Folk-Songs of Great Britain and America," which the reader might wish to obtain and explore. They also suggest traditional and authentic folk songs as the last group in their pronouncement, "Program Building for Young Singers." Because of melodic beauty, forthrightness, naturalness, and generally-limited range and technical requirements, folk songs, spirituals, and ballads are excellent practical choices in the early stages of vocal study. When mixed judiciously with the easy art song, they will do much to help build freedom, spontaneity, and pleasure in expression.

USE OF SONGS IN A FOREIGN LANGUAGE
(See also p. 148)

For a number of sound practical and psychological reasons, most experienced voice class teachers and many private teachers do not believe in the introduction of songs in a foreign language during the first year, especially for students with no background in the language concerned. Confidence, freedom, and naturalness of expression, and mastery of important fundamentals are difficult enough to establish through the medium of the familiar mother tongue, without the complication of trying also to sing significantly in a foreign language. Application of the five pure "Cardinal" Italian vowel sounds as the basis for improving the comparable English vowels is almost universally recommended at the beginning of vowel study, however.

In order to sound convicing when singing in a foreign language, a student first will obtain a good English translation, then with the aid of a dictionary, ascertain the meaning, correct pronunciation, and accent of each word. Recordings, when available,

---

[2]Graves, Richard M. "Singing for Amateurs." Oxford U. Press, 1954, p. 80.

[3]Mursell, James L. "The Psychology of School Music Teaching." Silver Burdette, 1931, p. 281.

should be listened to over and over as the foreign language text is observed. Then, just as in English, the text is read out loud until it is dramatically meaningful.

It is assumed that either or both the student and his teacher will have some academic or practical background in the pronunciation of either German or French before they are attempted in song. Italian is comparatively much more simple. Its rules are few, and experience so much more general in singing and hearing it by choirs and at sacred services, that an intelligent teacher and pupil should be able to master at least a fairly workable pronunciation without a formal course in the language. Knowledge of correct pronunciation is not enough for truly eloquent singing, however; it is important that meaning of words also be understood, in order that proper accent emphasis be given. Translation of each word can be obtained by having it written out by someone who understands the language or by looking it up in a good dictionary.

Art songs in the two song anthologies accompanying this course provide both the original language and a singable English translation. Normally, only the English translations would be sung during the first year of study, but the original language may be learned later if desired. A highly-select group of Old Italian, German, and French art songs are included in Song Anthology Volume II, together with hints regarding pronunciation. It is expected that those intending to continue beyond the second year in a serious study of voice will initiate their study of foreign language, if they have not already done so.

The Old Italian Song generally is emphasized in the second year of study. Those who wish to start its study earlier can do so by turning to Song Anthology Volume II or by purchasing a separate Old Italian song anthology. Italian is by far the easiest foreign language to learn to sing, and the Old Italian song is ideal technical material to follow easy English language songs which themselves feature a similar legato Bel-Canto style. There is a wealth of Old Italian songs interesting to the student and well adapted in technical requirements to the immature voice. They require free production, a refined, pure vowel leaning toward bright tone color, precise and elegant diction, finesse in phrasing, delicate portamento, light dynamics, and skillful use of legato. They are not only ideal technically to develop the voice at this stage but also are musical, a valuable adjunct to the concert repertoire, and far more interesting to students than vocalises possibly could be.

Students are admonished that *all* vowels in Italian are pronounced distinctly, given their full *pure* sound, and never slighted. In English songs only one vowel or dipthong is found on one note. This is not true of Italian songs where two or three vowel sounds are sometimes attached to one note, no matter how short. Each vowel is sounded distinctly, dividing the rhythm of the note involved equally between the vowels or emphasizing one or the other, as taste and tradition dictate.

The Old Italian song is unsurpassed for developing the quality of instrumental perfection in the voice; the folk song, and especially the Negro spiritual, is ideal in promoting naturalness, dramatic expressiveness, fervor, emotional intensity, and variety in tone color. Mastery of the Old Italian song style, and effective interpretation of the folk song and the Negro spiritual, are the best type of background to bring to the later study of more difficult art song and operatic aria literature. To plunge the pupil immediately into operatic or difficult art song literature without adequate foundation, as still is done by some teachers, is a serious if not a disastrous mistake. After the pupil has had an adequate foundation through study of the folk song, spiritual, easy art song, sacred song, Old English song, and Old Italian song, he then can work more safely in successive semesters on the various national schools of song, the oratorio, opera, and the more dramatic types of literature.

REPERTOIRE AND PUBLIC PERFORMANCE
(See also Part I, Chapters 12 and 13)

Before the vocal education of students can be considered fully rounded and complete, they should have in their repertoire representative examples from the following fields of song literature: Folk Song, Spiritual, and Ballad; Old Italian; Old English; Baroque; Classic; German Lieder; French Impressionistic; Russian; Scandanavian; Spanish; Contemporary and Modern; Oratorio, Cantata, and Sacred Songs; Grand, and Light Opera. The pupil is not expected to learn all the foreign languages involved, or to memorize all the songs studied, but ordinarily will sing the Russian, Scandanavian, and Spanish songs in English translations. The serious student of singing will learn, however, to sing the Italian, German, and French songs in their original tongue as well as in English.

While all well-trained singers should be familiar with the various styles and schools of song literature, the memorized repertoire of the particular student's public performance will avoid serious vocal limitations and reflect the better qualities of the voice at the time. It is advisable that pupils seldom, if ever, be forced to memorize and sing music unsuited to their type of voice, or to their physical, emotional, or personality limitations, in recital. Only music which is "kind" to the voice normally is put in the concert repertoire of the developing singer; if the published key is too high or too low, it should be transposed to a suitable range. There is nothing sacred about an original key, as some teachers seem to believe to the detriment of their pupil's voices and effectiveness in performance.

Students often have to be led for their own welfare to use good judgment in regard to a realistic appraisal of both their temporary and permanent limitations. For example, some are determined to make their voices either higher or lower than nature intended; others who do not have, and never can hope to attain, a dramatic, grand opera type of voice, persist in wanting to practice and sing the operatic arias because they prefer this type of music. There is, unfortunately, a prevalent idea among students and many teachers that one never can become a really fine singer unless grand opera can be mastered. This fallicious belief has discouraged many a promising concert, radio, or television artist and resulted in destroying the fine quality and charm of countless light, lyric voices.

TRANSLATIONS

The prejudiced attitude about translations of many vocal teachers and music critics in the United States is not prevalent in Europe. Some here take even the extreme attitude that, if a song cannot be sung in the original language, it should be omitted. More than once we have heard snobbish censure by would-be critics about vocalists singing Schubert's "Hark, Hark the Lark," and various songs of Haydn written originally to English texts because, according to the critics, they would sound so much better in the original German. Many other ridiculous examples of snobbishness in this regard could be cited.

It ought to be self-evident that, even if a song is interpreted eloquently in a foreign language, most members of American audiences cannot understand the words and *thus lose the unique advantage of singing over instrumental performance.* If the words are not understood, the song might perhaps better be played on an appropriate instrument, or even sung throughout on an ideal euphonious vowel.

What are the facts about the comparative aesthetic values of a song in its original foreign language and in a translation? First, there appears little doubt that most art songs do sound best in their original tongue and that there are many poor translations. The intelligent teacher quite often can suggest a better translation, especially in places where the English words are not euphonious, cause an unfortunate difference in phrasing, or have unaccented syllables and unimportant words falling on strong beats in the measure.

The facts are that there is also a growing number of excellent translations in which the original thought and mood are retained fully, and in which the poetic quality and euphony for singing are as good, or, in a few instances, even better, than in the original language. Some songs actually sound better to an unprejudiced listener in a fine English translation. This is particularly true of lyric legato songs set originally to a rough, gutteral, "consonantal" language like Russian or German that is ill adapted to the style. Such Bel-Canto type songs may well sound better in either the more euphonious Italian or English languages when a good poetic, singable, translation is provided. The fact that some songs actually may gain aesthetically through a good translation has been pretty well established through experiments before unprejudiced listeners. Experience in hearing tends to create prejudice, and a listener who has first heard a song in either the original language or in a particular translation is almost invariably prejudiced.

When students are singing in a foreign language, not only the general meaning as indicated by the English translation should be noted but also the specific meaning of each word. Key words, especially those that fall on climaxes and on accented beats, should be understood well if the singing is to be meaningful and not a mere prattling of nonsense syllables. This demands either previous knowledge of the language by the student through study, or slow and laborious reference to a foreign language dictionary, or a literal word translation furnished by the teacher.

Some successful teachers go a long way toward solving the foreign language problem for students by mimeographing the exact phonetic sound of each foreign language word under each word of the original language and, directly under this, providing the exact English meaning. Teachers of singing unable to do the translations and phonetic syllabification often can secure the needed help from teachers in the foreign language department of the school system. When choice phonograph records also are available for the foreign language songs being studied, the learning process can be greatly accelerated. Teachers themselves can make these records on tape or wax, or have advanced students do so, and file the records for future use.

How shall we judge a good translation? There are two opposed philosophies. One maintains that a translation shall be literal, or very nearly so, in order to be of high quality. The other philosophy holds that the central idea and mood of the original language must be retained but that it is far more important to obtain good poetry in English, and appropriate euphonious vowels for ease and beauty in singing, than to use an awkward, and perhaps ugly, literal translation. There appears to be few good singable translations when the first plan is used but a large number when the second philosophy is followed. This is true especially when the translator is sensitive to both good poetry and the affinity in singing between vowel color and mood on accented or sustained tones — using the rounder, darker vowel colors for more serious, sombre or quiet moods, and the brighter vowel colors for a gay or happy sentiment. A translation successful in following this philosophy throughout can be, and sometimes is, an improvement over the original language in this respect.

ANTHOLOGIES OR SHEET MUSIC?

Most vocal teachers agree that the most practical and economical solution to the problem of amplifying the songs included in any vocal course is the purchase of good song collections or anthologies. A number are now available in almost all schools of song and historical periods of vocal literature except the Baroque, Classic, and Modern periods. Contemporary songs are protected by copyright and are seldom available in song volumes; therefore, a few select contemporary or modern songs may well be included in sheet music form each year as a part of the student's repertoire. Such songs, although they may be musically inferior to the established classics available in collections, nevertheless often are considered something special by the pupil, resulting in more enthusiastic work. The teacher may well beware of neglect of the many fine contemporary songs by American and English composers or the exclusion of folk songs, ballads, spirituals, and sacred songs as a normal and desirable part of vocal study. This material is likely to be the most vital in creating and retaining interest with the average student. It should be mixed judiciously with art songs by the established composers of the past.

That no single anthology covering the Baroque and Classic periods has yet been published with English translations seems surprising, in view of the fact that all other past historical periods are covered by adequate editions. Some publishers state as their reason for lack of a song collection in this field that there is not enough song literature of sufficient musical worth and interest to singers to justify publication. After considerable research in vocal literature, we believe that this opinion is unjustified and that there is a real need for such a collection. In order to study literature of these periods adequately, it is necessary to purchase either a considerable number of separate songs in sheet music or several general collections, each of which contains a very few of the songs desired. Both solutions are expensive and unsatisfactory, especially for voice class work.

Where only two or three semesters of vocal study are offered, as is the case in most high schools, song collections or anthologies used need to be of a general nature covering a wide variety of types of vocal literature. When four years of study are available, as in most colleges and conservatories, there are many advantages after the first preliminary year of study to starting specialization or emphasis on songs of only one or two particular schools or historical periods each semester. This is the plan followed in our outline of a complete four-year vocal course — see p. 191. Style of each particular school or type of song can be studied and discussed more thoroughly, a common repertoire of most representative songs reviewed in class, select records played, and a better understanding and higher excellence in performance achieved, than if songs from all periods are attempted each semester.

From the standpoint of adoption for class use after the first year of study, or to supplement the songs included in any vocal course, the collection or anthology is of highest value if it is issued in more than one key edition. While a medium or medium-low key edition is likely to be most useful for ensemble class singing, a higher or a lower key edition will be better adapted to some individual students for use in solo work. Ideally, collections or anthologies designed for wide usage to serve all voice needs should be published in three editions: High, Medium, and Low. A number of collections are available in two editions — High and Low — but so far, no music publisher has recognized sufficiently the superior appeal and distinct practical advantages of the three edition plan to risk the added expense of its adoption.

JUDGING A SONG COLLECTION

Following are the principal criteria to keep in mind in judging a song collection or anthology for class adoption:

1. Number, worth, variety, difficulty, and probable appeal to students and audiences of the songs included.

2. Inclusion and quality of English translations.

3. Inclusion of the original foreign language text.

4. Inclusion of the original piano accompaniments and not a garbled or cut version in introductions, interludes, and postludes.

5. Attractiveness and practicality of the piano accompaniments.

6. Number of voice editions (High, Medium, and Low) published, and judgment of the editor in selecting the proper key and range in each addition to meet students needs best.

7. Care in editing — absence of errors and excellence of judgment in regard to dynamic, tempo, and phrase markings.

8. Size, clarity and attractiveness of print without crowding.

9. Durability, quality, and attractiveness of binding and paper.

10. Presence and quality of hints on interpretation of songs included.

11. Presence, accuracy, and clarity of suggestions for pronunciation of foreign languages included.

12. Comparative price.

Most low-priced editions are seriously lacking in a number of the desirable qualities listed. They often have garbled or condensed versions of the original music either in the piano accompaniments or in both the accompaniment and the vocal score. Such publications are high priced, even if given away. The best obtainable editions are usually cheapest in the long run.

OPERA AND ORATORIO ARIA SOURCES

No separate sheet music listings of opera or oratorio arias are given in the following listings, since it appears more practical to purchase separate anthologies in these fields for the specific type of voice concerned (See "Operatic Anthologies," and "Oratorio Anthologies," p. 226-227. Some operatic arias are included under the listing, "Songs with Special Instrumental Obbligato or Accompaniment," p. 313, however, while some oratorio arias are given under the headings, "Sacred Songs Recommended by Experienced Teachers and Vocal Authorities," p. 295, under songs for "Christmas Season and New Year," p. 304, and under songs for "Easter Season," p. 307.

Those wishing to sing separate arias from some of the more recent operatic works should write to the few firms specializing in this field for their catalogues, principally, Theodore Presser, G. Schirmer, Carl Fischer, G. Ricordi, Novello, and H. W. Gray.

The American Academy of Teachers of Singing have covered the matter of oratorio effectively in a pronouncement, "The Sacred Oratorio," published by Theodore Presser, list price $1.00. This pronouncement contains:

1. A brief historical outline of the sacred oratorio.

2. Recommended procedure for the study and performance of oratorio.

3. A discussion of tempi, appogiatura, and translations.

4. A representative list of eighteenth, nineteenth, and twentieth century sacred oratorios, with publishers indicated.

5. A representative list, with specific solo voices indicated, of the principal recitatives, arias, duets, trios, quartets, etc., from each oratorio.

SELECT SONGS FOR SPECIFIC TEACHING PURPOSES

(Note — Selected from "Expressive Singing," Song Anthology Volume I, and Song Anthology Volume II. This list expands the few select songs listed at the end of each lesson in Expressive Singing, Volume I.)

Tonal Beauty, Freedom, and Color.

All Through the Night (Welsh Air) — Arr. Christy, Vol. I, p. 143.

Tutu Maramba (Brazilian Berceuse) — Arr. Christy, Vol. I, p. 161.

O Calm of Night (In stiller Nacht) — Arr. Brahms-Christy, Vol. I, p. 139.

Thou'rt Lovely As a Flower (Du bist wie eine Blume) — Schumann, Vol. I, p. 63.

Dedication (Widmung) — Franz, Vol. I, p. 13.

A Legend — Tschaikovsky, Vol. I, p. 107.

Bread of Angels (Panis Angelicus) — Franck, Vol. I, p. 93.

O Rest in the Lord (from "Elijah") — Mendelssohn, Vol. I, p. 104.

O Lovely Peace (from "Judas Maccabaeus") — Handel, Vol. II, p. 140.

O Sleep, Why Dost Thou Leave Me? (from "Semele") — Handel, Vol. II, p. 147.

Pure Vowels, Dipthongs, and Pronunciation.

Out of My Soul's Great Sadness (Aus meinen grossen Schmerzen) — Franz, Vol. I, p. 15.

O Calm of Night (Suabian Folk) — Arr. Brahms-Christy, Vol. I, p. 139.

Passing By — Purcell, Vol. I, p. 54.

Away Over Yandro (Applachian Folk) — Arr. Christy, Vol. I, p. 147.

Bread of Angels (Panis Angelicus) — Franck, Vol. I, p. 93.

She Never Told Her Love — Haydn, Vol. I, p. 27.

Far Down in the Valley (German Folk) — Arr. Brahms, Vol. I, p. 136.

Dear Love of Mine (Caro mio ben) — Giordani, Vol. II, p. 38.

Virgin, Fount of Love (Vergin, tuto amor) — Durante, Vol. II, p. 35.

Sapphic Ode (Sappische Ode) — Brahms, Vol. II, p. 67.

Breath Control and Sostenuto.

Beautiful Savior (Crusader's Hymn) — Arr. Christy, Vol. I, p. 83.

Think on Me — Scott — Christy, Vol. I, p. 65.

Lonesome Valley (White Spiritual) — Arr. Christy, Vol. I, p. 91.

The Joys of Love (Plaisir d'amour) — Martini, Vol. I, p. 37.

The Lost Chord — Sullivan, Vol. I, p. 68.

Still As the Night — (Still wie die Nacht) — Bohm, Vol. I, p. 4.

The Lotus Flower (Die Lotusblume) — Schumann, Vol. I, p. 60.

Tomorrow (Morgen) — Strauss, Vol. II, p. 90.

After a Dream (Apres un Reve) — Faure, Vol. II, p. 102.

Secrecy (Verborgenheit) — Wolf, Vol. II, p. 96.

Lyric Legato.

Drink to Me Only with Thine Eyes (Old English) — Mellish, Vol. I, p. 42.

I Love Thee (Ich liebe dich) — Beethoven, Vol. I, p. 1.

She Never Told Her Love — Haydn, Vol. I, p. 27.

On Wings of Music (Auf flugeln Gesanges) — Mendelssohn, Vol. I, p. 45.

Wher'er You Walk — Handel, Vol. I, p. 24.

Lovely Celia — (Old English) — Munro, Vol. II, p. 10.

Nina (Nina) — Pergolesi, Vol. II, p. 51.

Well Thou Knowest (Tu lo sai) — Torelli, Vol. II, p. 57.

To Be Near Thee (Star vicino) — Rosa, Vol. II, p. 53.

Were My Songs with Wings Provided (Si mes vers avient des ailes) — Hahn, Vol. II, p. 117.

Articulation.

A Very Commonplace Story (Eein sehr gewohnliche Geschichte) — Haydn, Vol. I, p. 121.

Lithuanian Song (Lithauische Lied) — Chopin, Vol. I, p. 111.

Joshua Fit the Battle of Jericho (Spiritual) — Arr. Christy, Vol. I, p. 86.

The Old Woman and the Peddler (English Ballad) — Arr. Christy, Vol. I, p. 116.

A Tragic Story — Mozart, Vol. I, p. 126.

The Pretty Creature (Old English) — Wilson, Vol. I, p. 128.

Little Boy Blue — Nevin, Vol. I, p. 50.

Florian's Song — Godard, Vol. II, p. 110.

The Lass with the Delicate Air (Old English) — Arne, Vol. II, p. 1.

With Cunning Conniving (Che fiero costume) — Legrenzi, Vol. II, p. 41.

Portamento.

Shenandoah (Chantey) — Arr. Christy, Vol. I, p. 159.

Songs My Mother Taught Me (Als die alte Mutter) — Dvorak, Vol. 1, p. 7.

The Pretty Creature (Old English) — Wilson, Vol. I, p. 128.

Elegy (Elegie) — Massenet, Vol. II, p. 126.

Impatience (Ungeduld) — Schubert, Vol. II, p. 70.

To Be Near Thee (Star vicino) — Rosa, Vol. II, p. 53.

Speak Once More Dear (Pur dicesti, O bocca bella) — Lotti, Vol. II, p. 46.

Weep No More (from "Hercules") — Handel, Vol. II, p. 150.

Sapphic Ode (Sapphische Ode) — Brahms, Vol. II, p. 67.

The Lass with the Delicate Air (Old English) — Arne, Vol. II, p. 1.

Resonance and Sonority.

Verdant Meadows (Verdi prati, from "Alcina") — Handel, Vol. I, p. 19.

Sombre Woods (Bois épais) — Lully, Vol. I, p. 30.

The Sea — McDowell, Vol. I, p. 34.

The Miller of Dee (17th Century English) — Beethoven-Christy, Vol. I, p. 134.

The Lost Chord — Sullivan, Vol. I, p. 68.

I'll Not Complain (Ich grolle nicht) — Schumann, Vol. II, p. 83.

Impatience (Ungeduld) — Wolf, Vol. II, p. 70.

I Wept Beloved (J'ai pleuré un rêve) — Hüe, Vol. II, p. 120.

Dido's Lament (from "Dido and Aeneas") — Purcell, Vol. II, p. 170.

Secrecy (Verborgenheit) — Wolf, Vol. II, p. 93.

Accent.

Mister Banjo (Creole Folk) — Arr. Christy, Vol. I, p. 155.

The Old Woman and the Peddler (English Ballad) — Arr. Christy, Vol. I, p. 116.

Begone Dull Care (English Folk) — Arr. Christy, Vol. I, p. 151.

Joshua Fit the Battle of Jericho (Spiritual) — Arr. Christy, Vol. I, p. 86.

The Miller of Dee (17th Century English) — Beethoven-Christy, Vol. I, p. 134.

Sombre Woods (Bois épais) — Lully, Vol. I, p. 30.

Come unto These Yellow Sands (Old English) — Purcell, Vol. II, p. 13.

O Death Now Come (Lasciatemi morire) — Monteverdi, Vol. II, p. 168.

I Wept Beloved (J'ai pleuré un rêve) — Hüe, Vol. II, p. 120.

Ah, Poor Heart (Ah, mio cor, aria from "Alcina") — Handel, Vol. II, p. 159.

Agility, Velocity, Flexibility, and Ornamentation.

Faith in Spring (Frühlingslaube) — Schubert, Vol. 1, p. 56.

A Pastoral (Old English) — Monro, Vol. II, p. 8.

Speak Once More Dear (Pur dicesti, o bocca bella) — Lotti, Vol. II, p. 46.

Nina (Nina) — Pergolesi, Vol. II, p. 51.

Love Has Eyes (Old English) — Bishop, Vol. II, p. 5.

O Sleep, Why Dost Thou Leave Me — Handel, Vol. II, p. 147.

I Attempt from Love's Sickness to Fly — Purcell, Vol. II, p. 15.

Come Unto These Yellow Sands — Purcell, Vol. II, p. 13.

To Be Near Thee (Star Vicino) — Rosa, Vol. II, p. 53.

Sound the Trumpet — Purcell, Vol. II, p. 19.

Range.

None But the Lonely Heart (Nur wer die Sehnsucht kennt) — Tschaikovsky, Vol. I, p. 73.

The Lost Chord — Sullivan, Vol. I, p. 68.

The Pretty Creature (Old English) — Arr. Wilson, Vol. I, p. 128.

Still As the Night (Still wie die Nacht) — Bohm, Vol. I, p. 4.

Were My Songs with Wings Provided (Si mes vers avient des ailes) — Hahn, Vol. II, p. 117.

To You (Zueignuung) — Strauss, Vol. II. p. 93.

The Cradles (Les Berceaux) — Faure, Vol. II, p. 106.

O Divine Redeemer (Repentir) — Gounod, Vol. II, p. 129.

Orpheus with His Lute — Sullivan, Vol. II, p. 24.

All Soul's Day (Allerseelen) — Strauss, Vol. II, p. 86.

Dynamics.

1. Both *pianissimo* and *fortissimo*:

   I Love Thee (Ich liebe dich) — Grieg, Vol. I, p. 17.
   The Sea — MacDowell, Vol. I, p. 34.

Still as the Night (Still wie die Nacht) — **Bohm**, Vol. I, p. 4.

Elegy (Elegie) — Massenet, Vol. II, p. 126.

Secrecy (Verborgenheit) — Wolf, Vol. II, p. 93.

2. *Pianissimo*:

Tutu Maramba (Brazilian Berceuse) — Arr. Christy, Vol. I, p. 161.

O Calm of Night (Suabian Folk) — Arr. Brahms-Christy, Vol. I, p. 139.

The Exquisite Hour (L'Heure exquise) — Hahn, Vol. II, p. 114.

Evening Fair (Beau soir) — Debussy, Vol. II, p. 99.

Well Thou Knowest (Tu lo sai) — Torelli, Vol. II, p. 57.

The Captive (L'Esclave) — Lalo, Vol. II, p. 123.

I Dreamed That I Was Weeping (Ich hab' im Traum geweinet) — Schumann, Vol. II, p. 80.

3. *Fortissimo*:

I'll Not Complain (Ich grolle nicht) — Schumann, Vol. II, p. 83.

O Death Now Come (Lasciatemi morire) — Monteverdi, Vol II, p. 168.

I Wept Beloved (J'ai pleuré un rêve) — Hüe, Vol. II, p. 120.

Impatience (Ungeduld) — Schubert, Vol. II, p. 70.

To You (Zueignung) — Strauss, Vol. II, p. 93.

°ACB—   A. & C. Bone.
°Al—   Almanach de Co.
AMP—   Associated Music Publishers, Inc., 25 West 45th St., New York 19, N.Y.
AMS—   Amsco Music Corp., 240 W. 55th St., New York 19, N.Y.
APS—   Arthur P. Schmidt Music Co., c/o Clayton F. Summy Co., 1834 Ridge Ave., Evanston, Ill.
Ar—   Arrow Press, 10 E. 43rd St., New York, N.Y.
Aug—   Augener Ltd., c/o Broude Brothers, 115 W. 57th St., New York 19, N.Y.
APH—   Augsburg Publishing House, 426 S. 5th St., Minneapolis 15, Minn.
Ax—   Axelrod, c/o American Music Edition, 250 W. 57th St., New York 19, N.Y.
Baron—   M. Baron Co., P.O. Box 418, Oyster Bay, Long Island, N.Y.
Bel—   Belwin, Inc., 45 W. 23rd St., New York 10, N.Y.
BFW—   B. F. Wood Music Co., 24 Brookline Ave., Boston 15, Mass.
°BGB—   Bote and G. Bach.
BH—   Breitkopf & Hartel, c/o Associated Music Publishers, Inc., 25 W. 45th St., New York 19, N.Y.
BHks—   Boosey & Hawkes, Inc., P.O. Box 418, Lynbrook, L. I., New York.
°Blake—   Blake.
BM—   Boston Music Co., 116 Boylston St., Boston 16, Mass.
°BMC—   Bomart Music Co.
BMI—   Broadcast Music, Inc., c/o Associated Music Publishers, Inc., 25 W. 45th St., New York 19, N.Y.
Bor—   Borneman, c/o H. W. Gray Co., Inc., 159 E. 48th St., New York 20, N.Y.
Bourne—   Bourne, Inc., 136 W. 52nd St., New York 19, N.Y.
Broude—   Broude Bros., 115 W. 57th St., New York 19, N.Y.
By—   Boosey & Co., Ltd., Steinway Hall, 111-113 W. 57th St., New York, N.Y.
CCB—   C. C. Birchard & Co., c/o Summy-Birchard Co., 1834 Ridge Ave., Evanston, Ill.
CF—   Carl Fischer, Inc., 56-62 Cooper Square, New York 3, N.Y.
Ch—   John Church Co., c/o Theodore Presser, Bryn Mawr, Pa.
Chan—   Chantry Music Press, Ltd., P.O. Box 425, Fremont, Ohio.
Chap—   Chappell & Co., Inc., R.K.O. Bldg., Rockefeller Center, New York 20, N.Y.
Ches—   Chester, c/o Edward B. Marks Music Corp., 132 W. 52nd St., New York 19, N.Y.
Con—   Concordia Publishing House, 3558 S. Jefferson Ave., St. Louis, Mo.
Cons—   Consolidated Music Publishers, Inc., 240 W. 55th St., New York 19, N.Y.
CP—   Composers Press, Inc., 853 7th Ave., New York 19, N.Y.
Cur—   Curwen & Sons c/o G. Schirmer, Inc., 609 Fifth Ave., New York, N. Y.
DS—   Deiss Salabert, c/o Ricordi & Co., R.K.O. Bldg., New York 20, N.Y.
DBH—   De Sylva, Brown & Henderson, c/o Chappel & Co., Inc., R.K.O. Bldg., Rockefeller Center, New York 20, N.Y.
DLS—   D. L. Schroeder, Flushing, N.Y.
Du—   Durand, c/o Elkan Vogel Co., Inc., 1716 Sansom St., Philadelphia 3, Pa.
E—   Enoch & Sons, c/o Boosey & Co., Ltd., Steinway Hall, 111-113, W. 57th St., New York, N.Y.
ECS—   E.C. Schirmer Music Co., 221 Columbus Ave., Boston, Mass.

°Unable to obtain address; order from a large music jobber.

EHM—   Edwin H. Morris & Co., 1619 Broadway, New York 19, N.Y.
Elkan—   Henry Elkan, 1316 Walnut St., Philadelphia 7, Pa.
EV—   Elkan Vogel Co., Inc., 1716 Sansom St., Philadelphia 3, Pa.
Feist—   Leo Feist, Inc., 799 7th Ave., New York, N.Y.
FH—   Frederick Harris Co., c/o Western Music Co., Ltd., 570 Seymour St., Vancouver, B. C., Canada.
FM—   Forster Music Publishers, Inc., 218 S. Wabash Ave., Chicago, Ill.
Gal—   Galaxy Music Corp., 2121 Broadway, New York, N.Y.
GH—   Gamble Hinged Music Co., 312 S. Wabash Ave., Chicago 4, Ill.
GS—   G. Schirmer, Inc., 609 Fifth Ave., New York, N.Y.
H—   Handy Brothers Music Co., 383 Madison Ave., New York 17, N.Y.
Har—   Hargail Press, 130 W. 56th St., New York 19, N.Y.
Harms—   Harms, Inc., 619 W. 54th St., New York 17, N.Y.
HB—   Harcourt, Brace & Co., 383 Madison Ave., New York 17, N.Y.
HE—   Harmonia Edition Publ. Co., 22 W. 83rd St., New York 24, N.Y.
°Hi—   Higate.
HM—   Hall & McCreary Co., c/o Schmitt, Hall & McCreary, Park Ave. at 6th St., Minneapolis 15, Minn.
Hom—   Charles W. Homeyer & Co., 498 Boylston St., Boston, Mass.
Hu—   Hughes & Son, North Wales, Great Britain.
Hue—   Huegel, c/o Theodore Presser Co., Bryn Mawr, Pa.
Hunt—   R. L. Huntzinger, Inc., 124 E. 4th St., Cincinnati, Ohio.
HWG—   H. W. Gray Co., Inc., 159 E. 48th St., New York 17, N.Y.
IMC—   International Music Co., 509 5th Ave., New York 17, N.Y.
JF—   J. Fischer & Bro., 119 W. 40th St., New York 18, N. Y.
JJR—   J. J. Robbins & Sons, Inc., c/o Consolidated Music Publ. Co., 240 W. 55th St., New York, N.Y.
JM—   James McDermid, Fine Arts Bldg., Chicago, Ill.
JW—   Joseph Williams, c/o Mills Music, Inc., 1619 Broadway, New York, N. Y.
°Keane—   Keane.
L—   Lorenz Publ. Co., 501 E. 3rd St., Dayton 1, Ohio.
Leeds—   Leeds Music, Inc., 322 W. 48th St., New York 36, N. Y.
Mac—   Macmillan Book Co., 2459 Prairie Ave., Chicago 16, Ill.
Marks—   E. B. Marks Music Corp., 132 W. 52nd St., New York 19, N.Y.
MB—   M. Baron Co., 8 W. 45th St., New York 19, N.Y.
Mi—   Mills Music Co., 1619 Broadway, New York 19, N.Y.
MK—   Michael Keane, Inc., 113 W. 57th St., New York, N.Y.
Mlr—   Miller Music, Inc., c/o Big 3 Music Corp., 799 7th Ave., New York 19, N.Y.
MM—   Mercury Music, c/o Theodore Presser Co., Bryn Mawr, Pa.
°Morris—   Morris.
MPI—   Music Press, Inc., c/o Theodore Presser Co., Bryn Mawr, Pa.
M & R—   McLaughlin & Reilly, 45 Franklin St., Boston, Mass.
MS—   M. Senart, c/o Ricordi & Co., R.K.O. Bldg., New York 20, N.Y.
N—   Novello & Co., c/o British American Music Co., 235 S. Wabash Ave., Chicago 4, Ill.
NM—   New Music Press, c/o Theodore Presser Co., Bryn Mawr, Pa.
NMS—   New Music Society, c/o Theodore Presser Co., Bryn Mawr, Pa.
OD—   Oliver Ditson Co., c/o Theodore Presser Co., Bryn Mawr, Pa.
Ox—   Oxford University Press, c/o Carl Fischer, Inc., 56-62 Cooper Square, New York 3, N.Y.
P—   Peters Corp., Carnegie Hall, 881 7th Ave., New York 19, N.Y.
Pallma—   Frank Pallma, Beaumont, Calif.
PAS—   Paul A. Schmitt Music Co., 88 S. 10th St., Minneapolis, Minn.
Pat—   Paterson's Publications, Ltd., c/o Carl Fischer, Inc., 56-62 Cooper Square, New York 3, N.Y.
PI—   Peer International, c/o Southern Music Co., 1619 Broadway, New York, N.Y.
Pond—   William A. Pond, 18 W. 37th St., New York, N.Y.
R—   Robbins Music Co., c/o Big 3 Music Corp., 799 7th Ave., New York 19, N.Y.
RDR—   R. D. Row Music Co., Inc., 725 Boylston St., Boston, Mass.
Rem—   Remick Music Co., c/o Music Publishers Holding Corp., 488 Madison Ave., New York 22, N.Y.
Ric—   G. Ricordi & Co., Inc., R.K.O. Bldg., New York 20, N.Y.
RLC—   Ruart-LeRolle et cie, c/o Elkan Vogel Co., Inc., 1716 Sansom St., Philadelphia 3, Pa.
°Ro—   Rother
SB—   Stainer & Bell, c/o Galaxy Music Corp., 2121 Broadway, New York, N.Y.
Schott—   Schott, c/o Associated Music Publishers, Inc., 25 W. 45th St., New York 19, N.Y.

°Unable to obtain address; order from a large music jobber.

Schu—   Schuberth & Co., c/o Ashley Dealer Service, 39 W. 60th St., New York 23, N.Y.
Scr—   Scribner & Co., 597 5th Ave., New York, N.Y.
SF—   Sam Fox Publishing Co., R.C.A. Bldg., New York 20, N.Y.
Shawnee—   Shawnee Press, Delaware Gap, Pa.
Sil B—   Silver Burdett & Co., 45 E. 17th St., New York 3, N.Y.
Sim—   Simrock Co., c/o G. Schirmer, Inc., 609 Fifth Ave, New York, N.Y.
SMC—   Southern Music Publishing Co., 1619 Broadway, New York 19, N.Y.
Sp C—   Sprague-Coleman, c/o Leeds Music, Inc., 322 W. 48th St., New York 36, N.Y.
Sy—   Clayton F. Summy Co., 1834 Ridge Ave., Evanston, Ill.
*Taylor—   Taylor
*TJ—   Tischer & Jagenberg.
TP—   Theodore Presser Co., Bryn Mawr, Pa.
TS—   Templeton-Shawnee Press, Delaware Water Gap, Pa.
*U—   Universal
V—   Viking Press, 625 Madison Ave., New York 22, N.Y.
VB—   Volkwein Brothers, Inc., 623 Liberty Ave., Pittsburgh, 22, Pa.
*VP—   Valley Press.
Wei—   Weintraub Music, 853 7th Ave., New York, N.Y.
Wick   Wick Music Co., Minneapolis 6, Minn.
Wil—   Willis Music Co., 124 E. 4th St., Cincinnati 2,   Ohio.
Wit—   M. Witmark & Sons, c/o Music Publishers Holding Corp., 418 Madison Ave., New York 22, N.Y.
*WMW—   W. M. Wood.
*WR—   Winthrop Rogers.
WS—   White-Smith Publishing Co., c/o Edward H. Morris, 35 W. 54th St., New York 19, N.Y.
*WW—   William Wise.
*WWP—   Wa-Wau Press.

——————

   *Unable to obtain address; order from a large music jobber.

Song Collections and Anthologies

GENERAL

(Note-Collections in this listing contain a wide variety of different types and schools of vocal literature designed particularly for study by vocal students. See p. 220 for "Key to Publishers.")

Art Song Argosy — Ed. Breach, strong paper cover, GS
High and Low editions, 25 songs in English and original language, hints on interpretation and general suggestions to students.

Art Songs for School and Studio — Ed. Glenn & Spouse, paper cover, OD
Medium-High and Medium-Low editions, English and original language, hints on interpretation and teaching procedure, First Year Volume contains 25 songs, Second Year Volume includes 23 songs.

Boosey Vocal Albums — (No editor listed), paper cover, By
Volumes for Soprano, Mezzo-soprano, Contralto, Tenor, and Baritone.

Famous Songs — Ed. Krehbiel, paper cover, Ch
English and original language, volumes for Soprano, Alto, Tenor, and Bass with approximately 70 songs in each.

55 Art Songs — Ed. Spaeth & Thompson, paper cover, CCB
Medium voice, English only, first 14 songs are Old English.

50 Mastersongs — Ed. Finck (Musicians Library), both paper and strong paper board covers obtainable, OD
High and Low editions, English and original language.

56 Songs You Like to Sing — (No editor listed), strong paper cover, GS
Mostly medium and high voice keys, English and original language.

Foundational Repertoire for Singers — Ed. Prahl, paper cover, CCB
Medium-High and Medium-Low editions, English and original language in most instances, Vol. I includes 27 songs, Vol. II includes 25.

Gems of Antiquity — Ed. Nietzel, paper cover, Ch
Medium voice range, 38 songs in English and original language from the early historical period.

John Charles Thomas Album of Favorite Songs and Arias — (No editor listed), paper cover, GS
20 selections with English translations and original language, medium or medium high keys.

Marion Anderson Collection of Songs and Spirituals — (No editor listed), paper cover, GS
16 art songs with English translations and original language and 4 spirituals, medium voice key ranges.

New Anthology of American Songs — (No editor listed), paper cover, GS
Low and High editions, 25 songs by native American composers.

New Imperial Edition — Ed. Northcote, paper cover, BHks
Volumes for Soprano, Mezzo-soprano, Contralto, Tenor, Baritone, and Bass.

Pathways of Song — Ed. by La Forge and Earhart, paper cover, Wit.
High and Low editions, English and original language, Volumes I, II, II, and IV with 23-26 songs in each.

Seven Centuries of Solo Song — Ed. Woodside, paper cover, BM
High and Low editions, English and original language, historical comments, Volumes I, II, III, IV, V, and VI with 9-13 songs in each, covers historical period from 1240 to 1920.

Seven Songs — Henry Purcell, paper cover, BHks
Medium voice range, from "Orpheus-Brittanicus;" realization of figured bass by Benjamin Britten.

Singable Songs for Studio and Recital — Ed. Mason, paper cover, OD
High and Medium editions, English and original language, 30 songs, 14 of them contemporary.

The Singing Road — Ed. Ward, paper cover, CF
> High and Medium-Low editions, English and original language, hints on interpretation, and Italian pronunciation, select Vaccai and Marchesi exercises, Volumes I, II, and III, 9 songs in Volumes II and and III and and 21 in Volume I.

Song Classics — Ed. Parker, paper cover, Ch
> Volumes for Soprano, Alto, Tenor, and Bass with approximately 48 songs in each, English and original language.

Something to Sing — Ed. Baltzell & W. A. F., paper cover, OD
> Medium voice range, English and original language, 34 songs intended for first year study.

Standard Vocal Repertoire — Ed. Row, paper cover, RDR
> Medium voice range, English and original language, 22 songs.

A Treasury of Art Songs — Ed. Whitlock & James, paper cover, BM
> Medium voice range, English and original language, 14 songs by Mozart, Schubert, Mendelssohn, and Grieg with a short biography of each.

SACRED SONGS

Album of Sacred Songs — (No editor listed), paper cover, GS
> High Voice (Vol. 1384), Low Voice (Vol. 1385), 22 songs in each.

Album of Sacred Songs — (No editor listed), paper cover, GS
> High voice only, 21 songs.

Bach Songs and Arias — Ed. Prout, paper cover, Aug
> Volumes I and II with editions for Soprano, Contralto, Tenor, and Bass, 9-12 select arias and recitatives from Bach's sacred cantatas, English and original German texts.

Choice Sacred Songs — Ed. Wilmans, paper cover, OD
> High and Low editions, 26 songs.

Church and Home Collection of Sacred Songs — (No editor given), paper cover, TP
> Low voice, 19 songs.

Church Soloist — (No editor listed), paper cover, TP
> Low voice, 19 songs.

Devotional Solos for Church and Home — (No editor listed), paper cover, TP
> 18 songs in mostly medium and medium-high keys.

52 Sacred Songs You Like to Sing — (No editor listed), strong paper cover, GS
> Most keys best suited to medium or medium-high voice, a few for low.

Four Scriptural Songs — Brahms (Ed. Dies), paper cover, GS
> High voice (No. 1677), Low or Medium voice (No. 1678), English and original German texts.

Gems of Sacred Song — Ed. Marzo, paper cover, GS
> High voice (Vol. 1657), Low voice (Vol. 1656), 23 standard sacred songs for church service.

The Sacred Hour — Ed. Harrell, paper cover, CF
> High and Medium voice editions, 20 sacred songs especially suitable to Christian Science services.

Sacred Songs — Ed. Henderson, paper cover, Ch
> Vol. I, Soprano, 58 songs; Vol. II, Alto, 54 songs; Vol. III, Tenor, 53 songs; Vol. IV, Bass, 56 songs.

Sing Unto the Lord — Ed. Davis & Loring, paper cover, CF
> 20 songs in medium voice range.

Solos for the Church Year — Ed. Pfautsch, paper cover, Lawson & Gould,
> High and Low voice editions, 23 select songs for various occasions during the church year.

Songs for Worship — Arr. Brown, paper cover, CF
> 23 songs in medium voice range.

The Treble Voice Chorister — Ed. Heller, paper cover, HM
> 16 unison songs with optional second part, Medium-high range.

Twenty Sacred Songs — J. S. Bach, paper cover, N
> High or medium voice range, English translations only.

EARLY ITALIAN SONGS
(Note — All songs contain English translations)

Anthology of Italian Songs of the 17th and 18th Centuries — Ed. Parisotti, paper cover, GS
> Medium voice range, Vol. I (No. 290) 29 songs, Vol. II (No. 291) 30 songs.

Classic Italian Songs — Ed. Glenn & Taylor, paper cover, OD
> Medium High and Medium Low editions, Vol. I, 18 songs, Vol. II, 15 songs, hints on Italian pronunciation.

24 Italian Songs and Arias of the 17th and 18th Centuries — paper cover, GS
> Medium High edition (No. 1722), Medium Low edition (No. 1723).

OLD ENGLISH SONGS

55 Art Songs — Ed. Spaeth & Thompson, paper cover, CCB
Medium voice range, first 14 songs are Old English.
Henry Purcell Songs — Ed. Edmunds, paper cover, RDR
High and Low voice editions, 14 songs, realization of figured bass by John Edmunds.
Old English Melodies — Ed. Wilson, paper cover, By
21 songs in medium or medium-low range.
Reliquary of English Song — Ed. Potter, paper cover, GS
Medium voice range, Vol. I (No. 1250-1700) 52 songs; Vol. II, (1700-1800) 54 songs.

FRENCH IMPRESSIONISTIC AND MODERN SONGS

Anthology of Modern French Song — Ed. Spicker, obtainable with either paper or board cover, GS
High and Low voice editions, English translations and original French, 39 songs.
40 French Songs — Ed. Kagen, paper cover, IMC
Volumes I and II in High, Medium, and Low voice editions, 20 songs in each edition.
French Art Songs — Ed. Glenn & Taylor, paper cover, OD
Medium-High and Medium-Low voice editions, 20 songs each, English translation and original French, guide to French pronunciation and hints on interpretation.
Maggie Teyte Album of French Song — paper cover, GS
For high or medium-high voice, 19 songs.
Modern French Songs — Ed. Hale (Musicians Library), obtainable with either paper or board cover, OD
High and Low editions, Vol. I (Bemberg to Franck) 30 songs; Vol. II (Georges to Widor) 30 songs.

GERMAN LIEDER

Easy Classic Songs — Ed. Golde, paper cover, OD
Medium voice keys, 29 short and easy German Lieder, English translations, and original German.
Fifty Selected Songs of Schubert, Schumann, Brahms, Wolf and Strauss — (No editor listed), paper cover, GS
High Voice (Vol. 1754); Low Voice (Vol. 1755); English translations by Florence Easton and original German.
German Art Songs — Ed. Taylor, paper cover, OD
Medium-High and Medium-Low editions; English translations and original German, guide to German pronunciation and hints on interpretation, 16 songs.
100 Songs by 10 Masters — Ed. Finck (Musicians Library), obtainable with either paper or board cover, OD
High and Low editions; English translation and original German. Vol. I, 60 songs by Schubert, Schumann, Franz, Rubinstein, and Jensen. Vol. II, 40 songs by Brahms, Tschaikovsky, Grieg, Wolf, and Strauss.
Lotte Lehmann Album — Ed. Lehmann, paper cover, BHks
Mostly medium voice range; English translations and original German; 16 songs by Beethoven, Brahms, Mahler, Schubert, Schumann, Wagner, and Wolf marked with Madam Lehmann's own interpretation suggestions.

RUSSIAN SONGS

A Century of Russian Song (From Glinka to Rachmaninoff) — Ed. Schindler, paper cover, GS
Keys mostly for medium and high voice, English and German texts, 50 songs.
Masters of Russian Song — Ed. Schindler, paper cover, GS
Mostly for medium and high voice; Vol. I, 25 songs by Moussorgsky; Vol. II, 25 songs by six other Russian composers; English only.
Modern Russian Songs — Ed. Newman (Musicians Library), obtainable with either paper or board cover, OD
English and many songs in either German or French also. Vol. I (Alpheraky to Moussorgsky) 52 songs; Vol. II Moussorgsky to Withol.

SCANDANAVIAN SONGS

Modern Scandanavian Songs — Ed. Werrenrath (Musicians Library), obtainable with either paper or board cover, OD
High and Low voice editions, English and original language. Vol. I, songs from Alfven to Kjerulf. Vol. II, songs from Lange-Muller to Winge.

MODERN AND CONTEMPORARY

50 Art Songs from the Modern Repertoire — (No editor listed), paper cover, GS
Keys for most songs best for high or medium-high voice, some for medium; English and original language, composers of 15 nationalities represented.

A New Anthology of American Song — (No editor listed), paper cover, GS
High and Low editions; 25 songs by native American composers.

Songs by 30 Americans — Ed. Hughes (Musicians Library), obtainable with either paper or board cover, OD
High and Low editions; 30 songs.

GRAND OPERA

Coloratura Album for Soprano — Ed. Marzo, paper cover, OD
15 arias with English and foreign language text.

The Modern Operatic Album — (No editor listed), obtainable in either paper or cloth binding, Ric
Recitatives and arias from the more recent operas, English and the original language; Soprano volume, 32 arias; Tenor volume, 35.

Opera Songs — (No editor listed), paper cover, Ch
Vol. I, Soprano; Vol. II, Mezzo-soprano and Alto; Vol. III, Tenor; Vol. IV, Bass; English and original language; 32 to 35 arias.

Operatic Albums — (No editor listed), paper cover, Ric
No. 1, Contralto; No. 2, Mezzo-soprano; No. 3, Soprano; 6 arias in each; English and original foreign language texts.

Operatic Anthology — Ed. Spicker and Adler, paper cover, GS
Vol. I, Soprano; Vol. II, Alto; Vol. III, Tenor; Vol. IV, Baritone; Vol. V, Bass; 39 to 43 standard arias in each; English and original language texts.

Opera Repertoire for Coloratura Soprano — Ed. Pelletier, paper cover, TP
23 arias with English and original foreign language texts.

Songs from the Operas — (Musicians Library), obtainable in either paper or board cover, OD
Editions for Soprano, Mezzo-soprano, Alto, Tenor, and Baritone and Bass; English and original foreign language texts.

Star Songs from the Grand Operas — Collected and arr. by Lampe, paper cover, Rem
28 popular arias arranged in medium voice keys; English and original foreign language texts.

Verdi Operatic Albums — (No editor listed), paper cover, Peters
Soprano (2 volumes), 30 arias; Mezzo-soprano, 7 arias; Tenor, 23 arias; Baritone, 20 arias; Bass, 13 arias; German and the original foreign language texts.

LIGHT OPERA

Favorite Melodies from Gilbert and Sullivan — Arr. Treharne, paper cover, GS
28 songs from 8 operettas.

Gilbert and Sullivan Album — Ed. Schumann, paper cover, AMS
84 favorite songs from 8 operettas; cast of characters and brief setting of each song given.

Gilbert and Sullivan Songs — Ed. Frey, paper cover, R
86 songs from 11 of the Gilbert and Sullivan operettas.

A Treasury of Gilbert and Sullivan — Ed. Taylor, cloth cover, Simon and Schuster
102 songs from 11 operettas, carefully edited and beautifully illustrated.

Album of Song Hits by Friml — (No editor listed), paper cover, GS
12 favorite songs in medium voice keys from Friml operettas.

Victor Herbert Album of Selected Songs — (No editor listed), paper cover, Schu
8 songs in simplified arrangements from 3 operettas.

Victor Herbert Light Opera Songs — (No editor listed), paper cover, GS
11 songs from 3 operettas.

Victor Herbert Song Album — (No editor listed), paper cover, Wit.
Book I, 15 songs from 13 operettas; Book II, 10 songs from 7 operettas.

ORATORIO

Anthology of Sacred Song — Ed. Spicker, paper cover, GS
Vol. I, Soprano; Vol. II, Alto; Vol. III, Tenor; Vol. IV, Bass; 39 to 46 celebrated arias selected from oratorios by both the older and more recent composers; English and original language.

Handel Twelve Songs — Ed. Randegger, paper cover, HWG
Volumes for Soprano, Contralto, Tenor, and Baritone or Bass; 12 arias and recitatives from various oratorios in each volume.

Oratorio Songs — (No editor listed), paper cover, Ch
> Vol. I, Soprano; Vol. II, Alto; Vol. III, Tenor; Vol. IV, Bass; 32 to 35 arias in each.

Oratorio Repertoire — Ed. Douty, paper cover, TP
> Vol. I, Soprano; Vol. II, Alto; Vol. III, Tenor; Vol. IV, Bass; 24 to 26 arias in each.

SECULAR DUETS

Album of Duets — (No editor listed), paper cover, GS
> 15 duets for Soprano and Tenor.

Brahms Duets — (No editor listed), paper cover, Aug
> *Four Duets*, Op. 28, Contralto and Baritone; English and German texts.
> *Three Duets*, Op. 20, Soprano and Alto; English and German texts.

Canticle II, Abraham and Isaac — Britten, paper cover, BHks
> A long concert duet for Alto and Tenor.

The Ditson Collection of Soprano and Alto Duets — (No editor listed), paper cover, OD
> 22 standard duets; English and original language in most instances.

Duet Album — Ed. Morris and Anderson, paper cover, BHks
> 11 duets for high and medium voice.

Duette — Handel-Brahms, paper cover, P
> 2 sopranos, or soprano and alto; 6 long duets with Italian and German texts; 3 numbers for 2 sopranos and
> 3 for soprano and alto.

Duette — Schumann, (No. 2392), paper cover, P
> 34 original duets by Schumann in German; for one high or medium voice and one medium or low voice.

Folksongs and Other Duets — Selected by Gluck and Reimers, paper cover OD
> 4 songs for Soprano and Alto, 5 for Soprano and Baritone, and 8 for Mezzo-soprano or Alto and Baritone.

G. Schirmer Collection of Song and Duet Albums for Soprano and Tenor — (No editor listed), paper cover, GS
> 16 varied songs for voices of medium range; English and original foreign language texts.

19 Two-Part Songs — Mendelssohn, paper cover, Aug
> No's. 1-7, Soprano and Soprano; No's. 8-16, High and Low voice; No's. 17-19, Op. 77, Soprano and Soprano.

Operatic Duets — (No editor listed), paper cover, BHks
> Vol. I, Soprano and Mezzo-soprano; Vol. II, Soprano and Contralto or Mezzo-soprano.

Purcell Vocal Duets — Ed. Moffat, paper cover, Aug

Schirmer's Favorite Secular Duets — (No editor listed), paper cover, GS
> 15 favorite duets for various voice combinations.

Schumann Complete Duets — (No editor listed), paper cover, Aug
> English translations and original German.

Secular Duets for All Voices — (No editor listed), paper cover, TP
> 17 duets for various voice combinations.

16 Two-Part Songs — Mendelssohn, paper cover, GS
> English and original German texts.

Six Tuscan Folk Songs for Two Voices — Ed. Caracciolo, paper cover, GS

Soprano-Baritone Choruses — paper cover, HM

Soprano and Tenor Duets — (No editor listed), paper cover, OD
> 24 duets in English and original foreign language.

Twenty Choice Duets — (No editor listed), paper cover, OD
> 20 easy duets for various voice combinations.

Vocal Duets — Arr. Prahl, paper cover, ECS
> Vol. I and Vol. II, each with 24 varied songs for duet voices of medium range; English and many with original foreign language texts.

SACRED DUETS

Sacred Duets — (No editor listed), paper cover, OD
> 26 easy duets.

Sacred Duets for All Voices and General Use — (No editor listed), paper cover, TP
> 19 duets.

Sacred Duets for High and Low Voices — Ed. Shakespeare, paper cover, Ch
> 42 choice duets.

Sacred Duets for Two High Voices — Ed. Shakespeare, paper cover, Ch
> 42 choice duets.

20 Choice Sacred Duets — (No editor listed), paper cover, OD
> 20 easy to medium difficult duets for various voice combinations.

Collections for Bass Voice

(*Note — See also Opera, and Oratorio listings*)

Album of Bass Songs — (No editor listed), paper cover, GS
      21 bass solos.

The Artistic Basso — (No editor listed), paper cover, Wit
      19 concert favorites.

Bach Songs and Arias — Ed. Prout, paper cover, Aug
      Bass edition, Volumes I and II; 9-12 select arias and recitatives from Bach's sacred cantatas in each; English
      and original German text.

Bass Songs — Ed. Mason, paper cover, OD
      21 bass songs in English and original language.

A Collection of Songs — Ed. Ford and Erlebach, paper cover, BHks
      For bass or low baritone; 18 arias and recitatives from various oratorios.

Ezio Pinza Album of Concert Songs — (No editor listed), paper cover, GS
      14 songs for bass or low baritone; English and original language.

Famous Songs — Ed. Krehbiel, paper cover, Ch
      Bass Volume; approximately 70 songs in English and original language; many songs in a better key for baritone.

Favorite Bass Songs — Ed. Spicker, paper cover, GS
      22 favorite melodies for bass.

Sacred Songs — Ed. Henderson, paper cover, Ch
      Vol. IV for Bass; English and original language.

Six Purcell Songs for Bass — Ed. Kagen, paper cover, IMC
      Figured bass realization by Kagen.

Song-Classics — Ed. Parker, paper cover, Ch
      Bass Volume; 48 songs in English and original language, many of them better adapted to baritone.

Folk Songs, Spirituals, and Folk Ballads

ARRANGEMENTS OF FOLK SONGS OF GREAT BRITAIN AND AMERICA IN ENGLISH

(*Note*—Prepared by the American Academy of Teachers of Singing and used by permission. More recent collections and folk-song collections of a general nature added by the author.)

AMERICAN

*Bailey (Compiled Landeck) — Songs My True Love Sings, (32 varied numbers in medium or medium low range), Marks

Bartholomew — Mountain Songs of North Carolina, GS

*Bonds — Five Spirituals, Mutual Music Society

*Botsford — Botsford Collection of Folk Songs, GS Vol. I, Americas, Asia, and Africa; Vol. II, Northern Europe; Vol. III, Southern Europe. (Note — Also Available in complete edition with either paper or board cover.)

Brockway — Lonesome Tunes (Kentucky Mountain Songs), HWG

*Burleigh — Album of Negro Spirituals, (High and Low voice editions), Ric

Burleigh — (Many fine arrangements of Negro Spirituals, published separately), Ric

Calcord — Roll and Go (Songs of American Sailormen), WWN

Crosley — Book of Navy Songs, DP

*Davison and Surette — 140 Folk Songs, ECS

*Edmunds — Folk Songs (American, English, and Irish; 11 select folk songs in both High and Low editions), RDR

Fischer — 70 Negro Spirituals, OD

Foster, Stephen — Songs, GS

*Frey — Celebrated Negro Spirituals, (25 Spirituals in medium range), R

*Gellert and Siegmeister — Negro Songs of Protest (24 Spirituals, mostly medium range), CF

Handy — Blues, ACB

*Ives, Burl — Favorite Folk Ballads of Burl Ives, Vol. II, (17 folk ballads for low or medium voice with piano and guitar accompaniment), Leeds

*Ives, Burl — The Wayfarin' Stranger, Vol. I (21 folk songs for low or medium voice with piano, guitar, and ukulele accompaniment), Leeds

*Ives, Burl — Folio of Folksongs and Ballads, (13 recorded favorites for low or medium voice with piano, guitar, and ukelele accompaniment), Southern Music Publishing Co.

*Ives, Burl — Song Book (115 songs for medium or low voice with piano and guitar chords indicated), Ballantine Books

*Johnson — The Green Pastures Spirituals, CF

*Johnson and Brown — The Book of American Negro Spirituals, V

*Johnson, Hall — 30 Negro Spirituals (High and medium-high range), GS

*Johnson, Rosamund — Album of Negro Spirituals (26 spirituals in medium range), Marks

Johnson, Rosamund — (Two Volumes of Negro Spirituals), V

*Lansford & Stringfield — 30 & 1 Folk Songs from the Southern Mountains, CF

*Lloyd — Favorite American Songs, (46 folk and favorite songs in easy medium-low range), Simon & Schuster

*Lomax — Cowboy Songs and Other Frontier Ballads, Mac

Lumis & Farwell — Spanish Songs of Old California, GS

*Marias — Songs from the Veld (14 folk songs of South Africa), GS

Matteson — Beach Mountain Folk Songs and Ballads, GS

Monroe & Schindler — Bayou Ballads, GS

*Niles — Schirmer American Folk Song Series, Set 18, Ballads, Carols, and Tragic Legends, GS

*Niles — Schirmer American Folk Song Series, Set 27, The Shape — Note Study Book, GS

Niles — Seven Negro Exaltations, GS

Niles — Ten Appalachian Mountain Christmas Carols, GS

*Payne — Negro Spirituals (5 spirituals for low voice), GS

---

*Recommended by the author.

229

Pound — American Songs and Ballads, Scr

Powell — Five Virginia Folk Songs, JF

°Reddick — Roustabout Songs, (11 Ohio River Valley Songs for bass or baritone), Rem

°Richard Dyer-Bennett — A Collection of 20 Songs and Ballads (Piano and guitar accompaniment), Leeds

°Richardson — American Mountain Songs, (61 songs for medium voice and piano), Greenburg

Rickaby — Ballads and Songs of the Shanty Boy, HUP

Sandburg — American Songbag (Contains Colonial and Revolutionary Antiques, Frontier, Kentucky, the Lincolns, Erie Canal, Hobo, Blues, Great Open Spaces, Railroad and Work Gang Songs, Chanties, Lumberjack Songs, etc.), HB

°Sandburg — New American Songbag, (60 varied folk songs in a medium or medium low range), HB

°Schindler — Bayou Ballads, GS

Sharp, Cecil — American-English Appalachian Moun-Folk Songs, GS

Sharp, Cecil — Appalachian Nursery Songs (Two Volumes) N

°Shawnee Press — Your Favorite Negro Spirituals (30 varied spirituals in medium or medium-high range), Shawnee Press

Sires & Repper — Songs of the Open Range (Cowboy songs), CCB

Smith, Reed & Ruffy — American Anthology of Old World Ballads, JF

°Still — Twelve Negro Spirituals, TP

°Thiel & Heller — Chorus and Assembly (Includes 25 folk songs), HM

°Thomas & Leeder — The Singin' Gatherin', Sil B

°Wheeler — Kentucky Mountain Folk Songs, BM

°White — Forty Negro Spirituals, TP

°Wilson — Songs of the Hills and Plains (Mostly cowboy songs, medium voice range), HM

°Wilson, Leeder & Gee — Music Americans Sing (125 songs with many folk songs included, Sil B

°Woodside — Seven Centuries of Solo Song (Vol. IV is all folk songs), BM

°Wolfe — American Songster, CF

°Zanzig — Singing America, (Edition with piano) CCB

BRITISH (English)

Bantock — 60 Patriotic Songs of all Nations, OD

Bantock — 100 Folk Songs of all Nations, OD

Bantock — 100 Songs of England, OD

Barrett — English Folk Songs, N

°Britten — British Folk Songs, (Volumes I and II), BHks

Broadwood — English Traditional Songs, BHks

Fuller Sisters — English Folk Songs, N

Gardiner — Folk Songs (Hampshire), N

Gould & Sharp — English Folk Songs for Schools, Cur

Hadow — Songs of the British Isles, Cur

Hammond — Folk Songs (Dorsett), N

Karpeles — Folk Songs from Newfoundland (Vol I & II), N

Merrick — Folk Songs (Sussex), N

Sharp, Cecil — English Folk Carols, N

Sharp, Cecil — Folk Songs, Chanteys & Singing Games, N

Sharp, Cecil — Folk Songs from Somerset, N

Sharp, Cecil — Folk Songs (Various Countries), N

Sharp, Cecil — 100 Folk Songs, OD

Sharp, Cecil and Williams, Vaughan — Folk Songs (Vol. I & II), N

Somervell — Twelve French-Canadian Folk Songs, BHks

Williams, Vaughan — Six English Folk Songs, Ox

IRISH

Brennan — 4 Traditional Irish Songs, EV

Brewer — Irish Melodies, N

Fisher — 60 Irish Songs (High and Low editions), OD

Fogg — 3 Traditional North Country Songs, EV

Foster, Arnold — 12 Manx Folk Songs (Vol. I & II), SB

Fox, Milligan — 4 Songs of the Irish Harpers, GS

Harty, Hamilton — 3 Irish Folk Songs, Ox

Hatton & Molloy — Songs of Ireland, BHks

Hughes — Irish Country Songs (Vol. I & II), BHks

Moore, Thomas — Irish Melodies, OD

Spicker — Songs of the British Isles, GS

Stanford, C.V. — Anglo-Irish Folk Songs, SB

Stanford, C.V. — 50 Songs of Erin, BHks

Stanford, C.V. — 50 Songs of Ireland, BHks

Stanford, C.V. — Irish Melodies of Thomas Moore, BHks

Tours — Irish Melodies, N

Wood, Charles — Irish Countryside Songs (Vol. I & II), SB

SCOTCH

Diack — The New Scottish Orpheus (3 volumes), Pat

Hopekirk — 70 Scottish Songs (High and Low editions), OD

Karpeles — Folk Songs from Newfoundland, Ox

Kennedy-Fraser — Songs of the Hebrides, BHks

Kennedy-Fraser & Macleoud — Songs of the Hebrides (Published separately), Pat

Kennedy-Fraser — 12 Songs from the Hebrides, BHks

Kennedy-Fraser — 20 Scottish Songs (Vol. I & II), Pat

Pittman & Brown — Songs of Scotland, BHks

Ross & Moffat — Scottish Album (In Soprano, Mezzo, Contralto, Tenor, Baritone, and Bass editions), Pat

.... Favorite Scottish Songs (7 Volumes), Ox

WELSH

Davies, E. T. — Clarendon Series, Ox

Davies, Grace — 6 Welsh Folk Songs, Hu

Davies, W. Herbert — Folk Songs, Hu

Lewis, Lady Herbert — Folk Songs, Hu

Owen — Gems of Welsh Melody, Hu

Richards — Songs of Wales, BHks

Williams, W. S. Gynn — Welsh National Music and Dance, Hu

.... Welsh Melodies, BHks

FRENCH

°Tiersot — Sixty Folk Songs of France, OD

°Weckerlein (and others) — Echoes du Temps Passe, (A series of songs ranging from the twelfth to the sixteenth centuries), Durand et Cie, Paris

---

°Recommended by the author.

*Weckerlein (and others) — Echoes de France, (A series of songs ranging from the sixteenth to the eighteenth centuries), Durand et Cie, Paris

GERMAN

*Riemann (Editor) — Volumes I, II, III, and IV of Minnesinger Songs, (Folk songs, ballads, and some melodies of Bach and less well-known composers), Simrock, Berlin, Schott & Co.

---

*Recommended by the Author.

SEPARATE SOLO SONGS

(Sheet Music Editions)

A. RECOMMENDED SONGS FOR SPECIFIC VOICES

1. Vocal Solos from the 1961 Selective Music List of the National Interscholastic Music Activities Commission*

SOPRANO VOICE SOLOS

Grades I-II

Composer	Title	Publisher**
Besly	Second Minuet	BHks
Browning	Sleep, My Laddie, Sleep	HWG
Byars	The House Wren	HF
Cadman	Flowers of the Sun	Gal
Carpenter	The Sleep That Flits on Baby's Eyes	GS
Charles	Clouds	GS
Charles	When I Have Sung My Songs	GS
Clokey	The Rose	TP
Coombs	Four Leaf Clover	GS
Crist	Mistletoe	GS
Curran	Ho! Mr. Piper	GS
DeKoven	A Winter Lullaby	GS
Diller	How Your True Love To Know	CF
Dodson	Three Candles	BM
Edwards	By The Bend of the River	GS
Edwards	Stars of the Night, Sing Softly	GS
Fairchild	A Memory	BM
Giordani	Caro Mio Ben	GS
Guion	Mam'selle Marie	GS
Handel	Come Unto Him	GS
Handel	Thanks Be To Thee (in book)	GS
Haydn	Serenade	Wit
Ireland	If There Were Dreams to Sell	BHks
Kountz	Little French Clock	Gal
Mozart	Wiegenlied	TP,GS
Newman	Sicilian Lullaby	Wil
Niles	Black Is The Color of My True Love's Hair	GS
Niles	The Black Oak Tree	CF
Niles	Go Way From My Window	GS
Niles	I Never Had But One Love	CF
Paxson	Dodo (Lullaby)	HF
Reichardt	When The Roses Bloom	GS
Rogers	At Parting	GS
Schubert	Cradle Song	CF,GS,Wit
Scott	Blackbirds Song	Gal
Scott	The False Prophet	Hunt
Stanford	A Soft Day	Gal
Thayer	My Laddie	GS
Thompson	My Master Hath A Garden	GS
Thompson	Velvet Shoes	GS
Treharne	Corals	GS
Tschaikowsky	A Legend	GS
Walton	Song of Sleep	Leeds

*From "Selective Music Lists," Instrumental and Vocal Solos, 1961. Used by permission of the National Interscholastic Music Activities Commission of the Music Educators National Conference, 1201 Sixteenth Street, N.W., Washington 6, D.C.

**See p. 220 for "Key to Publishers."

Composer	Title	Publisher
Ward	The Roses' Cup	APS
Watts	Wings of Night	GS
Williams	Linden Lea	BHks
Wood	A Brown Bird Singing	Chap
Worth	Little Lamb	GS

Grades III-IV

Composer	Title	Publisher
Arlen	I Heard A Blackbird In A Tree	BHks
Arne	Polly Willis	CF,TP,GS,BHks
Barber	Sure, On This Shining Night	GS
Bassett	Take Joy Home	GS
Bax	I Heard A Piper Piping	Chap
Brahe	The Piper From Over The Way	Chap
Brahms	In Summer Fields	TP
Brahms	Sapphic Ode	CF,TP,GS
Bransen	Music of the Spring	Leeds
Bridge	Go Not, Happy Day	BHks
Browning	O Let Me Dream	GS
Cadman	A Redbird Sang In A Green Tree	Schu
Campbell	Wooden Ships	Gal
Carew	Love's Merchant	Chap
Charles	Let My Song Fill Your Heart	GS
Clokey	The Rose	TP
Coates	Bird Songs At Eventide	Chap
Coates	I Heard You Singing	Chap
Crist	April Rain	CF
Curran	Life	GS
Dougherty	Serenader	GS
Duke	The Bird (See Two Songs)	GS
Duke	Little Elegy	GS
Dungan	Can These Be Gone?	TP
Dungan	When I Sing Your Songs	TP
Dungan	When In My Heart	Ric
Dvorak	Songs My Mother Taught Me	CF,GS
Edwards	The Wild Rose Blooms	GS
Fenner	Spring Dropped A Song	Ric
Floyd	Ain't It A Pretty Night?	BHks
Floyd	Trees On The Mountain	BHks
Foote	An Irish Folk Song	APS
Giannini	Tell Me, Oh Blue, Blue Sky	Ric
Glen	The Mountain Linnet	BM
Godard	Chanson de Florian	GS
Goulding	Sweetest Moment	GS
Grieg	Solveig's Song	GS,Marks
Guion	The Hawk	CF
Hageman	The Night Has A Thousand Eyes	BHks
Hahn	Were My Songs With Wings Provided	GS
Haydn	Mermaids Song	TP
Head	Ships of Arcady	BHks
Homer	Sheep and Lambs	GS
Hopkinson	Beneath a Weeping Willow's Shade	TP
Hopkinson	My Love Is Gone To Sea	CF
Hue	To The Birds	BM
Kingsford	Comin' Thru The Rye	GS
Kingsley	The Green Dog	GS
Kramer	At Sunset	Gal
Lang	A Merry Roundley	BM
Lang	Spring Rhapsody	BM
Lehmann	If No One Ever Marries Me	BHks
Linley	No Flower That Blows	Row
Matthews	Night Song At Amalfi	EV

Composer	Title	Publisher
Maury	Some Girls Are Prettier	TP
McLain	My Choice	TP
Milkey	April Comes Early	BHks
Milligan	April, My April	APS
Moeran	The Lover and His Lass	N
Mozart	Non So Piu Cosa	GS
Niles	Careless Love	GS
Novello	Little Damosel	BHks
O'Hara	I Would Weave A Song For You	Wit
Perry	By The Sea	Gal
Peterkin	I Heard A Piper Piping	Ox
Purcell	Nymphs and Shepherds	TP,Ox,GS
Purvis	Discovery	EV
Quilter	Music, When Soft Voices Die	BHks
Rogers	The Time For Making Songs Has Gone	TP
Ronald	Down In The Forest	BHks
Ronald	O Lovely Night	BHks
Saar	The Little Gray Dove	GS
Sacco	Highland Song	BM
Salter	The Cry of Rachel	GS
Schubert	Faith in Spring	GS
Schumann	The Walnut Tree	AMP
Scott	Lullaby	Gal
Scott	Wailee, Wailee	TP
Serly	Forest Lullaby	Leeds
Shaw	Black Is The Color Of My True Love's Hair	TP
Shaw	He's Gone Away	TP
Shaw	If There Be Ecstasy	TP
Shaw	The Nightingale	TP
Shaw	Romance	TP
Singer	Folksong	CF
Spross	Will O' The Wisp	TP
Stevens	Barter	CF
Strickland	My Lover Is A Fisherman	TP
Thomas	A Maiden	GS
Tosti	Goodby	TP
Ware	Boat Song	TP
Weaver	Moon Harvesting	GS
Weaver	Praise The Lord	Gal
Wolf	The Old Woman	GS
Wolfe	Star of Courage	Baron
Woodman	An Open Secret	GS
Worth	Madrigal	Gal
Wragg	Song For Spring	Leeds

Grades V-VI

Composer	Title	Publisher
Bachelet	Chere Nuit	GS
Bantok	Silent Strings	BHks
Barber	Secrets of the Old	GS
Barraja	It Is May	Wit
Beach	Ah Love But A Day	APS
Beach	The Years At The Spring	APS
Bircsak	Hills of Spring	Pallma
Brahms	The May Night	GS
Brahms	Solitude In The Fields	APS
Campbell-Tipton	A Spirit Flower	GS
Castelnuovo-Tedesco	Recuerdo	CF
Charles	Remembrance	GS
Christie	Journey	TP
Clough-Leiter	My Lover He Comes On The Skee	BM
Creston	The Bird of the Wilderness	GS

Composer	Title	Publisher
Curran	Dawn.	GS
Curran	Rain.	GS
Delibes	Maids of Cadiz.	GS
Elgar	Pipes of Pan.	BHks
Gretchaninoff	Snowdrops	TP,BHks
Grieg	In The Boat	GS
Grieg	My JoHann	GS
Griffes	By A Lonely Forest Pathway.	GS
Guion	Love's Supremacy.	GS
Hageman	Do Not Go My Love	GS
Hageman	Fear Not The Night.	CF
Handel	Angels Ever Bright and Fair	TP,GS
Handel	Rejoice, O Daughter of Zion (in book)	GS
Harris	Winter.	Gal
Haydn	My Mother Bids Me Bind My Hair.	CF
Huerter	Until You Came.	TP
Klemm	Candles	CF
Kountz	The Sleigh.	GS
LaForge	No More Shall Sorrow.	CF
LaForge	Pastorale	Gal
Lie	Soft-Footed Snow.	BM
Liebling	Mother Dear	GS
Matthew	All Suddenly the Wind Comes Softly.	EV
Menotti	Lucy's Hello Aria	GS
Menotti	Lullaby (in book)	GS
Mozart	Alleluia.	TP,GS
Parks	Looking Across.	AMP
Puccini	Quando Mein Vo.	Blake
Purcell	Evening Hymn On A Ground.	N
Purcell	Hark the Echoing Air.	N
Rasbach	Mountains	GS
Raynor	The Loyal Lover	Ox
Roy	How Do I Love Thee.	GS
Rummel	Ecstasy	GS
Schubert	Du Bist Die Ruh'.	TP
Schubert	My Peace Thou Art	TP,GS
Scott	The Wind's In The South	Wil
Spross	Let All My Live Be Music.	Chap,TP
Turner	Enchanted Strings	BHks
Ware	Sunlight.	GS
Warren	Children of the Moon.	HF
Warren	When You Walk Through Woods	TP
Watts	Little Shepherd's Song.	Ric
Woodman	A Birthday.	GS

ALTO VOICE SOLOS

Grades I-II

Composer	Title	Publisher
Bartok	Tears of Autumn (in album).	GS
Brahms	Little Sandman.	CF,TP,GS
Brahms	Lullaby	TP
Branscombe	Blow Softly, Maple Leaves	HWG
Britten	The Ash Grove	BHks
Browning	Sleep, My Laddie, Sleep	HWG
Cadman	Lilacs.	TP
Carew	Everywhere I Look	Chap
Clayton	O Men From The Fields	BM
Del Riego	O Dry Those Tears	Chap
Del Riego	A Star Was His Candle	CF
D'Hardelot	I Know A Lovely Garden.	Chap

Composer	Title	Publisher
Diller	How Your True Love To Know	CF
Edwards	By The Bend of The River	GS
Edwards	Into The Night	GS
Elgar	Pleading	N
Faure	Aurore (in album)	GS
Forster	Rose In The Bud	Chap
Fox	My Heart Is A Silent Violin	CF
Franz	For Music	TP
Franz	Out of My Soul's Great Sadness	TP
Franz	Request	TP
Frazer	Only A Memory	BM
Gatty	Bendemeer's Stream	BHks
Greene	Sing Me To Sleep	BM
Hawley	Daisies	GS
Head	Star Candles	BHks
Huerter	Pirate Dreams	TP
Hulburt	Father We Thank Thee	Bourne
Kountz	Little French Clock	Gal
Manney	The Blue Hills Far Away	BM
Miller	Boats of Mine	HF
Moore	I Found A Flower	TP
Mozart	As Long As Children Pray	Wit
Mozart	Cradle Song	Wit
Mozart	Lullaby	Sy
Mozart-La Forge	Longing For You	Wit
Newman	Sicilian Lullaby	Wil
Niles	The Gambler's Wife	GS
Niles	The Lass From The Low Countree	GS
Quilter	Now Sleeps The Crimson Petal	BHks
Rasbach	Trees	GS
Reichert	In The Time of Roses	TP
Rich	American Lullaby	GS
Rogers	By The Sands of Old Dundee	TP
Rogers	Cloud Shadows	GS
Salter	The Pine Tree	GS
Schubert	Hedge Roses	CF,TP
Shaw	He's Gone Away	TP
Speaks	To You	GS
Taylor	Mayday Carol	JF
Thompson	Velvet Shoes	ECS
Willeby	Coming Home	TP
Woodin	Spring Is In My Heart Again	CMP
Woodman	I Am Thy Harp	GS

Grades III-IV

Composer	Title	Publisher
Brahms	Sapphic Ode	TP
Brewer	Fairy Pipers	BHks
Cadman	The Moon Behind The Cottonwood	GS
Carpenter	The Sleep That Flits On Baby's Eyes	GS
Carpenter	When I Bring You Colored Toys	GS
Cator	Pools of Quietness	GS
Charles	Sweet Song of Long Ago	GS
Charles	When I Have Sung My Songs	GS
Cox	To A Hilltop	APS
Curran	Nocturne	GS
Del Riego	Homing	Chap
D'Hardelot	Because	Chap
Duke	In the Fields	CF
Duke	Loveliest of Trees	GS
Dungan	Can These Be Gone?	TP
Dunhill	The Cloths of Heaven	Gal

Composer	Title	Publisher
Edwards	Evening Song	GS
Faure	The Cradles	BM
Ferrata	Night and The Curtains Drawn	JF
Franck	The Gathered Rose	TP
Franck	O Lord Most Holy	CF,BM,TP
Fraser-Simpson	Vespers	Chap
Gaul	Eye Hath Not Seen	GS
Gaul	Thou Art The Night Wind	TP
German	Charming Chloe	HWG
Giannini	There Were Two Swans	EV
Godard	Florian's Song	TP
Goulding	Sweetest Moment	GS
Gretchaninoff	Slumber Song	TP
Grieg	I Love Thee	CF,TP,GS
Grieg	Salveg's Leid	TP,GS
Grieg	A Swan	TP,GS
Guion	Pinto	CF
Hamblen	I Am Fate	TP
Handel	He Shall Feed His Flock	TP,GS
Handel	Where E're You Walk	CF,GS
Haydn	She Never Told Her Love	GS
Head	A Black Bird Singing	BHks
Head	Slumber Song of The Madonna	BHks
Hildach	Spring	CF
Homer	Sing Me A Song	GS
Horn	I've Been Roaming	TP,GS
Hughes	Kitty My Love	BHks
Hughes	O Men From The Fields	BHks
Keel	Trade Winds	BHks
Kernochan	Smuggler's Song	Gal
Kountz	The Sleigh	GS
Kramer	At Sunset	Gal
Kramer	Pleading	JF
Lully	Sombre Woods	BHks
Malotte	An Understanding Heart	GS
Malotte	A Little Song of Life	GS
Mana-Zucca	I Love Life	TP
Marriner	Exultation	TP
Martin	Come To The Fair	BHks
Martini	The Joys of Love	TP,GS
Mendelssohn	But The Lord Is Mindful Of His Own	TP,GS
Mendelssohn	Eye Hath Not Seen	TP
Mendelssohn	O Rest In The Lord	TP,GS
Mopper	Men	BM
Morgan	Clorinda	BHks
Niles	The Black Oak Tree	CF
Niles	I Wonder As I Wander	GS
Olmstead	Thy Sweet Singing	GS
Pergolesi	Nina	TP
Purcell	I Attempt From Love's Sickness To Fly	TP,GS
Purcell	If Music Be The Food Of Love	RDR
Quilter	June	BHks
Rachmaninoff	In The Silence Of Night	BHks
Rasbach	Overtones	GS
Reger	Virgin's Slumber Song	AMP
Repper	Where Lilacs Blow	Gal
Rogers	The Star	GS
Rogers	The Time For Making Songs Has Come	TP
Ronald	O Lovely Night	BHks
Sanderson	Break O'Day	BHks
Sanderson	Green Pastures	BHks

Composer	Title	Publisher
Sans Souci	Sing Again	APS
Schubert	Hark, Hark The Lark	TP,GS
Schubert	Linden Tree	CF,TP,GS
Schumann	The Lotus Flower	CF,TP,GS,Wit
Schumann	The Sandman	TP
Schumann	Thou Art So Like A Flower	AMP,CF,TP,GS
Secchi	When Two That Love Are Parted	BHks
Shaw	Black Is The Color Of My True Love's Hair	TP
Shaw	Romance	TP
Skiles	You Will Know My Love	CF
Taylor	Twenty-Eighteen	JF
Tharp	O Men From The Fields	Shawnee
Tschaikowsky	None But The Lonely Heart	TP,GS
Turner-Maley	Swift The Hours	TP
Tyson	Sea Moods	GS
Ware	Mammy's Song	TP
Warlock	As Ever I Saw	BHks
Watts	Blue Are Her Eyes	TP
Westherby	Danny Boy	BHks
Williams	Linden Lea	BHks
Williams, arr.	Phyllis Has Such Charming Graces	BHks
Youmens	Through The Years	TP

Grades V-VI

Composer	Title	Publisher
Bach	Bist Du Bir Mir	GS
Bach	My Heart Ever Faithful	TP,GS
Bach-LaForge	The Sheep Secure Are Grazing	CF
Bantock	Love's Secret	N
Brahms	May Night	GS
Brahms	Wie Melodien Zieht es Mir	TP,CF
Breuder	I Travel Alone	Bel
Bridge	Love Went A-Riding	BHks
Campbell-Tipton	The Crying of Water	GS
Campbell-Tipton	A Spirit Flower	GS
Carpenter	The Green River	GS
Clarke	Shy One	BHks
Debussy	Il Pleure Dans Mon Coeur	TP
Del Riego	Sun, Red Sun	Chap
Dichmont	Ma Little Banjo	GS
Dungan	Eternal Life	TP
Edwards	A Love Song	TP
Elgar	Is She Not Passing Fair	BHks
Foster	I Dream of Jeannie	CF
Fox	Hills of Home	CF
Franz	Abends	GS
Giannini	Sing To My Heart A Song	EV
Giannini	Tell Me, O Blue, Blue Sky	Ric
Grey	A Dream	TP
Griffes	By A Lonely Forest Pathway	GS
Hageman	At The Well	GS
Hageman	Music I Heard With You	Gal
Hageman	When I Am Dead, My Dearest	Gal
Handel	O Sleep, Why Dost Thou Leave Me	CF,TP,GS,Wit
Hayden	A Cypress Grove	Ox
Helms	Prairie Waters By Night	CF
Homer	Sheep and Lambs	GS
Hue	I Wept, Beloved	BM
Lalo	The Slave (in album)	CF,GS
Lehmann	Ah, Moon of My Delight	BM
Leoncavallo	Mattinata	Marks

Composer	Title	Publisher
MacDowell	Thy Beaming Eyes	TP
Montgomery	House With Nobody In It	Chap
Mozart	O Loveliness Beyond Compare	BHks
Murray	The Wandering Player	CF
Rachmaninoff	Lilacs	BM
Rasbach	Mountains	GS
Respighi	Nebbie	BM
Rogers	The Last Song	GS
Ronald	Prelude	BHks
Rosa	To Be Near Thee	Wit
Saint-Saens	Mon Coeur S'ouvre A Ta Voix	GS
Schubert	Der Erlkonig	Wit
Schubert	Maid of The Mill	GS
Schubert	Who Is Sylvia?	GS
Schubert	Wohin	GS
Schumann	Two Grenadiers	AMP
Scott	Think On Me	Gal
Serly	Let Us Haste To Kelvin Grove	SMC
Shaw	I'm Sad and I'm Lonely	TP
Sowerby	I Will Lift Up Mine Eyes	HWG
Sullivan	Take A Pair of Sparkling Eyes	Chap
Swift	Lullaby	BM
Touchette	My Glory	CF
Wagner	Traume	GS
Ware	This Day Is Mine	BM
Whitney	Nightfall	GS

TENOR VOICE SOLOS

Grades I-II

Arne	Preach Not Me Your Musty Rules	RDR
Bury	There Is A Lady	CF
Carpenter	May The Maiden	TP
Charles	My Lady Walks In Loveliness	GS
Charles	When I Have Sung My Songs	GS
Elgar	Is She Not Passing Fair	BHks
Handel-Somervell	Silent Worship	CF
Head	When I Think Upon The Maidens	BHks
Morgan	Clorinda	BHks
Purcell	Passing By	TP
Quilter	Now Sleeps The Crimson Petal	BHks
Schumann	Orpheus With His Lute	GS
Sinding	Sylvelin	GS
Sjoberg	Visions	Gal
Warlock	As Ever I Saw	BHks

Grades III-IV

Dello Joio	There Is A Ladye Sweet and Kind	CF
Duke	Evening	CF
Fox	Hills of Home	CF
Franck	Panis Angelicus	CF
Grieg	Ein Schwan	TP,GS
Grieg	Ich Liebe Dich	TP,GS
Handel	Where'er You Walk	TP,GS
Head	There's Many Will Love A Maid	BHks
Menotti	The Hero	GS
Niles	I Wonder As I Wander	GS
Rogers	The Star	GS
Schonberg	Erhebung (in album)	GS

Composer	Title	Publisher
Schumann	Thou'rt Lovely As A Flower	TP,GS
Warner	Hurdy Gurdy	CF
Wolf	Verborgenheit	GS

Grades V-VI

Campbell-Tipton	A Spirit Flower	GS
Handel	Comfort Ye (in book)	GS
Leoncavallo	Mattinata	Ric
Lie	Schnee	TP
Mendelssohn	If With All Your Hearts	GS
Mozart	Il Mio Tesoro	GS
Rossini	La Danza	GS

BARITONE-BASS VOICE SOLOS

Grades I-II

Andrews	Sea Fever	GS
Britten, arr.	The Ash Grove	BHks
Cadman	The Little Road to Kerry	TP
Cadman	The Song of The Mountains	TP
Charles	Oh, Little River	GS
Clarke	The Blind Ploughman	Chap
Dungan	Noonday Song	Gal
Flagler	Song of Ships	HF
Forsyth	Tell Me Not of A Lovely Lass	HWG
Fox	The Hills of Home	CF
Franz	Dedication	CF,TP,GS
Franz	Marie	TP
Gaul	On The Ragin' Canal	TP
Hawley	Molly's Eyes	TP
Homer	A Banjo Song	GS
Homer	Requiem	GS
Kennedy-Fraser	Road To The Isles	BHks
Kountz	What Shall I Ask?	Gal
Krouse	I Sing As I Sail	Wit
MacGimsey	Thunderin'-Wonderin'	CF
Martin	Wayfarer's Night Song	BHks
McCall	Westward Ho	Chap
Mineo	Jean	FM
Neidlinger	On The Shore	APS
Novello	A Page's Road Song	BHks
Old English	Drink To Me Only With Thine Eyes	BHks,TP
Robinson	Water Boy	BM
Salmon	Bells of The Sea	SF
Sanderson	Green Pastures	BHks
Schubert	Wanderer's Night Song	TP
Scott	The Old Road	GS
Shaw	Down By The Sally Gardens	GS
Speaks	Reveries	GS
Stanford	My Love's An Arbutus	TP,BHks
Stickles	The Open Road	TP
Watts	Blue Are Her Eyes	TP
Wellesley	Sing Me A Chanty	SF
Williams	Linden Lea	BHks
Williams	The Roadside Fire	BHks
Williams	Silent Noon (in album)	BHks
Wilson, arr.	The Sailor's Wife (Old English Melodies)	BHks
Wood	The Stars Looked Down	SF

Composer	Title	Publisher
Balfe	The Heart Bowed Down	TP
Bloomfield	Profundo's Delight	CF
Bury	There Is A Lady	CF
Cadman	The Builder	HF
Charles	Clouds	GS
Charles	The Sussex Sailor	GS
Charles	When I Have Sung My Songs	GS
Coburn	I'm Going A-Vagabonding	Pallma
Del Riego	Homing	Chap
Densmore	I Must Go Down To The Seas Again	BM
Dobson	Cargoes	GS
Duke	Loveliest of Trees	GS
Evans	I'm Neptune, King of The Sea	Cons
Flagler	Trader John	Harms
Forsyth	The Bellman	TP
Forsyth	God's Acre	CF
Foster	My Journey's End	GS
Franz	The Lotus Flower	TP
German	Rolling Down To Rio	HWG
Goreau	Shrimp Boy	Ric
Grieg	The Old Mother	TP
Griffes	An Old Song Resung	GS
Guion	Prayer	GS
Hamblen	The Restless Sea	TP
Hawley	Noon and Night	TP
Hodson	The Bold Banderlero	TP
Huhn	Courage	GS
Ireland	Sea Fever	Broude
Keel	Three Salt Water Ballads	BHks
Keel	Trade Winds	BHks
Kernochan	Smuggler's Song	Gal
Leoni	Tally Ho	GS
Lough	The Mendicant's Road Song	GS
Lully	Bois Epais	BHks
Malotte	The Homing Heart	GS
Malotte	My Friend	GS
Malotte	Up Stream	GS
Margetson	Tommy Lad	BHks
Menotti	The Hero	GS
O'Hara	I Have A Rendezvous With Life	Pallma
Paxson	The Rainbow Trail	GS
Perkins	The Good Ship Robador	Ric
Quilter	Go Lovely Rose	Chap
Robertson	The Jolly Roger	GS
Ronald	O Lovely Night	BHks
Sanderson	Friend O'Mine	BHks
Schubert	The Wanderer	GS
Scott	Soldier, Soldier, Will You Marry Me?	TP
Secchi	Love Me Or Not	BHks
Shaw	The Lamb	TP
Thompson	Velvet Shoes	Schu
Williams	Bright Is The Ring of Words	BHks
Wilson	Let Us Not Forget	Cons
Wilson	Pretty Creature	BHks

Grades V-VI

Composer	Title	Publisher
Allen	Eldorado	GS
Bach	Bist du Bei Mir (If Thou Be Near)	GS,Wit
Bridge	O That It Were So	Chap

Composer	Title	Publisher*
Buck	Sunset	GS
Cadman	The Brooklet	GS
Charles	My Lady Walks In Loveliness	GS
Dix	The Trumpeter	BHks
Handel	Thanks Be To Thee	JF
Henschel	Morning Hymn	CF, TP
Huhn	Invictus	APS
Lehmann	Myself When Young	BM
Liddle	How Lovely Are Thy Dwellings	BHks
Lippe	How Do I Love Thee	BM
MacDowell	The Sea	TP
Malotte	A Song of The Open Road	APS
Mendelssohn	Lord God of Abraham	TP
Moss	The Floral Dance	Chap
Mozart	Within These Temple Walls	BHks
Pergolesi	Nina	TP, GS
Peri	Invocazione di Orieo	TP
Russell	Vale	BHks
Sacco	Brother Will, Brother John	GS
Schubert	The Linden Tree	CF, GS
Schumann	Two Grenadiers	CF, TP, GS
Speaks	Shepherd, See Thy Horse's Foaming Main	HF
Spross	Let All My Life Be Music	TP
Tschaikowsky	Pilgrim's Song	GS
Verdi	Di Provenza Il Mar	GS
Walton	Mary	Leeds
Walton	Tang of The Sea	Harms
Wolfe	De Glory Road	GS

2. Songs Recommended for Specific Voices by Experienced Teachers and Vocal Authorities
 (NOTE - No German Lieder or French Impressionistic Art Songs are listed under this heading.)

SOPRANO

Composer	Title	Publisher*
Arne	The Lass with the Delicate Air	OD
Arne	Polly Willis	GS
Aylward	Deep in My Heart a Lute Lay Hid	Chap
Bantock	Yung Yen	Ric
Benkman	Silver Faun	GS
Bridge	O, That It Were So	Chap
Carew	Piper of Love	Chap
Carew	Tiptoe	Chap
Carmichael	Come and Trip It	BHks
Carpenter	Don't Ceare	GS
Carpenter	The Sleep That Flits on Baby's Eyes	GS
Chadwick	Song of the Robin Women (from "Shanewis")	GS
Coates	Bird Songs At Eventide	GS
Coombs	Four Leaf Clover	GS
Coombs	In the Dark, In the Dew	GS
Copland	I Bought Me a Cat	BHks
Copland	Long Time Ago	BHks
Curran	Ho! Mr. Piper	GS
Curran	I Know Rain	GS
Curran	Nocturne	GS
De Koven	A Winter Lullaby	GS
Diack	Little Jack Horner	Pat
Dungan	New Day	TP
Dunhill	Karoo Cradle Song	Mi
Dunhill	Snowdrops	Mi
Edwards	Gipsy Life	GS
Edwards	Out of the Dusk	GS
Edwards	The Song of the Brooklet	GS

*See p. 220 for "Key to Publishers."

Composer	Title	Publisher
Elgar	Moonlight	N
Elgar	Pleading	N
Gane	Joy	HWG
Gluck-Aslanoff	Fairest Maiden (L'adorable from "Iphignie in Aulis")	CF
Gorman	Love the Pedlar	BHks
Griselle-Young	The Cuckoo Clock	GS
Hadley	The Rose Leaves Are Falling Like Rain	GS
Handel	Care Selve (from "Atlanta")	BHks
Handel	The Elve's Dance	Pat
Handel	O Sleep, Why Dost Thou Leave Me (from "Semele")	OD
Hageman	Do Not Go My Love	GS
Hageman	Grandma's Prayer	GS
Hoffmeister	Wee Fiddle Moon	Hunt
Hopekirk, arr.	Turn Ye To Me	OD
Hopkinson	My Days Have Been So Wondrous Free	CF
Hopkinson	O'er the Hills Far Away	CF
Horsman	Bird of the Wilderness	GS
Horsman	In the Yellow Dusk	GS
Huerter	Pirate Dreams	TP
Kountz	Elf Dance	GS
Kramer	We Two	CF
Leoni	Little China Figure	GS
Leslie-Smith	Canterbury Fair	BHks
Martin	Wayfarer's Night Song	BHks
Maskowski	Springtime of Love	GS
Needham	Husheen	BHks
O'Hara	I Would Weave a Song For You	Wit
Olmstead	Thy Sweet Singing	GS
Reger	Virgin's Slumber Song	OD
Rich	American Lullaby	GS
Rogers	Cloud Shadows	GS
Rogers	Love's on the Highroad	GS
Salter	Come to the Garden Love	GS
Sanderson	The Valley of Laughter	BHks
Sarr	The Little Gray Dove	GS
Seiler	Butterflies	GS
Shaw, arr.	The Nightingale	TP
Sibelius	From the North	GS
Strickland	At Eve I Hear A Flute	GS
Tosti	Serenade	TP,GS
Treharne	A Widow Bird Sat Mourning for Her Love	GS
Veracini-A.L.	A Pastoral	BHks
Ware	From India	GS
Wells	The Elf Man	TP
Williams	Linden Lea	BHks
Woodman	My Dream Maker	GS
Young, arr.	Red Rosey Bush	CF
Zimbalist	Two Folk Songs of Little Russia	GS

ALTO OR MEZZO SOPRANO

Composer	Title	Publisher
Bantock	Wild Geese	Wi
Bantock	Yung Yang (Songs from the Chinese)	Ric
Barnett	A Caravan from China	GS
Bassett	Take Joy Home	GS
Bemberg	Hindoo Song	TP,GS
Bemberg	Nymphs and Fauns	GS
Berwald	Evening Song	OD
Carew	Tiptoe	Chap
Copland, arr.	Long Time Ago	BHks
Copland, arr.	Simple Gifts	BHks
Cox	To a Hill Top	GS
Del Riego	Homing	Chap
Davis, arr.	The Deaf Old Woman	Gal

Composer	Title	Publisher
Diack	Little Jack Horner	Pat
Dungan	Fish Seller	CF
Dunhill	Karoo Cradle Song	Mi
Dunhill	Snowdrops	Mi
Dunn	The Bitterness of Love	JF
Edwards	Evening Song	GS
Edwards	By the Bend of the River	GS
Elgar	Pleading	N
Elgar	Silent Noon	GS
Farley	The Night Wind	GS
Gretchaninoff	On the Steppe	OD
Grieg	I Love Thee	TP,GS
Grieg	In the Boat	TP,GS
Griffes	By a Lonely Forest Pathway	GS
Griffes	We'll to the Woods	GS
Guion	Mam selle Marie	GS
Guion	When You Smile	GS
Hageman	Grandma's Prayer	GS
Hadley	The Rose Leaves Are Falling Like Rain	GS
Handel	Dearest Lover (Cara Sposa)	Pat
Handel	Leave Me (From "Semele")	Pat
Handel	Weep No More	Pat
Hahn	The Green Cathedral	Ch
Hawley	Ah! 'Tis a Dream	GS
Hawley	Daisies	GS
Hawley	The Sweetest Flower That Blows	TP
Henschel	Morning Hymn	GS
Horsman	Bird of the Wilderness	GS
Horsman	In the Yellow Dusk	GS
Klemm	A Curious Thing	Gal
Kountz	Prayer of the Norwegian Child	GS
Kramer	We Two	CF
Lehman	Thoughts Have Wings	Chap
MacGimsey	Sweet Little Jesus Boy	CF
Manning	In the Luxembourg Gardens	GS
Manna-Zucca	The Big Brown Bear	GS
Menotti	The Hero	GS
Nevin	A Necklace of Love	TP
Old English	When Love Is Kind	GS
Protheroe	What Is Hid in the Heart of a Rose	OD
Rasbach	Debt	GS
Rasbach	Trees	GS
Rich	American Lullaby	GS
Rogers	Wind Song	GS
Roberton	All in the April Evening	Cur
Ronald	Down in the Forest	E
Salter	The Cry of Rachel	GS
Salter	The Pine Tree	GS
Sanderson	My Jewels	BHks
Sanderson	Quiet	BHks
Speaks	Little House o'Dreams	GS
Thayer	My Laddie	GS
Ware	Boat Song	TP
Ware	Hindoo Slumber Song	TP
Ware	Mammy's Song	TP
Ware	Joy of Morning	GS
Weatherly	Danny Boy	BHks
Whelpley	The Nightingale Has a Lyre of Gold	BM
Woodman	Ashes of Roses	GS
Young	The Cuckoo Clock	GS
Zimbalist	Chanson Triste	GS
Zimbalist	Two Folk Songs of Little Russia	GS

Composer	Title	Publisher
Bayly	Long Long Ago	TP
Bridge	E'en as a Lovely Flower	BHks
Bridge	Go Not Happy Day	BM
Brogi	Venetian Vision	Ric
Chadwick	Allah	APS
Clay	I'll Sing Thee Songs of Araby	GS
Clutsam	I Know of Two Bright Eyes	Chap
Coates	Bird Songs at Eventide	Chap
Coombs	In the Dark, in the Dew	GW
Coombs	Her Rose	GW
Copland (arr.)	Long Time Ago	BHks
Curran	Change o'Mind	GS
Curran	Nocturne	GS
De Rose	I Hear a Forest Praying	Chap
Dougherty	The Lady Who Loved a Pig	GS
Dungan	New Day	TP
Dunn	The Bitterness of Love	JF
Edwards	When I Am Gone Beloved	GS
Elgar	Pleading	N
Fontenailles	A Resolve	GS
Ford	A Prayer to Our Lady	Harms
Forrest (arr.)	He's Got the Whole World in His Hands	Mi
Fox	Hills of Home	CF
Fox	My Heart Is a Silent Violin	CF
Ganz	A Memory	GS
German	Charming Chloe	N
Glen	Twilight (Cello Obligatto)	BM
Guion	At the Cry of the First Bird	GS
Guion	The Cowboy's Dream	GS
Guion	Ride, Cowboy Ride!	GS
Handel	Total Eclipse (From "Samson")	Pat
Hadley	The Rose Leaves Are Falling Like Rain	GS
Hageman	Do Not Go My Love	GS
Hageman	In the Yellow Dusk	GS
Haydn	She Never Told Her Love	OD
Higgins	My Lovely Celia	BHks
Horsman	Bird of the Wilderness	GS
Horsman	In the Yellow Dusk	GS
Huhn	I Arise from Dreams of Thee	GS
Irish Folk	Down by the Sally Gardens	BHks
Klemm	A Hundred Little Loves	CF
Koemmenich	Was It in June?	GS
Kountz	The Sleigh	GS
Kramer	The Last Hour	Ch
Lehman	Ah Moon of My Delight (From "Persian Garden" cycle)	BM
Löhr	The Little Irish Girl	Chap
MacDowell	Thy Beaming Eyes	APS
Martin	Come to the Fair	BHks
McFeeters (arr.)	Hear the Nightingale Sing	Mi
McGill	Duna	BHks
Metcalf	Absent	APS
Morgan	Clorinda	BHks
Nevin	Little Boy Blue	BM
Nevin	When the Swans Fly	GS
Niles (arr.)	The Black Oak Tree	CF
O'Hara	Little Bateese	OD
Persichetti	I'm Nobody	EV
Piggot	Long Ago I Went to Rome	Mi
Protheroe	What Is There Hid in the Heart of a Rose	TP

Composer	Title	Publisher
Quilter	Now Sleeps the Crimson Petal	BHks
Rasbach	Trees	GS
Rogers	At Parting	GS
Rogers	The Time for Making Songs Has Come	TP
Russell	Young Tom O'Devon	Chap
Sanderson	Friend o'Mine	BHks
Shaw (arr.)	The Nightingale	TP
Sibelius	From the North	GS
Skiles	You Will Know My Love	CF
Smith	The Quest	Pond
Speaks	My Homeland	GS
Speaks	Over the Hills and Home Again	GS
Speaks	Sylvia	GS
Stanford	Trottin' to the Fair	BHks
Sullivan	Orpheus with His Lute	OD
Swedish Folk (arr. Burleigh)	The Dove and the Lily	Ric
Toselli	Serenata	BM
Tosti	A Vucchella	Ric
Weston	Lonesome Water	CF
Wilson	Phyllis Has Such Charming Graces	BHks
Wolfe	Betsey's Boy	GS
Wolfe	Short'nin' Bread	Flam
Wood	A Brown Bird Singing	Chap

BARITONE OR BASS-BARITONE

Composer	Title	Publisher
Bacon (arr.)	The Erie Canal	CF
Bantock	Wild Geese	Mi
Beethoven	In questa tomba oscura	OD
Bibb	Would God I Were a Tender Apple Blossom	GS
Boyce	The Song of Momus to Mars	Ox
Broadwood	Some Rival Has Stolen My True Love	BHks
Bush	The Eagle	TP
Cimara	Neath the Skies	GS
Charles	The Green Eyed Dragon	BHks
Charles	When I Have Sung My Songs	GS
Clay	Sands of Dee	GS
Coleridge-Taylor	Viking Song	TP
Copland (arr.)	Simple Gifts	BHks
Cowan	Border Ballad	BHks
Curran	Change o'Mind	GS
Day	Arise O Sun	Chap
Davis (arr.)	The Deaf Old Woman	Gal
DeKoven	Armorer's Song	GS
DeKoven	Prosit	GS
Densmore	I Must Down to the Seas Again	BM
Densmore	Roadways	TP
Dichmont	Ma Little Banjo	GS
Dix	The Trumpeter	BHks
Dobson	Cargoes	GS
Dungan	Fish Seller	CF
Dvorak-Fischer	Goin' Home	OD
Elgar	Pleading	N
Elgar	Silent Noon	GS
Edwards	The Fisher's Widow	GS
Flegier	The Horn	TP,GS
Forsythe	Tell Me Not of a Lovely Lass	N
Fox	Cowboy's Lament	GS
Fox	The Foggy Dew	GS
Fox	The Hills of Home	CF
Galloway	The Gypsy Trail	TP

Composer	Title	Publisher
Gilberte	Out of the Sweet Spring Night	CF
Griffes	An Old Song Resung	GS
Griffes	By a Lonely Forest Pathway	GS
Guion	The Cowboy's Dream	GS
Guion	Home on the Range	GS
Guion	Ride, Cowboy Ride	GS
Guion	Roy Bean	GS
Guion	What Shall We Do with a Drunken Sailor	GS
Hamblen	Celtic Fisher-folk Song	Chap
Hamblen	Restless Sea	GS
Hamblen	The Thief	Chap
Hammond	Pipes o'Gordon's Men	GS
Harris	The Wine Cup	GS
Hawley	Ah 'Tis a Dream	TP
Hawley	Singing of You	Ch
Hawley	Sweetest Flower That Blows	TP
Head	Ships of Arcady	BHks
Huhn	Invictus	BHks
Kernochan	Smuggle's Song	GS
Klemm	A Curious Thing	Gal
Koeneman	When the King Went Forth to War	GS
Kountz	Prayer of the Norwegian Child	GS
Kramer	We Two	CF
Leoni	Tally-Ho	GS
Lieurance	The Deserted Lodge	TP
Loewe	Edward	GS
Logan	Lift Thine Eyes	Ric
Lully	Sombre Woods (Bois épais)	BHks
MacDowell	The Sea	OD
McGill	Duna	BHks
Malloy	Punchinello	GS
Manna-Zucca	I Love Life	TP
Martin	Wayfarer's Night Song	BHks
Martini	The Joys of Love (Plaisir d'amour)	OD,GS
Neeham	The Fish Are in the Bay	GS
O'Hara	Give a Man a Horse He Can Ride	Hunt
O'Hara	Wreck of the Julie Plante	TP
Persichetti	I'm Nobody	EV
Piggot	Long Ago I Went to Rome	Mi
Protheroe	The Pilot	TP
Randolph	The Ragged Vagabond	Chap
Rasbach	Wanderer's Song	GS
Roberton	All in the April Evening	Cur
Roeckel	Happy Three	GS
Rogers	Boot and Saddle	GS
Russel	Young Tom O'Devon	Chap
Russian Folk Song	Song of the Volga Boatmen	GS
Salter	Remembrance	GS
Sanderson	Friend o'Mine	BHks
Sanderson	Quiet	BHks
Sanderson	Shipmates o'Mine	BHks
Sanderson	The Victor	BHks
Scott	The Old Road	GS
Skiles	You Will Know My Love	CF
Speaks	On the Road to Mandalay	GS
Speaks	Over the Hills and Home Again	GS
Speaks	Shepherd See Thy Horses Foaming Mane	HF
Speaks	Sylvia	GS
Stickles	The Open Road	TP
Sullivan	The Lost Chord	OD
Taylor	An Eating Song	JF

Composer	Title	Publisher
Taylor	An Eating Song	JF
Taylor	Captain Stratton's Fancy	GS
Tschaikovsky	Don Juan's Serenade	GS
Tschaikovsky	None But the Lonely Heart	GS., OD
Tschaikovsky	Pilgrim's Song	GS
Ward-Stephens	Fires	Chap
Watts	Alone	GS
Watts	Blue Are Her Eyes	OD
Weston	Lonely Water	CF
Whelpley	I Know a Hill	BM
Williams	Cavalier's Song	N
Wolfe	Betsey's Boy	GS
Wolfe	Blackberry Jam	TP
Wolfe	Sailormen	GS
Wolfe	Short'nin' Bread	Flam
Woodford-Finden	Kashmiri Song	BHks
Wood	When Dawn Breaks Through	Chap

B. List Nine of the American Academy of Teachers of Singing*

1. Songs for All Voices

OLD ITALIAN

Composer	Title	Key	Publisher**
Bononcini	Per la gloria d'adoravi	H.L.	OD
	(It. Anthol. Vol. II)		
		H.L.	GS
	(It. Anthol. Vol. II)	M.	GS
Caldara	Sebben crudele	H.L.	GS
	(It. Anthol. Vol. I)		
Giordani	Caro mio ben	H.M.L.	GS
	(It. Anthol. Vol. II)	M.	GS
	(It. Anthol. Vol. II)	H.L.	OD
		H.	CF
Paiseillo	Nel cor piu non mi sento	M.	GS
	(It. Anthol. Vol. I)		
	(It. Anthol. Vol. II)	H.L.	OD
Rosa	Star vicino	H.L.	GS
	(It. Anthol. Vol. I)	H.L.	OD
Sarti	Lungi dal caro bene	H.L.	GS
Scarlatti	O cessate di piagarmi	H.L.	OD
	(It. Anthol. Vol. II)		
	(It. Anthol. Vol. I)	M.	GS
Scarlatti	Sento nel core	H.L.	OD
	(It. Anthol. Vol. II)		

OLD ENGLISH AND FOLK

Composer	Title	Key	Publisher
Arne	Where the Bee Sucks	M.	GS
		H.M.L.	CF
		H.M.	OD
Bishop	Love Has Eyes	H.	GS
		M.	OD
		L.	Wit
Handel-Carmichael	Come and Trip It	H.L.	BHks
Irish Folk Song	Bendemeer's Stream	H.M.L.	BHks

---

*Used by permission. (The list presents what was felt to be only a representative sampling of available material most suitable for use, and was not intended to be inclusive in any sense.)

**See p. 220 for "Key to Publishers."

Composer	Title	Key	Publisher
Irish Folk Song....	.My Love's an Arbutus	M.L......	OD
Molloy	.Kerry Dance.	H.......	TP
		H.M......	OD
		H.L......	GS
Morley	.It Was a Lover and His Lass.	H.......	GS
		H.M......	OD
		H.......	TP
Morley	.Now Is the Month of Maying	H.......	GS
	(Reliq. Eng. Songs Vol. I)		
Munro..........	.My Lovely Celia.	H.L......	BHks
Purcell.........	.I Attempt from Love's Sickness	H.M......	GS
		H.L......	OD
Purcell.........	.Nymphs and Shepherds	H.M......	GS
		H.......	OD
Scotch Folk Song ...	.Turn Ye to Me.	M.L......	OD
Arr. Taylor......	.May Day Carol.	H.MH.Ml....	JF
Arr. Wilson......	.Ah Willow.	M.......	BHks
	(Collection)		
Arr. Wilson......	.Phyllis Has Such Charming Graces	H.L......	BHks

GERMAN LIEDER

Composer	Title	Key	Publisher
Beethoven........	.I Love Thee.	H.L......	GS
		M.......	CF
Franz..........	.Abends (Evening)	H.M......	GS
Franz..........	.Bitte (Entreaty)	H.L......	OD
		L......	Wit
Franz..........	.Widmung (Dedication)	H.M.L.....	GS
		M.......	CF
		H.L......	OD
Franz..........	.Gute Nacht (Good Night)	M.......	CF
		H.L......	OD
		L.......	Wit
Franz..........	.Marie.	M.......	GS
		H.L......	OD
Haydn..........	.She Never Told Her Love.	M.......	GS
Jensen	.Lehn Deine Wang.	H.L......	GS
		H.L......	CF
		H.L......	OD
Jensen	.Marie.	M.......	GS
		H.M......	OD
Mozart	.Warnung.	M.......	Aug
Reichardt........	.When Roses Bloom (In the Time of Roses).	H.M.L.....	OD,GS
		H.M.L.....	TP
Arr. Reimann	.Minnilied (Old German Folk Song)	M.......	Sim
Schubert	.Heidenröslein.	H.M.L.....	GS
		H.L......	CF
		H.M.L.....	OD
		M.......	TP
Schubert	.Who is Sylvia.	H.M.L.....	GS
		H.L......	CF
		M.......	TP
Schumann	.Die Lotusblume	H.L......	OD
		H.L......	CF
		H.M.L.....	GS
Schumann	.Du bist wie eine Blume	H.M......	GS
		H.L......	CF
		H.L......	OD
Schumann	.Volksliedchen.	H.L......	CF
		H.L......	OD

FRENCH

Composer	Title	Key	Publisher
Breton Folk Song	L'Angelus	M.L.	OD
Delibes	Bonjour Suzon	H.M.	GS
Martini	Plaisir d'Amour (The Joys of Love)	M.	TP
		H.M.	OD
		M.	GS
Massenet	Ouvre tes yeux bleu	H.M.L.	OD
		H.M.L.	CF
		H.M.	GS
Rousseau-Ferrari	Air sur trois notes	M.	Aug

AMERICAN, BRITISH AND GENERAL

Composer	Title	Key	Publisher
Aylward	House of Memories	H.M.L.	Chap
Branscome	I Bring You Heartease	H.M.	Sch
Brown	The Gift	H.L.	GS
Cadman	Land of the Sky-blue Water	H.ML.L.	WS
Chadwick	Allah	H.L.	Sch
Charles	Sweet Song of Long Ago	H.M.L.	GS
Clutsam	I Know of Two Bright Eyes	H.M.ML.L.	Chap
Cox	To A Hill Top	H.L.	Sch
Deis	Come Down to Kew	H.M.L.	GS
DeKoven	Winter Lullaby	H.M.	GS
D'Hardelot	I Know a Lovely Garden	H.M.L.	GS
Duke	Loveliest of Trees	M. or L.	GS
Edwards	Stars of the Night	H.M.	GS
Fairchild	A Memory	H. or M.	BM
Fox, J. Bertram	Wonder	H.L.	JF
Ganz	A Memory	H.L.	GS
German	Charming Chloe	H.	N
Gilberte	Two Roses	H.L.	CF
Klemm	Open My Eyes to Beauty	H.L.	Gal
Kountz	The Last Parting	L.	Gal
Kountz	A Sleepy Hollow Tune	H.M.L.	TP
Lehmann	Thoughts Have Wings	H.M.L.	Chap
Arr. Liebling	Lullaby of the Hills (Xmas)	M.	Gal
Maley	Fields of Ballyclare	H.M.L.	Hunt
Manning	In the Luxembourg Gardens	H.M.L.	GS
Martin	Come to the Fair	H.M.	BHks
Nevin	O That We Two Were Maying	H.M.L.	BM
Olmstead	If Love Were Like the Tune	L.	Gal
Rogers	At Parting	H.L.	GS
Rogers, J.	Cloud Shadows	M.	GS
Russell, K.	Vale	H.HM.L.	BHks
Russell, S. K.	Journey's End	H.M.L.	BHks
Sinding	Sylvelin	M.	TP
		M.	OD
		M.	CF
		H. or M.	GS
Scott-Perrenot	Think on Me	H.M.L.	Gal
Tosti	Serenata	H.MH.L.	Ric
		H.M.L.	CF
		H.L.	OD
Tschaikowsky	A Legend	M.	GS
Waring	Susan Simpson	M.	Sp-C
Whelpley	I Know a Hill	H.L.	BM
Woodman	I Am Thy Harp	H.L.	GS

2. Songs for Female Voice

Composer	Title	Key	Publisher
Arr. by A.L.	Come Sweet Morning	H.M.L.	BHks
Arne	Water Parted from the Sea	H.	SB
Besly	Second Minuet	H.L.	BHks
Besly	Three Little Fairy Songs	M.	Chap
Brahms	Sandman	H.L.	GS
		M.L.	OD
		M.	CF
Branscombe	Morning Wind	H.M.L.	APS
Carew	Love's a Merchant	H.M.	Chap
Carew	Sunday	H.L.	Chap
Chaminade	The Silver Ring	H.M.	GS
		H.M.L.	CF
		M.	TP
Chausson	The Charm		GS
	(Anthol. Modern French)		
Chopin	Maiden's Wish	M.L.	GS
		H.L.	CF
Clough-Leighter	Who Knows	M.	GS
Curran	Evening	H.L.	GS
Curran	Pastorale	H.L.	GS
DeKoven	Norman Cradle Song	M.	GS
Del Riego	Happy Song	H.M.	Chap
Durante	Vergin, tutta amor	M.	GS
Edwards	Little Shepherd's Song	H.M.L.	Mi
Farley	Night Wind	H.L.	GS
Foote	An Irish Folk Song	H.M.L.	APS
Foote	I'm Wearin' awa'	H.M.L.	APS
French Folk Song	Garden of Love		GS
(Arr. Ferrari)	(Collection)		
Gaul	Thou Art the Night Wind	H.L.	OD
German	Who'll Buy My Lavender	H.M.L.	BHks
Giorni	Cradle Song	M.	GS
Godard	Chanson de Florian (Florian's Song)	H.M.L.	GS
		H.L.	OD
		H.L.	CF
		H.	TP
Gretchaninoff	Slumber Song	H.L.	OD
		H.L.	CF
Grieg	First Primrose	H.L.	OD
		H.L.	CF
Guion	Mam'selle Marie	M.	GS
Hadley	My Shadow	M.	APS
Hahn	Si mes vers	H.M.L.	GS
		H.M.L.	CF
		H.M.	OD
		H.M.	TP
Handel	Here Amid the Shady Woods	H.	OD
	(Musicians Library)		
Haydn	Mermaid's Song	M.	TP
Head	Ships of Arcady	H.L.	BHks
Horn	I've Been Roaming	H.M.L.	OD
		M.	GS
Huerter	Pirate Dreams	H.M.L.	OD
Klemm	Little Moon	M.L.	OD
Klemm	The Little French Clock	H.L.	Gal
Klemm	Prayer of a Norwegian Child	M.L.	GS
Klemm	A Robin Sings in the Elmwood Tree	H.L.	GS
Lalo	L'Esclave	L.	GS
		H.L.	OD
		H.L.	CF

Composer	Title	Key	Publisher
Lang	Day is Done	H.M.L.	APS
Leoni	Birth of Morn	H.M.L.	Chap
Leoni	The Brownies	H.L.	BHks
MacDowell	The Blue Bell	M.	GS
MacDowell	The Clover	M.	GS
Mendelssohn	On Wings of Song	M.	GS
		H.	TP
		H.L.	CF
		H.M.	OD
Miller	Boats of Mine	H.M.L.	HF
Moore, Francis	Swing Song	H.L.	Hunt
Mozart	Voi che sapete (Marriage of Figaro)	M.	GS
		M.	OD
Mozart	Wiegenlied	H.M.	CF
		M.	TP
		H.	OD
		H.M.	GS
Neidlinger	Serenade	H.M.L.	GS
Arr. Paxson	Do-Do (Lullaby, Folk Song of the Pyrenees)	M. or L.	HF
Pelletier	In the Dark, in the Dew	H.M.	BM
Pergolesi	Se tu m'ami	H.M.	GS
Powers	The Night Has a Thousand Eyes	L.	Schu
Reger	The Virgin's Slumber Song	H.MH.M.L.	OD
Ronald	Love's on the Highroad	H.L.	GS
Ronald	Sunbeams	H.M.L.	BHks
Russell, S.K.	An Autumn Road	M.	Gal
Salter	Remembrance	M.L.	GS
Sans Souci	When Love is Sweet	H.M.ML.L.	Sch
Schubert	Cradle Song	H.M.L.	GS
		H.L.	CF
		M.	TP
		H. or M.	Wit
Strickland	My Lover is a Fisherman	H.L.	OD
Thayer	My Laddie	H.L.	GS
Thomas	Connais-tu ("Mignon")	M.	TP
		H.M.L.	GS
		H.M.	OD
		H.M.L.	CF
Vehanen	The Girl the Boys All Love (Finnish)	L.	Gal
Vehanen	Little Finnish Folk Song	L.	Gal
Ware	Boat Song	H.M.L.	TP
Wekerlin	Bergerettes		GS
	(Collection)		
Wekerlin	Willow Song		BHks
	(Collection)		
	(Collection)		GS
Wolff, E.	Fairy Tales	M.	GS
Woodman	April Rain	M.	GS
Woodman	Love's in my Heart	H.M.L.	GS

3. Songs for Male Voice

Composer	Title	Key	Publisher
Beethoven	In Questa Tomba	M.L.	GS
		L.	OD
Brahe	I Passed by Your Window	H.HM.L.	BHks
Branscombe	At the Postern Gate	H.M.	Sch
Arr. Burleigh	Hard Trials	M.	Ric
Arr. Burleigh	My Lord, What a Morning	H.L.	Ric
Bury	There is a Ladye	H.L.	CF

Composer	Title	Key	Publisher
Carpenter.	May the Maiden	H.L.	OD
Coates	Bird Songs at Eventide	H.M.	Chap
Densmore	I Must Go Down to the Sea Again.	H.M.L.	BM
Densmore	Roadways	M.L.	OD
Arr. Dett.	I'm So Glad Trouble Don't Last Always.	M.	TP
Dichmont	My Little Banjo.	H.M.L.	GS
Fisher, H.	Sittin' Thinkin'	H.M.L.	BHks
Fisher, Wm. A.	Under the Rose	H.M.L.	OD
Forsyth.	Tell Me Not of a Lovely Lass	L.	HWG
Foster	Carry Me Along	H.L.	CF
Fox, O.	Hills of Home.	H.MH.ML.L.	CF
German	Rolling Down to Rio.	H.M.	HWG
Gleeson.	The Little Hills	H.L.	Hunt
Handel	Ask If Yon Damask Rose	H.	Gal
Handel	Where'er You Walk.	H.L.	GS
		M.	JF
		H.L.	CF
		H.L.	OD
Harris, V.	A Man's Song	H.M.L.	GS
Harris, V.	The Hills of Skye.	H.L.	OD
Hatton	Tilda.	L.	BHks
Hawley	Noon and Night	H.M.L.	TP
Homer.	Banjo Song	H.M.L.	GS
Homer.	Requiem.	H.L.	GS
Huhn	Cato's Advice.	L.	GS
Huhn	Invictus	H.M.L.	APS
Huhn	A Secret from Bacchus.	H.M.L.	GS
Ireland.	Sea-Fever.	H.M.ML.L.	Aug
Keel	Trade Winds.	M.L.	BHks
Lehmann.	Myself When Young.	M.L.	BM
Margetson.	Tommy Lad.	H.M.ML.L.	BHks
McGill	Duna	H.HM.L.	BHks
Messager	Long Ago in Alcala	H.L.	GS
Messager	Maison grise	H.M.	Chap
Morgan	Clorinda	H.L.	BHks
Paine.	Matin Song	H.L.	OD
Pergolesi.	Nina	H.M.L.	GS
		H.M.L.	OD
Pessard.	L'Adieu du Matin	M.	OD
		H.M.L.	GS
Purcell, E.	Passing By	H.M.L.	GS
		H.L.	CF
		H.M.L.	OD
Radecke.	Aus der Jugendzeit	M.L.	CF
		M.	GS
Richardson, T.	Mary	H.M.L.	OD
Arr. Robinson.	Water Boy.	L.	BM
Russell, K.	Poor Man's Garden.	H.M.L.	BHks
Sanderson.	Green Pastures	L.	BHks
Schumann	Two Grenadiers	H.L.	OD
		H.L.	CF
		H.M.L.	GS
Scott.	The Old Road	H.L.	GS
Secchi	Love Me or Not	H.L.	BHks
Somervell.	A Kingdom by the Sea	M.L.	BHks
Speaks	Sylvia	H.M.ML.	GS
Speaks	To You	H.M.L.	GS
Stephenson	Ships that Pass in the Night	M.L.	BHks
Tosti.	Mattinata.	H.M.L.	GS
		H.M.L.	Ric
Vernon, Jos.	When That I Was.	H.L.	OD

(Musician's Library)

253

C. A List of Songs for High School Vocal Contests (or Solo Literature)

This list is compiled by the National Association of Teachers of Singing, Inc., Committee on Vocal Affairs, under the direction of the Advisory Committee on Vocal Education of the National Association, and is used by permission.

NOTE – Capital letters for keys indicate major, and small letters minor. In listing the range, capital letters are used for pitch names on the staff, and small letters for notes above or below the staff. Letters indicating the voices that might use the song are listed: S - Soprano, M - Mezzo, C - Contralto, T - Tenor, Bar - Baritone, and B - Bass. Volumes of songs are mentioned only when a song seems more readily available in certain keys in a collection than elsewhere.

Composer	Title	Keys	Voices	Publishers*
A. L. (arr.)	Come Sweet Morning	G(E-g or b♭)E,D	SMC	BHks
Bacon	The Erie Canal	d(d-C)	Bar B	CF
Barber	Daisies	F(c-F)D**	SMCT Bar	GS
Barber	Sure on This Shining Night	B♭(d-g)G	SMT Bar	GS
Bax	I Heard a Piper Piping	g(d-g)e	SM	Ox
Bishop	Love Has Eyes	B♭(F-g)F***	All	GS,TP,Wit
Brahe	As I Went A-Roaming	B♭(F-g)A♭G	SM	BHks
Brahms	The Little Sandman	B♭(F-g)G	SMC	GS
Brahms	The Little Sandman	G,E		TP
Brahms	(The Little Dustman)	G		CF
Brewer	The Fairy Pipers	C(F-g)B♭,A,G	SMC	BHks
Britten	The Ash Grove	A♭(d -F)F	All	BHks
Britten	O Can Ye Sew Cushions	A♭(E♭-a♭)	S	BHks
Bury	There Is a Lady	G(E-g)E	T Bar	CF
Buzzia-Peccia	Under the Greenwood Tree	A(E♭-a)G,F	SMT	TP
Carew	Love's a Merchant	F(d-a)E♭	S	Chap
Carpenter	The Green River	B(b-E)	M Bar	GS
Carpenter	The Sleep That Flits on Baby's Eyes	D(b-F♯)	SMT	GS
Cator	The Pool of Quietness	C(E♭-E)	M Bar	GS
Charles	Clouds	D♭(F-a♭)B♭,A♭	All	GS
Charles	Let My Song Fill Your Heart	D♭(C-E♭,g♭ or a♭)	SM	GS
Charles	When I Have Sung My Songs	F(d-g)D♭	All	GS
Clokey	The Rose	D♭(E♭-g♭)B****	SM	TP
Coates	Bird Songs at Eventide	B♭(F-g or b♭)G	SMCT Bar	Chap
Cox	To a Hilltop	E(E-g♯)D,C	SMCT Bar	APS
Dann	Whenever My Mary Goes By	G(D-g)	T	BHks
Deis	Come Down to Kew	G(d-F♯ or a)F,D	All	GS
DeKoven	A Winter Lullaby	B♭(d-F)A♭	SM	GS
Delibes	Bonjour Suson	F(c-F)E♭	All	GS
Densmore	Roadways	C(c-F)B♭	T Bar	TP
Dichmont	Ma Little Banjo	G♭(G♭-E♭)E	T Bar B	GS
di Nogero	My Love's a Dashing Muleteer	B♭(d-g)A♭	SM	APS
Dobson	Cargoes	F(d-F)E♭	T Bar B	GS
Dolmetch, arr.	Have You Seen but a Whyte Lillye Grow	F(E-F)D*****	T Bar	Wit
Dougherty	Across the Western Ocean	D(d-D)	Bar B	GS
Dougherty	Blow Ye Winds	C(c-D)	Bar B	GS
Dougherty	Bring My Lulu Home	B♭(c-E)	Bar	GS
Dougherty	Colorado Trail	E♭(c-E♭)	Bar B	GS
Douglas	Give Me a Ship	C(c-F)B♭	Bar B	CF
Elliot	Spring's a Lovable Lady	A(f♯-a)G,F,E♭	T Bar	Wit
Edmunds	Every Night When the Sun Goes In	F(c-F)D	All	BM
Edmunds	Jesus, Jesus, Rest Your Head	G(d-G)E♭,C	All	BHks
Edwards	Into the Night	G(G-F or g)F, E♭	All	GS
Edwards	By the Bend of the River	G♭(G♭-a♭ or b♭)E♭,C	All	GS
Engel	Sea Shell	G♭(E♭-E♭)	MCT Bar	GS

*See p. 220 for "Key to Publishers."
**In New Anthology of American Song (GS). Key of D in low voice edition.
***In Pathways of Song, Volume III (Wit). Key of F in low voice edition.
****In Art Songs, First Year (TP). Key of F in low voice edition.
*****In Pathways of Song, Volume III (Wit). Key of F in low voice edition.

Composer	Title	Keys	Voices	Publishers
Foote.	I'm Wearin' Awa'	D♭(d♭-F)B♭	All. . . .	APS
Forsyth. . . .	Tell Me Not of a Lovely Lass	C(c-C).	B. . . .	HWG
Forsyth. . . .	The Bellman.	G(E-g)E♭	T Bar. .	TP
Franz.	Dedication	A♭(E♭-F)G♭	All. . .	TP
Franz.	Dedication	A♭,F,E♭	All. . .	GS
Franck	Panis Angelicus.	A♭(A♭-F)F,D♭	All. . .	CF
Franck	Panis Angelicus.	G,E♭	All. . .	Wit*
Ganz	A Memory	G(E-g)D	All. . .	GS
Gatty.	Bendemeer's Stream	C(G-g)A♭,F. . . .	All. . .	BHks
Gaul	Eye Hath Not Seen. . . .	B♭(d-F)G. . . .	MC . . .	GS
German	Rolling Down to Rio. . . .	a(a-E)g	Bar B. .	HWG
German	Who'll Buy My Lavender	E(E-g♯)D,C. . . .	SMC. . .	BHks
Giordani . . .	Caro Mio Ben	F(E-g)E♭,C. . . .	All. . .	GS
Giordani . . .	Caro Mio Ben	E♭,D. . . .	All. . .	TP
Giordani . . .	Caro Mio Ben	E♭. . . .	All. . .	CF
Godard	Florian's Song	D(d-F♯)B. . . .	SMC. . .	TP
Godard	Florian's Song	D,C	SMC. . .	GS
Godard	Florian's Song	D,C	SMC. . .	CF
Gounod	Sing, Smile, Slumber	G(d-a)F,E♭. . . .	SM . . .	
Gretchaninoff.	Slumber Song	E(b or d♯-g♯)C. . .	SMC. . .	CF
Gretchaninoff.	Slumber Song	E,C . . .	SMC. . .	TP
Guion.	Mamselle Marie	E(d-E). . . .	M. . . .	GS
Handel	Where E'er You Walk. . . .	B♭(F-g)G. . . .	T Bar. .	TP
Handel	Where E'er You Walk. . . .	B♭,G. . . .	T Bar. .	CF
Handel	Where E'er You Walk. . . .	B♭,G,F. . . .	T Bar. .	GS
Handel	Where E'er You Walk. . . .	G♭(with recit.) . . .	T Bar. .	JF
Haydn.	Mermaid's Song	C(c-F). . . .	SM . . .	TP
Haydn.	My Mother Bids Me Bind My Hair	A(E-E)G	SMC. . .	CF
Haydn.	My Mother Bids Me Bind My Hair	A	SMC. . .	GS
Haydn.	My Mother Bids Me Bind My Hair	A	SMC. . .	TP
Head	When I Think Upon the Maidens. . . .	E♭(d-g)C. . . .	T Bar. .	BHks
Heurter. . . .	Pirate Dreams.	A♭(E♭-a♭)G♭,E♭. . .	SMC. . .	TP
Homer.	Sheep and Lambs. . . .	A♭(c-F♯)G♭. . . .	SMCT Bar	GS
Horn.	I've Been Roaming. . . .	F(E-a)E♭,C. . . .	SMC. . .	TP
Horn.	I've Been Roaming. . . .	E♭. . . .	SMC. . .	GS
Horn.	I've Been Roaming. . . .	D	SMC. . .	Ox
Hughes	Down By the Sally Gardens. . . .	E♭(E♭-F)D♭. . . .	SMT Bar.	BHks
Hughes	I Know My Love	F(c-F)E♭. . . .	SM . . .	BHks
Hughes	I Know Where I'm Going	A♭(G-E♭)G	SMC. . .	BHks
Ireland. . . .	Sea Fever.	a(E-g)g,f,e	T Bar B.	Aug
Keel	The Port of Many Ships . . .	d(c-E♭)	Bar B. .	BHks
Lang	A Merry Roundelay	G(d-b). . . .	S. . . .	BM
Lehman	If No One Ever Marries Me. . . .	D(d-a or F♯)C . . .	SM . . .	BHks
Liddle	An Old French Carol. . . .	F(F-F)D♭. . . .	All. . .	BHks
Liebling . . .	Mother Dear.	G(d-d). . . .	S. . . .	GS
Lully (A.L.) .	Sombre Woods	F(d-F)E♭. . . .	MC Bar B	BHks
MacDowell. . .	Thy Beaming Eyes	F(c-F)E♭. . . .	T Bar. .	APS
MacFayden. . .	Home	D(E-F♯)C♭	SMT Bar.	GS
Manning. . . .	In the Luxembourg Gardens. . . .	G(d-F♯)E♭	All. . .	GS
Martin	Wayfarer's Night Song. . . .	F(F-g or F)E♭,D . . .	T Bar B.	BHks
Martini. . . .	The Joys of Love	G(d-a)F	T Bar. .	GS,TP
Martini. . . .	The Joys of Love	F,E♭	T Bar. .	GS
Massenet . . .	Open Thy Blue Eyes	F(c-g)E♭	SMT Bar.	GS
Massenet . . .	Open Thy Blue Eyes	G,F,E♭	SMT Bar.	CF
Massenet . . .	Open Thy Blue Eyes	G,F	SMT Bar.	TP
Mendelssohn. .	On Wings of Song	A♭(E♭-F). . . .	All. . .	CF
Mendelssohn. .	On Wings of Song	A♭,F. . . .	All. . .	TP
Mendelssohn. .	On Wings of Song	A♭. . . .	All. . .	GS
Morgan	Clorinda	a(E-g)f	T Bar B.	BHks

*In Pathways of Song, Volume III (Wit).   Key of F in low voice edition.

Composer	Title	Keys	Voices	Publishers
Mozart	Cradle Song (Lullaby)	G(G-g)F	SM	GS
Mozart	Cradle Song (Lullaby)	G,F	SM	CF
Mozart	Voi Che Sapete	B♭(c-F)A♭	MC	CF
Mozart	Voi Che Sapete	B♭,A♭	MC	TP
Mozart	Voi Che Sapete	B♭,A♭	MC	GS
Munro	My Lovely Celia	G(d-g)E	T Bar.	B
Needham	Four Ducks on a Pond	F(c-F)D♭	All.	Shu
Newman	Sicilian Lullaby	F(c-F)	M.	Wil
Niles	Go Way from My Window	E♭(c-g)C	SMC.	GS
Niles	I Wonder as I Wander	C(E♭-g)G	All.	GS
Niles	Oh Waly Waly	f#(c#-F#)	SMT Bar.	CF
Novello	The Little Damozel	G(d-a)F,E♭,D	SMC.	BHks
Pennington	Come Along and Dance	D(d-g)C,B♭	SMT Bar.	CF
Pergolesi	If Thou Lov'st Me	g(c-g)f	SM	GS
Pergolesi	Nina	g(F-g)e,d	T Bar B.	GS
Pergolesi	Nina	f#,e,d	T Bar B.	TP
Purcell, E.	Passing By	A(F#-F#)G,F	T Bar.	TP
Purcell, E.	Passing By	A,D	T Bar.	CF
Purcell, E.	Passing By	A,G,E♭	T Bar.	GS
Purcell, H.	I Attempt from Love's Sickness to Fly	G(c#-E)	MC Bar B	GS
Purcell, H.	I Attempt from Love's Sickness to Fly	G,F	MC Bar B	TP
Purcell, H.	Nymphs and Shepherds	G(d-g)F	SM	GS
Purcell, H.	Nymphs and Shepherds	G	SM	Ox
Purcell, H.	Nymphs and Shepherds	G	SM	TP
Reger	Virgin's Slumber Song	A♭(A♭-a♭)G,F,E♭,D♭	SMC.	AM
Reichardt	In the Time of Roses	G(F#-g)E♭,D♭	All.	TP
Reichardt	In the Time of Roses	G,E♭,C	All.	GS
Reichardt	In the Time of Roses	G,E♭	All.	CF
Quilter	O Mistress Mine	G(d-g)G♭,E♭	T Bar.	BM
Robinson	Water Boy	e(d-D)	Bar B.	BM
Sacco	Brother Will, Brother John	F(c-F)	Bar.	GS
Sacco	Highland Song	G(d-g)	S.	BM
Sanderson	A Blackbird's Song	E♭(E♭-a♭ or b♭)	S.	BHks
Sanderson	Green Pastures	G(d-g)E♭	All.	BHks
Schubert	Cradle Song	A♭(E-F)F	SMC.	CF
Schubert	Cradle Song	A♭,G,F	SMC.	GS
Schubert	Hedge Roses	G(G-g)E	All.	TP
Schubert	Hedge Roses	G,E,D	All.	GS
Schubert	Hedge Roses	G,E	All.	CF
Schubert	Who Is Sylvia	A(E-F#)G,F	T Bar B.	GS
Schubert	Who Is Sylvia	G	T Bar B.	TP
Schubert	Who Is Sylvia	A, G	T Bar B.	CF
Schumann	The Lotus Flower	F(c-g)E♭,D♭	All.	GS
Schumann	The Lotus Flower	F	All.	TP
Schumann	Thou Art Like a Flower	A♭(G-F)G♭	T Bar B.	GS
Schumann	(Thou'rt Lovely as a Flower)	A♭,E	T Bar B.	TP
Schumann	(A Flower to Me Thou Seemest)	A♭	T Bar B.	CF
Scott	Lullaby	F(d-F)E♭,D♭	SMC.	Gal
Scott	The Blackbird's Song	F(d-g)E♭,D	SMT Bar.	Gal
Secci, arr.A.L.	Love Me or Not	G(d-a)E	SMT Bar.	BHks
Shaw	Black Is The Color of My True Love's Hair	f(c-F)	M Bar.	TP
Speaks	The Night Has a Thousand Eyes	C(G-F)A	All.	GS
Spross	Sunrise and Sunset	B♭(F-F)E	All.	TP
Stanford	My Love's An Arbutus	A♭(E♭-F)F	All.	TP
Stickles	Shepherd Play a Little Air	G(d-g)E♭	SM	HF
Storace-Wilson	The Pretty Creature	F(c-D or F)	Bar B.	BHks
Sullivan	The Moon and I (Mikado)	G(d-g)	S.	CF
Sullivan	When I Was a Lad (Pinafore)	F(c-F)B♭	Bar B.	TP
Tarrasch	Early One Morning	E(b-E)	M Bar.	CF
Taylor	The Loyal Lover	a(d-E)g	MC	JF
Taylor	Twenty-Eighteen	A♭(E♭-F)	T Bar.	JF

Composer	Title	Keys	Voices	Publishers
Thompson	Velvet Shoes	F(c-e)	M Bar.	ECS
Tosti.	Serenade	F(E-F)E♭,C.	T Bar B.	GS
Tosti.	Serenade	F,C	T Bar B.	CF
Tosti.	Serenade	C	T Bar B.	TP
Veracini	A Pastoral	F(c-g or a)E♭	S.	BHks
Veracini	A Pastoral	F	S.	GS
Warlock.	Yarmouth Fair.	G(d-g)E	T Bar.	Ox
Watts.	Blue Are Her Eyes.	f(F#-F#)d	SMT Bar.	TP
Wellesley.	Sing Me a Chantey with a Yo-Heave-Ho	G(b-E)F,E♭	Bar B.	SF
Whelpley.	I Know a Hill.	f(F-F)c#	All.	BHks
Williams	Linden Lea.	A(E-F#)G,F.	All.	BHks
Wilson	Mary of Allendale.	E♭(E♭-a♭)	T.	BHks
Woodman.	I Am Thy Harp.	F(c or E-G)D♭	All.	GS
Young.	Red Rosey Bush	F(F-F).	SM	CF
Young.	The Sleepy House	D(d-g)C,B♭.	SMC.	GS

D. List of Songs Used in the Voice Training Classes of the Rochester, New York, High Schools.*
   (H-High, L-Low, M-Medium Voice)

FIRST YEAR SONGS

Composer	Title	Voice	Publisher**
Brahe.	Bless This House.	H.M.L.	By
Branscombe	Morning Wind.	L.	APH
Brownell	Four Leaf Clover.	M.	HF
Burleigh	Just You.	H. L.	Ric
Clutsam.	I Know of Two Bright Eyes	H.M.L.	Chap
Coates	Bird Songs at Eventide.	H.M.L.	Chap
D'Hardelot	I Know a Lovely Garden.	M.L.	Chap
Dichmont	Ma Little Banjo	M.	GS
Dickson.	Thanks Be to God.	M.L.	By
Edwards.	Bring Back the Days	M.	OD
Edwards.	By the Bend of the River.	H. L.	GS
Edwards.	With the Wind and the Rain in Your Hair	M.L.	GS
Farley	I Am the Still Rain	M.	GS
Forster.	Mifany.	H.M.L.	Chap
Guion.	How De Do, Miss Springtime.	H.M.L.	GS
Hawley	Sweetest Flower That Blows.	H. L.	GS
Howe	Berceuse.	M.	GS
Keel	Tradewinds.	M.L.	By
Kjerulf.	Last Night the Nightingale.	M.L.	CCB
Kountz	Little French Clock	M.	Gal
Leone.	Secret of the Stars	H. L.	GS
Leoni.	Birth of Morn	H. L.	GS
Lieurance.	By the Waters of Minnetonka	H. L.	TP
Lohr	Where My Caravan Has Rested	H.M.L.	Chap
Maley.	Fields of Ballyclare.	H. L.	Hunt
Mana-Zucca	Big Brown Bear.	M.L.	GS
McGill	Duna.	M.L.	By
Mills-Lamon.	My Ain Folk	M.	By
Moore.	Alpine Bird Song.	H.	BM
Murray	I'll Walk Beside You.	M.L.	Chap
Nevin.	'Twas April	M.L.	BM
Newman	Sicilian Lullaby.	M.L.	Wil
Niles.	I Wonder As I Wander.	M.	GS

---

*Used by permission of Alfred Spouse, Director of Music, Rochester, N. Y. Rochester is one of the pioneer school systems in the United States to install voice class work in the high schools. The work there covers three years and is widely recognized for the excellent results achieved. This is the 1953 list of the songs recommended by the various voice teachers in the system and not a personal recommendation by Mr. Spouse.

**See p. 220 for "Key to Publisher."

Composer	Title	Voice	Publisher
Norton	Madcap Marjorie	H.M.	Chap
O'Hara	Give a Man a Horse He Can Ride	M.L.	HF
O'Hara	Two Little Stars	H. L.	Hunt
Old English	Drink to Me Only	H.M.L.	GS,OD
Reichardt	In the Time of Roses	M.L.	OD
Rodgers	You'll Never Walk Alone	M.L.	Wil
Rogers	Cloud Shadows	M.	GS
Rooney	Clang of the Forge	M.	GS
Russell	Children of Men	M.L.	HF
Russell	Ever in My Mind	H.	By
Sanderson	Friend O' Mine	M.L.	By
Speaks	Prayer Perfect	H.M.L.	GS
Speaks	Sylvia	M.L.	GS
Stratton	From Out the Long Ago	M.L.	GS
Wood	A Brown Bird Singing	M.L.	Chap
Woodforde-Finden	Kashmiri Song	H. L.	By

SECOND YEAR SONGS

Composer	Title	Voice	Publisher
Arne	Water Parted from the Sea	M.L.	N
Barker	Daisies, The	M.	GS
Bartlett	Dream, A	H.M.L.	OD
Bates	On the Nodaway Road	M.L.	Wit
Beach	Ecstasy	M.L.	APS
Beethoven	I Love Thee	M.	Wit
Besly	Bend Low Thine Ear	M.L.	WR
Bishop	Bid Me Discourse	H.	GS
Bishop	Love Has Eyes	H.	GS
Borowsky	Adoration	M.	GS
Brahe	Piper from Over the Way, The	H.M.	CF
Brewer	Fairy Pipers, The	H.	By
Broome	Moon Melody	L.	GS
Burleigh, arr.	By and By	M.L.	Ric
Burleigh, arr.	Deep River	M.L.	Ric
Burleigh, arr.	Didn't It Rain	M.L.	Ric
Cadman	Builder, The	M.L.	HF
Cadman	From the Land of The Sky Blue Water	H.	WS
Cadman	I Hear a Thrush at Eve	H.M.	WS
Cadman	Moon Behind the Cottonwood	L.	GS
Cain	Longing	L.	By
Carew	Love's a Merchant	H.	Chap
Carpenter	May the Maiden	M.L.	OD
Charles	House on the Hill	H.	GS
Charles	Let My Song Fill Your Heart	H.	GS
Charles	Over the Land Is April	H. L.	Hunt
Charles	Wish, A	M.L.	GS
Clarke	Blind Ploughman, The	M.L.	Chap
Coates	I Heard You Singing	H. L.	Chap
Combs	Four Leaf Clover	M.L.	GS
Coryell	Contentment	H.M.L.	BM
Coryell	Japanese Lullaby	M.	GS
Cox	Roads Lament, The	M.L.	APS
Cox	To a Hilltop	H. L.	APS
Curran	Dawn	H.M.L.	GS
Curran	Ho! Mr. Piper	H.M.	GS
Del Riego	Homing	H.M.L.	Chap
Del Riego	Slave Song	H.M.L.	Chap
D'Hardelot	Because	H.M.L.	Chap
Dichmont	Red Rose	M.	CF
Diller	How Your True Love to Know	M.	CF
Dobson	Cargoes	M.L.	GS
Dodson	Three Candles	H. L.	BM

Composer	Title	Voice	Publisher
Dougherty	Across the Western Ocean	M.	GS
Duke	Loveliest of Trees	M.L.	GS
Edwards	Into the Night	M.L.	GS
Edwards	Lady Moon	H.	OD
Enders	Travelin'	M.L.	GS
Fisher	Sittin' Thinkin'	M.L.	By
Fisher	Spanish Gold	M.L.	By
Foster	All on This Perfect Night	H.M.	BM
Fox	Hills of Home	M.L.	CF
Fox	White Is the Moon	M.	CF
Friml	Indian Love Call	H.M.	Harms
Gaul	Thou Art the Night Wind	L.	OD
German	Rolling Down to Rio	M.L.	HWG
Giannini	Tell Me O Blue, Blue Sky	H. L.	GS
Giordani	Caro mio ben	H.M.L.	OD
Gleason	Yellow Hills, The	H. L.	Hunt
Grieg	I Love Thee	H.M.L.	GS
Grieg	The Swan	M.L.	OD
Guion, arr	De Old Ark's a-Movenin'	M.L.	GS
Guion, arr	Man'selle Marie	M.	GS
Hahn	Were My Songs with Wings Provided	H.	GS
Hageman	Night Has a Thousand Eyes, The	M.L.	BHks
Hamblen	Nightfall	H. L.	GS
Harrby	Colette	H.	By
Hawley	Noon and Night	M.L.	Ch
Head	Money Oh!	L.	By
Homer	Banjo Song, A	H. L.	GS
Homer	Requiem	H. L.	GS
Hue	To the Birds	H.	BM
Huerter	Pirate Dreams	M.L.	OD
Hughes	Kitty, My Love	H. L.	By
Huhn	Courage	M.L.	GS
Huhn	Invictus	H. L.	APS
Hullah	Three Fishers	M.L.	GS
Jalowicz	Slow, Horses Slow	L.	By
Jerome	Open Road, The	M.L.	Rem
Klem	An Annapolis Lullaby	M.	EHM
Klem	Child's Prayer	H.M.L.	GS
Kountz	Elf Dance	H.	GS
La Forge	Dairy Maids, The (encore)	M.	HF
La Forge	Kitty of Coleraine	H. L.	Wit
La Forge	Little Star	H. L.	Ric
Leone	Birth of Morn	M.	Chap
Leoni	Tally Ho	H. L.	GS
Loughborough	How Lovely Is the Hand of God	M.L.	OD
MacMurrough	Shepherdess, The	H.	By
Malotte	For My Mother	H.M.L.	GS
Manna-Zucca	I Love Life	M.L.	Ch
Manna-Zucca	Top o' the Morning	H. L.	Ch
Manning	In the Luxembourg Gardens	H. L.	GS
Manning	Shoes	H.	GS
Margetson	Tommy Lad	H. L.	By
Metcalf	Absent	M.L.	APS
Mercanto	Fairy Story by the Fire	H.	JF
Messager	Long Ago in Alcala	L.	Chap
Morgan	Clorinda	H.	By
Morrison	Watchmaker's Shop, The	M.	Hunt
Nevin	Little Boy Blue	H.M.	Wit
Novello	Page's Road Song	H.	By
Oliver	Fairy Shepherd, The	H.	CF
Phillips	Open Your Windows to the Morn	H.	Chap

Composer	Title	Voice	Publisher
Phillips	Sing Joyous Bird	H.M.	Chap
Rich	An American Lullaby	H. L.	GS
Roberts	Sandman Is Calling You	H.	JF
Robinson	Water Boy	M.L.	BM
Rogers	At Parting	H. L.	GS
Rogers	Star, The	H.	GS
Rosenberg	Complete Misanthropist, The	M.	Gal
Rotoli	Fiore che langue	H.	GS
Roy	This Lovely Rose	H. L.	GS
Russell	Children of Men	H.	HF
Salter	Pine Tree, The	L.	GS
Sanderson	Captain Mack	M.L.	By
Sanderson	Green Pastures	M.L.	By
Sanderson	Shipmates o'Mine	M.L.	By
Skerrit	One Day As I Was Walking	H.	GS
Speaks	Morning	H.M.L.	GS
Speaks	On the Road to Mandalay	H.M.L.	Ch
Spross	Will o' the Wisp	H.	TP
Stevens	Barter	H.	CF
Stevens	Autumn	M.	CF
Stratton	May Magic	H.	BM
Strauss	One Day When We Were Young	M.	Feist
Strickland	Ma Lindy Lou	H. L.	GS
Stuart	Entreaty	H. L.	BM
Taylor	Twenty-Eighteen	H. L.	JF
Taylor, arr.	May Day Carol	M.L.	JF
Terry	Answer, The	M.L.	GS
Toselli	Serenade	H. L.	Ric
Tosti	Serenade	H.	GS
Vaughn	June Is in My Heart	H.	TP
Wallis	Close of Day	M.L.	BM
Wells	Flying Cloud, The	M.L.	GS
Whelpley	Nightingale Has a Lyre of Gold, The	H. L.	GS
Wilson	Come Let's Be Merry	M.L.	GS
Wolf	I Hear the Call of the Road	M,	HF
Woodman	I Am Thy Harp	M.L.	GS
Yon	Jesu Bambino	H.M.L.	JF
Young	Red Rosy Bush	M.	CF

THIRD YEAR SONGS

Composer	Title	Voice	Publisher
Arditi	Il bacio (The Kiss)	H.	GS
Bach-Gounod	Ave Maria	H.M.L.	GS
Barraja	It Is May	H.	Wit
Beach	Ah Love, But a Day	H.M.	GS
Bellini	L'Ombra	H.	Ric
Bishop	Lo! Here the Gentle Lark	H.	TP
Brahms	Wie Melodien ziet es	H. L.	SF
Burleigh	Woods of Finvara, The	H.M.	Ric
Cadman	Call Me No More	H. L.	GS
Cambell-Tipton	Crying of Water, The	H.M.L.	GS
Cambell-Tipton	Spirit Flower	H.M.L.	GS
Carpenter	Sleep That Flits on Baby's Eyes	H.M.L.	GS
Chadwick	Danza, The	M.L.	APS
Charles	Speak Not in Hate	M.L.	GS
Coryell	Medlar Tree, The	M.	BM
Crist	Evening	H.	GS
D'Hardelot	Dawn, The	H. L.	Chap
D'Hardelot	Wings	H.M.	Chap
Del 'Aqua	Vilanelle	H.M.	GS
Elgar	Twilight	H.M.	Ric

Composer	Title	Voices	Publisher
Enders	Russian Picnic	H. L.	GS
Engel	Sea Shell	M.	GS
Gaines	Robin in the Rain	H.	CF
Gardner	At Sunset	H.M.L.	Ch
Gay	Rain, Rain, Rain	H.M.L.	By
Golia	To a Sleeping Child	M.	OD
Griffes	By a Lonely Forest Pathway	H.	CF
Guion	At the Cry of the First Bird	M.	GS
Guion	Ride, Cowboy, Ride	H.M.L.	GS
Hageman	At the Well	H.	CF
Hageman	Christ Went Up Into the Hills	H. L.	GS
Hageman	Little Dancers, The	M.L.	By
Handel	He Shall Feed His Flock (Messiah)	M.L.	GS
Handel	I Know That My Redeemer Liveth (Messiah)	H.	GS
Hughes	Ballynure Ballad, A	M.	By
Klemm	Listen to Life	H.	CF
Klemm	London Rain	H.	GS
Kramer	Crystal Gazer, The	H. L.	OD
Kramer	Faltering Dusk, The	H. L.	OD
Kramer	For a Dream's Sake	H. L.	JF
La Forge	When Thy Dear Hands	H. L.	GS
Lehmann	Ah Moon of My Delight	H.	By
Leslie-Smith	Salt Water	M.	By
Lie	Soft Footed Snow	M.	BM
Malotte	Homing Heart, The	H.M.	GS
Malotte	Lord's Prayer, The	H.M.L.	GS
Malotte	O the First Delight	H. L.	GS
Malotte	Twenty-Third Psalm, The	H.M.L.	GS
Manna-Zucca	Nichavo	M.L.	GS
Massenet	My Heart At Thy Sweet Voice (from "Samson and Delilah")	M.L.	GS
Mendelssohn	If With All Your Hearts (from "Elijah")	H.	GS
Mozart	Alleluia (Exultate Deo)	H.M.	GS
Nickerson	Lizette, My Dearest One	H.M.	CF
Noel	Pastourelles (Pastoureaux)	H.	Gal
Olmstead	Evening Song	M.L.	GS
Phillips	Open Your Windows to the Morn	H. L.	Chap
Protheroe	Ah Love, But a Day	H. L.	GS
Purcell	Nymphs and Shepherds	M.	GS
Schubert	Linden Tree, The	H. L.	CF
Schubert	Serenade	H. L.	GS,CF
Spross	Let All My Life Be Music	H.M.	GS
Spross	Will O' the Wisp	H.	APS
Spross	Yesterday and Today	H. L.	TP
Strauss	Devotion	H. L.	GS
Strauss	Dreams in the Twilight	H. L.	GS
Thomas	Knowest Thou the Land (from "Mignon")	M.	GS
Tyson	Like Barley Bending	H. L.	GS
Von Flotow	Ah, So Fair (from "Martha")	H.M.	GS
Ware	Day Is Mine, The	H. L.	BM
Ware	This Day Is Mine	H.M.	BM
Warren	Wander Shoes	L.	HF
Watts	Little Shepherd Song, The	M.	Ric
Weaver	Moon Marketing	H.M.	GS

261

E. Selected Songs by American and British Composers

  1. Three Hundred Songs by American Composers - Lists No. 1, 2, and 3 Combined, American Academy of Teachers of Singing*
     (H - High, M - Medium, L - Low Key)

Composer	Title	Key	Publisher**
Allen	Eldorado	L	GS
Ardayne	Had I a Golden Pound to Spend	H	GS
Ardayne	Love's Island	H	GS
Barber	With Rue My Heart Is Laden	H L	GS
Barlow	The Rose-Tree	H L	GS
Barnett	Boat Song	H	GS
Barnett	In May	H M	OD
Bassett	Take Joy Home	H L	GS
Bauer	Only of Thee and Me	H L	APS
Bauer	Star-Trysts	H L	APS
Beach	Ah, Love, But a Day	H M L	APS
Beach	Fairy Lullaby	H	APS
Beach	Dark Garden	H L	APS
Beach	I Send My Heart Up to Thee	H M L	APS
Beach	I Shall Be Brave	H L	APS
Beach	The Year's at the Spring	H M	APS
Bennet	A Song	H L	Ric
Braine	Cherry Tree	H L	OD
Branscombe	By St. Lawrence Water	H L	APS
Branscombe	Hail, Ye Tyme of Holiedayes	H L	APS
Branscombe	I Bring You Heartsease	H L	APS
Branscombe	The Morning Wind	H M L	APS
Brockway	Lend Me Thy Fillet	M	GS
Buchanan	The Old Song	M	CF
Buck	Bedouin Love Song	H M	GS
Buck	Sunset	M	GS
Buck	When the Heart Is Young	H M L	OD
Bullard	Beam from Yonder Star	H M L	OD
Burleigh	Ethopia Saluting the Colors	H L	Ric
Burleigh	Her Eyes, Twin Pools	H	Ric
Burleigh	In the Woods of Finvara	H M	Ric
Burleigh	Jean	H M L	TP
Burnham	Sing Me a Song of a Lad That Is Gone	H L	GS
Busch	The Eagle	H M	OD
Cadman	Autumn Leaves	H L	BHks
Cadman	Four American Indian Songs	H L	WS
Cadman	Moonlight Song	H L	GS
Campbell-Tipton	The Crying of Water	H L	GS
Campbell-Tipton	If I Were King	H L	GS
Campbell-Tipton	Hymn to the Night	H L	N
Campbell-Tipton	The Spirit Flower	H M	APS
Carpenter	The Cock Shall Crow	M	GS
Carpenter	The Day Is No More	M	GS
Carpenter	Go, Lovely Rose	M	GS
Carpenter	The Green River	M	GS
Carpenter	May, the Maiden	H L	OD
Carpenter	On the Seashore of Endless Worlds	H	GS
Carpenter	The Sleep That Flits on Baby's Eyes	M	GS
Carpenter	When I Bring You Colored Toys	H M L	GS
Chadwick	A Ballad of Trees and the Master	H M L	GS
Chadwick	Allah	H M	APS
Chadwick	Before the Dawn	H M	APS
Chadwick	The Danza	H M	APS

*Used by permission American Academy of Teachers of Singing.
**See p. 220 for "Key to Publisher."

Composer	Title	Key	Publisher
Chadwick	Dear Love, When in Thine Eyes	H. L.	APS
Chadwick	He Loves Me	H.M.	APS
Chadwick	Oh Let Night Speak of Me.	H. L.	APS
Chadwick	Sweet Wind That Blows	H.M.	APS
Chadwick	Thou Art So Like a Flower	H.M.	APS
Charles	Clouds	H.M.L.	GS
Charles	My Lady Walks in Loveliness	H. L.	GS
Charles	Youth	H. L.	GS
Class	To You, Dear Heart	H. L.	AMP
Clough-Leiter	I Drink the Fragrance of the Rose	H.M.	OD
Clough-Leiter	My Lover He Comes on the Skee	H.M.	BM
Clough-Leiter	Possession	H. L.	GS
Clough-Leiter	Who Knows	M.	GS
Cohen	Alas That Spring Should Vanish with the Rose.	M.	Gal
Cohen	The Ballad of John Henry	M.	Gal
Coombs	The Dew Is on the Clover	H.M.L.	GS
Coombs	Her Rose	H.	GS
Crist	Evening	H.	GS
Crist	O Come Hither	H.M.	CF
Crist	The Way That Lovers Use	H.	CF
Curran	Nocturne	H.M.L.	GS
Damrosch	Danny Deever	M.	CH
De Golier	To a Sleeping Child	H. L.	OD
Deis	Come Down to Kew	H.M.L.	GS
Deis	Nocturne	H. L.	BM
De Leath	Wild Geese	M.	GS
Densmore	The Lamb	H.M.L.	GS
Densmore	Spring Fancy	H. L.	OD
Dichmont	Ma Littl' Banjo	M.L.	GS
Dobson	Cargoes	M.L.	GS
Dobson	Yasmin	M.	GS
Dunn	The Bitterness of Love	H.M.L.	JF
Engel	Sprig of Rosemary	M.	GS
Engel	Sea Shell	M.	GS
Fairchild	A Memory	H.orM.	BM
Farley	October End	H.	NM
Ferrata	Night and the Curtain's Drawn	H.M.	JF
Fisher	Gae to Sleep	H. L.	OD
Fisher	I Hear a Cry	H.M.L.	OD
Fisher	The Rose of Ispahan	H.M.	OD
Fiske	The Bird	H. L.	OD
Foote	An Irish Folk Song	H.M.L.	APS
Foote	Go, Lovely Rose	H. L.	APS
Foote	I'm Wearin' Awa'	H.M.L.	APS
Foote	The Lake Isle of Innisfree	H.	APS
Foote	On the Way to Kew	H. L.	APS
Forsyth	The Bell-Man	H.M.	OD
Forsyth	From the Hills of Dream	H. L.	OD
Foster	Jeanie with the Light Brown Hair	H. L.	JF
Fox, Bertram	Eventide	H.M.	JF
Fox, Bertram	Strings in the Earth	H. L.	JF
Fox, Bertram	Tears	M.L.	JF
Fox, Bertram	Wonder	H. L.	JF
Fox, Oscar	Hills of Home	H.M.L.	CF
Gaines	Wings of the Morning	H. L.	GS
Ganz	A Memory	H. L.	GS
Ganz	The Grave in France	M.L.	CF
Ganz	Woman's Last Word	H. L.	HWG
Giannini	Tell Me, O Blue, Blue Sky	H.	Ric
Gilbert	Pirate Song	M.	N
Golde	Awakening	H.M.	JF

Composer	Title	Key	Publisher
Grant-Schaffer	The Sea	H. L.	APS
Griffes	An Old Song, Re-sung	H.M.L.	GS
Griffes	By a Lonely Forest Pathway	H.M.L.	GS
Griffes	In a Myrtle Shade	H.	GS
Griffes	On the Beach of Waikiki	H.	GS
Griffes	Sorrow of Mydath	M.	GS
Griffes	We'll to the Woods and Gather May	M.	GS
Hadley	My Shadow	M.	APS
Hadley	My True Love	H. L.	CF
Hadley	The Time of Parting	H.M.L.	CF
Hageman	At the Well	H. L.	GS
Hageman	Christ Went Up Into the Hills	H. L.	CF
Hageman	The Cunnin' Little Thing	M.L.	GS
Hageman	Do Not Go, My Love	H. L.	GS
Hageman	Me, Company Along	H. L.	CF
Hammond	The Pipes of Gordon's Men	H. L.	GS
Hammond	When Thou Commandest Me to Sing	H. L.	TP
Harling	Divan of Hafiz (Cycle)	H. L.	BM
Harmati	Notre Dame de Sacre Coeur	M.	Gal
Harmati	Spring Night	H.	Gal
Harris, Edward	Moan	M.	JF
Harris, Victor	Daylight and Dusk	M.	OD
Harris, Victor	Hills o'Skye	H. L.	OD
Harris, Victor	Madrigal	H. L.	JF
Harris, Victor	Silver	H.M.	JF
Harris, Victor	Song from Omar Khayyam	H. L.	Schu
Hawley	Bedouin Love Song	M.L.	GS
Hawley	In a Garden	H.	JF
Hawley	Noon and Night	H.M.L.	TP
Hawley	Spring Night	H. L.	Ch
Herbert	I Love Thee	H.	CF
Herbert	The Song of Desire	M.	JF
Homer	Dearest	H.M.L.	GS
Homer	Requiem	H. L.	GS
Homer	Uncle Rome	H. L.	GS
Horsman	The Dream	H.	GS
Horsman	The Bird of the Wilderness	H.M.L.	GS
Horsman	The Shepherdess	H.M.	GS
Horsman	Thus Wisdom Sings	H.M.L.	GS
Horsman	You Are the Evening Cloud	H. L.	GS
Huerter	Pirate Dreams	H.M.L.	OD
Huhn	The Broken Song	H. L.	GS
Huhn	Invictus	H.M.L.	APS
Huhn	Israfel	H.M.L.	APS
Hutchinson	Gray Rain	H.	GS
Johns	I Cannot Help Loving Thee	H.M.L.	BM
Johns	Where Blooms the Rose	L.	BM
Josten	Cupid's Counsel	H.	GS
Josten	Summer Night	H.	GS
Josten	The Wind Flowers	H.M.	GS
Kelley	Israfel	H.	GS
Kelley	Lady Picking Mulberries	H. L.	GS
Kernochan	Lilacs	H.	Gal
Kernochan	King Charles	M.	Gal
Kernochan	Smuggler's Song	H. L.	GS
Kernochan	We Two Together	H.	Gal
Kountz	A Robin Sang in the Elm-wood Tree	H. L.	GS
Kramer	The Faltering Dusk	H. L.	OD
Kramer	For a Dream's Sake	H. L.	JF
Kramer	Clouds	H.	JF
Kramer	The Last Hour	H.M.L.	TP

Composer	Title	Key	Publisher
Kramer	Pleading	H. L.	JF
Kramer	Swans	H. L.	Ric
La Forge	Come unto These Yellow Sands	H.	GS
La Forge	Far Away	H. L.	GS
La Forge	Hills	H. L.	Ric
La Forge	I Came with a Song	H. L.	GS
La Forge	Song of the Open	H.M.	OD
Lang	Day Is Gone	H.M.L.	APS
Lang	Irish Love Song (Mavourneen)	H.M.L.	APS
Loeffler	To Helen	M.	GS
Luckstone	The Clown's Serenade	H.M.	TP
Lynes	He Was a Prince	H.M.L.	APS
MacDowell	A Maid Sings Light	H.M.	APS
MacDowell	The Blue-bell	M.	APS
MacDowell	Folk-song	M.	BH
MacDowell	The Gloaming Shadows Creep	H. L.	APS
MacDowell	Long Ago, Sweetheart Mine	H.M.	APS
MacDowell	Midsummer Lullaby	M.	BH
MacDowell	Slumber Song	M.	APS
MacDowell	Sweetheart, Tell Me (Op. 40)	H.	APS
MacDowell	The Robin Sings in the Apple Tree	M.	BH
MacDowell	The Sea	M.	BM
MacDowell	The Swan Bent Low	H. L.	APS
MacDowell	Thy Beaming Eyes	M.L.	APS
Macfarlane	Condescend	H. L.	GS
MacFayden	Inter Nos	H.M.L.	TP
Manney	Consecration	H.M.L.	OD
Manney	Heart of Gold	H.M.	OD
Manney	Orpheus with His Lute	H.M.L.	OD
Manning	Shoes	H. L.	GS
Manning	Hop-li, the Rickshaw Man	M.	GS
Matthews	A Morning in Spring	H.M.	OD
McKinney	Slower, Sweet June	H. L.	JF
Metcalf	Little House of Dreams	H.M.L.	APS
Miller	Boats of Mine	H.M.L.	HF
Neidlinger	Serenade	H.M.L.	GS
Nevin	Before the Daybreak	H.M.	BM
Nevin	O That We Two Were Maying	H. L.	BM
Nevin	'Twas April	H.M.L.	BM
Nevin	When the Land Was White	H. L.	BH
Osgood	On Eribeg Isle	H. L.	BM
Parker	Come, Oh Come, My Life's Delight	H. L.	TP
Parker	The Lark Now Leaves His Wat'ry Nest	H.	TP
Parker	Love in May	H.	TP
Parks	A Memory	H.M.L.	APS
Powell	Heartsease	H.	GS
Protheroe	Ah, Love, But a Day	H.M.L.	GH
Repper	Song Is Old	H.M.	OD
Rogers, James H.	At Parting	H. L.	GS
Rogers, James H.	Cloud-shadows	M.	GS
Rogers, James H.	The Last Song	H.M.L.	GS
Rogers, James H.	Love's on the Highroad	H. L.	GS
Rogers, James H.	The Time for Making Songs	H.M.	OD
Rogers, James H.	The Wind-song	H. L.	GS
Rogers, Withrop	Let Miss Lindy Pass	H. L.	GS
Rummel	Ecstasy	H.M.L.	GS
Rummel	June	H. L.	GS
Russell	In Fountain Court	H. L.	Wil
Russell	Sunset	H. L.	TP
Russell, Alex.	I Hold Her Hand	H.	GS
Russell, Alex.	Sacred Fire	H. L.	Ch

Composer	Title	Key	Publisher
Saar	The Little Gray Dove	H.M.	GS
Salter	Come into the Garden, Love	H. L.	GS
Salter	The Cry of Rachel	H. L.	GS
Salter	The Pine-tree	H. L.	GS
Salter	The Sweet of the Year	H.M.	APS
Schneider	Flower Rain	H. L.	Sum
Scott	The Wind's in the South	H.M.	Hunt
Seiler	Butterflies	H. L.	GS
Smith	Romany Love Song	M.	GS
Snodgrass	The Still of Evening	H.M.L.	Gal
Sowerby	Sweet Nymphs	M.	BM
Sowerby	What If I Never Spake	M.	BM
Spalding	On Her Dancing	H. L.	OD
Spalding	Rock of Rubies	M.	GS
Speaks	The Prayer Perfect	H. L.	GS
Speaks	Serenade	H. L.	GS
Speaks	Sylvia	H.M.L.	GS
Spier	The Pansy Flower	H.M.	OD
Spier	Thalatta (The Sea)	M.	JF
Spross	Come Down, Laughing Streamlet	H. L.	TP
Spross	Will o'the Wisp	H. L.	TP
Stickles	Who Knows	H.M.L.	Hunt
Strickland	My Lover Is a Fisherman	H. L.	OD
Taylor	A Song for Lovers	H.M.	JF
Taylor	Captain Stratton's Fancy	L.	JF
Taylor	The Rivals	H.M.	JF
Thayer	My Laddie	H. L.	GS
Tours	Mother o'Mine	H.M.L.	Chap
Treharne	Corals	H.	GS
Tureman	A Winter Sunset	L.	GS
Van der Stucken	O Come with Me in the Summer Night	H.M.L.	HF
Voorhis	A Little Song	H. L.	HF
Ware	Boat Song	H.M.L.	TP
Ware	Call of Radha, The	H.	TP
Ware	Come, Dance the Romaika	H.	HF
Ware	Stars	H. L.	GS
Ware	Wind and Lyre	H. L.	TP
Watts	Blue Are Her Eyes	H.M.	OD
Watts	The Little Shepherd's Song	H. L.	Ric
Watts	Pierrot	H.M.	OD
Watts	The Poet Sings	H.M.	OD
Watts	Transformation	L.	GS
Watts	Wings of Night	H. L.	GS
Weaver	Moon-marketing	H.M.L.	GS
Weaver, Powell	The Abbot of Derry	H. L.	GS
Weaver, Powell	The End of the Song	H.	Gal
Weil	Autumn-Spring	H.	GS
Wells	The Elf-man	H. L.	TP
Whelpley	A Forest Song	H.	BM
Whelpley	I Know a Hill	H. L.	BM
Whelpley	The Nightingale Has a Lyre of Gold	H.M.L.	BM
White	The Robin's Song	H.M.L.	CF
Whiting	Fuzzy-wuzzy	H. L.	GS
Wolfe	God's World	H. L.	GS
Wolfe	The Janitor's Boy	H. L.	GS
Wood	Ashes of Roses	H. L.	GS
Wood	Thy Name	H.M.	OD
Woodman	A Birthday	H. L.	GS
Woodman	An Open Secret	H. L.	GS
Woodman	I Am Thy Harp	H. L.	GS
Woodman	My Heart Is a Lute	H.orM.	GS

2. Recital Songs by American Composers - List No. 10 American Academy of Teachers of Singing*

 The American Academy of Teachers of Singing devotes this Tenth Song List to Recital songs by American composers. Its purpose in so doing is to emphasize the importance, musical worth and charm of the many vocal compositions contained in our native repertory, which are available to singers. Obviously, this list is not intended to appear as a complete catalogue of American song material, but simply to provide a comprehensive survey consisting of a selected number of songs that are representative and highly acceptable for inclusion in present day recital programs.

Composer	Title	Key	Publisher**
Ames	Spring Pool	M.	AMP
Ames	Nothing Gold Can Stay	M.	AMP
Barber	A Nun Takes the Veil	H.M.	GS
Barber	Rain Has Fallen	H.M.	GS
Barber	I Hear an Army	H.M.	GS
Beach	I Send My Heart Up to Thee	H.M.L.	APS
Beach	Ah Love, But a Day	H.M.L.	APS
Beach	My Star	M.L.	APS
Bibb	Rondel of Spring	H. L.	GS
Bloch	The Vagabond	M.	GS
Bloch	Psalm 22 for Baritone		GS
Bloch	Psalm 137 for Soprano		GS
Bloch	Psalm 134 for Soprano		GS
Bennett	A Song	H.	R
Bowles	David	M.	AMP
Cadman	The Moon Drops Low	H. L.	APS
Campbell-Tipton	The Crying of Water	H. L.	GS
Campbell-Tipton	Hymn to the Night	H. L.	N
Carpenter	Serenade	H. L.	GS
Carpenter	The Day Is No More	H. L.	GS
Carpenter	Water Colors	M.	GS
Carpenter	Silhouettes	M.	GS
Carpenter	Gitanjali (Cycle)		GS
Chadwick	O Let Night Speak of Me	H. L.	APS
Chadwick	Allah	H. L.	APS
Chadwick	Before the Dawn	H. L.	APS
Chadwick	Song from the Persian	H. L.	APS
Chadwick	Sweet Wind That Blows	H.M.	APS
Chadwick	The Danza	H.M.	APS
Chadwick	Thou Art to Me	M.	GS
Chadwick	A Ballad of Trees and the Master	H.M.L.	OD
Chandler	The Lamb	M.	AMP
Clark	The Seal Man	M.	BH
Clark	Shy One	M.	BH
Cowell	St. Agnes Morning	M.	MPI
Crist	By a Silent Shore	H.	GS
Crist	Evening	H.	GS
Crist	Dark King's Daughter	H.	CF
Crist	Into a Ship Dreaming	H.M.L.	CF
Crist	This Is the Moon of Roses	H. L.	CF
Davis	Nancy Hanks	H.	G
De Golier	To a Sleeping Child	H. L.	OD
Dello Joio	New Born	M.	CF
Dobson	Yasmin	M.	GS
Dobson	Cargoes	H. L.	GS
Duke	XXth Century	M.	VP
Duke	White in the Moon the Long Road Lies	M.	VP
Edmunds	Milkmaids	M.	MP
Elwell	Agamede's Song	H.M.	VP

*Used by permission American Academy of Teachers of Singing.
**See p. 220 for "Key to Publisher."

Composer	Title	Key	Publisher
Elwell	Suffolk Owl	H.	VP
Engel	The Sea Shell	M.	GS
Engel	A Sprig of Rosemary	M.	GS
Farwell	Drake's Drum	L.	WWP
Fergusson	Sonnet	M.	CF
Fiske	The Bird	H. L.	OD
Fox	Strings in the Earth	H. L.	JF
Fox	Two Cranes	M.	CF
Gilbert	Pirate Song	M.	N
Gilbert	Four Celtic Studies	H.M.	TP
Gilbert	Zephyrus	H.M.	TP
Gilbert	Salammbo's Invitation to Tanith	H.	WWP
Gilbert	Orlomonde	H.	WWP
Giannini	Tell Me, O Blue, Blue Sky	H.	Ric
Golde	To an Invalid	H.	JF
Griffes	Five Poems of Ancient China	M.	GS
Griffes	In the Myrtle Shade	H.	GS
Griffes	Symphony in Yellow	M.	GS
Griffes	An Old Song Re-sung	H.M.L.	GS
Griffes	The Lament of Ian the Proud	H. L.	GS
Griffes	Waikiki	H.	GS
Griffes	Thy Dark Eyes to Mine	H.	GS
Griffes	By a Lonely Forest Pathway	H.M.L.	GS
Hageman	Do Not Go My Love	H. L.	GS
Hageman	Don Juan Gomez	M.	Gal
Hageman	Music I Heard with You	H. L.	Gal
Hammond	The Pipes of Gordon's Men	H. L.	GS
Harmati	Spring Night	H.	Gal
Harmati	Notre Dame	L.	Gal
Harris	Agatha Morley	M.	CF
Harris	Song from Omar	H. L.	Schu
Heilner	The Traveler	M.	AMP
Homer	Pauper's Drive	L.	GS
Homer	Sheep and Lambs	H. L.	GS
Homer	Dearest	H.M.L.	GS
Homer	Fiddler of Dooney	L.	GS
Homer	The Last Leaf	H.M.L.	GS
Horsman	In the Yellow Dusk	H.M.	GS
Horsman	Bird of the Wilderness	H. L.	GS
Horsman	You Are the Evening Cloud	H. L.	GS
Horsman	Shepherdess	H.M.	GS
Huhn	I Mind the Day	H. L.	GS
Huhn	Broken Song	H. L.	GS
Ives	Charley Rutledge	M.	AR
Ives	The Greatest Man	M.	AR
James	Dearie	M.L.	CF
James	Evening	H. L.	GS
Josten	Christmas	H.	VP
Kernochan	We Two Together	H.M.	Gal
Kernochan	Ah Love, But a Day	M.	Gal
Kernochan	Lilacs	H.M.	Gal
Kramer	Dark and Wondrous Night	H.M.L.	OD
La Forge	Come unto These Yellow Sands	H.	GS
Lamont	Shule Agrah	H.	TP
Loeffler	Sonnet	M.	GS
Loeffler	To Helen	M.	GS
Loeffler	Four Songs with Viola	M.	GS

       1. La Cloche Fêlée
       2. "Dansons La Gigue!"
       3. "Le Son Du Cor S'Afflige Vers Les Bois"
       4. Sérénade

Composer	Title	Key	Publisher
Lucke	A Song on the Wind	H.	CP
MacDowell	The Sea	M.	BH
MacDowell	Confidence	M.	BH
Nordhoff	Time I Dare Thee to Discover	M.	AMP
Nordhoff	There Shall Be More Joy	M.	AMP
Nordhoff	Serenade	M.	AMP
Nordhoff	This Is the Shape of the Leaf	M.	AMP
Nordhoff	Tell Me, Thyrsis	M.	AMP
Nordhoff	White Nocturne	M.	OD
Nordhoff	Dirge for the Nameless	M.	AMP
Parker	The Lark Now Leaves His Wat'ry Nest	H. L.	TP
Patterson	Winter Rain	H.	WW
Posamanick	Croon for the Christ Child	H.	Gal
Protheroe	What Is There Hid in the Heart of a Rose?	M.L.	OD
Read	The Moon	M.	AMP
Read	Nocturne	M.	AMP
Repper	Song Is So Old	H.M.	OD
Rorem	A Song of David	M.	AMP
Rorem	A Psalm of Praise	M.	AMP
Russell	In Fountain Court	H. L.	Hunt
Rybner	Pierrot	H. L.	GS
Schneider	The Cave	H. L.	BHks
Spalding	On Her Dancing	H. L.	GS
Spalding	The Rock of Rubies	M.	GS
Taylor	A Song for Lovers	H.M.	JF
Taylor	Captain Stratton's Fancy	L.	JF
Shepherd	The Fiddlers	H.M.	VP
Shepherd	The Starling Lake	M.	VP
Thompson	Velvet Shoes	M.	ECS
Van Vactor	How Can I Sing Light-souled and Fancy Free?	H.	NMS
Warren	Silent Noon	H. L.	OD
Watts	Stresa	H.	OD
Watts	Little Shepherd's Song	H. L.	Ric
Weaver	Moon Marketing	H.M.L.	GS

3. Two Hundred Songs by Modern English and British Composers - Lists No. 5 and 6 Combined, American Academy of Teachers of Singing*
(H - High, M - Medium, L - Low Keys)

Composer	Title	Key	Publisher**
Aiken	Sigh No More	H.M.L.	SB
Allisten	Oh! For a Burst of Song	L.	BHks
A. L.	Marie Antoinette	H.	Chap
Aylward	Beloved, It Is Morn!	H.M.L.	Chap
Bantock	A Feast of Lanterns	H.M.L.	Gal
Bantock	Evening Song	L.	BH
Bantock	From the Tomb of an Unknown Woman	H.M.L.	EV
Bantock	Silent Strings	H. L.	BHks
Bantock	Song of the Bells	M.	BH
Bantock	Songs of the Genie	H. L.	BH
Bantock	The Parting	H. L.	BH
Bath	In a Gondola	H. L.	BHks
Bax	Christmas Carol	M.	Ches
Bax	I Heard a Piper Playing	H.M.	Ox
Besley	The Second Minuet	H. L.	BHks
Boughton	Fairy Song	H.M.	Gal
Boughton	The Love of Comrades	M.	Cur

*Used by permission American Academy of Teachers of Singing.
**See p. 220 for "Key to Publisher."

Composer	Title	Key	Publisher
Breville-Smith	Where My Dear Lady Sleeps	H.M.	BHks
Brewer	Fairy Piper	H.MH.ML.L.	BHks
Bridge	Come to Me in My Dreams	H. L.	WR
Bridge	E'en As a Lovely Flower	H. L.	BHks
Bridge	The Devon Maid	M.	WR
Bridge	Golden Hair	H. L.	Chap
Bridge	Go Not, Happy Day	M.	WR
Bridge	Isobel	H.M.L.	Chap
Bridge	Love Went A-Riding	H. L.	BM
Bridge	So Early in the Morning	H.	WR
Bright	Six Jungle Book Songs	H. L.	Gal
Carver	The House of Sleep	H. L.	EV
Clarke	Shy One	H. L.	BM
Clutsam	Songs from the Turkish Hills	H.M.L.	Chap
Coates	I Heard You Singing	H.M.L.	Chap
Coates	Sea Rapture	H. L.	Chap
Coleridge-Taylor	An Explanation	H.M.	APS
Coleridge-Taylor	Canoe Song	H. L.	N
Coleridge-Taylor	Corn Song	H. L.	BHks
Coleridge-Taylor	Eleanore	H.MH.ML.L.	N
Coleridge-Taylor	Life and Death	H.M.L.	APS
Coleridge-Taylor	She Rested by the Broken Brook	H. L.	OD
Coleridge-Taylor	Tell, O Tell Me	H.M.	APS
Coleridge-Taylor	When I Am Dead	H. L.	Au
Cowen	Snow-flakes	H.M.L.	BFW
Cowen	Border Ballad	H.M.L.	BHks
Davies	A Song of Innocence	H.	N
Davies	Hymn Before Action	M.	N
Davies	Our Lady of the Snows	M.	N
Davies	Requiem	M.	N
Davies	When Childer Plays	H.M.L.	BHks
Delius	Heimkehr	M.	Ox
Delius	Indian Love Song	H.	Ox
Delius	Three Lieder (Twilight Fancies; The Princess)	M.	TJ
Delius	Twilight Fancies	M.	Ox
del Riego	Happy Song	H.M.L.	Chap
Dunhill	The Cloths of Heaven	H. L.	SB
Elgar	After	H.M.L.	BHks
Elgar	In Haven (from Five Sea Songs)	H. L.	BHks
Elgar	The Pipes of Pan	H.M.L.	BHks
Elgar	Pleading	H.M.L.	HWG
Elgar	Sabbath Morning at Sea (from Five Sea Songs)	H. L.	BHks
Elgar	The Swimmer (from Five Sea Songs)	M.	BHks
Elgar	Twilight (Alto)	L.	N
Elgar	Where Corals Lie	H. L.	BHks
Fogg	Peace	H.M.L.	Gal
Foster	Rose in the Bud	H.MH.ML.L.	Chap
German	Charming Chloe	H.M.L.	HWG
German	Daffodils a-Blowing	H.MH.ML.L.	BHks
German	The First Friend	H.	N
German	My Song of the Sturdy North	M.L.	Schu
German	Restless River	H. L.	BHks
German	Rolling Down to Rio	M.L.	N
German	Sea Lullaby	H. L.	Chap
German	Who'll Buy My Lavender?	H.M.L.	BHks
Gibbs	Nod	M.	BM
Gibbs	A Song of Shadows	H.	WR
Goosens	Melancholy	M.	Ches
Goring-Thomas	A Love Lullaby	M.	GS
Goring-Thomas	Time's Garden	M.	GS
Greenhill	Autolycus Song	M.	BHks

Composer	Title	Key	Publisher
Harty	A Cradle Song	M.	N
Harty	At Sea	M.	BHks
Harty	The Blue Hill of Antrim	H. L.	BHks
Harty	By the Bivouac's Fitful Flame	M.	BHks
Harty	My Pagan Love	H.M.	BHks
Head	A Piper	H. L.	BHks
Head	The Dreaming Lake	H. L.	BHks
Head	Nocturne	H. L.	BHks
Head	Slumber Song of the Madonna	H. L.	BHks
Head	When I Think upon the Maidens	H. L.	BHks
Healy-Hutchinson	The Song of Soldiers	H. L.	EV
Henschel	The Angels Dear	M.	TP
Henschel	Morning Hymn	H. L.	GS
Henschel	The Spinning-wheel Song	M.	OD
Henschel	Spring	H. L.	BHks
Henschel	There Was an Ancient King (Op. 37, No. 1)	M.	Ro
Herbert	Lake Isle of Innisfree	H.M.	Gal
Holbrooke	Bonnie Dear	L.	Ric
Holst	The Heart Worships	M.L.	Gal
Holst	Weep You No More	M.	SB
Howells	Girl's Song	M.	WR
Hughes	Open the Door Softly	H.M.L.	E
Ireland	Hope, the Horn Blower	H. L.	BHks
Ireland	If There Were Dreams to Sell	H.M.L.	WR
Ireland	Sea Fever	H. MH.M.L.	Aug
Ireland	The Soldier	H.M.L.	WR
Johnson	An Offering	H. L.	Chap
Keel	Lullaby	H. L.	SB
Keel	Trade Winds	H. L.	BHks
Kellie	We Kissed Again with Tears	H.M.	GS
Lambert	A Barque at Midnight	H.M.L.	Chap
Lehmann	The Cuckoo	H. L.	BHks
Lehmann	Long Ago in Egypt	H. L.	Chap
Lehmann	Mirage	L.	BHks
Lehmann	Mother Sleep	H.M.	GS
Lehmann	Roses After Rain	H. L.	GS
Lehmann	Titania's Cradle	H.M.	OD
Lehmann	Thoughts Have Wings	H.M.L.	Chap
Liddle	The Garden Where the Praties Grow	H.M.L.	SB
Lidgey	A Widow Bird Sat Mourning	H.M.	Chap
Lohr	The Ringers	H.M.L.	Chap
Mallinson	Canoe Song	H.	FH
Mallinson	Eleanore	H. L.	FH
Mallinson	Sing, Break into Song	H. L.	FH
Mallinson	Slow, Horses, Slow	H. L.	FH
Mallinson	To Me at My Fifth Floor Window	M.	FH
Martin	Come to the Fair	H.M.L.	BHks
Morgan	Clorinda	H. L.	E
Needham	Hay-making	H.M.	BHks
Parry	Why So Pale and Wan, Fond Lover?	L.	N
Peel	The Early Morning	H. MH. ML. L.	Chap
Quilter	Cherry Valley	H. L.	EV
Quilter	Go, Lovely Rose	H.M.L.	Chap
Quilter	Now Sleeps the Crimson Petal	H. MH. ML. L.	BHks
Quilter	O Mistress Mine	H.M.L.	BHks
Quilter	Spring Is at the Door	H. L.	EV
Quilter	To Daisies	H.M.	BHks
Quilter	To Wine and Beauty	H. L.	EV
Quilter	Two September Songs	H. L.	EV
Ronald	A Little Winding Road	H.M.L.	E
Ronald	Down in the Forest	H. MH.M. ML. L.	E

Composer	Title	Key	Publisher
Ronald	Four Songs from the Hill	H. L.	E
Ronald	O Lovely Night	H.MH.ML.L.	E
Ronald	Prelude	H.M.L.	BHks
Ronald	Sun Beams	H.M.L.	E
Ronald	Wise Folly	H.M.L.	E
Russell	Vale	H.MH.ML.L.	BHks
Sanderson	Friend O'Mine	H.HM.HL.L.	BHks
Scott	A Picnic	H.	EV
Scott	A Roundel of Rest	H. L.	EV
Scott	Blackbird's Song	H.M.L.	Gal
Scott	Don't Come in Sir, Please	H. L.	EV
Scott	Lullaby	H.M.L.	EV
Scott	The Waterlilies	H.M.L.	EV
Scott	The Unforseen	H.M.L.	EV
Shaw	Bab-lock Hyth	H.	Cur
Shaw	Cuckoo	H. L.	Cur
Shaw	Down by the Sally Gardens	L.	Cur
Shaw	The Land of Heart's Desire	M.	Cur
Shaw	Song of the Palanquin Bearers	H. L.	Cur
Somerville	Sweet and Low	H.M.L.	BHks
Somerville	Shepherd's Cradle Song	H.M.	GS
Squire	Old Black Mare	M.L.	Chap
Stanford	Boot, Saddle, to Horse	M.	BHks
Stanford	Broken Song	H. L.	BHks
Stanford	Corymeela	L.	BHks
Stanford	I'll Rock You to Rest	H.MH.ML.L.	BHks
Stanford	King Charles	M.	BHks
Stanford	Marching Along	H.	BHks
Taylor	The Windmill	M.	Ox
Thomas	A Song of Sunshine	H.	TP
Thomas	Le baiser (A Memory)	H.MH.ML.L.	JW
Thomas	Summer Night	H. L.	GS
Thomas	The Willow	H.	TP
Thomas	Winds in the Trees	H.M.L.	BHks
Toy	The Inn	M.	Cur
Tours	The Three Singers	L.	BHks
Treharne	Corals	M.	GS
Walthew	April and I	H.M.L.	BHks
Walthew	Gleaner's Slumber Song	H. L.	BHks
Walthew	May Day	H.M.L.	BHks
Warlock	The Passionate Shepherd	H.M.	EV
Warlock	Sweet O' the Year	H.M.	EV
Warner	Dreams	H. L.	BHks
White	King Charles	M.L.	BHks
White	The Throstle	H.M.	GS
Willeby	Four Leaf Clover	H. L.	TP
Willeby	A June Morning	H. L.	GS
Williams	Linden Lea	H.M.L.	BHks
Williams	My Boy Johnny	H. L.	BHks
Williams	Road-side Fire	H.M.L.	BHks
Williams	Silent Noon	H.HM.HL.L.	GS
Williams	The Vagabond	H. L.	BHks
Williams	Youth and Love	H.M.	BHks
Wood	Ethopia Saluting the Colours	H.M.L.	BHks
Wood	O Captain, My Captain	H. L.	BHks
Wood, Haydn	A Brown Bird Singing	H.M.L.	Chap
Woodford-Finden	Old French Love Song	M.	BHks

4. Contemporary Songs by American Composers 1925-1950*
   (H - High, M - Medium, L - Low Voice)

Composer	Title	Voice	Publisher**
Allen	The Flight	H.	Gal
Allen	Vocalise	H.	Gal
Barber	Rain Has Fallen	H.M.	GS
Barber	Sleep Now	H.M.	GS
Barber	Monks and Raisins	M.	GS
Barber	Knoxville: Summer of 1915 (For Voice and Orchestra; Reduction for Piano by the Composer)	H.	GS
Bernstein	I Hate Music (Five Kid Songs)	H.	GS
Bernstein	Le Bonne Cuisine (Four Recipes)	H.	GS
Black, Jennie	The Pledge (A Wedding Song)	H.M.L.	GS
Bone, Gene and Howard	April Hill	H.M.	CF
Bone, Gene and Howard	Captain Kidd	H.M.	CF
Bone, Gene and Howard	Deborah	M.L.	CF
Bone, Gene and Howard	First Psalm	M.	CF
Bowles	Heavenly Grass	M.	GS
Bowles	Letter to Freddy	M.	GS
Bowles	Once a Lady was Here	M.	GS
Carr	Hosanna to the Son of David	H. L.	GS
Cator	Pool of Quietness	M.	GS
Chanler	The Children (cycle)	H.M.	GS
Chanler	The Lamb	H.M.	GS
Chanler	I Rise When You Enter	M.	GS
Creston	Bird of the Wilderness	H.M.	GS
Creston	Twenty-Third Psalm	H.M.	GS
Crist	The Mocking Fairy	M.	Gal
Davis	Folk Song Settings	M or L	Gal
	The Mill Wheel		
	Deaf Old Woman		
	The Soldier		
Davis	Nancy Hanks	H.	Gal
Davis	Christ Is Risen Today	M.	Gal
Dello Joio	The Assassination	M.L.	CF
Dello Joio	Lament	M.	CF
Dello Joio	There Is a Lady Sweet and Kind	M.	CF
Dello Joio	New Born	M.	CF
Diamond	Be Music, Night	H.M.	CF
Diamond	David Weeps for Absolom	H.M.	MPI
Dittenhaver	Lady of the Amber Wheat	H.	Gal
Dougherty	First Christmas	H.	GS
Dougherty	Love in the Dictionary	H.	GS
Dougherty	Loveliest of Trees	H.M.	GS
Dougherty	Declaration of Independence	M.	GS
Dougherty	Sea Chanties	M.L.	GS
Duke	A Piper	Very H.	GS
Duke	Bells in the Rain	H.	CF
Duke	Calvary	L.	CF
Duke	Miniver Cheevy	L.	CF
Duke	Loveliest of Trees	M.	GS
Duke	Wild Geese	H.	MPI
Duke	Two Songs: Little Elegy, The Bird	H.	MPI
Edmunds	The Lonely	M.	CF
Edmunds	Milkmaids	M.	MPI
Edwards	Little Shepherds Song	H.	Mi
Edwards	The Wild Rose Blooms	H. L.	GS

---

*Prepared by Miss Grace Leslie for the National Association of Teachers of Singing, Inc., and used by permission.
**See p. 220 for "Key to Publisher."

Composer	Title	Voice	Publisher
Finney	Poor Richard (a cycle of Songs to texts by Benjamin Franklin)	H.	GS
Foss	The Song of Songs (Biblical Solo Cantata for high Voice and orchestra or piano) (Movements II and IV may be sung separately in Recital)	H.	CF
Foster	My Journey's End	H.M.L.	GS
Guion	Mam'selle Marie	M.	GS
Guion	One Day	H.M.	GS
Hageman	Music I Heard with You	H. L.	Gal
Hageman	Voices	M.	Gal
Harris	Someone	M.	Gal
Harris	Holy Infant	M.	Gal
Harris, Roy	Fog	M.	CF
Helm	Prairie Waters by Night	M.	CF
Hively	Florentine Song	H. L.	GS
Hively	Prelude to Conversation	M.	Gal
Howe	Let us Walk in the White Snow	H.	CF
Howe	Ripe Apples	H.M.	GS
Ives	A Christmas Carol	L.	NM
Ives	Ann Street	M.	NM
Ives	Canon	H.M.	NM
Ives	Two Little Flowers	M.	NM
Kalmanoff	George Washington Comes to Dinner	M.	CF
Kingsford	Wall Paper (for a Little Girl's Room)	M.	GS
Kountz	Cynthia	H.M.	Gal
Kramer	Our Lives Together	H. L.	Gal
Lockwood	Oh Lady, Let the Sad Tears Fall	M.	MPI
Malotte	Mister Jim	M.	GS
Malotte	Only with Thine Eyes (Sacred Song)	H.M.	GS
Malotte	Sing a Song of Sixpence	H.M.	GS
Moore	Old Song	M.	CF
Moore	Under the Greenwood Tree	H.	CF
Niles	The Blue Madonna	H.	GS
Nordoff	Willow River	H.	GS
Nordoff	There Shall Be More Joy	M.	AMP
Read	Piping Dow the Valleys Wild	M.	Gal
Roy	This Little Rose	H.M.L.	Gal
Sacco	Brother Will, Brother John	M.	GS
Sacco	Luck of the Road	L.	GS
Shepard	Triptych (for Soprano Voice and String Quartette)		GS
Swanson	Joy	M.	Leeds
Swanson	The Negro Speaks of Rivers	M.	Leeds
Swanson	The Valley	L.	Leeds
Thompson	My Master Hath a Garden	M.	ECS
Thompson	Velvet Shoes (Elinor Wylie)	M.	ECS
Thomson	Preciosilla	H.	GS
	Recit. Cousin to Clare Washing; Aria: Please Be (Gertrude Stein)		
Warren	Light the Lamps Up	H.M.	GS
Warren	Who Calls	H. L.	CF
Warren	Snow Towards Evening	H.	GS
Whitney	Nightfall	M.L.	GS

5. Contemporary American and British Composers - List No. 12 American Academy of Teachers of Singing*

The tremendous upsurge in musical composition and the fact that song repertoire is divided among so many publishers make it difficult for vocal teachers to contact and become intimately acquainted with much of this literature. The American Academy of Teachers of Singing accordingly believes that the 12th Song List here presented, consisting of song material by American and British composers of the current era, will prove stimulating and otherwise rewarding through its reference and practical program usefulness to teacher, student and performer alike.

This listing of over three hundred vocal compositions, painstakingly selected from several thousand long and short works, reflects a flowering of recent individual musical creations, based on high aesthetic standards combined with a wealth of interesting poetry. It will be noticed that this compilation represents song material both simple and complex in form, of varying lengths, and embracing diversified harmonic and non-harmonic textures, suitable for study in the studio and use in recital. The brief, descriptive annotations are intended to serve as an informative guide as to the nature and purpose of each song, when making selections for programming and performance.

The names of approximately sixty of the composers included in this listing have not appeared in any previous song list issued by the American Academy, however some more widely known and important song compositions will be found among the newer material.

Composer — Title	Poet	Copyright	Range	Publisher**
ALLEN, ROBERT E.				
Vocalise		1949	E♭–G	Gal
The Flight	Teasdale	1950	F–A	Gal
(High mezzo or soprano, simple, fluent, flexibly conventional)				
AVSHALOMOV, JACOB				
The Glass Town	Reid	1957	B–G	Hi
(Atmospheric, singable contemporary idiom)				
BACON, ERNST				
Quiet Airs - from 12 short poems		1952		MM
Gentle Greeting	E. Bronte		C#–G	TP
The Little Stone	E. Dickinson		C#–G	
To Musique, to Becalme His Fever	Herrick		C#–G#	
(Not traditionally harmonic, vocal treatment logical)				
BARAB, SEYMOUR				
Four Songs		1955		BHks
Go, Lovely Rose	Waller		D–F#	
(Rhythmically and harmonically fluent)				
She's Somewhere in the Sunlight Strong	LeGallienne		E–G	
(Vigorous, appealing)				
Minstrel's Song	Chatterton		C–G	
(Harmonic in pattern, unhackneyed)				
I Can't Be Talking of Love	Mathews		C#–D♭	
(More conventional, Irish flavor, fresh)				
BARBER, SAMUEL				
Dover Beach (piano or string quartet)	Arnold	1936	B♭–F	GS
(Major concert material, sensitive, expressive)				
Sleep Now	Joyce	1939	E♭–A♭ / C–F	GS
(Slow, intense, subtle setting)				
Nocturne	Prokosch	1941	D#–G# / C#–F#	GS
(Broad, rich emotional tapestry)				
The Secrets of the Old	Yeats	1941	E♭–G / C–E	GS
(Requires clear delineation, rhythmically intriguing)				

*Used by permission American Academy of Teachers of Singing.
**See p. 220 for "Key to Publisher."

Composer — Title	Poet	Copyright	Range	Publisher
BARBER (cont.)				
Sure on This Shining Night.	Agee	1941.	D-G.	GS
(Sustained, mystic, poetic, dignified)			B-E	
Monks and Raisins	Villa.	1944.	D-F.	GS
(Enchanting, philosophical nonsense)				
*Rain Has Fallen				
*I Hear An Army				
*A Nun Takes the Veil (originally titled as Heaven-Haven in Musical Quarterly)				
BAUER, MARION				
Through the Upland Meadows.	Fletcher	1924.	E♭-A	GS
(Moderately big, harmonic, musically challenging)				
Swan.	Bailey	1947.	D-F.	AMP
(Simple, sincere, melodic)				
The Harp.	Bailey	1947.	C-E.	AMP
(Lyric, harmonic background)				
BAX, ARNOLD (Br)				
Oh Dear! What Can the Matter Be?.	Old Eng. . . .	1920.	D-E♭ . . .	Ches
(Delightful concert setting)				GS
Cradle Song	P. Colum	1922.	E-G. . . .	Ches
(Simple, touching)				Chap
BERGER, JEAN				
The Instruments	Dryden	1952.	C#-F#. . . .	RDR
(Modernly phonic, convincing, unequivocal)				BM
BERGSMA, WILLIAM				
Doll's Boy's A-Sleep, from "Six Songs".	E. E. Cummings . . .	1957.	E-B♭	CF
(Modern idiom)				
BERNERS, LORD (Br)				
Dialogue Between Tom Filuter and His Man by Ned the Dog-Stealer.		1924.	D-F.	Ches
(Characterization in the vernacular, effective)				GS
BERNSTEIN, LEONARD				
I Hate Music, a Cycle of Kid Songs for Soprano.	Bernstein.	1943.	C octave A .	Wit
III. I Hate Music				
V. I Just Found Out Today				
(Effective separately. Amusing divertissement, adroitly handled)				
Silhouette (Galilee).	Bernstein.	1951.	B♭-G#. . . .	GS
(English and Israeli, intensely descriptive)				
BESLY, MAURICE (Br)				
An Epitaph.	de la Mare . . .	1922.	A♭-E♭. . . .	Cur
(Subtle, slow, gentle)				GS
The Sleep That Flits on Baby's Eyes	Tagore	1922.	D-A#(C#) . .	Cur
(Violin optional with piano acc. Romantic for high lyric voice, not long)				GS
BLISS, ARTHUR (Br)				
The Buckle.	de la Mare	1922.	B-F#	Cur
(Rapid, strophic and attractive)				GS
Fair Is My Love, from "Serenade".	Spenser.	1930.	B♭-F	Ox
(Piano, or Baritone and Orchestra. Romantic, harmonic, sustained setting. Ends on high F piano)				
BOARDMAN, REGINALD				
Ancient Prayer.	Anon.	1955.	E-F#	GS
(Warm harmonic color reflects liturgical setting, eulogistic, maesotoso ending)				

*Included in previous Academy Song Lists.

Composer — Title	Poet	Copyright	Range	Publisher

BOUGHTON, RUTLAND (Br)

Immanence . . . . .Rodher . . . . 1919. .B-E. . . . . Cur
   (Impressionistic, acoustically effective in   GS
    an auditorium)

BOWLES, PAUL

Letter to Freddy. . . . . .Stein. . . . . . . 1935. .E♭-E♭. . . . GS
   (Delightfully set poem of Gertrude Stein)

Heavenly Grass. . . . . .Williams . . . . . 1946. .B-A. . . . . GS
   (Mystic, yearning)

Lonesome Man. . . . . .Williams . . . . . 1946. .D♭-E♭. . . . GS
   (Very rhythmic, moody)

Sugar in the Cane . . . . .Williams . . . . . 1946. .D-F$^\#$ . . . . GS
   (Vigorous, jazz in strict tempo)

Once a Lady Was Here. . . . . .Bowles . . . . . 1946. .C-E♭ . . . . GS
   (Marked "slowly and easily" - good soft-shoe
    timing, effective)

On a Quiet Conscience . . . . .Charles I. . . . . 1947. .E-F. . . . . MM
   (Harmonically difficult, not fast. Old   TP
    English text)

CARPENTER, JOHN ALDEN

The Green River . . . . .Douglas. . . . . 1912. .C$^\#$-E . . . . GS
   (Quiet, atmospheric, descriptive, rhythmic)

Looking-Glass River . . . . .Stevenson. . . . . 1912. .(A)B-D . . . GS
   (Atmospheric, smooth-paced classic)

*Serenade . . . . .Sassoon. . . . . 1921. .E♭-high C. . GS
   (Brilliant, powerful, Spanish idiom)   C-A

CASTELNUOVO-TEDESCO, MARIO

The Legend of Jonas Bronck. . . . . .Guiterman. . . . . 1941. .F-E♭ . . . . Gal
   (Bass-Baritone, colorful interpretive
    possibilities, standard harmonic background)

CHANLER, THEODORE

I Rise When You Enter . . . . .Feeney . . . . . 1945. .C$^\#$-G . . . . GS
   (Slangy and effective, uncomplicated
    harmonic background with good movement)

The Children. . . . . .Feeney . . . . . 1946. .C-F$^\#$ . . . . GS
   (Nine Songs. Short cycle requiring
   interpretive imagination. "The Wind" and
   "Grandma" are suitable for individual
   presentation)

COPLAND, AARON

Twelve Poems of Emily Dickinson . . . . 1951. . . . . BHks
   1. Nature, the Gentlest Mother. . . . . .B♭-G
     (Big, good length, pianissimo ending)
   2. There Came a Wind Like a Bugle . . . . .B-G
     (Fast, strong)
   3. Why Do They Shut Me Out of Heaven? . . . . .B♭-A♭
     (Moderate pace, short, forte ending)
   4. The World Feels Dusty. . . . . .A$^\#$-F$^\#$
     (Slow, short)
   5. Heart, We Will Forget Him. . . . . .B♭-G
     (Slow, soft ending)
   6. Dear March, Come In. . . . . .A-F$^\#$
     (Bright, lively, good length)
   7. Sleep Is Supposed to Be . . . . .B♭-2nd B♭
     (Moderately slow, big forte ending)
   8. When They Come Back. . . . . .C-F$^\#$
     (Fairly rubato, mood whimsy)

*Included in previous Academy Song Lists.

COPLAND (cont.)
    9. I Felt a Funeral in My Brain. . . . . .C#-G
        (Rather fast, declamatory, soft end)
    10. I've Heard an Organ Talk Sometimes. . . . . .B♭-F
        (Gentle, flowing, short)
    11. Going to Heaven . . . . .A-F
        (Fast, slow, soft ending declaimed)
    12. The Chariot .B-F#
        (Moderate pace, quiet ending. Free harmonic texture
        and key, dissonant, fluent, extensive range)
    Dirge in Woods. . . . . .Meredith . . . . . 1957. .D-B♭ . . . . BHks
        (Broad, flowing, wide range)

COWELL, HENRY
    The Donkey. . . . . .Chesterton . . . . 1947. .D-F#(A). . . MM
        (Harmonic but harshly dissonant, high   TP
        tessitura, needs dramatic color and
        interpretation)

CRESTON, PAUL
    The Bird of the Wilderness. . . . . .Tagore . . . . . . 1950. .F#-A . . . . GS
        (Sweeping, rich, harmonic color)

CRIST, BAINBRIDGE
    Girl of the Red Mouth . . . . .Macdermott . . . . 1918. .E-B♭ . . . . CF
        (Fast-moving, provocative)   C-G

DELLO JOIO, NORMAN
    The Assassination (Two fates discuss a human
        problem). . . . . .Hillyer. . . . . . 1949. .B♭-D . . . . CF
        (Declamatory, good length)
    Eyebright . . . . .J. Symonds . . . . 1954. .E♭-F . . . . CF
        (Free harmonic structure)
    Why So Pale and Wan, Fond Lover?. . . . . . .Suckling . . . . . 1954. .D-E. . . . . CF
        (Famous words imaginatively voiced)
    Meeting at Night. . . . . .Browning . . . . . 1954. .F-G. . . . . CF
        (Strong setting, quiet ending)
    The Dying Nightingale . . . . .Young. . . . . . . 1954. .D♭-G♭. . . . CF
        (Colorful)
    All Things Leave Me . . . . .A Symons . . . . . 1954. .F-F. . . . . CF
        (Liquid, simple)
    How Do I Love Thee? . . . . .Adapted from
        (Rich harmonic andante)   Elizabeth Browning. 1954. .D-G. . . . . CF

DIAMOND, DAVID
    David Weeps for Absalom . . . . .The Bible. . . . . 1947. .D-G(A) . . . MM
        (Fine strong lament)   TP
    Brigid's Song . . . . .Joyce. . . . . . . 1947. .E-G. . . . . MM
        (Simple, short, stark)   TP
    Even Though the World Keeps Changing. . . . .Rilke-Norton . . . 1948. .G-B♭ . . . . CF
        (Broad mystic paean to song)   C#-A

DITTENHAVER, SARAH LOUISE
    Lady of the Amber Wheat . . . . .Coleman. . . . . . 1944. .D-A♭ . . . .Gal
        ("After a Painting." Devotional, melodious,
        relatively high tessitura)

DOUGHERTY, CELIUS
    The K'e . . . . .Chinese. . . . . . 1944. .D-B. . . . . GS
        (Story-telling, simple)
    Loveliest of Trees. . . . . .Housman. . . . . . 1948. .E-G. . . . . BHks
        (Gracious melody, delicate harmonic   C-E
        treatment)
    Declaration of Independence . . . . .Gibbs. . . . . . . 1948. .C-C. . . . . GS
        (Child's testy declaiming)
    Love in the Dictionary. . . . . .Dougherty. . . . . 1949. .D-G. . . . . GS
        (Clever setting of dictionary definition of
        love)

Composer — Title	Poet	Copyright	Range	Publisher
DOUGHERTY (cont.)				
Oncet in a Museum (Two Ways)	Weaver	1953	D-G	RDR BM
(Philosophy expressed in the vernacular)				
DUKE, JOHN				
Shelling Peas	Jackson	1926	C-A♭ A-F	GS
(Lively, colorful. Rhythm uneven, harmonic, effective. Tests enunciation)				
*Loveliest of Trees	Housman	1934	C-D	GS
(Clear, simple, classic statement)				
The Bird	Wylie	1947	F-A	GS
(Simple lyric structure, sudden dynamic change)				
Bells in the Rain	Wylie	1948	E-G	CF
(Mood song, messa di voce climax)				
When I Set Out for Lyonesse	Hardy	1953	C-A♭ A-F	BM
(Pleasant, uncomplicated)				
In the Fields	Mew	1955	A-E	CF
(Mood song, slow, choral type. Pleasing, full of faith)				
DUNHILL, THOMAS F. (Br)				
To the Queen of Heaven	16th Century	1926	C-G	Cur GS
(Sustained and expressive)				
EDMUNDS, CHRIS. M. (Br)				
The Bellman	Herrick	1929	B♭-D	Cur GS
(Well-set impression of the Night-Watch passing as he calls his hours)				
EDMUNDS, JOHN				
The Faucon	Eng. 16th Century	1947	D-F	MM TP
(Unusual chording, stark, mystic)				
*Milkmaids	Anon	1947	D♭-G	MM TP
(Fresh, short, highly descriptive)				
The Lonely	Russell	1948	E♭-F	CF
(Lovely, gentle and sad mood)				
FERGUSON, HOWARD (Br)				
Discovery, Cycle of 5 Songs for Voice and Piano	Welch	1952	F -G(A)	BHks
1. Dreams Melting				
2. The Freedom of the City				
3. Babylon				
4. Jane Allen				
5. Discovery				
(Imaginative harmonic structure. A somewhat bitter-coated cycle)				
FINZI, GERALD (Br)				
Budmouth Dears	Hardy	1933	C#-A	Ox
(Exciting, taken from "A Young Man's Exhortation," ten songs for tenor and piano)				
Till Earth Outwears	Hardy	1958		WR
Seven Songs for High Voice and Piano				BHks
1. Let Me Enjoy the Earth			D -G♭	
2. In Years Defaced			C-A	
3. The Market Girl		1927	C-A	
4. I Look into My Glass			C-G	
5. It Never Looks Like Summer		1956	C-F	
6. At a Lunar Eclipse			E-A	
7. Life Laughs Onward		1955	C-G	
(A fourteen-minute cycle. Musically fluent, gracious to the voice, interesting Hardy poems)				

*Included in previous Academy Song Lists.

GLANVILLE-HICKS (cont.)
    3. Stars . . . . D–G
    4. Unlucky Love . . . . E–E
    5. Homespun Collars . . . . F#–A
        (Short songs, interesting delineation)

GOLDMAN, RICHARD FRANKO
    My Kingdom. .Stevenson. . . . . . 1948. .D–G. . . . . MM
        (Individual use of diatonic scale)   TP
    Two Poems of William Blake. . . . . 1952. .E–G. . . . . MM
        To a Lovely Mytle Bound   TP
            (Gracious, short, unusual, cool)
        The Shepherd
            (Religious, unusual)

GURNEY, IVOR (Br)
    Desire in Spring. . . . . .Ledwidge . . . . . 1928. .D–G. . . . . Ox
        (Charming description)   B–E

HARRIS, EDWARD
    *Agatha Morley. . . . . .Russell. . . . . . 1946. .C–D. . . . . CF
        (Descriptive, dry humor)

HARRIS, ROY
    Fog . . . . .Sandburg . . . . . 1948. .D–F. . . . . CF
        (Imaginative, free harmonic texture)

HARRIS, W. H. (Br)
    Piskies . . . . .Wilson . . . . . 1927. .B–E. . . . . Ox
        (Fluent, happy, whimsical)

HARTY, HAMILTON (Br)
    Sea-Wrack . . . . .O'Neill. . . . . . 1905. .C–F. . . . . BHks
        (Simple, traditional structure, dramatic,   Bb–Eb
        despondent)

HELM, EVERETT
    Prairie Waters by Night . . . . .Sandburg . . . . . 1940. .D–Eb . . . . CF
        (Colorful, atmospheric. Imaginative
        harmonic structure)

HINDEMITH, PAUL
    From "Nine English Songs 1942"
        On a Fly Drinking Out of His Cup. . . . . . .Oldys. . . . . 1944. .E–F. . . . . AMP
            (Serious, philosophical. Key feeling with
            use of unharmonic texture)
        The Whistlin' Thief . . . . .Lover. . . . . 1945. .D–F. . . . . AMP
            (Verse story, lively, declamatory, good
            "change of pace")
        Envoy . . . . .Thompson . . . . . 1945. .Eb–F. . . . . AMP
            (Serious, poetic mood, modal harmony)

HOWE, MARY
    Ripe Apples . . . . .Speyer . . . . . 1939. .Db–G . . . . GS
        (A philosophical song with sad ending.
        Imaginative harmony)
    When I Died in Berners Street . . . . .Wylie. . . . . 1947. .C–G. . . . . GS
        (Macabre verse-story of six reincarnations.
        Harmonic structure, freely imaginative)

HOWELLS, HERBERT (Br)
    Old Skinflint . . . . .Gibson . . . . . . 1920. .D–F. . . . . Cur
        (Modal, rhythmically strong tarantella.   GS
        Tinged with bitterness)

*Included in previous Academy Song Lists.

Composer — Title	Poet	Copyright	Range	Publisher

IRELAND, JOHN (Br)
From "Songs of a Wayfarer"
    I Was Not Sorrowful (Spleen)........Dowson.........1912 C-E♭.....BHks
      (Beautiful poetic sadness, lasting
      traditional harmonies)

IVES, CHARLES E.
From "Seven Songs"............Ives.........1932..D-F#.....Ar
    Walking (pub. separately)............1902.........AMP
      (Descriptive, effective, paces along)
From "Nineteen Songs"............1933.........NM
    Canon............Moore.........1894..D-F#(B)...TP
      (Fast, positive, brief)
    Two Little Flowers............1921..G♭-E
      (Almost simple, naive, sincere, short)
From "Thirty-Four Songs"............1933.........NM
    A Night Thought............Moore.........1895..B-D#.....TP
      (Quiet, slow, short)
    Ann Street............Morris.........1921..E♭-E
      ("Fast and noisily," amusing)
    The White Gulls............Morris.........1921..B-E
      (Quiet, mystic)
    *The Greatest Man............Collins.........1921..E-G
      (Active, personal, difficult)

JACKSON, FRANCIS (Br)
Tree at My Window............Frost.........1951..D-A.....Ox
    (Fluent, harmonically rich, rather moody
    and dramatic)

JACOBI, FREDERICK
Three Songs............Freneau.........1949.........VM
    I. On the Sleep of Plants (1790)............F#-G
      ("In the manner of a Folk-song."
      High tessitura)
    II. Elegy (1786)............E♭-B♭
      ("The Wild Honeysuckle." Romantic
      colonialism)
    III. Ode to Freedom (1795)............F-B♭
      (Early American flavor, varied and concise)

KAGEN, SERGIUS
Memory, Hither Come............Blake.........1948..D-F#.....MM TP
    (Unharmonic, expressive setting)
A June Day............Teasdale.........1950..F#-B♭.....Wei
    (Unconventional, graceful, good movement
    short)
Maybe............Sandburg.........1950..D-G.....Wei
    (Simple non-harmonic treatment, short
    effective story-telling)
Miss T.............de la Mare.........1950..E-E.....Wei
    (Amusing, uncomplicated, generally non-
    harmonic pattern)
All Day I Hear............Joyce.........1950..F-F#.....Wei
    (Dissonant, vigorous, quiet)
Let It Be Forgotten............Teasdale.........1950..F-F.....Wei
    (Unharmonic mood realized in quiet setting)
Sleep Now............Joyce.........1951..A-E.....Leeds
    (Unharmonic mood created by cohesive use of
    melody and dissonance)
From "Three Satires"............1956.........MM
    2. Yonder See the Morning Blink............Housman.........D-E.....TP
    3. How Pleasant It Is to Have Money............Clough.........C-E
      (Interesting, philosophical observations)

*Included in previous Academy Song Lists.

Composer — Title	Poet	Copyright	Range	Publisher

LEES, BENJAMIN
Songs of the Night . . . . Nickson . . . . 1958 . . . . BHks
  1. O Shade of Evening . . . . G♭-B♭
  2. A Star Fell in Flames . . . . A♭-A
  3. The Enemies . . . . F#-G
  4. A Whisper of Rain . . . . F-G
  5. Fall to the Night Wind . . . . F-B♭
  6. On Eastern Hills . . . . E♭-B
     (Highly impressive setting of distinctly original
      texts. 1, 2 and 5, 6 arr. for chamber orchestra
      of 13 solo instruments)

MOORE, DOUGLAS
Old Song . . . . Roethke . . . . . . 1950 . C-F . . . . . CF
     (Slow, paced mood of suspended action.
     Free use of harmonic structure)
Under the Greenwood Tree . . . . Shakespeare . . . . . 1950 . F-A . . . . . CF
     (Rhythmic, melodic)

MORGENSTERN, SAM
My Apple Tree . . . . Lorca-Honig . . . 1952 . F-A . . . . . CF
     (Free contemporary composition, clearly
     stated, unhackneyed)

NAGINSKI, CHARLES
Richard Cory . . . . Robinson . . . . . 1950 . A-G . . . . GS
     (Sophisticated, rhythmic, startling,
     dissonant, wide range)
The Pasture . . . . Frost . . . . 1950 . G♭-E♭ . . . . GS
     (Appealing child-approach, rhythmic
     description)
Under the Harvest Moon . . . . Sandburg . . . . . 1950 . D-E . . . . GS
     (Graceful melody, idyllic text)

NILES, JOHN JACOB
Go 'Way from My Window . . . . "Adapted, ... 1934 . C-G . . . . GS
     (Verse form, standard harmonic use,   J. J. Niles"
     appeal of traditional folk-song)
I Wonder as I Wander . . . . "Adapted, ... 1934 . E♭-G . . . . GS
     (Religious, gentle, appealing)   J. J. Niles"   B♭-D
Gambler's Lament . . . . Niles . . . . . . 1946 . B-E . . . . . GS
     (Dark, rhythmic, folk theme)
The Blue Madonna . . . . Niles . . . . . . 1948 . G-B♭ . . . . GS
     (Rhythm patterns tell unusual folk story)

NORDOFF, PAUL
Lacrima Christi . . . . Mannes . . . . . 1932 . C-F . . . . . MM
     (Slow, intense, dissonant harmonic pattern,   TP
     with key feeling)
Willow River . . . . Seifert . . . . . 1938 . D-G . . . . . AMP
     (Free harmonic use of fluent rhythm,
     extended melodic mood)
Embroidery for a Faithless Friend . . . . Prude . . . . . . 1945 . C-A . . . . . AMP
     (Fast, difficult of rhythm and enunciation,
     sharp, incisive)
*There Shall Be More Joy . . . . Ford . . . . . . 1938 . C#-F# . . . . AMP
     (Delightfully light, free harmonic pattern,
     happy song)

ORR, ROBIN (Br)
Three Chinese Songs . . . . tr. Waley . . . . 1947 . . . . Ox
  1. Tell Me Now . . . . Wang Chi . . . . C#-G

*Included in previous Academy Song Lists.

ORR (cont.)
  2. Plucking the Rushes. . . . . .Anon. . . . . .C#-D
  3. The Little Cart. . . . . .Ch'en Tzu-lung . . . . . . .F-E♭
      (Dramatic, free use of impressionistic
      harmony and rhythmic accent, effective
      pictorially. The first lends itself
      acceptably to transposition)

PERSICHETTI, VINCENT
  Emily Dickinson Songs
    Out of the Morning. . . . . 1958. .D-E. . . . . EV
    I'm Nobody. . . . . 1958. .D-E. . . . . EV
    When the Hills Do . . . . 1958. .D-D. . . . . EV
    The Grass . . . . 1958. .D♭-F. . . . . EV
        (Cameo-setting of four typical Dickinson poems)

PETERKIN, NORMAN (Br)
  I Heard a Piper Piping. . . . . .MacCathmbaoel. . . 1924. .G-F. . . . . Ox
      (Simple, haunting, tuneful)
  I Wish and I Wish . . . . .Campbell . . . . . 1925. .B-E. . . . . Ox
      (Song of wishfulness)
  The Bees' Song. . . . . .de la Mare . . . . 1940. .C-F#. . . . . Ox
      (Impressionistically onomatopoetic)
  The Tide Rises, the Tide Falls. . . . . .Longfellow . . . . 1943. .C#-G. . . . . Ox
      (Strong harmonic texture, moody, reflecting
      the unalterable ebb and flow of life)

PORTER, QUINCY
  Music When Soft Voices Die. . . . . .Shelley. . . . . . 1947. .D-E. . . . . MM
      (Slow, simple, non-harmonic, peaceful)   TP

RAWSTHORNE, ALAN (Br)
  Carol . . . . .Rodgers. . . . . . 1948. .D♭-F . . . . Ox
      (Harmonic tapestry, allegorical verse,
      ending on diminuendo high F)

READ, GARDNER
  Pierrot . . . . .Teasdale . . . . . 1943. .C-A. . . . . Gal
      (Simple, effective setting of well-known poem)
  When Moonlight Falls. . . . . .Conkling . . . . . 1945. .B♭-E . . . . Gal
      (Atmospheric setting of impressionistic poem,
      limpid and cool)
  Piping Down the Valleys Wild. . . . . .Blake. . . . . . . 1950. .D-E. . . . . Gal
      (Light, happy, modal setting)

ROREM, NED
  The Lordly Hudson . . . . .Goodman. . . . . . 1947. .D♭-G . . . . MM
      (Eulogistic, inspiring, fluent contemporary   TP
      freedom of setting)
  Alleluia. . . . . 1949. .B-G#. . . . Har
      (Free chordal structure in seven/eight time,
      developed to climactic conclusion)
  The Silver Swan . . . . .Jonson . . . . . . 1950. .E-high C . . PI
      (Free use of present-day harmony. Lyric,
      wide range melody, expressive)
  A Christmas Carol . . . ."almost 1500 A.D.". 1953. .C-F. . . . . EV
      (Light accompaniment, simple free use of
      harmonic texture)
  Spring. . . . . .Hopkins. . . . . . 1953. .C-A. . . . . BHks
      (Brilliant setting of colorful words
      requiring clarity of enunciation)
  Lullaby of the Woman of the Mountain. . . . . . .Pearse-MacDonagh . . 1956. .C-F#. . . . . BHks
      (Easily paced, loving mood, subtle harmonic
      structure)

Composer — Title	Poet	Copyright	Range	Publisher

ROREM (cont.)

Rain in Spring. . . . . .Goodman. . . . . . 1956. .A-E♭ . . . . BHks
    (Short, languidly flowing, delightfully
      descriptive text)

The Nightingale . . . ."about 1500 A.D.". . 1956. .C♯-F♯ . . . . BHks
    (Free modal use of old and picturesque
      verse)

ROSENBERG, EMANUEL

The Complete Misanthropist. . . . . .Bishop . . . . . . 1944. .C-F. . . . . Gal
  (I Love to Think of Things I Hate)
  (Light, simple and pungent)

ROWLEY, ALEC (Br)

Pretty Betty. . . . . .Anon. . . . . . 1927. .D♭-E♭. . . . Ox
    (Standard harmony in flexible measure
      enhancing the charm of homespun verse)

SACCO, JOHN

Rapunzel. . . . . .Crapsey. . . . . . 1941. .F♯-B♭ . . . BM
    (Free, romantic, ably sweeping, colorful and   C♯-F
      dramatic setting)

Brother Will, Brother John. . . . . .Welborn. . . . . . 1947. .C-F. . . . . GS
    ("With sly jocularity," an uncomplicated
      talkative verse song)

SCHUMAN, WILLIAM

Orpheus and His Lute. . . . . .Shakespeare. . . . 1944. .C-F♯ . . . . GS
    (Well-sustained, original setting, harmonically
      simple, fresh in feeling)

SCOTT, CYRIL (Br)

A Song of London. . . . . .Watson . . . . . 1906. .C♯-G . . . Elkin
    (Strong use of harmonic rhythmic groups,   B♭-E   Gal
      straightforward)

Our Lady of Violets . . . . .Hooley . . . . . 1920. .D-F♯ . . . . Elkin
    (Simple, religious, fluently harmonic)   B♭-E   Gal

SHAW, MARTIN (Br.)

Love Pagan. . . . . .Cripps . . . . 1919. .C-E♭ . . . . Cur
    (Vigorous declaration of coalminers love)   GS

*Down by the Sally Gardens. . . . . .Yeats. . . . . . 1919. .B-D. . . . . Cur
    (Classic concert setting)   GS

The Egg-Shell . . . . .Kipling. . . . . . 1919. .D-D. . . . . Cur
    (Fantasy, amusing but obtuse, typically   GS
      English use of harmonic structure)

SIEGMEISTER, ELIE

Johnny Appleseed. . . . . .R. Benet . . . . 1941. .B-E. . . . . MM
    (Colorful, modal)   TP

The Lincoln Penny . . . . .Kreymborg. . . . 1943. .B-E. . . . . Marks
    (Sincere, descriptive modal setting)

Nancy Hanks .R. Benet . . . . 1949. .D♭-F . . . . Marks
    (Reflective verse song, simple and sincere,
      declamatory)

SINGER, WERNER

Folksong. . . . . .London . . . . 1954. .C♯-E . . . . CF
  (Simple, colorful)

SLONIMSKY, NICOLAS

Gravestones at Hancock, N.H.. . . . . .Engravings . . . . 1946. .A♭-G . . . . Ax
  1. Vain World   TS
  2. Lydia
  3. Here Peacefully Lies the Once Happy Father

*Included in previous Academy Song Lists.

SLONIMSKY (cont.)
    4. A Lovely Rose
    5. In Memphis, Tenn.
    6. Stop, My Friends, As You Pass By
       (Six settings sharply etched, imaginative
       harmonic treatment)

STARER, ROBERT

Composer — Title	Poet	Copyright	Range	Publisher
Advice to a Girl	Teasdale	1951	D-G	Leeds
Dew	Teasdale	1951	E-A♭	Leeds
Silence	Lawrence	1951	B♭-E♭	Leeds
To Be Superior	Lawrence	1951	B-E♭	Leeds
'my sweet old etcetera'	Cummings	1956	A-E♭	Leeds

    (Spicy, interesting examples of atonal
    contemporary form)

SWANSON, HOWARD

Composer — Title	Poet	Copyright	Range	Publisher
Night Song	Hughes	1950	D-G	Wei

    (Freely unharmonic, sensitive mood, clear
    setting)

Composer — Title	Poet	Copyright	Range	Publisher
In Time of Silver Rain	Hughes	1950	F-A	Wei

    (Good texture, moves thematically in
    contemporary idiom)

Composer — Title	Poet	Copyright	Range	Publisher
The Valley	Markham	1950	D♭-F♭ B♭-D♭	Leeds

    (Structurally free, lovely, haunting,
    delicate)

Composer — Title	Poet	Copyright	Range	Publisher
I Will Lie Down in Autumn	Swenson	1952	D♭-C	Wei

    (Fatalistic mood, moderate pace, atonal)

Composer — Title	Poet	Copyright	Range	Publisher
Snowdunes	Swenson	1955	F♭-G	Wei

    (Slow-paced, atonal, expressive)

TATE, PHYLLIS (Br)
    Two Songs

Composer — Title	Poet	Copyright	Range	Publisher
1. The Falcon	15th Century	1948	C#-G	Ox

       (Accompaniment interpolated, simple,
       harmonic)

Composer — Title	Poet	Copyright	Range	Publisher
2. The Cock	14th Century	1948	C#-G	Ox

       (Fast, free verse form, clear, key feeling
       at end)

Composer — Title	Poet	Copyright	Range	Publisher
The Quiet Mind	Dyer	1948	A#-F	Ox

    ("Andante sereno," free use of harmonic
    structure)

TAYLOR, CLIFFORD S.

Composer — Title	Poet	Copyright	Range	Publisher
On a Certain Lady at Court	Pope	1954	E-G	AMP

    (Lively rhythm, free harmony)

THACKRAY, RUPERT (Br)

Composer — Title	Poet	Copyright	Range	Publisher
Neglectful Edward	Graves	1952	D-F	Ox

    (Dialogue in flexible harmonic setting)

THOMSON, VIRGIL

Composer — Title	Poet	Copyright	Range	Publisher
Dirge	Webster	1947	D-F	GS

    (Stark, rhythmic, effective)

TOYE, FRANCIS (Br)

Composer — Title	Poet	Copyright	Range	Publisher
*The Inn	Belloc	1925	C-E	Cur GS

    (Colorful, brilliant, a classic)

VALE, CHARLES (Br)

Composer — Title	Poet	Copyright	Range	Publisher
Litany to the Holy Spirit	Herrick	1950	A♭-F	Ox

    (Serious, spiritual setting)

VAUGHAN WILLIAMS, R. (Br)

Composer — Title	Poet	Copyright	Range	Publisher
Bright Is the Ring of Words	Stevenson	1905	G♭-E♭	By

    (Orthodox harmony. Calm, poetic mood)

*Included in previous Academy Song Lists.

VAUGHAN WILLIAMS (cont.)

Composer — Title	Poet	Copyright	Range	Publisher
From "Five Mystical Songs"	Herbert	1911	E♭-F	SB
4. The Call (Also pub. separately)			E♭-F	Gal
(Mystically beautiful)				
5a. Antiphon			F-F	
(Brilliant, heraldic, religious fervor)				
Four Hymns for Tenor, with Viola Obligato		1920		BHks
I. Lord! Come Away!	Taylor		D-B♭	
II. Who Is This Fair One?	Watts		E♭-A	
III. Come Love, Come Lord	Crashaw		G-G	
IV. Evening Hymn	Bridges		E-A	
(Modal treatment especially characteristic of Vaughan Williams)				
From "Three Poems by Walt Whitman"		1925		Ox
2. A Clear Midnight			E-F	
(Solemn and sustained)				
Two Poems by Fredegond Shove		1925		Ox
(Motion and Stillness)			C-D	
Four Nights			C♭-G♭	
(Sensitive moods, harmonically expressed)				
The Water-Mill	Shove	1925	E♭-F C-D	Ox
(Effective interweaving of words and modal sound)				
The New Ghost	Shove	1925	D-F	Ox
(Unusually sensitive description of the New Ghost meeting his Maker)				
The Twilight People	O'Sullivan	1925	B♭-E♭	Ox
(Mystic, lovely modal melody, sparse accompaniment)				
Two English Folk-Songs	Old English	1935		Ox
(For Voice and Violin only)				
1. Searching for Lambs			E-E	
(Quiet, simple verse form in five/four time)				
2. The Lawyer			C-E	
(Lively, three-verse story, unusual extended phrasing)				
The Pilgrim's Progress		1952		Ox
(Concert versions of Seven Songs from the Morality by the same composer)				
1. Watchful's Song (Nocturne)	Psalms and Isaiah		C#-E	
(Lovely, modal, religious)				
2. The Song of the Pilgrims	Bunyan		D-E	
(Allegro and maestoso, boldly assertive)				
3. The Pilgrim's Psalm	St. Paul and Psalms		D-F	
(Statement of faith, rhythmic and strong)				
4. The Song of the Leaves of Life and the Water of Life	Revelation		D-E	
(Beautiful, lyric movement and musical texture)				
5. The Song of Vanity Fair	Wood		C-F♭	
(Vigorous, exciting song of materialism, extremely difficult)				
6. The Woodcutter's Song	Bunyan		D-E	
(Peaceful, philosophic, quiet and lightly accompanied)				
7. The Bird's Song (The Lord Is My Shepherd)	Psalms		D♭-F	
(Quietly lyrical, light-hearted)				
In the Spring	Barnes	1952	C#-E	Ox
(Flowing melody, modern treatment of old dialect)				
Along the Field-		1954	C-A	Ox

VAUGHAN WILLIAMS (cont.)
    Eight Housman Songs for Voice and Violin
        I. We'll to the Woods No More
       II. Along the Field
      III. The Half Moon Westers Low
      IV. In the Morning
       V. The Sigh That Heaves the Grasses
      VI. Good-Bye
     VII. Fancy's Knell
    VIII. With Rue My Heart Is Laden
        (Novel duets, pleasing, uncomplicated)

WALTON, WILLIAM (Br)
    Three Songs . . . . .Edith Sitwell. . . . 1932. . . . . .Ox
      1. Daphne ("nello stile inglese") . . . . .C-A
      2. Through Gilded Trellises ("nello stile americano") . . . . .C#-A
      3. Old Sir Faulk ("nello stile americano"). . . . . .C#-G
        (Free use of very rhythmic and unharmonic
        structure, not simple songs)
    Under the Greenwood Tree. . . . . .Shakespeare. . . . . 1937. .D-G. . . . . .Ox
      (Fast-moving, simple setting in Old English
      style)

WARD, ROBERT
    Sorrow of Mydath. . . . . .Masefield. . . . . 1952. .E-A. . . . . .PI
      (Full rich harmonic use of modern texture)
    Ballad from Pantaloon . . . . .Stambler . . . . . 1957. .F-F. . . . . .Hi
      (Extended dramatic ballad, simply told)   Gal

WARLOCK, PETER (Br)
    From "Peter Warlock Song Album" . . . . BHks
      As Ever I Saw (Pub. separately) . . . . . . .Anon. . . . . . . 1919. .E♭-A♭
        (Interestingly phrased, pleasant)   D♭-G♭
      My Gostly Fader . . . . .XV Cen. Rondel . . . 1919. .E♭-F#
        (Early English text, simple setting)
    Good Ale. . . . . .15th Century . . . . 1922. .E♭-A♭. . . . Aug
      (Pleasing crescendo with abrupt ending to   C-F   Broude
      fourth verse)
    Piggesnie . . . . .16th Century . . . . 1922. .D-G. . . . . Aug
      (Moderately fast, requires enunciation)   B-E   Broude
    From "A Book of Songs". . . . . Ox
      Passing By. . . . . .Anon.. . . . . . . 1924. .D-G
        (Rich-sounding setting of complete poem)
      Sleep (Pub. separately) . . . . .Fletcher . . . . . 1924. .D-E♭. . . . .Ox
        ("To be...phrased according to the natural
        accentuation of the words," harmonic)
    The Singer. . . . . .Shanks . . . . . . 1925. .D-G. . . . . Aug
      (Unaffected lyricism)   Broude
    One More River. . . . . .Week-end Book. . . . 1927. .C-D. . . . . BHks
      (Unique setting of solo, vigorous, positive)
    Yarmouth Fair . . . . .From Norfolk . . . . 1927. .D-G. . . . . Ox
      (Descriptively delightful)   B-E
                                 A-D
    From "A Book of Songs"
      Cradle Song (Also pub. separately). . . . . .Phillip. . . . . . 1928. .D-F. . . . . Ox
        (Gentle, lilting, pleasing)
    The Fox .Blunt. . . . . . . 1931. .D-F#. . . . . Ox
      (Dramatic, colorful, slow, unusual harmonic
      treatment)

WATTS, WINTTER
    Miniver Cheevy. . . . . .Robinson . . . . . 1910. .B♭-F . . . . GS
      (Imaginative colorful musical setting,
      enhancing the text)

Composer — Title	Poet	Copyright Range	Publisher

WATTS (cont.)
    The Little Page's Song (XIII Cent.) . . . . . . .Percy. . . . . 1920. .G-A♭ . . . . . OD
      (Graceful, charming, atmospheric)

WISHART, PETER (Br)
    Two Songs . . . . 1953 . . . . .Ox
      1. Dirge. . . . . .Shakespeare. . . . . .E♭-F
        (Vocal statement, slow, sustained,
        frequently unaccompanied)
      2. The Mountebank's Song. . . . . .17th Century . . . . . . .E-A
        (Flamboyant, clever setting, effective)

F. Accredited and Acceptable Translations of Classic and Semi-classic Songs -- List No. 8 American Academy of Teachers of Singing*

This EIGHTH LIST is devoted -- not so much to songs -- as to acceptable and accredited translations. The composers covered by this list will be French, German and Russian. As far as possible -- the translations recommended by this list are published by American publishers. This has been done because of the difficulty and the expense of procuring foreign publications.

The singing of a song in translation may not meet the fullest realization of the composer's meaning -- but what is lost is more than offset by the practical use of our English language. Singing in the vernacular -- opens up to the singer a large field of song which would otherwise remain closed.

Composer	Title	Translator	Publisher**
Beethoven	Adelaïde	Mattulath	CF
Beethoven	Ich liebe dich	Mattulath	CF
Beethoven	In questa tomba	Mattulath	GS
Brahms	Der Schmied	Manney	OD
Brahms	Der Tod, das ist die kühle Nacht	Mattulath	CF
Brahms	Mainacht	Fox, Stuart Wilson & Strongways	Ox
Brahms	Feldeinsamkeit	England	OD
Brahms	Vergebliches Ständchen	Chapman	GS
Brahms	Sapphische Ode	Westbrook	OD
Bachelet	Chère Nuit	Osgood	GS
Debussy	Romance	Bliss Carman	BM
Debussy	Les Cloches	Bliss Carman	BM
Debussy	Mandolines	Bliss Carman	BM
Debussy	Beau Soir	Bliss Carman	BM
Du Parc	Invitation au Voyage	Bliss Carman	BM
Du Parc	Lament	Bliss Carman	BM
Du Parc	Soupir	Bliss Carman	BM
Du Parc	L'Extase	Parker	OD
Faure	Nell	Louise Baum	GS
Faure	Les Berceaux	Louise Baum	GS
Faure	Clair de Lune	Blaess	OD
Gretchaninoff	Over the Steppe	Taylor & Schindler	GS
Gretchaninoff	Berceuse	Taylor & Schindler	OD
Gretchaninoff	The Wounded Birch	Taylor & Schindler	GS
Grieg	Are They Tears, Beloved?	Taylor	JF
Grieg	Ein Traum	Manney	OD
Grieg	An einem Bache	Bullard	OD
Grieg	Eros	Dale	OD
Grieg	Solvejg's Lied	Westbrook	OD
Grieg	Ich liebe dich	Chapman	GS
Grieg	Mit einer Primula Veris	Cosler	OD
Grieg	Am schönsten Sommerabend	Manney	OD
Henschel	Morgen-Hymne	Baker	GS

*Used by permission American Academy of Teachers of Singing.
**See p. 220 for "Key to Publisher."

Composer	Title	Translator	Publisher
Jensen	Lehn' deine Wang'	Elson	OD
Jensen	O lass' dich halten	Baker	GS
Jensen	Mumuring Zephyr	Mattulath	CF
Jensen	Am Ufer des Manzanares	Manney	OD
Lalo	L'Esclave	Mattulath	CF
Liszt	Du bist wie eine Blume	Manney	OD
Liszt	Es muss ein Wunderbares sein	Manney	OD
Liszt	O quand je dors	Armbruster	OD
Massenet	Bonne Nuit	Burnett	OD
Massenet	Crepuscule	Audin	GS
Massenet	Ouvre tes yeux bleus	Mattulath	CF
Mendelssohn	Auf Flügeln des Gesanges	Wilson	Ox
Mussorgsky	Little Star so Bright	Taylor & Schindler	GS
Mussorgsky	Seminarian	Taylor & Schindler	GS
Mussorgsky	The Song of Solomon	Taylor & Schindler	GS
Mussorgsky	The Song of the Flea	Mattulath	CF
Mozart	Das Veilchen	Mattulath	CF
Rachmaninoff	In the Silence of the Night	Taylor & Schindler	GS
Rachmaninoff	The Song of Grusia	Taylor & Schindler	GS
Rachmaninoff	Floods of Spring	Hapgood	GS
Rachmaninoff	The Isle	Harris & Taylor	GS
Rachmaninoff	O Thou Billowy Harvest Field	Chapman	GS
Rimsky-Korsakoff	Song of India	Cowdray	GS
Rimsky-Korsakoff	The Nightingale and the Rose	Taylor	OD
Rubinstein	Du bist wie eine Blume	Chapman	GS
Rubinstein	Der Asra	Buck	GS
Rubinstein	Es blinkt der Thau	Westbrook	OD
Rubinstein	Die Lerche	Westbrook	OD
Schubert	Der Musensohn	Falk	Gal
Schubert	An die Musik	Grace Hall	OD
Schubert	Der Wanderer	Westbrook	OD
Schubert	Der Doppelgänger	Mattulath	CF
Schubert	Gretchen and Spinnrade	Mattulath	CF
Schubert	Haidenröslein	Mattulath	CF
Schubert	Wohin	Strongways & Wilson	Ox
Schubert	Litanei	Strongways & Wilson	Ox
Schubert	Der Tod und das Mädchen	Mattulath	CF
Schubert	Du bist die Ruh'	Mattulath	CF
Schumann	Die Lotosblume	Mattulath	CF
Schumann	Mondnacht	Mattulath	CF
Schumann	Der Nussbaum	F. F. Bullard	OD
Schumann	Du bist wie eine Blume	Manney	OD
Schumann	Marienwürmchen	Manney	CF
Schumann	Widmung	Mattulath	CF
Schumann	Wenn ich früh in den Garten geh'	Mattulath	CF
Schumann	Die beiden Grenadiere	Westbrook	OD
Schumann	Waldesgespräch	Mattulath	CF
Schumann	Dichterliebe	Westbrook & Bullard	OD
Schumann	Frauenliebe und-Leben	Baker	GS
Strauss, Richard	Morgen	Bernhoff	GS
Strauss, Richard	Zueignung	Bernhoff	U
Strauss, Richard	Die Nacht	Baker	GS
Strauss, Richard	Allerseelen	Baker	GS
Strauss, Richard	Ständchen	Baker	GS
Tchaikovsky	Don Juan's Serenade	Dale	GS
Tchaikovsky	Warum	Westbrook	OD
Tchaikovsky	Legend	Chapman	GS
Tchaikovsky	Pilgrim's Song	England	GS
Tchaikovsky	Nur wer die Sehnsucht kennt	Westbrook	GS
Wagner	Träume	Grace Hall	GS
Wolf, Hugo	Auch kleine Dinge	Manney	OD

Composer	Title	Translator	Publisher
Wolf, Hugo	Verborgenheit	Manney	OD
Wolf, Hugo	Weyla's Gesang	Boileau	OD
Wolf, Hugo	Das verlassene Mägdelein	Manney	OD
Wolf, Hugo	Fussreise	Manney	OD
Wolf, Hugo	Zur Ruh', zur Ruh'	Manney	OD
Wolf, Hugo	Er ist's	Henry C. Chapmann	GS

G. Sacred Songs

1. One Hundred Sacred Songs -- List No. 4 American Academy of Teachers of Singing*

At the end of the list we have included a number of excellent collections of sacred songs published by various houses -- including one published by the Boston Music Company devoted entirely to "Songs for Special Occasions," and one published by the Oliver Ditson Company devoted to solos for Christian Science Services.

(H - High, M - Medium, L - Low)

Composer	Title	Keys	Publisher**
Allitsen	Like as the Hart	H.M.L.	BHks
Andrews	Build Thee more Stately Mansions	H. L.	GS
Andrews	Blow Ye the Trumpet	H. L.	GS
Andrews	Twenty-Third Psalm	H. L.	GS
Bain	O Gathering Clouds	M.	Ox
Bainton	Ring out, wild bells	H. L.	CF
Barnby	O ye that love the Lord	L.	OD
Barnby	O Perfect Love (Wedding)	H.M.	OD
Barri	The Good Shepherd	H.M.	GS
Bartlett	O Little Town of Bethlehem (Xmas)	H.M.	GS
Bartlett	O Lord be Merciful	H. L.	GS
Beethoven	Song of Penitence	H.	GS
Berwald	More love to Thee, O Christ	M.	BH
Berwald	Give ear to my prayer	H. L.	APS
Brackett	Eyes that are weary	H.M.L.	BFW
Brahms	Four Sacred Songs	H. L.	Sim
Buck	Judge me, O God	L.	GS
Buck	O Savior hear me	H. L.	GS
Campion	Ninety and Nine	H.M.L.	GS
Chadwick	A Ballad of trees and the Master	H.M.L.	OD
Clokey	No Lullaby need Mary Sing	H. L.	JF
Coombs	O little town of Bethlehem (Xmas)	H. L.	GS
Cornelius	Three Kings (Xmas)	H.M.L.	BH
Corner-Liddle	Old Sacred Lullaby	M.	BHks
Diack	All in the April evening	H. L.	BHks
Dichmont	Peace I leave with you	H. L.	OD
Dressler	The Angel's Message (Xmas) (Violin)	H. L.	OD
Dunn	Come unto Him	H. L.	JF
Dvorak	Biblical Songs	H. L.	Sim
Fergusson	Does the road wind uphill? (C.S.)	M.	Gal
Fisher	Be ye comforted (Easter)	H.L. Bass	OD
Fisher	There were shepherds abiding in the fields	H.M.	OD
Foote	All's Well	H.M.L.	APS
Foster	O for a closer walk with God	H. L.	HWG
Franz	Sunday	H. L.	Ch
Fox	A Prayer	H. L.	GS
Franck	Bread of Life (Panis Angelicus)	H.M.	OD
Francke-Harling	Thine O Lord is the Greatness (C.S.)	H. L.	APS
Frey	In Thee, O God, do I put my trust	H. L.	OD
Gaines	A Christmas Alleluia (Xmas)	H. L.	JF
Gilbert	My Redeemer Lives	H. L.	JF

*Used by permission American Academy of Teachers of Singing.
**See p. 220 for "Key to Publisher."

Composer	Title	Keys	Publisher
Gounod	Forever with the Lord	H.M.L.	GS
Gounod	The King of love my Shepherd is	H.M.L.	GS
Gounod	O Divine Redeemer	H.M.L.	GS
Guion	Prayer	H.orM.L.	GS
Hageman	Christ went up into the Hills	H. L.	CF
Hammond	Invocation	H. L.	GS
Hammond	Behold the Master	H. L.	Ch
Harker	How beautiful upon the mountains	H.M.L.	GS
Hawley	All hail, risen King (Easter)	H.M.	TP
Hazelhurst	O leave your sheep	H.M.L.	E
Hildach	Easter triumphs	H. L.	JF
Homer	The sheep and the lambs	H. L.	GS
Huhn	Hear Me when I call	H. L.	GS
Hummel	Hallelujah	H.M.L.	Ric
Jacob	The Shepherd	M.	Ox
Kahn	Ave Maria	H. L.	GS
Kramer	Before the paling of the stars (Xmas)	H.M.orL.	JF
La Forge	Before the Crucifix	H.M.L.	GS
Liddle	The Lord is my Shepherd	H.M.L.	BHks
Liddle	How Lovely are Thy dwellings	H.M.L.	BHks
Malotte	The Lord's Prayer	H.M.L.	GS
Martin	The Holy Child	H.M.L.	E
Matthews	Emmaus	M.L.	OD
Matthews	Judge me, O God	L.	GS
Mozart	Jesu, Word of God (Ave Verum)	L.	Ch
Needham	Far from My Heavenly Home	M.	HWG
Neidlinger	Birthday of a King	H.M.	GS
Nevin	Jesu, Jesu Miserere	H.M.	GS
Parker	Come see the place (Easter)	H. L.	GS
Pughe-Evans	Lead, Kindly Light	H. L.	N
Rachmaninoff	Lead, Kindly Light	H. L.	GS
Randegger	Save me O God	H.M.	GS
Rogers	Out of the depths	H. L.	APS
Rogers	Great peace have They	H.M.	GS
Rogers	They that sow in tears	M.	GS
Salter	O Lord of Life	H.M.L.	GS
Schlosser	He that keepeth Israel	M.	GS
Schnecker	The Earth is the Lord's (Thanksgiving)	H. L.	Schu
Scott	Trust ye in the Lord	H. L.	Hunt
Scott	Come, Ye Blessed	H.M.L.	GS
Scott	Repent Ye	H.M.L.	GS
Scott	Like as a Father	H. L.	GS
Shelley	Abide with Me	H.M.L.	GS
Shelley	The Resurrection (Easter)	H.M.L.	GS
Speaks	The Pilgrim	H. L.	Ch
Speaks	The Lord is my Light	H.M.L.	GS
Spicker	Evening and morning	H.M.L.	GS
Spicker	In Thee, O God, do I put my Trust	L.	GS
Stainer	My Father and My King	H.	N
Thiman	My Master hath a Garden	H. L.	N
Thiman	The God of Love my Shepherd is	M.L.	N
Tours	Jesus, lover of my soul	M.L.	GS
Treharne	He that keepeth Israel	H.orM.L.	GS
Ware	The Cross (Lent)	H. L.	GS
West	The Lord is loving	H. L.	APS
West	God is our hope and strength	H. L.	APS
West	Like as the Hart	H. L.	APS
Wolf	Prayer	H.	OD
Wooler	Consider and hear Me	H.M.L.	OD
Yon	Go, happy soul (Funeral)	H. L.	JF

Composer	Title	Keys	Publisher
COLLECTIONS	Gems of Sacred Songs	H. L.	GS
	Album of Sacred Songs	H. L.	GS
	Sacred Songs for General Use	H. L.	BM
	Twelve Sacred Songs	H. L.	BM
	Sacred Songs for Special Occasions	H.	BM
	Treasury of Sacred Songs	H. L.	OD
	Solos for Christian Science Services	H. L.	OD
	Church Soloist	H. L.	TP
	Sacred Songs -- sop., alto, tenor, bass		Ch
	Oxford Book of Carols		Ox

2. General List of Newer Sacred Solos -- National Association of Teachers of Singing*
   (H - High, M - Medium, L - Low Voice)

Composer	Title	Keys	Publisher**
Andrews	The Shadow of Thy Wings	M.	HWG
Arno	Trust the Eternal	M.L.	CF
Baas	The Donkey (Palm Sunday)	M.	HWG
†Bach-Breck	Jesus from the Grave Is Risen	M.	CF
†Bach-Breck	Come Christians Greet This Day	M.	CF
†Bach-Breck	God Is Our Life	M.	CF
Bantock	The Lord's Prayer	H. L.	Marks
Banks	A Prayer of St. Francis	M.L.	HWG
Barker	Bless the Lord, O My Soul	H. L.	RDR
Bone, Gene & Howard	Thy Word Is a Lamp (Psalm 119; First Psalm)	M.	CF
Brown, Allanson	The Greatest of These Is Love		HWG
Brown, Russel J.	Great Peace Have They	M.	OD
Brown	23rd Psalm	H.	HWG
Browning	For I Am Persuaded	H.M.L.	CF
Browning	The Beautitudes	H.M.	CF
Charles	Incline Thine Ear	H. L.	GS
Charles	Psalm of Exaltation	M.	GS
Coenen	Come Unto Me	H.M.L.	Gal
Creston	23rd Psalm	H.M.	GS
Davis, Katherine	The Raising of Lazarus	M.	CF
Davis, Margaret	Revelation	H. L.	RDR
Delamarter	Break, New-Born Year	M.	Wit
Diack	Son of Mary	H. L.	Pat
Daugherty	The First Christmas	H.	GS
Duke	Calvary	L.	CF
Eville	Out of the Deep	H.M.L.	By
Erwin	I Will Lift Up Mine Eyes (Psalm 121)	M.	BMI
Freeman	My Salvation Shall Be Forever	H. L.	RDR
Gilbert	God of Righteousness	H. L.	Hunt
Goodhall	The Mountain		Gal
Gronham	An Understanding Heart (Prayer of Solomon)		Hunt
Hageman	Lift Thou the Burdens, Father	H.M.	Gal
Harris	The Holy Infant		Gal
Hart	The Miracles of Jesus	H.	GS
	1. The Healing of the Woman in the Throng		
	2. The Raising of the Son of the Widow of Nain		
	3. The Healing of Blind Bartimeus		
Hinchcliffe	Creation	M.	CF
Hinchcliffe	Tranquillity	M.	CF
Holst	The Heart Worships	M.L.	SB
Howe	The Christmas Story	M.	CF
Knowlton	Come Unto Me, All Ye That Labor	M.	Sy

*Used by permission National Association of Teachers of Singing.
**See p. 220 for "Key to Publisher."
†Note: These three numbers are adaptations to Chorales by J. S. Bach.

Composer	Title	Keys	Publisher
Kountz	What Shall I Ask	L.	Gal
LaForge	Bless the Lord	H. L.	CF
LaForge	Go and Sin No More	L.	Gal
LaForge	God Is Our Refuge	H.M.L.	GS
LaForge	Hast Thou Not Known	H.M.L.	
LaForge	I Love the Lord (Psalm 116)	M.	Gal
LaForge	The Lord Reigneth (Psalm XCIII)	H. L.	CF
LaForge	The Lord Reigneth	H.M.L.	GS
Lederer	Psalm 104	H.	CF
Lekberg	A Ballad of Trees and the Master	H.	Gal
MacKinnon	Sheep and Lambs	H.M.	HWG
McGill	Thine Eternal Peace	H. L.	GS
Maddox	For This I Pray	H. L.	Wil
Malotte	Only to Know		GS
Malotte	23rd Psalm	H.M.L.	GS
Malotte	Only with Thine Eyes	M.	GS
Malotte	Beautitudes	H. L.	GS
Marks	I Will Lift Up Mine Eyes (Psalm 121)	H. L.	
Marsh	The Lord Is My Light	H.M.L.	CF
Mitchell	The Tabernacle of God Is with Men	H.M.L.	Hunt
Moore	Silently Now We Bow	H. L.	TP
Mueller	A Prayer for Vision	M.	GS
O'Connor	Fulfilment	M.	CF
O'Connor	The Lord Is My Shepherd (Psalm 23)	M.	CF
O'Connor	Fill Thou My Life, O Lord	M.	CF
Ohlson	The Victory of Easter	H.M.	GS
Parker	Blessed Is The People (Psalms 89-119)	M.	CF
Paxson	He Was Alone (Lent)	H. L.	GS
Posamanick	A Song of Faith	H. L.	MK
Protheroe	Psalm 42, The Soul's Longing	H. L.	TP
Rolfe	Teach Me to Live	H.	BFW
Rorem	A Song of David (Psalm 120)	H.M.	AMP
Sacco	God's Time	M.	AMP
Saxton	My Soul Doth Magnify the Lord	H. L.	Gal
Scott	Consider the Lilies	H. L.	GS
Scott	Come Ye Thankful People	H. L.	GS
Scott	Messenger of Peace	H. L.	GS
Scott	When I Consider the Heavens	H. L.	Hunt
Shenk	The Lord's Prayer	H. L.	TP
Shenk	O Love That Wilt Not Let Me Go	H.M.L.	TP
Sowerby	Hear My Cry O Lord	Bass	HWG
Sowerby	The Lord Is My Shepherd	Bass	HWG
Sowerby	How Long Wilt Thou Forget Me (Psalm XIII)	Bass	HWG
Sowerby	I Will Lift Up Mine Eyes (Psalm 121)	Con. or Bar.	HWG
Stephenson	Psalm 103	M.	CF
Strong	He Rides Triumphant	H. L.	Chap
Thiman	Flower of Heaven (Christmas)	M.	E
Thiman	Jesus the Very Thought of Thee	M.L.	HWG
Thiman	Thou Wilt Keep Him in Perfect Peace		HWG
Thompson, Alan	Prayer for Easter Day	H.	BMI
Thompson, William	Come Unto Me	H. L.	OD
Tinturin	And When the Morn Was Come	M.	Mi
Townsley	Behold What Manner of Love	M.	F
Townsley	Upon a Hill (Lent)	H. L.	HF
Vale	Litany for the Holy Spirit	L.	Ox
Van Dyke	A Song from Isaiah (Pre-advent)		
Van Nuys	Whither Shall I Go	H.M.	GS
Voris	Song of Mothers (Mother's Day)	H.M.L.	HWG
Voris	O Calm of Soul		
Ward	O Brother Man, Fold to Thy Heart Thy Brother	H. L.	GS
Ward-Stephens	Shout Ye Seraphs	L.	GS

Composer	Title	Keys	Publisher
Warren	Blow Golden Trumpets	H. L.	HF
Warren	Hast Thou Not Known Me	H. L.	RDR
Warren	Because of Thy Great Bounty	L.	HWG
Way	Acquaint Now Thyself with Him (Job)	M.	Gal
Weaver	Assurance		Gal
Weaver	Build Thee More Stately Mansions, O My Soul		Gal
Weaver	Praise the Lord, His Glories Show	H.M.L.	Gal
Williams	Son of Man	L.	CF
Work	God, I Need Thee		

3. Sacred Songs Recommended by Experienced Teachers and Vocal Authorities

(Note - See also "Sacred Songs with Instrumental Obligato," p. 316, songs for the "Christmas Season," p. 304, songs for the "Easter Season," p. 307, and songs for "Funeral or Memorial Services," p. 310. Unless otherwise noted, the following songs are usually printed in more than one key. When ordering, type of voice and whether high, medium, or low range key is desired should be indicated.)

Composer	Title	Publisher*
Adams	The Holy City	BHks
Allisten	The Lord Is My Light**	BHks
Allisten	Psalm of Thanksgiving**	BHks
Ambrose	Come to My Heart Lord Jesus	OD
Arne	Trust the Eternal	
Ashford	Abide (Bass)	Ch
Ashford	My Task	L
Bach-Dickinson	God, My Shepherd Walks Beside Me**	HWG
Bach-Dickinson	Draw Near to Me (Bist du bei mir)	Wit, GS
Bach-Dickinson	My Heart Ever Faithful** (Soprano)	OD, GS, HWG
Bach-Dickinson	Thanks Be to God	By
Bach-Dickinson	Where Two or Three Together	P
Bach-Gounod	Ave Maria**	TP, GS
Bain	O Gathering Clouds**	Ox
Barbour	Where My Treasure Is	
Barri	At Benediction	GS
Barri	The Good Shepherd**	GS
Bartlett	O Lord Be Merciful	GS
Beethoven	Come to Me (Obbl.)	GS
Beethoven	Good Friend of Jesus Sake, Forbear (In questa tomba oscura) (Bass or Baritone)	OD
Beethoven	O What Is Man	TP
Beethoven	Song of Penitence ** (High)	GS
Bergh	Dear Lord and Father	Chap
Bitgood	Be Still and Know That I Am God	HWG
Bizet	Lamb of God (Agnus Dei)** (Lent)	OD, GS
Blair	He Restoreth My Soul	GS
Blair	Thou Wilt Light My Candle	HWG
Boatner (arr.)	Oh What a Beautiful City	GS
Bowling	He Shall Be Like a Tree	RDR
Brahe	Bless This House	By
Brahms	Four Serious Songs**	Sim
Bridges	The Lord Is My Shepherd	Chap
Brown	Great Peace Have They	OD
Buck	Fear Not Ye, O Israel	GS
Burleigh (arr.)	A City Called Heaven	R
Burleigh (arr.)	Deep River	Ric
Buxtehude-Dickinson	Lord in Thee Do I Put My Trust	HWG
Buxtehude-Dickinson	My Jesus Is My Lasting Joy** (High)	HWG
Buzzia-Pecia	Gloria**	BHks

*See p. 220 for "Key to Publisher."
**Recommended by the Voice Faculty of Westminster Choir College, Princeton, N. J.

Composer	Title	Publisher
Cadman	The Builder	HF
Cadman	The Silent Hour	MK
Campbell-Tipton	I Will Give Thanks Unto the Source*	BHks
Campion	The Ninety and Nine*	GS
Chadwick	Ballad of the Trees and the Master	TP
Chadwick	Hark, Hark My Soul	GS
Clarke	The Blind Ploughman	Chap
Clokey	Gifts	JF
Clokey	God Is Everything	JF
Coenan	Come Unto Me	TP,GS
Conway	He That Keepeth Israel	VB
Crerie	Hast Thou Not Known	VB
Curran	The Lord Is My Shepherd	GS
Dana	Flee As a Bird	OD
David	I Sought the Lord	JF
David	Let This Mind Be in You	GS
Davis	Let Not Your Heart Be Troubled	BFW
Davis	Trust in the Lord	Gal
Demarest	Hymn of the Last Supper	OD
Dett (arr.)	I'm Goin' to Thank God	JF
Dickinson	In the Day of Battle	HWG
Dickinson	Roads	HWG
Dickinson	Stainless Soldier on the Wall	HWG
Downey	Dear God Receive My Humble Plea	Gal
Dungan	Be Still, and Know	TP
Dungan	Show Me Thy Ways, O Lord	Chap
Dvorak	The Twenty-Third Psalm	Gal
Ebersole	Be Still and Know That I Am God	HWG
Effinger	I Shall Not Pass Again This Way	TP
Ellis	Seek Ye the Truth	OD
Fenner	When Children Pray	HF
Fisher (arr.)	Deep River	OD
Flick-Flood	Behold the Tabernacle	DLS
Foster-Gerson	The Souls of the Righteous	JF
Franck	La Procession	TP,GS
Franck	O Bread of Life from Heaven,* or O Lord Most Holy (Panis Angelicus)*	OD
Gaul	Eye Hath Not Seen (from the "Holy City")*	TP
Gaul	Prayer for Service	HF
Gaul	These Are They*	TP
Gluck	O Savior Hear Me*	GS
Gounod	Entreat Me Not to Leave Thee	GS
Gounod	Nazareth	OD
Gounod	O Divine Redeemer*	GS
Greenfield	The Hem of His Garment	GS
Guion	I Talked with God Last Night	GS
Guion	Mary Alone*	GS
Guion	Night	GS
Guion	Prayer*	GS
Hageman	Christ Went Up Into the Hills	GS
Hall	Lead My Feet	BMC
Hamblen	Beside Still Waters	BHks
Hamblen	Trust in Him	GS
Handel	He Shall Feed His Flock ("Messiah") (S, MS and Alto)	GS
Handel	How Beautiful Are the Feet ("Messiah") (High)	JF
Handel	I Will Magnify Thee	CF
Handel	O Had I Jubal's Lyre (Soprano)	OD
Handel	Praise the Lord	CF
Handel	Thanks Be to Thee*	JF,GS
Handel	When I Prayed to God (Largo from "Xerxes")	CF

*Recommended by the Voice Faculty of the Westminster Choir College, Princeton, N. J.

Composer	Title	Publisher
Harker	Consider the Lilies*	GS
Harker	How Beautiful upon the Mountains*	GS
Harker	O Love, That Will Not Let Me Go	GS
Harris	Give Thanks and Sing	BM
Harris	I Hear the Voice of Jesus Say	GS
Haydn-Dickinson	Lord to Thy Throne Would I Draw Nigh	HWG
Henschel	Morning Hymn*	GS
Hiller	Prayer*	GS
Holler	The King of Love	HWG
Holler	Now the Day Is Over	HWG
Holst	The Heart Worships*	SB
Homer	Sheep and Lambs*	GS
Hopkins	Let Not Your Heart Be Troubled	VB
Hosmer	He That Dwelleth	TP
Hummel	Hallelujah*	Ric
Humphries	Seek Ye the Lord	Wil
Humphries	The Lord Is My Shepherd	Wil
Hurst	Turn Thy Face from My Sins	Gal
James	Peace Be to This House	Hunt
Kennedy	A Song of Consecration	HWG
Kountz	Prayer of the Norwegian Child*	GS
LaForge	Have Mercy Upon Me	GS
LaForge	Suffer the Little Children	CF
LaForge	Teach Me, O Lord	CF
Lawrence	Let Us Break Bread Together*	M & R
Liddle	How Lovely Are Thy Dwellings*	BHks
Loeffler	Prayer	CCB
Loughborough	How Lovely Is the Hand of God	OD
Malotte	The Beatitudes*	GS
Malotte	The Lord's Prayer*	GS
Malotte	The Twenty-third Psalm*	GS
Mana-Zucca	Rachem	Ch
Manny	The Comforter	BWF
Marx	Adventide	AMP
Mascagni	Ave Maria (from "Cavalleria Rusticana)	GS
MacDermid	Arise, Shine, for Thy Light Is Come*	FM
MacDermid	He That Dwelleth in the Secret Place*	FM
MacDermid	Make a Joyful Noise	FM
MacDermid	The Ninety-first Psalm	FM
MacDermid	Perfect Peace	FM
MacDermid	The Spirit of the Lord Is Upon Me	FM
MacDermid	Whither Shall I Go from Thy Spirit	FM
McFeeters	A Psalm of Praise Redeemed	Mi
McGimsey	Sweet Little Jesus Boy*	CF
Mendelssohn	If with All Your Hearts* ("Elijah") (Tenor)	OD
Mendelssohn	But the Lord Is Mindful of His Own ("St. Paul") (Alto)	OD
Mendelssohn	Hear Ye, Israel* ("Elijah")	OD
Mendelssohn	Is Not His Word Like a Fire ("Elijah") (Bass or Baritone)	OD
Mendelssohn	It Is Enough ("Elijah") (Bass or Baritone)	OD
Mendelssohn	O God Have Mercy* (Bass)	GS
Mendelssohn	Lord God of Abraham* ("Elijah") (Bass or Baritone)	OD
Mendelssohn	O Rest in the Lord* ("Elijah") (Alto or Mezzo)	OD
Mendelssohn	O for the Wings of a Dove	OD
Mietzke	Callest Thou Thus, O Master	GS
Moe	The Greatest of These Is Love	Aug
Mozart	Alleluia* (Soprano)	Flam,GS
Mozart	Jesu, Word of God Incarnate* (Low)	Ch
Mozart	O Lord Our God	GS

*Recommended by the Voice Faculty of Westminster Choir College, Princeton, N.J.

Composer	Title	Publisher
Mueller	Christ of the Upward Way	HF
Mueller	Create in Me a Clean Heart	GS
Neidlinger	Spirit of God*	OD
Nevin	Into the Woods My Master Went	TP
Nevin	The Rosary (The Holy Hour)	BM
Newman	This Is My Prayer	BM
Noble	Souls of the Righteous*	HWG
Nordhoff	Lacrimi Christi	MPI
Norman	If I Forget to Pray	SMC
O'Hara	I Walked Today Where Jesus Walked*	GS
O'Hara	The Living God*	Hunt
O'Hara	The Waters of Thy Love	Wil
O'Hara	There Is No Death*	Hunt
Parker	Jerusalem	OD
Perry	God Shall Wipe Away All Tears	GS
Protheroe	The Builder	HF
Protheroe	Song of Redemption	OD
Randegger	Save Me O God	OD
Roberts	Seek Ye the Lord	GS
Roberton	All in the April Evening	Cur
Rogers	Great Peace Have They*	GS
Roma	God Shall Wipe Away All Tears	Wit
Rossini	Cujus Animam ("Stabat Mater") (Tenor)	OD
Ryder (arr.)	Let Us Break Bread Together	JF
Sacco	God's Time	GS
Saint-Saens	Thou, O Lord Art My Protector	GS
Sanderson	Green Pastures	BHks
Sateren	When God Made His Earth	APH
Saxton	My Soul Doth Magnify the Lord	Gal
Schlieder	O Lord Have Mercy	GS
Schubert	Ave Maria*	OD,GS
Schubert	Lord with Glad Heart I Praise Thee*	GS
Schubert-Dickinson	To the Infinite	HWG
Scott	Consider the Lilies*	GS
Scott	God Is a Spirit	OD
Scott	Light	GS
Scott	Like As a Father*	GS
Scott	The Voice in the Wilderness*	Hunt
Seaver	Just for Today	SF
Sowerby	Three Psalms for Bass	HWG
Sowerby	Three Songs of Faith and Penitence	HWG
Speaks	By the Waters of Babylon	GS
Speaks	Come Spirit of the Living God	GS
Speaks	His Perfect Love	GS
Speaks	How Long Wilt Thou Forget Me	GS
Speaks	Let Not Your Heart Be Troubled*	GS
Speaks	Living God	GS
Speaks	The Prayer Perfect*	GS
Speaks	Thou Wilt Keep Him in Perfect Peace*	GS
Spicker	Evening and Morning	GS
Stainer	My Hope Is in the Everlasting	TP
Stenson	The Prayer Perfect	SF
Stevenson	I Sought the Lord	OD
Stradella	Pity, O Savior, or O Lord Have Mercy*	GS
Sullivan	Come Ye Children ("Prodigal Son") (Tenor)	OD
Sullivan	Love Not the World	TP
Tate	Brother James Air	Ox
Thiman	The God of Love My Shepherd Is*	N
Thiman	In the Bleak Midwinter*	N

*Recommended by the Voice Faculty of the Westminster Choir College, Princeton, N. J.

Composer	Title	Publisher
Thiman	I Will Keep Him in Perfect Peace	N
Thiman	My Master Hath a Garden*	N
Thiman	Jesus, the Very Thought of Thee*	N
Thompson	My Master Had a Garden*	ECS
Tschaikovsky	A Legend	GS
Tschaikovsky	Pilgrim's Song*	GS
Van Etten	Behold, the Master Passeth By	OD
Vandewater	The Good Shepherd*	OD
Vandewater	The Penitent*	OD
Vandewater	The Publican*	OD
Van Dyke	Love	BHks
Van Nuys	Whither Shall I Go from Thy Spirit	GS
Vaneuf	Keep Close to God	OD
Verdi	Ave Maria	GS
Ward-Stephens	Blessed Are the Peacemakers	GS
Ware	The Cross*	GS
Warren	God Be in My Heart	TP
Weinberger	O Divine Work	HWG
Williams	Five Mystical Songs*	SB
Wise	The Lord Has Given Me a Song	GS
Wood	This Quiet Night	Mi
Wooler	Hear My Cry, O Lord	OD
Wolfe	British Children's Prayer	GS

4. Selected Sacred Songs for Each Sunday of the Year -- National Association of Teachers of Singing (Prepared by the Sacred Song Committee)**
   (H - High, M - Medium, L - Low Voice)

	Key	Publisher***
FIRST SUNDAY IN ADVENT		
Comfort Sweet, Lord Jesus Comes - Bach	Sop	Ox
Arise, Shine, For Thy Light Is Come - MacDermid	H.M.L.	FM
Comfort Ye and Every Valley ("Messiah") - Handel	Ten	GS
Repent Ye - J. P. Scott	H. L.	GS
Rejoice Greatly ("Messiah")	Sop	GS
SECOND SUNDAY IN ADVENT		
Prepare Thyself Zion ("Christmas Oratorio") - Bach	Alto	
How Beautiful Upon the Mountains - Harker	H.M.L.	GS
Fear Not Ye O Israel - Buck	H.M.L.	GS
Rejoice Greatly ("Messiah") - Handel	Sop	GS
THIRD SUNDAY IN ADVENT		
The Spirit of the Lord God Is Upon Me - MacDermid	H. L.	FM
Thus Saith the Lord and But Who May Abide ("Messiah") - Handel	Bass	GS
Arise, Shine, For Thy Light Is Come - MacDermid	H.M.L.	FM
He Shall Judge Thy People - LaForge	H.M.L.	GS
FOURTH SUNDAY IN ADVENT		
The Voice in the Wilderness - Scott	H. L.	Hunt
I Will Extol Thee - LaForge	H.M.	CF
Great Is the Holy One of Israel - Case	H. L.	HF
I Will Lift Up Mine Eyes (Psalm 125) - Ward-Stephens (In "Musical Settings of Selected Psalms")		
SUNDAY AFTER CHRISTMAS		
Behold What Manner of Love - Humphreys	H.M.L.	GS
The Christmas Story - Howe	M.	CF

*Recommended by the Voice Faculty of the Westminster Choir College, Princeton, N. J.
**Used by permission National Association of Teachers of Singing.
***See p. 220 for "Key to Publisher."

	Key	Publisher
SUNDAY AFTER CHRISTMAS (cont.)		
Heaven and Earth Rejoice and Sing	H.	HWG
He Shall Feed His Flock ("Messiah") - Handel	Alto.	GS
EPIPHANY SUNDAY		
They Brought Him Gifts - Nevin	H.M.	JF
They Call Him Jesus - Yon	H. L.	JF
Slumber Song of the Madonna - Head	H.M.L.	BHks
No Lullaby Need Mary Sing - Clokey	H. L.	JF
FIRST SUNDAY AFTER EPIPHANY		
How Lovely Are Thy Dwellings - Liddle	H. MH.ML. L.	BHks
Let This Mind Be in You - David	H. L.	GS
Be Still and Know That I Am God - Bitgood	H.M.	HWG
What Shall I Render Unto the Lord - LaForge	H.M.	GS
SECOND SUNDAY AFTER EPIPHANY		
Be Ye Kind One to Another - Davis	H. L.	Gal
Ye Are the Light of the World - LaForge	M.L.	GS
The Voice in the Wilderness - Scott	H. L.	Hunt
Repent Ye - Scott	H.M.L.	GS
THIRD SUNDAY AFTER EPIPHANY		
Come Ye Blessed - Scott	H.M.L.	GS
O Brother Man, Fold to Thy Heart Thy Brother - Ward	H. L.	GS
This is God's Love - O'Hara	H.M.L.	GS
This is My Commandment - Hamblen	H. L.	RDR
FOURTH SUNDAY AFTER EPIPHANY		
I Sought the Lord - Stevenson	H. L.	OD
Trust in the Lord with All Thine Heart - MacDermid	H. L.	FM
Give Me a Faith - Bitgood	H.M.L.	HWG
Have Mercy Upon Me O God - LaForge	H. L.	GS
SEPTUAGESIMA SUNDAY		
Thou Wilt Keep Him in Perfect Peace - Thiman	H.	HWG
Hast Thou Not Known - LaForge	H. L.	GS
O Master Let Me Walk with Thee - Speaks	H. L.	GS
O Master Let Me Walk with Thee - Matthews	L.	GS
SEXAGESIMA SUNDAY		
All This I Pray - Driggs	M.	TP
As the Rain Cometh Down - MacDermid	H. L.	FM
Love Not the World - Ward-Stephens ("Settings of Sacred Words")		
Christ of the Upward Way - Mueller	L.	HF
QUINQUAGESIMA SUNDAY		
Faith - Wilson	M.	CF
O Ye Who Seek the Lord - Cadman	H.M.	HWG
The Robe of Righteousness	H.M.	CF
This Is God's Love - O'Hara	H.M.L.	GS
FIRST SUNDAY IN LENT		
Lord Who Throughout These Forty Days - Lang	H.M.	GS
Today, If Ye Will Hear His Voice - Rogers	H. L.	APS
Trust in Him - Hamblen	H. L.	GS
Thou Wilt Keep Him in Perfect Peace - Thiman	H.	HWG
SECOND SUNDAY IN LENT		
Hear Me Speedily, O Lord - Vollenhaven	H. L.	GS
O God of Love - Gretchaninoff	Sop.	HWG
God Is My Strength - Hamblen		Chap
Give Me a Faith - Bitgood	H.M.L.	HWG
THIRD SUNDAY IN LENT		
Awake Thou That Sleepest - Ward-Stephens	H. L.	Chap
(In "Musical Settings of Sacred Words")		

	Key	Publisher

THIRD SUNDAY IN LENT (cont.)
    Behold What Manner of Love - Humphreys . . . . .H.M.L. . . . . . GS
    Think on These Things - MacGimsey . . . . M.L. . . . . . CF
    Search Me O God - Ward-Stephens . . . . .H. L. . . . Chap
        (In "Musical Settings of Selected Psalms")

FOURTH SUNDAY IN LENT
    Hear My Cry - Milligan . . . . .H.M. . . . . GS
    Hear My Cry O Lord - Wooler . . . . .H. L. . . . . . OD
    O Lord Be Merciful - Bizet . . . . .H. L. . . . . . GS
    Search Me O God and Know My Heart - Ward-Stephens . . . . .H. L. . . . Chap
        (In "Musical Settings of Selected Psalms")

FIFTH SUNDAY IN LENT (PASSION SUNDAY)
    Thou Wilt Keep Him in Perfect Peace - MacDermid . . . . . .H.M.L. . . . . . FM
    Great Is Our Lord - Cartwright . . . . .H.M. . . . . . Hunt
    For My Sake Thou Hast Died - Moore . . . . M. . . . . . . TP
    Art Thou the Christ? - O'Hara . . . . .H.M.L. . . . . GS

SIXTH SUNDAY IN LENT (PALM SUNDAY)
    Ride On, Ride On - Sterling . . . . .H. . . . . HWG
    Ride On, Ride On - Scott . . . . .H.M.L. . . . . . HF
    Hosanna to the Song of David - Carr . . . . .H. L. . . . . . GS
    Palm Sunday - Kountz .H. L. . . . . . GS

EASTER SUNDAY
    O Sing Unto the Lord a New Song - Gore . . . . .Sop. or Ten. . . . . JF
    Easter - Spier . . . . .H. . . . . HWG
    I Know That My Redeemer Liveth ("Messiah") - Handel . . . .Sop. . . . . . . GS
    First Easter Morn - J. P. Scott . . . . .H. L. . . . . . GS
    The Lord Is Risen ("Light of the World") - Sullivan . . . .H. L. . . . . . GS
    Come See the Place Where Jesus Lay - Parker . . . . .H. L. . . . . . GS
    Easter Triumph - Shelley . . . . .H.M.L. . . . . . TP

FIRST SUNDAY AFTER EASTER
    Peace I Leave With You - Dichmont . . . . .H. L. . . . . . OD
    My Redeemer Lives - Gilbert . . . . .H. L. . . . . . JF
    Spirit of God - Neidlinger . . . . .H.M.L. . . . . . OD
    Come Spirit of the Living God - Speaks . . . . .H. L. . . . . . GS

SECOND SUNDAY AFTER EASTER
    God My Shepherd Walks Beside Me - Bach-Dickinson . . . . . . .H. . . . . HWG
    The God of Love My Shepherd Is - Thiman . . . . M. . . . . . . HWG
    The Good Shepherd - van de Water . . . . .H. L. . . . . . OD
    My Shepherd - Jacob . . . . M. . . . . . . Ox

THIRD SUNDAY AFTER EASTER
    Song of David (Psalm 120) - Rorem . . . . M. . . . . . . AMP
    I Will Lift Up Mine Eyes (Psalm 121) - Parker . . . . L. . . . . . CF
    I Will Lift Up Mine Eyes (Psalm 121) - Lekberg . . . . . . .H. . . . . Wit
    I Will Lift Up Mine Eyes - Humphreys . . . . .H. L. . . . . . BM

FOURTH SUNDAY AFTER EASTER
    O Jesus, Lord of Mercy Great - Sowerby . . . . .Sop. . . . . . . HWG
    Laus Deo - Milford . . . . .H.M. . . . . . . HWG
    God Is Spirit - Ross .H. L. . . . . . GS
    I Will Not Leave Thee Comfortless - Row . . . . .H. L. . . . . . RDR

FIFTH SUNDAY AFTER EASTER
    Be Still and Know That I Am God - Bitgood . . . . .H.M.L. . . . . . HWG
    Let Not Your Heart Be Troubled - Davis . . . . .H.M.L. . . . . . BFW
    Behold the Former Things Are Come to Pass - Brown . . . . .H. L. . . . . . RDR
    Let Nothing Disturb Thee - Diamond . . . . M. . . . . . . AMP

SIXTH SUNDAY AFTER EASTER (FIRST SUNDAY AFTER ASCENSION)
    Praise the Lord ("Esther") - Handel . . . . .Sop. . . . . . . CF
    A Psalm of Praise - Rorem . . . . M. . . . . . . AMP

O Lord I Will Praise Thee - Marks .H. . . . . TP
Jesus Fount of Love - James . . . . .H. . . . . HWG

WHITSUNTIDE OR PENTECOST
I Will Not Leave You Comfortless - Row. . . . . .H. L. . . . . . RDR
Our Blest Redeemer - Timmings . . . . .H. . . . . HWG
I Love the Lord (Psalm CXVI) - LaForge. . . . . M. . . . . . . Gal
If Ye Abide in Me - LaForge . . . . .H. L. . . . . . GS

TRINITY SUNDAY
Praise God for Life Made New - Ward-Stephens. . . . . .H. L. . . . . . Chap
   (In "Musical Settings of Sacred Words")
Psalm 103 - Stephenson. . . . . M. . . . . . . CF
Sing Unto the Lord a New Song - MacDermid . . . . .H. L. . . . . . FM
A Psalm of Praise - McFeeters . . . . M. . . . . . . CF

FIRST SUNDAY AFTER TRINITY
God So Loved the World - MacDermid. . . . . .H.M.L. . . . . . FM
God So Loved the World - Fearis . . . . .H. L. . . . . . BM
If Ye Love Me - Gillingham. . . . . .H. L. . . . . . BM
Love Is of God - Charles. . . . . .H. . . . . GS

SECOND SUNDAY AFTER TRINITY
Love Never Faileth - Ward-Stephens. . . . . .H. L. . . . . . Chap
   (In "Musical Settings of Sacred Words")
Behold What Manner of Love - Humphreys. . . . . .H.M.L. . . . . . GS
Robe of Righteousness - Coryell . . . . .H.M. . . . . . . CF
God Is Our Life - Bach-Breck. . . . . M. . . . . . . CF

THIRD SUNDAY AFTER TRINITY
Let Not the Wise Man Glory in His Wisdom - MacDermid. . . . . .H. L. . . . . . FM
Let Nothing Disturb You - Diamond . . . . M. . . . . . . AMP
The Lord Is My Light - Allitson . . . . .H.MH.ML.L. . . . . . By
The Penitent - van de Water . . . . .H.M. . . . . . . OD

FOURTH SUNDAY AFTER TRINITY
Eternal Life - Dungan .H. L. . . . . . TP
For the Mountains Shall Depart - MacDermid. . . . . .H.M.L. . . . . . FM
O God, Father of Mercy - Burke. . . . . .H.M. . . . . . . R
Teach Me to Forgive - Ward-Stephens . . . . Hunt

FIFTH SUNDAY AFTER TRINITY
I Look for the Lord - Woodman . . . . M.L. . . . . . HWG
Let This Mind Be in You - David . . . . .H. L. . . . . . GS
Give Me a Faith - Bitgood . . . . .H. L. . . . . . HWG
Trust in the Lord with All Thine Heart - MacDermid. . . . . . .H. L. . . . . . FM

SIXTH SUNDAY AFTER TRINITY
Ye Are the Light of the World - LaForge . . . . GS
Faith, Hope, Love - Trued . . . . .H.M.L. . . . . . Schroeder
Blest Are the Pure in Heart - Harker. . . . . .H. L. . . . . . Hunt
God, Canst Thou Forgive - Brown . . . . .H. L. . . . . . Wil

SEVENTH SUNDAY AFTER TRINITY
Jesus My Savior Look on Me - Ed. Barnes . . . . .H. . . . . JF
Perfect Peace - Ed. Barnes. . . . . .H. . . . . JF
Blest Are They Which Do Hunger - Ward-Stephens. . . . . . . .H. L. . . . . . GS
For This I Pray - Maddox . . . . .H. L. . . . . . Wil

EIGHTH SUNDAY AFTER TRINITY
Thou Wilt Keep Him in Perfect Peace - Speaks. . . . . .H. L. . . . . . GS
In Thee O God Do I Put My Trust - Spicker . . . . M. . . . . . . GS
Incline Thine Ear - Charles . . . . .H. L. . . . . . GS
Trust Ye in the Lord - Scott. . . . . .H.M.L. . . . . . GS

	Key	Publisher

NINTH SUNDAY AFTER TRINITY

	Key	Publisher
The Ninety and Nine - Campion	H.M.L.	GS
The Penitent - van de Water	H. L.	OD
Light - Scott	H. L.	GS
I Heard the Voice - Harris	H. L.	GS

TENTH SUNDAY AFTER TRINITY

Build Thee More Stately Mansions - Andrews	H. L.	GS
My Redeemer and My Lord - Buck	H. L.	Ch
Love Not the World - Sullivan	M.	GS
Spirit of God - Neidlinger	H. L.	OD

ELEVENTH SUNDAY AFTER TRINITY

Repent Ye - Scott	H.M.L.	GS
The Publican - van de Water	H. L.	OD
Great Peace Have They - Rogers	H. L.	GS
How Beautiful Upon the Mountains - Harker	H. L.	GS

TWELFTH SUNDAY AFTER TRINITY

The Twenty-Third Psalm - Malotte	H.M.L.	GS
Come Ye Blessed - Scott	H.M.L.	GS
Love Never Faileth - Root	H. L.	Sy
The Shepherd - LaForge	H. L.	GS

THIRTEENTH SUNDAY AFTER TRINITY

O Brother Man, Fold to Thy Heart Thy Brother - Ward	H. L.	GS
Let This Mind Be in You - David	H. L.	GS
A Prayer of St. Francis - Banks	M.L.	HWG
Show Me Thy Task - Wooler	H.M.L.	Schroeder

FOURTEENTH SUNDAY AFTER TRINITY

Come Gracious Spirit - Morrison	L.	JC
Search Me O God - Ward-Stephens	H. L.	C
(In "Musical Settings of Selected Psalms")		
Great Peace Have They Which Love Thy Law - Rogers	H.M.	GS
If We Live in the Spirit - Barker	H. L.	CF

FIFTEENTH SUNDAY AFTER TRINITY

Consider the Lilies - Scott	H. L.	GS
Love Not the World - Ward-Stephens	H.M.	Chap
(In "Musical Settings of Sacred Words")		
Trust in the Lord with All Thine Heart - MacDermid	H. L.	FM
Love Not the World ("Prodigal Son") - Sullivan	Sop. and Alto.	OD

SIXTEENTH SUNDAY AFTER TRINITY

They Shall Run and Not Be Weary - MacDermid	H. L.	FM
Let This Mind Be in You - David	H. L.	GS
Consider, O My Soul ("St. John Passion") - Bach	Bass	Pat
Whither Shall I Go from Thy Spirit - MacDermid	H. L.	FM

SEVENTEENTH SUNDAY AFTER TRINITY

The Cross-Bearer - Guion	H.M.	GS
O Master, Let Me Walk with Thee	H. L.	GS
The Greatest in the Kingdom of Heaven - LaForge	H. L.	CF
They That Sow in Tears - Harker	H. L.	GS

EIGHTEENTH SUNDAY AFTER TRINITY

I See Him Everywhere - Turner-Maley	H. L.	GS
Like As an Hart Desireth the Waterbrooks	H. L.	GS
Water of Life - Olds	M.L.	CF
Fear Not Ye, O Israel - Buck	H.M.L.	GS

NINETEENTH SUNDAY AFTER TRINITY

I Sought the Lord - Stevenson	H. L.	OD
I Will Praise Thee with My Whole Heart - LaForge	H. L.	CF
Blest Are the Pure in Heart - Huhn	H. L.	GS
Great Peace Have They - Rogers	H.M.	GS

TWENTIETH SUNDAY AFTER TRINITY	Key	Publisher
For I Am Persuaded - Browning	H. L.	CF
Why Art Thou Cast Down - Spicker	H.M.L.	GS
Teach Me O Lord - LaForge	H. L.	CF
His Perfect Love - Speaks	H.M.L.	GS

TWENTY-FIRST SUNDAY AFTER TRINITY

He That Dwelleth - Meslin	H. L.	BHks
Let Not Your Heart Be Troubled - Speaks	H.M.L.	GS
God Is Our Life - Bach-Breck	M.	CF
In Faith I Shall Rise - Eville	H.M.L.	By

TWENTY-SECOND SUNDAY AFTER TRINITY

The Greatest of These Is Love - Bitgood	H.M.L.	HWG
Behold What Manner of Love - Townsley	M.	HF
This Is My Commandment - Hamblen	H. L.	RDR
Have Mercy Lord - Matthews	H.M.	EV

TWENTY-THIRD SUNDAY AFTER TRINITY

I Look for the Lord - Woodman	M.L.	HWG
Think on These Things - Miller	H. L.	RDR
Think on These Things - MacGimsey	M.	CF
Come Unto Me All Ye That Labor - Knowlton	M.	Sy

SUNDAY NEXT BEFORE ADVENT

Mighty Lord ("Christmas Oratorio") - Bach	Bass	GS
Fear Not Ye, O Israel - Buck	H.M.L.	GS
Hosanna to the Son of David - Carr	H. L.	GS
Arise O Lord - Hoffmeister	M.	GS

H. Songs for Special Occasions

(Note - Most songs listed are usually either in a medium key or printed in more than one key. When ordering, indicate whether high, medium, or low key is desired.)

CHRISTMAS SEASON AND NEW YEAR*

Composer	Title	Publisher**
Adam	Holy Night***	OD
Adam	Star of Bethlehem	TP
Andrews	I Heard the Bells on Christmas Day	Gal
Bach	Christmas Bells	TP
Bach	Haste Ye Shepherds (Tenor)	Ches
Bach	My Darkened Heart ("Christmas Oratorio") (Baritone or Bass)	Gal
Bach	Mighty Lord ("Christmas Oratorio") (Baritone or Bass)	Gal
Bach	Prepare Thyself, Zion ("Christmas Oratorio") (Mezzo or Alto)	Gal
Baldwin	Little Lordeen	Wit
Bax	A Christmas Carol*** (High)	Ches
Beach	Around the Manger	TP
Berger-Bos	A Miracle Came to Me	GS
Berlin	White Christmas	Berlin
Beyer-Bos	A Miracle Came to Me	GS
Black	In the Sky a Wondrous Star	HWG
Black	So Appears Thy Natal Day	HWG
Brahms	Geistliches Wiegenlied (Mezzo or Alto) (Viola & Piano)	GS
Brahms-Dickinson	Virgin's Cradle Song	HWG
Buck	The Night Song of Bethlehem	

---

*See "Ave Marias" by Gounod, Schubert, Verdi, etc., in previous listing and also "Sacred Songs with Special Instrumental Obligato," p. 316.

**See p. 220 for "Key to Publisher."

***Recommended by the Voice Faculty of the Westminster Choir College, Princeton, N. J.

Composer	Title	Publisher
Buck	The Virgin's Lullaby	GS
Burleigh	Little Child of Mary	Ric
Bush	I Saw a Maiden Fair	HWG
Candlyn	The Song of Mary	HWG
Chaminade	Christmas Carol of the Bells	GS
Carr	As on the Night	GS
Christiansen	Lullaby on Christmas Eve	APH
Clokey	No Lullaby Need Mary Sing*	JF
Clokey	Storke	JF
Coerne	A Rhyme for Christmas Tide	OD
Conant	In the Bleak Midwinter	Gal
Daniels	In a Manger Lowly	GS
Davies	Still There Is Bethlehem*	Pat
De Koven	The White Christ (Low)	GS
Delamater	Break New-Born Year (New Year)	Wit
Del Riego	A Star Was His Candle*	CF
Densmore	The Lamb	GS
Diack	Song of Mary*	BHks
Dickinson	Away in a Manger	HWG
Dickinson	Joseph, Tender Shepherd*	HWG
Dickinson	The Shepherd's Story (High)	HWG
Dickinson	Still There Is Bethlehem*	HWG
Dietrich	God of Love	BHks
Downey	With the Shepherds	JF
Dunhill	The Queen of Heaven	GS
Eakin	What of the Midnight Long Ago	Gal
Engel	Christmas Call	BM
Elmore-Reed	Come All Ye Who Weary	JF
Evans	The Virgin Had a Babe	BHks
Faure	Noel	GS
Fisher	To Us in Bethlehem City	JF
Gaines	A Christmas Lullaby	JF
Ganschow	Sleep, Gentle Jesus	APH
Gaul (arr.)	Carol of Provincetown (Portuguese)	HWG
Gaul (arr.)	Go Tell It on the Mountains (Spiritual)	OD
Gaul (arr.)	Shepherds and the Inn	OD
Geibel	Angel's Refrain	TP
Gevaert	Sleep of the Infant Jesus	BM
Gounod	Nazareth*	TP
Gounod	Ring Out Wild Bells (New Year)	TP
Grandi-Clokey	O Fair Art Thou	JF
Grieg	Christmas Song	Aug
Hageman	Christmas Eve*	Gal
Hamblen	Mary's Slumber Song	Chap
Handel	Arias from the "Messiah":	
	But Who May Abide* (Bass or Baritone)	OD
	Come Unto Him* (Soprano)	OD
	Every Valley* (Tenor)	OD
	How Beautiful Are the Feet (Soprano)	OD
	O Thou That Tellest Good Tidings* (Soprano)	OD
	Rejoice Greatly* (Soprano)	OD
Harker	Calm on the Listening Ear of Night*	GS
Harker	A Child Is Born in Bethlehem	GS
Harker	There's a Song in the Air	GS
Harris	The Feast of Christmas	Ox
Hatch	Child Jesus	GS
Head	Little Road to Bethlehem	BHks
Head	Slumber Song of the Madonna	By
Head	Small Christmas Tree	BHks

*Recommended by the Voice Faculty of the Westminster College, Princeton, N. J.

Composer	Title	Publisher
Head	Star Candles	By
Head	The Three Mummers	By
Homer	Mary's Baby	GS
Huhn	A Child Is Born in Bethlehem	GS
Ireland	The Holy Boy*	BHks
Ives	A Christmas Carol	NM
Jewell	The Vision of the Shepherds	APS
Joseph	O Young Carolers	JF
Kountz	The Sleigh	GS
Kramer	Before the Paling of the Stars*	JF
Kramer	Dark and Wondrous Night	OD
Kramer	This Is the Day Christ Is Born	TP
Kreisler	Shepherd's Madrigal	CF
LaForge	And There Were Shepherds Abiding*	CF
Lehmann	No Candle Was There and No Fire	Chap
Liddle	An Old French Carol	BHks
Lockwood	Joseph, Dearest Joseph	AMP
Lubin	The Carnal and the Crane	GS
Lynn	Gently, Little Jesus	OD
Martin	The Holy Child	E
Martin	Saint Nicholas Day in the Morning	E
Marx	The Song of Mary	AMP
Massenet	Légende de la sauge	Hengel
Matthews	Voices of the Sky	GS
McGimsey	Hallelujah	CF
McGimsey	A New Christmas Morning	CF
McGimsey	Sweet Little Jesus Boy*	CF
McKinney	The Holy Mother Sings (Soprano)	JF
Montani	The Rose and the Lily*	GS
Mueller	Our Christmas Day	GS
Murphy	The Holy Mother Sings	GS
Neidlinger	The Birthday of a King	Sy
Neidlinger	The Manger Cradle	GS
Niles (arr.)	Carol of the Birds	GS
Niles (arr.)	The Cherry Tree	GS
Niles (arr.)	Our Lovely Lady Singing	CF
Niles (arr.)	The Silent Stars	CF
Niles (arr.)	Sweet Marie and Her Baby	GS
Niles-Horton (arr.)	Appalachian Carols:	
	I Wander As I Wander	GS
	Jesus, Rest Your Head	GS
Owen	Lute Book Lullaby (Alto)	HWG
Pasker-de Brant	Christ Today Rejoices Men	CF
Piety-Bailey	Bethlehem Beloved	HWG
Proctor	I Light the Blessed Candles (New Year)	GS
Prokoff	Christmas Cradle Song	Chap
Protheroe	Mary's Treasure	BM
Quilter	An Old Carol	BHks
Ravel	Noel des jouets	Mathot
Reed	Come All Ye Who Weary	JF
Reger	The Virgin's Cradle Song*	AMP
Rich	Beneath a Southern Sky	JF
Riemann-Dickinson	Joseph Tender, Joseph Mild	HWG
Rodney	A Dream of Bethlehem	E
Rogers	Candlelight	GS
Rogers	The Shepherds of Judea	OD
Rorem	A Christmas Carol	EV
Rotoli	Glory to God	TP
Russell	Child Redeemer	Gal
Sacco	The Holy Day	BM
Saint-Saens	Expectans Dominum ("Christmas Oratorio") (Alto or mezzo)	GS

*Recommended by the Voice Faculty of the Westminster College, Princeton, N. J.

Composer	Title	Publisher
Salter	Mary's Manger Song	GS
Salter	The Virgin's Lullaby	GS
Sateren	Three Oxen	Aug
Schelley	Christmas	GS
Schloss-McKinney	Bells of Noel	JF
Schubert	They Sang That Night in Bethlehem*	GS
Scott	Following the Star	GS
Shaw	Old Christmas*	Cur
Speaks	There's a Song in the Air*	GS
Stickles	King of Love Proclaim	Chap
Stults	Song the Angels Sang	TP
Taylor	Christmas Folk Song	HWG
Thiman	As Joseph Was a-Walking*	Aug
Thiman	In the Bleak Midwinter	N
Thompson	The Knight of Bethlehem*	N
Thorp	Come Mary Take Courage	Gal
Trunk	Mary	AMP
Van Dyke	Lullaby (Soprano)	JF
Warlock	Bethlehem Dawn	BHks
Warlock	The First Mercy	By
Warner	A Song of Seven Lambs	APH
Weld	The Christ Child	CF
Wentzel	Lamkins (Cello and Piano)	HWG
West	It Cam Upon a Midnight	Sy
Whitehead	The Croon Carol	CF
Williams	In Bleak Midwinter	HWG
Wolfe	The Mother Sings	CF
Wright	A Babe Lies in His Cradle (Seventeenth Century)	GS
Yon	Jesu, Bambino*	JF

EASTER SEASON, PALM SUNDAY**

Composer	Title	Publisher
Adams	Man of Sorrows	BM
Ambrose	He Is Risen	TP
Bach	Hochgelobter Gottesohn (Cantata 6) (Alto or mezzo) (English horn, or viola or violin)	N
Bach	Jesus from the Grave Is Risen	CF
Bantock	Easter Hymn	Ches
Barnes	Easter	GS
Berwald	As It Began to Dawn	GS
Buck	My Redeemer and My Lord	Ch
Byles	Wood of the Cross	TP
Cadman	Hail Joyous Morm	Wil
Champion	The Ninety and Nine	GS
Coleridge-Taylor	Easter Morn	BHks
Coombs	The Conquerer	GS
Curran	The Crucifixion	GS
Curran	The Resurrection	GS
Davis	Christ Is Risen Today	Gal
Deesler	The Joyful Eastertide	GS
Denie	Easter Song	APS
De Rose	I Heard a Forest Praying	Chap
Diack	All in the April Evening	By
Dickinson	Roads (Palm Sunday or General)	HWG
Dubois	God My Father ("Seven Last Words")	GS
Dungan	Eternal Life	TP
Edwards	Awake! Arise!	TP
Eville	Ride On! Ride On in Majesty (Palm Sunday)	BHks
Faure	Crucifix	BM

*Recommended by the Voice Faculty of the Westminster Choir College, Princeton, N. J.
**See also "Sacred Songs with Special Instrumental Obligato," p. 316.

Composer	Title	Publisher
Faure	The Palms (Palm Sunday)	OD,BM,GS
Fisher	Be Comforted, Ye That Mourn	TP
Fisher (arr.)	Crucifixion (Spiritual)	GS
Gaul (arr.)	Ride on, King Jesus (Palm Sunday)	OD
Geibel	Hail Glorious Morn	TP
Gore	O Sing Unto the Lord a New Song (High)	JF
Granier	Hosanna* (Palm Sunday)	TP
Hall Johnson (arr.)	Ride on King Jesus (Palm Sunday)	CF
Handel	Arias from the "Messiah":	
	He Was Despised (Alto)	OD
	I Know That My Redeemer Liveth* (Soprano)	OD
	The Trumpet Shall Sound (Baritone or Bass)	OD
Harker	As It Began to Dawn	GS
Heyser	The Wondrous Cross	TP
Hildach-McKinney	Easter Triumph*	JF
Huhn	Christ Is Risen	APS
Huhn	Easter Triumph	BM
Humphries	Alleluia	TP
Jordan	Christ the Lord Is Risen Today	TP
Knapp	Open the Gates of the Temple	CF
Kountz	Palm Sunday	GS
LaForge	Before the Crucifix	GS
Lawrence	They Led My Heart Away	M and R
Manney (arr.)	Were You There When They Crucified My Lord	OD
McCollin	Into the Woods My Master Went	JF
McFarlane	On Wings of Living Life	GS
McFadyen	Easter Lilies	TP
McGimsey	I Was There When They Crucified My Lord	CF
Morgan	The Way of the Cross	BM
Mozart	Alleluia*	Flam, CF,GS
Nevin	At the Cross	Ch
Nevin	The Holy Hour	BM
Nordoff	Lacrimi Christi	NPI
O'Hara	Could I Have Held His Nail-pierced Hands	GS
O'Hara	I Walked Today Where Jesus Walked	GS
O'Hara	There Is No Death	Chap
O'Hara	They Have Not Taken My Lord Away	CF
Ohlson	The Vigils of Mary (Lent or Advent) (High Soprano)	GS
Parker	Come See the Place Where Jesus Lay	GS
Protheroe	The Trees and the Master	BM
Rachmaninoff	Christ Is Risen	Gal
Roberton	All in the April Evening	Cur
Rossini	Christ the Victor	JF
Rossini	Inflammatus ("Stabat Mater")	GS
Salter	Gethsemane	GS
Scott	Angels, Roll the Rock Away	Hunt
Scott	Christ Is Risen	HF
Scott	The First Easter Morn*	GS
Scott	Ride On! Ride On! (Palm Sunday)	HF
Shaw	Easter Carol*	Cur
Shelley	Easter Triumph	Cur
Shelley	The Resurrection*	GS
Shelley	Victory	GS
Speaks	In the End of the Sabbath	GS
Spier	Easter	HWG
Sterling	Ride On, Ride On (Palm Sunday) (High)	HWG
Stults	Resurrection Song	TP
Stults	Voice Triumphant	TP
Sullivan	And God Shall Wipe Away All Tears*	GS
Sullivan	The Lord Is Risen	OD

*Recommended by the Voice Faculty of the Westminster Choir College, Princeton, N. J.

Composer	Title	Publisher
Thiman	My Master Hath a Garden	ECS
Topliff	Consider the Lilies	TP
Turner	Hail Your Risen Lord	GS
Vaughan-Williams	Easter	Gal
Yon	Christ Triumphant	JF
Yon	O Faithful Cross	JF
Yon	Our Paschal Joy	JF

LENT

Composer	Title	Publisher
Bedell	Two Songs for Lent	HWG
Bitgood	Give Me Faith	HWG
Bizet	Agnus Dei (Lamb of God)	OD,GS
Bizet	O Lord Be Merciful	GS
Burleigh (arr.)	Were You There (Spiritual)	Ric
Cartwright	Great Is Our God	Hunt
Chadwick	A Ballad of the Trees and the Master	OD
Diack	All in the April Evening	By
Gounod	There Is a Green Hill Far Away	OD
Gretchaninoff	O God of Love (Soprano)	HWG
Guion	At the Cry of the First Bird	GS
Hageman	Christ Went Up into the Hills	CF
Hamblen	God Is My Strength	Chap
Hamblen	Trust in Him	HWG
Humphries	Behold What Manner of Love	GS
LaForge	Before the Crucifix	GS
Lang	Lord Who Throughout These Forty Days	GS
MacDermid	Thou Wilt Keep Him in Perfect Peace	FM
MacGimsey	Think on These Things	CF
Milligan	Hear My Cry	GS
Moore	For My Sake Thou Hast Died	TP
Niles (arr.)	I Wonder as I Wander	GS
O'Hara	Art Thou the Christ	GS
Rogers	Today, If Ye Hear His Voice	APS
Thiman	Thou Wilt Keep Him in Perfect Peace	HWG
Tschaikovsky	A Legend	GS
Van Vollenhaven	Hear Me Speedily, O Lord	GS
Ward-Stephens	Two Songs from "Musical Settings of Sacred Words":	
	Awake Thou That Sleepest	Chap
	Search Me O God	Chap
Wooler	Hear My Cry, O Lord	OD

MOTHER'S DAY

Composer	Title	Publisher
Austin	I Have a Dream	Ric
Ball	Mother Machree	Wit
Bishop-Page	Home Sweet Home	TP
Brown-Deis	Glorious Day	GS
Burleigh	Little Mother of Mine	Ric
Cadman	Candle Light	
Caldwell	Mother My Own	BHks
Clokey	When Mother Sings	TP
Collinson-Hill	Once More to Touch Her Fragile Hand	GS
Dvorak	Songs My Mother Taught Me	TP,CF,GS
Grieg	The Old Mother	OD
Grimm	A Prayer for Mother's Day	JF
Hadley	Beautiful Mother	CF
Kramer	Mother O'Mine	CF
Liebling	Mother Dear (Soprano)	GS
McGimsey	To My Mother	CF
Malotte	For My Mother	GS
Schindler	Mother My Own	BHks
Sterling	Dear Little Mother O'Mine	FM

Composer	Title	Publisher
Test	Little Mother Dear	BHks
Thomas	Mother	BM
Tours	Mother O'Mine	Chap
Treharne	Mother My Dear	HF
Ware	To My Mother	CF
White	My Mother	Ric
Willeby	Coming Home	TP

FUNERAL OR MEMORIAL SERVICES*

Composer	Title	Publisher
Allisten	The Lord Is My Light	BHks
Ambrose	O Come to My Heart Lord Jesus	OD
Bach	Come Kindly Death (Komm süsser Tod)	CF
Bach	Draw Near to Me (Bist du bei mir)	CCB,GS
Bach-Gounod	Ave Marie	TP,GS
Bizet	Lamb of God (Agnus Dei)	OD,GS
Buxtehude-Dickinson	Lord in Thee Do I Put My Trust	HWG
Burleigh (arr.)	A City Called Heaven (Spiritual)	R
Byles	Prayer for Courage	TP
Campion	The Ninety and Nine	GS
Chadwick	Ballad of the Trees and the Master	TP
Coverley	This Day	TP
Cowles	Crossing the Bar	TP
DeKoven	Abide with Me	
DeKoven	Recessional	Ch
Dichmont	Peace I Leave with You	TP
Dortch	They That Trust in the Lord	TP
Dvorak-Fisher	Goin' Home	OD
Felton	Be Near Me Father	TP
Fisher	Be Comforted, Ye That Mourn	TP
Franck	Bread of Tears**(Panis Angelicus)	OD
Klein	Fine Words	Chap
Geibel	Hail Glorious Morn	TP
Gounod	Cross of Calvary	BM
Gounod	Forever with the Lord	BM
Gounod	Gentle, Holy Savior	BM
Gounod	There Is a Green Hill Far Away	OD
Guion	My Eternity	CF
Handel	I Know That My Redeemer Liveth ("Messiah") (High)	GS
Hamblen	Lead Kindly Light	BHks
Hahn	There Is My Home	TP
Harker	O Love That Wilt Not Let Me Go	GS
Haydn-Dickinson	Lord to Thy Throne Would I Draw Nigh (Cello obbl. optional)	HWG
Homer	Requiem	GS
Jewell	In My Father's House Are Many Mansions	TP
Knapp	Open the Gates of the Temple	CF
Lindsay	Come unto Me	TP
Malotte	The Lord's Prayer	GS
Marks	Thy Will Be Done	TP
Moore	Come Weary Soul	TP
Mowrey	Tears of God	Hunt
O'Hara	There Is No Death	Chap
Parker	Jerusalem	TP
Pochon	Crossing the Bar	
Protheroe	The Trees and the Master	BM
Sevenoak	Rock of Ages	
Shelley	Abide with Me	
Shenk	O Love That Wilt Not Let Me Go	TP
Speaks	Heaven Is My Home	TP
Steinel	Home to Thee, Lord	TP
Stor	With God	TP

*See also all "Ave Marias" in previous listings.
**Recommended by the Voice Faculty of the Westminister Choir College, Princeton, N. J.

ARMISTICE DAY, MEMORIAL DAY AND PATRIOTIC OCCASIONS

Composer	Title	Publisher
Alberti	A Nation's Prayer	EV
Bergen	In Flanders Fields*	GH
Bone-Fenton	Prayer for a Waiting World	CF
Bowles	An American Hero	Ax
Cadman	Glory*	Gal
Candyln	O God of Armies	HWG
Chadwick	He Maketh Wars to Cease	HWG
Carpenter	The Home Road*	GS
DeKoven	Recessional*	APS
Dix	The Trumpeter*	By
Dungan	Eternal Life	TP
Elgar	Land of Hope and Glory	By
Foster	The Americans Come*	JF
Howe	To the Unknown Soldier	GS
Lester	Greater Love Hath No Man*	CF
Handel	Arm, Arm Ye Brave (from "Judas Maccabaeus")	TP
MacDermid	Land of Mine*	FM
Mark-Andrews	Resurrection*	GS
Mowry	Tears of God*	Hunt
O'Hara	Guns*	DBH
O'Hara	My Country*	HF
O'Hara	There Is No Death*	Chap
Schubert-O'Hara	The Unknown Soldier*	GS
Steffe	Battle Hymn of the Republic	
Ward-Stephens	Christ in Flanders*	Chap
Ward-Stephens	Phantom Legions*	Chap

THANKSGIVING

Composer	Title	Publisher
Allisten	A Psalm of Thanksgiving	BM
Allisten	Praise to the Lord	OD
Barnaby	The Soft Southern Breeze	OD
Costa	It Is a Good Thing to Give Thanks	OD
Costa	I Will Extol Thee	GS
Cowan	Thanksgiving	BHks
Curran	Blessing	GS
Faure	Bless the Lord, O My Soul	BM
Fitzgerald	We Thank Thee	Chap
Gaeng	Praise the Lord, O My Soul	OD
Hall	God's Love Is Everywhere	APS
Ireland	Thanksgiving	BHks
LaForge	Hymn of Thanks and Praise	GS
Lansing	I Will Praise Thee, O God	OD
Lynes	The Earth Is the Lord's	APS
MacDermid	Make a Joyful Noise	FM
McFeeters	A Song of Praise	CF
McNellis	Thanksgiving	APS
Secchi	Lift Up Your Heads	OD
Warren	Because of Thy Great Bounty	HWG

WEDDINGS

Composer	Title	Publisher
Aylward	Beloved, It Is Morn	Chap
Bach	My Heart Ever Faithful	TP
Barnaby	O Perfect Love	OD
Beethoven	I Love Thee	GS
Black	The Pledge	GS
Bohm	Calm As the Night	TP
Bond	I Love Thee Truly	BM

*Suggested by the Chicago Singing Teacher's Guild.

311

Composer	Title	Publisher
Burleigh	O Perfect Love	TP
Cadman	At Dawning	OD
Carmichael	Star Dust	Mi
Clokey	Wedding Suite (Solo voice and organ)	JF
Clough-Leiter	Possession	GS
Coenen	Come Unto Me	TP
Deer	Before Thine Altar	BMC
De Koven	O Promise Me	TP,CF
Delius	So White, So Soft, Is She	BHks
Dello Joio	How Do I Love Thee	CF
Densmore	If God Left Only You	OD
Dickson	Thanks Be to God	E
Diggle	A Wedding Prayer	GS
D'Hardelot	Because	Chap
Dunlap	Wedding Prayer	GS
Fox	O Perfect Love	CF
Galbraith	Holy Spirit, Breath of Love	APS
Gaul	Entreat Me Not to Leave Thee	HWG
Geehl	For You Alone	Schu
Gounod	Entreat Me Not to Leave Thee	GS
Grieg	I Love Thee	OD,HWG,GS
Hammond	O Perfect Love	TP
Handel	Wher'er You Walk	CF,GS
Herbert	O Sweet Mystery of Life	Wit
Herbert	Thine Alone	Wit
Hopkins	How Do I Love Thee	TP
Huhn	I Love Thee	GS
Kiecker	Bless Our Vows	Wick
Kramer	Love's Litany	Ws
Leoncavallo	Matinnata	GS
Lippe	How Do I Love Thee	BM
List	Love Dream	TP
Lucas-Moya	Song of Songs	Chap
MacDonald	Nuptial Benediction	TP
Malotte	The Lord's Prayer	GS
Manney	Consecration	OD
McDowell	Thy Beaming Eyes	APS
Mendelssohn	Wedding Hymn	TP
Moffatt	I Love My Love	APS
Murray	I'll Walk Beside You	Chap
Nevin	The Wedding Morn	BM
O'Hara	Your Eyes Have Told Me So	GS
Romberg	One Alone (from "Desert Song")	Wit
Romberg	Serenade (from "Desert Song")	Wit
Ronald	Love I Have Won You	E
Ronald	Here at Thine Altar, Lord	N
Rosas	Wedding Song	GS
Rowley	Here at Thine Altar	N
Sacco	With This Ring	BVC
Sanderson	Until	BHks
Saxe	Wedding Bells	BVC
Schumann	Du Ring an Meinen Finger	GS
Schumann	Thou Art Like a Flower (Du bist wie eine Blume)	TP,GS
Schumann	Widmung (Dedication)	CF
Schutz	Wedding Song	Chap
Sharp	Possession	OD
Sowerby	O Perfect Love	HWG
Spohr	Rose Softly Blooming	TP
Stanton-Jeffries	With You to Bless	AMP
Strauss	Seitdem dein Aug' in meines schoute	Schott
Thompson	Velvet Shoes	GS

Composer	Title		Publisher
Willan	O Perfect Love		HWG
Williams	A Wedding Prayer		HWG
Woodman	I Am Thy Harp		GS
Youmans	Through the Years		Mlr

I. Songs with Special Obligato or Instrumental Accompaniment

(Note - Most songs have piano accompaniment also and in many instances the special instrumental obligato is optional. It will be noted that many of the leading modern composers are in this list.)

SECULAR

Composer	Title	Instruments	Published Keys*	Publisher**
Albieff	The Russian Nightingale	Flute	H	GS
Barber	Dover Beach	String quartet	M	GS
Bartlett	The Day Is Ended	Violin	HML	OD
Bartlett	Love's Rhapsody (L'Amour)	Cello	H	GS
Beach	Mirage	Violin, cello	H	TP
Beach	Rendevous	Violin	H	TP
Beethoven	12 Scotch and Irish Songs (Two volumes for voice, violin, cello, and piano)			MM
Bemberg	Hindoo Song (Chant Hindou)	Violin or cello	L	TP
Benedict	Gipsy and the Bird	Flute	H	TP,GS
Benedict	The Wren (La Capinera)	Violin or flute	H	GS
Benjamin	Three Impressions	Voice and string quartet		Cur
Benjamin	Four Impressions	Mezzo S and string quartet		Cur
Berger	Four Sonnets by Louis de Camoens	Piano or string quartet	M	GS
Bergman	Pastorale	Contralto, flute, alto recorder		Schott
Bergman	Nine Christmas Carols	Voice, recorder, piano		Schott
Bergman	John Brown's Body	Voice, 2 sop., sop., alto recorder, or ad. lib 3 violins, viola, cello		Schott
Bishop	Echo Song	Flute	H	GS
Bishop	Lo! Hear the Gentle Lark	Flute	H	TP,CF,GS
Bochau	You Are the Dawning of Dreams	Cello	H L	Ric
Bohm	Happiness of Love (Liebesglück)	Violin or flute	H	GS
Bonner	Opus 10 1. La Chanson du Porc-epic 2. La Compainte de Monsieur Benoit 3. Chameaux 4. Paysage de Neige	Medium Voice, flute, clarinet, bassoon, harp, piano		Ches
Brahms	Two Songs, Op. 91 1. Longing at Rest 2. Cradle Song of the Virgin	Contralto, viola, cello, piano		Sim
Britt	O Turtle Dove So Mournful	Harp or piano, cello	H	GS
Britten	Serenade, Op. 31	Tenor, horn, strings		BHks
Britten	Les Illuminations (Nine Songs)	Voice and orchestra		BHks
Brown	Spring Greeting (Waltz Song)	Violin	H	GS
Copland	As It Fell upon a Day	Soprano, flute, clarinet		Ar
Crist	Remember	Violin	H	CF
Curran	Nocturne	Violin	HML	GS
Davies	Six Pastorales, Op. 15	4 solo voices, string quartet, piano		Cur
Davies	Prospice	Baritone and strings		Cur
Densmore	Longing Dear for You	Violin or cello	HML	TP

*H – High, L – Low, M – Medium voice; if no key is mentioned, medium voice is assumed.
**See p. 220 for "Key to Publisher."

Composer	Title	Instruments	Published Keys	Publisher
Densmore	Voice and the Flute	Flute		TP
Denza	Your Voice	Violin or cello	H	TP
D'Indy	Madrigal, Op. 4	Soprano and cello	HML	GS
Francaix	1. Priere du Soir	Medium voice and guitar		Hue
	2. Chanson			Schott
Goodeve	Fiddle and I	Violin	H L	TP
			HML	GS
Gounod	Sing, Smile, Slumber	Violin or cello	ML	TP
Gounod	Tell Me Beautiful Maiden	Violin, flute or cello	ML	TP
Grainger	The Two Corbies	2 violins, 2 violas, 2 cello and 1 double bass	M	GS
Grainger	Willow Willow	Guitar or harp, string quartet	M	GS
Grant	Stars of the Summer Night	Violin	M	GS
Gruenberg	The Daniel Jazz, Op. 21	Tenor, piano, 2 violins, viola, cello, clarinet, trumpet		UE
Gruenberg	The Creation, Op. 23	Voice and same instr. as above		UE
Gurney	Ludlow and Teme (Seven Songs)	Voice, string quartet, piano		SB
Gurney	The Western Playland	Cycle for voice, string quartet		SB
Gurney	Lights Out (Cycle)			SB
Hadley	Make Me a Song	Cello	H	GS
Hadley	When I Go Away from You	Violin and cello	H L	CF
Handel	Hush Ye Pretty Warbling Quire	Sop., recorder, 2 violins, cello, piano		Schott
Handel	8 German Arias	Sop., violin, piano, cello ad lib.		
Handel	Liebliche Walder	Sop., obbl. violin, piano		BGB
Handel	22 Italian Duets and Trios	Voice with harpsichord, cello		Bor
Handel	Flammende Rose	Sop., violin, cembalo, bass		Con
Handel	Suesse Stille	Sop., tenor, flute, bass		GS
Handel	Meine Seele Hoert	Sop., flute, or violin, keyboard		GS
Heinrick	The Bony Fiddler (Der Knochenmann)	Violin	M	GS
Heinrick	Heigho! We'll Dance Today	Violin	L	GS
Heinrick	Night	Violin	M	GS
Holmes	Night Comes and the Day Is Done	Violin or cello	H L	GS
Holst	Four Songs, Op. 35	Voice and violin		MB
	1. Jesu Sweet (Sacred)			
	2. My Soul Hath Nothing But Fire and Ice			
	3. I Sing of a Maiden			
	4. My Leman Is True			
Holst	Savitri, Op. 25 (A Chamber Opera)	Flutes, English horn, hidden chorus		MB
Honneger	Chanson de Ronsard d'Anderson	Voice, flute, string quartet		MS
Kücken	Heaven Hath Shed a Tear (Der Himmel hat eine Thrane geweint)	Violin or clarinet, flute or cello	H L	
Kreisler	Oh, Cease Thy Singing Maiden Fair	Violin or cello	H	GS
Lachner	Thou Everywhere (Uberall du)	Violin, flute, or cello	H	GS
LaForge	Menuet varié	Flute	H	GS
Lekeu	Nocturne	Voice and string quartet		RLC
Lieurance	Remembered	Violin	M	TP
Lieurance	She Stands Smiling	Violin or flute	H	TP
Loeffler	Four Poems, Op. 5	Voice, viola, piano		
Loeffler	Serenade	Viola	M	GS
Milhaud	Psalm 129	Baritone and 2 pianos		U
Milhaud	Le retour de l'Enfant Prodique, Op. 56	Five voices and 21 instruments		U
Milhaud	Machines Agricoles, Op. 56	Voice and 7 instruments		U
Milhaud	Catalog de Fleurs, Op. 60 (7 Songs)	Voice and 7 instruments		Du
Milhaud	Caramel Mou, Op. 68	Voice and small jazz band		Me
Milhaud	Cocktail, Op. 69	Voice and 3 clarinets		AL

Composer	Title	Instruments	Published Keys	Publisher
Milhaud	Sixth Symphony, Op. 79	Vocal quartet, oboe, cello		U
Milhaud	Quatre Poemes de Catulle	Voice and violin		Hue
Milhaud	Adages, Op. 120	Vocal quartet, instruments		Du
Milhaud	Liturgie Comtadine, Op. 125	Voice, small orchestra		Hue
Milhaud	Pan et Syrinx, Op. 130 (6 numbers)	Sop., baritone, vocal quartet 5 instruments		DS
Moderati	I Lived Forlorn	Harp and violin	H	GS
Moir	Parted or Near	Violin	H	GS
Nin	Le Chant du Veilluer	Mezzo sop., violin, sax, piano		ME
Poulenc	Rapsodie Negre	Voice, flute, clarinet, string quartet		MB
Poulenc	Cocardest Bestiaire	Voice, string quartet, flute clarinet, bassoon		Ches
Proch-LaForge	Theme and Variations	Flute	H	CF
Reinicke	Greeting to the Woods	Violin, flute, or cello	H	GS
Robaudi	Bright Star of Love	Violin, flute, or cello	H L	GS
Rachmaninoff	Oh, Cease Thy Singing Maiden Fair	Violin	H	CF
Rachmaninoff	When Night Descends in Silence	Voice, violin, piano		CF
Ravel	Trois Poems de Mallarme	Voice, string quartet, 2 clarinets, 2 flutes, piano		Du
Ravel	Chansons Madecasses	Voice, flute, cello, piano		Du
Ravel	Don Quixotte a Dulcinee	Baritone and small orchestra		Du
Riegger	Frenetic Rhythms (Modern Dance Music)	Voice, 3 woodwinds, piano		BMP
Riegger	Music for Voice and Flute	Medium voice, coloratura sop., flute		BMP
Riegger	La Belle Dame Sans Merci	4 solo voices and chamber orchestra		BMP
Ross	At Twilight	Violin	HM	GS
Sarr	Of Days Without My Own	Violin	M	GS
Sarr	Two Flowers	Violin	H	GS
Saint-Saens-Salzedo	A Swan's Song	Harp, piano, cello	HML	GS
Schönberg	String Quartet in F Minor, Op. 10	3rd and 4th movements with soprano		U
Schönberg	Serenade, Op. 24	String quartet with deep male voice in 4th movement		U
Schönberg	Herzgewache, Op. 20	Sop., celesta, harmonium, harp		U
Schonberg	Lied der Waldtaube	Voice and chamber orchestra		U
Schonberg	Pierrot Lunaire	Voice, piano, flute, piccolo, clarinet, bass clarinet, violin, viola, cello		U
Schubert-Dies	Serande (Standchen)	Violin, flute, or cello	H	GS
Schubert-Dies	The Shepherd on the Rock (Der Hirt auf dem Felsen	B Flat clarinet, violin or flute	H	GS
Scott	Nocturne	Cello	M	GS
Shelley	Another Day	Violin	HML	GS
Shelley	Ever True	Violin or cello	HML	GS
Shepperd	My Love Went Sailing	Violin or cello	H L	GS
Slater	Mountain Flowers	Violin or cello	ML	GS
Stravinsky	Pastorale (Vocalise)	Sop., oboe, English horn, clarinet in A, bassoon		Schott
Stravinsky	Pribautki Songs	Voice, flute, oboe or English horn, clarinet, bassoon, violin, celoviolo, cb		Ches
Stravinsky	Berceuses du Chat	Female voice, 3 clarinets		MB
Terry	Song Is So Old	Violin	ML	GS
Thomas	Time's Garden	Cello	M	GS
Thrane-LaForge	Norwegian Echo Song	Flute	H	CF

Composer	Title	Instruments	Published Keys	Publisher
Tirindelli	A Voice from Afar (Canto Gontano)	Violin	H	Ric
Tirindelli	Love's Symphony	Violin	H	Ric
Tirindelli	Mistica	Violin, cello, harmonium	H	Ric
Toch	The Chinese Flute, Op. 29	Sop., 14 solo instruments		Schott
Toch	Poems to Martha, Op. 66	Baritone, string quartet		Schott
Tosti	Beauty's Eyes	Violin	M	GS
Tosti	Chanson de l'adieu	Violin	M	GS
Tosti	Good-Bye	Violin	HML	Ric
Villa-Lobos	Bachianas Brazileiras #5	Sop. and an orchestra of cellos		AMP
Villa-Lobos	Poem de L'enfant et de sa mere	Voice, flute, clarinet, cello		AMP
Villa-Lobos	Suite	Voice and violin		AMP
Vogrich	Arabian Song	Violin, cello	H	GS
Warlock	Sorrow's Lullaby	Sop., baritone, string quartet		Ox
Warlock	The Curlew*	Voice, string quartet, flute, English horn		Ox
Weber-Liebling	Invitation to the Dance	Flute	H	GS
Webern	Geistlicher Volkstext	Voice and 3 instruments		Ar
Webern	Two Songs, Op. 8	Voice, violin, viola, vlc., horn, trumpet, celeste		Ar
Webern	Six Songs, Op. 14	Voice, clarinet, violin, cello, harp		Ar
Williams	On Wenlock Edge (Cycle)	Tenor, string quartet, piano		BHks
Williams	Two English Folk Songs	Voice and violin		CF
Williams	Nine Housman Songs	Voice and Violin		CF
Williams	Merciless Beauty	Voice, 2 violins, cello		Cur
Woodman	In Arcady	Violin	ML	GS
Wright	Fidelity	Violin	HML	Ric

SACRED

Composer	Title	Instruments	Published Keys	Publisher
Adam	O, Holy Night	Violin, cello	HML	OD
Bach	I Follow with Gladness (from "St. John Passion")	Flute or violin	Sop	Pat
Bach	On My Shepherd I Rely	Oboe or violin	Sop	Pat
Bach-Engel	Arioso	Violin, piano, organ	H L	BM
Bach-Gounod	Ave Maria	Violin, cello	HML	OD,GS
Barnes	Love Divine	Organ; piano, violin opt.	H	OD
Bartlett	Day Is Ended	Violin	ML	TP
Bishop	Pretty Mocking Bird	Flute	H	Ric
Bizet	Lamb of God (Agnus Dei) (Lent)	Violin or cello	HML	OD,GS
Blackwell	Rest	Cello	HM	Ric
Braga	Angel's Serenade (La Serenata)	Violin or cello	HML	OD
Buxtehude-Dickinson	Lord in Thee Do I Put My Trust	2 violins		HWG
Buxtehude-Dickinson	My Jesus Is My Lasting Joy	2 violins		HWG
Coombs	My Defender	Violin	M	BM
Coombs	Star of the East (Christmas)	Violin	HML	GS
Denza	Si vous l'aviez compris	Violin or cello	HML	Ric
Dressler	The Angel's Message (Christmas)	Violin	HML	OD
Faure	The Palms (Les Rameaux) (Palm Sunday)	Violin	ML	OD
Franck	O Lord Most Holy (Panis Angelicus)	Violin or cello; harp or piano	H L	BM
Geibel	The Angel's Refrain (Christmas)	Violin	H L	TP
Gillingham	Supplication	Violin	H L	BM
Granier	Hosanna (Easter)	Violin	HML	OD
Gray	Dream of Paradise	Violin or cello	H	TP
Handel	Love Ye the Lord (Largo from "Xerxes")	Violin	ML	OD
Haydn-Dickinson	Lord to Thy Throne	Cello		HWG

*Won a Carnegie Award.

Composer	Title	Instruments	Published Keys	Publisher
Holst	Four Songs, Op. 35	Voice and violin		MB
	1. Jesu Sweet			
	2. My Soul Hath Naught But Fire and Ice			
	3. I Sing of a Maiden			
	4. My Leman Is So True			
Johnson	Angels Sing On	Violin	H	BM
Marsh	The Lord Is My Light	Violin	H MH M	CF
Montani	The Virgin at the Crib (Christmas)	Violin	HM	GS
Mascagni	O Loving Father	Violin	H	TP
Roberts	Ave Maria (Christmas)	Violin or cello	M	BM
Santiago	Ave Maria (Christmas)	Violin	H	TP
Scarlatti	Christmas Cantata	Sop., string quartet, piano		Ox
Schelley	The Holy Child (Christmas)	Violin		GS
Shackley	In the Dawn of Early Morning (Easter)	Violin	L	TP
Spross	I Do Not Ask, O Lord	Violin	H L	TP
Tschaikowsky	How Long Wilt Thou Forget Me	Violin	L	TP
Vannah	Tears of Christ	Violin	M	TP
Williams	Four Hymns	Tenor, viola, strings		Cur
Yon	Gesu Bambino (Christmas)	Violin or cello	H L	JF

OPERATIC

Composer	Title	Instruments	Published Keys	Publisher
David	Thou Brilliant Bird (Charmant oiseau) (from "La Perle du Bresil")	Flute	H	GS
Donizetti	Mad Scene (from "Lucia di Lammermoor")	Flute	H	CF,GS
Donizetti	O Could We Lightly Fly (from "Lucia di Lammermoor")	Flute	H	CF
Gounod	Little Swallow (Waltz Song from "Mireille")	Flute	H	CF
Grétry-LaForge	The Pretty Warbler with All Her Brood. (from "Zemire et Agor")	Flute	H	GS
Herbert	Aurora Blushing Rosily (from "The Madcap Duchess")	Violin	H	GS
Meyerbeer-Liebling	That's the Tune (from "L'Etoile du Nord")	Special cadenza for voice and two flutes	H	GS
Mozart	Her I'll Love (from "L'amero Saro Castante")	Violin	H	TP
Mozart-Dies	Faithful Heart Enraptured (from "Il Re Pastore")	Violin or flute	H	GS
Mozart-LaForge	Variations	Flute	H	CF
Napravnik	Lullaby (from "Harold")	Viola or cello	M	GS
Saint-Saens	My Heart at Thy Sweet Voice (from "Samson et Delila")	Violin or cello	ML	TP
Strauss	Fledermaus Fantasy (Excerpts from "Die Fledermaus")	Flute	H	CF
Thomas	Know'st Not That Fair Land (from "Mignon")	Violin or cello	H	GS
Verdi	Ave Maria (from "Otello")	Violin or cello	HM	GS

J. Duets*

SECULAR DUETS

Composer	Composition	Voices**	Publisher***
Allitsen	In Our Boat	MS & B	
Ardite	A Night in Venice (Una notte a Venezia)	S & T	
Balfe	Excelsior	A & B	
Bainton	The Nymph's Song	S & A	JW
Blumenthal	Venetian Boat Song	S & A	
Bohm	Soft Vernal Night (Lenzige Nacht)	S & A or T & B	CF
Bohm	Still As the Night (Still wie die Nacht)	S & A	OD
Bohm	Recollection of Spring	H & L	CF
Brahms	The Little Sandman	S & A	WR
Brahms	The Gipsies (Les bohemiennis)	S & MS	GS
Bridge	Evening Primrose	S & A	Ox
Bridge	The Graceful Swaying Wattle	H & L	WR
Buck	A Carol of St. Bridgit	H & L	Arnold
Buck	The Windmill	H & L	Arnold
Cadman	At Dawning	A♭ for H & M; F for M & L	TP
Caracciolo	Nearest and Dearest (Tuscan Folk)	S & A	GS
Chaminade	Oui, mon ami est charmante	S & MS	GS
Delius	Streamlet's Slumber Song	H & L	Ox
Densmore	Starry Night	S & A	OD
Dunhill	Full Fathom Five	T & B	Arnold
Dvorak-Fisher	Goin' Home	S & A	TP
Dyson	To the Thames	H & L	Arnold
Gade	Lightly Borne on Music's Wing	S & S	GS
Gibbs	Dream Pedlary	H & L	Ox
Gibbs	Five Eyes	H & L	WR
Godard	A Summer Night (Nuit de ete)	S & S	GS
Goetze	Still As the Night (Still wie die Nacht)	S & B or A	OD
Golde	Was It You	S & T or B	GS
Gounod	Beautiful Night (Par une belle nuit)	S & A	GS
Goya (arr.)	The Swallow ("La Golondrina," Mexican Folk)	H & L	OD
Graben-Hoffman	Messengers of Spring	S & B	GS
Graben-Hoffman	My Boat O'er the Tide	MS & B	GS
Graben-Hoffman	I Feel Thy Angel Spirit	S & B	GS
Handel	Fairy Folk	S & A	Ox
Handel	When You Marry Me	S & B	Pat
Hawthorne	Passage Bird's Farewell (Abschied der Vogel)	S & B	TP
Hildach	Passage Bird's Farewell	H & M; M & L	GS
Holst	Clouds O'er the Summer Sky	H & L	N
Holst	The Corn Song	H & L	Arnold
Holst	The Song of Ship Builders	T & B	N
Holst	The Song of the Lumber Men	T & B	Arnold
Howells	Golden Lullaby	H & L	Arnold
Howells	The Tinker's Song	H & L	Ox
Huhn	The Hunt	T & B	GS
Ireland	Aubade	H & L	N
Ireland	Full Fathom Five	T & B	N
Ireland	In Praise of May	S & A	N
Ireland	There Is a Garden in Her Face	H & L	N
Jensen	O Lay Thy Cheek on Mine (Lehn' deine Wang an meine Wang)	S & T	Ox

*See also duet collections, p. 227.

**S – Soprano, MS – Mezzo Soprano, A – Alto, T – Tenor, B – Baritone, or High Bass, H – High, M – Medium, L – Low. In many cases a Tenor may be substituted for Soprano and Baritone for Mezzo Soprano or Alto.

***See p. 220 for "Key to Publisher."

Composer	Composition	Voices	Publisher
Kountz	The Sleigh	H & M or L	GS
Küchen	O Swallow, Happy Swallow	S & A	GS
Ley	Up the Hillside	H & L	Arnold
Lovering	At Night	H & L	Ox
Lucantoni	Bright As the Bow of Promise (Il bacio)	S & S	GS
Mana-Zucca	I Love Life	S & A	TP
Massenet	Joy (Joie)	S & A	GS
Marzials	Go Pretty Rose	S & T	TP
Mendelssohn	May Bells and Flowers (Maiglöckchen und die Blümelein	S & A	GS
Mendelssohn	On Wings of Music (Auf flugeln des Gesanges)	S & A	OD
Morley	It Was a Lover and His Lass	H & L	N
Oliver	In Old Versailles	S & T; A & T	CF
Paganucci	Columbina	H & L	N
Parker	Hark, to the Mandoline	S & A	TP
Pinsuti	Love On (Ama)	S & B	N
Pinsuti	Pearls of Love (Due Perle)	S & A	GS
Purcell	Shepherd, Shepherd	S & B	N
Purcell	Sound the Trumpet	H & L	N
Rubinstein	Pass Lightly	S & A	GS
Rubinstein	Wanderer's Night Song	S & A	GS
Saint-Saens	Le Soir (Barcarolle)	MS & T	GS
Saint-Saens	The Unfortunate (El desdichado)	S & S	GS
Schindler	La Camargo (Eighteenth Century Minuet)	S & B	GS
Schubert	Serenade	S & T or A; H & L	TP,GS,CF
Schoebel	Come, Love, Come	S & T	TP
Schumann	The Fall of the Leaf (Herbstlied)	S & A	N
Schumann	Pluck Ye Roses	H & L	N
Stanford	The Lark's Grave	S & A	Cur
Thomas	My Bark	S & A	GS
Thomas	My Heart Greets the Morn (Mon coeur, lève Toi)	S & T	GS
Thomas	Neath the Stars (Sous les etoiles)	S & T; MS & B	GS
Weidt	The Minstrel and His Child	B or T & B	CF,GS
Widor	J'étais seul pres dés flots	S & A	GS
Willeby	Coming Home (Mother's Day)	S & A	TP

SACRED DUETS*

Composer	Composition	Voices	Publisher
Adam	O Holy Night (Cantique de Noel) (Christmas). (Optional violin or cello obligato)	S & A	OD
Ambrose	One Sweetly Solemn Thought (Funerals)	S & A	TP
Bach	Thou Crownest the Year	H & L	SB
Bartlett	O Lord, Remember Me	S & A	GS
Berger	Little Christmas Song	S & B	TP
Buck	Acquaint Thyself with Him	S & T; A & B	GS
Buck	Be Good Comfort	S & T; A & B	GS
Chadwick	A Ballad of the Trees and the Master	H & L	OD
Chaminade	Angelus (L'Angelus)	MS & B	
Coombs	The Angel of Light (Christmas)	A & T	GS
Coombs	The Dawn of Hope (Christmas)	S & A	GS
Coombs	O How Amiable Are Thy Dwellings	MS & B	GS
Coombs	The Radiant Star (Christmas)	T & B	GS
Del Riego	Thank God for a Garden	H & L	Chap
Dubois	I Will Ever Bless Thy Name (Ecce Panis)	S & B	JF
Faure	Charity	S & T	GS
Faure	The Crucifix	S & A or T & B	CF,GS
Franck	The Virgin by the Manger (Christmas)	S & A	GS
Gounod	The Cross of Calvary (Ave Maria)	S & A and Ms & T	GS

*See also Sacred Duet collections, p. 227.

Composer	Composition	Voices	Publisher
Gounod	Forever with the Lord	S & A and MS & B	GS
Gounod	Glory to Thee, My God	S & A and MS & B	GS
Gounod	Guardian Angel	S & MS	GS
Gounod	Heavenly Love	S & A	GS
Gounod	O for a Closer Walk with God	S & T	TP
Gounod	Ring On, Sweet Angelus	MS & B	GS
Gounod	There Is a Green Hill Far Away (Good Friday)	S & A	TP
Gounod	Until Day Breaks	H & L	GS
Granier-McKinney	Hosanna (Easter)	S & A	JF, GS
Hammond	Behold, the Master Passeth By (Lent)	H & L	Ch
Handel	He Shall Feed His Flock, and Come Unto Him (from "Messiah") (Christmas or general)	Solo S & Solo A	TP, Pat
Handel	O Lovely Peace (from "Judas Maccabaeus")	S & A	OD
Hageman	Christ Went Up into the Hills	H & L	CF
Harker	How Beautiful Upon the Mountains	H & L	GS
Harker	O Paradise (Funerals)	S & T	CF
Harker-Riegger	God Shall Wipe Away All Tears	S & A	GS
Huhn	Be Thou Exalted	S & T and A & B	GS
Huhn	High in the Heavens	H & L	GS
Kerr	In Juda's Land (Christmas)	Two medium voices	TP
Knapp	Open the Gates of the Temple (Easter)	S & A	CF
Leo	From Your Heavenly Throne	H & L	GS
Lester	Rejoice in the Lord (Easter)	S & A	CF
MacFarlane	O Love Divine	S & A	GS
Malotte-Dies	The Lord's Prayer	S & A, S & T, A & B	GS
Matthews	Lord, I Have Loved the Habitation of Thy House	A & B	OD
Matthews	The Lord Is My Shepherd	S & T	OD
Mendelssohn	I Waited for the Lord	S & MS	OD, GS
Nevin	Twilight (Day Is Dying in the West)	S & A or S & S	OD
O'Hara	I Walked Today Where Jesus Walked	S & A, S & T, A & B	GS
Rathbun	I Heard the Voice of Jesus Say	A & B	TP
Reinicke	A Christmas Carol (Christmas)	H & L	N
Roberts	If with All Your Hearts	S & T	TP
Rossini	Where's the Cold Heart So Unfeeling (Onis est Homo)	S & A	TP
Rubinstein	The Angel	S & A	GS
Schnecker	My Faith Looks Up to Thee	T & B	GS
Smart	The Lord Is My Shepherd	S & A	OD, CF
Scott	Art Thou Weary	S & A or T & B	GS
Shelley	Easter Vespers (Easter)	H & L	GS
Shelley	Hark! Hark My Soul	S & A	GS
Shelley	Noel of the Bells (Christmas)	H & L	GS
Shelley	Savior, When Night Involves the Sky	H & L	GS
Spross	I Love Thee Lord	H & L	Ch
Stainer	Love Divine, All Love Excelling	S & T	TP, CF, GS
Van de Water	Day of Days (Easter)	S & A	TP
Van de Water	Night of Nights (Christmas)	A & B, S & T	TP
Verdi	Ah! Remember Me (from "Requiem")	S & MS	GS
Warren	Magdalene	S & A	CF

OPERATIC DUETS

Composer	Composition	Voices	Publisher
Bellini	Deh! con te li prende (Take Them with Thee) ("Norma")	S & S	GS
Bellini	Mira, O Norma (Hear Me Norma) ("Norma")	S & MS	TP
Bellini	Prende, l'anel ti dono ("La Sonnambula")	S & T	Ric
Bizet	Parle moi di ma mère ("Carmen")	S & T	
Boito	Lontano, lontano (Afar from Pain) ("Mefistofele")	S & T	GS, Ric

Composer	Composition	Voices	Publisher
Delibes	Déjà les hirondelles (The Swallows Gaily Singing) ("Le Roi l'a Dit")	S & MS.	GS
Delibes	Sous le dome é pais ("Le Roi l' a Dit").	S & MS or A	GS
Donizetti	Ah! l'alto ardor (Ah, Noble Love) ("La Favorita").	S & Baritone.	GS
Donizetti	Sulla tomba che rinserra ("Lucia di Lammermoor").	S & T	Ric
Donizetti	Torami a dir che m'ami ("Don Pasquale").	S & T	Ric
Leoncavallo	Silvio! a quest' ora ("I Pagliacci") (Silvio! In the Daytime)	S & Baritone.	GS
McCay	Il addio (The Farewell) ("Egypt").	S & T	GS
Mozart	Là ci darem la mano (Nay, Bid Me Not Resign Love) ("Don Giovanni").	S & Baritone.	TP,GS,Ric
Mozart	La Dove Prende (Smiles and Tears) ("Magic Flute") Giovanni").	S & S	TP
Mozart	Sull' aria (Sweet Zephyr) ("Le Nozze di Figaro").	S & S	GS
Offenbach	Night, O Night of Love ("Tales of Hoffman").	S & MS or A	OD,GS
Ponchiello	L'amo come il fulgor del crealo.	S & MS.	Ric
Puccini	Bimba dagli occhi pieni di malia ("Madame Butterfly")	S & T	Ric
Puccini	O Mimi, tu più non torni ("La Bohème") (Ah, Mimi False)	T & B or Baritone	Ric
Puccini	O soave fancuilla (Lovely Maid in Moonlight) ("La Bohème")	S & T	Ric
Puccini	Sono andati ("La Bohème").	S & T	Ric
Puccini	Tutti i fior (Every Flower) ("Madame Butterfly")	S & MS.	Ric
Puccini	Tu, tu amore ("Manon Lescaut").	S & T	Ric
Puccini	Vogliatemi bene ("Madame Butterfly") (Note - In Two Keys, D♭ and E♭)	S & T	Ric
Tsaikovsky	Tis Evening ("Pique-Dame").	S & A	GS
Thomas	Legeres hirondelles (O Lightly Flitting Swallows) ("Mignon").	S & Baritone.	GS
Verdi	From "Aida":		
	Fu la sorte dell'armi	S & MS.	GS
	Morir! si pura e bella.	S & T	GS,Ric
	Riverdrai le foreste.	S & Baritone.	GS
Verdi	From "Falstaff"		
	Labbra di foco.	S & T	Ric
Verdi	From "La Forza del Destino":		
	Amica in vita e in morte.	T & Baritone.	Ric
	Col sangue sol cancellasi	T & Baritone.	Ric
	Piu tranquilla l'alma sento	S & Bass.	Ric
	Solenne in quest ora (In This Solemn Hour)	T & B	TP,Ric
Verdi	From "La Traviata":		
	Libiam ne'lieti calici.	S & T	Ric
	Un di felice, eterea.	S & T	Ric
	Pura siccome un angelo.	S & Baritone.	Ric
	Parigi, o cara.	S & T	TP,Ric
Verdi	From "Il Trovatore":		
	Se m'ami ancor.	MS & T.	Ric
	Si la stanchezza m'opprime (Home to Our Mountains	A or MS & T	GS
	Qual voce! Come! Tu donna	S & Baritone.	Ric
Verdi	From "Rigoletto":		
	Figlia! mio padre! A te' d'appresso.	S & Baritone.	Ric
	Signor ne principe io lo vorrei	S & T	Ric
	Tutte le feste al tempio.	S & Baritone.	Ric

Bibliography

Alda, Frances. *Men, Women and Tenors.* Houghton Mifflin, 1937.

Anderson, Marion. "Some Reflections on Singing." (an interview) Etude, 1939, Vol. 57.

Anderson, Virgil. *Training the Speaking Voice.* Oxford University Press, 1942.

Armstrong, William G. "On the Treatment of Vocal Registers." Etude, 1939, Vol. 57.

Bachner, Louis. *Dynamic Singing.* L. B. Fischer, 1944.

Bartholomew, Wilmer T. "The Paradox of Voice Teaching." Journal of the Acoustical Society of America, Vol. II, 1940.

Bjorling, Jussi. "Good Singing Is Natural." (an interview) Etude, 1937, Vol. 55.

Bowen, George Oscar. "Voice Training in the High School." Music Supervisors National Conference Yearbook, 1947.

Bowen, George Oscar and Mook, Kenneth C. *Song and Speech.* Ginn and Co., 1952.

Breach, William. *Art Song Argosy.* G. Schirmer, 1937.

Brown, Ralph Morse. *The Singing Voice.* Macmillan Co., 1940.

Bushell, Sidney. "Covered Tone." Etude, 1939, Vol. 57.

———. "Fifteen Minutes of Stimulating Vocal Practice."

———. Etude, 1940, Vol. 58.

———. "Poise: an Essential of Good Singing." Musician, 1939, Vol. 44.

Butler, Harold L. "Salient Changes in Voice Teaching in the Past 50 Years." Etude, 1928, Vol. 46.

California-Western Conference Curriculum Committee. "Voice Training in Classes." Music Educators Journal, May-June, 1945.

Callan, Emily Jean. "High School Voice Classes." School Music, Nov. 1930.

Castagna, Bruna. "Good Singing Must Be Natural." (an interview) Etude, 1939, Vol. 57.

Chambers, Lawrence B. *A Critical Survey of Unison Octavo Music for Voice Students.* M. A. Thesis, Ohio State University.

Christy, Van A. *Glee Club and Chorus.* G. Schirmer, 1936.

Clark, Wallace. "Breathing." Etude, 1930, Vol. 48.

Clippinger, David Alba. *The Clippinger Class Method of Voice Culture, Ditson, 1932.*

———. "Collective Voice Training." MSNC Yearbook, 1935.

———. *The Head Voice and Other Problems.* Ditson, 1917.

———. "The Human Instrument." Etude, 1929, Vol. 47.

———. "On Becoming Musical." Music Supervisors National Conference Yearbook, 1933.

———. "School Music." (Vocal Department) Chicago, Jan. 1935.

Clippinger, David Alba and Others. "Vocal Forum." Music Teachers National Association Proceedings for 1936, Vol. 31.

Coleman, Henry. "The Amateur Choir Trainer." Oxford University Press, 1932.

Conklin, Maurice. *Fundamental Vocal Technic.* Dorrance and Co., 1936.

Combs, William Baker. *The Voice in Singing; Its Care and Development.* The Author, 1938.

Cooke, James Francis. *How to Memorize Music.* Theodore Presser, 1948.

Dassert, Dean (Mme). *Sound Sense for Singers.* J. Fischer and Brothers.

De Bruyn, John. "The Oldest Authentic Voice Method." Etude, 1940, Vol. 59.

Della Chiesa, Vivian. "Successful Singing." (an interview) Etude, 1942, Vol. 60.

Dengler, Clyde. "Class Vocal Methods — High School Level." M E N C Yearbook, 1937.

Dodds, George and Lickly, James Dunlop. *The Control of Breath.* Oxford University Press, 1935.

Downing, William B. *Vocal Pedagogy*. Carl Fischer, 1927.

Dragonette, Jessica. "The Mental Approach to Singing." (an interview) Etude, 1940, Vol. 58.

Drake, Raleigh M. "How to Memorize Music Economically." Music Educators Journal, May 1939.

Dykema, Peter. *Music for Public School Music Administrators*. Bureau of Publications, Teachers College, Columbia University, 1931.

Dykema, Peter and Gehrkens, Karl. *The Teaching and Administration of High School Music*. C. C. Birchard and Co., 1941.

Ferguson, George. "Class Instruction in Singing." Music Supervisors Journal, Feb. 1932.

———. "Singers' Basic Equipment." Musician, 1940, Vol. 45.

Fields, Victor Alexander. *The Singer's Glossary*. Boston Music Co., 1952.

———. *Training the Singing Voice*. Kings Crown Press, 1947.

Garcia, Manuel. *Hints on Singing*. A Aschenburg and Co., 1894.

Garnetti-Forbes, Elena. *My Views on Voice Production*. The Author, 1941.

German, Francis. "What a Judge Has Learned at Contests." Music Educators Journal, Sept.-Oct., 1952.

Glenn, Maybelle and Spouse, Alfred. *Art Songs for School and Studio*. Ditson, 1934.

Grace, Harvey. *The Training and Conducting of Choral Societies*. Novello and Co., 1938.

Graves, Richard M. *Singing for Amateurs*. Oxford University Press, 1954.

Graveure, Louis. "New Theories of Vocalism." (an interview) Etude, 1931, Vol. 49.

Grove, Grace J. "On the Development of the Vowel." Etude, 1937, Vol. 55.

Greene, Henry Plunkett. *Interpretation in Song*. Macmillan, 1940.

Gunderman, John and Schumacher, Bernhard. *Manual for the Music Reader for Lutheran Schools*. Concordia, 1933.

Hall, John Waller and Brown, Ralph M. *What Every Singer Should Know*. .Vocal Science Publishing Co., 1928.

Hathaway, Helen. *What Your Voice Reveals*. E. P. Dutton.

Haywood, Frederick. *Universal Song*, G. Schirmer, 1933, 1942.

———. "The Value of Voice Culture Classes for Senior High School Students." Etude, April 1929.

———. "Voice Culture Classes." Music Supervisors Journal, Feb. 1929.

Henley, Homer. "Training the Male Voice." Etude, 1936, Vol. 54.

Henderson, Mrs. Archibald M. *Speech and Song*. Macmillan, 1933.

Henderson, W. J. *The Art of Singing*. Dial Press, 1948.

Herbert-Caesari, Edgar F. "Opening the Mouth in Singing." Etude, Jan. 1938.

———. *The Science and Sensations of Vocal Tone*. J. M. Dent and Sons, 1936.

Hesser, Ernest G. "Historical Data — High School Voice Classes." Dec. 1928.

Hoffman, Franz. "Recitative." The Journal of the Choral Conductors Guild of California, Feb. 1953.

Howerton, George. *Technic and Style in Choral Singing*. Carl Fischer, 1957.

Jeffries, Arthur. "For the Untrained Singer." Etude, 1933, Vol. 51.

———. "The Natural Voice." Etude, 1934, Vol. 52.

Johnson, Edward. *Styles in Singing*. Doubleday Doran, 1941.

Jones, Archie N. "The Basis of Choral Interpretation." The Supervisors Service Bulletin, Jan. 1932.

———. *Technic in Choral Conducting*. Carl Fischer, 1948.

Judd, Percy. *Singing Technique*. Oxford University Press, 1931.

Kagen, Sergius. *Music for Voice*. Rinehart & Co., 1949.

———. *On Studying Singing*. Rinehart and Co., 1950.

Key, Pierre Van Rensselaer. *Teach Yourself to Sing*. Reader Mail, Inc., 1941.

Kirkland, H. S. *Expression in Singing*. Richard G. Badger, 1916.

Klingstead, Paul T. *Common Sense in Vocal Pedagogy as Prescribed by the Early Italian Masters*. Edwards Brothers, 1941.

Kortkamp, Ivan A. "Compensating for Flatting." Educational Music Magazine, Sept.-Oct. 1940, Vol. 20.

———. "Tone Color Artistry." California Choral Conductors Guild Choir Guide, May-June, 1949.

Krone, Max T. *The Chorus and Its Conductor*. Neil J. Kjos, 1945.

Laine, Juliette. "A Cure for Hoarseness After Singing." Etude, 1934, Vol. 52.

Lamperti, Carlo. *Improving Your Voice*. Vantage Press, 1954.

Lamperti, G. B. *The Technics of Bel Canto*. G. Schirmer, 1905.

Lee, Marjorie Evelyn. *Voice Classes in Secondary Schools*. Master's Thesis, University of Illinois, 1946.

Lehmann, Lilli. *How to Sing*. Macmillan, 1929, 3rd revised edition.

Lehmann, Lotte. *More Than Singing*. Boosey and Hawkes, 1945.

Litante, Judith. *A Natural Approach to Singing*. Wm. C. Brown Co., 1959.

Lloyd, Robert. *The Robert Lloyd Tone System*. Herr Wagner Publishing Co., 1929.

Marchesi, Blanche. *The Singer's Catechism and Creed.* J. M. Dent and Sons, 1932.

Marifioti, P. Mario. *Caruso's Method of Voice Production.* Cadica Enterprises, 1950 (original copy 1922).

McClosky, David Blair. *Your Voice at Its Best.* Little, Brown and Co., 1959.

McKinney, Howard D. and Anderson, W. R. *Music In History.* American Book Co., 1940.

Metfessel, Milton. "The Vibrato in Artistic Voices." University of Iowa Studies in the Psychology of Music, 1932, Vol. I.

Meyer, Edmund J. *Vocal Reinforcement.* Boston Music Co., 1913.

Mursell, James L. *Education for Musical Growth.* Ginn and Co., 1948.

———. *Human Values in Music Education.* Silver Burdett & Co., 1930.

———. *Music and the Classroom Teacher.* Silver Burdett & Co., 1951.

———. *Music in American Schools.* Silver Burdett and Co., 1943.

———. *The Psychology of Music.* W. W. Norton, 1937.

———. "We Need Music." Music Supervisors National Conference Yearbook, 1932.

Mursell, James L. and Glenn, Maybelle. *The Psychology of School Music Teaching.* Silver Burdett & Co., 1931.

Music Educators National Conference. *Music Educators Source Book.* 1947.

———. *Music Rooms and Equipment.* 1957.

Negus, V. E. *The Mechanism of the Larynx.* C. V. Mosley Co., 1929.

New York Singing Teachers Association. *Its Story.* Theodore Presser, 1928.

Nicoll, Irene and Dennis, Charles M. *Simplified Vocal Training.* Carl Fischer, 1940.

Novahec, Hazel B. (editor) *Music Education Source Book.* Music Educators National Conference, 1945.

Oblensky, Alexis. "Passing from the Conscious to Subconscious Control." Musician, April 1930, Vol. 35.

Parisotti, Allessandro. *Anthology of Italian Song.* G. Schirmer, 1894.

Pease, E. R. Garnett. *The Singing Voice.* Pitman and Sons, Ltd., 1933.

Peterson, Paul W. *Natural Singing and Expressive Conducting.* John F. Blair, 1955.

Philip, Frank. *Philosophy of Vocal Culture.* Schribners, 1930.

Pierce, Anne E. and Liebling, Estelle. *Class Lessons in Singing.* Silver Burdett and Co., 1937.

Pons, Lily. "Fame Overnight." (an interview) Etude, 1931, Vol. 49.

Roberton, Sir Hugh. "Adjudicators and Adjudication." Supervisors Service Bulletin, May 1934.

Roma, Lisa. *The Science and Art of Singing.* G. Schirmer, 1956.

Ross, William Ernest. *Sing High, Sing Low.* Brown and Ross, 1948.

Rubin-Rabson, Grace. "The Psychology of Memorizing." Music Educators Journal, Jan. 1950.

Schumann-Heink, Ernestine. "You Can Sing — If You Will." (an interview) Etude, 1934, Vol. 52.

Scott, Charles Kennedy. *Word and Tone.* J. M. Dent and Sons, 1933, (Volumes I and II)

Seashore, Carl E. "A Beautiful Voice." Music Educators Journal, Feb. 1938, Vol. 24.

———. "New Approaches to the Science of Voice." Scientific Monthly, Vol. 49.

———. *Psychology of Vibrato in Both Voice and Instrument.* University of Iowa Studies in the Psychology of Music, Vol. III, 1936.

———. "Variability of Pitch in Artistic Singing." Music Teachers National Association Proceedings for 1938, Vol. 33.

Shakespeare, William. *Plain Words in Singing.* Putnam, 1938.

Shaw, W. Warren. *Authentic Voice Production.* Lippincot, 1930.

———"Modern Trends in Voice Class Instruction." M E N C Yearbook, 1936, Vol. 29.

Silva, Giulo. *Advise to Beginners in Singing.* G. Schirmer, 1917.

Skiles, Wilbur Alonza. "Learning to Rule the Unruly Tongue." Etude, 1934, Vol. 52.

Smallman, John and Wilcox, E. H. *The Art of A Cappella Singing.* Ditson, 1933.

Smith, Joseph. *Voice and Song.* G. Schirmer, 1907.

Spouse, Alfred. "High School Voice Class Demonstration." Music Supervisors National Conference Yearbook, 1930.

———. "Voice Classes in the High School." Music Publishers Journal, March-April, 1944.

———. "Voice Classes in the Senior High School." Music Supervisors Journal, Feb. 1930.

Stanley, Douglas. *The Science of Voice.* Carl Fischer, 1939, 3rd. edition.

———. *Your Voice,* Pitman Publishing Corp., 1945.

Stephens, Percy Rector. "Fundamentals That Govern Singing." Musician, Jan. 1934, Vol. 39.

Storey, Barbara and Barnard, Elsie I. *A Key to Speech and Song.* Blackie and Son, 1940.

Street, George Hotchkiss. *Pure and Easy Tone Production.* The Author, 1927.

Stueckgold, Grete. "If You Were My Pupil." (an interview) Etude, 1935, Vol. 53.

Taylor, Bernard U. *Group Voice.* G. Schirmer, 1936.

———. "Group Voice Instruction." Music Teachers National Association Proceedings for 1937.

Tibbett, Lawrence. "Should I Change Teachers?" (an interview) Etude, 1935, Vol. 35.

———. "There Is No Open-Sesame." (an interview) Etude, 1940, Vol. 58.

Tkach, Peter. *Vocal Technic.* Neil J. Kjos, 1948.

Trusler, Ivan and Ehret, Walter. *Functional Lessons in Singing.* Prentice-Hall, Inc., 1960.

Turner, Louise. *A Study of Song Literature for Solo Voices in Secondary Schools.* M. A. Thesis, University of Iowa, 1939.

Vennard, William. *Singing, the Mechanism and the Technic.* Edwards Brothers, 1950.

Wagner, Richard. *On Conducting.* William Reeves, 1897.

Ward, Arthur E. *Music Education for the High Schools.* American Book Co., 1941.

Waters, Crystal. *Song, the Substance of Vocal Study.* G. Schirmer, 1930.

Weer, Robert Lawrence. *My Views on Voice Production.* The Author, 1941.

Westerman, Kenneth U. *Modern Phonetization.* Edwards Press, 1945.

Wharton, Florence C. *Rotary Voice Method.* Augsburg Publishing House, 1937.

White, Ernest George. *Sinus Tone Production.* J. M. Dent and Sons, 1938.

Wilcox, John C. *The Living Voice.* Carl Fischer, 1935.

———. "Why Do They Sing Off Pitch?" Etude, Jan. 1937.

Wilson, Harry Robert. *Artistic Choral Singing.* G. Schirmer, 1959.

———. "Establishing the Resonance." Organ and Choral Guide, Feb. 1952, Vol. 5.

———. *Music in the High School.* Silver Burdett and Co., 1941.

———. *The Solo Singer,* Carl Fischer, 1941.

———. "What! Another Voice Book?" California Choir Guide, Vol. 4, No. 9.

Winslow, Robert W. "The Psychology of Musical Memory." Music Educators Journal, Jan. 1949.

Witherspoon, Herbert. *Singing.* G. Schirmer, 1925.

———. *Thirty-Six Lessons in Singing for Teachers and Students.* Meissner Institute of Music, 1930.

Wodell, Frederick W. *Choir and Chorus Conducting.* Theodore Presser, 1919.

———. "The Proper Training and Use of the Voice of Persons of School Age." Etude, 1929, Vol. 47.

Wronski, Thaddeus. *The Singer and His Art.* D. Appleton and Co., 1921.